Christopher Joseph Hansen

World Construction via Networking

The Storytelling Mechanics of the Marvel
Cinematic Universe

[transcript]

Dissertation an der Philosophischen Fakultät der Universität Siegen.

Bibliographic information published by the Deutsche Nationalbibliothek
The Deutsche Nationalbibliothek lists this publication in the Deutsche Nationalbibliografie; detailed bibliographic data are available in the Internet at https://dnb.dnb.de

© 2024 transcript Verlag, Bielefeld

All rights reserved. No part of this book may be reprinted or reproduced or utilized in any form or by any electronic, mechanical, or other means, now known or hereafter invented, including photocopying and recording, or in any information storage or retrieval system, without permission in writing from the publisher.

Cover layout: Kordula Röckenhaus, Bielefeld
Cover illustration: Kohji Asakawa / Pixabay (modified)
Printed by: Majuskel Medienproduktion GmbH, Wetzlar
https://doi.org/10.14361/9783839470985
Print-ISBN: 978-3-8376-7098-1
PDF-ISBN: 978-3-8394-7098-5
ISSN of series: 2703-013X
eISSN of series: 2703-0148

Christopher Joseph Hansen
World Construction via Networking

Lettre

Christopher Joseph Hansen is a scholar specializing in literary studies, media studies, transmediality, and narratology. He holds a master's degree in transnational literary studies from Universität Bremen and completed his Ph.D. thesis at Universität Siegen. His research interests include the interplay of media, narrative structures, popular culture, and creative writing.

Acknowledgments

I want to express my deepest gratitude to Prof. Dr. Anja Müller and Prof. Dr. Daniel Stein for their unwavering guidance, invaluable insights, and relentless commitment to excellence. Their mentorship has made this Ph.D. project possible and has been instrumental in shaping its course. I am profoundly thankful for their expertise and support.

I would also like to thank the entire English Department of the University of Siegen. They provided an inspiring academic environment and access to resources, discussions, and ideas, greatly enriching my research journey. Within this context, special thanks go to my colleagues Kieron Brown, Katrin Becker, and Alessandra Boller, who, outside of stimulating discussions and shared insights, provided a sounding board for dealing with the unexpected and usually unmentioned pitfalls of completing a Ph.D. project. I am honored to have had the opportunity to meet and work with such dedicated and talented individuals.

Finally and most importantly, I would like to thank my wife, Anna-Maria von Kentzinsky, who endured months of my uncertainty and more rewatches of the MCU than a sane person should be legally submitted to, and my mother, Sue Hansen, who never questioned the validity of my path and always encouraged me to do something out of the ordinary. I am eternally grateful for their unwavering love, encouragement, and understanding throughout this challenging endeavor. Their steadfast support sustained me during the long hours of research and writing, and I am deeply fortunate to have them in my life.

Contents

Introduction 11

1 The Foundation 21
1.1 Foundational Terms 21
    1.1.1 Narrative 21
    1.1.2 World 23
    1.1.3 Network 29
1.2 Foundational Theories – The Good, The Bad, and The Ugly 36
    1.2.1 The Good 36
    1.2.2 The Bad 49
    1.2.3 The Ugly 57
1.3 Foundation for a New Terminology 60

2 The Universe Model 67
2.1 Definition of Narrative Entity and Manifestation 72
    2.1.1 Narrative Entity 72
    2.1.2 Manifestation 74
2.2 Elements of Governance 76
    2.2.1 Index Manifestation 77
        2.2.1.1 Example Index Manifestation 86
        2.2.1.2 Differing Versions of Index Manifestations: Civil War vs. Civil War: Warzone ... 91
        2.2.1.3 Manifestation – Narrative Entity Feedback Loop 94
    2.2.2 Transformation Triggers 97
        2.2.2.1 Shared Narrative 105
        2.2.2.2 Example Transformation Trigger 110
        2.2.2.3 Autonomy through Index Collection 117
    2.2.3 Narrative Reliance 120
        2.2.3.1 The Three Types of Audiences 123
        2.2.3.2 Example Narrative Reliance 125

    2.3 Classification of Relationships 130
        2.3.1 Shared Universe 132
        2.3.2 Multiverse 135
        2.3.3 Company Universe 137

3 The Mechanics 141
3.1 The MCU Network 142
    3.1.1 The MCU Films 143
        3.1.1.1 Phase 1 143
        3.1.1.2 Phase 2 157
        3.1.1.3 Phase 3 171
        3.1.1.4 Network Spanning Connections 194
        3.1.1.5 MCU-conclusion 209
    3.1.2 The Marvel Netflix Universe (MNU) 211
        3.1.2.1 Daredevil, Season 1 (2015) 212
        3.1.2.2 Jessica Jones, Season 1 (2015) 213
        3.1.2.3 Daredevil, Season 2 (2016) 215
        3.1.2.4 Luke Cage, Season 1 (2016) 216
        3.1.2.5 Iron Fist, Season 1 (2017) 218
        3.1.2.6 The Defenders (2017) 220
        3.1.2.7 The Punisher, Season 1 (2017) 222
        3.1.2.8 Jessica Jones, Season 2 (2018) 223
        3.1.2.9 Luke Cage, Season 2 (2018) 224
        3.1.2.10 Iron Fist, Season 2 (2018) 227
        3.1.2.11 Daredevil, Season 3 (2018) 228
        3.1.2.12 The Punisher, Season 2 (2019) 229
        3.1.2.13 Jessica Jones, Season 3 (2019) 230
        3.1.2.14 Network Spanning Connections 231
        3.1.2.15 MNU Conclusions 241
    3.1.3 The ABC Series 243
        3.1.3.1 Agents of S.H.I.E.L.D. (2013-2020) 243
        3.1.3.2 Agent Carter (2015-2016) 245
        3.1.3.3 Conclusion ABC Series 246
    3.1.4 The Marvel Relationships 246
        3.1.4.1 MNU/MCU Relationship 246
        3.1.4.2 ABC/MCU Relationship 251
        3.1.4.3 MNU/ABC Relationship 266
        3.1.4.4 The Roxxon Corporation/Stark Industries 269
    3.1.5 Lack of Connection 271
3.2 Understanding the Mechanics of *The Marvel Cinematic Universe* 275
    3.2.1 From Personal to Global to Cosmic and Beyond:
        Managing Expansion and Escalation 275
        3.2.1.1 The Foundational Phase: Constructing a Network 277
        3.2.1.2 The Expansion Phase: Maintaining and Adding to the Network 280
        3.2.1.3 The General Structure of Shared Universe Expansion 286

	3.2.2	It's All Too Much: The Need for Clustering	293
		3.2.2.1 The Process of Clustering	295
		3.2.2.2 Connecting Clusters	298
		3.2.2.3 Cluster Relationships (Shared Universes in a Multiverse Relationship)	301
	3.2.3	Escalating the Network: Audience Creation and Maintenance	304
		3.2.3.1 Crafting Fandoms: Creating an Informed Audience	305
		3.2.3.2 Making Everybody Happy: Balancing Audience Types	308
		3.2.3.3 Limited Audience: The Escalation of Expansion	310
		3.2.3.4 Bigger Threats: The Escalation of Spectacles	311
	3.2.4	Endings and Beginnings Forever	314
		3.2.4.1 Levels of Ending	316
		3.2.4.2 Types of Endings and Beginnings	319
		3.2.4.3 Continuing Forever	322

4 Reflections 323
4.1 Reflection on Practice: A short look at other Universes 323
4.1.1 The Arrowverse: Keeping the Comic Structure 323
4.1.2 DCEU: Working without a Foundation 326
4.1.3 Discworld: Shared Universe in Novels 329
4.1.4 Other Universes 330
4.2 Reflection on Theory: Researching Universes 331
4.2.1 Value for Aesthetic Analysis 332
4.2.2 Value for Cultural Analysis 334

Afterword 341

References 345
Primary Sources 345
    Film 345
    Series 347
    Comics 354
    Books 355
    Internet 356
Secondary Sources 356
    Internet 359

Introduction

With the mainstream's growing acceptance of worlds and storytelling spread among several different texts – e.g., films, television series, novels, and comics – this Ph.D. project conducted at the University of Siegen under the tutelage of Prof. Dr. Anja Müller and Prof. Dr. Daniel Stein originally began with the premise that new and old cultural values hid within the larger structures governing deliberately related texts forming a singular world. The focus on structure grew out of the realization that many discussions concerning phenomena such as the Marvel Cinematic Universe (MCU) and its comic book source operated with decisively post-structuralist approaches or with a limited view of the overall larger worlds. The initial project mistakenly presumed that one of the theoretical fields concerned with such phenomena had mapped out the narrative framework underlining the organization of such phenomena. While several approaches describe singular aspects of the MCU's proliferation and theorize how such a structure may emerge, none has attempted to distill and define these processes. The lack of such research appears quite surprising, as within the field of popular literature confined narratives – meaning those limited to a singular text or form of expression – seem to become rather the exception than the rule. Most notable properties produce sequels or prequels, contain elements of a larger franchise, or appear to lay the foundation for further expansion. The success of popular properties almost appears directly linked to the number of installments it produces or has the potential to produce. The notable recognition of the MCU with a more mainstream audience only highlights this development of not only popular franchises but also fictional worlds constructed from the interrelation of several different texts. Its success has started to influence a fair number of other products of popular literature. Warner Brothers attempted to adapt DC comic properties in a similar fashion, creating the DC Extended Universe (DCEU); Star Wars has not only launched a continuation of the original movies' storyline but also started to brand some of their other narrative products as "A Star Wars Story" with *Rogue One*[1] as the first installment; Universal Studios released *The Mummy*[2] in 2017 with the explicit intention of creating an MCU-like connected network of films derived from famous monster and horror characters. These efforts are not

---

1 *Rogue One: A Star Wars Story*. Directed by Gareth Edwards. Lucasfilm Ltd. 2016
2 *The Mummy*. Directed by Alex Kurtzman. Performances by Tom Cruise. Universal Pictures. 2017

limited to film. The Arrowverse, the MCU Netflix productions, and Star Wars TV shows adapted a similar notion for television. Despite this growing occurrence, associated theories and fields of study have only partly addressed how the storytelling structure of such franchises operate, usually focusing on philosophical or post-structural approaches concerned with the mental creations of a world, the potential spread across media, and their contents' meaning for society and culture. While all these approaches have come to some interesting results – often through crosspollination – they overlook the potential benefits of a structural approach to the underlying mechanics governing the interrelation of such a phenomenon. Realizing that research into storyworlds, vast narratives, seriality, transmediality, and intertextuality tackled the influences among different texts but made no attempt at deriving such a governing structure, this project's goal shifted to the development of a structural model. While such a model allows for the description of cultural assertions in the formation of such a network – the project's initial goal – it may also provide new means of grasping the interrelation between different texts in general and better determining their relationship. Even though this project does not delve into these possibilities, a structural model could also serve to evaluate the potential success of franchises based on interrelated texts.

On a more theoretical level, a focus on the interrelation of texts as a means to create a coherent world necessarily has to rethink general conceptions already put forward by post-structural approaches. Equally, it may have to reevaluate basic principles of narration to accommodate the interaction between different singular plot structures within a more extensive network of texts. Focused on a specific type of relationship and its ability to create the perception of a unified world, constructing a model requires some manner of describing a specific collection of texts in distinction to other potential relationships – such as intertextual ones or categorizations by author, theme, genre etc. – as well as a manner of considering their type of interrelation. With worlds created within the superhero genre – specifically the MCU and Marvel comics – at the center of the Universe Model, the inclusion of specific materials arises from different texts' contribution to a unified fictional space. The potentially direct interaction of the involved texts' setting and plot mark their relationship as uniquely different from those focused on the sole acceleration of meaning or categorization by similarities. Due to the prominence of transmediality, franchises involving texts with direct relationships are often visualized in a core/periphery manner[3]. This approach assumes the existence of some central text, which for some reason have greater prominence and usually also a guiding function for all others. While this view accurately represents the franchises from which transmediality was initially derived, the interactions between different texts within the broader superhero genre do not operate with a universally acknowledged central core text guiding the form and formation of the material around it. Instead, these franchises seem to work with distinct degrees of relationships, which form clusters within a wider collection of material. The most straightforward manner to consider these patterns is as a network, in which the distance between different properties denotes the overall degree of their interaction. As such, this research rethinks phenomena such as the MCU as networks of texts

---

[3] See, for example, Jenkins (1992/2006), Bacon-Smith (1991), Mittell (2014), Urbanski (2013)

creating a unified world, thereby declaring a limited corpus within networks of this kind and avoiding any assumed prominence towards any specific central text.

The unique nature of such a network equally raises questions concerning the interaction between texts and their audiences. All relevant information constituting the overall world is spread across several texts. Therefore, a model describing the interrelation of texts meant to coordinate them in a network has to consider a diverging engagement with the different materials contributing to a complete comprehension of the associated world. A singular text can operate with some assurance that an audience engages with it as a whole and, therefore, has the chance to absorb all necessary information to comprehend its overall content. In contrast, a text constructed to operate in a network – as singular issues in a superhero comic network, for example – cannot rely on its audience's engagement with all necessary materials. Aside from differing levels of knowledge, the potential for diverging degrees of engagement potentially creates alternate expectations toward a text within such a network. While an audience without any knowledge from other parts of the network engages with one of its texts, expecting it to work independently, devoted followers may expect some more or less obvious connection to other materials within the same network. As we know, literary products do not work unidirectionally but operate via the interaction of an audience and the text at hand. Therefore, the question arises: How do texts in such networks deal with an audience's fluid knowledge base, especially when that knowledge base potentially creates divergent viewing habits and expectations? Thus, any model establishing a structure for a network of texts should consider differing knowledge bases for the audiences engaging with its singular texts. Hereby, this differing knowledge base should be specifically associated with information provided from texts in the network itself.

Within different approaches to the comprehension of narration, considerations of time have always been complex. Most approaches to time in fiction grapple with the relationship between the passage of time in the 'real' world and in fiction. Concepts such as story time, time of the narrated, and Erzählte Zeit grasp time within narration itself, covering the presumed time between the actions and events taking place in a text. Discourse time, time of narrating, and Erzählzeit cover the time required to tell the story at hand. These relatively simple two-tier systems invite intriguing intricacies, especially considering the potential for plots to rearrange events into a non-temporally consecutive order, thereby creating a more complex relation between story time and discourse time. Considerations of time become even more multifaceted when the events and actions of several different plots from different texts relate to one another by formally occurring within a presumably unified world and when the publication of these texts does not occur simultaneously and across different media. Within the context of a network, classic approaches to time in fiction become convoluted when confronted with a causal relation between events from separate texts. To avoid complications, a model approaching a world created from a network of texts should focus on the notions of state and alteration over temporality, as the state of the world and the way it changes is of far greater importance than the potential time in which these changes occur. This focus on a state should not be limited to the state of the world – in the sense of the state of the setting – but equally apply to the state of the network – in the sense of the relationships between the different relevant texts – as alterations to the network, including a changing number of relevant texts, have a significant influence on understanding a world's constitution. In other words, in addition to the world, the model should apply the notion of state and alteration to the network of texts as well. This approach allows an analysis to describe the state of a network and its associated world between two events, independent from the events' precise textual source within that network. A simple compare and contrast between either state then reveals the degree and type of influence a singular event may have had within the development of the world and its associated network.

As previously mentioned, the general type of phenomenon presented by the MCU and superhero comics in general has been discussed extensively from a post-structuralist and cultural studies perspective. These approaches have yielded interesting results, applying their specific concepts to the overall phenomenon or by transferring insight from adjacent research. These specific approaches, however, operate firmly within the notions of their principal field, using their specific terminology. To derive a structure for a network of texts creating a unified world, this discussion must lean on the insight gained from these other fields, dominantly transmediality – including some adjacent concepts – and narratology. Hereby, the research attempts to combine insights from competing or otherwise unrelated principles. To avoid confusion and potential misinterpretation, a model for a network of texts creating a unified world should operate with its own terminology derived from existing research but defined in distinction from already established concepts. Aside from providing a new perspective on aspects surrounding a network of texts, offering an alternative set of terms and refining established principles represents one of this research's contributions to current scholarly discourse. Within the process of understanding the mechanics governing more extensive networks of texts, this research introduces and defines new terminology for categorizing and describing the interaction between texts and worlds derived from them. This terminology partly arises from scholarly research, with some terms derived from the fan discourse surrounding the established superhero genre. By developing the terminology from a combination of academic thinking and fan engagement, the overall structure will more directly represent the reality of such a network's system of narration, organization, and management. Hereby, the research will not go against currently established principles but use their ideas and notions as an academic baseline. These academic principles can then augment and clarify fan terminology to create a better sense of categories to describe and understand the different levels and relationships within such networks.

Ultimately, the purpose of this research project is to develop the Universe Model by uncovering the structure that governs the networks of texts that create the sense of a unified world – such as the Marvel Cinematic Universe – in consideration of its audiences' divergent knowledge base. To grasp the specifics of such a phenomenon, the development entails the emergence of new terminology derived from various fields. Equally, due to the interaction of several plots and several different release dates, such a structure should avoid any direct consideration of time and, instead, focus on the state of the unified world, contemplate the interrelation of text as a network, and consider questions of audience engagement. In other words, this research provides a new model and terminology to grasp a network of texts forming a unified world and rethinks established notions and concepts in the process of its development. To this end, this paper is split into four sections: 1) a discussion of relevant contributions to the overall conception, 2) the development of the model's basic units by advancing established principles from narratology, proving their viability through a direct application to material from Marvel Comics, 3) the application of the previously developed principles to the MCU to unearth its general structure organizing the overall emergence and expansion of the franchise, and finally 4) a discussion of potential further developments of the model through an application to other similar research objects as well as its potential use for overall research.

Consisting of three chapters, the (1) *Foundation* section establishes a theoretical foundation for the following discussion. Its first chapter debates and defines three essential key terms underlying further deliberation of the model – narrative, world, and network. As either of these terms has multiple partly contentious uses within various fields, their definition will help clarify this research's specific view on either. In the course of these definitions, other principles typically associated with these concepts also receive clarification. Within this process, narrative is broken down into a straightforward combination of setting and plot. World is generally based on Ryan's storyworld concept, which is advanced through the adaptation of principles from Wolf's imaginary world approach and notions of transfictional world-building. Avoiding a standard link and node approach, this paper adapts a simpler notion of Latour's Actor-Network-Theory to define its conception of network. The second chapter engages different poststructuralist theories concerned with expanding narrative structures to identify important underlying aspects. Hereby, the chapter dominantly focuses on notions derived from transmediality and some adjacent principles – such as storyworld, remediation, re-imagination, and seriality. As one of transmedia storytelling's chief concerns is the proliferation of franchises, its insights provide a good basis for developing a structure explaining the expansion process. The chapter approaches the field by first appropriating parts useful to developing a structural model, followed by a discussion and reconstitution of some principles to better suit the task at hand, and finally, a disregard of some of the theory's aspects. A third chapter formulates the basis for new terms, leaning on a mixture of academic uses and applications within fan theory. Combined, the first section provides the general basis for developing a model.

Leaning on the previous discussion, the (2) *Model* section develops the basic principles and terms to describe the specific mechanics used to create and manage relationships between different texts. To this end, section two contains three chapters, each tackling different elements of the model. A brief explanation of the final Universe Model's operation precedes the definition of its singular parts. This description at the beginning of the section employs the terminology defined in the following chapters. The first chapter – *Definition of Narrative Entity and Manifestation* – describes the basic units of the overall model, distinguishing between a discursive notion and a physical manifestation of each story. The elaboration arises from further considerations of the previously discussed theories in the specific context of the superhero genre. With the basic units in place, the following chapter – *Elements of Governance* – defines the principles used within different texts to create and manage their interrelation as well as the general development of the associated fictional world. These principles are dominantly distilled from traditional narratology. A direct application of each new principle to examples from the Marvel superhero comics through a close reading then shows their validity and process of operation. Superhero comics are chosen for these initial applications because they – especially those published by DC and Marvel – employ a form of cross-textual storytelling with a continuous expansion through the creation of new material representative of the overall phenomenon the Universe Model attempts to describe. Essentially, the superhero comic's internal interdependence and its coherent speed of production provide abundant examples of interrelated texts. While examples from different genres and other media exist, none has employed the same complex interrelation of different stories for as long and to the same degree as the superhero comic. Within this context, these specific analyses will focus on a comic book Event. The Event employed in the superhero genre – or superhero Event – does not relate to narratology's conception of the term – meaning an action or act performed by an agent. The superhero Event usually denotes a significant alteration to the unified world, which influences the setting and plot of several different related comic series within a set number of publications. As such, several narratological 'events' occur within the context of a superhero Event. More importantly, the sequences of events related to a superhero Event cascade outward from a main plotline, necessarily creating causal relations between plots of different series set within the same world. In other words, Events within the superhero genre affect a larger section of their overall world and, therefore, provide an excellent basis to test the applicability of the Universe Model's basic concepts. The Event *Civil War* provides the general research material for this chapter. It was chosen due to the general plot's later adaptation to the Marvel Cinematic Universe – the main research object – its prominent influence over several different running series at the time, and a notable number of texts exploring alternate outcomes of the Event. The final chapter – *Classification of Relationships* – introduces terms to classify the relationship between different texts. Here, fan terminology is contextualized with the previously established principles to derive a general categorization of differing relationships between texts. To this end, the chapter will draw on existing definitions and research where available and codify fan perception in any other case.

With the basic principles established, the (3) *Mechanics* section attempts to identify and understand the mechanics governing and maintaining the development of a network of texts that creates the sense of a unified world. To this end, the newly established concepts are applied to a larger subsection of the overall Marvel Cinematic Universe to generate a more definite description of its network. Engaging with a considerable amount of material, the analysis of the MCU is conducted in four separate stages, each corresponding to its own chapter. The first three stages each classify a different subset of the overall material by applying the previously established principles. Categorized by the medium and most prominent venues of publication, the analysis establishes a network from each subset, illustrating the relationship between its singular texts and the techniques used to create a sense of interrelation. Hereby, the first stage focuses on the MCU's cinematic releases, meaning the films prominently associated with it; the second stage describes the different streaming series originally produced for and released on the streaming platform Netflix – often referred to as the Marvel Netflix Universe (MNU); and the third stage engages with material associated with the American Broadcasting Company (ABC). In the fourth stage, these separate networks are interrelated, setting up the overall network. Building on the description of the overall MCU network, this section's second chapter – *Understanding the Mechanics of The Marvel Cinematic Universe* – derives general strategies employed to create a unified world, manage its constant expansion, initiate and maintain a specialized audience while attempting to please a wider one, and set up the network to potentially forever add new releases. This section analyzes the Marvel Cinematic Universe, in contrast to material from Marvel comics, because the latter has continuously published and developed new material since 1961 for the same universe, partly even adapting characters and plots from previous iterations of the company. Besides the problem of retrieving all relevant material to derive the overall structure of its network at any point in time, no subsection of Marvel comics' publications was conceived and remained independent from the main world created in their regular titles. In other words, finding a smaller, more manageable network of texts that remains autonomous from all its other publications and the associated world is nearly impossible within the genre of superhero comics. At the time of writing, the MCU provides the ideal research object for the discovery of governing principles, as it contains enough material to require such principles but not so many to make a general overview nearly impossible.

After the analysis, the (4) *Reflections* section considers potential advancements of the model and its value for future research. The former discusses other potential objects that seem to operate with a similar structure to the MCU but carry significant differences in either their dominant medium of representation or the presumed process of creation and expansion. Within this discussion, singular chapters speculate how the engagement with these different objects could advance the model and how it could explain their specific structure. In a second chapter – *Reflection on Theory* – this research considers the potential use of the Universe Model in research, pointing out notable processes within the MCU supporting difficult cultural norms of Western society. The overall discussion is completed with a short afterword.

Within this frame, the research focuses on material published by Marvel because of the number of publications and the unique relationship between the cinematic and the comic iterations of their world. In the medium of comics, Marvel offers one of the two most notable, extensive, and longest-running networks of texts that create a unified world. In addition, Marvel currently provides a more manageable alternate cinematic version of such a network, which spreads across a variety of media. Hereby, the unique relationship between the world created in the comics and the world created in the films provides a significant opportunity.

> "This relationship is not adequately explained by the traditional logics of adaptation or transmedia storytelling alone; rather, the Marvel Cinematic Universe primarily embraces a logic of transfictionality, which Richard Saint-Gelais has defined as an intertextual relation that 'neither quotes nor acknowledges its sources. Instead, it uses the source text's setting and/or inhabitants as if they existed independently' (2005, 612). The Marvel Comics Universe is thereby positioned as both complementary to and diegetically separate from the films."[4]

---

4   Jeffries, Dru. "The Worlds Align: Media Convergence and Complementary Storyworlds in Marvel's Thor: The Dark World". *World Building. Transmedia, Fans, Industries.* Marta Boni (ed.), Amsterdam University Press, 2017. 287–303. Page 288

The nature of the MCU as equally related but existing separately from its comic book source allows this paper to draw general conclusions for the structural operation of more extensive networks by analyzing a more manageable one. At the same time, it reasonably allows the transference of basic techniques derived from the comics to the general operations of the MCU. In other words, this specific relationship between the two networks allows the analysis to derive some global principles in the management of the networks they represent. Because this research paper concentrates on the overall structure underlining the organization of the entire network and moments of direct interrelations of singular texts within it, the amount of material is inevitably quite extensive. To limit the research material, the analysis of singular moments of direct interrelation focuses on material related to a specific superhero Event. This paper favors superhero Events over specific graphic novels for the simple reason that, within the superhero canon, Events are created with a plot device that echoes further than a single character, plotline, or series[5].

The *Civil War* Event, for example, starts when the superhero team "New Warriors" accidentally destroys a school, killing over 600 civilians, 60 of whom were children. The catastrophe prompts the government to issue the Superhuman Registration Act, which forces all super-powered individuals to register and train with the government. In response, the superhero community divides into two factions: advocates under Iron Man and adversaries under Captain America. The implementation of a Superhuman Registration Act, as well as the resulting conflict, have a narrative impact on all major and minor super-powered characters inhabiting Marvel's main Shared Universe. As such, the full range of comic material for this research formally includes the full scope of the *Civil War* comic Event, which includes publications with the **Road To Civil War**, **Civil War**, and **Casualties of War** taglines, as well as the miniseries offering alternate versions of this superhero Event. In detail, the comic side formally comprises of the following titles: *New Warriors #1–6* (2005), *Civil War #1–7* (2006), *New Avengers #21–25* (2006), *Ms. Marvel #6–8* (2006), *Captain America #22–25* (2006), *Iron Man #13–14* (2006), *Fantastic Four #538–543* (2006), *Black Panther #19–25* (2006), *Civil War: Frontline #1–11* (2006), *She-Hulk #8–9* (2006), *Civil War: Young Avengers & Runaways #1–4* (2006), *Heroes for Hire #1–3*(2006), *Civil War: Choosing Sides* (2006), *Punisher War Journal #1–3*(2006), *Civil War: The Return*(2006), *Amazing Spider-Man #532–538*(2006), *Sensational Spider-Man #28–24*(2006), *Friendly Neighborhood Spider-Man #11–16*(2006), *Thunderbolts #103–105*(2006), *Wolverine #42–48*(2006), *X-Factor #8–9*(2006), *Cable & Deadpool #30–32*(2006), *Civil War: X-Men #1–4*(2006),*Moon Knight #7–12*(2007), *Civil War: War Crimes* (2007), *Ghost Rider #8–11* (2007), *Iron Man/Captain America: Casualties of War "Rubicon"* (2007), *Civil War: The Confession* (2007), *Civil War: The Initiative* (2007), *Fallen Son: The Death of Captain America – Wolverine* (2007), *Fallen Son: The Death of Captain America – Avengers* (2007), *Fallen Son: The Death of Captain America – Captain America* (2007), *Fallen Son: The Death of Captain America – Spider-Man* (2007), and *Fallen Son: The Death of Captain America – Iron Man* (2007)[6]. Alternate worlds based on the

---

5   Jenkins and Ford discuss and present the range, impact, and meaning of such superhero Events, specifically *Civil War*, in *Managing Multiplicity in Superhero Comics*.
6   Instead of working with the singular issues, this research accesses the entire material from a special collection box sets containing all of the mentioned issues except *Civil War: Warzone*. To al-

same superhero Event occur in *What If? Civil War* (2008), *What If? Fallen Son* (2009), and *Civil War: Warzone#1–5* (2016).

As the cinematic material does not have superhero Events in the same manner superhero comics have, the MCU material for this research is organized around their formal medium of release. Specifically, the analysis looks at the films, the Netflix series, and the ABC series. Hereby, the overall scope has been limited to contain only the material published within the general timeframe of the Infinity Saga, as the film concluding the saga and several character's larger story arc – *Avengers: Endgame* – is generally perceived as the final of the cumulative works of all previously released MCU films. This leaves the research with an overall network consisting of 23 films, six streaming series with a total of 13 seasons, and two television series with a total of nine seasons. *Iron Man* (2008), *The Incredible Hulk* (2008), *Iron Man 2* (2010), *Thor* (2011), *Captain America: The First Avenger* (2011), *Marvel's The Avengers* (2012), *Iron Man 3* (2013), *Thor: The Dark World* (2013), *Captain America: The Winter Soldier* (2014), *Guardians of the Galaxy Vol.1* (2014), *Avengers: Age of Ultron* (2015), *Ant-Man* (2015) *Captain America: Civil War* (2016), *Doctor Strange* (2016), *Guardians of the Galaxy Vol.2* (2017), *Spider-Man: Homecoming* (2017), *Thor: Ragnarok* (2017), *Black Panther* (2018), *Avengers: Infinity War* (2018), *Ant-Man and The Wasp* (2018), *Captain Marvel* (2019), *Avengers: Endgame* (2019), and *Spider-Man: Far From Home* (2019) constitute the entire film material. *Marvel's Agents of Shield* (2013–2020) and *Marvel's Agent Carter* (2015–2016) are the ABC series, while *Marvel's Daredevil* (2015–2018), *Marvel's A.K.A Jessica Jones* (2015–2019), *Marvel's Luke Cage* (2016–2018), *Marvel's Iron Fist* (2017–2018), *Marvel's The Defenders* (2017), and *Marvel's The Punisher* (2017–2019) comprise the series from the streaming service. As the overall material is quite extensive and the individual plots have little bearing on the overall structure, the discussion excludes summaries of each text, only including specific explanations directly required for the comprehension of the presented argument.

---

low other researchers to review any mentioned instance, all citations have been made as if they emerged from the singular issue comic to avoid a need to access this specific collector's edition.

1 The Foundation

1.1 Foundational Terms

1.1.1 Narrative

Defined, re-defined, and applied in various approaches to literature, the term 'narrative' is a contentious one. According to Geralt Prince's *Dictionary of Narratology*, narratives are perceived "as a particular mode of knowledge", as a "structure or product, [...][which] exhibit six basic macrostructural elements", as "not only a product, but also a process", as requiring "a continuant subject and constitut[ing] a whole", and as a "verbal representation"[1] by different scholars. Within this range of conceptions, the "[n]arrative has traditionally been defined as the representation of a sequence of events"[2] with scholars like Greimas understanding concepts such as canonical narratives as "the representation of a series of events oriented in terms of a goal" and scholars such as Labov, Prince, and Rimmon-Kenan viewing narratives as "the representation of at least two real or fictive events (or one state and one event), neither of which logically presupposes or entails the other."[3] The simple conception of narrative as a sequence of events can emerge in different forms. As Ryan explains in her discussion on Interactive Drama:

> "In its common usage, the term subsumes two concepts whose distinction constitutes a cornerstone of structuralist narratology: narrative can mean a discourse reporting a story, as well as the story itself. Even in its "story" sense, narrative is an ambiguous term. It can be conceived: (a) as a representation of events involving common or related participants and ordered in a temporal sequence ("the king died, then the queen died"); (b) as an interpretation of events invoking causality ("the king died, then the queen died of grief"); or (3) [sic!] as a semantic structure meeting certain formal requirements, such as a salient theme, a point, and a development leading from equilibrium to crisis to a

---

[1] Prince, Gerald. *Dictionary of Narratology*. Nebraska: University of Nebraska Press, 2003. Page 58ff.
[2] Ryan, Marie-Laure. "Semantics, Pragmatics, and Narrativity: A Response to David Rudrum." *Narrative*, vol. 14 no. 2, 2006, p. 188–196. Project MUSE, doi:10.1353/nar.2006.0006. Page 188
[3] Prince, Gerald. *Dictionary of Narratology*. Nebraska: University of Nebraska Press, 2003. Page 58ff.

new form of equilibrium (see Chatman 45–48). I will call the first type sequential narrative, the second type causal, and the third type dramatic, since it corresponds rather closely to the Aristotelian concept of plot."[4]

Regarding a story or plot as a sequence of events, Ryan identifies the story as a base component of the narrative. Exploring the categorization of Interactive Drama – meaning virtual reality and MOO/MUD[5] games – as narratives, she describes such interactive games as providing a setting and absolute freedom of action but lacking a formally guiding plot. While she focuses on the need for a guiding script to order actions within such interactive environments, Ryan – via Reid – unwillingly points towards the importance of a setting in the conception of a narrative.

> "As Elizabeth Reid observes, 'the MUD [and also the MOO] system provides users with a stage but it does not provide them with a script' (170). In the MOO, interactivity consists mainly of a free-flowing, open-ended conversation with other characters. It can take up a narrative form when characters activate standard cultural scripts, such as courting, making love, and building together a house, or when they spontaneously engage in a game of make-believe revolving around virtual objects (such as creating a pet and playing with it). But even when interaction develops spontaneously into narrative action, the responsibility for the users' aesthetic gratification rests heavily on their own performances. MOO sessions can be a tremendous waste of time if users cannot find cooperative and imaginative partners."[6]

Ryan's discussion indicates that in the case of Interactive Drama, a stage – albeit an empty stage – has to be already present for actions as part of events to take place. More importantly, the later section of the quote highlights that interactivity requires characters. Essentially, actions need someone/something to perform them but equally require someone/something for them to be performed upon. As actions are parts of events and narratives contain sequences of events, it necessitates that settings as a collective of characters, places, and props also constitute an essential component of narratives. As such, this paper considers a narrative as a combination of a setting – in this instant, referring to characters, places, and props – and a sequence of events, which may form a story or plot. This is not a groundbreaking conception, as either component already is part of the general view of narrative. In *Story and Discourse: Narrative Structure in Fiction and Film*[7], Chatman defines a story as consisting of two fundamental constituents: event and ex-

---

4   Ryan, Marie-Laure. "Interactive Drama: Narrativity in a Highly Interactive Environment." *MFS Modern Fiction Studies*, vol. 43 no. 3, 1997, p. 677–707. Project MUSE, https://doi:10.1353/mfs.1997.0065. Page 683

5   Multi-user domain – a text-based multiplayer roleplay game, taking place in a real-time created virtual world.

6   Ryan, Marie-Laure. "Interactive Drama: Narrativity in a Highly Interactive Environment." *MFS Modern Fiction Studies*, vol. 43 no. 3, 1997, p. 677–707. Project MUSE, https://doi:10.1353/mfs.1997.0065. Page 681ff

7   Chatman, Seymour. *Story and Discourse: Narrative Structure in Fiction and Film*. Cornell: Cornell University Press, 1978.

istent. An existent is defined as "an ACTOR or an item of SETTING."[8] As Ryan describes a Narrative as "a discourse reporting a story, as well as the story itself"[9], narratives naturally have to consist of events and existents, as narratives are based on the conception of story. However, most applications and concepts focus on the aspect of event, taking the presence of an existent as a given, apparently forgetting its vital role in the formation of a narrative. As the following discussion leans on this dual nature, the excursion into Ryan's exploration of Interactive Drama highlighted the importance of setting and how it is often overlooked in favor of events and actions.

Aside from understanding a narrative as a combination of events and existent, the upcoming discussion equally requires a conception of each story as a creator of a corresponding discourse. Generally, all discussions of narrative acknowledge the existence of a corresponding discourse to an existing story as in "the famous two tier structuralist model, narratives can be said to have two parts: STORY and DISCOURSE."[10] Ryan earlier also pointed out that a narrative could be "a discourse reporting a story". As such, every narrative contains a discourse, which in some form relates to the events and existents constituting a story that directly corresponds with a narrative.

In other words, narratives consist of three parts: a sequence of events, a collection of existents, and a corresponding discourse. To reiterate, further discussion on narrative operates with a conception of the term as a combination of setting – in lieu of the term existent – which here is understood as the collection of characters, places, and props – and a plot or story, which here – in violation of Chatman's definition of story – dominantly denotes a sequence of events or actions. This narrative additionally always creates a corresponding discourse.

1.1.2 World

On the surface, the conception of a world created in fiction is deeply intertwined with the concept of narrative. However, while worlds, to some degree, hinge on a narrative, it is essential to note that narrative and world are two distinct concepts that need to be defined and understood separately, as Mark J.P. Wolf points out. "Recognizing that the experience of a *world* is different and distinct from that of merely a *narrative* is crucial to seeing how worlds function apart from the narratives set within them, [...]."[11] Even though these are two different conceptions, they remain dependent on one another and interact meaningfully. Within world construction, narratives serve as a basic structure through which processes of definition and specification are guided. "Naturally, *narrative* is the most common form of structure, and the one that usually determines which ele-

---

8 Prince, Gerald. *Dictionary of Narratology*. Nebraska: University of Nebraska Press, 2003. Page 28, original emphasis
9 Ryan, Marie-Laure. "Interactive Drama: Narrativity in a Highly Interactive Environment." *MFS Modern Fiction Studies*, vol. 43 no. 3, 1997, p. 677–707. Project MUSE, doi:10.1353/mfs.1997.0065. Page 683
10 Prince, Gerald. *Dictionary of Narratology*. Nebraska: University of Nebraska Press, 2003. Page 59, original emphasis
11 Wolf, Mark J.P. *Building Imaginary Worlds: The Theory of Subcreation*. New York: Routledge, 2012. Page 11, original emphasis

ments in a world are most defined and developed or at least mentioned."[12] The reverse is equally true; narratives inherently build worlds. "Narrative is a form of world building: it creates miniature worlds, which, in the arts and media in particular, have a world(view)-modeling function."[13] Within the context of the discussion presented in this paper, the relationship between narrative and world is important, as narrative provides an organizational function within world representation and creation. More importantly, this organizational function also determines the sprawl of a coherent world across different texts or even the relationship between different worlds. "Narrative, then, holds a world together at different scales, as it structures individual works that make up a world, links different works set in a world and, occasionally, links separate worlds together in multiverses."[14] Because of the pervasive influence of narrative on world and vice versa, conceptions of either are conflated easily and often. Approaching world as an extension of the previously set definition of narrative, world essentially can be understood as an elaborate form of setting. Describing world solely as a setting diminishes its potential complexity. However, such a description highlights a world's possible independence from a full narrative. As a setting, world is a key component of narrative, providing characters, places, and props for a plot or story to occur, but similarly can exist independent from that story. "The case of world without story is much more feasible than the case of stories without worlds."[15] Ryan's assertion reiterates the relationship between world and narrative, with the former as a complex setting, explaining how any conception of world relates to this definition of narrative. While a world operates as a setting within the concept of narrative, it amounts to much more due to its sheer complexity and grander presence in an audience's mind as something more than the mere collection of objects on screen, descriptions in a novel, or items on a stage.

Attached to fields of research and a specific understanding of our (real) world, a variety of different world principles have emerged over the years. Narratology focuses on a world's extension as part of narration, creating principles such as storyworld, narrative world, and diegetic world. Approaches in philosophy, in contrast, concentrate on the relation of these imagined worlds with our own reality, creating conceptions such as possible world, subcreated world, secondary world, and fictional world. Other fields, such as media studies (transmedia world) and cosmology (many-world model), developed world conceptions relevant to their specific inquiries. Not entirely separate from one another, the different notions of world – specifically from narratology and philosophy – have influenced each other meaningfully. Ignoring the cosmological assertions as outside our purview and folding media concerns into those of narratology[16], world principles within

---

12 Wolf, Mark J.P. *Building Imaginary Worlds: The Theory of Subcreation*. New York: Routledge, 2012. Page 154, original emphasis
13 Wolf, Werner. "Lyric Poetry and Narrativity: A Critical Evaluation, and the Need for 'Lyrology'". Narrative, vol. 28 no. 2, 2020, p. 143–173. Project MUSE, https://doi:10.1353/nar.2020.0008. Page 145
14 Wolf, Mark J.P. *Building Imaginary Worlds: The Theory of Subcreation*. New York: Routledge, 2012. Page 154, original emphasis
15 Ryan, Marie-Laure. "The Aesthetics of Proliferation". *World Building. Transmedia, Fans, Industries*. Marta Boni (ed.), Amsterdam University Press, 2017. 29–46. Page 40
16 An approach actively pursued by David Herman.

the humanities generally develop out of one of two traditions: a cognitive and an ontological one.

> "As the Czech narratologist Jiří Koten observes, the narratological concept of world can be traced back to two lines of ancestry. When we speak of storyworld, the influence comes mainly from cognitive approaches to narrative (Herman 2009), while, when we speak of fictional world, the influence comes from schools and disciplines interested in the ontological status of imaginary entities: philosophy of language, formal semantics, and, more particularly, possible worlds theory (Pavel, Doležel, Ryan 1991)."[17]

Either of these traditions and singular world conceptions have contributed to a more extensive understanding of worlds in fiction.[18] As the discussion in this paper later advances its overall view with principles of transmediality, its initial understanding of world is based on an approach generally related to that field of research. Existing on the intersection between cognitive narratology and transmediality, Ryan's storyworld provides the basis for this paper's conception of world. Mark Wolf's imaginary world includes a greater part of most theoretical approaches, as the principle deals with the general manner in which worlds emerge through fiction. As such, the principle helps to expand and clarify any initial approach. Any perception of world developed here should also acknowledge the specific relationship between Marvel comics and the MCU. Notions from Dru Jeffries's transfictional worldbuilding grasp such a relationship. Developed in relation to transmediality, Ryan's storyworld is dominantly concerned with the mentally imagined world created through a person's interaction with a narrative (or the traditional understanding of a story).

> "As narratology expanded from literature to other disciplines and media, it became more and more reliant on the concept of world. In its current narratological use, 'world' is no longer the elusive sum of the meanings conveyed by a text, nor the sum of the ideas of an author, but the very concrete space projected by stories, literally, a 'storyworld'."[19]

The conception of a world as a concrete space allows a storyworld to contain elements beyond those solely presented in a text, as it encompasses the totality of a story, which, according to transmedia and transnarrative approaches, is not limited to a specific text. In a discussion of a structure of interacting texts potentially creating a world, the notion of an imagined world as a concrete space is, in so far, useful as it opens up the concept to achieving a sense of wholeness or completeness by adapting characteristics from outside a primary text. As storyworld derives from transmediality, Ryan considers mainly transmedia expansions or other forms of transmedia sprawl in this context. The notion

---

17   Ryan, Marie-Laure. "The Aesthetics of Proliferation". *World Building. Transmedia, Fans, Industries.* Marta Boni (ed.), Amsterdam University Press, 2017. 29–46. Page 32
18   Most of the different world conceptions as well as their general contribution to a general understanding of world are discussed in detail in Mark Wolf's publication on world building.
19   Ryan, Marie-Laure. "The Aesthetics of Proliferation". *World Building. Transmedia, Fans, Industries.* Marta Boni (ed.), Amsterdam University Press, 2017. 29–46. Page 31

is particularly useful considering the potential of interacting texts to create a coherent world.

The principal notion of a fictional world as a complete space, however, does not limit such a process to a transmedia form of expansion. Theoretically, it does not even limit such an adaptation to texts concerned with Ryan's specific stories or even texts at all. A concrete space technically entails an understanding that this space is complete within the realm of a person's experience or perception of a world[20]. Due to the nature of storytelling, this completeness is never captured within any given representation within a text, most likely not even in the collection of all texts from such a storyworld. Instead, missing information is substituted with cultural knowledge, speculation, or assertion derived from other but similar worlds, theoretically allowing audiences to establish a sense of completeness. Assuming that part of a storyworld's concrete space is completed with knowledge residing outside its actual texts also opens up the potential for the interaction between different (types of) texts and narratives – meaning a process of leveling out contradictions, considering potential influences of events in one text on another, or using backstory in one text to explain something in another – to provide information to complete such a world. In other words, storyworld allows for a conception of world not limited by its textual representation and authorial intent, permitting the acknowledgment of an audience's assertions from their own experiences and from interactions between texts on the world's formation. In addition to its characteristic as a concrete space, Ryan includes the potential for a storyworld to change via the influence of events.

> "A storyworld is not just the spatial setting where a story takes place, it is a complex spatio-temporal totality that undergoes global changes. Put more simply, a storyworld is an imagined totality that evolves according to the events told in the story. To follow a story means to simulate mentally the changes that take place in the storyworld, using the cues provided by the text."[21]

This apparent ability of events to evolve or alter an established storyworld directly corresponds to the separation of setting and story/plot established in the definition of narrative. Storyworld provides a basic understanding of world not limited by its immediate textual representation and authorial intent, allowing for other influences in the formation of a world and a general notion that a world can be altered through the application of events.

Several approaches to storyworld discuss how a world can be completed outside of its direct textual representation, elaborating on the previously mentioned cultural knowledge, speculation, or assertion derived from other but similar worlds. While these notions exist, they are not codified parts of the concept of storyworld. Focused on comprehending the entire process and details of world-building in fiction, Wolf's term, imag-

---

[20] The Universe Model adapts the concept of experience as a building block from Fludernik's concept of Natural Narratology. While Fludernik employs this idea to narratives in general, the use here is limited to the conception of world and places a greater emphasis on filling in information none of the given text may provide.

[21] Ryan, Marie-Laure. "The Aesthetics of Proliferation". *World Building. Transmedia, Fans, Industries*. Marta Boni (ed.), Amsterdam University Press, 2017. 29–46. Page 32

inary world, includes most of these aspects. Describing his imaginary world as "often transnarrative, transmedial, and transauthorial in nature"[22], Wolf distills the potential influence of overarching narratives, the interaction between media, and diverging claims of authority into his conception. Aside from including these aspects of world-building, imaginary world also advances the perception of a concrete space, tying its actuality directly to a sense of experience.

> "The term 'world', as it is being used here, is not simply geographical but *experiential*; that is, everything that is experienced by characters involved, the elements enfolding someone's life (culture, nature, philosophical worldview, places, customs, events, and so forth), [...]."[23]

Combining this perception of world with storyworld – thereby conceiving of a world as a singular concrete space experienced by characters – separates each representation of a world from the actual nature of that world. In other words, while the world may be a singular concrete space, its representation in a text merely reflects a (set of) character's experiences of that world. Considering the potential for a world to exist transnarratively, transmedially, and transauthorially, a view of textual representation as biased through a character's experiences dissolves any potential separation of segments of the potentially same world solely based on types of representation. For example, while *Caravan of Courage: An Ewok Adventure*[24] as a children's movie has a child-like representation of the Star Wars Universe and *Rogue One: A Star Wars Story*[25] as essentially a war movie has a violent and desperate view of the same world, these different representations do not exclude the possibility that each film is set in the same concrete space but represent different experiences of that space. A relationship to the same world may appear evident in a case like Star Wars, in which most textual representations operate with a similar set of aesthetics and, until recently, were guided by a dominant authorial force. However, the superhero genre works with potentially very different sets of aesthetics, very different rules governing the specific narratives, and various authorities influencing singular textual representations.

As such, understanding that a concrete space can be experienced differently in alternate textual representations is vital for the conception of a unified world created from a network of texts. Notions of magic and sorcery, for example, govern the narrative of *Doctor Strange*, while notions of technology and science govern the narrative of Iron Man. Additionally, various authors have tackled either narrative in a variety of media. Despite these differences, these narratives presumably and potentially represent the same world. Such a difference in individual narratives, while representing the same concrete space, is possible because either narrative merely shows a version of that space experienced by

---

22   Wolf, Mark J.P. *Building Imaginary Worlds: The Theory of Subcreation*. New York: Routledge.2012. Page 14
23   Wolf, Mark J.P. *Building Imaginary Worlds: The Theory of Subcreation*. New York: Routledge.2012. Page 25, original emphasis
24   *Caravan of Courage: An Ewok Adventure*. Directed by John Korty. Lucasfilm and Korty films. 1984
25   *Rogue One: A Star Wars Story*. Directed by Gareth Edwards. Lucasfilm Ltd. 2016

a specific set of characters. As such, adapting Wolf's imaginary world allows for the networking of very different representations of the same world. More importantly, the combination of storyworld and imaginary world allows for the perception of a world as a concrete space potentially assembled from the collection of various experienced worlds – as the subsection of a world as represented in a text – simultaneously acknowledging such an experienced world's individual existence as well as its part in the formation of a larger concrete world. The combination of storyworld and imaginary world, therefore, leaves us with a potentially transnarrative, transmedial, and transauthorial conception of world, which is constituted from different experiences of that world in some textual form, in which events may materially and experientially alter it.

While this concept covers most concerns for further discussions of a world created through the networking of different texts, focusing on the superhero genre, specifically the MCU and its comic book source, warrants the additional adaptation of another principle.

> "But the MCU is also significantly distinct from these properties insofar as it doesn't adapt a finite story revolving around a stable set of characters. Where the Harry Potter films adapted the story told in J.K Rowling's novels, the MCU adapts the ongoing storyworld created over decades of Marvel Comics publishing."[26]

Concerned dominantly with questions of adaptation, Jeffries brings up a distinctive and essential relationship between the world created in Marvel comics and the one created in the MCU, namely that the latter imitates processes and ideas from the former to build a distinct world, which simultaneously leans on tropes, symbols, and information generated through decades of comic publication. "What is really being adapted from comics, then, is ultimately not stories at all but rather an approach to world-building and media franchising."[27] This distinct relationship further influences the considerations in this paper on two accounts: (1) It allows for a separate analysis of the comic superhero and the film superhero to unearth underlying principles and structures governing such networks of texts. (2) It highlights an additional source through which a world such as the MCU and Marvel comics may generate information to fill in gaps left unresolved by the text within the network itself. The former (1) is important as the superhero comic provides a more established example of a network of texts creating a singular concrete space formed from different experiences of that world, but – over decades – has amassed an amount of material, which makes deriving a structure underpinning their interaction impossible. Knowing that the MCU adapted the comic's "approach to world-building and media franchising" allows for the analysis of the MCU as a more manageable source to derive such a structure while looking at the comics for the basic techniques used to interrelate different texts or even narratives. The latter (2) leads Jeffries to describe part of the MCU's

---

26 Jeffries, Dru. "The Worlds Align: Media Convergence and Complementary Storyworlds in Marvel's Thor: The Dark World". *World Building. Transmedia, Fans, Industries.* Marta Boni (ed.), Amsterdam University Press, 2017. 287–303. Page 288

27 Jeffries, Dru. "The Worlds Align: Media Convergence and Complementary Storyworlds in Marvel's Thor: The Dark World". *World Building. Transmedia, Fans, Industries.* Marta Boni (ed.), Amsterdam University Press, 2017. 287–303. Page 288

construction as "transfictional world building—that is, world-building characterized by the creative transformation of and continued engagement with another preexisting storyworld"[28]. Aside from directly addressing the relationship between the two primary objects discussed here, transfictional world-building acknowledges an additional source, which may fill in information not provided by the texts directly associated with the world at hand. Going off of Jeffries's definition, a transfictional world, in this context, then derives some of its substance through the engagement with knowledge and understanding from another pre-existing world. With the general network approach and the primary research material in mind, including the notion of transfictional world into this paper's overall conception appears reasonable. As such, further discussions perceive "world" as a potentially transfictional, transnarrative, transmedia, and transauthorial concept constituted of different textual experiences of that concrete space, in which events may alter the world materially and experientially.

1.1.3 Network

More so than 'narrative' or 'world', the term 'network' invokes a sense of intuitive comprehension, especially when attached to an apparently distinctive description of what is networked. For this reason, all preceding discussions use the term without a definition, assuming an intuitive knowledge of the overall idea. The intuitive conception of 'network' also includes a preconceived notion of its usefulness within an analysis. "In simple terms, the network is "a structure composed of links and nodes," which expresses a "proliferating multiplicity that at once enables and challenges our very capacity to think" (Jagoda 3)."[29] As McBean indicates via a quote from Jagoda, the simple formation of network as a structure of "links and nodes" already propagates an expansive understanding of a subject. This straightforward application, however, has led to a multiplicity of uses and definitions in several fields.

> "Who says everything is a network? Everyone, it seems. In philosophy, Bruno Latour: ontology is a network. In literary studies, Franco Moretti: Hamlet is a network. In the military, Donald Rumsfeld: the battlefield is a network. (But so too our enemies are networks: the terror network.) Art, architecture, managerial literature, computer science, neuroscience, and many other fields--all have shifted prominently in recent years toward a network model. Most important, however, is the contemporary economy and the mode of production. Today's most advanced companies are essentially network companies. Google monetizes the shape of networks (in part via clustering algorithms). Facebook has rewritten subjectivity and social interaction along the lines of canalized and discretized network services. The list goes on and on."[30]

---

28 Jeffries, Dru. "The Worlds Align: Media Convergence and Complementary Storyworlds in Marvel's Thor: The Dark World". *World Building. Transmedia, Fans, Industries.* Marta Boni (ed.), Amsterdam University Press, 2017. 287–303. Page 291
29 McBean, Sam. "The Queer Network Novel." *Contemporary Literature*, vol. 60 no. 3, 2019, p. 427–452. *Project MUSE* muse.jhu.edu/article/763824. Page 430
30 https://cultureandcommunication.org/galloway/network-pessimism, retrieved July 29th, 2021

As with all overused terms, the application in such a wide range of fields dilutes any universal conception. While not leaving it useless, the term becomes too ambiguous for general academic discourse. Even when only considered in a specific field, the term may have to contend with several other traditions inside and outside the presumed area of research. Bruno Latour points out such problems when discussing the adaptation of 'network' for sociology.

> "The word network is so ambiguous that we should have abandoned it long ago. And yet the tradition in which we use it remains distinct in spite of its possible confusion with two other lines. One is of course the technical networks—electricity, trains, sewages, internet, and so on. The second one is used, in sociology of organization, to introduce a difference between organizations, markets, and states (Boyer 2004). In this case, network represents one informal way of associating together human agents (Granovetter 1985).
> When (Castells 2000) [sic!] uses the term, the two meanings merge since network becomes a privileged mode of organization thanks to the very extension of information technology. It's also in this sense that Boltanski and Chiapello (2005) take it to define a new trend in the capitalist mode of production."[31]

Such multiplicity of meanings is not limited to the social sciences; the field of literary study similarly has adapted and adjusted the notion of a network in multiple ways to suit whatever specific analysis they wanted to perform.

> "Literary scholars have carried out a similar pattern of projection and re-projection as some adopt the social network from early studies in sociology, while others take an approach founded in linguistics. For example, Murray Pittock applies the 'social network' to argue for ethnic Scottish influence on Lord Byron, while Takeshi Moriyama traces the patterns of aesthetic conversations in Tokugawa-era Japan. [...] This sense of a teeming excess, an unmappable complexity, also undergirds some literary scholars' understanding of recent narrative trends: Rita Barnard argues that the novel *Ghostwritten* and the films *Crash* and *Babel* strive toward a more 'humanist' globalism (209) by conjuring local humanist qualities in a globally-networked context. Her analysis applies the 'network' to characters and their interactions, but Andrew Strombeck takes a different approach. Operating from D.A. Miller's analysis of narration as discursive discipline, Strombeck sees narration *itself* as a network-like system for control and management (283, 289)."[32]

Narratology even considered the application of networks within the structure of literary texts and attempted to use it to describe postmodern narratives. Equally, models based on semiotics and communication employ networks to capture the interaction between mind and text in the reading process.

---

[31] Latour, Bruno. *Reassembling the Social: An Introduction to Actor-Network-Theory.* Oxford: Oxford University Press, 2005. Page 129

[32] Kilgore, Christopher D. "Rhetoric of the Network: Toward a New Metaphor." *Mosaic: a journal for the interdisciplinary study of literature,* vol. 46 no. 4, 2013, p. 37–58. *Project MUSE,* doi:10.1353/mos.2013.0044, Page 39ff

"[...] structuralist narratology has already attempted to map story as assemblages of lines and points, in the kernel-and-satellite model advanced by Gerald Prince (83), and in Emma Kafalenos's conceptual tree-diagrams of causality (7). Communications, semiotic, rhetorical, and cognitive models have attempted in different ways to map the reading process according to a similarly network-friendly system, producing an increasingly nuanced model of the interactions between minds and texts. I would suggest that the texture-map concept should make possible an integrative narratological theory that can portray the spatiotemporal dimensions of story, text, and interpretation, giving even seemingly 'shapeless' postmodern texts a discernable—and analytically transparent—legibility."[33]

Within the context of this research, another notable network approach to literature emerges in the form of Janet Murray's concept of hyperserial. While not directly using the term 'network', hyperserial conceives of a "story web" within a text. Each of these elements contains the potential for a grander engagement with a main narrative or even the creation of a subsequent parallel narrative.

"The compelling spatial reality of the computer will also lead to virtual environments that are extensions of the fictional world. For instance, the admitting station seen in every episode of ER could be presented as a virtual space, allowing viewers to explore it and discover phone messages, patient files, and medical test results, all of which could be used to extend the current storyline of provide hints of future developments. ... In a well-conceived hyperserial, all minor characters would be potential protagonists of their own stories, thus providing alternate threads within the enlarged story web."[34]

While hyperserial helps with the description of singular texts creating a larger whole[35], it does so mainly on an intradiegetic level, considering new technology only in regard to its potential to flesh out otherwise less prominent parts of a world or narrative, but ignoring the text, the audience, and the producers as a potential part of a network. Most hyperserial approaches to creating a larger whole from a collection of singular texts appear to focus solely on characters as possible means of interrelation. While the multiplicity of use hinders a universal definition for 'network', it also highlights the term's potential within the analysis of literature. Aside from allowing a description of relationships on several levels, some scholars argue that modern literature in itself has adapted the notion of networks.

"Jagoda argues that since the 1990s, the network has pervaded television shows, films, video games, and novels. While there were network novels before the 1990s, it was

---

33 Kilgore, Christopher D. "Rhetoric of the Network: Toward a New Metaphor." *Mosaic: a journal for the interdisciplinary study of literature*, vol. 46 no. 4, 2013, p. 37–58. Project MUSE doi:10.1353/mos.2013.0 044, Page 53
34 Quoted in Wolf, Mark J.P. *Building Imaginary Worlds: The Theory of Subcreation*. New York: Routledge, 2012. Page 8.
35 As for example in Johnston, Sarah Iles. "The Greek Mythic Story World." *Arethusa*, vol. 48 no. 3, 2015, p. 283–311. *Project MUSE*, doi:10.1353/are.2015.0008.

during this decade that 'the popularization of the Internet altered the public perception of information technology and transformed networks into an even more prominent metaphor of contemporary life' (Jagoda 43). Scott Selisker similarly notes that much twenty-first-century American literature draws on the network form to explore the infrastructures of the present and as a means to consider 'individual and collective agency, by modeling action through the dynamic networks of characters' interactions' (212)."[36]

The wide range of applications makes the concept of network useful for the research at hand, as it attempts to not only uncover narrative techniques used to create a singular coherent world from generally different narratives but also wants to consider the potential influence of an audience on such a process. Concerning narrative techniques, the universal applicability of network may allow a description of various levels of interrelation. Relationships of different narratives can technically occur on the level of character – the manner in which such networks are most often considered (i.e., Thon's "Transmedia Character: Theory and Analysis") – on the level of events, on the level of ownership (i.e., Harvey's "Taxonomy of Transmedia Storytelling"), on the level of genre, on the level of brand, and so on. While no concept can (and probably should not) describe all these relationships at once, it is helpful to consider the combined influence of these levels on the emergence of something like the MCU. Equally, the impact of an audience or a community engaging with the singular texts and the world created by their interaction can be described via several constellations of engagement.

Aside from the relationship between mind and text mentioned in the quote earlier, theoretically, there are networks of individuals and communities. A definition of network should generally be able to grasp all of these levels without relying on the most rudimentary conception of the term and equally without going through the process of combining and, thereby, muddling several different definitions. One of the most comprehensive approaches to a theoretical and general conception of network comes in the form of Bruno Latour's Actor-Network-Theory, which was adapted to the analysis of literature by Rita Felski. To garner universal applicability, the Actor-Network-Theory breaks down the notion of network into two main components, actors and attachments, collectively considered mediators. Among these components, attachment is regarded as the more important, despite its absence from the name. "So, an actor-network is what is made to act by a large star-shaped web of mediators flowing in and out of it. It is made to exist by its many ties: attachments are first, actors are second."[37] The greater importance of attachment arises from the notion that, essentially, the existence and meaning of everything, according to Actor-Network-Theory, is defined along its relations with other actors.

"In actor-network theory, by contrast, the stress lies on the making of ties rather than the breaking of ties. Attachment is a key concept, defined as an affective state, a social principle, and an ontological fact. That attachment is an affective state means that we

---

36   McBean, Sam. "The Queer Network Novel." *Contemporary Literature*, vol. 60 no. 3, 2019, p. 427–452. Project MUSE muse.jhu.edu/article/763824. Page 431
37   Latour, Bruno. *Reassembling the Social: An Introduction to Actor-Network-Theory*. Oxford: Oxford University Press, 2005. Page 217

cannot 'not care' about certain phenomena, and that such preferences set the tone for our engagement in the world. That it is a social fact means that we no longer organize social analysis around oppositions of structure versus agency or text versus context, but instead trace out the coalescing of actors into constellations, networks, and groupings. And that it is an ontological reality means that our existence is only possible via our reliance on countless coactors. Left to our own devices, we would swiftly sink into the abyss of nonexistence; relations are not just modes of regulation but inescapable conditions of being. 'We need no longer distinguish between the restrained and the liberated,' observes Latour, 'but instead between the well and the poorly attached.' It is not that a Latourian model does not allow for disjuncture, disagreement, or detachment—the opposite is true—but that such acts of disassociation themselves depend on prior ties or bonds. We detach from something because we are more attached to *something else*: even if only to an image of the intellectual as a lonely or embattled figure-in-exile."[38]

Considering that everything finds meaning and definition via its interrelations is particularly useful in evaluating singular texts forming a constellation and creating the sense of a singular world, as the sense of a coherent setting partly arises out of the compatibility and tension between the different representations of an experienced world within a given text. The Actor-Network-Theory (ANT) values attachments as the basis for deriving each element's value within its network. Hereby, this value does not arise out of the static existence of such a relationship but via the assumption that each actor operates as a mediator[39] towards every interrelated element.

> "I would define a good account as one that traces a network. I mean by this word a string of actions where each participant is treated as a full-blown mediator. To put it very simply: A good ANT account is a narrative or a description or a proposition where all the actors do something and don't just sit there. Instead of simply transporting effects without transforming them, each of the points in the text may become a bifurcation, an event, or the origin of a new translation. As soon as actors are treated not as intermediaries but as mediators, they render the movement of the social visible to the reader."[40]

Operating as mediator, each actor within a network necessarily alleviates differences, defines relations, and alters the meaning of all collective actors attached to it. This reinforces the notion that attachments or relations are far more critical in the conception of a network than the actors themselves. "At the most basic level, ANT is a form of relational

---

38 Felski, Rita. "Comparison and Translation: A Perspective from Actor-Network Theory." *Comparative Literature Studies*, vol. 53 no. 4, 2016, p. 747–765. Project MUSE muse.jhu.edu/article/648800, Page 760, original emphasis
39 Latour and Felski discuss at length the process of translation, which is performed by each mediator in the context of a network. As the discussion here is more concerned with the structure used to create and maintain such a network of interrelation and world-building, in contrast to the universal transformation of each text within a network through processes of interaction, I chose to omit any discussion on these processes of translation.
40 Latour, Bruno. *Reassembling the Social: An Introduction to Actor-Network-Theory*. Oxford: Oxford University Press, 2005. Page 128

thinking: one that requires close-up (myopic) investigation, exhaustive (workaholic) description, and close to the ground (trail-sniffing) analysis."[41] While attachments are more important to the Actor-Network-Theory, actors serve as the second vital component of this conception of network. Within this context, the theory itself defines actor in broad terms:

> "What is an actor? For ANT, it is anything that makes a difference. My coffee mug makes a difference in delivering a stimulant to my befogged brain; its handle makes a difference by inviting me to pick it up in certain ways. A rock makes a difference by causing the water running downstream to flow around it rather than over it, while its overhanging side makes a difference in providing shelter for tiny water creatures. 'Actor' thus refers to acting-as-agency, not acting-as-theatrical-performance. Agency, meanwhile, has nothing to do with consciousness, will, or intention (a common source of misunderstandings of ANT), let alone with autonomy or independence; rather, it refers to the coordinated actions that link human and/or nonhuman actors."[42]

Generally, the concept of actor in this context connects directly to the previously mentioned notion of a mediator in the sense that it has an altering function on another actor within the same network. As Felski's examples indicate, the term actor in this instant is not limited to a conscious person or, considering a narrative structure, a character. In essence, actor is not bound to entities usually ascribed some form of conscious agency. Instead, everything with a transformative effect on its environment – meaning other actors in the same network – technically can be an actor.

> "Latour basically enables object-agency by radically disavowing the subject-object dichotomy: We – humans – have never been modern, and thus we have no business claiming an ontological advantage over non-human entities, 'nature', 'objects', or however we wish to call or (sub)divide this 'other' realm. Which is not really another realm at all."[43]

Considering non-conscious objects as actors advances the potential applicability of the notion of network without compromising its definition. In the context of this research, this consideration frees any network drawn between intradiegetic elements from solely focusing on characters, allowing for other elements of setting to influence a process of interrelation. Objects as actors also allow a direct and transformative relation between not only different literary products – i.e., films, novels, comics etc. – but also allow for the inclusion of objects such as merchandise into the potential development of such a network. As such, Actor-Network-Theory derives an understanding of network, which

---

[41] Felski, Rita. "Comparison and Translation: A Perspective from Actor-Network Theory." *Comparative Literature Studies*, vol. 53 no. 4, 2016, p. 747–765. Project MUSE muse.jhu.edu/article/648800, Page 748

[42] Felski, Rita. "Comparison and Translation: A Perspective from Actor-Network Theory." *Comparative Literature Studies*, vol. 53 no. 4, 2016, p. 747–765. Project MUSE muse.jhu.edu/article/648800, Page 748

[43] van Oenen, Gijs. "Interpassive Agency: Engaging Actor-Network-Theory's View on the Agency of Objects." *Theory & Event*, vol. 14 no. 2, 2011. Project MUSE, doi:10.1353/tae.2011.0014.

is composed of two main components: actors and the attachment between actors. In contrast to the node-and-link conception of network, these two components are set in a clear theoretical context. Either part of this conception attempts to perceive a network as a process of mutual mediation in which the interconnection transforms each part of the network itself.

> "What ANT does offer literary studies are new ways of thinking about connectivity. An emphasis on relations is not new in literary studies (which has, over recent decades, challenged the idea of literature's autonomy by variously emphasizing intertextuality, discursive networks, ideology etc.). What is different, however, is ANT's view of these relations: in particular, its emphasis on connection as co-creation rather than as limit or constraint. For ANT, mediation does not subtract from the object but adds to the object; that I discuss Mrs. Dalloway with my fellow students, read articles about it, watch the movie of The Hours, buy a mug emblazoned with a Virginia Woolf quote, has the effect of making the novel more real, not less real."[44]

Within this conception of network, it is essential to note that Actor-Network-Theory does not consider the network itself an object or principle worth of study. Instead, it considers it merely a tool in service of description and analysis. A tool specifically designed to potentially be expansive and inclusive, when necessary, but assumes that every part within the network contains some transformative function.

> "A network, in ANT, does not imply a network-y shape, that is, a web of interconnected horizontal lines. Nor does it have any special affinity with the Internet, computers, or technical networks. Rather, a network simply is an assembly of actors that share information and coordinate action. It has no necessary size, shape, or scale. A network can be made up of soccer players, a ball, the rules of the game, and cheering spectators, or of chemicals, postdocs, hypotheses, and a lab report. At the same time, a network is not so much something we find as something we make; it is the pencil rather than the object drawn; it is a means of checking how much 'energy, movement, and specificity our own reports are able to capture.' Network, in this sense, is shorthand for including as many actors as feasible in our research, the researcher included, and tracing the complexities of their interactions."[45]

As such, all future mentions of network lean on the Actor-Network-Theory approach to the term network, conceiving it as an analytical tool constructed from actors – which are all things that can alter other actors within the network in some way, shape, or form – and the attachments between these actors.

---

44   Felski, Rita. "Comparison and Translation: A Perspective from Actor-Network Theory." *Comparative Literature Studies*, vol. 53 no. 4, 2016, p. 747–765. Project MUSE muse.jhu.edu/article/648800, Page 749ff
45   Felski, Rita. "Comparison and Translation: A Perspective from Actor-Network Theory." *Comparative Literature Studies*, vol. 53 no. 4, 2016, p. 747–765. Project MUSE muse.jhu.edu/article/648800, Page 748ff

1.2 Foundational Theories – The Good, The Bad, and The Ugly

While the emergence and conception of an imaginary world created out of networked texts is relatively new, conceptions concerning the constitution of worlds through fiction and theories on interactions between different elements in such a construction are not. Transmediality, or transmedia storytelling as its notion of practical application, discusses the relationships of separate media in the construction of a coherent world. Deriving from post-structuralism, the theory covers many aspects influencing the construction of a fictional world. In its fluid and all-encompassing view, however, transmediality also lends itself poorly to the systematic deconstruction and understanding of a specific imaginary world, especially when the construction of this world employs a (supposedly) novel approach. Still, current research into any object or expansive narrative structure employing more than one medium or some tangible form of seriality cannot circumvent the use of transmediality. As Linder explains:

> "Although transmediality has always been part of serialization, it has arguably acquired a new-found dominance in contemporary culture, where traditional (and often technological) boundaries between media are rapidly changing and, in some cases, even dissolving."[46]

With this assumed universal presence, basing a model meant to describe the construction of an imaginary world via the networking of different literary products on insights of transmediality makes sense. Hereby, it is necessary to distinguish applicable insights from limiting ones and include a specific view of world creation in fiction.

Jenkins, who originated transmediality in his seminal publication *Convergence Culture*, defines the concept as simply "across media" and as a "way of talking about [media] convergence as a set of cultural practices"[47]. The latter indicates the wide and fluid application of the concept, which grants several understandings of world, world constructions, and its relation to varying parts of media consumption and production. As such, the entire conception of transmediality contains aspects applicable to the evaluation of a world as a network. However, it equally contains elements requiring redefinition as well as elements to be excluded from direct usage. Therefore, the following chapters review tenets of transmediality and related theoretical concepts, evaluating the applicability of their assertion for the theoretical model formulated throughout this paper.

1.2.1 The Good

Attempts at focusing transmedia research on narratives are not new. Most prolific are combinations of transmediality and narratology.

---

[46] Lindner, Christoph. "Foreword". *Serialization in Popular Culture*. Rob Allen and Thijis van den Berg (Ed.). New York: Routledge 2014. page X

[47] http://henryjenkins.org/2011/08/defining_transmedia_further_re.html (retrieved June 29th, 2021)

"Transmedial narratology is premised on the assumption that, although narrative practices in different media share common features insofar as they are all instances of the narrative text type, stories are nonetheless inflected by the constraints and affordances associated with a given medium (e.g., print texts, film, comics and graphic novels etc.). Unlike classical narratology, transmedial narratology disputes the notion that the story level of a narrative remains wholly invariant across shifts of medium. However, it also assumes that stories do have 'gists' that can be remediated more or less fully and recognizably — depending in part on the semiotic properties of the source and target media."[48]

While transmedia narratology acknowledges the interaction between source narrative and target medium, it still assumes an unchangeable essence within a given story. Herman connects the notion mainly to the process of remediation. According to him, transmedia narratology "disputes the notion that the fabula or story level of a narrative (= what is told) remains wholly invariant across shifts of medium (= an aspect of how that "what" is presented)"[49]. Despite this potential for variance, Herman argues that the central core of a story "can be remediated more or less fully and recognizably"[50]. While the approach of transmedia narratology acknowledges variation in narration across media, it underplays the potential for changes within Herman's 'gist'. The continuous addition of narrative and non-narrative material, as well as chains of re-imagination (a re-imagination of a re-imagination of a re-imagination) or remediation, necessarily influence all aspects of a story; even a perceived core cannot remain insulated from a process of constant retelling. Herman's transmedia narratology underestimates the influence of continuous serialization, continued remediation, and narrative expansions, which all may add to the narrative structure in a manner (I would argue) that necessarily alters its perceived core essence. Continuously expanding and re-inventing stories across generations (as in the case of various superhero stories) indicate that within the context of constant recreation, instability is a crucial feature of what is understood as an essential core. A well-documented example is the perceived essence of Superman – the character and aspects surrounding his story. The original conception of Superman published in *Action Comics #1* only had unbelievable strength and could leap 1/8th of a mile. He also lacked most of the now-associated support characters, and instead of the "American Way", the character championed socialist values, supporting striking workers and forcing corrupt mine owners to adhere to regulations. This version, however, differs significantly from how the essence of a Superman story is perceived today. The character's abilities alone have become far more complex; flight, heat vision, x-ray vision, and a slew of other powers are central markers of a Superman narrative. Other characters, places, and concepts are intertwined in any current interpretation, such as The Daily Planet, Jimmy Olsen, Lois Lane, Lana Lang etc. As the Superman story was remediated and re-imagined over decades, its 'gist' changed, taking on, altering, and losing different character-

---

48   Herman David. "Narrative Ways of Worldmaking". *Narratology in the Age of Cross-Disciplinary Narrative Research*. Ed. Sandra Heinen and Roy Sommer. Walter de Gruyter GmbH. Berlin: 2009. 71–87, Page 85
49   Herman, David. *Storytelling and The Science of Mind*. Cambridge: MIT Press, 2013
50   Herman, David. *Storytelling and The Science of Mind*. Cambridge: MIT Press, 2013

istics[51]. Even if we only consider the last 15 years of the character's portrayal, notions of its essence have changed meaningfully. Specifically, the introduction of biological offspring as a part of the essence appears to have become a current fixture[52]. Predictably, Superman story's perceived core essence will further change with upcoming reimaginations and remediations. This alteration of core aspects through constant serialization and chains of re-imagination is part of nearly all long-running superhero characters. While operating with the assumption that these essential cores remain recognizable in their malleability within the context of transference, a better approach for understanding the creation of worlds as well as the expansion of such narratives is to understand such narrative as having a malleable core essence in the constant process of alteration or transformation, due to its essential nature of continual recurrence in ever-new retellings (of itself and within other networked storyworlds) as well as the discourse surrounding it.

Transmediality's view of core and periphery in the formation of stories and world is not limited to a narrative's internal construction and general understanding. While transmedia storytelling generally propagates an egalitarian understanding of the different texts that contribute to a story or world, various scholars of transmediality have recognized some need for a distinctive evaluation of a text's importance. As Mittell has argued:

"Despite the growing ubiquity of transmedia, we need to avoid confusing general transmedia extensions with, the more particular mode of transmedia storytelling. Nearly every media property today offers some transmedia extensions, such as promotional websites, merchandise, or behind-the-scenes materials. These forms can be usefully categorized as *paratexts* in relation to the core text, whether a feature film, video game, or television series."[53]

Transferring Herman's view of transmedia narratology to the evaluations of texts within transmedia products, Mittell essentially realizes a form of hierarchy. Hereby, he determines core texts as the one(s) carrying the actual narrative – the novel, television show, film, comic – and "paratexts that function primarily to hype, promote, and introduce a text [...]"[54]. The core-and-paratext approach reasonably dissolves the assumption that the influence of each text within a transmedia franchise carries the same impact on the formation of a fictional world surrounding it. However, such a simple two-tier system overlooks potential gradations among all texts involved in such a network. Assuming the

---

51   For further information on the history of Superman and the character's development, I advise reading Ian Gordon's *Superman – The Persistence of an American Icon*.
52   Whereas the personality and identity of these offspring seem still very much in flux. Jason White from *Superman Returns* (2006) lacks all personality other than being Superman's son. Jonathan and Jordan Kent from *Superman & Lois* are presented as angsty teens. And Jon Kent from the current DC comic publication appears as a responsible bisexual teenager.
53   Mittell, Jason. "Strategies of Storytelling on Transmedial Television". *Storyworlds across Media*. USA: University of Nebraska Press, 2014. 253–277. Page 254, original emphasis
54   Mittell, Jason. "Strategies of Storytelling on Transmedial Television". *Storyworlds across Media*. USA: University of Nebraska Press, 2014. 253–277. Page 254

perception of a fictional world hinges mainly on its discursive nature – as implied earlier – a potential hierarchy between different core texts may emerge. Hereby, such a hierarchy may arise from the public's awareness of each text and its specific content. Hassler-Forest mentions current developments within the production of popular narratives that equally require a more flexible understanding of a core text.

> "Increasingly, such franchises *no longer revolve around a single central text* with related texts and products relegated to the peripheral status of 'spin-off' or 'merchandise.' Instead, franchises are now often defined by a recognizable central brand (with its associated copyrighted logo), *allowing for an assortment of texts to fulfill different roles in relation to each other.*"[55]

Hassler-Forest points not only toward the possibility of several core texts for a single transmedia franchise but also the potential for each text to fulfill a different function within a central brand. The notion of "an assortment of texts to fulfill different roles in relation to each other" essentially rethinks Mittell's core text as a core network, which contains various 'core' texts under a central brand organizing them. Hereby, the assertion that each text fulfills a different role towards another implies the existence of hierarchy within this network. However, such a hierarchy does not seem absolute or linear as one text at the same time might fulfill the function of a central core text within one relationship but serve in a paratext-like capacity within another. Such a fluid hierarchy is not limited to the core texts in the notion of a transmedia franchise but equally affects Mittell's paratext. Similar to the different core texts, the influence of a singular paratext may rest on the public's awareness of its existence and the existence of its content. While the influence of a trailer or a movie poster on the subsequent engagement with the associated film is inarguable, such an influence is rendered void when nobody perceives the paratext, or it is overshadowed by another text related to the overall franchise. Equally, a paratext does not only stand in some relation to a singular or collection of core texts but also in some relation to other paratexts that share its central brand. While the hierarchy between the presumed core text and paratext appears generally clear, the hierarchy within either group appears somewhat fluid and determined by each text's general influence on the discourse surrounding the specific brand. Generally, transmediality, despite claims of viewing all texts as equal, naturally tends towards acknowledging a hierarchy within the different texts forming a central brand or a transmedia franchise. While overall fluid, due to changing functions towards one another and altering levels of engagement, a universal distinction between some form of core texts and some form of paratexts remains.

Considering Herman's 'gist' and Hassler-Forest's central brand, transmediality implies the existence of an overarching, agreed-upon essence, which later guides the form of a textual manifestation. As already discussed, this essence is not invariant and subject to potential change. More importantly, while guiding any textual form based on it, this

---

55   Hassler- Forest, Dan. "The Walking Dead: Quality Television, Transmedia Serialization and Zombies". *Serialization in Popular Culture*. Ed. Rob Allen and Thijis van den Berg. New York: Routledge, 2014. 91–105. Page 97, my emphasis

essence allows for various expressions in textual form, leading to the creation of several types of texts. This dialectic creates a natural duality to the existence of every fictional world or story: a discursive essence as part of public imagination and a physical manifestation as expressed in textual form. The consideration of literature in this form is not new and has been described by several scholars with a variety of theoretical approaches. Transmediality advances this view through the notion that multiple texts can arise from such an essence and that a singular essence can provide the basis for numerous differing core texts and central brands. In other words, the discursive conception may be applied to the creation of one or more central brands, which in turn potentially create a network of core texts. While the potential for several central brands compounds the complexity of a shifting hierarchy among different texts, this view of the relationship between discursive essence and textual manifestation is still limited because it assumes a singular essential 'gist' instead of considering the potential of multiple essences created as feedback to the multiple textual manifestations. Transmedia storytelling approaches the notion of differing textual manifestations of the same discursive essence in some of its conceptions of storyworld. Mittell points towards the distinction of storyworlds by categorizing different texts based on the same essence as 'What Is' texts and 'What If' texts. Mittell supposes 'What Is' transmedia as follows:

> "'What Is' transmedia seeks to extend the fiction canonically, explaining the universe with coordinated precision and hopefully expanding viewers' understanding and appreciation of the storyworld. This narrative model encourages forensic fandom with the promise of eventual revelations once all the pieces are put together."[56]

Comparatively, he understands 'What If' texts as distinct alternates to an existing storyworld.

> "This approach to transmedia poses hypothetical possibilities rather than canonical certainties, inviting viewers to imagine alternative stories and approaches to storytelling that are distinctly not to be treated as potential canon. The goal for 'What If?' transmedia is to launch off the mothership into parallel dimensions, with connections foregrounding issues of tone, mood, character, or style more than continuing with canonical plots and storyworlds."[57]

While grasping the potential of one essence to beget several alternate storyworlds through different textual manifestations, Mittell's 'What Is'/'What If' distinction focuses on instances in which a clear canonical original is easily determined. The principle, however, proves shortsighted when such a clear hierarchy between the texts is not apparent. Cases of re-imagination – specifically reboots – for example, do not necessarily invite a clear distinction between a canonical original and a 'What If' interpretation. Arguably, audiences who have seen the 1978 television series *Battlestar Galactica* when it originally

---

[56] Mittell, Jason. "Strategies of Storytelling on Transmedial Television". *Storyworlds across Media*. USA: University of Nebraska Press, 2014. 253–277. Page 273

[57] Mittell, Jason. "Strategies of Storytelling on Transmedial Television". *Storyworlds across Media*. USA: University of Nebraska Press, 2014. 253–277. Page 273

aired will rather perceive that version as the canonical original and consider the 2004 series a 'What If' offshoot. Audiences who experience the reboot first may have a different view on the matter.[58] As such, this perception of the creation of multiple storyworlds from the same essence arises dominantly out of the assumption that each narrative has only a singular discursive essence. In his approach, Mittell acknowledges that the distinction between 'What is' and 'What if' "can best be seen as vectors or tendencies rather than as distinct categories, with fluidity and blur between the dual approaches."[59] Without a clear distinction of an essence's different textual interpretations into a 'What Is' or 'What If' category, the potential feedback of each text into the discursive understanding of the essence becomes more complicated, as aspects that were meant to serve as "hypothetical possibilities rather than canonical certainties" suddenly are handled as canonical fiction, "explaining the universe [...] and [...] expanding viewers' understanding and appreciation of the storyworld." The loss of a clear hierarchy between two such interpretations can have two distinctive developments. The 'What If' iteration enters a general discourse as canonical, leading to the adaptation of certain elements into the narrative's perceived essence. Or the 'What If' interpretation is considered a unique storyworld of its own, giving rise to a new 'gist', which may be related and connected to its forbearer, but is generally considered a new essence. Herman's transmedia narratology recognizes how the shift in media, and therefore in the "semiotic environment"[60], also creates different storyworlds even if based on the same essence or 'gist'.

> "Transmedial narratology thus begins with the assumption that, although stories conveyed via different media share common features insofar as they are all instances of the narrative text type, storytelling practices are nonetheless inflected by the constraints and affordances associated with a given semiotic environment. Sets of constraints and affordances interact in multimodal storytelling, or forms of narration that recruit from more than one semiotic channel to evoke storyworlds."[61]

Through the focus on shared core aspects between different narratives, Herman acknowledges the potential emergence of different transmedia storyworlds from the same source. Still, he overlooks the potential effect different "semiotic environments" – which I understand as different media and culture-related potentials to manifest the 'gist' of a narrative – may have on the constitution and development of a discursive essence. In other words, while Herman recognizes that the expression of the same essence through different media may lead to additional, singular storyworlds, he does not discuss the potential of these different storyworlds to either reform the original essence or, more importantly, to create a completely new one, which relates to the 'original' but is distinctive enough to make it an entity of its own. While adaptations of different superhero properties to the medium of film and television potentially provide such an

---

58   Considering the perception of reboots and their relationship with a perceived original, I advise reading Heather Urbanski's *The Science Fiction Reboot*.
59   Mittell, Jason. "Strategies of Storytelling on Transmedial Television". *Storyworlds across Media*. USA: University of Nebraska Press, 2014. 25–277. Page 274
60   Herman, David. *Storytelling and The Science of Mind*. Cambridge: MIT Press, 2013, Page 106
61   Herman, David. *Storytelling and The Science of Mind*. Cambridge: MIT Press, 2013. Page 106

occurrence, as the storyworlds of DC characters in the Arrowverse or diverse Batman films are vastly different from those of their comic counterparts, this aspect is better presented by the Japanese adaptation of the Spider-Man property[62]. In this version, a young motorcycle racer named Takuya Yamashiro sees a space warship fall to Earth. Takuya's father, a space archaeologist, is killed while investigating the spaceship. Trying to find his father, Takuya discovers the dying last warrior of Planet Spider, Garia. He was hunting Prof. Monster and his evil Iron Cross Army. Garia injects Takuya with some of his own blood, which gives Takuya spider-like powers, and gives Takuya a bracelet that activates a spider protector costume, shoots web-lines, and controls his ship (which can also transform into a giant battle robot called "Leopardon"). Using his powers, Spider-Man fights Professor Monster's army and other threats to Earth. The shift in semiotic environment renders the property nearly incompatible with the presumed original, necessarily creating a new discursive essence distinct from the essence usually associated with the traditional Spider-Man format.

As the discussion of Mittell's and Herman's view indicates, the potential existence of multiple worlds from a similar source inherently contains the potential of creating several similar, related essences or 'gists'. Hereby, Mittell's assertion of multiple storyworlds is based on the reinterpretation of a 'gist' to explore alternate versions to a presumed original, and Herman's multiple storyworlds arise from the different potential affordances and possibilities of a 'semiotic environment' created by the individual medium. Somewhat expanding on these views, Ryan and Thon mention the existence of different storyworld types in their potential variety of utilization of media and their possible engagement with the audience.

> "Nowadays we have not only multimodal representations of storyworlds that combine various types of signs and virtual online worlds that wait to be filled with stories by their player citizens but also serial storyworlds that span multiple installments and transmedial storyworlds that are deployed simultaneously across multiple media platforms, resulting in a media landscape in which creators and fans alike constantly expand, revise, and even parody them."[63]

With this approach, they understand storyworld types as a formal expression, meaning that storyworlds may appear in a serial, transmedia, and multimodal formation. The combination of all three views – Mittell, Herman, and Ryan/Thon – implies not only the existence of several worlds but equally hints at a potential direct relation of worlds created from the same essence.

---

62 *Spider-Man (Japanese:* スパイダーマン*).* Created By Shozo Uehara and Susumu Takaku. Toei Company. 1978–1979

63 Ryan, Marie-Laure and Jan-Noel Thon. "Introduction". Storyworlds across Media. USA: University of Nebraska Press, 2014. 1–24. Page 1

1 The Foundation

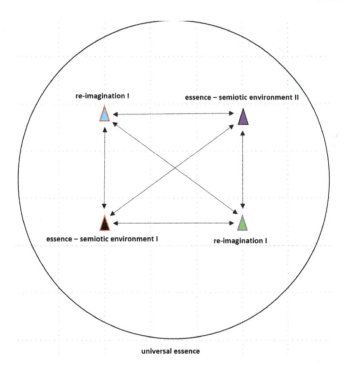

This and all following illustrations were produced by the author.

While, as argued, Mittell's 'What If' approach may express an entirely different version of an already existing textual manifestation, these differing worlds are related through a shared essence. Similarly, according to Herman, due to the difference in 'semiotic environments', the expression of the same essence in two different media creates singular worlds which are equally related. Connecting these conceptions to Ryan and Thon's storyworld types interrelates Herman's and Mittell's view by assuming them as multiple expressions of a singular world. Assuming that "every story has its own storyworld (except in transmedial projects, where the representation of a world is distributed among many different texts of different media)"[64] denotes that in the case of a transmedia storyworld, each expression of a story's 'gist' essentially is the same storyworld. In other words, the textual manifestation of the same story as adaptation in the medium of film and the medium of video games feed into a singular universal storyworld encompassing all elements of either expression. This conception contradicts Herman's and Mittell's approach, which signifies the creation of differing storyworlds due to either the influence of a unique 'semiotic environment', the re-imagination of the story, or potentially the combination of both. However, it is possible to assume that either view is simultaneously accurate. While the different singular textual manifestations create distinct worlds corresponding solely to aspects within that representation, each textual manifestation feeds into an overarching world, which includes and negotiates the elements of all textual representations. This view connects singular worlds directly

---

64   Ryan, Marie-Laure. "Story/World/Media – Tuning the Instruments of a Media-Conscious Narratology". *Storyworlds across Media*. USA: University of Nebraska Press, 2014. 25–49. Page 32

to a universal one, but it equally ties the distinct worlds to one another through their interrelation with a universal concept of their individual form. More importantly, if we previously assumed that each textual manifestation of an essence could create its own individual discursive 'gist' that generally corresponds to the singular world created for it, the universal world corresponds to the first or foundational essence. As such, the discursive essences of the different textual manifestations equally link to one another, existing simultaneously as singular entities and within a universal conception encompassing all their aspects.

The combined view of transmediality and storyworld establishes a general understanding of world creation in particular – and fiction creation on a more universal level – as a relationship between a potential network of discursive 'gists' and a potential network of core texts. Within this context, the discursive network revolves around a central essence, while the network of texts operates with a fluid hierarchy. Within this conception, its discursive nature implies a transformability of the essence. Similarly, the conception of differing core texts or even differing networks of core texts hinges to some degree on the re-imagination of existing material, equally implying a potential for variability. In either case, the alteration requires a human element, which either creates a re-imagination or participates in the discourses surrounding them. Different approaches to transmediality are conscious of the complex interaction between texts, their producers, and active participants. Bringing up transmediality's need to acknowledge Herman's different 'semiotic environments' in an attempt to remain 'media-conscious', Stein and Thon indicate a general tendency of theoretical approaches such as transmedia storytelling to include elements outside the actual text.

> "One way or another, though, in order to remain 'media-conscious,' such a transmedial narratology would still have to acknowledge both similarities and differences in the ways in which conventionally distinct media such as literary texts, films, or comics narrate. Moreover, it should be noted that current narratological practice tends to be methodologically inclusive insofar as exploring narrative representations 'beyond the literary text' often goes hand in hand with a particular attention to narrative's cultural and historical contexts as well as a concern for the cognitive processes involved in making narrative meaning."[65]

While "cultural and historical contexts as well as a concern for the cognitive processes" each are valid and important fields of concern in the comprehension and interpretation of literary texts on their own, combining these aspects in a conception of audience and producer appears more useful in the development of a structural model. Several theoretical fields concerned with the research of literary texts assume that producers inherently include cultural and historical assumptions in the formation of any textual manifestation of an essence. Equally, similar notions exist for the evaluation of an audience's interpretation of any given text. Within these fields, research is usually conducted to unearth

---

65 Stein, Daniel and Jan-Noel Thon. "Introduction: From Comic Strips to Graphic Novels". *From Comic Strips to Graphic Novels*. Göttingen: De Gruyter, 2013. 1–26. Page 1

hidden elements of culture or history or to discuss interesting misappropriation or misinterpretation of texts due to differing contexts between producer and audience. Rather concerned with the relationship between text and discourse, a closer look at how transmedia storytelling perceives an ideal and functional relationship between these three elements – producer, text, and audience – appears more fruitful than focusing on singular contexts. In his approach towards a transmedia understanding of fictionality, Zipfel ties producer and audience engagement with a text as intermediary to institutionalized practices.

> "'An institutional practice [...] is *constituted* by a set of conventions and concepts which both regulate and *define* the actions and products involved in the practice. [...] An institution, in the relevant sense, is a rule-governed practice which makes possible certain (institutional) actions which are defined by the rules of the practice and which could not exist as such without those rules' (256, original emphases). Lamarque and Olsen also argue that 'any attempt to explain how fictive stories are told and enjoyed in a community, without deceit, without mistaken inference, and without inappropriate response, seems inevitably to require reference to co-operative, mutually recognized, conventions' (37)".[66]

As Lamarque and Olsen point out, any story requires some convention or mutual agreement to function. Zipfel further argues that the whole notion of fictionality is not only based on such an institutionalized practice but that both sides – producer and audience – rely on these conventions to fulfill the narrative effect of a story.

> "Dealing with fictional works thus involves some kind of mutual agreement between producers and audiences. Or, to put it more precisely, the specific attitude of audiences is triggered because they recognize the intentions of the producers that the audience should adopt a fictionspecific attitude, that is, the attitude that has been outlined in what has been said about games of make-believe. Moreover, the general make believe conventions that define the institutional practice of fiction in a transmedial understanding can be considered as a frame that allows for fiction-specific representational conventions-that is, conventions that regard the particular ways in which fictional worlds can be presented in a specific art form or medium."[67]

Aside from providing the framework for a fictional interaction and how specific media may present a textual manifestation, such a mutual agreement may also extend to any type of world or worlds employed in the representation of an essence. In other words, institutionalized practices in the production of fiction also determine if an essence may manifest in several different 'What If' versions and what form these may take. Equally, an unspoken mutual agreement creates a framework that governs if an essence may manifest in the form of a serial, a transmedia, or even only a singular world. As such, it also

---

[66] Zipfel, Frank. "Fiction Across Media: Towards a Transmedial Conception of Fictionality". *Storyworlds across Media*. USA: University of Nebraska Press, 2014. 103–125. Page 108

[67] Zipfel, Frank. "Fiction Across Media: Towards a Transmedial Conception of Fictionality". *Storyworlds across Media*. USA: University of Nebraska Press, 2014. 103–125. Page 108

reasonably determines which aspects of a textual manifestation feed back into the overall essence and which remains a sole part of a singular, specific essence. As Zipfel points out, all formal aspects potentially governed by such a mutual agreement hinge on an audience's recognition of a producer's intention. As such, the producer's initial ability to create any imaginable textual manifestation relates to some degree to the ability to trigger a "specific attitude" in the audience. Audiences' recognition of the producer's intention initiates the mutual agreement or, more precisely, gives an audience a chance to decide if they want to engage with the proposed framework. While such a step is essential concerning fictionality in general and the engagement of specific genres and re-mediations in particular, it bears even more weight regarding a serial or transmedia representation. In the former case, the producer's intention primes an audience for genre- or media-specific aspects within the textual manifestations of an essence. The film *Pride + Prejudice + Zombies*[68], for example, invokes solely by its title a parody-oriented reinterpretation of Jane Austen's novel, which should contain – due to the mention of zombies – aspects of horror and post-apocalyptic fiction. However, while the producer's intention in such a case prepares an audience to expect the use of dim lighting, an apocalyptic aesthetic of Victorian England, and fantastical combat combined with a generally known 'gist' of *Pride and Prejudice*, it still only projects the expected engagement with one film. In case of serial or transmedia storytelling, the producers' intention necessarily includes a projected expectation for audiences to engage with several different texts or even several different types of text, meaning that, in addition to a mindset, the producers' intent broadcasts some need for the audience to engage with several different texts, potentially across several different media. Superhero comics carry such an expectation, as singular issues usually relate to others within the same series, and singular series in some form relate to others within a larger world. Quintessentially, the producers' intent weighs heavier in case of transmedia and serial storytelling as it denotes a more significant effort on the side of the audience. As such, the producers' ability to manifest an essence into a textual form of their choosing partly comes with the responsibility of projecting the correct attitude the audience must take to engage with this specific interpretation. If a potential audience participates in this mutual agreement, it acknowledges not only the producer's intention but also the producer's authority to imagine, add, subtract, and alter aspects of a 'gist' in their textual manifestations, as the projected intention creates some range of expectations such alterations may take. However, while audiences need to accept the producer's authority in forming a textual manifestation, they serve as gatekeepers towards the creation and alteration of any part of an essence. Audiences' gatekeeping position does not arise out of the audience's evaluation of the textual manifestation's perceived quality. Instead, it arises out of acknowledging any of the text's presented aspects as a current definitive form of the associated essence. In other words, audiences constantly re-invoke certain textual interpretations of an essence, thereby gradually determining a new definite state of that essence. As these interpretations regularly emerge in discourse, they gradually become part of the 'gist' of that particular story. The entire notion here goes back to Barthes's idea that a form of stereotypical knowledge created through

---

[68] *Pride + Prejudice + Zombies*. Directed by Burr Steers. Lionsgate. 2016

1 The Foundation 47

the most current discourse dominates the audience's understanding of what is true for a specific narrative. Herman explains Barthes's principle:

> "For Barthes (1966/1977), people's stereotypical knowledge about the world allows them to chunk narrative discourse into action-sequences; these sequences are elements of a broader experiential repertoire based on recurrent patterns of behavior (*quest, betrayal, revenge* etc.). Hence, action-sequences afford heuristics for interpreting the conduct of narrative agents, whose doings trigger the inference that they are engaged in some culturally salient behavioral pattern or another."[69]

Within this frame of thinking, textual manifestations offer additions or alterations to the current discourse surrounding a narrative, allowing for the potential emergence of new "stereotypical knowledge" of a narrative. However, the audience determines if and in what form new "stereotypical knowledges" emerges from a textual manifestation by deciding which aspects of the new textual manifestations warrant recurring repetition. As such, the audience takes on the role of a managing force in the overall formation of worlds, as any following textual manifestation engages with the most recent discourse. Within the frame of transmedia storytelling, Harvey also grants the audiences such a position.

> "What differentiates varieties of transmedia storytelling from one another is the extent to which such consistency is managed by the owners of the property in question and by other active agents in the transmedial process. Crucial to these processes are the relative power of the various active agents involved in the transmedia storytelling process to deploy, erase, or otherwise alter existing world-internal elements of the franchise in question."[70]

Harvey's focus on active agents – or Jenkins's focus on *participatory culture* – is characteristic for transmedia research. Active audiences[71], which make their opinions known via various channels accessible these days, are an influencing factor as their specific contribution to the overall discourse often carries further than that of other audiences. However, this focus on audiences that directly engage with producers or every aspect of a world underplays the potential influence of 'passive agents'. Harvey and Jenkins determine an audience's power in the formation of a narrative by its active contribution to the narrative and its structure through processes like fan fiction, message boards, and other forms of direct engagement. While I do not want to downplay the potential of direct engagement, this view diminishes an audience's constant repetition of an essence's aspects without the deep investment of time and effort inherent to members of a *participatory*

---

[69]   Herman, David. *Storytelling and The Science of Mind*. Cambridge: MIT Press, 2013, Page 124
[70]   Harvey, Colin. *Fantastic Transmedia*. London: Palgrave Macmillian, 2015, Page 279
[71]   I am aware that Charlotte Brunsdon and David Morley developed the same term to describe an audience's ability to create their own meaning when engaging with a television program. A principal Morley discusses in *Television, Audiences, and Cultural Studies* (1992). This use of the term, however, bears no relation to Brunsdon and Morley's usage. Instead, it is meant to provide a median between Harvey's 'active agent', presumably an individual, and Jenkins's *participatory culture*, presumably the entire culture surrounding a franchise, as an active group engaged with a franchise.

culture. True and truly informed fans of the *Star Wars* franchise may know that Princess Leia Organa is a force wielder (as implied in *The Empire Strikes Back*[72] and mentioned in *Return of the Jedi*[73]) who trained under her brother's tutelage in the novels of the expanded universe. However, this notion never entered the wider discourse surrounding the Star Wars narrative, leaving a mainstream audience bewildered when the character wields this mystical power in *The Last Jedi*[74]. While an active audience operated with an essence in which far more aspects of different textual manifestations have taken hold, a wider passive audience, meaning one that had interacted mainly with the most well-known core texts and only had singular opportunistic discussions about the material, operated with a less defined, but equally definitive, essence of the same world. As such, the audience's influence is not limited to the direct engagement of its 'active agents' but equally does not operate as a central monolith. Instead, the diversity within an audience creates and supports the network of different essences of a singular story, as each audience member operates with a different discourse concerning the same essence. In other words, because of their different levels of engagement, the different audiences form different discourses and essences concerning properties like Star Wars. Problematic engagements with textual manifestations, as described earlier, arise because the different audiences each bring only their own essence to a textual manifestation. Concerned dominantly with an active audience from a *participatory culture*, transmediality does not consider the existence of several potentially competing discourses surrounding a singular storyworld created by different types of audiences. Instead, it approaches mismatches in engagement via audiences' degrees of knowledge. As Kukkonen points out in her description of comic book storytelling: "When readers imagine a storyworld – its setting, characters, and events – the fictive text elicits meaning-making processes that draw on readers' experience, their knowledge about the actual world, and their knowledge about contexts of relevance in cultural memory."[75] Within this context, this experience includes their general knowledge surrounding the textual manifestations of larger franchises. Jenkins already spoke about the establishment of specific knowledge in relation to a franchise and the interaction among fans concerning the dissemination and stabilization of such information. Because Jenkin's approach focuses on fan culture and fan interaction, he describes the process as 'knowledge communities' in *Convergence Culture*[76]. Focusing on fan cultures requires no gradation of these 'knowledge communities', merely a gradation of knowledge among participants. When we, however, consider the potential of multiple discourses, which may not only contain different degrees, but different types of knowledge, the notion of a gradation of knowledge among 'knowledge communities' necessarily turns into different types of 'knowledge communities'. Hereby, these different types of audiences

---

[72] *The Empire Strikes Back*. Directed by Irvin Kershner. Performances by Carrie Fisher, Harrison Ford, and Mark Hamil. Lucasfilm Ltd. 1980

[73] *Return of the Jedi*. Directed by Richard Marquand. Performances by Carrie Fisher, Harrison Ford, and Mark Hamil. Lucasfilm Ltd. 1983

[74] *Star Wars: The Last Jedi*. Directed by Rian Johnson. Performances by Carrie Fisher, Adam Driver, and Mark Hamil. Lucasfilm Ltd. 2017

[75] Kukkonen, Karin. *Studying Comics and Graphic Novels*. Singapore: Wiley Blackwell, 2013, Page 105

[76] Jenkins, Henry. *Convergence Culture*. New York: New York University Press, 2006

necessarily connect to the different discourses surrounding a narrative, leaving a transmedia approach with several audience types.

At this point, research in the field of transmediality introduced the conceptual idea that narratives are not confined to the medium or frame of their original representation, opening the door to a view that allows for a complex understanding of the interrelation of discourses, audience types, and textual manifestations. Therefore, in this view, narratives exist as two associated networks – a network of core texts and a network of their associated essences or 'gists' – as each text within a network necessarily creates a discursive essence of itself. The network of essences additionally is encompassed by a metadiscourse of the singular conceptions of the same narrative. Each existing discourse technically denotes the existence of several associated audience types with varying degrees and types of knowledge and experience. The combination of these principles generates the general foundation for understanding narratives with multiple texts and potentially multiple discourses. Hereby, transmediality focuses on the notion of a multi-text storyworld with a central text but does not consider a world created through the interaction of several diverse core texts. Even the network of core texts developed in this discussion arises from various interpretations of the same source material, meaning, for example, the relationship of the different iterations of Batman throughout the decades. However, transmediality does not present the notion of core texts from multiple sources forming an overarching storyworld, as the worlds created by variations of the superhero genre. While the conceptions developed in this chapter provide a good foundation for developing a model to grasp the creation of an imaginary world through a network of texts, it is still necessary to disregard some aspects of transmediality before pursuing such a model.

1.2.2 The Bad

As discussed in the previous chapter, transmediality generally holds an egalitarian perspective on media, texts, and discourses included in the formation of a world or even a narrative. In other words, transmedia storytelling assumes that all parts of a transmedia narrative, without regard to the media relation or narrative complexity, hold similar levels of influence on the process of world-building. While some researchers – specifically the ones quoted previously – acknowledge that this idea represents idealized circumstances and countered this notion, common transmedia storytelling practice and theory neglect the influence of perceived hierarchies on a narrative's expansion, changes, and alteration. However, outside of proving impractical in application, this view contradicts the general reality of production. In his essay on transmedia television, Mittell discusses this very problem.

> "This definition of transmedia storytelling problematizes the hierarchy between text and paratext, for in the most ideally balanced example, all texts would be equally weighted rather than having one being privileged as 'text' while others serve as supporting 'paratexts.' However, in the high-stakes industry of commercial television, the financial realities demand that the core medium of any franchise be identified and privileged, typically emphasizing the more traditional television form over newer modes of online textuality. Thus in understanding transmedia television, we can

identify the originating television series as the core text with transmedia extensions serving as paratexts."[77]

While he limits his distinction to two levels, a core text and a paratext, Mittell points out that the economic realities of literature production do not allow for the assumption of an egalitarian view of different texts. As the textual manifestation in some media is far more costly than in others, attempts at getting a return-on-investment lead to a greater effort on the producers' side to make such an expensive production an essential text within a transmedia franchise. In other words, an expensive film will entice its producer to market it aggressively in an attempt to reach a wider audience. As a wider audience consumes it, the film's likelihood of becoming an essential or core text in a transmedia construction is exponentially higher, as it is part of a wider discourse. A comic book, in contrast – as an example of a less expensively produced medium – does not induce the same effort in marketing, as it can generate its return on investment on a far narrower audience, therefore limiting its chance to influence the larger discourse in the same manner as a film would. Instead, such texts as comics remain the dominant source for a specialized fan base. The "financial realities" mentioned here not only influence the focus and means of production but equally have bearing on the audiences' side. As Jenkins pointed out in *Convergence Culture* and *Textual Poachers*, the control of transmedia narratives is not purely dependent on a producing entity. Audiences, through a form of selective consumption, influence the general development of such narratives. While personal interest guides this selective consumption, the range and potential of economic access necessarily plays a part in the engagement with different transmedia texts.

> "We are confronted with all sorts of images (posters, computer games, and video-screens), as well as social and economic artifacts (the choice of films offered and the pricing strategy for tickets and refreshments). These do not simply provide context for the film itself; they take part in the constitution of the medium of film as we understand it in the United States today."[78]

Bolter and Grusin argue here that the constitution of a medium does not solely lie in the elements within the medium but equally in its context. Considering the economic context, each medium within a transmedia interaction also alters its relationship with other media by its accessibility and form of accessibility to specific audiences. The initial characteristic naturally is the cost of engagement. Gaining access to a textual manifestation is associated with some form of monetary effort. Hereby, this cost is not necessarily limited to accessing the text itself. As the previous quote indicates, refreshments are a social artifact of the constitution of a film and, therefore, may increase its economic barrier, as such a purchase may be socially expected. While access to a film is not limited to the social event of going to the cinema, other means to view a film usually rely on a pre-established infrastructure. In other words, while an audience could engage with a

---

[77] Mittell, Jason. "Strategies of Storytelling on Transmedial Television". *Storyworlds across Media*. USA: University of Nebraska Press, 2014. 253–277. Page 255
[78] Bolter, Jay-David and Richard Grusin. *Remediation: Understanding New Media*. Cambridge: The MIT Press, 1999. Page 65

film at home, this type of engagement requires a personal television and some means of obtaining the film, either by a streaming service or via a DVD. The use of either option requires the existence of another prerequisite in the form of internet access or an associated playing device. Each of these requirements necessarily create some form of economic barrier, which an audience has to overcome to partake in the consumption of a text and its subsequent discourse. The differing accessibilities of each medium create a necessary hierarchy between the different textual forms. However, assuming this hierarchy solely relates to the collected cost required to access each medium is short-sighted, as the nature of these costs is different between media. For example, purchasing an internet connection, a smart television, and access to a streaming service is more expensive than purchasing a movie ticket. Still, the previous expense provides constant access to a library of content, while the latter offers a one-off experience. Such a distinction within the conception of world constructed from several core texts implies a greater likelihood of further engagement with other texts broadcasted across the same infrastructure. In other words, an audience that already has established the necessary infrastructure to engage with texts from a specific medium is likelier to engage with other texts in the same medium, as there is a 'more direct line' between textual manifestation and audience. Depending on cultural values and general social assumptions, these types of access may also automatically denote the potential size of an audience. These distinctions may appear redundant in the case of films, as most films initially released for cinema eventually make their way to a streaming platform and/or onto a physical recording medium. However, these considerations influence the relationship between all types of media. Gamers have the necessary equipment to engage with a textual manifestation that takes the form of a video game, while non-gamers are less likely to have such an infrastructure in place. The classic comic book reader will have a designated distributor (usually a comic book shop) that funnels the singular issues of different series on the day of publication towards them. In contrast, somebody without this resource will have to expend additional effort to find the comic that expands on a movie. As such, audiences will tend to engage with a medium they already can access or have a system in place to access. This tendency is not limited to economic considerations but is likely compounded by social reality and skills developed through habit. Becoming a voracious reader, after all, partly hinges on a social environment that supports the constant consumption of novels (or at least does not dissuade the behavior) and the ability to read for hours regularly. Conversely, having such a social environment and reading ability likely leads to the consumption of novels as a preferred medium. According to Harvey's recount of Beddows's research into the transmedia engagement with the television series *Buffy – The Vampire Slayer*, the tendency to remain with the initial medium emerges within her initial interviews.

> "Beddows draws upon her own research and that of Elizabeth Evans's into *Spooks* transmedia to suggest that 'consumers may not be as comfortable about shifting their consumption patterns across media as traditional theories of transmedia storytelling would suggest', positing an inevitable shift in tone as a concomitant effect of moving between different media platforms (2010:147). For instance, she cites one of her participants, Jeremy 10, as experiencing difficulties when reading *Buffy* novels, the

interviewee suggesting that the problem might lie in the conversion of inherently visual material into prose (2010:147)."[79]

The difficulty in shifting from one mode of communication to another appears as a natural conclusion of a process of habitual engagement. The economic and social means to engage regularly with a specific medium arguably teaches and solidifies an individual's ability to decode and evaluate a medium's storytelling pattern. As such, audiences habitually engaging with a particular narrative in a specific medium may have some difficulty rethinking a familiar storytelling pattern into a different one. Beddows's suggestion that a world or narrative may be inherently tied to a medium's mode of representation, as *Buffy – The Vampire Slayer* is considered "inherently visual material", creates another barrier in an egalitarian view of media. Assuming the essence or 'gist' of a narrative is formed via a discourse sparked or influenced by its textual manifestation, it is reasonable to assume that this medium's modes of communication affect the definite characteristics of that very narrative. In other words, when a narrative initially emerges in a visual form, visual components will most likely define some of its essence's presumably fixed characteristics. As such, every transposition of a narrative into another medium requires some form of translation, which necessarily invokes the shift in tone mentioned by Beddow[80]. Audiences who have mentally formed a definitive essence of the narrative may not be able to reconcile a new version containing all the necessary changes required by the storytelling patterns of a different medium. While this view does not exclude the possibility of transmedia extension – as such extensions do exist – it does create a venue of likelihood for transmedia expansion. Harvey points out that a section of the (fan) audience will engage with all transmedia elements of a franchise, circumventing such problems and limitations.

> "My own research suggests that attitudes and motivations amongst those who *do* wish to engage with transmedia material differ considerably. One fan relates how he or she isn't 'the biggest fan of reading, but really wants to continue Buffy', so chose to buy the motion-comic version of Season 8 (buffffy 2013). Another fan provides a list of important canonical developments in the comic series to assist other 'uninformed' fans who don't wish to read the comics (nerd4hire 2007)."[81]

The existence of such an audience and their willingness to engage with every material form of a franchise explains transmediality's assertion that all media in a transmedia expansion are equally meaningful. Focusing on members of Jenkins' *participatory culture*, which presumably makes every attempt to engage with every material form of their favorite franchise, automatically compensates for any barrier from previously described economic, social, and habitual contexts. The removal of such barriers allows for the evaluation of each part of a transmedia franchise as equally impactful and meaningful in the formation of a world or any other aspect of a transmedia franchise. However, while this

---

79   Harvey, Colin. *Fantastic Transmedia*. London: Palgrave Macmillian, 2015, p.128ff
80   Concerning the specific problems and changes such 'translations' from one medium to another could invoke, I advise reading Linda Hutcheon's *A Theory of Adaptation*.
81   Harvey, Colin. *Fantastic Transmedia*. London: Palgrave Macmillian, 2015, p.129, original emphasis

view of media may be valid for a *participatory culture* or Harvey's 'active agent', it is questionable to assume that every narrative's commercial success and cultural impact solely hinges on this type of audience.

Comparatively expensive media cannot solely rely on a specialized audience, as their production cost requires a broad level of engagement to generate a necessary return on investment. Equally, the transference of specific symbols to a larger culture requires constant repetition within a wider discourse, meaning that only in cases in which a narrative-specific *participatory culture* dominated or, at least, intersected with every other non-related discourse such a transference could occur. A singular specific media iteration of a narrative is more likely to engage a broader audience, which includes a *participatory culture* but does not solely consist of one. This wider audience then carries such specific symbols through discourse into the larger culture. While the existence of an active audience fuels and commercially justifies a transmedia expansion, its very tendency to overcome barriers between different media renders it immaterial for the evaluation of such an expansion. The willingness to engage with any material form of a franchise firmly places any decision concerning that expansion in the hands of an associated producer. A passive audience – in this instance, meaning one that is interested in engaging with the meaningful elements of a transmedia franchise but unwilling to expend undue effort towards that end – may influence the course of such transmedia expansions by different media's ability to cater to their already existing social, economic, and habitual contexts. In other words, the likelihood of a passive audience engaging with the transmedia expansion increases with a presumed similarity between the perceived inherent medium and the medium of its transmedia proliferation. Assuming a film as the perceived inherent medium, the barrier to a television series as a medium of expansion appears the lowest, as a television series operates with mostly the same modes of communication, requires one of the infrastructures by which film is also accessible (for example a streaming service), and both hold a similar social standing. Comics and video games have a lower likelihood of engaging a passive audience as a means of expansion in such an instance. Video games can adapt a film's visual and sound components. Still, these necessarily have to be altered into some form of animation to fit the interactive nature of a computer game. The game's interactive manner of engaging an audience equally demands a different infrastructure. As discussed earlier, comics also require a different infrastructure, but the difference in modalities has a more significant impact. While comics may adapt some of the visual characteristics of film, the medium requires their transfer into a drawn form. In contrast to video games, which can counter the shift to animation through the inclusion of other modes related to film, such as dialogue, sound effects, music, and editing, comics have to translate such effects into the modes of comic narration, such as panel structure, written dialogue, and onomatopoeia. Additionally, both media operate with a different social context than film and television series. While such considerations will not dominate the process of transmedia expansion in the same manner an existing infrastructure, viable return on investment outside of its transmedia function, and cost of production does, the tendency of a passive audience to engage with the more familiar over the completely new does have some bearing on the expansion of a world across media. A tendency to consume the same or similar media indicates that audiences also rather pull the material for a unified world created through the interrelation of different texts from a collection of comparable outlets. Such a preference does not preclude that an audience may engage with a franchise transmedially when the content evokes enough interest to warrant the effort. Still, it indicates that a network of texts spread across different media is more likely to engage a broader audience when the various media within this process dominantly share more similarities than differences.

Dissolving the presumed egalitarian relationship between different media and assuming a fluid hierarchy based on the audience's means of engagement, the producer's reasonable interest, and the dominantly perceived essence of the narrative allows for a more precise evaluation of the potential function of different textual manifestations within a network of texts creating a world. Such an evaluation, however, is not only determined by the medium but equally by a text's function within the broader construction of a world. Transmediality and storyworld assume that every text within a transmedia expansion, by its nature, functions as a fully narrative text, meaning that it naturally contains an exposition of setting – characters and places – and some form of plot – actions and events. However, the creation of a world may rely on non-narrative texts, which in this instance refers to texts that contain descriptive or expositive elements but lack the component of plot. The term non-narrative by no means assumes that these descriptive aspects are not part of narrativity. Instead, it highlights the difference between actions/events, which may alter the world, and characters/places, which collectively create a coherent space for these events to occur. Both are crucial elements to a world's creation, coherence, and change.

> "The commonsense notion of *storytelling* assumes the centrality of narrative events, where a story consists of 'what happens.' Certainly, events are crucial ingredients of any story, but a narrative also comprises two additional components that are crucial to transmedia storytelling – characters and settings. A television series works to create a sustained narrative setting, populated by a consistent set of characters who experience a chain of events, with all three factors combining to forge a coherent storyworld. A primary feature of serialized television is that these facets are cumulative and consistent in the storyworld, with everything that happens and everyone we see as a part of this persistent narrative universe. Such cumulative persistence is one of the chief ways that serial storytelling is defined against episodic television."[82]

While Mittell highlights the importance of a setting for a world's consistency, coherence, and persistence, he only hints at the role of actions and events for its alteration. This distinction of setting as the element of consistency and coherence as well as event as a catalyst for changes within a serial narrative helps to understand and better evaluate the mechanics governing transmedia and non-transmedia worlds. However, to that end, such a concept has to engage with the general understanding of worlds as a narrative. Ryan describes a "narratological concept of storyworld" by pointing out two specific characteristics.

---

[82] Mittell, Jason. "Strategies of Storytelling on Transmedial Television". *Storyworlds across Media*. USA: University of Nebraska Press, 2014. 253–277. Page 256

"First, it is something projected by individual texts, and not by the entire work of an author, so that every story has its own storyworld (except in transmedial projects, where the representation of a world is distributed among many different texts of different media). Second (and this point may seem obvious), it requires narrative content, so the applicability of the concept of storyworld to lyric poetry is questionable."[83]

The previously presented arguments on the limitations of transmediality's media-focus also advance Ryan's view of transmedia storyworlds. A world not only can comprise several texts from the same medium, but considering the previously discussed social, economic, and habitual context, presumably is more likely to exist in a mono-media form over a transmedia one, as audiences are more likely to engage with a network of texts from the same medium. Every serialized single media product (comics, book series, television) provides proof of the possibility for a non-transmedial, multi-text world. Even if the episodes of these series are not considered singular texts of their own, the existence of film series and spin-offs proves the potential for the existence of a single world in multiple texts from the same medium. Equally, not every story necessarily has a world of its own, as the overall concept of the superhero genre is a singular world in which multiple different stories occur. Even if superhero comics potentially provide the best counterexample, the general assertion that different texts create a unified world in which a multitude of stories take place includes phenomena such as the previously mentioned spin-offs. A storyworld neither has to be told transmedially nor through a singular work. Concerning Ryan's second characteristic, the previous assertion that narrativity contains two essential components creates the need to add the word 'potential' to the definition. A world does not require narrative content, but "[…] it requires" the potential for "narrative content […]"[84].

This alteration might appear inconsequential concerning worlds from inherently narrative products like novels or films because common perception assumes that literary products do not just give us descriptions of a world without any actions. However, they actually do. With the advent of expansive world video games like *World of Warcraft* and world-oriented franchises like *Star Wars*, *Star Trek*, and *Harry Potter*, a continuous number of non-narrative literary products describe or advance the setting of an existing world without employing a full narrative. Products like *Fantastic Beasts and Where to Find Them*[85] (the book, not the film), *Star Trek: Shipyards*[86], or *Star Wars: Galactic Atlas*[87] are not narrative in the sense that their primary purpose is descriptive. They describe areas, animals, or other elements of a world but do not convey actions or events that change its current perceived status. They might, however, include explanations of events that inform how the current status of a world came to be. The distinction between narrative products

---

[83] Ryan, Marie-Laure. "Story/World/Media – Tuning the Instruments of a Media-Conscious Narratology". *Storyworlds across Media*. USA: University of Nebraska Press, 2014. 25–49. Page 32
[84] Ryan, Marie-Laure. "Story/World/Media – Tuning the Instruments of a Media-Conscious Narratology". *Storyworlds across Media*. USA: University of Nebraska Press, 2014. 25–49. Page 32
[85] Rowling, Joanne. *Fantastic Beasts and Where to Find Them*. London: Arthur A. Levine Books, 2001.ß
[86] Robinson, Ben and Marcus Riley. Star Trek Shipyards: 2294 to the Future – The Encyclopedia of Starfleet Ships. Hero collector, 2021
[87] McDonagh, Tim. *Star Wars: Galactic Atlas*. Egmont UK Limited, 2016

altering the current state of the world and elements that are mainly descriptive is of even more relevance for literary products with the purpose of providing merely a setting for participants to create their own narrative. While fan fiction is proof that popular literature fulfills this function, Pen&Paper Roleplaying Games, like *Dungeons&Dragons*, *Shadowrun*, and *Das Schwarze Auge*, mainly exist as descriptive literary products with the potential for a narrative, because they serve as the basis for a game of make-believe in which players can freely create their own story within and for a given world. By releasing material merely describing new surroundings, backstory, or characters, a literary product may only add to a world without altering the existing setting. Adding specific actions or events then fashion a plot within this setting, whoever provides them. Hereby, these actions and events, in addition to creating the plot, potentially alter the state of the overall world via their impact on different aspects of the setting. Obi-wan revealing to Luke that Leia is his sister in *Return of the Jedi*[88], for example, fundamentally alters the relationship between the two characters. A more obvious example may be the death and, therefore, subsequent removal of a character from the current iteration of a world.

While the potential for a literary product to function solely as a means of exposition and without the inclusion of any action or event does occur, the reverse, meaning a literary product without the element of description, appears unlikely, as the potential for actions is dependent on the existence of characters to perform such actions as well as characters and objects actions can be performed upon. As true as this relationship between setting and action is, it may be helpful to consider the function of some literary products as dominantly providing actions concerning their influence on a world. Every literary product requires some form of exposition to establish its setting for the overall plot. However, in the context of a world with several texts, such an exposition potentially only re-iterates an already established setting without adding any meaningful new aspect. While such a re-iteration is important for the narrative at hand, and constant repetition solidifies the conception of a specific setting, this does not add any new setting to the overall world. Within an understanding of a world's establishment and development, the repetition of an already established description, therefore, is of lesser importance in relation to the greater whole. This view allows for singular literary products within an established world to function as a vessel of pure action, in the sense that their impact on the world lies with the alteration of parts of the established setting in contrast to the creation of a new one. Considering television series with an overarching plot and generally stable setting, singular episodes may fulfill such a function. The first few episodes of *Buffy – The Vampire Slayer*'s fifth season, for example, do not introduce new elements to the overall setting. The exposition of all episodes outside the first, which establishes the characters' new normal after Buffy's death in the previous season, is generally limited to the current threat of the week. Otherwise, the episodes operate dominantly with the established setting – primarily characters – and alter these through singular actions, which form plots. As such, while containing some necessary exposition concerning world establishment and development, these texts rather hold a transformative function. A similar observation could probably be made concerning most series with a generally stable setting and

---

[88] *Return of the Jedi*. Directed by Richard Marquand. Performances by Carrie Fisher, Harrison Ford, and Mark Hamil. Lucasfilm Ltd. 1983

overarching plot, as most plot structures focus on the effect of action over introducing new elements toward their end. Pen & Paper roleplaying games mostly release material that merely serves the expansion of a world by extending its setting; most episodes of a series alter the world through the application of actions and events. These examples, of course, provide an extreme illustration for such a separation of setting and plot. Literary products will usually contain both elements to generate a functioning narrative. However, the distinction provides an important indication regarding the influence of singular literary products for the establishment and development of a world, as it allows deciphering if a literary product dominantly establishes a setting or dominantly changes one. Combined with an audience's tendency to follow a specific line of expansion across different media, this principle may permit a meaningful description of the perceived essences or 'gists' of a world for different audiences. In other words, the connection of both principles enables researchers to develop a general understanding of the perception of worlds for different audiences based on their most likely engagement with new material across media and the type of information each of these materials provide in regard to that world.

As Thon points out, current literary and media studies tend to use transmediality as an overarching term for a variety of narrative and cultural practices concerned with storytelling[89]. While he sees the potential for a refocused transmedia perspective, a comprehensive approach to the analysis of narrative interactions used for the creation of a world should not focus on transmedia models of narrative. Instead, research should examine narrative phenomena and strategies that govern the establishment and development of worlds. With this focus on narrative aspects, the approach has to acknowledge media-specific limitations and affordances as well as differences in audiences' willingness to participate. Additionally, such an analysis would have to conceive of functions each literary product may have in the formation of the overall world and how a lack of knowledge concerning an individual text may reframe the understanding of it.

1.2.3 The Ugly

Transmediality offers a basis for thinking of a narrative structure as a network of essences connected to a network of texts. Countering some of transmediality's core assumptions provides a more hierarchical formation of media and a clear conception of potential functions singular texts may have in the previously mentioned network. These views on transmedia storytelling are helpful for the development of a model concerned with grasping the creation of an imaginary world through the interrelation of different texts. However, transmediality's generally still fluid nature makes it a problematic basis for developing a model. In a white paper for the Transmedia Hollywood Conference in 2012, Geoffrey Long advocated for a higher form of transmedia criticism. This call simultaneously points out an inherent malleability within individual conceptions and applications of transmediality:

---

89   Thon, Jan-Noel. "Subjectivity across Media: On Transmedial Strategies of Subjective Representation in Contemporary Feature Films, Graphic Novels, and Computer Games". *Storyworlds across Media*. USA: University of Nebraska Press, 2014. 67–102. Endnote, Page 93

"Measuring transmedia success objectively will require some form of transmedia metrics, to tell us which transmedia experiences are gathering audiences, retaining audience attention, converting new audiences in one medium into fans that pursue the experience into additional media, and so on. Alas, we're not there yet. For now, we must satisfy ourselves with subjective forms of success, observing tactics adopted by various transmedia experiences and evaluating how well they appear to function in the service of the whole."[90]

While a higher form of transmedia criticism has emerged, it arguably is not founded on a more explicit definition of transmediality. Instead, new insights generated through the application in research emerged. Much of this research arises from transmediality's malleability and the potential to adapt it to different subjects at hand. As such, a higher form of transmedia criticism coincides with an increasing tendency to connect transmediality with other conceptions to describe a transmedia experience. A development Long encourages:

"Simply put, we don't yet know enough about transmedia to communicate firm, definitive truths about it that we already hold. However, this demonstrates the value of engaging in such analysis now, while general understanding of – and the creative practices in – transmedia is still relatively malleable. We should engage in earnest transmedia criticism now to gain a clearer focus, a better understanding, and ideally both a broader audience for transmedia and deeper, richer, more engaging, more profitable, and generally better transmedia experiences overall."[91]

Even though such an approach provides fruitful insight into the cultural influence and appropriation of transmedia franchises[92], this development supports contested conceptions of transmedia storytelling within the field, as many researchers may generally agree on which objects can be classified as transmedia but not on what such a classification encompasses completely. The processes of re-mediations, reboots, and re-imaginings further compound the concept's flexibility in regard to a general application. All these terms may fall under the umbrella of transmediality but, in practice, describe vastly different relationships between an old, presumable original franchise and its new iterations. As Rippl and Etter illustrate in their essay on the relation between inter- and transmediality within graphic narratives, Ryan "frequently uses the terms "remediation" and "transmedial narration" as synonyms"[93]. Presumably, Ryan is aware of the difference between these approaches, but the interchangeable usage implies a disregard for either concept's finer distinctions. Within the same paragraph, Rippl and Etter also point out that the insertion of remediation into the concept of transmediality entangles the transposition of a

---

90 http://henryjenkins.org/blog/2012/03/how_to_ride_a_lion_a_call_for.html, retrieved July 8th, 2021
91 http://henryjenkins.org/blog/2012/03/how_to_ride_a_lion_a_call_for.html, retrieved July 8th, 2021
92 For example Hassler-Forest's analysis of political identities applied to the Star Wars franchise in his essay "Transmedia Politics: Star Wars and the Ideological Battlegrounds of Popular Franchises".
93 Rippl, Gabriele and Lukas Etter. "Intermediality, Transmediality, and Graphic Narratives". *From Comic Strips to Graphic Novels*. Göttingen: De Gruyter, 2013. 191–218. Page 203

narrative from one medium to another with transmediality's original focus of describing a singular narrative spread across different media. This blank assertion of remediation and transmedia narration as the same fails to recognize a distinction between the advancement of an existing narrative (transmedia narration) and the retelling of an existing narrative (remediation/re-imagination) as well as each principle's distinctly different relationship with a perceived original. Narrative extensions add elements – settings and plot – that expand on a specific core text or network of core texts. While such an expansion theoretically can refer to a retelling of a core text and, therefore, inform and influence an understanding of the perceived original, the general conception of a transmedia franchise denotes that such an expansion rather refers to new material – meaning a new setting or new plot – that increases the overall substance associated with an entire complex. Transmedia franchises, such as *Star Wars* and *Star Trek*, do not constantly release retellings of their existing core material but regularly add texts that expand on the existing information of the world by exploring previously unexplored aspects of the franchise. Re-mediation, in contrast, retells an established narrative in another medium, adapting to some degree the existing setting and plot. This new version of the narrative may alter an audience's view of the previous original, but it does not necessarily add any setting or plot to that original. In essence, the process of transmedia narration expands or enlarges an established world; the process of remediation – and re-imagination by extension – creates a new separate world, which is related to the one created by the original but does not share the same imaginary space. The relationship between concepts like re-imagination/remediation and transmediality concerning their perceived association, their actual usage, and their potential conflation in discourse highlights the problem of transmedia storytelling as an analytical tool. Within the current range of use, transmedia storytelling can be nearly anything as long as it encompasses the sprawl of a singular narrative across several different media. This flexibility does not make transmediality useless; instead, its usefulness arises less as an analytical theory of its own but as an expansion of other theoretical frames. Within the discussion on transmediality presented in these pages, the principle has been related to narratology, fictional worlds, interpretative communities, and audience conception as a whole. Other publications connect notions of transmediality with politics, social identity, and culture. Transmedia storytelling's aversion to a more straightforward, more precise definition and distinction from other, similar theories allows it to serve as a bridge between large popular franchises and theoretical fields, which have no manner of grasping such a narrative structure. However, it also forces a continuous debate on the range and understanding of transmediality. A debate Long regards as rather positive.

> "This isn't to say that pushing and pulling at the boundaries of a definition isn't a worthwhile pursuit – such experimentation is what leads to the expansion of any enterprise, and often leads to the creation of wholly new types of things."[94]

---

94 http://henryjenkins.org/blog/2012/03/how_to_ride_a_lion_a_call_for.html, retrieved July 8th, 2021

Considering transmediality's potential to serve as a bridge between different theories and objects, the constant shifting of boundaries of a definition truly allows for its expansion. The constant shifting, however, makes it useless as an analytical tool concerning governing structures within expansive franchises. While various transmedia analyses related to other theories exist, a purely transmedia analysis of objects is exceedingly rare. In common practice, transmediality is used to describe an object or phenomenon and less used to understand the internal mechanics that govern such a franchise. As such, transmediality is not directly applicable to the development of a model meant to grasp the narrative techniques governing more extensive franchises but provides a set of basic assertions concerning the formation and development of such franchises. These basic assertions, however, require some relation to other theoretical conceptions to allow for further analysis of any larger narrative structure as presented in the comic superhero genre or the Marvel Cinematic Universe.

Following the malleability of transmediality and its need to connect to other theoretical principles, this chapter previously unearthed a basic understanding of the relationship between the texts constituting a franchise, the discourses surrounding their essence or 'gist', and the relationship between producers and audiences through these networks by focusing on notions of transmedia narratology and storyworld. Going against some of transmediality's established considerations revealed a system to perceive a hierarchy between different media in the expansion of a transmedia franchise and come to a general conception of setting and plot as basic elements for the establishment and development of worlds. Finally, understanding transmediality's need for another theory to operate as a direct analytical tool creates a demand for adding ideas and terminology from other fields to give transmedia storytelling's concept of thinking some directly applicable means of analysis.

1.3 Foundation for a New Terminology

Diving into and partly rethinking transmediality provides a reasonable basis for perceiving worlds as networks of different texts and associated discourses. To unearth the mechanics that govern such a network, a model needs to set and define these principles in a manner that lends itself to direct application. Hereby, the greater part of a new terminology arises from combining the previously discussed transmedia thinking patterns with principles of basic narratology. The combination derives a set of terms focused on describing the procedures relevant to the establishment and management of a network of texts. While the current state of narratology and transmediality nearly covers most aspects necessary to describe the mechanics of such a network, the combination retains some difficult terms best replaced. Additionally, it has a set of blind spots requiring some new terms. To fill these gaps, the model borrows and (re-)defines expressions derived from the fan culture surrounding the superhero genre. While these terms lack refinement, they attempt to grasp the phenomenon that conventional scholarly approaches overlook. Additionally, the model requires the creation of entirely new expressions to grasp principles not covered by either narratology, transmediality, or fan discourse. The following section presents a basic conception of each new and fan term. Hereby, these understandings, similar to the previously developed conception of transmediality, serve as the basis for later clarification within the development of the actual model.

Because the superhero genre and its associated worlds have, since their inception, offered a more complex (and convoluted) interaction of settings and plots than any other narrative, the fan culture around them has naturally developed terms to communicate and debate differences in a variety of superhero iterations. Reworking fan terminology for academic use is not a new idea. Equally, Jenkins makes a case for the strength of his knowledge communities – meaning fan communities in this instance – and their specific form of communication in his analysis of fan cultures and fan interaction. Both instances acknowledge the potential and advantages of terminologies from fan discourses. However, while these terms exist, their use primarily hinges on the current discourse surrounding them. As some phenomena – such as Shared Universes – enter a wider perception, the meaning of these terms tends to become more fluid and often adaptive to a subject matter at hand. In other words, while more strongly related to the complexity of expansive narrative structures, fan terms lack the clear distinction necessary for academic discourse or direct application. With each term in a constant state of flux, this paper takes on the most academic definition of each fan term and points out the principal difficulties of these definitions.

Outside of direct fandom, the comic historian Don Markstein made the only published effort at defining a Shared Universe in the 1970s. In his essay THE MERCHANT OF VENICE meets THE SHIEK OF ARABI[95], he postulates five defining criteria to grasp a Shared Universe. (1) His first criterion is an interrelation through chains of interaction. If two characters (A and B) have met, they are in the same universe; if the second character (B) meets a third (C), the first (A) and third (C) character exist in the same universe. (2) Within this chain of interaction, Markstein excludes connections via real people — as real people (such as the current president) regularly appear in comics and could create a false sense of interrelation. He provides the example of Superman (a DC property) and the Fantastic Four (a Marvel property) occupying the same universe if real people provided a connection. Superman met John F. Kennedy in *Superman #170* from 1964, and The Fantastic Four met Neil Armstrong in *Fantastic Four #98* from 1970. As Armstrong and Kennedy are part of the same universe (our reality), the chain of interrelation would lead to the conclusion that Superman and The Fantastic Four equally exist in the same universe, which is not the case as they are owned by the two competing superhero comic companies. (3) Markstein also excludes characters "that do not originate with the publisher" as superhero comics often make use of characters without ownership, such as heroes from Greek Mythology. As with real people, this might create a connection between characters from different properties; for example, each Marvel and DC use a version of the character Hercules. This dual use, however, does not create a connection between elements of DC comics and Marvel comics. Addressing the different renditions of public domain characters such as Hercules or the fictionalization of real people, Markstein suggests that (4) these specific versions of real people and public domain characters can serve as connections. (5) Finally, he specifies his notion of interaction by defining a meeting between characters as them appearing together on-panel in a story.

---

95 https://www.toonopedia.com/universe.htm. Retrieved August 24th, 2021

Markstein's definition operates with several limitations and difficulties. For one, he presumes the existence of a Shared Universe solely on the interaction of characters, excluding other means of indicating a direct relation, such as the possibility of a character engaging with the setting associated with another character or the appearance of a marked object with another marked object in the same panel. In other words, he does not consider Superman standing in the Batcave or Batman holding a piece of Kryptonite a connecting moment. Equally, he excludes the potential of a setting's arrangement for connective purposes. A panel showing a piece of kryptonite standing on a pedestal in the Batcave implies an interrelation between Superman and Batman without using any character. While a distinction in interrelation created with presumably the same or directly related elements – be they fictionalized elements of the real world or versions of public domain elements – needs addressing, tying the distinction to the authority of the publisher neglects the potential importance of audiences' understanding and discourse in the successful formation of a Shared Universe. In addition to limitations created through publisher and character focus, the definition also carries an unnecessary media focus when it uses the appearance in a (comic) panel as the basis for its understanding of interrelating characters. As such, Markstein's definition provides a reasonable initial definition of a Shared Universe but requires some adaptation to the principles of transmediality and better relations to narratological classifications when adapted for a narrative model of worlds created via networked texts.

While a direct, usable definition of Shared Universe for the application in literature exists, the adaptation of the term Multiverse appears slightly more complex. Originally a concept of theoretical physics, the term is more prominent as a feature of Science-Fiction literature. Its origin and the manner of its use in fiction make it challenging to define for the purpose of this discussion, as its roots in theoretical physics are far more complex than any manner in which this model would approach the notion. However, the use of Multiverse in fiction, as grasped by fans, apparently attempts to give the term some scientific validity by adapting principles from theoretical physics. This tendency retains some of the complexity of the term's origin, which marks it as too multifaceted for the model at hand. As such, it appears useful to employ the most basic definition. Merriam-Webster defines Multiverse as "a theoretical reality that includes a possibly infinite number of parallel universes"[96]. Assuming for a fictional context that a universe relates to the previously defined Shared Universe, a Multiverse merely describes the conception of a world in which several similar but somehow as distinct identifiable settings exist simultaneously. Aside from adapting the various problems of Markstein's Shared Universe definition, this conception of Multiverse neglects to conceive of a manner in which these alternate settings may be presented. Formally, a Multiverse could occur in a singular text when a setting includes two distinguishable universes, and it could occur among a collection of texts when different texts represent different interpretations of the same setting. Any adaptation of Multiverse as part of an analytical model for literary texts needs to evaluate these different interpretations of a Multiverse as operating within a text and across texts. Additionally, it has to set up a manner in which the relationship between different Shared Universes can be evaluated. Like Shared Universe, the current conception of

---

96   https://www.merriam-webster.com/dictionary/multiverse, retrieved July 12th, 2021

Multiverse provides a usable understanding of the term but requires adjustment along narratological and transmedia principles to operate within the proposed model.

Following the principal conceptions of Shared Universe and Multiverse, this paper proposes a new term along the universe line. Within fan discourses, Shared Universes and Multiverses are encapsulated under the ownership of one publisher or media conglomerate. These assumptions of ownership often appear subdivided along the lines of released media. Respectively, all narrative worlds owned and maintained by Marvel Comics are considered part of the 'Marvel Universe' as all narrative worlds and products maintained by DC Comics is generally referred to as the 'DC Universe'. A good example for the necessity of this distinction is superhero characters from a team known as the Squadron Supreme. DC Comics' Justice League inspired the entire team and singular members of the Squadron directly and purposely mirror members of the League. However, all characters of the Squadron Supreme are properties of DC Comics' chief competitor, Marvel. Due to the reality of intellectual property, the likelihood of both teams interacting directly appears relatively low – albeit not impossible, as both companies could come to some agreement, which would integrate their separate worlds. However, the Squadron Supreme and the Justice League remain related to one another on an intertextual level through their intentional similarities.

In other words, while changes to Superman alter the interpretation of the character Hyperion – the Squadron's version of Superman – and vice versa, the two characters (outside of special licensing agreements) cannot interact with one another because different companies own them. This is very different for other Superman-inspired characters like Shazam or Mr. Majestic – both owned by DC Comics – who may alter any interpretation of Superman on an intertextual level but can also interact with the character directly.

As the previous analysis of transmediality and this example point out, the economic realities of literature production have some influence on the establishment and development of a world. Specifically, the question of ownership or intellectual property may create borders or advance the potential interaction of different settings. Because these matters determine some potential interactions, realities of ownership deserve due consideration in a model meant to describe the mechanics governing imaginary worlds constructed from the interrelation of different texts. Leaning on the notion of Shared Universe as a potentially fixed setting and Multiverse as the collection of several Shared Universes, the term Company Universe shall cover a collection of Multiverses and Shared Universes related solely by them being the property of a singular company or media corporation.

Continuing along questions concerning the relationship between different texts leads to the other area requiring a new term. Within a model conceived as a network of texts, it becomes conceivable that singular texts within a network rely on knowledge from another text, meaning that the narrative – plot and setting – in a text requires some information from another to fulfill its potential. Hereby, this fulfilled potential equally refers to plot that requires outside information to make sense as well as an alternate interpretation created by additional knowledge. Continuing the previous example, the intertextual relationship between Hyperion and Superman works through a reader's knowledge of both characters. However, as this relationship remains intertextual, no reader of a plot revolving around either character requires any knowledge from the others' source, as an intertextual relationship denotes an increased range of interpretation but no greater dependence on one another. In contrast, singular issues of a comic series rely heavily on information presented in earlier issues, as a plot is split across several installments of the same series. While these examples cover the extremes, a variety of conceivable reliance within a perceived network of text can occur. A text may rely only on their direct sequels – meaning those directly bearing their name – or equally rely on any other texts in the same network. A narrative may be split among a series of otherwise unrelated texts, creating a narrative spread across the network. Singular plot points in one text may require some knowledge of another text. A model designed to grasp more extensive franchises of popular texts requires some manner to comprehend and evaluate the different degrees to which one text of a network may rely on another. However, there is no conception evaluating the relationship between texts as a dependency concerning the 'completion' of a narrative. As such, the Universe Model will introduce the notion of *Narrative Reliance* to describe the manner in which one text requires knowledge from another. To that end, the model will adapt Jenkins's concept of *knowledge community* to evaluate such dependencies, leaning on the transmedia base established previously.

The final new term equally emerges from the discussion of transmediality. Up to this point, this conception of transmedia storytelling has referred to the discourses and the associated core conceptions of different narratives by adapting Herman's term 'gist' or alternatively referring to it as essence. While either term conveys a general idea, they are insufficient in further constructing an analytical model. While this conception of a 'gist' is related to the discourse surrounding an individual textual iteration, they remain distinct mental formations.

> "This performance of transmediality thus is seen to depend upon a series of active feats of universalization, which construct the overarching transmedial entity even as they construe its severability from the intermedial moments of contact and reference among the concrete media productions that launch them. While each individual image and story about Spider-Man is concrete, the abstract transmedial entity is kept alive as a collective imagination among the participants involved in that performance."[97]

Packard's "abstract transmedia entity" stretches across several iterations of its formation, creating a set of collective criteria that exist independently of the discourse surrounding the text. As an analytical model of a network of text constructed from longstanding "abstract transmedia entities" has to acknowledge the difference between "active feats of universalization" surrounding the core essence of a narrative and the discourse potentially only surrounding a specific text, it requires a singular term to grasp this core essence as an individual element. Based on Packard's wording and shifting away from such an entity's relationship with the different media representing its text and refocusing on its inherent narrative elements, the Universe Model will refer to these universalized core essences as *Narrative Entities*. A *Narrative Entity*, therefore, contains an ab-

---

[97] Packard, Stephan. "Closing the Open Signification: Forms of Transmedial Storyworlds and Chronotopoi in Comics". *StoryWorlds: A Journal of Narrative Studies*, Volume 7, Number 2 University of Nebraska Press, 2015. 55–74. Page 62

stract conception of all elements of setting and plot inherently associated with a specific narrative.

With *Narrative Entity*, the model contains three entirely new terms – *Narrative Entity*, *Narrative Reliance*, and Company Universe. They combine with the notion of Shared Universe and Multiverse to provide the basis for five new terms for a Universe Model that describes how a network of texts creates interrelation and a unified world.

2 The Universe Model

Broken down to the simplest principle, all narrative techniques surrounding the management of a network of *Narrative Entities* revolve around building, strengthening, weakening, and severing connections between different textual manifestations. However, this rather simple notion reaches untold levels of complexity when put into practice. Defined and explained in detail following the overview of the model, the narrative techniques used to manage these different connections come down to the implication of a unified *Index Manifestation* (the elements of a setting), the acknowledgment of *Transformation Triggers* (actions causing alterations to a setting), and the construction of *Trigger Waves* (chains of *Transformation Triggers*) arching across several different texts. Evaluation of these connections through *Narrative Reliance* serves as a tool to determine the strength of a connection made by these narrative techniques. Overall, the resulting network serves as a model that represents the argued relationships between multitudes of interdependent *Narrative Entities*. The Universe Model also allows for an overview of the changes made through *Transformation Triggers*. The representation of the network operates with the units *Narrative Entity*, Shared Universe, Multiverse, and Company Universe. *Narrative Entities* are moveable elements within the Universe Model. Ideally, one *Narrative Entity* provides the model's center, serving as a fixed point of orientation. Depending on the research, any *Narrative Entity* can serve as the center. Circles around the center provide a classification for the relationship between various *Narrative Entities* as in Shared Universe, Multiverse, Company Universe, or purely intertextual relationships. Multiple *Narrative Entities* are placed within the Universe model to describe their relationship to one another.

Example model: With four *Narrative Entities* in mind, the Universe Model would be set up with one *Narrative Entity* at its center (NEC) and then draw one circle around it. Every other *Narrative Entity* in that circle is in a Shared Universe relationship with the NEC. A wider circle with the NEC at its center represents the area at which a *Narrative Entity* stands in a Multiverse relationship with the NEC and with most *Narrative Entities* within the Shared Universe circle. A final circle around the NEC contains the *Narrative Entities* in a Company Universe relationship. Every *Narrative Entity* outside the final circle may only have an intertextual relationship to the NEC, and most other *Narrative Entities* represented within the model. To place other *Narrative Entities* into the model (NE1, NE2, NE3), we compare the *Index Manifestations* of each *Manifestation* of these *Narrative Entities*.

Index Manifestations – singular aspects of a setting – create relationships between different *Narrative Entities* by the detail and multiplicity of their representation. The interconnection created through *Index Manifestations*, hereby, remains the easiest to register, classify, and evaluate. As such, the combination of all *Index Manifestations* within different *Narrative Entities* declares the position of each *Narrative Entity* within the Universe Model. For example, if the exact same representation of the character Spider-Man appears within *Manifestations* of different *Narrative Entities*, these *Narrative Entities* are related to one another. This relationship is strengthened by the coherent representation of Spider-Man across all of these appearances as well as through other aspects of setting and character equally transposed in the same manner. Hereby, it should remain clear that every *Transformation Trigger* potentially changes the state of an *Index Manifestation* and the state of information of every Index Manifestation, potentially altering the relationship between different *Narrative Entities*. In other words, the evaluation of coherence of, for example, Spider-Man is dependent on changes made to the representation of the character in the course of a narrative. As such, each network merely represents the relationship between *Narrative Entities* based on shared *Index Manifestations* between consecutive *Transformation Triggers*. Additionally, despite the egalitarian notion of transmediality, Jenkins conceded that the type of media influences an audience's engagement. Extending on that notion, I presume that the representation of an *Index Manifestation* presented in the same medium is more closely related than representations of the same *Index Manifestation* presented in different media. The notion of a media-based link arises from the assumption that audiences are more likely to engage with an extension presented in the same medium. On the level of representation, a stronger connection between similar or the same *Index Manifestation* within the same medium also arises from the unity in representation. As described, the greater the unity of detail of different representations of *Index Manifestation*, the greater the connection. In other words, the representation of Spider-Man within the same medium is more likely to share the same details to the same degree than representations across different media. Using the same means of representation allows for a more unified representation of the same *Index Manifestation*.

Within the setup presented, a *Narrative Entity* that shares some similar part of comparable *Index Manifestations* with the NEC would be placed within the Shared Universe zone. Assuming NE1 and NEC share many *Index Manifestations*, which are in representation and detail mostly the same, and NE2 equally shares a smaller number of equally detailed represented *Index Manifestations*, both NE1 and NE2 are placed into the Shared Universe zone. Hereby, the distance between NEC and NE1 is shorter than the distance between the NE2 and the NEC because the greater number of shared *Index Manifestations* relates the former two more closely to one another than the latter two. The distance between NE1 and NE2 is determined by the number of equally detailed representations of *Index Manifestations* between them. Assuming they share a lesser number than NE1 and NEC but a greater number than NE2 and NEC, the distance between them would be greater than the former (NE1-NEC) but lesser than the latter (NE2-NEC). NE3 initially shares only a few *Index Manifestations* with the other three *Narrative Entities*. However, its *Manifestation* comprises of another medium than the other three. As such, its *Index Manifestations* are represented by other means than those of NEC, NE1, and NE2. This already sets NE3 apart from the other three. Because the comparable *Index Manifestation* also differs in its representation beyond the medium's capacity, NE3 slips further away from the NEC. At this stage, it might be in a Shared Universe relationship with the NEC, however, only tangentially. As such, NE3 ends up on the border between Shared Universe and Multiverse. As with the relationship between NE1 and NE2, the distance between NE3 and the other two *Narrative Entities* depends on the shared *Index Manifestations* between them.

Independent from their position within the Universe Model, *Index Manifestations* can change under the influence of *Transformation Triggers*. Because every *Transformation Trigger* has the potential to alter the state of an *Index Manifestation* and, therefore, the overall network, research in this manner can be bogged down by a systematic analysis of the network between every *Transformation Trigger*. Organizationally, it is easier to process the changes in collections of *Transformation Triggers* in the form of, for example, an episode, a film, or an entire series. Aside from their transformative capacity, *Transformation Triggers* also directly interlink *Narrative Entities*. Hereby, the focus of interrelation should start with the effects of *Shared Narratives* – a series of *Transformation Triggers* across different texts organized into a plot – on the overall network. Textual manifestations of *Narrative Entities* hosting a *Shared Narrative* move closer together as they carry an overarching plot in some form. In contrast to *Shared Narratives*, *Trigger Waves* represent chains of causality not directly linked to one specific *Index Manifestation*. As such, they describe events and changes across texts and *Index Manifestations*, drawing different *Narrative Entities* together, but to a lesser extent than a *Shared Narrative*.

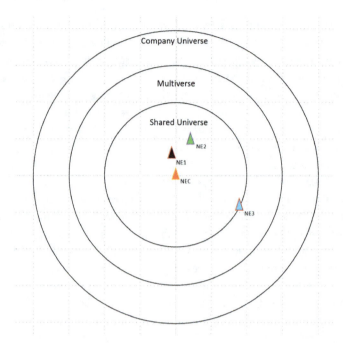

It is easy to assume that the Universe Model represents the relationship of *Narrative Entities* at the end of each text in regard to the incorporation of *Transformation Triggers*. As such, the *Index Manifestation* should be analyzed at the end of all current alterations. However, the introduction of new textual manifestations could alter existing relationships. Assuming that NE1 and NE2 have a *Shared Narrative*, they would move closer together. A chain of *Transformation Triggers* may also draw NE1 closer to NEC. Without any link through *Transformation Triggers* aside from comparable alterations to *Index Manifestation*, NE3 moves slightly down the border between Shared Universe and Multiverse to maintain the relationship with all other *Narrative Entities*.

Finally, connections hinge on the audiences' knowledge, interpretation, and identification. Because the audiences' ability and willingness to recognize an implied relationship is more difficult to argue, *Narrative Reliance* works with a notion of the audience targeted. In essence, *Narrative Reliance* allows arguing the necessity of connecting a given text to another by looking at the need for outside information to comprehend the given content. It allows researchers to determine the strength of these connections without involving the full spectrum of audiences' interpretations. To have more tangible means of arguing such connections, this paper defines three types of audiences – a casual audience, an informed audience, and a skilled audience – regarding different levels of *Narrative Reliance*. Established interrelations are tested against the audience types, evaluating the need for knowledge from another source to understand how dependent one text might be on another *Narrative Entity* and the network as a whole. If the evaluation shows a need for knowledge from another source, *Narrative Entities* necessarily draw closer together. In contrast, a lesser need for dependency keeps the *Narrative Entities* in place, and non-existing dependency even inches *Narrative Entities* apart. Hereby, the relationship between texts from the same *Narrative Entity* generally is assumed to be necessarily dependent on one another (as well as connected through a shared *Index Manifestation* and potential *Trigger Waves*) that the representation of their relationship can be considered superfluous.

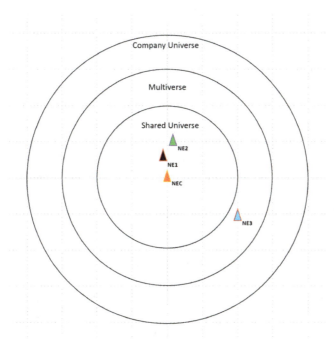

Assuming that the plot of NE2 requires some understanding of the *Shared Narrative* and, therefore, direct knowledge of the content of NE1's text, it would play against a casual audience, favoring an informed one. This draws the NE1 and NE2 closer together. As a chain of *Transformation Triggers* connects NEC with NE1 and NE2, knowledge of their relationship engages an informed audience. However, assuming the plot of NE1 and NEC do not require knowledge from NE2, both can sustain a casual audience while enhancing the experience of an informed one, fixing the relationships between NE1 and NEC as well as NE2 and NEC into place. As NE3 uses texts from another medium than the other *Narrative Entities*, it has no connection through *Transformation Triggers*, and its interrelations with other *Narrative Entities* hinge on the skill to see those connections, NE3's relationship to the other *Narrative Entities* serves only a skilled audience. Requiring a skilled audience to identify the relationship moves NE3 further away from not only NEC but also the other two *Narrative Entities*, pushing it into a Multiverse relationship with NEC as well as NE1 and NE2.

Of course, no single aspect, either a single *Transformation Trigger* or a single *Index Manifestation*, makes a connection or a distinction alone. The amount and type of connections establish the nature and level of a relationship, which constantly changes with addition (or subtraction) of more texts, leaving the example a snapshot of the network of *Narrative Entities*. Additionally, the visual representation of the model shown here operates with idealized parameters. Many *Narrative Entities* with many complex interrelations – as employed in the upcoming analysis – require a more sophisticated visual representation to maintain correct distances between their elements within the network. However, as a three-dimensional interactive visual representation is difficult to print on paper, the analysis will use the same visual representation used in this example to approximate the relationships between different *Narrative Entities* within the presented network.

2.1 Definition of Narrative Entity and Manifestation

As the example above indicates, while the Universe Model approaches the development of a network via the analysis of material presented in different texts, it describes these relationships via the mental projection and the discourses surrounding these ideas. The discussion develops alternative terminology and definitions to distinguish the association between the discursive network created by different texts' content and other conceptions of discourse in literary research.

2.1.1 Narrative Entity

Established research into narrative world construction operates with a notion of coherence. Transmediality, as Jenkins proposed it, operates on the idea of a coherent world spread across several platforms. Ryan's storyworld concept, leaning on transmediality, assumes the production of one world within one medium with aspects of transmedia extension advancing the understanding of that world. Mark J.P. Wolf's concept of imaginary worlds uses Tolkien's notion of sub-creation to explain how different sources are used to establish a functioning world. All these approaches assume that worlds can only exist and rise in an established coherent form. Even if traditionally contradictory elements are involved in this fictional universe – such as magic in a science-fiction setting or steampunk elements in a space opera – this approach to worlds assumes that such perceived contradictions are or will be smoothed out through a systematic explanation and organization of the setting. The world of *The Legend of Korra*[1] combines elements of steampunk and Asian fantasy. Still, the world provides explanations and an internal logic to incorporate either into a coherent backdrop. The imaginary spaces created out of the interconnected tales forming the network of classic superhero comics as well as, more recently, the MCU does not arise from such an inherent consistency but has to find ways to renegotiate all its elements in its formation.

A network of different tales brings together contradictory elements after the backdrop of the singular tales has already been established. As such, the imaginary space created through a network cannot incorporate contradictory elements easily. As each tale within the network eventually returns to its own themes and rules, a universal incorporation of all affordances might not even be desirable. A famous example in the realm of Marvel Comics is the odd coexistence of Mutants from the *X-Men* series and other properties with super-powered individuals. Within Marvel Comics (and most other iterations

---

1   *Avatar: The Legend of Korra*. Created by Michael Dante DiMartino and Bryan Konietzko. Nickelodeon Animation Studio, 2012–2014

of the same universe), Mutants are presented as a diasporic species emerging within the human population. Using an emerging species as a source of superpowers, *X-Men* tales often revolve around notions of racism, minority community, and bigotry. As such, *X-Men* tales, to a degree, rely on clearly distinguishing Mutants from the rest of society. Within Mutant-centric stories, possessing superpowers serves as a clear marker of Mutanthood, and aside from employing some form of scanning device, no other means of clear identification is given for the entire species. However, the *X-Men* comics exist in a network forming a unified world with other super-powered individuals with a variety of explanations concerning the source of their powers – the Fantastic Four and Spider-Man (accidents), Captain America and the Hulk (human augmentation), the Inhumans and the Eternals (extraterrestrial interference) etc. As Mutants do not all have the same superpowers – showing a variety typical for the genre – and lack a unifying physical marker distinguishing them from other groups of superpowered individuals, the entire network has to contend with a paradox. The paradox is that the general population of the Marvel Comic Universe can distinguish between Mutant groups and other superpowered individuals without any clear distinctive marker of identification, especially as Mutants are not the only superpowered species of the Marvel Comic Universe. This understanding serves as an explanation why hate groups only harass and act against Mutants while leaving all other groups of superpowered individuals to their own devices. This inconsistency arises from differences in theme and focus of the singular tales related to the same network. *The Fantastic Four* comic revolves mainly around ideas of family and the adventures of exploration. *Spider-Man* comics focus on personal responsibility, sacrifice, and guilt. *The Hulk* comics usually explore the duality of the individual and humanity as a whole. All these tales have no use for the application of some form of racial markers or a clear distinction from Mutants, meaning that incorporation of this contradiction only arises when the *X-Men* comics interact with another tale, and, even then, it would only arise if the status of Mutants as *the Other* is significant for the story at hand. The idea behind this example extends to other contradictory elements within the Marvel Comic network, such as the clear focus on science and technology in *Iron Man* comics and magic in *Dr. Strange* comics. The existence of these parallel, sometimes opposing, backdrops requires a less coherent understanding of worlds than established research currently provides. Instead of assuming that a world is conceived as a collection of parts making a coherent whole, this research approaches imaginary worlds as a network of parts that invites an understanding of it as a whole without compromising its individual units. As such, the model has to balance two notions of world within the overall representation. It requires (1) a representation of a coherently formed world with a coordinated and thematically guided setting created for a specific property and (2) the notion of a unified world created by the interrelation of different properties. The word 'entity' describes an "existence [...] considered as distinct [...] or self-contained."[2] With the understanding that the collective discursive understanding associated with a specific overall narrative – such as that of the X-Men, Dr. Strange, or Captain America – essentially is self-contained and, therefore, solely provides the necessary material to manifest a singular world for that specific

---

[2] https://www.dictionary.com/browse/entity, retrieved August 25th, 2021

property, this paper describes such singular discursive understandings as *Narrative Entities*.

As the representation of a specific world, a *Narrative Entity* consists of the unified elements, such as settings, characters, symbols, and themes associated with that world. Continuing the previous example, the *Narrative Entity* of *the X-Men* comics contains mainly Mutants and Mutant-hating characters, has Mutant/human relations, the 'Xavier Institute of Higher Learning', and a fictional version of the US as backdrop, and revolves mostly around themes of *Otherness*. In contrast, the *Narrative Entity* of *Dr. Strange* consists of magical and demonic characters, has an interdimensional and fantastic background, and revolves mostly around themes of hubris. Within the discussion of networks of superhero comics, singular *Narrative Entities* are usually associated with one specific or a team of 'Hero' characters. Within the Universe Model, this research will refer to different *Narrative Entities* by the name of the titular character(s) combined with the word narrative (e.g., Thor Narrative, X-Men Narrative etc.).

In its conception, *Narrative Entity* is meant to exist as a primarily discursive collection of ideas, describing a world's potential and its potential for a story. However, it does not inherently have to carry a tale within its composition but has the potential for a narrative. As such, material previously described as non-narrative can equally form a *Narrative Entity*, even if they have no classically produced narratives. The potential for a tale can be realized when different parts of the *Narrative Entity* are manifested in some form of text.

2.1.2 Manifestation

As a discursive conception, *Narrative Entity* requires a material form to relate, add, subtract, or alter its elements. More importantly, it requires some form of expression for an audience to experience the *Narrative Entity* before it can become part of personal imagination and public discourse.

Building on Saussure, Seymour Chatman, in *Story and Discourse*, distinguished between a content level linked to story and a level of expression related to discourse. Applied to the Universe Model presented in this paper, *Narrative Entity* would mostly coincide with Chatman's notion of story, as it holds the singular parts that make up the content. Following Chatman's principle of narrative, *Narrative Entity* needs to be balanced out by an element of expression, which links the narrative to a discourse and audience. Splitting both principles into substance and form, he determines that the 'Substance of Expression' is "Media insofar as they can communicate stories"[3]. He terms the collection of all these means of expression Manifestation. Chatman's principle of Manifestation is not concerned with narrative transmission because his model relegates these aspects to his notion of 'Form of Expression'. This separation between a physical object carrying the discourse and the structure transferring the narrative to the discourse coincides with this researcher's assertion of narrative and non-narrative material contributing to the construction of a world. As such, Chatman's term describes all means used to manifest aspects of a *Narrative Entity* into the real world. *Story and Discourse* does not define the

---

3   Chatman, Seymour. *Story and Discourse: Narrative Structure in Fiction and Film*. Cornell: Cornell University Press, 1978. Page 24

range and limit of a Manifestation closely other than its capability to "communicate a story". This liberal definition covers all means by which narratives are classically transported and through which they are consumed, e.g., a Graphic Novel, a film, a season of a series, a novel, oral storytelling etc. While this range of Manifestation suffices for the research presented here, it appears useful to expand the term to include objects, which can manifest aspects of a *Narrative Entity* but not necessarily tell a story. Books and other material meant to be descriptive but not narrative (e.g., compendiums for roleplaying games or handbooks explaining the makeup of a world) are obvious choices for inclusion. These materials are already part of Chatman's definition of Manifestation as they could communicate a story but do not use that capability. Merchandise presents a far more contentious candidate. While statues of characters, posters of fictional landscapes, and props representing objects from a fictional world do not communicate a story (in the way Chatman understands), they do manifest some specific notion of a *Narrative Entity* into a physical form. In his analysis of Japanese media culture, Marc Steinberg postulates that "the anime media mix simultaneously creates (1) the character merchandise as the material object, (2) the world to which the character merchandise belongs, and (3) the character as immaterial connective agent [...]."[4] This interrelation between merchandise and its fictional origin describes the relation between a *Narrative Entity* and its Manifestation. While Steinberg focuses on the enterprise of merchandise creation – hence the simultaneousness of merchandise and narration production – a temporally removed order would not change the necessary link between the collective understanding forming a *Narrative Entity* and a piece of merchandise appearing as a Manifestation of it[5]. As such, *Manifestation* describes any physical object related to a *Narrative Entity*, including classic storytelling media, merchandise, and purely descriptive background information.

Within this dialectic relationship of *Narrative Entity* and *Manifestation*, it is essential to understand that paths of influence and means of creation are not unidirectional. In further discussing the concept, Chatman clarifies that "manifestation must be distinguished from the mere physical disposition of narratives"[6]. Based on the work of Roman Ingarden, he makes a distinction between the 'real object', which is the physical novel or film, and the 'aesthetic object', which "is a construction (or reconstruction) [of the real object] in the observer's mind."[7] As the *Narrative Entity* formed the basis for its *Manifestation*, ideas constituting the *Narrative Entity* clearly inform the *Manifestation*. However, the reconstruction in the observer's mind equally influences the understanding of that *Narrative Entity*, potentially altering, adding, or removing some of its elements. Various

---

4 Steinberg, Marc. *Anime's Media Mix: Franchising Toys and Characters in Japan*. Minneapolis: University of Minnesota Press, 2012. Page 200

5 In his essay "Narratology and Media(lity)", Werner Wolf shows via the analysis of sculptures that singular objects such as statues arguably do contain some form of conceptual narrativity in itself. His relation of the sculpture capturing a specific moment or emotion of a larger story supports the notion that objects such as merchandise equally serve as *Manifestations* to traditionally more literary objects, as they carry and operate with the discourse idea of a *Narrative Entity*.

6 Chatman, Seymour. *Story and Discourse: Narrative Structure in Fiction and Film*. Cornell: Cornell University Press, 1978. Page 26

7 Chatman, Seymour. *Story and Discourse: Narrative Structure in Fiction and Film*. Cornell: Cornell University Press, 1978. Page 27

changes to long-running serial superhero stories provide numerous examples of such interrelation. As the Superman narrative transitioned to radio in 1940, this *Manifestation* of the *Narrative Entity* adapted greater parts of the action inherent to it but required some means to dramatize the actions beyond the use of a narrator. Equally, the radio show needed to convey the idea that Superman's heroics were a secret and that he performed them mostly alone. As the medium of radio lacks a visual component, this *Manifestation* of the Superman Narrative introduced Jimmy Olsen, a young photographer, to comment on, describe the action, and provide somebody the hero could talk to apart from his love interest. With repeat appearances in the radio show, Jimmy Olsen gradually became part of the Superman Narrative as audiences reconstituted the *Narrative Entity* with the character as a fixture in it. In 1941, comic *Manifestations* of the Superman Narrative included Jimmy Olsen, and the character has appeared in several *Manifestations* of this *Narrative Entity*.[8] This interrelation between *Narrative Entity* and *Manifestation* allows for the analysis of what Chatman describes as real objects – meaning novels, radio shows, comics etc. – to determine the relationship between different *Narrative Entities*, as the *Manifestation* influences the *Narrative Entities* and the potential relationship between them.

With *Manifestation* describing every physical object tied to a *Narrative Entity*, I am aware that the concept is vague and problematic for use in research. Any series has smaller elements, such as films, comics, or seasons. These elements equally can be split into smaller parts such as scenes, pages, and singular episodes. These smaller parts can also be broken down further until singular symbols and objects appear as their smallest unit. Encompassing and distinguishing all these different levels of a *Narrative Entity* gives *Manifestation* broad applicability, which in turn extends the Universe Model's range of research in the constitution of worlds in fiction and their interrelation. However, when used in analysis, the exact range of reference potentially becomes unclear as *Manifestation* can refer to several levels. Especially in the case of series, *Manifestation* might refer to a single episode, an entire season, or the complete series, depending on the focus of a research project. As such, each research project should determine what range *Manifestation* encompasses within their network before conducting their analysis.

2.2 Elements of Governance

As the different units within the Universe Model describe distances between *Narrative Entities*, a key component for understanding world-construction through an interrelation of *Narrative Entities* hinges on determining connections and their influence on the relative distance between different *Narrative Entities*. Three essential elements allow for determining the separation and connection of different narratives. *Index Manifestation* describes the elements within a *Narrative Entity*, which serve as the basis for connection and distinction. *Transformation Triggers* relate to the alteration these relationships may

---

8   For further information on the influence of the radio show and other iterations of Superman on the current understanding of this *Narrative Entity*, I advise reading Tim DeForest's article "Faster than a Speeding Bullet: Superman" from *Storytelling in Pulps, Comics, and Radio*.

undergo. Finally, *Narrative Reliance* deals with the need and necessity to identify connections for an audience to reasonably decode the *Manifestation*'s content.

2.2.1 Index Manifestation

As the genesis of *Manifestation* as a physical object born out of a *Narrative Entity* includes static objects such as merchandise, the question arises if smaller elements presented within a *Manifestation* could be understood as *Manifestations* themselves. In other words, if Harry Potter wands sold as merchandise count as *Manifestations* of the Harry Potter Narrative, are the wands shown in the Harry Potter films (which themselves are *Manifestations*) not also a *Manifestation* of that *Narrative Entity*? The short answer is yes: Following the definition of *Manifestation*, the film, series, or novel created from a *Narrative Entity* is comprised of smaller *Manifestations* within it. As such, each larger *Manifestation* is nothing else than a network of smaller *Manifestations* attached in an influencing context to one another. However, while physical objects – the one in another *Manifestation* as a narrative product and the one in the real world in the form of merchandise – arise as a representation of a *Narrative Entity*, the realm and context of their existence differentiate their status and meaning for that *Narrative Entity*. A merchandise object exists with some immanence to an audience, as it is a tangible and attainable prop within the real world. The *Manifestations* shown within a film, series, or novel lack this immanence because they are enshrined within that film, series, or novel. More importantly, *Manifestations* presented as part of another *Manifestation*'s setting exist in an intrinsic relationship with one another. The tight-knit network created by the interaction of these smaller *Manifestations* forms the setting of films, series, and novels. As such, the long answer makes them similar elements differentiated by the place and form of their creation. While the setting within a larger *Manifestation* comes into existence by the same means and relates to the same notion as a narrative product, their place of existence and their direct relation to one another gives them the means to influence the discourse surrounding them and, therefore, alter the *Narrative Entity*. A practical example is the relationship between Mjolnir, Thor's Hammer, as *Manifestation* within *Thor: Ragnarok*[9] and its *Manifestation* as a piece of merchandise. When the merchandise *Manifestation* of the Hammer shatters (because somebody tried to use it in a mock fight), no alteration to the *Narrative Entity* occurs. Because the merchandise *Manifestation* is not part of a network forming a film (or other medium communicating a story) of the *Narrative Entity*, the change to its representation does not add to the larger discourse surrounding it. Hence, it becomes 'just' a broken *Manifestation* from the *Narrative Entity*. When, however, Mjolnir is shattered within the network of *Manifestations* forming *Thor: Ragnarok* (i.e., Mjolnir shatters in course of the film), the alteration has two distinct directions of influence, towards other parts of the network and the discourse surrounding the *Narrative Entity*. As Mjolnir carries the idea that it holds part of Thor's power and ties him to his heroic identity, the hammer's destruction forces a new understanding of the character or its redefinition without this specific object. Equally, all the alterations set off by Mjolnir's destruction, including its

---

[9] *Thor: Ragnarok*. Directed by Taika Waititi. Performances by Chris Hemsworth, Tom Hiddleston, and Cate Blanchett. Marvel Studios, 2017.

demolition, carry into a discourse about the *Narrative Entity* as its observers reconstitute the *Narrative Entity* mentally after witnessing the event in the film. As such, these two types of *Manifestation* are meaningfully different and predictably have a different impact on a network of *Narrative Entities*.

Leaving the term *Manifestation* for physical objects in the real world (such as books, films, and merchandise), the elements making up the *Manifestation* of a *Narrative Entity* in film, series, or novel require renaming and a clear definition. In his essay "An Introduction to The Structural Analysis of Narrative", Roland Barthes similarly argues for understanding narratives as a collection of smaller units by viewing narration through the lens of linguistics. In his model, Barthes determines three levels of a story, one of which contains the units making up a story. The level of functions further divides into smaller units, which he terms *functions* and *indices*. Describing it as "functional in term of actions"[10], he ties the term *function* to its inherent use for the procedure of a present narrative. His example is that the purchase of a gun pertains to its use later in the story. Overlaying Barthes's notion of units with the idea of smaller *Manifestations* described here, the notion of *functions* proves important for the continued operation of a plot. *Narrative Entities* exist as a discursive collection of assertions with the potential for a narrative and, therefore, the need for a plot. However, they are not a narrative yet; their singular components solely have the potential to attain Barthes's notion of *function* but are not a *function* in themselves. This potential is only realized when these smaller *Manifestations* appear as part of a film, series, or novel. Here, any might gain some *function* as it has become part of a plot and might serve to propel the action forward. Note that this gained *function* exists in service of that particular plot but serves no direct purpose for the *Narrative Entity*. This potential for a *function* over the presumption of a fixed *function* is important because it entails that every individual component of a *Narrative Entity* can manifest in nearly every position within a given plot. Considering the exchange of these singular elements between different *Narrative Entities* in the process of creating a network, the ability to take on a different *function* allows for a different usage within alternative plots. While the character Batman, for example, takes on the mantle of the protagonist within a Batman comic, he may not be able to take on the same *function* within a comic in which his protégé, Robin, is the protagonist. Instead, the same character may take on the *function* of Mentor (to use Campbell's terminology). In contrast, Roland Barthes's *indices* "are truly semantic units, [...] [that] refer to a signified [...]"[11]. Contrary to *functions*, *indices* relate to the meaning of a unit. While Barthes considered this solely for a narration at hand, the notion lends itself to the description of a *Narrative Entity*. Each element of a *Narrative Entity* solely exists to provide meaning to that *Narrative Entity*. Captain America's shield within the Captain America Narrative is a signifier for the presumed indestructibility of American values and its protective nature. Several works have pointed out how the character of Steve Rogers/Captain America is a signifier for presumed American ideals. Therefore, Captain America and his shield serve as semantic units that provide meaning

---

10   Barthes, Roland. "An Introduction to the Structural Analysis of Narrative". *New Literary History, Vol. 6, No. 2, On Narrative and Narratives*, 1975. 237–272, Page 247
11   Barthes, Roland. "An Introduction to the Structural Analysis of Narrative". *New Literary History, Vol. 6, No. 2, On Narrative and Narratives*, 1975. 237–272, Page 247

to the overall *Narrative Entity* of Captain America. As such, Roland Barthes's notion of *index* proves highly adaptable to a model concerned with describing a world constructed by networking different *Narrative Entities*. Within the context of the Universe Model, a *Narrative Entity* consists of a collection of *indices*, which refer to Chatman's concept of an aesthetic object signified towards that *Narrative Entity*. As such, *indices* naturally encompass notions of characters, sets, and props. However, *indices* can also refer to musical scores, sound effects, as well as *Narrative Entity*-specific words, phrases, and sayings. The musical score for *Superman: The Movie*[12] by John Williams and the phrase "Faster than a speeding bullet" from the 1945 opening of *The Adventures of Superman* radio show are examples of non-object indices, generating meaning for the Superman Narrative. In addition, *indices* should also include the backstory explaining or contextualizing sets, props, and characters before their first representation within a *Manifestation*. While characters and sets inherently have such an assumed backstory, treating it as an *index* of its own makes it easier to distinguish backstory from events and actions. The distinction might prove rather important for creating an exact model of a network of *Narrative Entities*, as different versions of similar *Narrative Entities* exist. In this context, backstory is to be understood as the explanation attached to another *index* as reasoning for specific aspects of that *index*. In other words, backstory tells the recipient why a character (in its first representation) has a drinking problem, wears an eye patch, or is attached to a specific symbol. Like *Narrative Entities*, *indices* are purely collections of ideas constituted to an aesthetic object in people's minds. In the same fashion, the term *index* does not refer to the physical object presented within a *Manifestation*, as the physical version of an *index* presented in a film, series, or novel already is an interpretation of an *index*'s qualities. To differentiate *indices* from the smaller elements constituting the *Manifestation* of a *Narrative Entity*, *Index Manifestation* will refer to the manifestation of *indices* from a *Narrative Entity*.

As *indices* manifest in a film, series, or novel, they exhibit characteristics different from the potentially fluid notion they held within a *Narrative Entity*. *Index Manifestations* become part of a specific setting and, equally, the medium presenting it. The incorporation into a specific setting and a representing medium demands some interpretation of an *index*'s characteristics, some supplementation to its representation, the potential acquisition of a *function*, and the potential incorporation of some additional meaning. As a part of a narrative, an *Index Manifestation* might need to take on utilities specific to the tale it is a part of. However, it is necessary to clarify that these additions do not supersede or replace the *index*'s original meaning. Instead, they exist aside one another. In his discussion of *indices* and *functions*, Barthes explains that "a unit can at the same time belong to two different classes [meaning *functions* and *indices*] [...]"[13]. While the potential of taking on an additional *function*, the same holds true for any additional meaning placed on an *Index Manifestation*. For example, in the film *Captain America: Civil War*[14], Captain America's

---

12   *Superman: The Movie*. Directed by Richard Donner. Performance by Christopher Reeves and Gene Hackman. Warner Bros. 1978
13   Barthes, Roland. "An Introduction to the Structural Analysis of Narrative". *New Literary History*, Vol. 6, No. 2, *On Narrative and Narratives*, 1975. pp. 237–272, Page 250
14   *Captain America: Civil War*. Directed by Anthony Russo and Joe Russo. Performances by Chris Evans and Robert Downey Jr. Marvel Studios, 2016

shield receives the additional meaning of representing the relationship between Tony Stark and Steve Rogers. This meaning is generated when the film reminds the audience of Steve Rogers's and Howard Stark's (Tony's father) history – which includes the latter giving the former the shield – and when Tony Stark reiterates that his father created it. The moment Captain America drops his shield, he symbolically drops his relationship with Tony, but equally, the protection of American ideals it holds from its general relation to the Captain America Narrative. This combination of signification arises again when Tony Stark offers the shield back in *Avengers: Endgame*,[15] and Steve Rogers is reluctant to accept it. While additional meaning can arise from a narrative's need for that meaning, an *Index Manifestation* can also take on new meaning due to the interpretation of an *index*'s characteristics or a necessary supplementation to the *index*'s representation. Either of the two aspects depend on the medium in which an *index* is manifested and its notions of representation from the *Narrative Entity*. All *Narrative Entities* engage with an audience through one or several *Manifestations*. Each *Manifestation* influences the notion of different *indices* constituting a *Narrative Entity*, thereby creating specific affordances to the representation of these *indices*. *Manifestations* of superheroes are famously and dominantly visual, as they are intractably tied to comics and have often been adapted to audio-visual media. As such, many notions concerning their representation equally are visual in nature, which influences the range of interpretation an audio-visual *Manifestation* may take, as some key visuals are part of each *index*. Equally, a purely written *Manifestation* of superheroes, like a novel, would need to transfer these visual characteristics to the written affordances of a novel. The reversal would hold true for a *Narrative Entity* dominantly formed by written *Manifestations* like the Guards Narrative from Terry Pratchett's Discworld series. The *Narrative Entity* mostly finds representation in its book series, which in turn gives the Guards' *indices* a lexical quality. Therefore, any audio-visual *Manifestation* of the Guards Narrative has to transfer the lexical characteristics into a visual form[16]. This relationship between notions of the *Narrative Entity* and the manifesting medium additionally creates the need to add aspects to the *Index Manifestation* that are not part of the *index* to accommodate a medium's needs. For example, the lexically dominant Guards Narrative contains no precise and intricate visual form of its characters. The novel *Manifestations* often use hints and metaphors to conjure a visual image. However, when the *Narrative Entity* manifests in a visual medium, it necessarily needs to create a visual *Index Manifestation* of these characters. To do so, the visual *Manifestation* has to, for one, interpret the lexical characteristics but also supplement visual elements necessary for a visual representation not covered in the *index*'s lexical nature.

The changes made to *Index Manifestations* due to media affordances and re-interpretation pertain to an interesting problem concerning the interrelation of different *Narrative Entities* and the comparability of different *Manifestations* of the same *Narrative Entity*. They call into question the comparability of different *Index Manifestations* of the same *index* as every representation of it necessarily combines identifying but malleable features with new ones specific to a *Manifestation*. The combination of influence on the final form of

---

15   *Avengers: Endgame*. Directed by Anthony Russo and Joe Russo. Marvel Studios, 2019
16   Adaptation Studies deals specifically and more thoroughly with the alteration of representation due to a shift in medium. For more detail, I recommend Linda Hutcheon's *Adaptations*

an *Index Manifestation* demands the identification of different elements constituting it. In his essay "Narrative Ways of Worldmaking", David Herman uses the term *semiotic cue* to describe elements "in a given narrative medium to design blueprints for creating and updating storyworlds."[17] He continues to relate the different forms a *semiotic cue* can take in different media. Hereby, his description of *semiotic cues* in the storytelling mechanics of different media coincides with the affordances of media in the manifestation of *indices* described earlier. However, he employs a simplified view of a fictional world, which he describes as "the characters, situations, and events (what this book terms storyworld)"[18] in *The Basic Elements of Narratives*. While Herman's definition of a fictional world and his notion of a *semiotic cue* are fundamentally correct, either is focused on the process of world creation through narration (meaning the process of storytelling).

As the model in this research attempts to describe worlds as a network, Herman's understanding of world and the smaller parts formulating it appears too limited. *Semiotic cues* relate the textual form of a narrative representation of a fictional world to the elements constituting what he refers to as storyworld. As such, the term can be linked to the notion of *Index Manifestation*. *Indices* serve to constitute the notion of a fictional world in the form of a *Narrative Entity* and can manifest in the form suited to the representing medium. However, to grasp an *Index Manifestation* in a manner useful to determine the relationship of multiple *Narrative Entities*, it is not enough to understand that *Index Manifestations* function like *semiotic cues*. Instead, it is necessary to perceive them as a collection of semiotic affordances, meaning the meaning-making possibilities and requirements of their general environment. In other words, the final *semiotic cues* of an *Index Manifestation* arise through the potential and demands created through the intersection of discourse and production process. By its nature, every *Index Manifestation* is constructed from three sources determining the final collection of its *semiotic cues*, its *index*, the medium in which it is manifested, and attempts at distinguishing it from other *Index Manifestations* created from the same *index*.

The influence of the former two has been discussed in the adaptation of *indices* into *Index Manifestations*. As described, an *Index Manifestation* carries the characteristics of the *indices* forming it. For example, every version of the character Batman, by virtue of the Batman Narrative, has to wear a stylized bat costume with a bat symbol across the chest, employ a multitude of gadgets, and fight crime to carry the label of this superhero persona. Equally, the *Index Manifestation*, for one, realizes these *indices* but, more importantly, adds elements in accordance with its representing medium. Staying with Batman, a cinematic version of the character requires an actor. The choice of actor introduces elements to the *Index Manifestation* that are not inherently part of the *Narrative Entity's index*, such as the appearance of physical age and build, the color of his eyes, level and type of attractiveness, and so on. Additionally, actors might add *semiotic cues* of their own, created through previous roles, a perception of their private lives, and their status within the film industry. The third influence on an *Index Manifestation*'s final form arises

---

17 Herman David. "Narrative Ways of Worldmaking". *Narratology in the Age of Cross-Disciplinary Narrative Research*. Ed. Sandra Heinen and Roy Sommer. Walter de Gruyter GmbH. Berlin: 2009. 71–87, Page 75
18 Herman, David. *The Basic Elements of Narrative*. London, Wiley-Blackwell: 2009, Page 17

out of a potential need to determine a relationship – a clear distinction or some implied connection – to previous (or future) manifestations of the same *indices*. As a *Narrative Entity*'s *indices* provide merely one of three components, each *index* can manifest several times, forming different representations of itself. While all these representations relate to the same *index*, they do not necessarily represent the same *Index Manifestation*. Different media affordances might create distinctly contradictory representations, excluding the possibility of a unified perception. Similarly, *functions* placed onto a representation due to narrative affordances might create contradictions between multiple *Index Manifestations*. Independent from the circumstances of adaptation altering the representation of an *index*, contextual factors like a cultural or temporal transposition of the *Narrative Entity* might require a conscious distinction from one *Index Manifestation* to another. As such, each *Index Manifestation* contains, in addition to the *semiotic cues* formed from its *indices* and the affordance of the representation medium, unique features distinguishing it from other representations of the same material. Depending on the number and specificity of features describing the *index*, these distinguishing *semiotic cues* can range from a singular interpretation of features to the change, subtraction, or addition of elements. An example of the former is the different interpretations of the Bat symbol in each cinematic iteration of the character, while a detraction of Batman's usual scientific genius and an altered relationship with the League of Shadows in Christopher Nolan's adaptation of the *Narrative Entity*[19] is an example of the latter. It is prudent to mention that no *Index Manifestation* can be clearly separated into smaller parts, which then can be sorted into these three categories – *index*, medium, and rendition. As the example of the Bat symbol already hints, singular aspects of an *Index Manifestation* can serve in more than one capacity. Still, as the Universe Model attempts to describe the relationship between different *Narrative Entities* and their *Manifestations*, as well as the means by which they form a shared fictional world, it is necessary to describe features to separate different representations of the same *Index Manifestation*.

To that end, this model describes the *semiotic cues* of *Index Manifestations* in terms of *index cues*, *media cues*, and *rendition cues*. Hereby, *index cues* are the manifestation of the discursive aspect identifying a *Narrative Entity* or a part of it, previously described as an *index*. Within the realm of superheroes, the appearance of costumes, weapons, superpowers, or specific symbols signifying the *Narrative Entity* or part of it are *index cues*. *Media cues* describe aspects of the formation of an *Index Manifestation* arising out of the potential and/or need of the specific medium in which the *Narrative Entity* is presented. The association of a character with a specific musical score is a *media cue* of audio-capable media. A non-audio-capable medium may adapt the idea of that specific musical score by invoking the idea lexically or visually. However, the lexical alteration then is a *media cue* for the non-audio-capable medium. *Rendition cues* describe specific interpretations or alterations added to an *Index Manifestation* to indicate its relationship to other *Index Manifestations* from the same *index* (potentially in the same medium). Superman in Mark Waid's *Kingdom Come*[20], for example, is marked as a distinctly older version of the 'typical'

---

19   *Batman Begins*. Directed by Christopher Nolan. Performances by Christian Bale and Liam Neeson. Warner Bros. Pictures, 2005
20   *Kingdome Come*. by Mark Waid. Illustrated by Alex Ross. DC Comics 2008 (1996)

Superman by the addition of grey temples in his usually black hair. The different nature of this rendition is enhanced with a black and red S-symbol in contrast to the more common yellow and red version.

As such, an *Index Manifestation* is constituted of three types of *semiotic cues*, which represent (1) the influence of collective expectation (*index cue*), (2) the needs of the medium (*media cue*), and (3) its attempts at unique identification (*rendition cue*), and it serves as the representation of one part of a *Narrative Entity* (*index*) within a network of other *Index Manifestations*. This understanding of the manifestation of a *Narrative Entity* provides the possibility to compare different appearances of the same *index* relatively precisely, thereby allowing for the description of their potential relationship outside of being derived from the same *Narrative Entity*. Every noticeable difference distinguishes one representation from another, while equally, every similarity ties them closer together. For example, the two versions of the character Spock – from *Star Trek: The Original Series*[21], which aired in 1966, and the 'new' *Star Trek*[22] film from 2009 – display a distinction of interpretation while acknowledging some inherent expectations towards the character. The existence of *index cues* in each representation relates the two versions. Both Leonard Nemoy's 'original' Spock and Zachery Quinto's 'new' Spock share not only the name but also the marks of a fictional species (Vulcan), the heritage of being half-human, a specific haircut, and an overemphasis on pursuing emotionless and logical behavior. A difference between the two versions is created through the addition of *rendition cues* to Zachery Quinto's Spock that specifically contradict Nemoy's version. Nemoy's Spock has a deep connection and friendship with Kirk; Quinto's Spock cannot stand him. Nemoy's Spock adheres forcefully to the ideal of logical behavior and decision-making, while different levels of emotion constantly break through the logical façade of Quinto's performance. Nemoy's Spock's primary relationships on the Enterprise are with Captain Kirk and Leonard 'Bones' McCoy; Quinto's Spock has a romantic liaison with Saldana's Nyota Uhura. Equally, the actors representing the characters serve as *rendition cues*, as they (willingly or unwillingly) highlight a difference in iteration and carry additional meaning from their previous performances and public persona with them. The backstory of Quinto's Spock provides another *rendition cue* as that *Index Manifestation* is placed before any of the events of *Star Trek: The Original Series* had taken place, and the events of the 2009 *Star Trek* actively contradict the backstory of Nimoy's Spock. If some of the events that influenced the 'old' Spock had been introduced to the 'new' one's backstory, the versions would have been more closely related. Aside from the previously mentioned ones, each of these iterations of *Star Trek* also creates a series of *rendition cues* as a product of their time. With a $150 million production budget, the 2009 film presents a sleek, realistic-looking version of the whole *Narrative Entity*, built on modern CGI and fast-paced editing. In contrast, the entire run of *Star Trek Manifestations* in which Nemoy appeared worked with physical models in a small space. While the last point highlights the question which version of Nemoy's Spock (the early one from the series or the one shown in films) is compared to Quinto's Spock, this example shows how the application of specific

---

[21] *Star Trek: The Original Series.* Created by Gene Roddenberry. Norway Corporation, Desilu Production and Paramount Television, 1966–1969
[22] *Star Trek.* Directed by J.J. Abrams. Spyglass Entertainment and Bad Robot Productions. 2009

semiotic cues (notable *index cues* and *rendition cues*) create the possibility of clearly identifying the elements relating and distinguishing *Index Manifestations* created from the same *index*. However, these *Index Manifestations* are tied to the same *Narrative Entity* and, therefore, do not serve as a means to interrelate *Narrative Entities* in so much as they allow an understanding which *semiotic cues* might ultimately serve as *index cues*. To interrelate *Narrative Entities*, an *Index Manifestation* with unaltered *index cues* and *rendition cues* has to appear in *Manifestations* of two different *Narrative Entities*.

While the definition of an *Index Manifestation* postulates that it has to appear within a network of *Index Manifestations*, the definition purposely does not state that all *Index Manifestations* within the network forming a *Manifestation* have to arise from the same *Narrative Entity*. In other words, the *index* of one *Narrative Entity* can manifest in another *Narrative Entity's* film, series, or novel. Such appearances have occurred in several literary genres throughout time with diverse purposes, depending on the *function* associated with the transposed *Index Manifestation*. Aside from such superhero properties and ancient myths, the manifestation of an otherwise unrelated *index* has occurred, for example, in *Mask of the Musketeers*[23] (in which Alexander Dumas's Musketeers encounter Johnston McCully's Zorro) or *House of Frankenstein*[24] (in which Count Dracula's corpse and the Wolf Man appear). Cross appearances naturally relate different *Narrative Entities* with one another. These interrelations remain marginal if the transposed *Index Manifestation* lacks a corresponding *Manifestation* based on its own *Narrative Entity* or does not reappear with the same *semiotic cues* in the *Manifestation* of another *Narrative Entity*. Instead, it initiates a discourse and gradually builds a case for including the transposed *index* among the first *Narrative Entity's* indices. A stronger interrelation between two different *Narrative Entities* occurs when an *Index Manifestation* appears in a *Manifestation* of either *Narrative Entity*. Hereby, a similarity in representation is crucial to the connection as the use of different *rendition cues* and an altered interpretation of *index cues* in either version could call a connection between these particular *Manifestations* and, therefore, the corresponding *Narrative Entities* into question. As the example with the two Spocks has shown, the application of different *rendition cues* can create distinctive representations. In this case, this distinction (among others) is deliberate, as the 2009 film attempts to highlight its reboot[25] status and separate itself from the events shown in the original series, as both versions of Spock appear in the 2009 film. Similarly, different versions of *Index Manifestations* in different *Manifestations* are used for the same purpose. The re-interpretation of several superheroes in DC's *Elseworlds* imprint or Marvel's *What If* series operate with such an assertion to create stories outside of their normal running series. Each of these Graphic Novels deliberately creates an *Index Manifestation* with distinct *rendition cues* and re-interpretations of *index cues* to mark them as separate from the versions appearing and interrelating different *Narrative Entities* within the comic company's main network of *Narrative Entities*. For example, while presenting several re-imagined versions of DC

---

23   *Mask of the Musketeers*. Directed by Luigi Capuano. Jonia Film. 1963
24   *House of Frankenstein*. Directed by Erle C. Kenton. Universal Pictures Company, Inc. 1944
25   For a deeper understanding of the interrelation between a reboot and a presumed original as well as the effects of seriality on the reboot process consult Urbanski's *The Science Fiction Reboot*

characters, the *Elseworlds* Graphic Novel *Kingdom Come* uses specific *rendition cues* to create distinct versions of Superman, Batman, and Wonder Woman in order to separate its story from DC's main series and world. Conversely, using several coinciding *index cues* and *rendition cues* can serve as a method of interrelation through *Index Manifestations*. Hereby, the determination as the same iteration hinges on the consistency of *semiotic cues* in their level of detail within the possible range of the representing media. In this case, the level of detail describes a degree of adherence of each following presentation of a *semiotic cue* to a former one, ensuring recognition across different *Manifestations*. The adherence to detail does not have to be exact but cannot diverge so much that an attempt at recognition might fail. Hereby, detail in representation is influenced by the interaction between potentially different media. Every medium can generate (in one form or another) an *Index Manifestation*'s *semiotic cues* in their respective modes. The significance lies more in a medium's ability to recreate the level of detail in the production or reproduction of specific *semiotic cues*. A good example of this phenomenon is a character's physical and facial representation. Film is tied to a necessarily high level of visual detail in its attempt to convey a sense of realism, even in a fantastic genre. Comics, due to their reliance on drawings for the visual part of their narration, have much greater control over the amount of and the exact nature of detail. Novels can deliver detailed descriptions of a visual representation but require far greater effort to reach the instant clarity of a drawing or a cinematic representation. Within the medium of film (excluding animation, which in this instance is more akin to comics), the representation of (human) characters relies on the use of actors. As actors are real, physically present people, they carry a high level of detail. The Hollywood star system economically and somewhat narratively relies on an audience recognizing specific actors in specific roles. The recognition value of actors simplifies the interrelation of *Narrative Entities* by sending the same actor as the same character through different *Narrative Entities*. Due to their drawn nature, comics have the potential to associate a character with a specific actor. They can tie the comic representation closer to a film representation by including specific details associated with an actor playing the character. Purely written narration could relate expected *semiotic cues* to an actor but cannot relay the detail of a visual representation. Instead, it would have to refocus on the details of *semiotic cues* more easily captured with words. Considering this difference, the ability to connect different *Narrative Entities* changes among and across media. Media with a visual component can form Shared Universes more easily than purely written narratives because they need less effort to make subtle connections. The representation of an *Index Manifestation* in film can appear within the shot of a different *Narrative Entity*'s *Manifestation*. While the economic and logistical reality of film production may prove a significant hindrance, narratively speaking, film – and by extension, TV series – have the advantage that they can have a specific actor as a specific character draped in all necessary *semiotic cues* wander through several *Narrative Entities* to interrelate them, because the level of detail naturally remains the same. Similarly, studio sets, shooting locations, props, and costumes can be reused or rebuilt. Without the same complexities in production, comics can equally easily relate different *Narrative Entities*. With direct control over the level of detail in visual representation, comics cannot only connect different *Narrative Entities* but deliberately choose to avoid connections or determine potential degrees of connection. Simplified representations demand a focus on a detailed depiction of specific *semiotic cues*, which allows for connections even between different styles of drawing. Detailed representation can elicit transmedial connections with film or serve as a mark of distinction. Written narration necessarily has to describe *Index Manifestations* in enough detail for an audience to recognize the aspect, and they often must do so independently from its importance in a specific scene. This might be why book adaptations of otherwise cinematic material often skip descriptions, mostly serving an audience that already engaged with the visual material. Similar observations can be made for other modes of storytelling across different media, limiting the notion of the universality of media transition argued by transmedia storytelling. Nevertheless, *Index Manifestation* is left with two means of interrelation. (1) Different *Manifestations* of the same *Narrative Entity* can connect via the use of a similar *Index Manifestation* with the same *index cues* while creating distinction via divergent *rendition cues* (Nimoy's Spock vs. Quinto's Spock). (2) The appearance of an *Index Manifestation* bearing the same *index cues* and *rendition cues* in the *Manifestations* of different *Narrative Entities* allows for the interrelation of these *Narrative Entities* (as frequently used in superhero comics).

2.2.1.1 Example Index Manifestation

Within my definition of *Index Manifestation*, I explained that the connection hinges on a unity of representation bound to the detailed and recognizable use of *semiotic cues*. Specific similarities within the *Index Manifestation* are required to equate two different representations. In other words, the relationship between the version of Spider-Man shown in the pages of *Civil War* and the pages of *The Amazing Spider-Man* can be described along the lines of similar and detracting *semiotic cues*, specifically a similar use of *index cues* and *rendition cues*. While the notions of interrelation due to similarity in representation affect all parts of *Index Manifestation*, the following example will focus on characters because they are the prominent feature of superhero narrative (to the degree that all titles are named after them) and provide more readily accessible instances for analysis. However, the same principles can help identify any *Index Manifestation* connecting *Manifestations* or *Narrative Entities*.

Focusing on the comic event *Civil War*, we can identify the relationship of multiple series through their exchange of *Index Manifestations*. All *Index Manifestations* related to Mark Miller's *Civil War*[26] publication appear directly in that miniseries and their own titles. The producer's conscious intent to interrelate the narratives of other running series and *Civil War* is directly related via a tagline atop the singular issues, declaring the solo-titles connection to the superhero Event. As it would be too time-consuming and too extensive to describe the connection created by every character, the example will focus on three: Captain America, Iron Man, and Spider-Man. The character selection automatically entails that the example will only make statements about the relationship between the *Civil War* mini-series, *Captain America #22–24*[27], *Iron Man #13–14*[28], *The Amazing Spi-*

---

26 *Civil War*. Created by Mark Millar. Illustrated Steve McNiven. Marvel Comics, 2006–2007
27 *Captain America #22–24*. Written by Ed Brubaker. Illustrated by Mike Perkins. Marvel Comics, 2006–2007
28 *Iron Man #13–14*. Written by Daniel and Charles Knauf. Illustrated by Patrick Zircher. Marvel Comics, 2006–2007

der-Man #532–538[29], New Avengers #21–25[30], Fallen Son: The Death of Captain America – Spider-Man[31], Fallen Son: The Death of Captain America – Avengers[32], and Fallen Son: The Death of Captain America – Iron Man[33]. Iron Man and Captain America appear in The Amazing Spider-Man title, creating a connection between three Narrative Entities: the comic's Spider-Man, Iron Man, and Captain America Narrative. Spider-Man equally appears within the pages of the New Avengers series.

Aside from showing that superhero comics employ the notion of Index Manifestations to interrelate Manifestations, the analysis indicates a degree of divergence different representations of the assumed same character may sustain across multiple, presumably connected, comic series. In other words, the analysis may reveal to what degree the representation of a singular character may differ between different series and yet still provide a connection[34]. Within this context, it is necessary to acknowledge that the medium comic has specific affordances that influence adherence to detail. As the issues of each series have different artists (each with their own style), each representation of the same character necessarily carries some expected level of divergence, which does not interfere with an assumed coherence of representation. A more detailed style may contain additional structure on uniforms, more precise features in faces, and/or a collection of smaller elements in a scene that a more cartoonish style may not include. Similarly, an artist employing a more angular drawing style may favor drawing machinery – like the Iron Man armor – with more edges, while another favors a round and sleek approach to the representation of technology. Despite these differences related to an artist's style, there is an assumed coherence in the appearance of similar Index Manifestations. In other words, despite being drawn differently, the representations of Iron Man, Captain America, and Spider-Man appearing in various series are assumed to be the same version of that character due to some coherence of representations undiluted by the style of drawing. As such, this analysis will ignore differences in representation reasonably related to the drawing style as an acceptable divergence created by a characteristic of the medium.

---

29 The Amazing Spider-Man #532–538. Written by J. Michael Straczynski. Illustrated by Ron Garney. Marvel Comics, 2006–2007

30 New Avengers #21–25. Written by Brian Michael Bendis. Marvel Comics, 2006–2007

31 Fallen Son: The Death of Captain America – Spider-Man. Written by Joeb Loeb. Illustrated by David Finch. Marvel Comics, 2007

32 Fallen Son: The Death of Captain America – Avengers. Written by Joeb Loeb. Illustrated by Ed McGuinness. Marvel Comics, 2007

33 Fallen Son: The Death of Captain America – Iron Man. Written by Joeb Loeb. Illustrated by John Cassaday. Marvel Comics, 2007

34 In his seminal essay "Transmedia Characters: Theory and Analysis", Thon describes the relationships between what he calls local work-specific characters and characters as part of a global transmedia character network. His approach focuses on the relationship and interaction between differing versions of the same character (e.g. Batman from Christopher Nolan's trilogy and Batman from the Adam West television series) and the audience's overall perception or remembrance of these transmedia characters. In contrast, the presented analysis (and model) is concerned with a presumed relationship between different texts via the recognition or distinction of multiple character representations. As such, this analysis is more concerned with the means and moment in which two representations of a character become two distinct versions of a character instead of what elements of specific representation becomes a defining feature of its general transmedia perception.

The superhero genre contains some inherent elements that support the recognition of characters across several forms of artistic representation. It favors clear symbols and images as well as unique abilities and names. Additionally, the genre evokes an expected interrelation between series. Such an expectation may prime an audience to seek out presumed connections and forgive a mismatch in representation across series (to some degree). The material at hand invokes a direct relationship between the different series via a shared tagline mentioning the larger Civil War Event. Assuming the comic's producers intended an interrelation between the series and a presumed audience would accept such a relationship as given, each analysis will first mention aspects consistent across representations within the material, followed by the descriptions of divergences. To avoid confusion in the case of characters with more than one form of representation, each version is approached as a singular character. Following this pattern, the analysis first looks at representations of Iron Man, followed by the representation of his civilian identity, Tony Stark. Captain America appears dominantly in his uniform. As such, there is no analysis of Steve Rogers. Three iterations of Spider-Man occur within the material at hand: the Iron Spider version, the classic version, and a symbiote version. Each version is analyzed singularly in that order.

The consistent aspects of Iron Man's representation include a gold/yellow-and-red color scheme with the character's facemask, biceps, and sections of the upper legs adorned in gold/yellow. A diamond-shaped emblem decorates the center of his chest, and a small triangle rests on his forehead right atop the facemask. When the armor emits light/energy, it always emits it from the chest emblem, the eyes, and a circle in the lower arm close to the elbow. Even when a representation of Iron Man emits no energy/light, these sections remain visible and identifiable. Alterations in the color of energy/light emitted and the additions of energy vents signify notable changes in the character's representation. While the energy/light often carries a yellow tinge, that color is mixed with orange in *Iron Man* #13–14 and with red in *Civil War* #1 and *Civil War* #6. In *New Avengers* #23, the armor emits a purely blue energy/light without any yellow tinge. The representation of the armor in *Iron Man* #13 contains two additional elongated and narrow energy vents on each lower arm. *Civil War* #6 displays a similar feature in addition to having three of the same vents on each upper leg of the armor. The representation of Iron Man within the material implies that aspects such as color scheme and chest emblems have to remain consistent across representations of the presumed same character. In contrast, less noticeable aspects of a representation, such as the color of the energy/light and the details concerning the armor's ventilations may change.

Throughout the material, Iron Man's civilian identity, Tony Stark, appears as a Caucasian man with black, short hair, blue eyes, and a short van Dyke-style beard. Wearing a suit or pieces of a suit seem inherent to the character's representation. However, while Tony Stark mostly wears a suit in his representations, the suit does not remain consistently the same. Dominantly, the character appears in a black suit and tie with a white shirt. Presented in *Iron Man* #14 and *Civil War* #3, this attire is also implied in *New Avengers* #25, in which the character wears only black trousers and a white shirt. An inverted version of this outfit – meaning a white suit with a black shirt – without a tie appears in a brief representation of Tony Stark in *Civil War* #3 on page 4. In *Amazing Spider-Man* #532, the character wears a grey suit with a blue shirt and no tie. While a suit appears as the character's default attire, he does appear in other types of clothing when the circumstance warrants different clothing. For example, battling doubt and depression in *Iron Man* #13, Tony Stark temporarily dresses down to jeans, a t-shirt, and a bathrobe. This version also has stubble on his cheeks but maintains the identifiable short van Dyke beard. The representation of Tony Stark implies that traditionally constant features – such as hair and eye color – as well as identifiable features – such as a style of beard – have to remain coherent across representations. While there is some liberty in the choice of attire, it has to adhere to a sense of associated style. However, even this character-related style can be broken in specific circumstances and remains within a single issue.

Throughout the material at hand, Captain America appears in his superhero uniform. Remaining largely consistent, the uniform has a red-white-and-blue color scheme, with the latter covering the cowl, the upper portion of the chest and shoulders, and the entire hip-and-leg section. The cowl has a large white A on its forehead and a small wing on each temple. A white star sits in the center of the character's chest. The blue section of the torso always includes some indication of armor, usually in the form of a fish scale pattern. The arms below the shoulders are white and lead into a set of red gloves covering a greater part of the forearms. The lower torso is covered in vertical red-and-white stripes. The character wears a belt and a pair of red pirate boots. Aside from the uniform, Captain America is traditionally marked by his iconic shield. The shield appears in nearly every panel with the character. It is round with a blue disc at its center, which is surrounded by first a white, then a red circle. A large white star adorns the shield's center. Without his cowl, Captain America is presented as a blond Caucasian man with blue eyes. The representation of the character remains consistent throughout the material, nearly to a fault. The only difference in representation arises in the presence and absence of pouches. While most re-presentations of the character contain pouches on the belt, this feature is missing in *New Avengers* #22 and *Civil War* #1. Similar to the previous two analyses, this one implies that minor alterations to the representation of a superhero persona do not interfere with identification and connection across *Manifestations* as long as the general appearance remains the same. Furthermore, the analysis implies that the number and form of characteristics, which must remain consistent, may vary from *Index Manifestation* to *Index Manifestation*. While Tony Stark requires merely a few features and Iron Man requires some larger indicators, the representation of Captain America appears to entail an extensive collection of aspects, as each representation in the material adheres to a rather precise set of visual characteristics.

Spider-Man shifts through three versions of his superhero persona, representing a shifting alliance within the larger conflict underlining the material and his reaction to its outcome. Peter Parker, Spider-Man's civilian identity, received the Iron Spider armor from Tony Stark when he became Stark's assistant previous to the material analyzed here. Within the context of the Civil War event, the Iron Spider armor is generally considered a symbol of Spider-Man's allegiance to Iron Man. In line with this relationship, it imitates a muted version of Iron Man's color scheme. Dominantly red, the armor contains arm and leg guards, large eyes, a disc on the back, and an angular, stylized spider symbol on its chest with legs reaching around the torso, all in a dark gold/yellow. In some instances, the armor displays three mechanical spider legs attached/emerging from the disc on its back. The representation of the Iron Spider armor remains mostly consistent throughout its appearances within the material. The one exception is a lack of armguards when the character appears in the background of the second panel of page three in *Iron Man #13*. Notable changes to the armor's representation only occur after a fight with Iron Man shortly before Spider-Man switches his allegiance. The Iron Spider armor sustains damage to a lower section of the mask, which is displayed in *Amazing Spider-Man #536* and *Civil War #5*. Following his break with Iron Man, Peter Parker reverts to using his classic Spider-Man outfit. Prior to this change in allegiance, this version of the character made a short appearance in the press conference in which Spider-Man revealed his civilian identity. The conference is shown in *Spider-Man #532/#533* and *Civil War #2*. The classic Spider-Man outfit in the material at hand follows established *semiotic cues*. It has a red-and-blue color scheme. Large white eyes with a black rim cover part of the red mask. A small black spider symbol adorns the center of the character's mostly red chest, and a large and red stylized spider symbol sits in the center of blue on his back. Black lines run across the outfit's red sections, forming the image of a net. The character appears several times without a mask, notable at the before-mentioned press conference and an impromptu television appearance in *Amazing Spider-Man #537*. Without his mask, the character is shown as a Caucasian man with light brown hair and brown eyes. All representations of the classic Spider-Man outfit remain consistent throughout the material. This consistency even includes the display of light brown hair peeking out underneath a broken mask in *Iron Man #14*. After the resistance to the Registration Act loses, Captain America is assassinated, and Peter Parker's Aunt May is shot, Spider-Man switches into the cloth version of his symbiote outfit. As this alteration occurs only after the primary Event conflict ends, this version of Spider-Man dominantly appears in the material concerned with the event's aftermath, namely *Civil War #7*, *Fallen Son: The Death of Captain America – Spider-Man*, *Fallen Son: The Death of Captain America – Iron Man*, and *Fallen Son: The Death of Captain America – Avengers*. Held in black, the symbiote outfit has large white eyes and a white spider symbol on the chest and back. The spider's legs connect along the side of the torso. A white square covers the back of the character's hands. The representation of the symbiote outfit stays consistent throughout the material. The only exception is the lack of the white square on the back of the character's hand in *Fallen Son: The Death of Captain America – Iron Man*, in which Spider-Man appears in the background of two panels on page 15. The consistency of representation of the different versions of Spider-Man throughout the material underscores previous indications. When the overall representation remains clear, alterations of more minor details seem to have no determent on the interrelating effect of an *Index Manifestation*. However, the analysis of Spider-Man in general also implies that adherence to a consistent representation becomes essential when an *Index Manifestation* transforms in the course of an overarching narration, as only a singular inconsistency occurs for two of the three versions, which only arises when the character is in the background.

Generally, the analysis indicates that *Index Manifestations* used to interrelate different *Manifestations* must maintain a general consistency of representation across different appearances. However, this consistency does not have to be absolute, allowing for alteration of an *Index Manifestation*'s details. Hereby, more noticeable and signifying aspects of representation – costumes, color schemes, symbols, meaningful gear – appear less flexible to change than less prominent aspects – street clothing, meaningless equipment, details in design. This correlation between noticeable and less prominent features indicates why superheroes may lend themselves well to the creation of a network of *Narrative Entities*. The genre's representation of character often includes unique and noticeable symbols, color schemes, and signifying behaviors. Despite such an inherent advantage within superhero characters, the connection of different *Manifestations* via the transposition of recognizable *Index Manifestations* operates in conjunction with other techniques, reinforcing the unity of different representations. Snippets of dialogue allude to a unity in character by including some signifier not part of the character's visual representation or by referring to the character's presence in another *Manifestation*. The addition of references to other comic series within a running narration – such as the reference to *Daredevil #93* and *Civil War #7* on pages nine and ten of *Amazing Spider-Man #538* – serve a similar purpose. The use of helpful dialogue to reinforce interrelating effects indicates that the transposition of *Index Manifestations* is not the only means of creating a network but that it operates in conjunction with other techniques.

2.2.1.2 Differing Versions of Index Manifestations: Civil War vs. Civil War: Warzone

Having a notion in what manner an *Index Manifestation* can change without compromising its connective ability, the question arises: what degree of changes have to be made to an *Index Manifestation* to mark it as a distinctly different iteration of the same collection of *indices*? Several *What If.?*-publications considered different outcomes and developments for superhero Events and, therefore, intentionally created alternate versions of familiar *Index Manifestation*. While the *What If...?*-version shares some *semiotic cues* with the presumed original, they are meant to exist as an alternative interpretation, usually outside of the network housing a presumed original. As a widely noticed event, *Civil War* spawned *What Ifs* creating alternate versions of the known *Index Manifestations*. *Civil War: Warzone*[35] created an alternative universe to the dominant network of *Narrative Entities* and significant alternatives to existing *Index Manifestations*. In this *Manifestation*, the presented backstory describes the destruction of St. Louis triggered by the political divide of the original *Civil War*'s Registration Act. The destruction of a major city did not occur during the original Civil War event. Creating two separate nations in the wake of this outcome, Iron Man governs the Iron in the East, while Captain America leads the Blue in the West. A comparison between the *Civil War* Event in its entirety and its *What If...?* alternate *Civil War: Warzone* provides a good indication of the degree of alterations needed to create a distinct alternative of an existing *Index Manifestation* as well as the relationship of such an alternative to a presumed original. For the sake of simplicity and synergy, the comparison of the *Index Manifestation* will focus on the same characters as the previous example. The analysis will start with Steve Rogers/Captain America and Tony Stark/Iron Man, followed by Peter Parker/Spider-Man. The previously discussed versions of these characters appear on the first ten pages of *Civil War: Warzone* before the comic uses alternate versions of these *Index Manifestations*. With a focus on the effects of an alternate

---

35 *Civil War: Warzone*. Written by Charles Soule. Illustrated by Leinil Francis Yu. Marvel Comics, 2016

representation of similar characters, the following analysis does not repeat an analysis of the *Index Manifestations* in this section of *Civil War: Warzone*.

As symbols of the political divide between the heroes, the characters Steve Rogers and Tony Stark play a similarly important role within this alternative timeline to their counterparts in the 'original' *Civil War* Event. Neither Tony Stark nor Steve Rogers goes by their original superhero monikers. Steve Rogers is referred to as General Rogers. Tony Stark has taken on the title of President. A visual representation of greater age accompanies the alteration in title. This specifically goes against the standard procedure of the serial superhero comic, which continuously shifts timelines to keep characters in their mid-30s. *Rendition cues* of Steve Rogers include informal military field gear and a slightly more military-type buzz cut than the usual version. Roger's military angle folds more into the visual representation of his civil identity than it usually does. While Captain America always had an association with the military, his costume – the Captain America outfit – was somewhat regarded as his field uniform. Within his entire appearance in the *Civil War* material at hand, the character never wears any version of a military field uniform. The presumed superhero version of the character still sports signifying *index cues*, specifically the star on his chest, the A on his cowl, and his iconic shield. However, he has lost all other aspects of the visual representation mentioned in the previous analysis. His new uniform is held in green/grey with blue armor over it. In essence, Steve Rogers wears a blue chest plate, arm guards, knee guards, and cowl/helmet in a rendition of his superhero costume over a military field uniform. While the shield remains presumably unaltered, it is often drawn in shadow, covering its traditional features other than the white star at its center. The star, however, does not remain consistent throughout the graphic novel. The retention of specific *index cues* marks the character as Captain America. Still, the changes to the overall representation appear to mark him as a different iteration of the more widely known version. Something similar can be said about the representation of Tony Stark in *Civil War: Warzone*. The character still wears a suit and retains a short van Dyke beard. However, this suit has a red tie and is reminiscent of the attire associated with American politicians. As mentioned in the previous analysis, some form of a suit is an overall mark of the character. The alteration of his hair color to a nearly white, contrasting the black of the usual depiction, and the alteration of eye color to a light brown provide more significant alterations to Tony Stark's depiction. As with Steve Rogers, the retention of the suit and the beard mark the character as Tony Stark, while the change in hair color indicates that this is a different version. Similarly, the Iron Man armor contains a set of *rendition cues*. Within the previous material, Iron Man's armor is a full-metal body suit with a closed helmet and a red-and-yellow color scheme. He also sports a diamond-shaped chest insignia. While the Iron Man of the Warzone comic equally retains the original color scheme on a full-body armor, it also appears generally translucent with a helmet, which allows a view of Tony Stark's face. Additionally, this armor uses a circular chest piece in contrast to the diamond-shaped one and contains four circular energy vents along the abdomen. The release of energy occurs only along the five circular markings on the chest but in no other place. The representations of General Rogers and President Stark in *Civil War: Warzone* indicate that retaining a few simple *index cues* is sufficient to identify a character as a manifestation from a specific *Narrative Entity*. Within this context, the material implies that no specific *index cue* carries more importance than any other, as General Rogers is linked to Captain America via the use of specific symbols while sacrificing the associated color scheme. President Stark, on the other end, retains Iron Man's color scheme but does not retain other established symbols of his armor. The limited use of *indices* to relate different versions of a character also implies that changes to a more significant part of an *Index Manifestation* denote an alternate iteration of a known character.

The alterations to Peter Parker/Spider-Man appear more substantial than the other two characters. On a visual level, the character retains a shirt with the blue-and-red color scheme of his former classic Spider-Man costume. While the distribution of color imitated this classic representation, the shirt lacks any other associated symbol. He also maintains his brown hair and eyes. However, he now has a military buzz cut. Aside from these previously mentioned *index cues*, this representation also employs some additional ones not explored in the previous analysis, such as the use of his web-shooters and the hand position associated with it. The existence of a wrist-mounted device to shoot webs has long been an established aspect of Spider-Man, as has the gesture of pressing his middle and ring finger into the palm of his hand while keeping the other three digits stretched outward. The relationship between this hand gesture and the use of his webs occurs clearly on page 21 of *Amazing Spider-Man* #533, page 17/18 of *Amazing Spider-Man* #534, page 14 of *Amazing Spider-Man* #537, page 14 of *New Avengers* #21, and page one of *New Avengers* #24. These instances also indicate the character's typical use of webs in combat and as a means of transportation. A similar relationship between the hand gesture, the use of webbing, and this character appears on page two of *Civil War: Warzone* #3. Peter Parker employs the hand gesture when he threatens one of Spider-Man's old foes, Flint Marko/Sandman, on page 13 of *Civil War: Warzone* #2. A generally more military appearance provides clear *rendition cues* for this iteration of the character. Aside from the haircut, Peter Parker wears green combat pants and military boots. Straps fasten pouches to his legs and belt, some reminiscent of military holsters. In addition to the military association, this Peter Parker is marked by a silver-metallic backpack containing mechanical wings usually associated with Sam Wilson/The Falcon. A set of straps holding the device runs across his chest and converges in a metallic plate, which hides Peter's original Spider symbol. As with the previous two characters, this manifestation of Peter Parker retains a relation to the *Narrative Entity* by using implications of *indices* related to the Spider-Man Narrative. At the same time, the clear avoidance of a more significant part of the *Narrative Entity*'s *indices* and their replacement with other significant and signifying *rendition cues* clearly distinguish this specific Peter Parker from other manifestations of the character, specifically the one presented in the 'original' publications.

The analysis of all three *Index Manifestations* indicates that a rendition of a character requires only a few *index cues*, as either character employs only a limited number of clear *indices* to identify them as a manifestation of a specific character. A similar observation holds true for the application of *rendition cues*. The examples imply that only a few clear distinctions from established *Index Manifestations* are required to mark a character as a different iteration. The combination and type of *index cues* and *rendition cues* potentially also determine the relationship of these specific character iterations with others. In this case, specifically, Spider-Man's *rendition cues* relate the version from *Civil War: Warzone* to the version of the character from *Civil War*, as the *rendition cues* all relate in some form to a notion of Captain America, reiterating Spider-Man's changed loyalties from the 'original' *Civil War*. This apparent flexibility in the creation of an *Index Manifestation*'s rendition, not only in its representation but also in its potential relationship with other iterations born from similar *indices*, stands in stark contrast to the apparent consistency of *semiotic cues* required in the use of *Index Manifestations* as means of interrelating the *Manifestations* of different *Narrative Entities*.

2.2.1.3 Manifestation – Narrative Entity Feedback Loop

While this research focuses on the interrelation of *Narrative Entities* via the interrelation of their *Manifestations* and does not attempt to explain or discuss the alteration of the discourse surrounding *Narrative Entities* and, therefore, their potential transformation in public perception, it is necessary to acknowledge such a process to clarify the range and meaning of an analysis. As earlier defined, *Manifestations* and *Index Manifestations* do not exist in a unilateral relationship with their respective *Narrative Entities*. When a *Manifestation* engages with an audience, it influences the audience's understanding and perception of the *Narrative Entity*, thereby altering the *Narrative Entity*'s and its *indices*' composition. While this influence and impact of a *Manifestation* can vary greatly and range from effectively non-existent to dominating the view of its *Narrative Entity* for several generations, there is no denying that such an influence does exist. The development of several superheroes is littered with examples of *indices* added, removed, and changed due to the creation and popularity of a *Manifestation*. The most famous (and often used) example is the changes to the Batman Narrative due to its different iterations created throughout the years. Here, the focus often falls on the *Narrative Entities* transformation from its campy 1960s version featuring Adam West to the grave 'darker' version created by Tim Burton in 1989 and by the 1990s animated series. As this research only uses *Narrative Entities* as a source for classifying distinctive and similar *semiotic cues* from one another, such changes remain irrelevant to the network described. However, the feedback loop created between a *Narrative Entity* and all of its *Manifestations* is neither necessarily linear nor does a newer *Manifestation* necessarily 'overwrite' previous assertions with its representation. Linear, in this case, refers to the creation of a new interpretation of a *Narrative Entity* only after a former interpretation has run its course and its potential influence has settled within public discourse. While such a linear production of *Manifestations* of *Narrative Entities* does exist, it proves more the exception than the rule in today's media-, story-, and franchise-saturated world. The phenomenon of parallel existing iterations of a *Narrative Entity* competing for acknowledgment, however, is prominent in the various *Manifestations* of superhero properties. As different superhero narratives find their way into film and television series, their comic counterparts never stop production. As such, multiple competing *Manifestations* exist concerning the alteration of a *Narrative Entity*. That the interpretation of one *Manifestation* does not 'overwrite' the interpretation of another *Manifestation* becomes abundantly clear when new interpretations illicit discussions concerning its validity and the 'true nature' of a *Narrative Entity*. Similarly, that the different interactions do not develop entirely independently becomes obvious when either adapts prominent aspects from their competitor, like a comic adapting the likeness presented in film or the film taking on aspects of recent comic storylines. The simultaneous existence of several *Manifestations* of the same *Narrative Entity* and the lack of continual replacement of its indices' *interpretation* creates a problem for the notion of *Narrative Entity* as presented and used. Up to now, the Universe model operated under the assertion of one unified *Narrative Entity* for all corresponding *Manifestations*, assuming each would alter it but ultimately leave a singular one in place. However, discussions concerning the 'true nature' of different *Narrative Entities* and the simultaneous existence of multiple interpretations highlight the possibility of several *Narrative Entities* operating with the same subset of *indices* while simultaneously maintaining individual *indices* for singular interpretations, defining them as unique. Returning to the example of Batman, the different *Manifestations* of the Batman Narrative paired with their interaction with different audiences means that there is more than one *Narrative Entity* that could be considered the Batman Narrative. Each *Manifestation* (the Tim Burton version, the animated version, the Adam West version) creates its own *Narrative Entity*. These *Narrative Entities* are all connected to one another and a universal *Narrative Entity* of Batman via the application of similar *indices* while creating distinction by adopting new *indices* as uniquely their own.

Combining the notion of a feedback loop with the notion of *semiotic cues*, the alteration of a *Narrative Entity* amounts to the transformation of *media cues* and/or *rendition cues* to *index cues* in public discourse, making them ultimately *indices* of the *Narrative Entity*. While a discussion of and research into the exact mechanics to facilitate such a transition and determine its degree would constitute its entirely own project, we can assume that when subsets of a larger population engage with different *Manifestations* of the same *Narrative Entity*, the chance arises that contradictory *media cues* and *renditions cues* become part of a *Narrative Entity*'s *index*, due to parallel running discourses and differing perceptions. In other words, as a group of people engages with a specific *Manifestation* of a *Narrative Entity*, this version can become the dominant interpretation of that *Narrative Entity* for that subset of people. Due to this dominance, some *rendition cues* and *media cues* of that specific interpretation may enter the discourse as definitive characteristics of the *Narrative Entity*, becoming *index cues*. However, as another *Manifestation* with different *rendition cues* and (potentially) *media cues* exists, another group might have engaged with that other version in a similar fashion, introducing an entirely different set of new *index cues* to the overall discourse. Such a situation creates an interesting question concerning the nature of a *Narrative Entity* as the collection of basic notions concerning a potential world: How does a *Narrative Entity* deal with such a potentially diverse perception of its existence? Only three solutions come to mind: 1) accept and incorporate the contradiction, 2) adapt and favor aspects of one interpretation over another, or 3) create a subcategory of the *Narrative Entity* in question. The former two outcomes indisputably have occurred. The Batman Narrative, for example, includes the fixed *index* of Batman as a solitary, cautious, and distrustful crimefighter aside from the similarly fixed *index* of the Bat-family, which includes a slew of young men and women he has taken on as partners and protégés, with the character Robin being the most notable. The introduction of Harley Quinn in the 90's *Batman: The Animated Series*[36] contradicted the exchangeability of Joker's associates por-

---

36 *Batman: The Animated Series*. Created by Eric Radomski and Bruce Timm. DC Entertainment and Warner Bros. Animation. 1992–1995

trayed in the 1989 Batman[37] film, especially in his disregard for his mistress, Alicia. This contradiction was solved by adapting Harley Quinn as a fixture of the Batman Narrative. It altered the Joker's disregard into a sociopathic need to assert control over his associates, favoring the series' interpretation over the films. This alteration became such a fixture that the Joker received a new sidekick named Punchline when Harley Quinn switched to heroism in the comics[38]. While the former two solutions occur, either process of transformation cannot have transpired immediately. For an undefined amount of time, multiple versions of the *Narrative Entity* must have existed simultaneously as their rise and fall in public discourse gradually determines if and which place their *semiotic cues* might have within the overall constitution of the *Narrative Entity*. As such, the third solution must have occurred as a precursor to the former two. Temporarily, the *Manifestation* of a *Narrative Entity* does not directly feed back into the *Narrative Entity* itself but creates a sub-entity of that specific *Manifestation*. This sub-entity exists because the audience first reconstitutes an aesthetic object from the object they witnessed, creating the idea of a *Narrative Entity* closely related to the *Manifestation* at hand. Due to the manner of its creation, the sub-entity remains connected to both the *Manifestation* and the *Manifestation*'s original *Narrative Entity*. The *Narrative Entity*, in turn, provides a relationship to other sub-entities of its own *Manifestations*. Within public discourse, these sub-entities provide a different notion of the *Narrative Entity*, which can be negotiated until a new status quo concerning the original *Narrative Entity*'s *indices* is reached (which potentially might never happen).

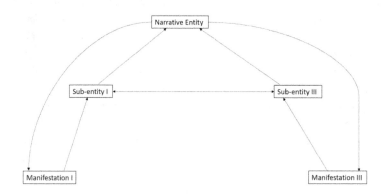

As already mentioned, the process of altering the *indices* of a *Narrative Entity* is only of marginal interest to this research. However, because this research describes the creation of a world via a network created with films and series associated with the MCU, it should be clear that the analysis does not refer to the larger *Narrative Entity* of the singular narratives, which would represent the understanding of each narrative in the context of all its

---

37   *Batman*. Directed by Tim Burton. Performances by Michael Keaton, Jack Nicholson, and Kim Basinger. Guber-Peters Company. 1989

38   Concerning the diverse meanings and development of villains and their relationships in superhero comics, I advise reading Nao Tomabechi's *Supervillain Comics: The Significance of Supervillains in American Superhero Comics*. (forthcoming).

Manifestations. Instead, this research discusses the sub-entities of each narrative. In other words, the analysis does not speak about the Thor Narrative but the MCU Thor Narrative. The clarified status has implications for the evaluation of different *semiotic cues*. As specific *media cues* and *rendition cues* remain the same throughout all the MCU *Manifestations* for a specific *index*, they might be classified as an *index cue* instead. The change occurs to the question of differentiation. With the description of the network focused on different sub-entities, *rendition cues* do not serve as a means of distinguishing between the films and the comics but as a means to separate appearances within the films. However, while understanding the network as one of sub-entities instead of *Narrative Entities* influences the results concerning the cultural impact of the MCU and any future view on the comics, the alteration has no impact on overarching results concerning the mechanics of creating and managing a network of *Narrative Entities* to the end of creating an imaginary world.

2.2.2 Transformation Triggers

Networks of *Narrative Entities* are created by comparing the composition of an *Index Manifestation*, appearing in *Manifestations* specific to each *Narrative Entity*. Hereby, the relationship is determined by the similarities and distinctions between *Index Manifestations* created from the same *Narrative Entity* or the appearance of a stable *Index Manifestation* within the *Manifestations* of several *Narrative Entities*. While this view allows for the creation of a network, employing it alone assumes an unrealistic stability of *Index Manifestations* within any given narrative structure. As such, the Universe Model requires some means to incorporate and negotiate alterations to *Index Manifestations*. In his essay "Action, Action, Description and Narrative", Teun A. van Dijk tackles "a general theory of action" to find "partial insight into the structure of narrative discourse."[39] In his work, van Dijk proceeds to define acts or actions as a "being in a state i," in which "x intentionally brings about a state j under the purpose k."[40] He continues discussing the meaning of state change to clarify his understanding of action. Here, van Dijk concludes that a state change "*takes place* or *occurs*, if one or more objects acquire or lose certain properties or mutual relations" and determines that "[s]tate changes will be called *events*."[41] Understanding that van Dijk's research considers a state "a set of objects characterized by a certain number of properties [...]"[42], his approach to *events* is easily adaptable to the mechanics of the Universe Model. Basically, van Dijk's notion of state directly corresponds to the principle of *Index Manifestation*. As he is mainly interested in the relationship between actions and narrative discourse, van Dijk does not dwell on a deep understanding of his notion of state. Correlating state to Kripke's version of *possible world*, he clarifies

---

39 van Dijk, Teun A. "Action, Action, Description and Narrative". New Literary History. Vol. 6, No. 2, On Narrative and Narratives, 1975, pp. 273–294. Page 273
40 van Dijk, Teun A. "Action, Action, Description and Narrative". New Literary History. Vol. 6, No. 2, On Narrative and Narratives, 1975, pp. 273–294. Page 277
41 van Dijk, Teun A. "Action, Action, Description and Narrative". New Literary History. Vol. 6, No. 2, On Narrative and Narratives, 1975, pp. 273–294. Page 278, original emphasis
42 van Dijk, Teun A. "Action, Action, Description and Narrative". New Literary History. Vol. 6, No. 2, On Narrative and Narratives, 1975, pp. 273–294. Page 277

that his notion of act or action affects "fragments of worlds"[43]. Considering that an *Index Manifestation* is the representation of an *index*, which is the smaller part of a *Narrative Entity* serving as the basis for creating a world, the notion of *Index Manifestation* can directly replace van Dijk's 'state' term. Combining van Dijk's definition of act with the terminology presented here, "being in the state i" would correlate with an *Index Manifestation* with a fixed set of *semiotic cues*, while his "state j" equals the same *Index Manifestation* with the addition, subtraction, or alteration of one or several *index cues*, *media cues*, or *rendition cues*. As such, the Universe Model can adapt part of van Dijk's understanding of action to describe changes to *Index Manifestations* due to the *events* affecting them within the course of a plot. As the interrelation between *Narrative Entities* relies on comparability, the Universe Model is more concerned with the fact that a change to *Index Manifestations* occurs rather than the question of the change's facilitator or a determination of its level of success. Therefore, van Dijk's principle of action includes too many aspects outside this model's concern.

Adapting such an understanding of *event* into the network requires clarification concerning its level of encompassment and its potential degree of influence. Starting with the latter, van Dijk already described that an *event* included changes to an immanent representation of an *Index Manifestation* in contrast to the permanent alterations this paper's definition requires. As such, things like opening a book, raising an arm, or walking across the room are included in van Dijk's *event* but violate the definition based on *Index Manifestation* because neither caused any alteration to a *semiotic cue*. However, as the model is not concerned with changes in service of action, discussing the relevance of non-transformative changes to *Index Manifestations* appears counterproductive. Instead, the Universe Model refocuses *events* on their transformative capability and evaluates them along those parameters. Existing as a collection of *semiotic cues*, a degree of change within an *Index Manifestation* theoretically is measurable by comparing the number of altered *semiotic cues* in relation to unaltered ones. This measurement corresponds to an *event*'s degree of influence, giving *events* a potential degree of influence that encompasses all of an *Index Manifestation*'s *semiotic cues*, none of them, and any number in between. While this range of transformation might seem broad, it covers all potential changes an *Index Manifestation* might undergo. Although no change does not warrant a reevaluation of the relationship between previously related *Index Manifestations*, smaller and larger changes require some level of reassessment.

Similar to their degree of influence, the effect of an *event* is not limited to a singular *Index Manifestation*. For one, as *Index Manifestations* are defined as existing within a network of other *Index Manifestations*, changes to one can cause a chain reaction across the presented network. A slew of genres, revenge stories and hero tales among them, lean on the fact that the changed status of a character can motivate/cause change in another. Van Dijk describes this process as a *causal chain*, in which "an event E_i causes (directly) an event E_j, if – all other things being equal – E_j would not occur without the previous occur-

---

[43] van Dijk, Teun A. "Action, Action, Description and Narrative". *New Literary History*. Vol. 6, No. 2, On Narrative and Narratives, 1975, pp. 273–294. Page 278

rence of E_i."[44] While his description of the process serves his understanding of action, it remains applicable to our developing re-conception of Dijk's *event* when the *causal chain* is adapted to the basis of altered *semiotic cues*. Adopting van Dijk's formula, the Universe Model perceives a *causal chain* as follows: An *event* E_1 causes an alteration to an *Index Manifestation* I_1, the alteration to I_1 triggers a new *event* E_2; E_2 causes an alteration to a new *Index Manifestation* I_2, which again causes a new *event* E_3, and (potentially) so on. As in van Dijk's case, the alteration of I_2 is directly related to E_1 if E_2 would not have occurred without the changes to I_1.

Aside from influencing different *Index Manifestations* via a *causal chain*, events can also directly affect several *Index Manifestations* simultaneously. Existing in a network, *Index Manifestations* within a *Manifestation* do not only relate to one another causally but equally stand in some form of imagined spatial relationship. In other words, the network of *Index Manifestations* denotes a relationship of action between the indices and a relation in space. Perceiving the network of *Index Manifestations* as an implied relation in an imaginary space entails the potential for an *event* to affect several *Index Manifestations* directly and simultaneously. Considered spatially, van Dijk's *events* need to be viewed in two parts to understand their level of encompassment. A notion of potential alterations has to be related to the process of actual alterations. As an *event* is defined along the lines of its effect on *Index Manifestations* and not an occurring action, its range of influence cannot be argued across the nature of the action producing it. Instead, the number (or spatial equivalent denoting a number) of *Index Manifestations* potentially altered serves as the basis for its range. Hereby, this potential lies in the representation of *Index Manifestations* in the occurrence of the *event* as well as any description of it. For example, a fight between two characters shown in a solitary ring solely has the potential of altering the two characters and the props within the scene. If the same sequence includes an audience, the *event*'s potential range extends to the audience. If the venue changes to a battlefield of war, the *event*'s potential influence includes the social and national entities engaged in that war. As the word potential and the previous description of an *event*'s degree of influence implies, an *Index Manifestation*'s presence within the range of *event* does not automatically entail a change to it, especially considering that an alteration of *Index Manifestations* is defined as additions, subtractions, and alterations of *semiotic cues*. As such, the level of encompassment is evaluated by the detraction of non-altered *Index Manifestations* from all *Index Manifestations* within the range of potential alteration. While an *event* operates with a degree of influence and a level of encompassment, these two principles contain no fixed correlation. Furthermore, the degree of influence is not fixed in either type or degree when the event affects more than one *Index Manifestation*. When the Joker creates two simultaneous explosions in Christopher Nolan's *The Dark Knight*[45], the event has varying degrees of influence. As the two explosions are presented not only as timed together and prepared in the same fashion (barrels connected with wires), with the only difference

---

44 van Dijk, Teun A. "Action, Action, Description and Narrative". *New Literary History*. Vol. 6, No. 2, On Narrative and Narratives, 1975, pp. 273–294. Page 278
45 *The Dark Knight*. Directed by Christopher Nolan. Performances by Christian Bale, Heath Ledger, and Maggie Gyllenhaal. Warner Bros. Pictures. 2008

being the lightening and Batman as well as Jim Gordon rushing to save the characters endangered by the impending *event*, the outcome has a vast level of encompassment. Aside from the mentioned characters, sets and props in proximity to an explosion are obviously changed by it. Focusing on Rachel Dawes, Harvey Dent, and Batman, it becomes clear how different the effect of one *event* can be on several *Index Manifestations*. Rachel Dawes dies in the explosion. While this alteration of an *Index Manifestation* triggers a series of other *events* in a *causal chain*, the *event*'s direct effect is her removal as an *Index Manifestation* from the network and her reattribution as a new *semiotic cue* to other *Index Manifestations* (foremost characters). The explosion's direct effect on Harvey Dent is the addition of his half-burned face and damaged suit as an *index cue* indicating his transformation into his villainous persona 'Two-Face' and as a *rendition cue* due to the unique version of his disfigurement in relation to other interpretations of the character. Batman undergoes no direct alteration due to the explosion, but, like other characters, he is greatly influenced by *events* triggered along a *causal chain*, as he has to contend with a new villain and the notion of a lost future with Rachel Dawes. Overall, within the Universe Model, an *event* causes an alteration to one or more *Index Manifestations* with a potentially individual set of changes depending on the *event* and the *Index Manifestation* impacted by the *event*. As the manner and form in which the term *event* is used within the Universe Model differs significantly from its use in current research, it is prudent to alter the name to distinguish it from more established uses like by Herman, Coste, and Chatman or other principles built upon it like the notion of *eventfulness*. Considering that the main line of definition and the main view of *event* within this discussion and its further use lies in its ability to trigger a transformation in an *Index Manifestation*, the notion of *event* developed here is referred to as a *Transformation Trigger*.

Taking on the alteration of *semiotic cues* and concurrently *Index Manifestations* for understanding a network of *Narrative Entities* automatically influences the view on narrative structure and plot. A focus on the state of different parts of the network delegates the cause and action to the background. While notions of actions remain in place, they provide nothing more than a means of evaluating changes to *semiotic cues*. This demotion of the action and focus on transformation within the network determines a view of time, which, instead of being defined in any relation to the time passing in reality, is based on a spatial understanding. In the *Dictionary of Narratology*, Prince briefly defines time as "[t]he period or periods during which the situation and events presented (*story time*, time of the *narrated, Erzählte Zeit*) and their presentation (*discourse time*, time of *narrating, Erzählzeit*) occur."[46] This essential and widely known definition grasps time in fiction by comparing it to a human experience, with the former basing the sense of time in narration on comparable occurrences and the latter grasping the time it takes to perceive that occurrence in a given text. Within the use of *Transformation Triggers*, the conception of time becomes spatial because time in fiction moves in accordance with the causal order of the transformed versions of the same network. Considering the beginning of any *Narrative Entity*'s *Manifestation*, a network of *Index Manifestations* with fixed *semiotic cues* is created as a representation of the world at hand. This stable world embodies T_0, the

---

46   Prince, Gerald. *Dictionary of Narratology*. Nebraska: University of Nebraska Press, 2003. Page 99, original emphasis

set iteration of the presented world. When the first *Transformation Trigger* occurs, some *semiotic cues* within the larger networks are altered, which (potentially) changes the relationship between *Index Manifestations* within it. As such, the new network expresses an altered version of the presented world; it represents the version conjured through the application of a specific *Transformation Trigger* on the previous network. This second world embodies T_1, the first altered iteration of the presented world. With the second *Transformation Trigger*, a second altered iteration of the network emerges, which then embodies T_2. This process can continue as long as *Transformation Triggers* can be applied to the network. Like the panels of a comic, each iteration represents a state of existence, with each iteration connected through the idea of a transformative action between them. Within this view, it is notable that previous networks do not cease to exist. As long as they are accessible, audiences and researchers can return to them.

Equally, as with a comic book page, the spatial manner of thinking about time in fiction allows for comparisons of iterations of the same network separated by several *Transformation Triggers*. This spatial view of time provides important features for the use of the Universe Model. Foremost, it allows for a precise determination of the network of *Narrative Entities* described in relation to all *Manifestations* and their *Transformation Triggers* influencing the makeup of the network. Secondly, it separates collections of meaningful actions from collections of hollow actions. Meaningful actions, in this instance, refer to actions that can be classified as *Transformation Triggers*. In other words, they are actions that cause changes within an *Index Manifestation*, potentially altering the network. Hollow action, in this context, relates to actions or sequences of actions that occur but do not directly alter any *semiotic cue* of an *Index Manifestation*. Classic examples of sequences of hollow actions in film are fight/combat or love scenes. In either case, the initial or final action might constitute a *Transformation Trigger*. However, all actions in between do not alter the *semiotic cues* and, therefore, the network directly, primarily providing a spectacle over narrative content. The third important aspect is that the spatial view of time allows an understanding of the interrelation of different *Narrative Entities* across time in the same manner as across space. In relating different *Narrative Entities*, the intradiegetic notion of distance and the intradiegetic means of traversing and communication across distance affect the potential of *Index Manifestations* to influence and relate to one another. Simply put, if two *Index Manifestations* are separated from one another by a galaxy with no means of communication and/or traveling that distance, it becomes more difficult for them to form or interact within a network. Conversely, forming a network is much more likely when the *Index Manifestations* appear in an imagined close proximity. If we consider the established view of time in literature, the relation of *Index Manifestations* has to be evaluated spatially and temporally. The latter demands that an analysis of interrelation considers potential long *causal chains* and fills in a timeline to evaluate potential connections. Viewing time as spatial within the context of the model allows for the definition of a different time as a different place. As such, the connection between *Index Manifestations* can also be determined by the intradiegetic means of traversing and communicating across these different spaces. Aside from simplifying any argument concerning a lack of interrelation, this understanding also compensates for the existence of time travel, which is common in certain types of speculative fiction. This changed view on narrative structure permits a more straightforward analysis of *Manifestations* for the purpose of interrelating them and determining their relationship.

The dominant means by which *Transformation Triggers* influence a network is its effect on *Index Manifestations*. Hereby, it provides a legitimate reason for the consistent (or inconsistent) representation of an *Index Manifestation* despite a difference in appearance between two or more representations. In other words, when Captain America appears in an issue of Iron Man, changes his costume in one of his own issues, and then appears in an issue of Spider-Man, the *Transformation Trigger* of changing his costume provides the reason why the version of Captain America in the Iron Man comic and the version of Captain America in the Spider-Man comic can be considered the same, despite differing *semiotic cues*. A *Transformation Trigger* can provide such a reason because it automatically becomes backstory within the altered network. As described earlier, *Index Manifestation* refers to characters, sets, props, musical scores, sound effects, unique words, phrases, and sayings. However, it equally refers to the aspect of backstory. Backstory usually explains the state of an *Index Manifestation*, or a network of *Index Manifestations*, before any *Transformation Trigger* has occurred. This distinction serves to separate events that explain the state of an *index* (backstory) from events that generate changes to an *Index Manifestation* (*Transformation Triggers*) in the course of a plot. As mentioned, *Transformation Triggers* provide a reason for the changed state of a *semiotic cue*, thereby splitting a narrative structure into several networks between such *Transformation Triggers*. However, this view of narrative structure as a series of singular networks demands that an analysis continuously reaches for an aspect situated outside of the actual network to justify the network's constitution. In other words, to explain the state of a network, an analysis would always have to refer back to different moments of alteration. However, every network that has undergone an alteration due to a *Transformation Trigger* has to adopt that trigger as backstory, as it explains the state of the network or a specific *Index Manifestation*, which is the definition of backstory. As such, every *Transformation Trigger*, in addition to directly altering the *semiotic cues* of an *Index Manifestation*, becomes a new *index* of the *Narrative Entity* itself. Aside from maintaining the separation of different networks, this adoption of *Transformation Triggers* into the network as backstory serves several other purposes. For one, it secures the order of a network's different states as each following network includes all previous *Transformation Triggers* as backstory. The network with the most *Index Manifestations* classified as backstory always stands later in the chain. Secondly, the adoption of *Transformation Triggers* as backstory counters the potential need to go back and revise the transformative effect of a *Transformation Trigger* because the narrative reveals something significant about the event later. As backstory is an *index* like any other, its *Index Manifestations* contain the same three types of *semiotic cues* – index cues, media cues, and rendition cues. Suppose a revelation alters the meaning of a backstory created from a previous *Transformation Trigger*. In that case, this revelation is nothing more than a new *Transformation Trigger*, which alters the *semiotic cues* of an existing *Index Manifestation* that happens to be a backstory. This line of thinking may appear unnecessary and overly complicated. Still, it allows for determining a network relationship in the order of a plot instead of the order of the story – in this case, meaning the *fabula* – which otherwise would have to be reconstituted for an analysis. More importantly, in the case of several *Manifestations*, it allows for an analysis maintaining the order of publication, even if a later publication contradicts the representation of an earlier one. Finally, this adoption of *Transformation Triggers* as *indices* provides the potential to link the *Narrative Entity* of long-running series to their outdated *Manifestations* by relating certain backstory *indices* to *Transformation Triggers* within those *Manifestations*. In practice, *Narrative Entities* can be related to one another because the backstory of one *Narrative Entity* has a corresponding *Transformation Trigger* in the *Manifestation* of another *Narrative Entity*.

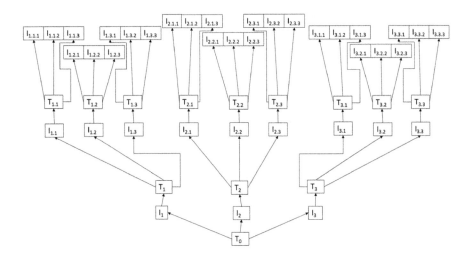

Aside from serving as a connection via becoming a backstory *index*, *Transformation Triggers* have another means of interrelating different *Narrative Entities*: *Trigger Waves*. Van Dijk's notion of *causal chains* can also be adapted to the principle of *Transformation Triggers*. Instead of perceiving chains of *events* as attached by the causal relation of events, consecutive *Transformation Triggers* operate on waves of reaction due to the changes in an *Index Manifestation*. Laying the new terminology over the description for the adaptation of *events* presented earlier, the idea of a chain of *Transformation Triggers* would follow a certain pattern. A *Transformation Trigger* T_1 causes an alteration to an *Index Manifestation* I_1; in consequence, the alteration to I_1 triggers a new *Transformation Trigger* T_2; T_2 causes an alteration to a new *Index Manifestation* I_2, which again causes a new *Transformation Trigger* T_3 and (potentially) so on. The alteration of I_2 is directly related to T_1 if T_2 would not have occurred without the changes to I_1. While a chain of *Transformation Triggers* can occur linearly, causally related changes are more likely to occur in waves. *Transformation Triggers* have been defined as potentially affecting multiple *Index Manifestations*. Equally, the emergence of a second *Transformation Trigger* within a causal order is related to the changes made to the previously affected *Index Manifestation*. As a *Transformation Trigger* potentially can affect multiple *Index Manifestations*, each *Transformation Trigger* could initiate several new *Transformation Triggers*. Continuing the process, each of the new *Transformation Triggers* could alter several *Index Manifestations*, which each could trigger new *Transformation Triggers*. Understanding this difference, the previously mentioned formula has to be adjusted: T_0 alters I_1, I_2, I_3. I_1, I_2, and I_3 each trigger a new

Transformation Trigger T_1, T_2, and T_3. T_1 alters $I_{1.1}$, $I_{1.2}$, $I_{1.3}$. T_2 alters $I_{2.1}$, $I_{2.2}$, $I_{2.3}$. T_3 alters $I_{3.1}$, $I_{3.2}$, $I_{3.3}$. Each of these nine altered *Index Manifestations* potentially continue onward to create a *Transformation Trigger*, $T_{1.1}$, $T_{1.2}$, $T_{1.3}$, $T_{2.1}$, $T_{2.2}$, $T_{2.3}$, $T_{3.1}$, $T_{3.2}$, $T_{3.3}$, which in turn potentially further alter other *Index Manifestations* and so on. While this description is artificial in nature as it assumes a gradual expansion by a constant power of three and a *Transformation Trigger* can alter any number of *Index Manifestations* – including ones that have already been altered in the process – it still demonstrates the difference between chaining van Dijk's *events* and chaining *Transformation Triggers*. The former continues as a linear series. The latter expands in a wave of causally linked transformations. As such, the consecutive generating of *Transformation Triggers* is referred to as a *Trigger Wave*. The change in description and view is necessary because, while a *Trigger Wave* may appear as a linear *causal chain*, it can expand in a series of several causal lines, which run parallel, cross, merge, interfere with one another, and halt at different points. The image of a wave causing a set of new waves, which expand alongside and into one another, covers all of these potential linear developments. Such a view is important when researching the interrelation of *Narrative Entities* in a network. While the transposition of singular *Index Manifestations* between two *Narrative Entities* might operate linearly concerning potential *Transformation Triggers*, the notion of a network contains the potential of one event affecting numerous members of that network, especially when the network contains *Manifestations* built on the use of *Index Manifestations* from different *Narrative Entities* like films such as *The Avengers*[47]. Furthermore, such a network necessarily will have different lines of narration, which potentially run parallel, cross, merge, and interfere with one another. *Trigger Waves* do not necessarily run for all eternity (whereas they could as long as new *Manifestations* continue to react to previous alterations) but stop when the alteration of the final *Index Manifestations* does not cause a new *Transformation Trigger*. It is necessary to point out that narratology's usual view of acts or actions does not overlap with *Transformation Triggers*. While an action can cause changes to an *Index Manifestation*'s *semiotic cues*, it does not have to. Following the notion of action that includes simple movements and acts like raising one's hand, most actions will not serve as *Transformation Triggers* but instead stand in service of a required *function* (Barthes's term). As such, it is reasonable to assume that a *Trigger Wave* is not endless, but because even if every alteration to an *Index Manifestation* caused a (re-)action, this action is not necessarily a *Transformation Trigger*. Concerning the interrelation of *Narrative Entities*, *Trigger Waves* operate in the same manner singular *Transformation Triggers* do, with one difference: Every backstory *index* is, by its nature, automatically linked to another backstory *index* explaining a preceding state. Backstory *indices* created from *Trigger Waves* are also linked to the *index*'s one or several semiotic cues that caused its original *Transformation Trigger* because the backstory's final form and conceptualization are based on its source. As such, the backstories generated from *Trigger Waves* form a net of dependencies, which lies over the actual network, tying singular *Narrative Entities* together.

Independent from all the forms a *Transformation Trigger* can take, it connects *Narrative Entities* mostly via its means of becoming backstory. Backstory based on *Transformation Triggers* then interrelates *Narrative Entities* by two means: (1) explaining changes made to

---

47   *The Avengers*. Directed by Joss Whedon. Marvel Studios, 2012

an *Index Manifestation* and (2) creating a net of interlinked backstory *indices* across different *Narrative Entities*. While these two means are the dominant manner in which *Transformation Triggers* relate *Narrative Entities*, they do not provide the most meaningful manner of interrelation. Instead, a direct combination of *Transformation Triggers*, one *Index Manifestation*, and a classic plot structure creates one of the most substantial means of tying *Narrative Entities* together.

2.2.2.1 Shared Narrative

While not denoting them with a sense of complete randomness – as a sense of continued causality generates the different changes – the principle of *Trigger Waves* is far from a coherent and classic structure usually used for the classification of a plot. However, employing a plot structure to the notion of a *Trigger Wave* seems counterproductive, as classic plot structures have been built around the same linear notion Barthes used for his understanding of events and actions. As plot functions around a cohesive order of sequences, the spreading structure of a *Trigger Wave* contradicts an amalgamation with a plot. Still, adding plot structures to the Universe Model is necessary. Aside from the apparent need to interlay the plot of a *Manifestation* with the network of *Narrative Entities*, the Universe Model specifically has to cover the existence of overarching plot structures. Story franchises inherently contain the notion of a plot spanning several *Manifestations*. This notion is associated more with series but has also been part of film franchises. Within a world created through a network of *Narrative Entities*, the idea of an overarching plot becomes even more important, as it technically does not have to contain itself to *Manifestations* of the same *Narrative Entity* but can spread across any participant within the same network. A plot structure stretched across *Manifestations* of several *Narrative Entities* would also tie these *Narrative Entities* closer together because the complete comprehension of that plot ties to an engagement with several *Narrative Entities*. As such, the Universe Model requires a combination of the principles of a *Trigger Wave* and a classic plot structure.

As the spreading wave configuration, which can continuously create further waves, is antithetical to the linear form of a plot, it is necessary to create a plot structure based on a *Trigger Wave* or find some sense of linearity within the process of a *Trigger Wave*. While the former is conceivably possible, it would take an entire additional monography to build and argue an entirely new understanding of plot. As it is easier to find linearity within a wave structure, the Universe Model will seek to maintain the greater part of a traditional plot structure by applying it to a linear causality created in the course of different *Trigger Waves*. As the argument for a *Trigger Wave* contained the possibility for such a wave to form linearly, it appears sensible to apply any notion of plot to such linear cases. However, assuming that an overarching plot structure could only occur if a *Transformation Trigger* solely causes one *Index Manifestation* to change, which in turn creates a *Transformation Trigger* that in itself only affects one *Index Manifestation*, is too limiting. Instead, finding singular elements that allow drawing a line through the emerging wave structure is more reasonable. While finding different means of drawing such a line is possible, the simplest is to focus on one clear presence, meaning a specific *Index Manifestation*. As *Trigger Waves* are built on the mechanics of a *Transformation Trigger*, grasping them within a narrative structure is tied to the changes made to an *Index Manifestation*. As such, it is easy to draw a line through *Trigger Waves* by focusing on the changes made to and caused by one specific *Index Manifestation*.

With a line through any number of potential waves of transformations, it is necessary to adapt a plot structure to the processual notion of a *Trigger Wave* as a series of *Transformation Triggers* and build its status in relation to the overall network. The latter is necessary because, in contrast to a regular plot structure, the plot structure applied here does not exist in isolation. The general approach to determining and identifying a plot presumes its existence within a closed unit, usually within some form of text – e.g., novel, film, series, or oral tradition. While the meaning of a narration's elements could change due to discourse, and the structure might change through the adaptation to another means of telling, the plot structure exists only within a singular text or a clear, linear series of texts. Within a network of *Narrative Entities*, the understanding of such a structure has to grow to incorporate not only its existence aside other plots but also a form independent from the traditionally presumed boundaries set by a text. Keeping this in mind, a plot tied to a specific *Index Manifestation* does not only have to situate singular elements within the plot structure of all the *Manifestations* it appears in but also may have to evaluate its relation to other overarching plots, which may pass through the same *Manifestation(s)*. Additionally, as the plot structure is tied to a specific *Index Manifestation*, the position and relations of that *Index Manifestation* within the overall larger network also become important. The adaptation to the notion of change inherent to *Transformation Triggers* means that the notion of an overarching plot within the Universe Model has to relate each stage of a plot to changes within its *Index Manifestation*, the *Transformation Triggers* caused by that change, and another change caused by the reflection of that *Transformation Trigger*. In other words, each element has to contain the elements of a *Trigger Wave* but with a focus on changes made to a specific *Index Manifestation*. With the understanding that an overarching plot has to be located within the larger network and adapted to the Universe Model's focus on alterations over actions, a traditional plot structure can be adapted to the overall model. While it is reasonably possible to adapt any form of plot structure, this research will adopt a simplified understanding of *Freytag's Pyramid* because it is one of the oldest and most prominent plot structures, is based on Aristoteles's three-part structure, and "has often been used to characterize (various aspects of) PLOT in narrative"[48]. While *Freytag's Pyramid* exists in interpretations of various complexity, this research will adapt the basic version along its five parts: *Exposition, Rising Action, Climax, Falling Action*, and *Catastrophe/Denouement*. Using the basic definition given in Gerald Prince's *Dictionary of Narratology*, *Exposition* is "[t]he presentation of the circumstances obtaining before the BEGINNING of the action."[49] Within the context of a traditional plot structure tied to a single *Manifestation*, this definition entails a complete presentation of the overall world, including characters, set, props, and so on, as it pertains to the narrative at hand. Focused on a single *Index Manifestation* presented within a network of *Index Manifestations*, which again exists within a larger network of *Narrative*

---

[48] Prince, Gerald. *Dictionary of Narratology*. Nebraska: University of Nebraska Press, 2003, Page 36, original emphasis

[49] Prince, Gerald. *Dictionary of Narratology*. Nebraska: University of Nebraska Press, 2003, Page 28, original emphasis

Entities, *Exposition* necessarily pertains to a presentation of the plot's *Index Manifestation*'s position within the overall network as well as its constellation of *semiotic cues*. In other words, an *Exposition* phase within this plot structure solely serves to present the *Index Manifestation* in question and locate it within the larger network. Hereby, the *Exposition* does not have to play out within a single film, series, or novel but may find its presentation across several. In the same way, the *Exposition* in a traditional plot structure can be "provided after the beginning or the action has been set forth"[50]; the same can hold true for the *Exposition* within such an overarching plot structure.

With a clear understanding of the *Index Manifestation* and its place within the network, the *Index Manifestation* moves into the *Rising Action* of *Freytag's Pyramid*. Referring to this part also as the rising movement, Gustav Freytag describes the *Rising Action* as an exciting force or inciting event, which forces the constellation created within the *Exposition* towards the *Climax*. Hereby, the *Rising Action* can occur in one or several stages.[51] The assertion of a set overall situation and a reliance on a notion of action over an understanding of transformation makes the adaptation of *Rising Action* to the mechanics of the Universe Model more difficult. On the level of the situation, Freytag's original theory operates with the assertion that the *Exposition* has explained and set all elements into place. However, within a network that by its definition appears as a new iteration in irregular intervals and a conception of *Exposition* focused on one element within this large network, such an assertion cannot be made. Similarly, a model based on changes to its various elements has to consider a continued series of changes for a continued rise instead of assuming a series of actions. An overarching plot structure focused on the relation of one *Index Manifestation* within the *Manifestations* of different *Narrative Entities* has to consider the *Rising Action* as a process of changes due to that specific *Index Manifestation*'s involvement with these different *Manifestations*. In other words, within a network and transformative understanding, the *Rising Action* within the Universe Model interweaves the overarching *Index Manifestation* with the *Manifestations* of one or several *Narrative Entities* by creating a process of change and counter-change between the network at hand and the overarching *Index Manifestation*. Viewing the two elements as separate until they engage allows them to interact at different stages with one another. As such, the *Exposition* of the *Index Manifestation* that operates in an overarching plot can already have occurred (in a different *Manifestation*) when the *Exposition* for the plot of a specific *Manifestation*, in which the specific *Index Manifestation* appears, takes place. More importantly, it frees the overarching plot structure from setting the entire stage but leaves it to focus on the specific stage for one *Index Manifestation*. As with the original *Rising Action*, this process of interweaving can occur in different stages, and, within the idea of an overarching *Index Manifestation*, these stages can occur within several *Manifestations* from multiple *Narrative Entities*. The fact that the *Rising Action* within this overarching plot structure can occur in different *Manifestations* highlights that procedural change towards a *Climax*, in this in-

---

50   Prince, Gerald. *Dictionary of Narratology*. Nebraska: University of Nebraska Press, 2003, Page 28
51   Freytag, Gustav. *Technique of the Drama*. Translated by E.J. McEwan. Scott, Foresman and Company, 1900 https://archive.org/details/freytagstechniquoofreyuoft/page/124/mode/2up?q=125., Page 125

stance, is not tied to an overall network but solely to the development of that one *Index Manifestation*.

As such, the *Climax* equally is tied to that *Index Manifestation*. Defined as "the culminating point in a progressive intensification" and "the highest point of the RISING ACTION"[52], the *Climax* within the structure presented here is the most significant change to the *Index Manifestation* within the entire plot structure. With the *Rising Action* understood as a series of changes and counter-changes, the *Climax*, as the end of intensification, also has to adhere to a process of transformation as "the place in the piece where the results of the rising movement come out strong and decisively"[53]. While the transformations of the *Rising Action* formally are limited to the *Index Manifestation* and the network of *Manifestations* it passes through at that moment, the transformation created by the *Climax* can reverberate throughout the larger network significantly and meaningfully. As such, the *Climax* of such an overarching plot structure tied to an *Index Manifestation* requires an evaluation of the network as a whole within the context of a monumental change, which leads to the *Falling Action*.

In his work *Technique of the Drama*, Freytag defines the *Falling Action* as the counter beat to the *Rising Action* and attributes the use of a limited number of characters and scenes to the rising movement.[54] Determining any number of characters within this context of a network is difficult, as the overall number of characters at any given moment is dictated not only by the overarching plot but equally by the plot structure of the specific *Manifestation* in which the *Falling Action* of the overarching plot occurs, as well as the needs of the larger network. Adapting a limited number of scenes, however, is very well possible. Freytag's understanding of the *Falling Action* as a counterbeat to the *Rising Action* is more problematic. As he devised his plot structure for tragedies, Freytag follows his *Climax* with a reversal, "a tragic force"[55] which overthrows the hero. While the plot cannot and should not rise further after the *Climax*, understanding the *Falling Action* as the process of tragically tearing down the *Index Manifestation* the plot structure is ascribed to would limit the applicability too much for the use within a larger network. Instead, this plot structure should focus on the fact that "[s]uspense must now be existed in what is new. For this, new forces, perhaps new rôles[sic!], must be introduced, in which the hearer must acquire interest."[56] While Freytag probably refers to the intro-

---

52   Prince, Gerald. *Dictionary of Narratology*. Nebraska: University of Nebraska Press, 2003. Page 14, original emphasis

53   Freytag, Gustav. *Technique of the Drama*. Translated by E.J. McEwan. Scott, Foresman and Company, 1900 https://archive.org/details/freytagstechniqu00freyuoft/page/124/mode/2up?q=12 5., Page 128

54   Freytag, Gustav. *Technique of the Drama*. Translated by E.J. McEwan. Scott, Foresman and Company, 1900 https://archive.org/details/freytagstechniqu00freyuoft/page/124/mode/2up?q=12 5., Page 133

55   Freytag, Gustav. *Technique of the Drama*. Translated by E.J. McEwan. Scott, Foresman and Company, 1900 https://archive.org/details/freytagstechniqu00freyuoft/page/124/mode/2up?q=12 5., Page 130

56   Freytag, Gustav. *Technique of the Drama*. Translated by E.J. McEwan. Scott, Foresman and Company, 1900 https://archive.org/details/freytagstechniqu00freyuoft/page/124/mode/2up?q=12 5., Page 132

duction of new *Index Manifestations*, it makes more sense to understand the need for new forces and new roles as the reorganization of the network after the dramatic change to the *Index Manifestation* associated with the overarching plot structure. In other words, the alteration created by the *Climax* is so significant that it requires the entirety of the *Falling Action* to re-evaluate the *Index Manifestation*'s place within and the subsequent effects on the overall network. As such, the *Falling Action* contains nothing else but a series of *Trigger Waves* created by the *Climax* and, through the process, relocates the *Index Manifestation* within the overall network. Describing the *Falling Action* in such a manner necessarily redefines Freytag's *Catastrophe*, which formally ends the plot structure. With Freytag's focus on tragedy, his original plot structure predetermines an ending containing the logical destruction of a hero. In his writing, he focuses on the character's demise and the need for a grand destruction on stage against the "modern tender-heartedness" of his time's modern poets and playwrights. The focus on a grand destruction has no direct use for a plot structure, which is interwoven into a larger network, especially as the network will continue, even after the plot specific to an *Index Manifestation* has ended. In various versions of *Freytag's Pyramid*, *Catastrophe* has been replaced with the more flexible notion of *Denouement*, which usually is defined as "the end of a story [...] or the end result of a situation"[57] or "as the resolution of the issue of a complicated plot in fiction."[58] This understanding of *Denouement* is easily applicable to the notion of a plot structure tied to a specific *Index Manifestation*. Essentially, the *Denouement* marks the first appearance of the *Index Manifestation* within a new stabilized representation in relation to the network, in contrast to the continued *Trigger Wave* forming the *Falling Action*. As the overarching transformative influence of the entire plot has ended, the appearance of the *Index Manifestation* in a new stabilized context formally ends the running plot. As this plot's structure is embedded into a larger network, which necessarily has a variety of further plots within and across *Manifestations*, the occurrence of the *Denouement* within one plot has no necessary influence on the continuation of the overall network. Equally, it does not necessarily end the existence or importance of the *Index Manifestation* related to it but solely finalizes the plot structure, leaving the *Index Manifestation* to continue within the network in any form its collection of *semiotic cues* and position within the network theoretically allows.

The combination of the different steps developed here forms a plot structure that can exist within another network, interact with the plot of a *Manifestation*, and tie *Narrative Entities* together by spreading its process across various *Manifestations*. As, presumably, the application of such an overarching plot serves to tighten the relationship between networked *Narrative Entities*, it makes sense to focus on its spread across *Narrative Entities*. Therefore, this iteration of the plot structure shall be referred to as a *Shared Narrative*, in which the word 'share' denotes the narratives split across the *Manifestations* of different *Narrative Entities*. Structured along the traditional dramatic structure of *Freytag's Pyramid*, a *Shared Narrative* contains five phases. The *Exposition* introduces and establishes a specific *Index Manifestation* and contextualizes it within the network. Renaming *Rising Action* to *Rising Transformation*, the second phase interweaves the *Shared Narrative*'s *Index*

---

57 https://dictionary.cambridge.org/dictionary/english/denouement?q=Denouement, retrieved August 30th, 2021
58 https://literarydevices.net/denouement/, retrieved August 30th, 2021

Manifestation with the *Manifestations* of one or more *Narrative Entities* by creating a process of change and counter-change between the network and the overarching *Index Manifestation*. A series of *Rising Transformation* sequences eventually lead to the *Climax*, which is a grand change to the *Index Manifestation*, redefining it and its position within the larger network. The *Trigger Waves* created by the *Climax*'s grand transformation are resolved in the fourth phase. As the structure focuses on the transformative effect of the *Climax* across the network, this plot structure will refer to the *Falling Action* as *Climax Waves*. The *Denouement* represents the final phase of the *Shared Narrative*. It ends the structure by presenting the state of the *Index Manifestation* and its place within the network after the *Climax Waves*. *Shared Narratives* may spread out each of these phases across several *Narrative Entities*. They may also allow for the continued use of the *Index Manifestation* after the plot has been completed.

Concerning their ability to draw *Narrative Entities* together, *Shared Narratives* create a dependency between the *Manifestations* of different *Narrative Entities* due to the reliance of each of the *Shared Narrative*'s phases on one another. With each phase (or even sections of each phase) in a different *Manifestation*, the full comprehension of the plot surrounding that one *Index Manifestation* depends on an engagement with each *Manifestation*, which necessarily draws the associated *Narrative Entities* closer together. However, while the *Shared Narrative* can singularly tie any number of *Narrative Entities* to one another, it also sets the *Manifestations* it appears in into a linear relationship. As the phases function along a causality of presentation and change to one specific *Index Manifestation*, it necessarily orders the appearance of that *Index Manifestation* linearly. Spreading the phases out across different *Manifestations*, therefore, forces these *Manifestations* into the same order as the related phases within that specific *Shared Narrative*. The effect is strengthened by the collapse of the *Transformation Triggers* running along the *Shared Narrative* into backstory *indices* of its *Index Manifestation*. In other words, the additional number of *semiotic cues* the *Index Manifestation* collects during the *Shared Narrative* also forces the different *Manifestations* into a specific order.

2.2.2.2 Example Transformation Trigger

In the simplest terms, *Transformation Triggers* contribute to the interrelation of different *Manifestations* and their corresponding *Narrative Entities* by providing a link between changed representations of the same *Index Manifestation*. Hereby, the link between *Manifestations* arises from the presumed coherence of an *Index Manifestation* and a presumed causal link between subsequent *Transformation Triggers*. In other words, *Transformation Triggers* serve the process of interrelation by providing a reason for an altered representation of an *Index Manifestation*, which appears in different *Manifestations*, and by continuing a series of changes stretching across several *Manifestations*. In practice, these simple terms take on complex forms, as the changes to an *Index Manifestation* can be subtle or overt, and the causal relation between *Transformation Triggers* may be singular, immanent, and short, or multifaceted, delayed, and long, or anything in between. The following analysis shows how superhero comics employ *Transformation Triggers* to interrelate *Manifestations* and which expression the genre generally favors. Any aspect mentioned in the previous analysis of *Index Manifestations* concerning other means by which the genre supports the interconnected nature of their comics equally applies in this case.

Dominantly concerned with the application of *Transformation Triggers*, the analysis of the *Civil War* Event focuses on one specific *Index Manifestation* and the relation of its subsequent changes to the process of interrelation. Additionally, the analysis looks at the causal link between alterations to various *Index Manifestations* and one inciting *Transformation Trigger*. The latter specifically highlights the principle of a *Trigger Wave* as it occurs within a network of superhero comics. A discussion of the research material first looks at the wave of changes caused by the 'Stamford Incident' followed by a discussion of the *Index Manifestation* of Peter Parker/Spider-Man. The analysis of the character attempts to show how *Transformation Triggers* serve to connect altered versions of the same *Index Manifestation* appearing in different *Manifestations*. Hereby, the initial example deals with minor and limited changes, which do not affect any pervasive *semiotic cues*, as well as the ability of *Transformation Triggers* to induce more noticeable alterations. The analysis is then expanded with the notion of a *Shared Narrative* to provide a look at that technique's usage within superhero comics. This chapter ends with a short evaluation of the network of backstory created at the end of the Civil War Event and its potential influence on the creation of *Manifestations* following the research material.

The capital 'E' Event in superhero comics generally operates in the manner of a *Trigger Wave*, as usually a singular occurrence has to affect and influence several different *Narrative Entities*. As such, comic Events employ singular alterations to one or more *Index Manifestations*, which in turn provokes the alteration of one or more other *Index Manifestations*, which again provokes the alteration in one or more further *Index Manifestations*, and potentially so on. Within the research material, the 'Stamford Incident' provides an example of an initial *Transformation Trigger*, invoking further *Transformation Triggers* across several other series. Occurring in *Civil War #1*, the 'Stamford Incident' refers to an explosion caused by a superhuman conflict between the team of young superheroes filming a reality TV show – the 'New Warriors' – and a group of recently escaped supervillains. The explosion kills over 600 people, 60 children among them. This *Transformation Trigger* also removed all but one of the current members of the superhero team 'New Warriors' and a collection of supervillains from the network, effectively ending that iteration of the *New Warriors* series. Additionally, the incident altered Robert Baldwin/Speedball's powers[59]. The deaths of civilians, specifically children, alter the public's perception of superheroes. News reports question the freedom and status of superheroes within overall society[60]. This new antagonistic stance is personified in the character Miriam Sharpe. Created for the Civil War Event, the mother of a Stamford victim attacks Tony Stark at the memorial service, accusing him of bearing responsibility for her son's demise[61]. The altered state of Robert Baldwin's powers leaves him helpless when arrested for the 'Stamford Incident'.[62] Effectively, the *Transformation Trigger* removed some *Index Manifestations*, altered one *Index Manifestation*, and changed the relationship between the larger

---

59   Civil War: Frontline #1 "The Accused, Part One". Written by Paul Jenkins. Illustrated by Steve Lieber. Marvel Comics, 2006. Page 11
60   Civil War #1. Written by Mark Millar. Illustrator Steve McNiven. Marvel Comics 2006. Page 13/15
61   Civil War #1. Written by Mark Millar. Illustrator Steve McNiven. Marvel Comics 2006. Page 13
62   Civil War: Frontline #1 "The Accused, Part One". Written by Paul Jenkins. Illustrated by Steve Lieber. Marvel Comics, 2006. Page 11

society and a smaller community. These alterations cause further *Transformation Triggers*. Miriam Sharpe's public accusation influences Tony Stark's position on registering and regulating the superhuman community. Johnny Storm/The Human Torch ends up in a coma[63] when a mob, representing the antagonistic public, assaults him outside a nightclub[64]. The new public stance on superhumans causes S.H.I.E.L.D. to anticipate an upcoming need for "an Anti-Superhuman Response Unit", for which they want to recruit Steve Rogers/Captain America. Reacting to the change of S.H.I.E.L.D.'s position towards his community, Steve Rogers alters his loyalty to the organization, setting the character up as the face and leader of the anti-registration rebellion[65]. All of these changes invoke another series of *Transformation Triggers*, which alter the state of multiple *Index Manifestations* and the larger network. Tony Stark's new stance on registration positions him to agree with the U.S. government's decision to pass the Superhuman Registration Act and to reveal his secret identity to the president[66] and later the public[67]. This alteration also demands a change to the *Index Manifestation* of Peter Parker, as Tony Stark expects Spider-Man to reevaluate his stance on his own secret identity[68]. The combination of the emerging Superhuman Registration Act and the hospitalization of Johnny Storm alters the relationships among the members of the Fantastic Four, leaving them in discord[69]. To some degree, all of these Trigger Waves feed back into Congress passing the Superhuman Registration Act and the President signing it into law. Its passage constitutes another *Transformation Trigger*, which affects many *Narrative Entities* within the network. Therefore, it starts a similar series of *Trigger Waves*, which effectively separates the superhero community into two opposing sides, one pro-registration side under Iron Man and one anti-registration side under Captain America. Concerning the character of Robert Baldwin/Speedball, the intersection of passing the law and his previous arrest – possible due to the loss of his powers – results in his imprisonment without a trial, which marks the loss of his civil liberties[70]. The latter alteration deserves special mention because it results from the intersection of both larger *Transformation Triggers*, providing an example of the potential intersection of *Trigger Waves* to influence one *Index Manifestation*. Overall, continuing *Trigger Waves* alter several *Index Manifestations* within this network of *Narrative Entities* either directly or subsequently. Further alterations to the characters of the Fantastic Four Narrative led to greater division and a temporary disbanding of the

---

63 *Fantastic Four #538*. Written by J. Michael Straczynski. Illustrated by Mike McKone. Marvel Comics, 2006. recap page
64 *Civil War #1*. Written by Mark Millar. Illustrator Steve McNiven. Marvel Comics 2006. Page 17
65 *Civil War #1*. Written by Mark Millar. Illustrator Steve McNiven. Marvel Comics 2006. Page 23
66 *Amazing Spider-Man #532*. Written by J. Michael Straczynski. Illustrated by Ron Garney. Marvel Comics, 2006. Page 7/8
67 *Civil War: Frontline #1 "Embedded, Part One"*. Written by Paul Jenkins. Illustrated by Ramon Bachs. Marvel Comics, 2006. Final page
68 *Amazing Spider-Man #532*. Written by J. Michael Straczynski. Illustrated by Ron Garney. Marvel Comics, 2006. Page 10
69 *Fantastic Four #538*. Written by J. Michael Straczynski. Illustrated by Mike McKone. Marvel Comics, 2006.
70 *Civil War: Frontline #2 "The Accused, Part Two"*. Written by Paul Jenkins. Illustrated by Steve Lieber. Marvel Comics, 2006. Page 3

team; further alterations to the public view on superheroes and Robert Baldwin directly cause him to take on a new superhero identity; further changes to the *Index Manifestation* within the conflict creates Spider-Man's shift in loyalty. Of course, all these waves of alteration continue further down the research material and, frankly, far beyond it. The point of this analysis was to show that superhero comics not only employ the notion of *Trigger Waves* but that these waves spread across numerous *Manifestations*, relating their individual network of *Index Manifestations* and the associated *Narrative Entities* to one another. Furthermore, it highlights that *Transformations Triggers* do not induce changes singularly or linearly but potentially towards all *Index Manifestations* within its network. As such, *Transformation Triggers* can interfere with a currently running plot, suddenly end a plot or even the continued release of further *Manifestations* for a *Narrative Entity*, start a new plot or *Manifestation*, and potentially invoke any combination of these effects.

Superhero comics employ *Transformation Triggers*, especially Events and their subsequent *Trigger Waves*, for all the mentioned effects. Hereby, *Transformation Triggers* interconnect different *Manifestations* by providing a link between altered representations of the same *Index Manifestation*. This allows the two representations to interrelate two *Manifestations* in the same manner a completely unchanged *Index Manifestation* would. A prolific example highlighting how the explanation for minor changes to an *Index Manifestation* can connect different *Manifestations* is the physical conflict between Iron Man and Spider-Man and the latter's escape through the sewers presented in *Civil War #5/6* and *Amazing Spider-Man #535/536*. Here, *Transformation Triggers* occurring at different stages of the conflict explain the altered state of the Iron Spider armor within several *Manifestations*. The initial physical confrontation begins on page 21 of *Amazing Spider-Man #535* when Iron Man tackles the titular hero through a wall. The confrontation continues in *Civil War #5* on page four. The first *Transformation Trigger* occurs at the end of this sequence, when a group of soldiers fire at Spider-Man, pushing him through a reinforced window and out of the building on page seven of the same issue. For one, the *Transformation Trigger* provides an initial explanation for Spider-Man crashing into a hotdog cart on the street at the beginning of *Amazing Spider-Man #536*. Additionally, the subsequent *Trigger Wave* provides a reason for the first alteration to the representation of the Iron Spider armor. The *Index Manifestation* appears now with the lower section of its mask torn, revealing parts of Peter's face underneath it[71]. The sequence ends with Spider-Man fleeing into the sewers on page six of the same issue. The character reappears with the broken mask, traveling in the sewers on page nine of *Civil War #5*. Within this sequence, two members of the Thunderbolts – a group of supervillains forcefully recruited into the government – catch up with him. Their attack tears and breaks most of the Iron Spider armor. The extent of damage visible on page 15 of the same issue implies the armor's decommission in the near future. With a *Transformation Trigger* explaining the loss/disappearance of the Iron Spider armor, Peter Parker reappears in civilian clothing on page seven of *Amazing Spider-Man #536*. An editor's note on the same page supports the notion that the previously mentioned *Transformation Triggers* influence the depiction of Peter Parker in this instance. On page 18 of the same issue, Aunt May returns Peter's classic

---

71 *Amazing Spider-Man #536.* Written by J. Michael Straczynski. Illustrated by Ron Garney. Marvel Comics, 2006. Page 2–6.

outfit to him. This *Transformation Trigger* explains a significant change in the representation of an *Index Manifestation*, namely why Spider-Man appears in his classic outfit in subsequent *Manifestations*, including further issues of *Civil War* and in *Iron Man #14* on page 16. Intradiegetically, these sequences spread across two *Manifestations* explain why Peter Parker stops using the Iron Spider armor and returns to his classic suit, thereby creating a direct link between the two different representations of the same *Index Manifestation* within the given network. Maintaining a coherent representation of the Iron Spider armor throughout a series of minor changes strengthens the interrelation between *Manifestations*. Hereby, the coherence appears as a helpful indicator of the potential split between a *Transformation Trigger* and the actual representation of the alteration across *Manifestations*. The general insight of this analysis is that the different *Manifestations* of superhero comics are not only related via a coherent representation of *Index Manifestations* but also via the coherent acknowledgment of certain changes made to them, independent of the *Manifestation* in which they occurred.

The interrelation of *Manifestations* via the acknowledgment of changes made to *Index Manifestations* finds its highest form in the application of a *Shared Narrative*, as these changes interact to create a plot structure across multiple *Narrative Entities*. Spider-Man's shift in loyalty within the research material is a good example of a *Shared Narrative* spread across two separate *Manifestations*[72]. In the context of Spider-Man's *Shared Narrative*, the Exposition occurs in Amazing Spider-Man #532 and *Civil War #1*. As superhero comics are a perpetually serial genre, this *Exposition* dominantly establishes the *Index Manifestation*'s position within the larger network because *semiotic cues* already have been established prior to the research material. Within the context of this *Shared Narrative*, Peter Parker/Spider-Man's relationship with Tony Stark and the idea of a Registration Act provides the basis for future developments. The two characters' relationship is partly characterized by Peter referring to Tony as 'boss'[73]. His loyalty to Tony Stark emerges most significantly in his deference to the latter's position on a Superhuman Registration[74] Act[75]. This deference directly conflicts with Peter's personal view[76] on the matter[77]. The hierarchy between these two positions is set when Peter agrees to Tony's ultimatum to unmask and register under the new law[78]. The *Exposition* sets the relation between the *Index Manifestation* and two parts of the network, another character and an upcoming *Transformation*

---

72   Arguably, the *Shared Narrative* covers four *Manifestations* as the *Sensational Spider-Man* and the *Spider-Man* series arguably include some *Transformation Triggers* playing into the *Exposition* and the *Rising Transformation*. However, as these additional series and *Amazing Spider-Man* arise from the same *Narrative Entity*, their inclusion would not have added anything meaningful to the example.
73   Amazing Spider-Man #532. Written by J. Michael Straczynski. Illustrated by Ron Garney. Marvel Comics, 2006. Page 2
74   Amazing Spider-Man #532. Written by J. Michael Straczynski. Illustrated by Ron Garney. Marvel Comics, 2006. Page 10
75   Amazing Spider-Man #532. Written by J. Michael Straczynski. Illustrated by Ron Garney. Marvel Comics, 2006. Page 20
76   Civil War #1. Written by Mark Millar. Illustrator Steve McNiven. Marvel Comics 2006. Page 20
77   Amazing Spider-Man #532. Written by J. Michael Straczynski. Illustrated by Ron Garney. Marvel Comics, 2006. Page 7
78   Amazing Spider-Man #532. Written by J. Michael Straczynski. Illustrated by Ron Garney. Marvel Comics, 2006. Page 10

Trigger. Hereby, the *Shared Narrative* clarifies that Peter's loyalty to Stark exceeds his reservation towards the upcoming law. The *Rising Transformation* initiates when Spider-Man reveals his identity on national television at the end of *Amazing Spider-Man #532* and *Civil War #2*, which continues at the beginning of *Amazing Spider-Man #533* and *Civil War #3*. While *Civil War* deals with this alteration's effect on the superhero community, *Amazing Spider-Man* shows the changes to Peter's personal life. The latter's ramification includes personal and physical attacks by the perceived public, endangerment of his wife by 'Captain America's number 1 fan'"[79], and legal actions by Peter's former employer, J. Jonah Jameson[80]. The more significant ramification is that Tony uses Spider-Man's registered status to include him in a task force designed to hunt down unregistered heroes without consulting Peter[81]. The character's association with Iron Man's task force set its relationship to other *Index Manifestations* within the same network. However, it also indicates a beginning shift in the hierarchy between Peter's loyalty to Tony Stark and his position on the Registration Act. The *Rising Transformation* continues with the death of Bill Foster/Giant-Man at the hands of Ragnarok – a clone of Thor created by Tony Stark and Reed Richards. This *Transformation Trigger* invokes further alteration in Peter's evaluation of his loyalty to Tony Stark. Directly following the battle in which the *Transformation Trigger* occurs, Spider-Man (Iron Spider) says: "I thought you know what you are **doing**, Tony."[82] The following conversation with Hank Pym/Yellowjacket and Janet van Dyne/Wasp indicates that Peter's waning confidence is accompanied by a reassertion of his misgivings[83] concerning the Registration Act[84]. This shift in perspective invokes a change in the character's relationship with the other pro-registration heroes[85]. Peter Parker's altered perception of Tony Stark's moral and general competence leads him to demand a tour of the secret holding facility constructed by Iron Man and Mister Fantastic[86]. Effectively a fictional version of Guantanamo Bay, the Negative Zone Prison's extralegal status combined with Iron Man's veiled threats towards Peter and his relatives[87] erodes the remainder of Spider-Man's trust[88]. This *Transformation Trigger* leads to the previously analyzed fight between Iron Man and Spider-Man as well as the escape of Aunt May and Peter's wife, Mary

---

79 *Amazing Spider-Man #533*. Written by J. Michael Straczynski. Illustrated by Ron Garney. Marvel Comics, 2006. Page 20/21.
80 *Amazing Spider-Man #533*. Written by J. Michael Straczynski. Illustrated by Ron Garney. Marvel Comics, 2006. Page 12.
81 *Amazing Spider-Man #533*. Written by J. Michael Straczynski. Illustrated by Ron Garney. Marvel Comics, 2006. Page 22
82 *Civil War #4*. Written by Mark Millar. Illustrator Steve McNiven. Marvel Comics, 2006. Page 12, original emphasis
83 *Civil War #4*. Written by Mark Millar. Illustrator Steve McNiven. Marvel Comics, 2006. Page 13
84 *Civil War #4*. Written by Mark Millar. Illustrator Steve McNiven. Marvel Comics, 2006. Page 14
85 *Civil War #4*. Written by Mark Millar. Illustrator Steve McNiven. Marvel Comics, 2006. Page 19 / *Civil War #5*. Written by Mark Millar. Illustrator Steve McNiven. Marvel Comics, 2006. Page 8
86 *Amazing Spider-Man #535*. Written by J. Michael Straczynski. Illustrated by Ron Garney. Marvel Comics, 2006. Page 3
87 *Amazing Spider-Man #535*. Written by J. Michael Straczynski. Illustrated by Ron Garney. Marvel Comics, 2006. Page 12
88 *Amazing Spider-Man #535*. Written by J. Michael Straczynski. Illustrated by Ron Garney. Marvel Comics, 2006. Page 19

Jane Watson, from Stark Tower. Here, Peter dissolves his loyalty to Tony Stark and the pro-registration side. However, he has not yet turned against his former allies but merely separated from them. That shift occurs with the *Climax* when the character announces his opposition to the registration act and his support for the anti-registration rebellion[89]. At this turning point, Peter Parker/Spider-Man arrives at the peak of the *Shared Narrative*, as all but the character's relationship with his wife and aunt are rearranged, and his visual representation has reverted to his classic outfit. The *Shared Narrative*'s *Climax Waves* begins with Spider-Man's acceptance to the anti-registration side in *Amazing Spider-Man #537* and his determination to be part of their operation[90], specifically their assault on the Negative Zone prison. Spider-Man's fate is now tied to the success or failure of the anti-registration group, more specifically, the fate of Captain America. Additionally, the combination of this *Transformation Trigger* with previous changes leaves Mary Jane Watson, Peter's wife, and Aunt May in an endangered position. Spider-Man's identity and his loss of government protection are publicly known, and his involvement with the rebellion draws him away from them. The final *Climax Wave* comes in the form of Captain America's surrender in *Civil War #7*. Here, the Event's larger conflict formally ends with Spider-Man's loyalties on the losing side, which again alters the *Index Manifestation*'s position within the overall network of *Index Manifestations* and its direct representation. The following *Denouement* resolves the outcome of all the changes made to the *Index Manifestation* within the *Shared Narrative*. Spider-Man's shift in loyalty forces him to remain in the underground movement even after the general conflict has ended. An appearance of Spider-Man in his black outfit juxtaposed with a letter by Reed Richards[91] indicates the character's continued status as a rebel and fugitive. Due to his public status outside of government protection, an assassin hired by the Kingpin – one of New York's foremost crime lords in Marvel Comics – manages to find the hiding place of Peter's family. He shoots and fatally wounds Aunt May[92]. As a direct reaction to the outcome of his choices (and the death of Captain America in *Captain America #25*), Spider-Man makes a final shift in representation to the black Spider-Man outfit. The *Shared Narrative* effectively ties the two *Manifestations* to one another by spreading plot points across *Amazing Spider-Man* and *Civil War*. Assuming this *Shared Narrative* represents a general application of the principle in superhero comics leaves the impression that *Shared Narratives* dominantly tie *Narrative Entity*-specific *Manifestations* into *Manifestations* that function as a team narrative. A glance at other potential *Shared Narratives* within the Civil War Event, specifically the Fantastic Four, Ms. Marvel, and the Thunderbolts, supports this notion. However, whether this is consistently true within the overall superhero genre in comics may require additional research.

Generally, this analysis shows that *Transformation Triggers* dominantly interconnect different *Narrative Entities* by providing a link between altered representations of the

---

[89] *Amazing Spider-Man #536*. Written by J. Michael Straczynski. Illustrated by Ron Garney. Marvel Comics, 2006. Page 19

[90] *Civil War #6*. Written by Mark Millar. Illustrator Steve McNiven. Marvel Comics, 2006. Page 9

[91] *Civil War #7*. Written by Mark Millar. Illustrator Steve McNiven. Marvel Comics, 2007. Page 24

[92] *Amazing Spider-Man #537*. Written by J. Michael Straczynski. Illustrated by Ron Garney. Marvel Comics, 2007. Final page.

same *Index Manifestation*. Hereby, this link can appear as a simple singular change or as a consecutive series of changes spread across multiple *Manifestations*, which ultimately form a plot surrounding a specific *Index Manifestation*. Additionally, *Transformation Triggers* relate different *Narrative Entities* by being told within each of the *Narrative Entity*'s *Manifestation*, as, for example, in the case of Spider-Man's unmasking, which appears equally in *Civil War* and *Amazing Spider-Man* but also finds mention/occurs in other *Manifestations* associated with this Event. *Transformation Triggers* also relate different *Manifestations* via consecutive *Trigger Waves* reaching across several *Manifestations* created in their wake. It should be remarked that the collection of these *Trigger Waves* necessarily creates a situation in which the current state of an *Index Manifestation* can be traced along several lines of *Transformation Triggers*. Just by the nature of *Trigger Waves*, these lines may necessarily cross paths within an *Index Manifestation*, representing changes that require more than one *Transformation Trigger* to explain. In effect, these overlapping lines of *Transformation Triggers* collapse into a network of backstory, which carries over into future *Manifestations* of the network of *Narrative Entities*. The overall Civil War Event is an excellent example of this phenomenon, as all the changes made to numerous *Index Manifestations* throughout different materials inform the state of the network in any *Manifestation* about the network released after it. May it be Spider-Man's status as a fugitive, Aunt May's presence in a hospital, Bucky Barnes's inner conflict about taking on the Captain America identity, or Tony Stark's position as the new director of S.H.I.E.L.D.

2.2.2.3 Autonomy through Index Collection

As discussed in the chapter 'Manifestation-Narrative Entity Feedback Loop', the different adaptations of a *Narrative Entity* can create sub-entities in the number of existing *Manifestations* due to the audience creating an aesthetic object from the *Manifestation* first. In other words, a discursive interpretation of a film, book, or series exists between the actual object and the original *Narrative Entity*, which provides the basic *indices* . The need for a separation between a sub-entity and *Narrative Entity* lies in the evaluation of *rendition cues* and *media cues* as defining characteristics for the overall *Narrative Entity* or as a signifier for a specific interpretation of it. While understanding this distinction is important, it overlooks the potential accumulation of *semiotic cues* and, thereby, the creation of a more significant division between the sub-entity and the *Narrative Entity*.

The influence of *Transformation Triggers* in their various forms, including *Trigger Waves* and *Shared Narratives*, on *Index Manifestations* in the spatial view of time within the model has been discussed in every instance. However, while it is clear that the different *Transformation Triggers* collapse into backstory *indices*, which relate to the *Manifestation* of the *Narrative Entity*, the explanation never clarifies which *Narrative Entity* the backstory relates to and how its *semiotic cues* are comprised in its representation within the *Manifestation*. In other words, while we know what happens to *Transformation Triggers*, we cannot say where they go and what form they ultimately have or take. However, either is relevant concerning the relationship between sub-entity and *Narrative Entity* as well as the development of any network created on the representation within any *Manifestation*. Concerning the placement of backstory *indices* created from *Transformation Triggers*, the answer initially appears obvious: As a part of the procedural changes within a *Manifestation*, these types of backstory *indices* are directly linked to an audience's creation of an aesthetic object and, therefore, these backstory *indices* necessarily become part of the associated sub-entity. While this procedure is generally accurate, it simplifies potentially more complex interactions between *Manifestation*, sub-entity, and *Narrative Entity*. Although backstory *indices'* existence within a *Narrative Entity* generally explains the state of other *indices*, such as characters, sets, props, and so on, their potential manifestation is as multifaceted as any other *index*. Specifically in the case of backstory, its adaptation to a *Manifestation* could take the form of a snippet of dialogue explaining the state it caused, it could appear in a series of objects and actions hinting at its actual form, or the backstory and the *semiotic cue* or *index* it is connected to is not adapted initially, but becomes part of a series of *Transformation Triggers*. Specifically, adaptations of a superhero's origin story make use of the latter. This complexity means that in understanding the location of backstory *indices* created through *Transformation Triggers*, it is necessary to distinguish between those arising solely from the *Manifestation* and those adapted from an *index* within the original *Narrative Entity*. Backstory *indices* created solely from *Transformation Triggers* in the *Manifestation* predictably move to the sub-entity, in which they reside in the same fashion as the interpretation of any other *index*, awaiting the final decision concerning their inclusion in the overall *Narrative Entity*. Backstory *indices* adapted from the *Narrative Entity* appear in the *Manifestation* in the same complexity as any other adapted *index*. In its final form, meaning when all *Transformation Triggers* or hints required have been presented within the *Manifestation*, a backstory *Index Manifestation* contains a collection of *index cues*, *rendition cues*, and *media cues*. As with any other *Index Manifestation*, the specific version of the backstory containing all these *semiotic cues* becomes part of the sub-entity, awaiting the process of discourse deciding on the transference to the overall *Narrative Entity*. Although the process appears the same, the additional step of adaptation from an existing *index* alters the relationship between the sub-entity and the *Narrative Entity* as well as the influence over the sub-entity's constitution. In the case of an adapted backstory *index*, the overall number of *indices* between the *Narrative Entity* and the sub-entity essentially remain the same. The constitution of the backstory *index* will have changes within the sub-entity as every interpretation will alter, add, and subtract some *semiotic cues*, but the *index* will have a correspondent within the *Narrative Entity*. In contrast, backstory *indices* created without this relation to the *Narrative Entity* add an element to the sub-entity, differentiating it from the *Narrative Entity* outside of alternate *semiotic cues*. Furthermore, as any original backstory *index* emerged from a *Transformation Trigger*, it implies the existence of a set of additional changes to other *indices* within the sub-entity. As such, while some backstory *indices* retain a relation to the *Narrative Entity*, they all become part of the sub-entity and take on the form presented in the *Manifestation*.

A distinction between backstory *indices* with a previous version in the *Narrative Entity* and those without might appear insignificant. However, as the constitution of a *Narrative Entity* within the discourse rests on the existence of its *indices*, a process that changes their number and escalates the alteration to existing *indices* within the corresponding sub-entity becomes relevant. As the understanding of a *Narrative Entity* is not only determined by its *indices* but the existence of these *indices* in a specific constellation (its network), the addition of new *indices* inherently carries the risk of changing the sub-entity to something perceived as distinctly different. Still, suppose the number of new elements remains low. In that case, the dominance of the *Narrative Entity*'s *indices* will create a clear relation between it and the sub-entity because its dominant and defining aspects are directly related to those of the *Narrative Entity*. However, when the number of new *indices* outgrow that of those provided by the original *Narrative Entity*, the possibility that the sub-entity is dominantly defined and understood as something different from the original *Narrative Entity* increases. The reason for this is essentially two-fold. Effectively, new and established *indices* stand in constant competition concerning the determination of a sub-entity's status within public discourse. While the prominence of a singular *index* or part of the *semiotic cue* associated with its manifestation might hold sway in determining that perception, the sheer difference in number might give one side more prominence simply because the presence of one overwhelms the other. The second influence comes in the form of a necessarily altered constellation. The incorporation of several new *indices* requires an establishment of their position within the network of *indices* forming the sub-entity, which necessarily and gradually ties established *indices* to new ones, subverting original interrelations. This alteration again distinguishes the sub-entity from its original *Narrative Entity* and renditions of the *Narrative Entity* with a greater focus on original *indices*. The result of such a competition between original and new *indices* is prominently visible when adaptations of superhero properties into film or television are compared to the 'alternate universe' versions presented in DC's *Elseworlds* imprint or Marvel's *What If*-line. Adaptations to film retain a strong association with the original *Narrative Entity* by mostly using interpretations of the original *indices*. Examples of this can be seen in the film adaptations of the Superman Narrative from 1978, 2006, and 2013. *Superman: The Movie* from 1978 formally adds two new *indices*, in the form of the characters Otis, played by Ned Beatty, and Eve Teschmacher, played by Valerie Perrine, as henchmen for Gene Hackman's Lex Luthor. Additionally, the film introduces two henchmen for Terence Stamp's General Zod, Sarah Douglas's Ursa, and Jack O'Halloran's Non (both only become truly relevant in this film's sequel). Otherwise, the film operates with *Index Manifestations* based solely on the *indices* of the original *Narrative Entity*. Similarly, *Superman Returns*[93] from 2006 mostly employs *Index Manifestations* created from the original *Narrative Entity* with three exceptions: James Marsden's Richards White (Perry White's nephew and Lois Lane's fiancé within the film), Parker Posey's Kitty Kowalski (a new henchman for Kevin Spacey's Lex Luthor), and John [Lane] (Lois Lane's and implicitly Superman's son). With the exception of Christopher Meloni's Col. Nathan Hardy, *Man of Steel* from 2013 makes no addition to the overall indices of the original *Narrative Entity*. Even if the plots of each film could be considered new backstory *indices*„ the overall numbers favor the material derived from the original *Narrative Entity*. In contrast, comic re-imaginations of the Superman Narrative, like *Superman: Speeding Bullets*[94] and *Superman: Secret Identity*[95], replace or add to the original *indices* to create a distinctly alternate version. *Superman: Speeding Bullets* tells the Superman story in which the Wayne family from the Batman Narratives

---

[93] *Superman Returns*. Directed by Bryan Singer. Performances by Brandon Routh and Kevin Spacey. Warner Bros. Pictures, 2006

[94] *Superman: Speeding Bullets*. Written by J.M. DeMatteis. Illustrated by Eduardo Barreto. DC Comics, 1993

[95] *Superman: Secret Identity*. Written by Kurt Busiek. Illustrated by Stuart Immonen. DC Comics. 2004

(instead of the Kent family) finds the boy in the spaceship. As such, the story makes more use of the *indices* of the Batman Narrative than the Superman Narrative, merely retaining Perry White, Lois Lane, and one mention of the Daily Planet. *Superman: Secret Identity* detaches even more prominently from the original *Narrative Entity*. Telling the story of a boy who coincidently is named Clark Kent and suddenly finds himself with the powers of Superman, this *Manifestation* uses none of the original Superman Narrative *indices*, only alluding to the place their *indices* would take within the usual Superman mythos. While the introduction of new *indices* is not the only way to create a sub-entity with the tendency to become its own *Narrative Entity* instead of folding into the original (an abundant use of *rendition cues* may accomplish the same task), setting up a greater number of new *indices* in relation to original *indices* will rather separate the sub-entity than retain a relation to the *Narrative Entity* originating it. This is of relevance because if the *Manifestation* of a *Narrative Entity* continuously employs new *Transformation Triggers* through new or unassociated storylines, it necessarily adds new *indices* in the form of backstory to the sub-entity, gradually diminishing the relation between the sub-entity and the *Narrative Entity*.

Assuming this process as true that the continued collection of differing *indices* will gradually separate a sub-entity from the *Narrative Entity* spawning it creates an alternate outcome to the eventual adaptation of the sub-entity into the formation of the *Narrative Entity*, it conjures the possibility for the sub-entity to become a distinct *Narrative Entity* of its own, which might share features with its original but remains a singular *Narrative Entity*, nonetheless. While this helps explain and classify the relation between adaptation, re-interpretations, and re-imaginations or in- and out-continuity material, if you so will, this effect has other significance for the Universe Model and the research presented here. It presumes that continued seriality, due to the continuous production of new backstory *indices*, has little other choice than to eventually become a *Narrative Entity* of its own when it does not solely exist as the adaptation of another serial, storylines and all. Within the larger complex of the Universe Model, this also means that a clarification concerning the discussed *Narrative Entity* or sub-entity is in order, and relationships might have to be redefined within the process of continued seriality. It also means that different sub-entities can continually distinguish themselves from others while maintaining a relationship with their original *Narrative Entity*.

2.2.3 Narrative Reliance

Within literary fiction, we can consider two ways in which one narrative may rely on another. The first and most apparent one lies with traditional serial relation. All forms of sequels, prequels, and serials rely to some degree on the audience knowing some portion of a preceding reference text. The second is an adaptation or form of re-imagination. Here, even though the related *Index Manifestations* differ from the presumed original, each version informs the other, allowing meaning generated by one version to compensate for narrative shortcomings or deviations. Something similar can be said about the relationship between Mittell's mothership texts and their satellites. In either case, the crosspollination of meaning equally enriches the range and understanding of each element within the narrative beyond the actual text. As the model presented here concerns itself with various means of interconnecting *Narrative Entities* through *Index Manifestations* and *Transformation Triggers*, an idea of the relationship between the content of a *Manifestation* and a need for an audience to obtain knowledge from another appears crucial. However, while the Universe Model has to use the two classic dependencies, its understanding of such a reliance must be more nuanced.

In the case of a linear serial relationship – like a television series or a prequel/sequel relation – which generally revolves around a stable set of recurring *Index Manifestations* influenced (only) by the *Transformation Triggers* within this linear serial, dependency and interconnection act in unison. *Back to the Future Part II*[96] expects the audience to accept the *Index Manifestation* as explained, understand the events as a continuation, and ideationally relate and compare scenes to the first film. Something similar counts for the relationship between *Back to the Future Part III*[97] and its two predecessors. Due to the title and the marketing as a sequel, the connection is overstated, and a necessary knowledge or understanding of the earlier films can be expected. However, such potential dependencies do not follow the same obvious pattern within a complex network of Narrative Entities with different parallel, linear, and crossing Shared Narratives. While marketing does broadcast the relationships between these texts to a degree, the interconnection is not and cannot be as obviously presented as with classic sequels because the different *Manifestations* relate in varying complex ways. Although they can be, these relationships do not have to be causally linear. Consequently, knowledge or understanding of another *Manifestation* cannot be expected in the same fashion. This lack of overt dependency necessarily leads to a more complex approach to storytelling and a more complex approach to the use of *Shared Narratives* and *Trigger Waves*; as such, interdependency has to be addressed.

Most theoretical conceptions and interpretations related to intertextuality equally apply to *Narrative Reliance*. However, where intertextuality works with an infinite, non-chronological network of all text ever created to advance the range of interpretation for a singular text, *Narrative Reliance* hinges on the idea that one *Manifestation* requires information given within another *Manifestation* to not only advance meaning but to allow for some degree of overall comprehension. In this point, *Narrative Reliance* differs from Intertextuality. While Kristeva's Intertextuality assumes that the knowledge of one text informs the content of another, she does not argue that the comprehension or enjoyment of one text is (or might be) dependent on another text. Concerning the analysis and description of relationships such as allusions, parodies, or homages, an understanding of text interrelation purely in the intertextual sense is sufficient. However, within the confinement of not only a Shared Universe, a *Shared Narrative*, or even complex seriality, connections do not only work as allusions but, in some scenarios, simply require information given in another text. In other words, while Intertextuality assumes that the interrelation of texts enriches meaning but is not necessary for its comprehension, *Narrative Reliance* assumes that there might be a need for information from another text to comprehend a

---

[96] *Back to the Future Part II*. Directed By Robert Zemeckis. Performances by Michael J. Fox and Christopher Llyod. Amblin Entertainment and Universal Pictures, 1989

[97] *Back to the Future Part III*. Directed By Robert Zemeckis. Performances by Michael J. Fox and Christopher Llyod. Amblin Entertainment and Universal Pictures, 1990

given narrative. The narrative relies on the audience bringing knowledge from that other text to bear.

In essence, *Narrative Reliance* allows arguing the necessity of making a connection between *Manifestations* by looking at the need for information given in another *Manifestation*. Hereby, the need for information can range from a *Transformation Trigger*, which makes sense of a sudden change in a *Manifestation* or informs a continuing *Trigger Wave*, to a mere allusion, which contextualizes new information. In this, the distance between different *Manifestations* and *Narrative Entities* hinges on the degree to which one text relies on another. If the overall plot of a *Manifestation* can absolutely not be understood without information given in the *Manifestation* of another *Narrative Entity*, these two *Narrative Entities* are closely connected. Conversely, if a *Manifestation* offers information that enriches the understanding of another *Manifestation*, the related *Narrative Entities* have a more distant relationship.

As any determination of information needed for an assumed full comprehension (in another text or otherwise) might be contentious, the Universe Model requires more tangible means of evaluating such a need. For this purpose, the Universe Model employs a notion of Jenkins' *knowledge community* to create the idea of three types of engaged audiences. Hereby, the understanding of these engaged audiences is purposely disassociated from the notion of fan as well as *participatory culture*. This focus on the overall non-participatory but engaged audience does not diminish the importance of fans (in Jenkin's definition) in the research of popular literature or culture. However, using a *knowledge community* casts a broader net and includes various degrees of engagement and influence on the narrative. More importantly, it disengages the question of personal or subcultural authorization practices, as described by Stein and Kelleter[98], in favor of an information-based understanding of audience engagement. Academic engagement with fan letters, reactions to authors, fan forum boards, and fan fiction has shown several versions of appropriation of material and aspects of popular literature. Fans have taken charge of their fandom. They claim not only ownership but also the right to determine the representation of the material. Research into fan appropriation has shown that the processes of appropriation, the recombination of fan material, and the struggle over ownership with the actual producers have a somewhat marginal influence on the success of mass media franchise products reliant on a large audience. Looking at the complex and expansive nature of a network of *Narrative Entities*, like the MCU, and its success or failure, the assumption that this outcome rests solely on the engagement of a dedicated fan base appears rather unlikely. While the focus on and influence of fandom on such networks is valuable and tangible, a larger network with a more complex presentation of its *Manifestations* requires less the understanding of fans and more an understanding of a "silent majority"[99], which makes up its audience. As a "vocal minority", fans hold value for the

---

[98] Kelleter, Frank und Daniel Stein. "Autorisierungspraktiken seriellen Erzählens". *Populäre Serialität: Narration – Evolution –Distinktion*. Frank Kelleter (Ed.). Bielefeld: transcript Verlag, 2012. 259–290

[99] I am aware of this phrase's political use and its controversy in relation to Nixon's popularization of the term in his television address regarding the demonstrations against the Vietnam War. In this instance, the term is only meant to express the potential dichotomy between a smaller and more expressive subsection of a larger group and the less expressive rest of the same group without

direct engagement with *Manifestations* – in the form of processes of speculation, the creation of fan fiction as narrative extensions, and even as experts and marketers towards non-fan audiences – but ultimately the "silent majority" determines the success, expansion, and overall form of a network of *Narrative Entities*, simply due to the influence and distribution of economic power. However, the "silent majority" is more difficult to read or predict, as they will react to the received material without broadcasting their reaction beyond their imminent social group. Academics and producers require more patience and work to account for the silent majority's reaction. While fans can act as representatives of a larger audience, they still hold a special status and, as such, unique views on their specific fandom. As such, *Narrative Reliance* includes notions of knowledge communities solely based on necessary knowledge and previous engagement but avoids a definition of these groups via fan commentary.

2.2.3.1 The Three Types of Audiences

As both the previous chapters on *Index Manifestations* and *Transformation Triggers* indicate, connections rely to some degree on the audience's understanding and/or knowledge of a *Narrative Entity* or their respective *Index Manifestations*, as well as the potential and intent of creating an interrelation. This *Narrative Reliance* varies from relationship to relationship and carries different value within each *Manifestation*. Hereby, the aspects for variations of *Narrative Reliance* are always present within the different texts. However, we require a notion of different communities to discuss the effect created by them. By speculating on a required level of knowledge of and interest in making specific connections between narratives, it is possible to distinguish various "interpretative communities" (as Stanley Fish calls them) or "knowledge communities" (Jenkins' term). Hereby, the audience does not actively declare the amount of *Narrative Reliance* within a text, but the type of audience targeted for a specific text regulates the degree of dependency. In other words, the assumed target audience determines to what degree a text depends on information from another text within the same complex.

The intention of interrelating texts on the producers' side has some relevance. Hereby, I am not referring to the apparent result of the producer's intention, which is the application of the techniques mentioned in this research. Instead, the audience's awareness of the producer's intention has a more ambiguous role. As the narrative mechanics to create interconnections between different texts can range from very blunt to unbelievably subtle, a fair number of cases might require the audience to "be in on it" to make the connection. Understanding that producers actively broadcast their intention concerning the connection of text allows us to assume an ideal audience, which attempts to and successfully follows clues pointing towards such an interrelation. Such an informed audience can be understood in a similar manner as Wolfgang Iser's "ideal reader". The informed audience is, in a sense, the producer's ideal audience. It does not only engage with all texts (including marketing material and transmedial extensions as Harvey understands them) but also actively looks for connections. This informed audience might take the producer's stated intention over the actual narrative

---

including any potential moral, political, or ideological association sometimes connected to this phrase.

processes within the text. As such, the audience explains away inconsistencies and elevates connections beyond their actual strength. This type of audience understands all aspects of *Narrative Reliance* of a given network, as they have not only engaged with the necessary material but usually followed the pattern (probably several times and in various combinations) the producers laid out. The informed audience generally lacks the narrative instinct to recognize connections outside a prepared pattern. In other words, the informed audience learned and understood the intricacies of a specific network of *Narrative Entities* but does not have the capacity to engage with networks of *Narrative Entities* universally. Hereby, it is necessary to understand that an informed audience is not necessarily synonymous with an audience comprised of fans. Derived from the word fanatic, a fan is defined as an admirer and supporter of a thing (in this case, a franchise). As discussed by Stein[100], this admiration includes a self-titled authority of the thing and judgment of who can include themselves within the category of fan. The informed audience, on the other hand, is defined by their ability to realize and understand the interrelation between different *Manifestations*. While it is easier to presume the presence of at least a mild interest, any degree of emotional connection does not play into the inclusion into an informed audience. As the definition of the informed audience runs along the line of ability, and the definition of a fan runs along the line of an emotional attachment, an informed audience can include fans, and fans can be comprised of an informed audience, but a member of an informed audience does not have to be a fan, and a fan does not have to be part of an informed audience.

As the producers' communication and intentions theoretically cultivate an ideal audience, which looks for and understands all the producers' narrative attempts, conversely, there has to be an audience that engages with the text without knowing of the producer's intention or even purposely ignores it. As such, any model including notions of different audiences has to consider those audiences with no expectation of interrelation between different *Manifestations*. This casual audience engages with a *Manifestation* for other reasons than its association with a network and presumably has overlooked, ignored, or simply disregarded such an interrelation. The casual audience may not only lack the actual information from another text but also the knowledge that there is another text. As such, this type of audience is most susceptible to the potential adverse effects of *Narrative Reliance*. *Manifestations* requiring information from another source might irritate members of the casual audience, as the content of the *Manifestation* will make the least sense to them. This irritation, however, indicates a strong relationship between certain *Manifestations* and, therefore, *Narrative Entities*. Conversely, a *Manifestation* that disregards engaging an uninformed casual audience relies more heavily on another text within the network.

A third type of audience arises out of the disengagement of the producer's intention to interrelate different *Narrative Entities* and the ability to recognize the narrative techniques used to connect *Manifestations*. In other words, the third audience has developed the ability to understand and recognize connections without requiring a producer to point out the attempt. Following this line of thinking, this skilled audience represents

---

100 Stein, Daniel. "Superhero Comics and the Authorizing Function of the Comic Book Paratext". *From Comic Strips to Graphic Novels*. Göttingen: De Gruyter, 2013. 155–190

a group that has engaged with interconnected texts in the past and developed a basic understanding of how such networks usually work. They engage a network of *Narrative Entities* with the skills to identify narrative techniques, building the connections between different texts without following the producers' guidance. The disassociation of the knowledge of these techniques and the producers' intention allows the skilled audience to see the interrelation between texts as they are presented. In some cases, a skilled audience's evaluation can lead to an unwanted interrelation, like the notion of the Pixar Universe[101], which interrelated the Pixar films into a coherent universe, despite the producers' stated opposition to such a relationship. As the opposite of the casual audience, interrelations between *Manifestations* arguably only a skilled audience could make indicate a weak relationship between those *Manifestations*.

Following the impact of a broadcast of the producer's intention, the Universe Model ends up with three basic types of audiences: casual, informed, and skilled. Within that framework, the distance between Manifestations shortens if a casual audience recognizes the reliance on another text. If the informed audience would identify the reliance, the *Narrative Reliance* does not change the relationship between the *Manifestations*. If only a skilled audience builds a reliance, the distance increases. Hereby, it should be noted that the existence of each audience type is speculative and serves as a baseline for a philosophical discussion. This works in accordance with the artificial nature of the audience types, which are all idealized and neglect the fact that individuals may belong to several groups depending on the franchises or even different parts within the same network of *Narrative Entities*. The approach remains legitimate as it merely evaluates the relationship of different texts from the audience's point of view and acknowledges possible unwanted effects within a complex narrative structure.

2.2.3.2 Example Narrative Reliance

While the superhero comic might have started the process of creating an informed audience at the start of each major age – The Golden Age, The Silver Age, The Bronze Age etc. – the superhero comic published from the mid-90s forward basically worked with an elite, specialized audience, which, even pre-internet, gradually collected the information needed to maneuver the complex network created by the genre. Through reading back issues, conversing with more experienced readers in comic shops, buying explanatory compendiums, and later employing the internet, the active readership of superhero comics effectively trained themselves to become a skilled or at least an informed audience to engage with *Manifestations* from this respective network of *Narrative Entities*. Different scholars have sufficiently discussed the Avant-Garde nature of the superhero comic and its surrounding subculture[102]. The inability to engage with a casual audience partly lies with the applied narrative techniques but also comes down to the nature of the medium and its specific form of publication. While the medium comic has proven a great versatility and the capability to alter its overall length, either taking the form of a graphic

---

101 https://www.thepixartheory.com
102 Concerning the perceived specialization and exclusivity of the superhero comic readership, I recommend reading Matthew Pustz's *Comic Book Culture: Fanboys and True Believers* and John Fiske's *Understanding Popular Culture*.

novel or limiting itself to a "mere" comic strip, the serial issue-based booklet remains the superhero comic's most common form of publication. The relatively cheap issue-based publication allows the superhero narrative to maintain a large and complex network of ever-changing *Narrative Entities* because it allows for the simultaneous representations of several *Narrative Entities* and *Shared Narratives* in various interactions. The stable cost of producing its visuals greatly simplifies the expansion of the network and the interconnection of its elements. However, different running series, overlapping *Index Manifestation*, parallel and crossing *Shared Narratives*, and the simultaneous use of different versions of the same *Index Manifestation* can easily confuse even ambitious readers. The ease of expansion and interrelation create a complexity that makes it nearly impossible for the uninformed to read even one series from a larger superhero comic publisher casually. The only potential exception is a casual reader with regular access to an informed one. It is not difficult to argue that the superhero comic generally targets an informed or skilled audience. The means by which *Transformation Triggers* facilitate interrelations between different *Manifestations* inherently alludes to a reliance between different texts, underscoring the superhero comic's favor for an informed audience. As *Transformation Triggers* link representations of the same *Index Manifestation*, knowledge of a *Transformation Trigger*'s existence may be required to understand sudden alterations in a running series – if the changes occurred in another *Manifestation*. As such, the relationship of alterations described in the analysis of *Transformation Triggers* indicates some inherent *Narrative Reliance* within the material constituting the Civil War Event. In addition, the Event overall also relies on knowledge provided by additional material outside the associated tagline.

To provide a better understanding of the use of *Narrative Reliance* in superhero comics, the following evaluation of *Narrative Reliance* takes a broad look at the relationship between the *Manifestations* constituting the Civil War Event – meaning those comic book issues sporting the *Civil War* tagline at the time of their publication – and selected outside material. Within this context, the focus lies on indications alluding to a degree of outside knowledge or source, while an overview of the outside material provides all necessary information to recognize the relationship. On the simplest level, *Civil War* generally relies on basic knowledge concerning the state of its *Index Manifestations* at the beginning of the Event, specifically concerning *Index Manifestations* related to a specific series. In other words, *Manifestations* related to the Event rely to some degree on the audience knowing most of the involved characters without any meaningful explanation, especially in cases of *Index Manifestations* that come from a longer-running series contributing to *Civil War*. General examples of this phenomenon are the lack of introduction or exposition on the numerous superhero characters appearing within the comics. Neither the origins nor the direct range of abilities of the two main characters – Captain America and Iron Man – are discussed. Instead, the *Manifestation* operates as if these aspects are common knowledge and require no further deliberation. In other words, Civil War relies on an audience that has read *Narrative Entity*-specific *Manifestations* of either character or knows these specific aspects before engaging with the material. Other, less prominent superhero characters appear in a similar fashion. The *Manifestations* employ associated *semiotic cues*, helping an informed audience to identify the characters, but it never provides any clear exposition or explanation for the superheroes involved, instead relying on an audience's previous engagement with material containing that information. The clearest example of reliance on issues of a running series feeding into the Event in the context of this research is the *Index Manifestation* of Peter Parker/Spider-Man. Similar to most other superhero characters, none of the *Manifestations* with the *Civil War* tagline explain or retell the current representation of the character – the source and type of his powers, the basis of his morality, the unique nature of his secret identity, the specifics of his relationship with his aunt and wife, his living situation, or his current use of the Iron Spider armor. Several notable changes in the publications prior to the actual *Civil War* material formed this representation. Spider-Man switches from his traditional (classic) outfit to the Iron Spider armor in *Amazing Spider-Man #529*[103]. Peter, his wife, and his aunt move into Avengers (Stark) Tower in *Amazing Spider-Man #518*[104]. Spider-Man becomes an Avenger in *New Avengers #1–3*[105]. Aunt May discovers Peter's secret identity and learns to accept his double life in *Amazing Spider-Man (Vol.2) #31–38*[106]. These alterations explain the *Index Manifestation*'s current state as it appears in the beginning pages of the *Civil War* material. Excluding direct references to these changes to the Spider-Man Narrative within issues related to *Civil War* indicates a reliance on an audience with specific knowledge of these *Transformation Triggers*. In the instant of a famous character as Spider-Man, disregarding any specific acknowledgment of these *Transformation Triggers* even significantly excludes casual audiences. Due to the *Narrative Entity*'s long existence and several retellings over the last 15 years, the Spider-Man Narrative and several of its *semiotic cues* have arguably trickled down into general (pop-)culture. As such, a casual audience from a U.S. or even wider Western background will more likely identify the *semiotic cues* of this *Narrative Entity* – such as the classic blue-and-red Spider-Man outfit – and may understand the hero character's appearance in another *Manifestation* without any meaningful explanation. However, as such *Transformation Triggers* add and alter some *semiotic cues*, the likelihood of a casual audience relating the altered version to the more commonly known one decreases, making the lack of exposition in this instance an even more notable means of exclusion. While Spider-Man is an obvious example, its reliance on previous *Manifestations* to make sense of the character's current state highlights how large parts of the overall Event rely on outside knowledge. Concerning running comic series that dedicate singular issues to larger Events, it becomes clear that *Civil War* operates as a node, which briefly escalates the interrelation between several series but, in turn, relies significantly on audiences carrying knowledge from each series into the larger Event.

Similar to its reliance on previous issues of the series that contribute to its constitution, the Event also relies on information from *Manifestations* not directly tied into it – meaning, in this instance, a comic series without issues bearing the *Civil War* tagline. An

---

[103] *Amazing Spider-Man #529*. Written by J. Michael Straczynski. Illustrated by Ron Garney. Marvel Comics, 2006

[104] *Amazing Spider-Man #518*. Written by J. Michael Straczynski. Illustrated by Mike Deodato Jr. Marvel Comics, 2005

[105] *New Avengers #1-#3*. Written by Brian Michael Bendis. Illustrated by David Finch. Marvel Comics, 2004

[106] *Amazing Spider-Man (Vol. 2) #31–#38*. Written by J. Michael Straczynski. Illustrated by John Romita Jr. Marvel Comics, 2001

obvious and straightforward example of such a reliance is the appearance of the superhero team New Warriors at the beginning of *Civil War #1*. Traditionally, this superhero team consists of teenage and young adult characters and often serves as a junior counterpart to the Avengers. In the six-issue miniseries of their third volume, *New Warriors*, the team is cast as the stars of their own reality TV show. Despite appearing only on the first six pages of *Civil War #1* within the overall Event, the New Warriors play a significant role in the overall narrative. Their televised fight against several supervillains in Stamford, Connecticut, sparks the Event's overall conflict, as described in the analysis of *Trigger Waves*. Within the confines of the six pages, the members of the New Warriors appear more concerned with the television aspect than the superhero aspect of their current status[107]. This apparent focus on fame leads them to engage a set of enemies "totally out of [their] league". Despite becoming the prime example for superhero irresponsibility, the only surviving New Warrior member, Robert Baldwin/Speedball, constantly claims no wrongdoing by his team in *Civil War: Frontline "The Accused"*[108]. In this case, the evaluation of the New Warrior's behavior depends slightly on an audience's general engagement with different *Manifestations*. The six-issue mini-series *New Warriors*[109,110] published from August 2005 to February 2006, prior to the start of Civil War, explains the team's current constellation, its reason for and status as reality TV stars, the origin of its need to take on a set of more dangerous supervillains, and the relationship between the characters. The latter two aspects significantly inform Robert Baldwin's decisions in *Civil War: Frontline "The Accused"*[111]. While the team's status as reality show stars regularly appears in conversations within *Civil War*, the meaning and root cause of this status is never retold within the Event, relegating such information to an outside source. However, a lack of knowledge concerning the New Warriors does not impede comprehension of the overall narration, allowing a casual audience to engage with the Event without prior knowledge concerning this specific *Narrative Entity*. Instead of exclusivity, an informed audience enters the Civil War Narrative with an additional perspective informing the evaluation of the New Warriors and later Robert Baldwin. This addition of information and perspective grants the informed audience a more complex view of the representation and evaluation of the *Narrative Entity* within the pages of *Civil War*. A less obvious but insightful example for the Civil War Event's reliance on outside *Manifestations* is its relationship with the Thor Narrative. *Thor #80–85*[112], published from August to December 2004, temporarily removed the entire Thor Narrative from Marvel comic's main network. These issues

---

107 *Civil War #1*. Written by Mark Millar. Illustrator Steve McNiven. Marvel Comics, 2006. Page 2
108 *Civil War: Frontline #1-#11 "The Accused"*. Written by Paul Jenkins. Illustrated by Steve Lieber. Marvel Comics, 2006 – 2007
109 *New Warriors #1-#6*. Written by Zeb Wells. Illustrated by Skottie Young. Marvel Comics. 2005–2006
110 The graphic novel collecting the six-issue miniseries does contain a Civil War tagline and is marketed as a prelude to *Civil War*. However, the original publications did not sport any reference to the larger Event. No Civil War reference appears on the original covers and the graphic novel shows the Civil War connection only on its cover and on its front matter page.
111 *Civil War: Frontline #1-#11 "The Accused"*. Written by Paul Jenkins. Illustrated by Steve Lieber. Marvel Comics, 2006–2007
112 *Thor #80-#85*. Written by Michael Avon Oeming and Daniel Berman. Illustrated by Andrea DiVito. Marvel Comics, 2004

contained a story detailing the fall of Asgard and its people's destruction before the publications of *Civil War*. During *Civil War*, Marvel did not release any *Manifestation* of the Thor Narrative directly related to its main network. Only singular *Index Manifestations* associated with that *Narrative Entity* remained – specifically a character known as Beta Ray Bill and the character Jane Foster. Despite the absence of a Thor Narrative at the time, an *Index Manifestations* informed by the character Thor appears in the pages of *Civil War*. Not the Thor Narrative's actual hero character, this Thor is a clone created by Tony Stark, Reed Richards, and Hank Pym and fights on the pro-registration side of the conflict. As the Civil War Event does not contain any *Narrative Entity*-specific *Manifestation* related to the Thor Narrative, all discussions and reactions concerning the clone necessarily relate back to information given in previous Thor *Manifestations*. Conversations evaluating the clone's behavior, specifically his lack of morality[113] necessarily refer to and rely on knowledge of previous Thor *Manifestations*. Similarly, a full comprehension of some characters' reactions[114] to seeing Thor equally expects some knowledge of the fall of Asgard, as presented in *Thor #85*. More than in the case of the New Warriors, *Civil War* relies on an audience's knowledge of the Thor Narrative, as the immediate reaction of other characters requires some understanding of the *Narrative Entity*'s status and general relationships within the network, allowing an informed audience to recognize the emotional impact and sense of betrayal and hubris within the scene. Generally, however, a casual audience most likely understands the flow of the overall plot without this additional information, turning the Thor clone solely into another superhuman combatant without any specific dramatic effect.

In either of the presented cases, the Civil War Event includes attempts at alleviating a sense of lacking information, either by hinting at explanations via dialogue or editor's notes or by creating a scene in which the additional information provides insight or emotional gravity. While any lack of knowledge from outside *Manifestations* does not hinder a general comprehension of the overall situation in most singular scenes, the combination of all the varying degrees of *Narrative Reliance* within the larger Event indicates a reliance on an informed audience. In essence, the overall comic superhero genre requires a readership that can untangle sections of the larger Event of which it has no prior knowledge by employing some degree of previous information collected from earlier *Manifestations*. In other words, superhero comics expect their readers to deduce missing information by bringing their knowledge of various *Narrative Entities* to bear. As such, the overall Event appears more targeted towards an informed audience. This result coincides with the general perception and understanding of superhero comics as an Avant Garde genre, which expects its audience to have or seek out some degree of specialized knowledge. More importantly, this example hints that the superhero genre employs *Narrative Reliance* in two forms: (1) It leans heavily on outside information when it can reasonably assume that an active readership has engaged with sections of previous material, as in the case of running series contributing to an Event. Arguably, a significant amount of the Civil War

---

113 *Civil War #4*. Written by Mark Millar. Illustrator Steve McNiven. Marvel Comics, 2006. Page 9 + Page 14
114 *Civil War #4*. Written by Mark Millar. Illustrator Steve McNiven. Marvel Comics, 2006. Page 2

readership at the time of the Event's publication were readers of one or several series contributing to the *Civil War*. (2) In case a readership's engagement with previous material is less certain – as with the *New Warriors* and *Thor* – the superhero genre appears to employ some degree of reliance to create multiple viewpoints or a more significant emotional impact, but not as necessary means to comprehend the overall plot.

2.3 Classification of Relationships

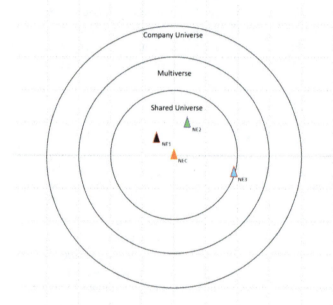

With *Narrative Entities* as the notion of a narrative in public discourse and *Manifestation* as its physical appearance for an audience to engage, the Universe Model has elements to determine and discuss the specific nature of the relationship between narratives. Hereby, the Universe Model assumes that the relationship between narratives exists on the level of the *Narrative Entity*, created through techniques employed within the *Manifestations* of these *Narrative Entities*. In other words, the network as a notion of world is a purely discursive construct, created as an expansive aesthetic object by the audience's engagement with different *Manifestations*. This discursive nature entails that the relationships discussed in the Universe Model always refer to the idea, the *Narrative Entity*, over the material form of the *Manifestation*.

As the network described here is founded on the premise that the interrelation between different *Narrative Entities* can construct a unified world as a shared space in which narration can occur, it makes sense to describe the relationship between the *Narrative Entities* in a spatial sense. In essence, the network describes the relation of different *Narrative Entities* with the understanding of their proximity within an imaginary space, which then declares the likelihood of the interaction of their diverse *indices* within a *Manifesta-*

tion. As such, *Narrative Entities* can exist in such proximity to one another that an interaction of *indices* in some way, shape, or form is expected, very likely, unlikely, unusual, only imaginably, purely speculative, or out-of-question. As an entanglement of narratology and network theory in such a manner is novel, neither field provides any good terminology to describe such a relation. However, interacting indices within their *Manifestation* occurred in superhero comics early in their inception. The *World's Finest Comics*, which told stories featuring elements of the Batman and Superman Narrative, was first published with the title *World's Best Comics* in 1941. The series itself was part of the *New York World's Fair Comics* from 1940, which also featured stories from either *Narrative Entity*[115]. As such, culture and discourses surrounding superhero comics created an undefined terminology to grasp a relationship between different *Narrative Entities* in a network. Shared Universe and Multiverse are two terms potentially describing a relation that implies the interaction of *indices* from different *Narrative Entities* ranging from expected to unusual. They do not cover the potential for the interaction of *indices* as only imaginable or out-of-question. However, neither discourses surrounding superhero comics nor current research use any terminology, which inherently covers a lower-tier likelihood for the interaction of *indices* of different *Narrative Entities*. In line with the terms Shared Universe and Multiverse, this research proposes the term Company Universe for an imaginable or purely speculative interaction of the *indices* from different *Narrative Entities*. The term is meant to imply that while such interactions may not exist in any *Manifestation*, the reality of Intellectual Property (IP) may allow for speculation on their existence. While any relation that categorically excludes the interaction of *indices* from different *Narrative Entities* does not require inclusion into the Universe Model, it must be acknowledged that the relationships categorized here are discursive in nature. As such, despite a presumed impossibility of *index* interaction, different *Narrative Entities* do not necessarily have no relationship. According to Kristeva's principle of Intertextuality, all texts exist in a constant network of meaning-generation. While her approach pursues very different objectives than those presented in this research, it is necessary to acknowledge that *Narrative Entities* with no definable relationship pertaining to the Universe Model still exist in an intertextual meaning-making context. As such, every relationship that does not fall within the former three categories (Shared Universe, Multiverse, Company Universe) automatically can be considered in an Intertextual one.

Visually, the Universe Model would represent different relationships between *Narrative Entities* by using associated symbols in a presumed proximity to one another. Hereby, the symbols sit in a series of circles, which each represent the potential relationship between *Narrative Entities*. Within this collection of ever wider circles, one *Narrative Entity* provides the center, serving as a proverbial north star for others in the network to be evaluated against first before then set into context with other elements. Within this complex, the first circle drawn around this center shows a Shared Universe relation, the second circle provides a Multiverse relation, and the final one shows a Company Universe relation.

---

115   For more on the early history of superhero comics and the emerging interaction between different characters, I advise reading Kurt Mitchell's and Roy Thomas's *American Comic Book Chronicles: 1940–1944*

Every *Narrative Entity*, which moves beyond the final circle, interacts with the center and other elements within the network on an Intertextual level.

2.3.1 Shared Universe

Returning to Don Markstein's definition of Shared Universe – (1) Shared Universes are created through characters' chains of interaction; (2) real people cannot provide chains of interaction; (3) equally characters "that do not originate with the publisher" cannot provide a chain of interaction; (4) specific, fictionalized versions of real people and public domain characters can serve as connection; (5) a meeting between characters is defined as them appearing on-panel together – it becomes clear that the use of *indices* and the focus on *Narrative Entity* over its actual *Manifestation* resolve some of the problems created by this definition. Replacing Markstein's focus on character with the principle of *indices* allows for a variety of representative features to illicit a connection between *Narrative Entities*, independent from their actual form or function within a *Manifestation*. As such, Superman standing in the Batcave, Batman holding a piece of Kryptonite, or a piece of Kryptonite displayed on a pedestal in the Batcave carry a similar connective effect as the appearance of Superman and Batman in the same panel would, as each of these elements represent specific *indices* of their respective *Narrative Entity*. Within the same vein, the use of *indices* equally removes the necessary distinction between the appearances of different interpretations of public-domain characters within different contexts. As a *Narrative Entity* consists of a collection of *indices*, the connection via a public-domain character (or any other public-domain *index*) is only possible if the public-domain character has become part of one of the *Narrative Entities* it is meant to relate. However, when it has become part of a *Narrative Entity*, it has developed defining connections with other *indices* in that *Narrative Entity*, which form it into a specific rendition suitable to that network of *indices*. In other words, it had to change to fit into the notion of that specific *Narrative Entity*. As such, an unwilling connection through multiple uses becomes impossible, as each use of a public-domain *index* that could facilitate a connection entails its own rendition within a *Narrative Entity*. Markstein's Hercules example postulates the potential mistake of assuming Marvel characters sharing the same universe as DC characters because both interacted with Hercules in their comic. To avoid this mistake, he excludes such public-domain figures from any connecting potential. However, the two Hercules are not the same version of that character (alas, they are not even comparable to the 'original' ancient Greek version) because they have formed links with other *indices* within their respective networks and, therefore, developed a subset of defining *rendition cues*. Marvel's Hercules made his first appearance with the Avengers and built an association with Thor and the Hulk, which influenced his visual representation and his characteristics. He shares a problem with rage and a sense of loss with the Hulk, as well as a love of combat and traditional viewpoints with Thor. Each aspect serves to relate him with the slew of *indices* associated with the Avengers Narrative and influences his visual representation. Either interpretation has tied the character to actions in larger Marvel Events concerning these characters, most notably the destruction of a Thor clone during *Civil War #7*[116]

---

[116] *Civil War #7*. Written by Mark Millar. Illustrator Steve McNiven. Marvel Comics, 2006. Page 15/16

and becoming the protagonist in *The Incredible Hulk* comic – renamed *The Incredible Hercules*[117], but continuing the original issue numbering – after the *World War Hulk*[118] Event. In contrast, DC's Hercules is tied to the Wonder Woman and Aquaman Narrative through their shared connection to Greek mythology. With less direct involvement in DC storylines, Greek mythology dominates this Hercules's visual representation, wearing a type of armor associated with ancient Greece. He appears as Wonder Woman's proud brother (Zeus sired both of them), who has given up on heroics and begets all his possessions to her after his death[119]. While both characters share the same inspiration, assuming they could relate different *Narrative Entities* solely due to their shared source is unreasonable, as either Hercules exists as a separate and different rendition defined by their existence in a specific network of *indices*. This idea of different renditions affirms Markstein's assertion that fictionalized versions public domain characters can serve as connection. Markstein's assumption concerning the potential connection of *Narrative Entities* via elements of the real world appearing in fiction equally dissolves within the existing explanation.

The interrelation via reality does not apply in fiction due to the limited means of fictional representations in contrast to the encompassing version of reality and the potential uniqueness of a fictional *Narrative Entity*'s network. Every representation in a *Manifestation* is a detraction from the actual presence, as no medium conveys the full scope of reality. As such, no fictional representation can fully overlap with a real-world occurrence, even if the occurrence provided the basis for the *index*, which is fictionally represented. As discussed in detail in the chapter on *Index Manifestation* and exemplified by the explanation on public-domain *indices*, interrelation rests on a certain unity of representation within different *Manifestations*. As any media representation of reality by its nature is a detraction from what is considered real, representation of an aspect of reality is never the same as that aspect of reality itself. In other words, because the representation of John F. Kennedy in a Superman comic is a representation, it is by its nature a version of John F. Kennedy, which plays on specific ideas held about the actual person (*semiotic cues*) and, therefore, differs from the 'original'. As the real John F. Kennedy and the representation of John F. Kennedy effectively are different manifestations of an *index*, the real John F. Kennedy cannot serve as a bridge for an interrelation for Superman, who only interacted with the representation of John F. Kennedy. Aside from its status as representation, an *index* based on an element of reality still appears in a network of fictional *indices*, meaning it potentially has to change to adhere to the needs of the *Narrative Entity* in which it appears. While an *index* created from reality is not as malleable as a public-domain *index* because reality provides more defining facts, it potentially has to adjust to other *indices* in a *Narrative Entity*. In the case of a superhero narrative, a politician might have to have a stance on superhero vigilantism or their status as part of law enforcement. Taking on such a characteristic further differs the representation from the original, as the original does not share that characteristic. Additionally, the focus of a *Narrative Entity* also removes principles of ownership from the formation of a Shared Universe and removes

---

117 *The Incredible Hercules* #113-#141. Written by Greg Pak and Fred van Lente. Marvel Comics, 2008–2010
118 *World War Hulk*. Written by Greg Pak. Illustrated by John Romita Jr. Marvel Comics, 2007–2008
119 *Wonder Woman* #31. Written by James Robinson. Illustrated by Carlo Pagulayan. DC comics, 2017

any definition via a media affordance suggested by Markstein's definition. As the interaction of *indices* exists independently from any medium, any medium formally can create a Shared Universe as long as it can facilitate such an interaction. The removal of ownership comes due to the discursive nature of a *Narrative Entity* and, therefore, a network composed of it. While this does not remove ownership altogether, as the owners of a *Narrative Entity*'s IP control the creation of its *Manifestation*, it spreads some of the creating power to the audience, who has to facilitate the representations in *Manifestations* into the idea of a Shared Universe.

While the basic terminology and the elements of governance set up in the Universe Model recontextualize aspects of Markstein's definition, this recontextualization does not fundamentally help to find a definition in the context of this model. Within the Universe Model, a Shared Universe implies an expected or likely interaction between *indices* from different *Narrative Entities*. When focused on text, such an expected interaction of *indices* arises out of the sense of entanglement already existing between the *Manifestations* of various *Narrative Entities*. This sense of entanglement is created through the specific application of the governing elements in a connecting manner. *Index Manifestations* appear outside of a *Manifestation* of their *Narrative Entity*; *Transformation Triggers* influence *Index Manifestations* outside their own source; *Trigger Waves* wander through *Manifestations* of several *Narrative Entities*; *Shared Narratives* run through multiple *Manifestations*; and *Manifestations* rely on others for comprehension and context. In other words, the greater use a collection of texts has made of the techniques described earlier, the greater the sense of entanglement and the greater the expectancy that different *indices* from the same network will interact in some shape or form. As such, a Shared Universe relationship between two or more *Narrative Entities* can be described in relation to the amount and efficiency in which the elements of governance are employed to connect their *Manifestations*. A definition along the amount and efficiency of techniques for a Shared Universe relationship makes sense in the context of the Universe Model. Yet, it is difficult to determine a clear number of interrelating techniques described here to use as a threshold determining the moment of transference from a non-Shared Universe relationship into a Shared Universe one. This difficulty arises out of a troublesome evaluation of each technique's efficacy, the significant influence of paratextual contexts, and the amount as well as the diversity of material at hand to research such a threshold. As implied in the various discussions concerning the elements of governance, an audience's perception of a *Narrative Entity* and their level of engagement with the *Manifestation* of the *Narrative Entity* greatly influences the overall notion of any relationship it forms with another. The efficacy of any technique used to connect different *Narrative Entities* partly hinges on an audience's ability to recognize these aspects. While the concept of *Narrative Reliance* covers a *Manifestation*'s overall dependence on another *Manifestation*, it does so by evaluating the totality of connecting elements used in relation to the rest of a plot. Assessing the effectiveness of singular connecting techniques via the audience conceptually is more difficult, as it would directly require data generated from an audience's experiences. Additionally, it is more complex to derive a sufficient notion of audience groups in the same manner this research did for *Narrative Reliance*. Each technique for the creation of a network does not operate with the same requirements concerning the comprehension of its purpose and knowledge of other *Manifestations*. Generally, creating a clear threshold necessitates some form of data generation from audiences and the various texts. The need for data from the engagement with various texts highlights an additional problem. The number and diversity of Shared Universes currently in circulation are limited and mostly tied to comics or comic adaptations. Of these, the greater part falls into some version of the superhero genre. This limited amount of specific material hinders the evaluation of techniques and their number to create the sense of a Shared Universe because they do not allow a good separation of technique, genre, and audience type. Finally, the complicated link between attempts at interrelation presented within a text and the marketing of these attempts equally might influence the efficacy of the techniques used. While at the current date, it is unclear how public mentions of a producer's intention influence an audience's reaction to such connections, it is inarguable that such a mention does influence their perception and effectiveness. May it encourage audiences to look for the smallest hints of interrelation or aggravate them into disregarding a text as nothing but an attempt at a franchise? As such, finding a clear threshold at this date appears impossible. However, the relative relations between two *Narrative Entities* still have to be evaluated to be determined as a Shared Universe. Within the context of this research, the Universe Model will use a general level of overall comparison. In other words, the threshold will be determined in relation to the number and efficacy of connections already used within the overall network. As such, the relationships described within the network exist all in comparison to one another. The Shared Universe moniker, therefore, describes a high use of narrative techniques to interrelate different *Narrative Entities* by implying that further interactions between their *indices* are likely to occur.

Within the Universe Model, Shared Universe represents an array of close relationships multiple *Narrative Entities* formally can have. The breadth of these close relationships necessarily grows out of the expectancy of *index* interaction. As such interaction naturally facilitates the rise of further means of interrelation, *Narrative Entities*, which already exist in a Shared Universe context, are more likely to increase their interrelation in future *Manifestations*. Therefore, the range of Shared Universe relationships tends to be greater than that of Multiverse and Company Universe relationships.

2.3.2 Multiverse

The term Multiverse generally encompasses the idea that other universes exist aside our own (in physics) or aside a perceived main universe (in fiction). As such, the term already carries certain notions concerning the construction of a fictional world. While these notions parallel certain understandings of world creation through networking numerous *Narrative Entities*, they do not automatically coexist with the narrative techniques and the Universe Model. To decipher the difference, it is necessary to separate the notion of Multiverse perpetuated mostly in speculative fiction from its notion based on narrative techniques within the Universe Model.

As the term Multiverse holds a specific understanding within speculative fiction, the use of the term within the Universe Model needs to be distinguished from that classic perception. In other words, the notion of a Multiverse as a narrative technique and the notion of a Multiverse as part of the setting associated with a specific genre requires clarification. The latter describes a setting consistent of (several) alternate versions of a *Narrative Entity*'s familiar *indices*. This genre-focused understanding of Multiverse does not require a *Narrative Entity* (or *Manifestations*) of its own but can exist solely as part of a perceived 'main' *Narrative Entity*. Examples of this type of Multiverse exist in several instances of speculative fiction. Star Trek famously created its Mirror Universe (an alternate Universe in which the Federation is a dictatorial regime) and used it in nearly all of its series at some point. The episode "Brave New Metropolis"[120] from *Superman: The Animated Series*, as well as the episodes "Legends"[121] and "A Better World"[122] from the *Justice League* animated series, employ the notion of a Multiverse in this fashion. In either Multiverse, a darker and more dangerous rendition of the *Narrative Entity*'s usually more noble interpretation of their *indices* is introduced. The Mirror Universe represents an aggressive, mistrustful, and opportunistic world, which counters the *Star Trek* Universe's optimistic future of peace, cooperation, and exploration. In "Brave New Metropolis", a parallel universe version of Metropolis is a dictatorship in which Lex Luthor and Superman rule together. A "Better World" involves a parallel world version of the entire Justice League known as the Justice Lords, which enforce their brand of law ruthlessly. Aside from direct contrast through darker versions, this Genre Multiverse also allows the introduction of alternate versions of familiar *indices*. The episode "Legends" from *Justice League* introduced an entirely new set of *indices* based on Golden Age concepts of DC heroes (dominantly the Justice Society of America characters). In the episode, four Justice League members are accidentally transported to a parallel world and encounter the Justice Guild of America in a setting reminiscent of a 1960s superhero narrative. More recently, the television series *The Flash* also makes use of this type of Genre Multiverse when they introduce alternate realities within the series, referred to as Earth-2. Essentially, this notion of Multiverse serves mainly to expand the number of *indices* within a *Narrative Entity*. As such, the notion of Genre Multiverse dominantly serves as an expansion of the regular setting by introducing alternate versions of already established *Index Manifestations*.

In contrast to this notion of Multiverse as an extra set of *indices* based on alternate versions of familiar *indices*, the narrative notion of Multiverse describes a relationship between Narrative Entities between a Company Universe and a Shared Universe. Within the Universe Model, the term Multiverse operates similarly to Shared Universe but denotes a use of connecting narrative techniques between *Narrative Entities* in smaller numbers and/or with less efficacy. As with the term Shared Universe, Multiverse is tied to a likelihood of *indices* interacting with one another in future *Manifestations* of the involved *Narrative Entities*. While a Shared Universe indicates an expected or, at least, very likely interaction of *indices* from different *Narrative Entities*, a Multiverse relation designates a relationship between *Narrative Entities* in which the interaction between their *indices* is unlikely or unusual but not out of the question. In other words, a relationship on a textual

---

120 "Brave New Metropolis". *Superman: The Animated Series*. Directed by Curt Geda. Season 2, episode 12. Warner Bros. Animation, 1997

121 "Legends". *Justice League*. Directed by Dan Riba. Season 1, episodes 18 & 19. Warner Bros. Animation, 2002

122 "A Better World". *Justice League*. Directed by Dan Riba. Season 2, episodes 11 & 12. Warner Bros. Animation, 2002

level exists through the use of a few connecting narrative techniques, but a few additional usages are required to create a certainty concerning the potential of interaction. As with the Shared Universe relationship discussed previously, determining clear thresholds for when two *Narrative Entities* pass into or out of a Multiverse relation is difficult. Equally, the solution is a general level of overall comparison. Hereby, each relationship is placed in context to existing ones and evaluated along the potential of all techniques described previously. Multiverse, then, is distinguished from Shared Universe by the use of connecting narrative techniques that mostly imply the potential for *indices* to interact but scarcely verify this implication by creating an actual interaction of *indices*. As the explanations above show, the genre-notion of Multiverse generally serves as an expansion of setting beyond its usual limitations in non-speculative genres. In contrast, the notion of a Narrative Multiverse provides a model for understanding the relationship between multiple *Narrative Entities*, independent from the existence of a Genre Multiverse within the *Manifestation* or *Narrative Entity*. While each use of the term describes very different ideas within the realm of fiction, representation through a Genre Multiverse may often overlap with the state of connection created through a Narrative Multiverse. As a Narrative Multiverse only implies a potential for interaction, the limited potential for contact inherent to most representations of a Genre Multiverse often coincides with a limited use of connecting narrative techniques. Still, while they often might coincide, either version of Multiverse is not dependent on the other. The *Manifestations* of different *Narrative Entities* may set up a Genre Multiverse between them, but any form of regular and constant interaction of their *indices* will set them in a Shared Universe relationship within the Universe Model. Conversely, the *Manifestations* of different *Narrative Entities* may imply their existence in the same genre universe, but when they never more than imply a relationship to one another, they exist in a Narrative Multiverse relationship within the Universe Model. As such, it is necessary to acknowledge that both versions of Multiverse describe different ideas and that they can exist independently from one another.

2.3.3 Company Universe

While Shared Universe holds an expected or likely interaction for *indices* of different *Narrative Entities* and a Narrative Multiverse implies that such an interaction is unlikely or unusual, the level of Company Universe denotes it barely imaginably or purely speculative. This improbable but speculated connection between *Narrative Entities* arises from a combination of little to no use of the techniques described in this paper and a perceived relation due to some real world contextual relation. The former aspect follows the logic for determining a Shared Universe or Multiverse. When two or more *Narrative Entities* make no direct use of the more complex techniques described previously (such as *Trigger Waves*) and even employ more direct techniques sparingly, in the background, and/or with some range of obfuscation, the connection between them effectively becomes nothing else than an allusion. Defined as "something that is said or written that is intended to make you think of a particular thing or person"[123], allusions provide no direct connection to another text other than serving as a reminder of that text's existence. Such a reminder

---

123   https://dictionary.cambridge.org/dictionary/english/allusion. Retrieved September 2nd, 2021

invites comparisons, potential viewpoints for interpretation, and speculation of a deeper connection between the mentioned *Narrative Entities*. Ultimately, allusions do not provide a direct interrelation in the same manner a clear combined use of specific narrative techniques would. More importantly, allusions can be ignored concerning the range of interaction of *indices* in future *Manifestations* of the participating *Narrative Entities*. The implications created by the use of narrative techniques on a Narrative Multiverse and Shared Universe level, in contrast, narrow the potential range of interactions. However, while the narrative techniques used within a text do not imply a relationship, *Narrative Entities* set in a Company Universe context still invoke an imagined potential for a more direct connection. This imagined potential arises from a pre-existing relationship surrounding the *Narrative Entity* or a contextual factor linking them outside of any relation created within a text. While concerns of ownership are not the only contextual factor in this regard, they appear to be the most common within the current Western understanding of literary production. The prolific status of ownership arises from the potential to create a *Manifestation* including *indices* from various, otherwise unrelated, *Narrative Entities*. Intellectual properties existing under a uniform owner are more likely to appear in each other's *Manifestation* because there are no legal hurdles and competing economic interests. An interesting example is the relationship between the MCU and Marvel properties licensed by other companies, namely 21st Century Fox and Sony Pictures. In the source material, all characters of the X-Men Narratives and all characters associated with The Avengers Narratives occupy the Shared Universe presented within the *Manifestations* of Marvel Comics. Due to Marvel's licensing agreement with 21st Century Fox (negotiated before Disney acquired Marvel Entertainment), these properties exist in two separate networks of *Narrative Entities* within the medium of film. For the longest time, the MCU and Spider-Man also operated in separate networks as all aspects of the Spider-Man Narrative were licensed to Sony Pictures[124]. The distinction in this case muddied over the years as Disney renegotiated its licensing agreement with Sony Pictures and bought larger parts of 21st Century Fox. However, the need for such re-negotiations and acquisitions, as well as the drama surrounding the potential disappearance of Tom Holland's Spider-Man from the MCU,[125] show how the legal reality and the audience's perception of these realities influence the formation of a network of *Narrative Entities*. Additionally, it highlights that the perception of ownership appears to weigh heavier than the burdens of a legal and economic reality[126]. The company presented as the owner usually appears more relevant than the actual complexities of intellectual property rights. While Disney acquired Marvel Entertainment in August of 2009, and several cooperative projects have been released, the MCU films are seldom directly associated with the Disney image or logo. Disney does

---

124 For a quick overview of the financial development of Marvel Productions and the varying shifts of Intellectual Property rights, I advise reading Sean Howe's article "Avengers Assemble!" published by Slate.
125 In 2019, after the success of *Spider-Man: Far From Home*, Sony and Disney had a public disagreement concerning the future funding and payout of Spider-Man films. This dispute created a fear that the *Narrative Entity* might leave the MCU and compromise both the network and the Spider-Man Narrative created in the films. The drama disappeared when Disney and Sony came to an agreement.
126 For a more in-depth description and a way of classifying the influence of ownership on perceived networks of texts, I advise reading Colin B. Harvey's *A Taxonomy of Transmedia Storytelling*.

not actively hide their relationship with Marvel (Disney stores carry MCU merchandise, and Disney+ contains all Marvel films). Still, it keeps the brands separate by releasing the MCU films without overt Disney branding. In the same manner, Disney also avoids any direct networking between Star Wars (which it acquired in December 2012) and its other properties. Independent from the actual context linking them, *Narrative Entities* related to the level of Company Universe merely share a vague relationship created by allusions and external circumstances.

3 The Mechanics

Having a general model to represent the changing relationships between different *Narrative Entities*, the analysis should look at a collection of objects after a set of *Transformation Triggers*. As mentioned, the inclusion of *Transformation Triggers* makes the Universe Model a synchronous representation of a diachronic process. As such, each analysis has to acknowledge not only the number of *Manifestations* and *Narrative Entities* involved but equally determine the point of comparison along the line of all *Transformation Triggers*. In this, any set moment along the line of *Transformation Triggers* works as long as they remain comparable. The obvious points of comparison appear either structural (within the same point in the plot) or temporal (within some comparable time of publication).

Independent from the number of *Narrative Entities*, one forms the center of the Universe Model, allowing a determination of the relative distance between the different objects. Hereby, the center should be chosen relative to the argument and the suspected interrelation of *Narrative Entities*. An interest in the relationship between more famous *Narrative Entities* with less successful ones might set the most successful *Narrative Entity* at its center. Research interested in the development of interrelations over time might place the earliest *Narrative Entity* at the model's center; research interested in the use of comparable *semiotic cues* might place a prototypical *Narrative Entity* at its center. The analysis should be conducted in stages depending on the number of *Narrative Entities* and the types of interrelations represented within the Universe Model, starting on the lowest level first and shifting upward when lower relationships have been established. The definition of lower and higher, here, again rests on actual research and the objects of analysis chosen. However, the default assumption is that lower levels of interrelation also mean closer. As such, in case of a large number of objects, (1) presumed clusters of *Narrative Entities* should be established first, followed by (2) an analysis of the relationship of such pre-established clusters, and, if different clusters from the first level prove to form a set of grouped constellations of their own, (3) these relationships should be reanalyzed.

In this research, *Manifestation* mainly refers to films, entire seasons of series, and complete Graphic Novels.

3.1 The MCU Network

The overall Marvel Cinematic Universe contains several *Narrative Entities* presented across different media. If we include all transmedia extensions and follow the declaration of its producers, the MCU spreads across films, streaming series, television series, comic books, short films, and digital series. At the time of this writing, these divisions contain 25 cinematically released films, 13 streaming series with a total of 23 seasons, three television series with a total of ten seasons, 33 comic book series with a total of 72 single issues, five short films, and two digital series. The MCU is too vast to be thoroughly analyzed within the pages of this paper. As new *Manifestations* are continuously added, research at this point in time might not be able to grasp the entire span of such a network. As such, the network presented here will be limited to the cinematically released films forming the so-called 'Infinity Saga', two of the television series (*Agents of S. .I.E.L.D.* and *Agent Carter*), and the streaming series collectively referred to as the Marvel Netflix Universe (MNU).

The research excludes comics, digital series, and short films because each serves mainly as a transmedia extension to a singular *Narrative Entity* and has little additional bearing on the interrelation between different *Narrative Entities*. While one short film – *A Funny Thing Happened on The Way to Thor's Hammer*[1] – arguably has a more significant influence on connecting two MCU films, it only expands on one *Index Manifestation*, which appears and is characterized in several *Narrative Entities*. The effects of transmedia extensions have been sufficiently researched and discussed by several scholars cited earlier. As such, this research decided to exclude these from its discussion, focusing primarily on the core material of the films and notable material released as a series.

Agent Carter and *Agents of S.H .I.E.L.D.* were included because both continue the story of *Index Manifestations* presented within the MCU films. This starting relationship provides a good case study for potential changes in the relationship of *Narrative Entities* due to an alteration of the representing medium. Additionally, the alteration in relationship might provide insight into the process of narration in changing relations to their origin. The MNU series provides an example of a parallel-developing network, which is meant to relate to the MCU. As such, the MNU provides a singular case study for the development of interrelations between established networks within the idea of a complex network.

The core of the research will revolve around the 23 films of the 'Infinity Saga'. Arguably, these films provide the primary starting point and the core material for the wider MCU. Understanding the mechanics of the interrelation between the singular films could provide the basis for understanding the mechanics governing wider networks forming a coherent sense of a world.

---

1 *A Funny Thing Happened on The Way to Thor's Hammer*. Directed by Leythum. Marvel Studios, 2011

3.1.1 The MCU Films

The first of four sections focus on the material that gives this particular network its name. The Marvel films began with the release of *Iron Man*[2] in 2008, with the final release of the 'Infinity Saga' being *Spider-Man: Far From Home*[3] in 2019. The 'Infinity Saga', a collective term for 23 films, is categorized into three distinct phases. The analysis will describe the interrelation of each *Narrative Entity* within a larger network in relation to these phases. Hereby, each section examines the *Manifestations* in order of release, adding a description and discussion of complex aspects spread across several films like *Shared Narratives* and *Trigger Waves* at the end of each phase. Additionally, an examination of potential *Shared Narratives* spread across the entirety of all 23 films, or several phases, will follow the discussion of the singular phases.

3.1.1.1 Phase 1

The MCU's Phase 1 contains six films. The first two installments of Iron Man, as well as the first installments of Captain America and Thor. Additionally, it includes the first team narrative in the form of *The Avengers* and the singular *Manifestation* devoted to the *Narrative Entity* of the Hulk.

3.1.1.1.1 Set up of Phase 1

As the beginning of the network, the MCU's Phase 1 has no previous collection of *Transformation Triggers* or *Index Manifestations* to consider. However, each film is the *Manifestation* of an already existing *Narrative Entity*, as different comic books, television series, and films have introduced aspects of them to public discourse. Most of the singular films serve as an introduction to a *Narrative Entity*, with the exception of *Iron Man 2*[4], which is the only sequel within the phase, and *The Avengers*, which is the introduction to a *Manifestation* utilizing several *Narrative Entities*.

A notable contextual influence on the setup of the first phase is Disney's acquisition of Marvel Comics (including all its subsidiaries) in 2009. The transfer of ownership might explain an odd skip in release dates as *Iron Man 2* was released two years after *Iron Man* and *The Incredible Hulk*[5], making 2009 the only year without an MCU film appearing in cinemas since the start of the franchise[6]. More importantly, the sudden shift in ownership and, therefore, parts of management might have influenced the decision to repeat an already established *Narrative Entity* instead of focusing on introducing new ones exclusively.

---

2 *Iron Man*. Directed by Jon Favreau. Performances by Robert Downey Jr., Gwyneth Paltrow, Terrence Howard, and Jeff Bridges. Marvel Studios, 2008
3 *Spider-Man: Far From Home*. Directed by Jon Watts. Performances by Tom Holland, Jake Gyllenhaal, and Zendaya. Marvel Studios, 2019
4 *Iron Man 2*. Directed by Jon Favreau. Performances by Robert Downey Jr., Gwyneth Paltrow, Don Cheadle, Sam Rockwell, and Mickey Rourke. Marvel Studios, 2008
5 *The Incredible Hulk*. Directed by Louis Leterrier. Performances by Edward Norton, Liv Tyler, William Hurt, and Tim Roth. Marvel Studios, 2008
6 Until the year 2020, in which Disney opted to skip another year, due to the effects of the corona pandemic.

3.1.1.1.2   Iron Man (2008)

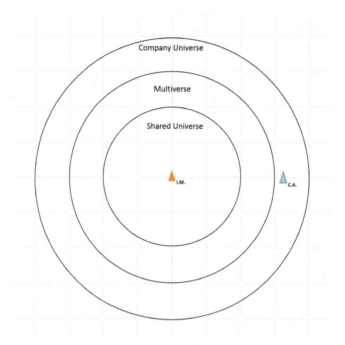

Because it is the first publication within the network, *Iron Man* mostly operates as a standalone film with only allusive connections to other *Narrative Entities*. The most significant part of its interrelation with other *Manifestations* of the MCU lies in its introduction of *Index Manifestations*, later used to connect to other *Narrative Entities* in the form of Clark Gregg's Phil Coulson and Samuel L. Jackson's Nicholas Fury. However, *Iron Man* does start with a potential relation to a Captain America Narrative. At 01:25:22, an incomplete rendition of Captain America's shield appears in the background. As this manifestation of an *index* from the Captain America Narrative merely hints at its actual form, holding incomplete *index cues*, it cannot rise above an allusion. While the shield's appearance alone does not connect the MCU's Iron Man Narrative to the MCU version of the Captain America Narrative, this short allusion reminds an audience that the same company owns the two properties. The combination of an allusion with contextual information of ownership places the Narrative Entities in a Company Universe relationship at this stage. Additionally, the two *Narrative Entities* are known to interact with one another within their formative medium (comic). While knowledge of these interactions might be limited to a subsection of a mainstream audience, it justifies a slight decrease in the distance as the context of the source material increases the likelihood of future interaction of their *indices*.

Independent from direct connections formed in the film, *Iron Man* implies the idea of a network of *Narrative Entities* by mentioning *The Avengers*, which in the source material is a team formed by heroes from multiple *Narrative Entities*.

3.1.1.1.3 The Incredible Hulk (2008)

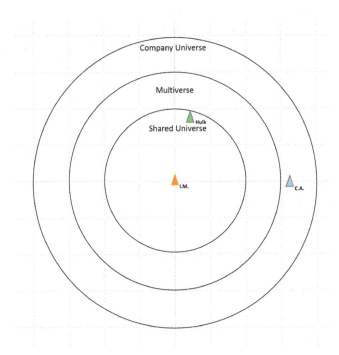

This *Narrative Entity* ties specifically to the MCU version of the Iron Man Narrative and alludes to an undefined version of the Captain America Narrative. The interrelation to the Iron Man Narrative relies on the appearance of one specific *Index Manifestation* and the allusions to another. Robert Downey Jr.'s Tony Stark/Iron Man appears in the film's post-credit scene with William Hurt's Thaddeus "Thunderbolt" Ross (the movie's main antagonist)[7]. Robert Downey Jr. retains the same hairstyle and beard from the first film. Additionally, their conversation alludes to Tony Stark's Iron Man armor[8]. The appearance of Tony Stark, played by the same actor in the same representation, forms the most vital link between the two *Narrative Entities*. The mention of the suit underscores the unity of the representation. While not directly linked to any specific *Narrative Entity* but a part of the overall network, the secret agency S.H.I.E.L.D. (The Strategic Homeland Interventions, Enforcement, and Logistic Division) already appears in *Iron Man*. *The Incredible Hulk* furthers its relation to the Iron Man Narrative by mentioning the organization and the appearance of the S.H.I.E.L.D. logo in a digital database. However, as the logo was not shown on screen in *Iron Man*, its presence only supports the connections made through the other techniques. Blueprints of the more fantastic weapons shown in *The Incredible Hulk* carry the Stark Industries logo. Hereby, the logo is the same in both

---

[7] For screenshots of Tony Stark/Iron Man's appearances within the MCU consult https://marvelcinematicuniverse.fandom.com/wiki/Iron_Man/Gallery

[8] *The Incredible Hulk*. Directed by Louis Leterrier. Performances by Edward Norton, Liv Tyler, William Hurt, and Tim Roth. Marvel Studios, 2008. 01:45:29

films. Aside from the blueprints, the Stark company logo also appears on the Crysync container,[9] holding a later attempt at recreating the super soldier serum. The combination of all these connections, but dominantly the appearance of an established *Index Manifestation* in the form of Robert Downey Jr.'s Tony Stark/Iron Man, set the two MCU versions of these *Narrative Entities* in a Shared Universe relationship. However, as their connection is solely based on an exchange of *Index Manifestations*, the relationship is not close.

A mention of the super soldier program in two instances – the previously mentioned post-credit scene and a separate conversation[10] – creates a relation to a Captain America Narrative, as such a program is an established *index* of that *Narrative Entity*. The super soldier program gives Steve Rogers his powers, making him Captain America in every *Manifestation* of that *Narrative Entity*. However, as this *Index Manifestation* only appears in dialogue and has no unified representation in the MCU at this point, the mentions serve primarily as an allusion similar to the allusion in *Iron Man* – whereas this case is more overt. As such, the Captain America Narrative equally stands in a Company Universe relation with the MCU version of the Hulk Narrative. The same contextual considerations as made for *Iron Man* draw them slightly closer together.

As the mere existence as allusion does not change with *The Incredible Hulk*, the film also does not affect the relationship between the MCU versions of the Iron Man Narrative and the Captain America Narrative, keeping them at the previous distance. Both the MCU version of the Iron Man Narrative and the Hulk Narrative exist in a similar relationship with the Captain America Narrative.

3.1.1.1.4 Iron Man 2 (2010)

Iron Man 2 alludes to two *Narrative Entities*. Both allusions are based on the manifestation of an *index* associated with the respective *Narrative Entity*. The film reiterates the allusion to a Captain America Narrative via the appearance of Captain America's shield. As with its representation in *Iron Man*, the *Index Manifestation* indicates its association via incomplete *index cues*. As this is the only connection to a Captain America Narrative, it only reiterates the previous relationship, neither decreasing nor increasing the likelihood of more significant interaction between their *indices*. Thor's hammer, Mjolnir, appears in the film's post-credit scene[11]. As this *Index Manifestation* is given no further context, explanation, or association within *Iron Man 2*, it merely alludes to a version of the Thor Narrative. However, the representation of Mjolnir is the same within both *Iron Man 2* and *Thor*[12], which will affect the relationship between the two *Narrative Entities* in that *Manifestation* later. Additionally, however, Mjolnir crashing on Earth initiates Phil Coulson's departure from the plot of *Iron Man 2*. As the *Trigger Waves* leading up to this change

---

9   *The Incredible Hulk*. Directed by Louis Leterrier. Performances by Edward Norton, Liv Tyler, William Hurt, and Tim Roth. Marvel Studios, 2008. 00:45:06
10   *The Incredible Hulk*. Directed by Louis Leterrier. Performances by Edward Norton, Liv Tyler, William Hurt, and Tim Roth. Marvel Studios, 2008. 00:32:51
11   For screenshots of this *Index Manifestation*'s appearances in the MCU consult https://marvelcinematicuniverse.fandom.com/wiki/Mj%C3%B8lnir/Gallery
12   *Thor*. Directed by Kenneth Branagh. Performances by Chris Hemsworth, Tom Hiddleston, and Natalie Portman. Marvel Studios, 2010

necessarily have to occur in *Thor*, the MCU version of the Iron Man Narrative shares a stronger connection with a Thor Narrative than with a Captain America Narrative at this point. The interrelation due to a *Transformation Trigger* in combination with the actual appearance of an *Index Manifestation* draws the Thor Narrative into a Multiverse relationship with the MCU version of the Iron Man Narrative because a more significant interaction between their *indices* appears more probable at this stage than with the Captain America Narrative. Interestingly, this connection implies that parts of the *Transformation Triggers* initiated in *Thor* must have occurred parallel to the *Transformation Triggers* of *Iron Man 2*, implying the potential of parallel-running storylines within the same network.

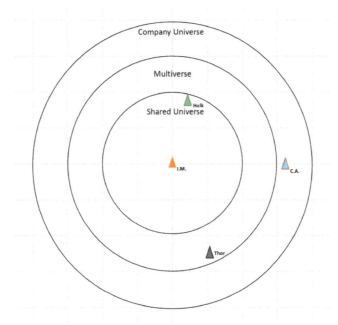

As the film mentions both *Narrative Entities*, it equally sets a Thor Narrative and a Captain America Narrative into a relationship. As the *Index Manifestations* only appear in this *Manifestation* but do not interact with one another, and the *Trigger Wave* caused by *Thor* has no bearing on a Captain America Narrative, the two *Narrative Entities* will have a Company Universe relationship. The context influencing previously described Company Universe relationships within this research equally applies to this one. As *Iron Man 2* does not mention the MCU version of the Hulk Narrative, only an association with the Iron Man Narrative ties either to one another. Therefore, the Thor Narrative holds a greater distance from the Hulk Narrative than any other *Narrative Entity* within the network. Nothing changes the relationship between the Captain America Narrative and the Hulk Narrative.

3.1.1.1.5 Thor (2010)

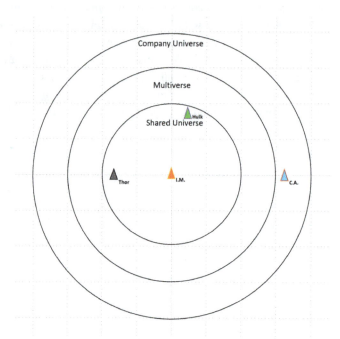

Aside from interrelations created by including S.H.I.E.L.D. and Clark Gregg's Phil Coulson, *Thor* mostly relates to the MCU Iron Man Narrative and a Captain America Narrative. Directly, the film connects to the Iron Man Narrative when Maximiliano Hernández's Agent Jasper Sitwell asks his colleague Phil Coulson if the Asgardian Destroyer – a mystical battle armor – is "one of Stark's"[13]. Indirectly, *Thor* connects to the MCU version of the Iron Man Narrative via Mjolnir. The representation of Thor's hammer is the same within *Iron Man 2* and *Thor*[14]. Aside from the actual prop, the similarity continues through mirroring the *Iron Man 2* post-credit scene within the running plot of *Thor*. The *Index Manifestation*, Mjolnir, is shown in a small crater surrounded by a group of locals. Mjolnir appearing in the same constellation within both films implies that both representations refer to the same *Index Manifestation*. While this is a substantial connection, it also relies on a minimally engaged audience, as the connection hinges on a scene that appears after the credits, meaning after the actual movie has already ended. As such, the MCU version of the Thor Narrative is pulled into a Shared Universe relation with the MCU version of the Iron Man Narrative but maintains some distance as its strongest connections rely on a minimally informed audience. In the same manner that *Iron Man 2*

---

[13] *Thor*. Directed by Kenneth Branagh. Performances by Chris Hemsworth, Tom Hiddleston, and Natalie Portman. Marvel Studios, 2010. 01:21:21

[14] For screenshots of this *Index Manifestation*'s appearances in the MCU consult https://marvelcinematicuniverse.fandom.com/wiki/Mj%C3%B8lnir/Gallery

relates to *Thor*, *Thor* sets up a relationship with *Captain America: The First Avenger*[15] through the appearance of the Tesseract in its post-credit scene[16]. However, as the Tesseract is not explicitly related to any Captain America Narrative, its appearance has no direct influence on the relationship at this point, paying off in the latter film. As such, the Thor Narrative presented here has only a distant and allusive relationship with any Captain America Narrative set up through its connection with Iron Man at this point. More notable, the post-credit scene initiates a *Trigger Wave* leading into the plot of *The Avengers* by showing Tom Hiddleston's Loki's influence on Stellan Skarsgard's Erik Selvig to study the Tesseracts, as Loki later uses it to bring an alien army to earth.

By moving into a Shared Universe relationship with the MCU version of the Iron Man Narrative, the MCU version of the Thor Narrative necessarily closes some distance to the Hulk Narrative presented in this network. While they operate in a Shared Universe via the Iron Man Narrative as a proxy, these versions of the Thor Narrative and the Hulk Narrative still exist in a Multiverse relationship because there is no indication of their *indices* interacting other than the shared relation to a proxy.

3.1.1.1.6   Captain America: The First Avenger (2011)

The final *Narrative Entity*-specific *Manifestation* of Phase 1, *Captain America: The First Avenger*, connects exclusively to the MCU's Iron Man and Thor Narrative. The setup of these interrelations is significant because these three *Narrative Entities* are often directly associated with the Avengers in the comics. The movie connects to the MCU version of the Iron Man Narrative due to the use of an *Index Manifestation* of Howard Stark, Tony Stark's father. Howard Stark is part of the super soldier program, which gives Steve Rogers/Captain America his extraordinary abilities. In the film, he provides Steve Rogers with his costume and signature shield. However, instead of John Slattery – who plays the character in *Iron Man 2* – Dominic Cooper portrays a younger version of Howard Stark. Following the notion that connections arise from a degree of similarity, the potential connection provided via these two versions of the same *index* appears more complicated than a simple transposition of an *Index Manifestation*. As the representation of Howard Stark in *Captain America: The First Avenger* is meant to be a younger version of the one shown in *Iron Man 2*, as the plot of the film takes place during World War II, the changed *media cue* in the form of a different actor makes sense. However, such a significant shift in *media cue* in combination with the addition of some *rendition cues* – as the character has to be adapted to its age and the period – requires additional or even other means of interrelation between the two *Index Manifestations*. Using details in representation to link them proves difficult, as Slattery's appearance in *Iron Man 2* is limited to a less-than-three-minute recording. Contrasted with Cooper's version, no similarity outside of the name, the association with a secret organization – S.H.I.E.L.D. for Slattery and the S.S.R., the former's precursor, for Cooper – and the company Stark Industry remains. Aside from using different actors, each representation wears an attire

---

15   *Captain America: The First Avenger*. Directed by Joe Johnston. Performances by Chris Evans, Hayley Atwell, and Hugo Weaving. Marvel Studios, 2011
16   For screenshots of this *Index Manifestation*'s appearances in the MCU consult https://marvelcinematicuniverse.fandom.com/wiki/Tesseract/Gallery

appropriate for their respective period. Each also speaks and behaves differently. Only the style of hair and the mustache appear significantly similar[17]. Generally, Dominic Cooper's Howard Stark constructs fewer similarities with the representation of Howard Stark in *Iron Man 2* than with the representation of Tony Stark in either Iron Man film. The similarity between Howard Stark and Tony Stark is best exemplified by their similar style of introducing new and advanced technology[18], which in either case includes showmanship and attractively dressed, dancing women. Howard Stark is shown to be a lady's man as he kisses one of the showgirls on stage, and his penchant for women is mentioned in dialogue, which mirrors Tony Stark's representation in either of the previous Iron Man films. Dialogue in *Iron Man* mentions Tony Stark's success with women several times and shows him seducing a reporter[19]. The manner in which Gwyneth Paltrow's Pepper Potts deals with the reporter the following day implies a certain regularity to such occurrences. Similar to Tony Stark's tendency to try technology without reasonable experimentation – he tests his armor's flight capability without preparation or safety protocols – Cooper's Howard Stark blows up a lab because he disregards the potential danger of an unknown substance[20]. While *Captain America: Civil War* later mentions a *Transformation Trigger* explaining the changes between the two representations, the two renditions are not directly linked via their manifestation within the films. Instead, they are related by the context of the MCU, meaning the understanding that there is an attempt at interrelation and an association between Tony Stark and Howard Stark through similarities in action. The unambiguous differences of each *Index Manifestation* lower the connection the use of a transferred *Index Manifestation* would usually provide, giving the two Howard Starks merely a level of allusion, a reasonable and singularly relatable one, but still merely an allusion. As such, the relationship between the MCU Iron Man Narrative and the MCU Captain America Narrative at this point amounts to a Multiverse one because the presence of a Howard Stark increases the chance for the *indices* of each *Narrative Entity* to interact. The relationship between the *Narrative Entities* surpasses the Multiverse stage due to the appearance of Samuel L. Jackson's Nick Fury in the film's post-credit scene. The influence of that aspect will be discussed in the chapter on overarching elements.

In *Thor*'s post-credit scene, the Tesseract manifests as a cube with a blue glow and a white center. Lightning wanders from its center to the outside in either appearance[21]. It follows the same representation as in *Captain America: The First Avenger*. The unity of the Tesseract's representations provides a clear, unambiguous interrelation between the

---

17   For screenshots of Howard Stark's appearances (Slattery and Cooper) in the MCU consult https://marvelcinematicuniverse.fandom.com/wiki/Howard_Stark/Gallery

18   *Captain America: The First Avenger*. Directed by Joe Johnston. Performances by Chris Evans, Hayley Atwell, and Hugo Weaving. Marvel Studios, 2011. 00:11:59

19   *Iron Man*. Directed by Jon Favreau. Performances by Robert Downey Jr., Gwyneth Paltrow, Terrence Howard, and Jeff Bridges. Marvel Studios, 2008. 00:08:54

20   *Captain America: The First Avenger*. Directed by Joe Johnston. Performances by Chris Evans, Hayley Atwell, and Hugo Weaving. Marvel Studios, 2011. 01:15:36

21   For screenshots of this *Index Manifestation*'s appearances in the MCU consult https://marvelcinematicuniverse.fandom.com/wiki/Tesseract/Gallery

two films. *Captain America: The First Avenger* tries to deepen the relationship by indicating an Asgardian origin for the Tesseract's hiding place on Earth. Odin, Asgard's ruler and Thor's father, is mentioned by name. Similarly, a representation of the world tree Yggdrasil from Norse mythology appears within the movie's setting and is mentioned in dialogue[22]. Yggdrasil also appears in dialogue within *Thor* but has a different representation. As such, while *Captain America: The First Avenger* relates directly to *Thor* through the Tesseract, every other connection remains merely on the level of an allusion. As with the Mjolnir example in *Iron Man 2*, the Tesseract draws the two *Narrative Entities* into a Multiverse relationship. However, the additional constant allusions to *indices* associated with the Thor Narrative create a slightly closer relationship with the Captain America Narrative than the sole appearance of an *Index Manifestation*.

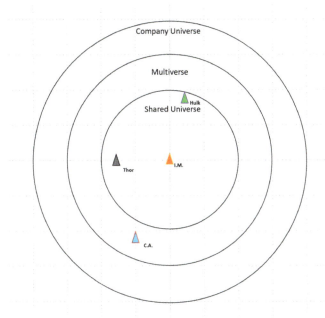

Captain America: The First Avenger makes no effort and shows no further indication of an interrelation with the MCU version of the Hulk Narrative. The connection between the two *Narrative Entities* closes a bit because the occurrence of an MCU *Manifestation* of a Captain America Narrative re-contextualizes allusions made in *The Incredible Hulk* to a super soldier program. However, the decreased distance is minimal.

Aside from existing *Narrative Entities*, *Captain America: The First Avenger* initiates the potential for a Black Panther Narrative to become part of this network. The potential is minimal and hinges solely on the mention of a fictional metal, vibranium. As part of Captain America's shield and mined exclusively in Black Panther's homeland, this *index* has ties to both *Narrative Entities*, whereas it carries greater importance for the Black Panther

---

22   *Captain America: The First Avenger*. Directed by Joe Johnston. Performances by Chris Evans, Hayley Atwell, and Hugo Weaving. Marvel Studios, 2011. 00:06:43

Narrative. When discussing the prototype of Captain America's shield in *Captain America: The First Avenger*, the metal is mentioned by name and given as the reason for the weapon's extraordinary properties. While no other aspect of a Black Panther Narrative finds mention in the film, the appearance of an *index* so uniquely tied to that *Narrative Entity* creates the potential for it to appear in the MCU. However, similar to the mention of the Captain America Narrative in *The Incredible Hulk*, any connection to a part of the MCU network remains on the Company Universe level, specifically with the MCU's Captain America Narrative. As such, the connection requires mention but does not appear directly in the network at this point.

3.1.1.1.7 The Avengers (2012)

Literary products based on the collaboration of characters from different sources have a prominent function within the conception of a world built from the interrelation of Narrative Entities. In Marvel comics, publications focused on the Avengers always feature a team of 'heroes' collected from other *Narrative Entities*. This nature of the product makes them a connective node because the structure of the subsequent story necessarily interrelates *Index Manifestations* from various *Narrative Entities*. Following this 'tradition' of a team narrative, *The Avengers* features the specific *Index Manifestations* presented in previous *Manifestations* from the network discussed in this research. While smaller aspects in representation change, each appearance retains the necessary *index cues*, marking them as a version of that figure, and, more importantly, their *rendition cues* mark them as the established MCU version. Prominently, the actors for nearly all characters remain the same and appear with generally the same grooming and mannerisms. Changes to the semantically charged wardrobe (most notably in the case of Chris Evan's Steve Rogers) retain all notable *semiotic cues* associated with the character[23]. Merely Mark Ruffalo's Bruce Banner is a significant departure from the previously established *Index Manifestation* when Edward Norton played the character in *The Incredible Hulk*. With the change of actor, other aspects of the representation changed as well, such as mannerisms and wardrobe. The most notable alteration exists in the representation of Bruce Banner's alter ego. 'The Hulk' in *The Incredible Hulk* walks mostly upright, has a V-shape torso, a dehydrated physique with clear muscle definition and veins, as well as an overall dirtier and darker presence. *The Avengers*' Hulk supports his weight on his knuckles, has a square torso, thicker muscles, and lacks the dark shadows and dirt of the other representation. While either maintains the necessary *index cues* for the Hulk, they use different *rendition cues*. Due to the motion capture technology used to link the facial features of the respective actors to each representation, the use of different actors also influences each representation of the Hulk. More significant in this departure in representation within *The Avengers*, however, is the lack of other *Index Manifestations* from the Hulk Narrative. Aside from the other Avenger member, Scarlett Johansson's Natasha Romanoff, who appears in *Iron Man 2* (played by the same actress displaying the same style of combat and similar wardrobe)[24], Gwyneth Paltrow's Pepper Potts[25] appears as one specific *Index Manifestation* from the MCU's Iron Man Narrative. Similarly, the MCU's Thor narrative provides not only the main villain in the form of Tom Hiddleston's Loki (played by the same actor displaying established *semiotic cues*)[26] but also adds the character of Stellan Skarsgard's Erik Selvig[27]. *Thor* also connects to *The Avengers* via Jeremy Renner's Clint Barton, who has a short cameo in the earlier film[28]. Even though the MCU's Captain America narrative has a greater difficulty connecting directly to the team narrative because the main character was transported from the end of the Second World War to the present, it does add material from its *Manifestation* to *The Avengers*. Weaponry used by the antagonist organization Hydra in *Captain America: The First Avenger* appears in the team narrative, as does the Tesseract[29], which powered them. As such, all these *Narrative Entities* are drawn into a close Shared Universe relationship because the film generates apparent anticipation concerning the interaction of the different *indices* in future *Manifestations*. The exception

---

23 For screenshots of Steve Rogers/Iron Man's appearances within the MCU consult https://marvelcinematicuniverse.fandom.com/wiki/Steve_Rogers/Gallery
24 For screenshots of Natasha Romanoff/Black Widow's appearances within the MCU consult https://marvelcinematicuniverse.fandom.com/wiki/Black_Widow/Gallery
25 For screenshots of this character's appearances within the MCU consult https://marvelcinematicuniverse.fandom.com/wiki/Pepper_Potts/Gallery
26 For screenshots of this character's appearances within the MCU consult https://marvelcinematicuniverse.fandom.com/wiki/Loki/Gallery
27 For screenshots of this character's appearances within the MCU consult https://marvelcinematicuniverse.fandom.com/wiki/Erik_Selvig/Gallery
28 For screenshots of this character's appearances within the MCU consult https://marvelcinematicuniverse.fandom.com/wiki/Hawkeye/Gallery
29 For screenshots of this *Index Manifestation*'s appearances in the MCU consult https://marvelcinematicuniverse.fandom.com/wiki/Tesseract/Gallery

to an expected interaction of *indices* lies with *The Incredible Hulk*'s version of the Hulk Narrative. The absence of any direct *Index Manifestation* from the Edward Norton version and the presence of a distinctly different iteration of the Narrative Entities's titular character pushes the relationship of this version of the Hulk Narrative into a Company Universe with the rest of the network. At the same time, Mark Ruffalo's manifestation of the character becomes an *index* to the overall network without carrying any other *index* from an overall Hulk Narrative connected to the MCU or otherwise.

The Avengers further relates the different *Narrative Entities* by taking note of *Transformation Triggers* from the *Manifestations* within the network. Steve Roger's presence in the film and his lack of understanding concerning modern culture and technology directly relate to his sudden shift in time caused by his crash at the end of *Captain America: The First Avenger*. Similarly, the interactions between Steve Rogers and Howard Stark color the interactions between Tony Stark and Steve Rogers[30]. Furthermore, S.H.I.E.L.D.'s application of Hydra technology and the Tesseract is explained as a reaction to the organization's helplessness in the face of the Asgardian Destroyer in *Thor*[31]. As such, *The Avengers* also interrelates the different *Narrative Entities* by acknowledging the effect of singular *Transformation Triggers* and connections created through *Trigger Waves*. The acknowledgment of *Transformation Triggers* is most noticeable in the case of the MCU's Thor Narrative, in which the main character's access to Earth was cut off due to the destruction of the Rainbow Bridge – the Bifrost – at the *Climax* of *Thor*. Instead of ignoring this change to an *Index Manifestation*, *The Avengers* offers an alternate explanation for Thor's journey[32]. Despite the distance created by the different versions of the Hulk, *The Avengers* even hints at *Transformation Triggers* from *The Incredible Hulk*. Specifically, the film refers to the presumed control Bruce Banner gained over his transformation. A sub-theme in *The Incredible Hulk*, the notion of meditation regularly appears in the film to display Bruce Banner's constant pursuit of control over his emotions – chiefly his anger and excitement – and, therefore, his transformation into the Hulk. *The Incredible Hulk* ends with Bruce Banner implicitly initiating his transformation in a completely serene environment through meditation. The voluntary nature of the change arises from a shot of Edward Norton's Bruce Banner grinning as his eyes turn to a bright (radioactive) green. The theme of Bruce Banner's involuntary to voluntary transformation is picked up in *The Avengers*. Snippets of dialogue refer to Bruce Banner's secret[33] for constantly remaining calm[34]. He also scares people by displaying anger without transforming. While he changes once involuntarily, Bruce Banner displays the ability to initiate the change willingly[35]. That he has this ability links this version of the character to a *Transformation Trigger* (or a similar version of this *Transformation Trigger*) presented in *The Incredible Hulk*. While *The Avengers* significantly decreases the distance between the *Narrative Entities* through the interaction of usually

---

30   *The Avengers*. Directed by Joss Whedon. Marvel Studios, 2012. 00:59:10
31   *The Avengers*. Directed by Joss Whedon. Marvel Studios, 2012. 01:08:05
32   *The Avengers*. Directed by Joss Whedon. Marvel Studios, 2012. 00:44:50
33   *The Avengers*. Directed by Joss Whedon. Marvel Studios, 2012. 00:16:33
34   *The Avengers*. Directed by Joss Whedon. Marvel Studios, 2012. 00:56:41
35   *The Avengers*. Directed by Joss Whedon. Marvel Studios, 2012.01:51:30

unassociated *Index Manifestations* and smaller *Trigger Waves*, it does so by necessarily creating a narrative that relies on information provided in texts outside of the *Manifestation* at hand. None of the mentioned characters are introduced, nor are relationships put into context. Instead, the film alludes to information audiences should have gathered from earlier *Manifestations*. Tony Stark's romantic relationship with Pepper Potts is presented as a given, and her position as CEO of his company is only implied. Personal and professional relationships of characters of the MCU version of the Iron Man and Thor Narrative with S.H.I.E.L.D. Agent Phil Coulson are implied but never explained, even though his death prompts the heroes into action. Thor's conversation with Loki refers to revelations and *Transformation Trigger*s of *Thor* but offers no clarification[36]. To comprehend all actions and relationships, a film traditionally includes some form of exposition. However, *The Avengers* opts to rely on an informed audience, which gathered all necessary knowledge from earlier *Manifestations* or hopes for an audience with the ability to accept unexplained portions of the narration. These acknowledgments draw the *Narrative Entities* closer to one another, as the team narrative's reliance on previous information implies that these interactions between *indices* of different *Narrative Entities* will carry into future *Manifestations*, leaving the MCU's Iron Man, Captain America, and Thor Narrative in an overall close Shared Universe relationship. With a new version of the Hulk, the Hulk Narrative, as presented in *The Incredible Hulk*, shifts to a Multiverse relationship bordering on a Company Universe relationship.

3.1.1.1.8 The Special Case of Hulk and War Machine

Within my definition of *Index Manifestations* and how they help connect *Narrative Entities*, I greatly emphasize the retention of *semiotic cues* through similarity in representation. Specifically concerning the MCU's Phase 1, two problematic characters warrant discussion in this regard, namely Bruce Banner/Hulk and James "Rhodey" Rhodes/War Machine. Within the overall network of the MCU films, two different actors portrayed each character. Terrence Howard played James "Rhodey" Rhodes in *Iron Man* and was replaced by Don Cheadle, who portrayed the character in all further MCU appearances. Similarly, Edward Norton played Bruce Banner/Hulk in *The Incredible Hulk*, but Mark Ruffalo assumed the part for all subsequent appearances in the MCU. Suppose details in the representation of Index Manifestation are of such importance for a sense of interrelation and continuity. How does the change of an actor not call the overall efficacy of such a means of interrelation into question? As the analysis of *The Avengers* indicates, to some degree, it can. However, that analysis also pointed towards altered *rendition cues* to Bruce Banner and the Hulk other than the actor. In contrast, the transfer from Terrence Howard to Don Cheadle appears nearly without impact. Within the Universe Model presented in this research, using different actors decreases the interrelation between *Narrative Entities* within the network, as the change potentially marks a different rendition of the same *index*. However, even though uniquely noticeable, a new actor represents merely a singular alteration in a constellation of *semiotic cues*, which exists in a network of other established *Index Manifestations*. Specifically in the case of the MCU version of the Iron

---

36 *The Avengers*. Directed by Joss Whedon. Marvel Studios, 2012. 00:45:12

Man Narrative, the alteration of one *rendition cue* is countered by the overwhelming retention of previously established *semiotic cues* in related *Index Manifestations*. Outside of James "Rhodey" Rhodes, *Index Manifestations* from the first movie retain their overall characteristics. When changed, the alterations occur in the course of a *Transformation Trigger* presented directly in *Iron Man 2*. Robert Downey Jr. portrays Tony Stark, Gwyneth Paltrow plays Pepper Potts, Clark Gregg reappears as Agent Coulson and even Samuel L. Jackson returns as Nick Fury. Even minor characters like Jon Favreau's Happy Hogan contribute to a stable rendition. Most sets and props equally manifest in the same form in *Iron Man 2*. Tony's house is the same. Stark Industries' main office also preserves its overall appearance. The overabundance of retained *semiotic cues* throughout *Manifestations* of the MCU's Iron Man Narrative clarifies that Don Cheadle's James Rhodes is meant to represent the same character as Terrence Howard's James Rhodes, indicating that the coherence of the overall representation does not hint at a singular *Index Manifestation* or even a singular *semiotic cue*, but on the consistency of the overall network.

Because there is no direct sequel to *The Incredible Hulk*, the change from Edward Norton to Mark Ruffalo presents a more complicated case. As the analysis of *The Avengers* shows, *The Incredible Hulk* ends up in a Multiverse/Company Universe relationship with the MCU film network. Excluding Bruce Banner/Hulk, the only other *Index Manifestation* from *The Incredible Hulk*, which reappears in other MCU *Manifestations*, is William Hurt's General Thaddeus "Thunderbolt" Ross. *Captain America: Civil War* features the character as the US. Secretary of State, and he makes a brief appearance in *Avengers: Infinity War*[37]. However, while the same actor portrays the character, the change in title already indicates other changes to the *Index Manifestation*'s *semiotic cues*. While the precise shifts in relation between the overall network and the version of the Hulk Narrative presented in *The Incredible Hulk* are discussed in the analysis of *Captain America: Civil War* and *Avengers: Infinity War*, suffice it to say that the reoccurrence of the one *Index Manifestation* does not alter the relationship drastically when it is set against a collection of other moments of interrelation. The overall lack of returning *Index Manifestations* from *The Incredible Hulk* gives the shift in actor a more significant impact. While the potential ramification of the change in the case of James 'Rhodey' Rhodes is cushioned by a stable constellation of established *Index Manifestations*, the change of actor in the case of Bruce Banner nearly ostracizes the former version of the Hulk Narrative because the evaluation of connection and rendition is solely based on one *Index Manifestation*.

These two shifts in actor highlight the relation of singular elements of an overall network concerning interrelation. In either case, the change in actor appears as the most visible and dissonant feature in the attempt at interrelating different *Narrative Entities* within the medium of film. However, the very different result and impact of these changes relies on the reaction to subsequent networks surrounding such a shift. Its relation to other stable aspects within its network can compensate even such visible and radical changes to an *Index Manifestation*. In contrast, the placement of such a change within an entirely new environment allows for a detachment from all previously established parts. On a universal level, this sets the efficacy of any interrelation effort or, subsequently, the stability of a network in relation to the size of the overall network –

---

37   *Avengers: Infinity War*. Directed by Anthony Russo and Joe Russo. Marvel Studios, 2018

potentially down to the degree of the *semiotic cues* within singular *Index Manifestations* – as well as the overall consistency of the networks' various elements. These aspects also only unfold their fortification of the network through constant repetition in one form or another. In other words, a regularly repeated and consistently presented set of *Index Manifestations* gives the network – and singular versions of the *Narrative Entity* in it – some semblance of stability in the face of one *Index Manifestation*'s radical re-interpretation, which is the reason the shift of actor in James Rhodes's case did not influence the overall network as much as in the case of Bruce Banner. This relationship between a higher number of consistent elements and a lower number of inconsistent elements may also explain how more extensive networks compensate for logical inconsistencies, forgotten *Transformation Triggers*, and the general viability of retcons within larger networks.

3.1.1.2 Phase 2

Similar to Phase 1, Phase 2 consists of six films. The first three films continue *Narrative Entities* from the previous phase with *Iron Man 3*[38], *Thor: The Dark World*[39], and *Captain America: The Winter Soldier*[40]. Two films, *Guardians of the Galaxy*[41] and *Ant-Man*[42], introduce new *Narrative Entities* to the network, leaving *Avengers: Age of Ultron*[43] as a *Manifestation* drawing from several *Narrative Entities*.

3.1.1.2.1 Set up of Phase 2

Phase 1 *Transformation Triggers* – through causing *Trigger Waves* – influence every Phase 2 *Manifestation* in some form. *Manifestations* continuing established *Narrative Entities* necessarily acknowledge their predecessor. *Trigger Waves* informing and determining the composition of *Index Manifestations* in *The Avengers* carry influence into the wider network. In other words, each sequel placed in Phase 2 must acknowledge changes made to their setting in their predominant prequel and the team narrative preceding them.

Narrative Entities added to an existing network must acknowledge some elements that constitute the network at their point of arrival. Such an acknowledgment necessarily entails that the new *Narrative Entity* establishes some form of relation with the recognized *Narrative Entities* of the network. In other words, each new *Narrative Entity* has to acknowledge an existing one when it joins a network.

Within the context of the MCU films, all *Narrative Entities* of Phase 2 (established and new alike) must acknowledge one alteration to the overall network: the battle against an

---

38 *Iron Man 3*. Directed by Shane Black. Performances by Robert Downey Jr., Gwyneth Paltrow, Don Cheadle, Ben Kingsley, and Guy Pearce. Marvel Studios, 2013
39 *Thor: The Dark World*. Directed by Alan Taylor. Performances by Chris Hemsworth, Tom Hiddleston, Natalie Portman, and Christopher Eccleston. Marvel Studios, 2013
40 *Captain America: The Winter Soldier*. Directed by Anthony Russo and Joe Russo. Performances by Chris Evans, Scarlett Johansson, and Sebastian Stan. Marvel Studios, 2014
41 *Guardians of the Galaxy*. Directed by James Gunn. Performances by Chris Pratt and Zoe Saldana. Marvel Studios, 2014
42 *Ant-Man*. Directed by Peyton Reed. Performances by Paul Rudd, Michael Douglas, and Evangeline Lilly. Marvel Studios, 2015
43 *Avengers: Age of Ultron*. Directed by Joss Whedon. Marvel Studios, 2015

alien invasion in New York at the end of *The Avengers*. Through the Avengers' public battle, the entire (seen and unseen) *Index Manifestations* bound to Earth are confronted with two definite and influential redefinitions of society. This *Transformation Trigger* not only presents the world with proof of alien life and its potential as a larger threat to humanity but equally with the existence and capabilities of 'enhanced' humans. As such, films of the second phase have to negotiate the idea of a more complex world to maintain the notion of interrelated *Narrative Entities*.

3.1.1.2.2 Iron Man 3 (2013)

As the first second phase film, *Iron Man 3* focuses on renegotiating the *Index Manifestations* of its *Narrative Entity* in light of *Trigger Waves* started in *The Avengers*. As this renegotiation focuses on the elements of the Iron Man Narrative, *Index Manifestations* of other *Narrative Entities* make no appearance, with one exception. Mark Ruffalo's Bruce Banner appears in the movie's post-credit scene, which links to the character leaving with Robert Downey Jr.'s Tony Stark at the end of *The Avengers*. As the discussion on the changes made to the character implies, this appearance does not link the MCU's Iron Man Narrative to the Hulk Narrative established by *The Incredible Hulk*, but more to the *Transformation Triggers* of the team narrative.

More substantial than direct interrelation through an exchange of *Index Manifestations* are the connections created through *Trigger Waves*. The most significant are the changes to the *Index Manifestation* of Tony Stark. In his appearance in *The Avengers* and throughout *Iron Man* and *Iron Man 2*, Robert Downey Jr.'s portrayal focuses on Tony Stark's disregard and obnoxious personality, as well as his irresponsibility and egotistical nature. These characteristics become apparent in his disregard for Terrence Howard's James "Rhodey" Rhodes's time in *Iron Man* when he arrives three hours late for a scheduled plane departure[44]. The subsequent conversation on a plane directly addresses Tony Stark's lack of responsibility and respect for others[45]. This general egoism, or lack of regard for the impact of his actions, continues when he shuts down the weapon-manufacturing branch of Stark Industries. Instead of phasing out production, offering alternative revenue streams, or even giving his board of directors any advance notice, he calls an immediate press conference in which he declares his intention, causing panic among stockholders, his employees, and his military liaison. This pattern of behavior repeats itself in his refusal to share details on the miniaturized arc-reactor and the Iron Man armor in *Iron Man 2*, where he declares the privatization of world peace[46]. The selfish behavior continues in *The Avengers* when Tony Stark hacks into the S.H.I.E.L.D. database[47], is combative towards Steve Rogers, and attempts to get Bruce Banner to turn into the Hulk. *Iron Man 3* reminds the audience of this version of Tony

---

44 *Iron Man*. Directed by Jon Favreau. Performances by Robert Downey Jr., Gwyneth Paltrow, Terrence Howard, and Jeff Bridges. Marvel Studios, 2008. , 00:12:49
45 *Iron Man*. Directed by Jon Favreau. Performances by Robert Downey Jr., Gwyneth Paltrow, Terrence Howard, and Jeff Bridges. Marvel Studios, 2008. 00:13:14
46 *Iron Man 2*. Directed by Jon Favreau. Performances by Robert Downey Jr., Gwyneth Paltrow, Don Cheadle, Sam Rockwell, and Mickey Rourke. Marvel Studios, 2010. 00:16:33
47 *The Avengers*. Directed by Joss Whedon. Marvel Studios, 2012. 00:58:09

Stark as the film begins with a flashback set in 1999 – before the events of *Iron Man*. By showing him ignoring a fellow scientist and giving a lecture while drunk, the film retells a version of Tony Stark before *The Avengers*. However, in the present, Tony Stark has changed due to the 'Battle of New York' – the Avengers' defense against alien invaders. The character shows greater concern with the state of the world. He fears losing the people he cares about (namely Pepper Potts)[48]. Additionally, Tony Stark displays all the telltale signs of PTSD. J.A.R.V.I.S mentions that he has not slept for 72 hours. When he sleeps, he has nightmares of his near-death experience in *The Avengers*. Confronted with reminders of the incident, Stark suffers anxiety attacks, which cause him to seek protection in his armor. He shows concern for and bonds with a young boy, who receives new equipment from him at the end of the film. The tendency to disregard the effect of his actions on others remains in place after the 'Battle of New York' from *The Avengers*, but the basis for his actions changes drastically. While his egotistic behavior in *Iron Man* and *Iron Man 2* mainly served the retention of his legacy, his personal enjoyment, or the acknowledgment as a hero, after *The Avengers*, Tony Stark expands his motivation to the protection of his loved ones and the world at large. *Iron Man 3* presents this alteration in his behavior because of the posttraumatic stress disorder he incurred due to the events of *The Avengers*. Because Tony Stark is the focus of this particular *Narrative Entity*, this alteration to his overall motivation (and parts of his personality) creates a strong relationship between *Iron Man 3* and *The Avengers*. As *The Avengers* is not a *Manifestation* of its own *Narrative Entity* (in this context) but a connective node of the *Narrative Entities* in the network, this relationship reaffirms the relationship established in the team narrative and acknowledges the direct influence different *Narrative Entities* within the network can have on one another.

Remarkably, the *Transformation Triggers* of *The Avengers* equally influence the general threat and theme of the Iron Man films. While the first two films revolve around Tony Stark dealing with and redefining his legacy (his company's in *Iron Man*, his father's and his own in *Iron Man 2*), *Iron Man 3* refocuses on the threat of a larger and more complex world and how a man like Tony Stark can deal with it. The threats of the first two films are people misusing technology the main character claims dominance over. With his superhero status based on machinery, Tony Stark matches such threats as both serve the *Narrative Entity*'s general themes (dangerous technology and their policing). In contrast, *Iron Man 3* introduces super-powered threats to the MCU's Iron Man Narrative. Because Tony Stark solves a problem for Rebecca Hall's Maya Hansen, who worked on the Extremis formula, and his mistreatment of Guy Pearce's Aldrich Killian created the movie's villain, the theme of legacy and taking responsibility for your actions remains a part of this *Manifestation*. However, unlike previous threats, the super-powered Extremis soldiers are not an extension of Tony Stark/Iron Man. Jeff Bridges's Obadiah Stane/Iron Monger – the villain from *Iron Man* – is a leading executive and a member of the board of directors of Stark Industries. He also builds a mock version of Tony Stark's suit. In the same film, the Ten Rings terror organization uses Stark weaponry. In *Iron Man 2*, Mickey Rourke's Ivan Vanko/Whiplash employs the arc-reactor technology (which powers the Iron Man

---

48   *Iron Man 3*. Directed by Shane Black. Performances by Robert Downey Jr., Gwyneth Paltrow, Don Cheadle, Ben Kingsley, and Guy Pearce. Marvel Studios, 2013. 00:21:29

armor), and Sam Rockwell's Justin Hammer tries to develop technology in a direct reaction to the Iron Man armor's existence. Instead of an extension of Tony Stark, the super-powered antagonists of *Iron Man 3* are an extension of the close relationship between the different *Narrative Entities* after *The Avengers*. While the MCU's Iron Man Narrative does not offer a direct basis for the threat of artificially created super-powered individuals, the MCU's Captain America and Hulk Narrative do. Their films contain directly augmented humans as super-powered antagonists in the form of Hugo Weaving's Johann Schmidt/Red Skull (*Captain America: The First Avenger*) or Tim Roth's Emil Blonsky/Abomination (*The Incredible Hulk*). Specifically, the idea of artificial human enhancement is a prominent feature of any Captain America Narrative. As such, the notion of super-powered antagonists spills over from other *Narrative Entities*. Using enhanced humans in contrast to people abusing technology as the main threat in *Iron Man 3* anchors the MCU's Iron Man Narrative into a larger and more complex world than the previous Iron Man films. More prominently, it forces the *Narrative Entity* (in this case, through its hero character) to redefine itself in relation to the elements of other *Narrative Entities*. Due to the acknowledgment of not only each *Narrative Entity's* existence but also their general themes and *Index Manifestations*, the Iron Man sequel or even any other MCU sequel necessarily has to address its place in the established network after *The Avengers* . In *Iron Man 3*, this notion of engaging a larger world appears directly in Tony Stark's PTSD, which is triggered by reminders of the aliens and the wormhole from *The Avengers*, but equally in the unusual shift of antagonists. The acknowledgment of a unified world created by the interrelation of *Narrative Entities* also informs Tony Stark's general coping mechanisms. When in the face of "gods, aliens, other dimensions", Tony Stark realizes that he is "just a man in a can" and does "what [he] knows. [He] tinkers."

Overall, *Iron Man 3* does not change the relationship between the established *Narrative Entities*, leaving all interrelations in place. Instead, it is more prominently concerned with negotiating the new status quo forced through the close interaction of *Narrative Entities* in *The Avengers*.

3.1.1.2.3 Thor: The Dark World (2013)

Similar to *Iron Man 3*, the second *Manifestation* of the MCU's Thor Narrative is mostly concerned with negotiating the state of its *Index Manifestations* regarding *Trigger Waves* started in *The Avengers*. Due to the galactic and mystical nature of this *Narrative Entity* contrasting it to others at this stage in the network, the renegotiation does not have the same impact as in the case of *Iron Man 3*. Still, the distribution of interrelating techniques appears to follow a comparable pattern. The transposition of *Index Manifestations* is limited, while a greater focus is placed on changes to *Index Manifestations* of the MCU's Thor Narrative due to *Trigger Waves*.

Concerning appearances of transposed *Index Manifestations*, Chris Evans appears as an illusion of Steve Rogers, created by Loki. While only on-screen for 15 seconds, the illusion wears the Captain America uniform from *The Avengers* and carries the character's trademark shield[49]. Loki also refers to him as one of Thor's new companions, which al-

---

49   For screenshots of the movie consult https://marvelcinematicuniverse.fandom.com/wiki/Thor:_The_Dark_World/Gallery

ludes to the *Transformation Triggers* of *The Avengers*. Furthermore, S.H.I.E.L.D. appears in more minor instances within the movie. Kate Denning's Darcy Lewis refers to them as she tries to phone for help,[50] and Natalie Portman's Jane Foster uses a measuring device with the S.H.I.E.L.D. sigil printed on it. The most intriguing *Index Manifestation*, however, connects *Thor: The Dark World* with *Guardians of the Galaxy*. Benicio Del Toro's Taneleer Tivan/The Collector appears in the film's mid-credit scene and reappears within the plot of *Guardians of the Galaxy*[51]. As with all post- and mid-credit scenes so far, the *Index Manifestation* of Taneleer Tivan/The Collector connects to a later released *Manifestation*. A more precise analysis of the character and the interrelation created follows in the discussion on *Guardians of the Galaxy*.

Dr. Erik Selvig and Loki represent the film's strongest connection due to *Transformation Triggers*. Shown as a respected astrophysicist in *Thor*, Stellan Skarsgard's Erik Selvig is recruited by S.H.I.E.L.D. to work on the Tesseract in the post-credit scene of *Thor*. Loki magically subjugates him within *The Avengers*, using Erik Selvig's expertise for his invasion plan. Saved at the end of *The Avengers*, Dr. Selvig reappears in *Thor: The Dark World* as mentally unstable. He is seen in a television report running naked around Stonehenge[52] and is later held by the police for psychiatric evaluation[53]. A bag of prescription medication he collects upon his release from the hospital implies that he uses pharmaceuticals to deal with his mental and emotional state. When asked if he is all right, he replies that he "had a god in [his] brain"[54], which directly refers to the means of his subjugation. As such, his entire representation continues a series of *Transformation Triggers* from *Thor* through *The Avengers* into *Thor: The Dark World*. Something similar can be said about Tom Hiddleston's Loki. Loki appears first as the antagonist in *Thor* and falls off the Rainbow Bridge into a portal in the void of space. He reappears as the main antagonist in *The Avengers*. After his defeat, Thor takes him back to Asgard. While the character does not change significantly through the *Transformation Triggers*, his relations and position within this *Manifestation* of the MCU's Thor Narrative do. A prince at the beginning of *Thor*, he has been mourned at the beginning of *The Avengers*. When Loki asks if Thor mourned him, the latter replies that they all did[55]. His return and defeat in *The Avengers* explain Loki's presence in Asgard's prison, an aspect that would otherwise appear as a break in continuity between *Thor* and *Thor: The Dark World*. As such, Loki also follows a series of *Transformation Triggers* stretched across three different *Manifestations*.

On a smaller level, the relationship between Natalie Portman's Jane Foster and Thor is equally altered through a *Trigger Wave* started in *The Avengers*. At the end of *Thor*, both

---

50   *Thor: The Dark World*. Directed by Alan Taylor. Performances by Chris Hemsworth, Tom Hiddleston, Natalie Portman, and Christopher Eccleston. Marvel Studios, 2013. 00:55:55
51   For screen shots of all appearances of this character within the MCU consult https://marvelcinem aticuniverse.fandom.com/wiki/Collector/Gallery
52   *Thor: The Dark World*. Directed by Alan Taylor. Performances by Chris Hemsworth, Tom Hiddleston, Natalie Portman, and Christopher Eccleston. Marvel Studios, 2013. 00:16:30
53   *Thor: The Dark World*. Directed by Alan Taylor. Performances by Chris Hemsworth, Tom Hiddleston, Natalie Portman, and Christopher Eccleston. Marvel Studios, 2013. 00:56:11
54   *Thor: The Dark World*. Directed by Alan Taylor. Performances by Chris Hemsworth, Tom Hiddleston, Natalie Portman, and Christopher Eccleston. Marvel Studios, 2013. 01:11:41
55   *The Avengers*. Directed by Joss Whedon. Marvel Studios, 2012. 00:45:12

characters are shown as separated romantic interests because Thor has to destroy the Rainbow Bridge to save one of the nine realms and cannot return to Earth. Despite his romantic interest, Thor does not seek out Jane Foster in *The Avengers*, only acknowledging that S.H.I.E.L.D. keeps her out of harm's way[56]. This lack of interaction (and presumed damper on their romantic relationship) is addressed in *Thor: The Dark World*, when Jane Foster is shown in an attempt at dating somebody else. The neglect of her character in *The Avengers* and all implications connected to her absence arise again when she and Thor are reunited. Jane Foster slaps him and accuses him of leaving her waiting and crying. When he explains his reasons in the same dialogue, she mentions that she saw him on television fighting in New York.[57] While this example does not alter the overall dynamic between different *Index Manifestations*, it does highlight that a *Manifestation* within a network has to resolve the effects of *Trigger Waves* in one form or another.

Similar to *Iron Man 3*, *Thor: The Dark World* does not affect the relationship between the established *Narrative Entities* within the network. Instead, it focuses on reestablishing its own *Index Manifestations* in the network of the *Narrative Entity* under the effects of the *Trigger Waves* permeating the overall MCU network. In other words, it is prominently concerned with negotiating all its elements with the new status quo created by the stronger interrelation with other *Narrative Entities*. In contrast to *Iron Man 3*, the second Thor film does not try to merge larger changes made by the interrelation into its *Manifestation*, but instead, it attempts to mitigate the effects of such *Trigger Waves*, as most of the *Index Manifestation* circumvents the most lasting effects from *The Avengers*.

3.1.1.2.4 Captain America: The Winter Soldier (2014)

Similar to the previous two films, *Captain America: The Winter Soldier* focuses on renegotiating the changes to its own *Index Manifestation* due to *Trigger Waves* started in *The Avengers* over establishing or reestablishing connections with the *Narrative Entities* in the MCU network. As such, the inclusion of transposed *Index Manifestations* is limited, while a relation to the network through *Transformation Triggers* and *Trigger Waves* appears more prominent.

Overall, the film builds connections via the use of *Index Manifestations* from the MCU's Iron Man Narrative. These appear primarily through intimations in dialogue and the film's background, as well as the use of Scarlett Johansson's Black Widow and Samuel L. Jackson's Nick Fury. Two exceptions are the appearance of Loki's scepter in the film's mid-credit scene and the prominent use of Cobie Smulder's Maria Hill. The scepter Loki used to mind-control people in *The Avengers* reappears in the mid-credit scene of *Captain America: The Winter Soldier*. The representation of the *Index Manifestation* on screen marks it as the same scepter in either film[58]. This specific object connects the MCU's Captain America Narrative dually with the team narrative, as the scepter appears in both

---

56   *The Avengers*. Directed by Joss Whedon. Marvel Studios, 2012. 01:01:30
57   *Thor: The Dark World*. Directed by Alan Taylor. Performances by Chris Hemsworth, Tom Hiddleston, Natalie Portman, and Christopher Eccleston. Marvel Studios, 2013. 00:26:20
58   For screenshots of this *Index Manifestation*'s appearances within the MCU consult https://marvelcinematicuniverse.fandom.com/wiki/Scepter/Gallery

The Avengers and the later-released *Avengers: Age of Ultron*. In the same manner, the appearance of Maria Hill ties the MCU's Captain America Narrative directly to the team narrative, as she only appeared in *The Avengers* previously[59]. Aside from a connection to *The Avengers*, the second Captain America film most prominently relates to the MCU's Iron Man Narrative. The Helicarriers' redesigned propulsion system is attributed to Tony Stark in dialogue[60]. Equally, after the fall of S.H.I.E.L.D., Cobie Smulder's Maria Hill takes an interview in an office with a Stark Logo on the door. The *Index Manifestations* of Black Widow and Nick Fury also prominently relate the MCU's Captain America and Iron Man Narrative with one another. Aside from *The Avengers*, Samuel L. Jackson's Nick Fury, up to this point, only appeared in *Manifestations* related to either the MCU's Iron Man Narrative or the MCU's Captain America Narrative[61]. While having a greater prominence in the Iron Man Narrative due to his involvement with the plot in *Iron Man 2*, Nick Fury balances out his appearances with a more prominent role in *Captain America: The Winter Soldier*, strengthening the connection between the two Narratives. As Scarlett Johansson's Natasha Romanoff/Black Widow only appeared in *The Avengers* and *Iron Man 2* previously, the character also connects the Captain America Narrative with the team narrative and the MCU's Iron Man Narrative[62]. The two *Index Manifestations* (Nick Fury, Black Widow) in *Captain America: The Winter Soldier* are overarching elements that form *Shared Narratives* across several *Manifestations*. As such, they will be discussed in detail in future chapters.

Like its two preceding *Manifestations*, *Captain America: The Winter Soldier* mostly focuses on renegotiating its *Index Manifestations* into the context of the larger changes created by *The Avengers*. In contrast to the former two, which either elaborate or mitigate the effect of *Trigger Waves* of the team narrative, the second Captain America film uses the *Transformation Triggers* from *The Avengers* to establish a wide range of new *Index Manifestations* for this particular narrative. The need for new *Index Manifestations* in the case of the MCU's Captain America Narrative does not arise from a *Transformation Trigger* of *The Avengers* but from the ending of *Captain America: The First Avenger*. At the end of that film, Steve Rogers ends up in a form of suspended animation in 1945. He awakes 70 years later in modern-day New York. This *Transformation Trigger* necessarily alters or removes nearly all *Index Manifestations* associated with that film's Second World War setting. Only two *Index Manifestations* from the first Captain America film reappear in *Captain America: The Winter Soldier*, Hayley Atwell's Peggy Carter, and Sebastian Stan's Buchanan "Bucky" Barnes. Peggy Carter reappears in a video segment of a documentary presumably filmed

---

59   For screenshots of this character's appearances within the MCU consult https://marvelcinematicuniverse.fandom.com/wiki/Maria_Hill/Gallery
60   *Captain America: The Winter Soldier*. Directed by Anthony Russo and Joe Russo. Performances by Chris Evans, Scarlett Johansson, and Sebastian Stan. Marvel Studios, 2014. 00:16:30
61   For screenshots of Nick Fury's appearances within the MCU consult https://marvelcinematicuniverse.fandom.com/wiki/Nick_Fury/Gallery
62   For screenshots of Natasha Romanoff/Black Widow's appearances within the MCU consult https://marvelcinematicuniverse.fandom.com/wiki/Black_Widow/Gallery

in 1953[63] and as an old woman with dementia[64]. Buck Barnes appears as the Winter Soldier mentioned in the title. Otherwise, *Captain America: The Winter Soldier*, in contrast to the previous two films of the second phase, has to rebuild an *index* network for the MCU's Captain America Narrative. It does so by appropriating and expanding on the organization S.H.I.E.L.D. Gradually established throughout the first phase, S.H.I.E.L.D. becomes a prominent and central part of the overall MCU in *The Avengers*. Events in the first team narrative also appear to alter the status of the organization from an utterly secretive entity to a semi-public one, similar to the CIA. With no existing network of *Index Manifestations* to return to, like Thor and Tony Stark, Chris Evan's Steve Rogers/Captain America became a permanent operative of S.H.I.E.L.D. after *The Avengers*. As such, a more significant part of newly established *Index Manifestations* within the film is associated with the organization. Emily VanCamp's Sharon Carter, Robert Redford's Alexander Pierce, and Frank Grillo's Brock Rumlow all have positions within S.H.I.E.L.D. This connection extends to transferred *Index Manifestations*, such as Maria Hill, Natasha Romanoff/Black Widow, and Nick Fury, who are all established S.H.I.E.L.D. Agents. This sudden tie between the MCU's Captain America Narrative and S.H.I.E.L.D. warrants mention because it is a reaction to two intersecting *Trigger Waves*, the end of *The Avengers* and the end of *Captain America: The First Avenger*. Binding the MCU Captain America Narrative into an *Index Manifestation* of S.H.I.E.L.D. arises from the need to negotiate unresolved changes, Steve Rogers/Captain America's loss of his former environment, and the altered state of the world from *The Avengers*. As such, *Captain America: The Winter Soldier* highlights the second phase's need to renegotiate an established Narrative Entity's position in the network after a considerable alteration and shows how different transformations might intersect within a network of *Narrative Entities*.

The interrelation of *Captain America: The Winter Soldier* with *The Avengers* via *Transformation Triggers* also exists within the film's plot, as its threat arises out of S.H.I.E.L.D.'s reaction to the attack on New York. Nick Fury's 'Project Insight' is based on three Helicarriers with automated weapons linked to spy satellites. The system was designed to eliminate potential enhanced threats preemptively. Fury mentions that he convinced the world security councils that they "needed a quantum surge in threat analysis". Fury also mentions that Project Insight puts S.H.I.E.L.D. "for the first time ahead of the curve."[65] As such, the creation of the object of conflict and the threat in the film arises directly in relation to a *Transformation Trigger* from *The Avengers*, which revealed to the MCU's public that they live in a more dangerous world than they previously suspected.

---

[63] For screenshots of Peggy Carter's appearances in the MCU consult https://marvelcinematicuniverse.fandom.com/wiki/Peggy_Carter/Gallery

[64] *Captain America: The Winter Soldier*. Directed by Anthony Russo and Joe Russo. Performances by Chris Evans, Scarlett Johansson, and Sebastian Stan. Marvel Studios, 2014. 00:20:16

[65] *Captain America: The Winter Soldier*. Directed by Anthony Russo and Joe Russo. Performances by Chris Evans, Scarlett Johansson, and Sebastian Stan. Marvel Studios, 2014. 00:17:16

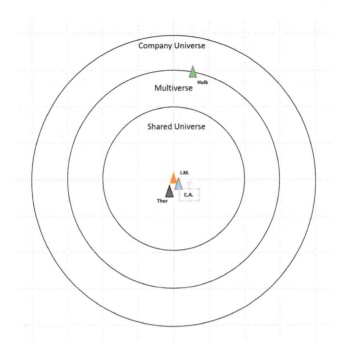

Overall, *Captain America: The Winter Soldier* strengthens the relationship between the MCU's Captain America Narrative and the MCU's Iron Man Narrative. More importantly, however, it leans on several *Trigger Waves* by taking on an overarching *Index Manifestation* (S.H.I.E.L.D.), which formally was not directly associated with a specific *Narrative Entity* and made it part of its own *index* network. It does so to remove S.H.I.E.L.D. from the MCU film network as the organization is destroyed at the end of the film. However, the film provides an example of resolving multiple changes to a network within a *Narrative Entity*-specific *Manifestation*. With one eye on the third Captain America film, it appears that this is the overall function of the Captain America Narrative within the MCU film network.

3.1.1.2.5 Guardians of the Galaxy (2014)

Guardians of the Galaxy (renamed *Guardians of the Galaxy Vol. 1* after the release of its sequel) introduces the first new *Narrative Entity* to the MCU film network since the end of Phase 1. Within a potential spectrum of interweaving and relying on a network's existing elements, this *Manifestation* only tangentially connects to the overall network. Specifically, the film solely relates to the MCU's Thor Narrative via an *Index Manifestation* presented in *Thor: The Dark World*. Benicio del Toro's Taneleer Tivan/The Collector appears in the mid-credit scene of *Thor: The Dark World* and reappears in the *Guardians of the Galaxy*. The representation remains consistent between both films[66]. The recurrence of a surrounding specifically heightens the recognition value of this *Index Manifestation*. In either representation, the Collector is shown with the same alien servant played by Ophelia Lovi-

---

66 For screen shots of all appearances of this character within the MCU consult https://marvelcinem aticuniverse.fandom.com/wiki/Collector/Gallery

bond, the same 'shop' containing chambers holding different alien species. Additionally, the character's motivations align with those implied in *Thor: The Dark World*. In the latter, after receiving the Reality Stone for safekeeping, the Collector says: "One down, five to go."[67] This snippet of dialogue implies an interest in collecting all Infinity Stones, and the motivation reemerges when he appears prominently as the prospective buyer for the Power Stone in *Guardians of the Galaxy*. The *Narrative Entity* also connects to the larger Shared Universe via the *Shared Narrative* involving Thanos and the Infinity Stones. However, aside from the *Index Manifestation* of the Collector, *Guardians of the Galaxy Vol.1* shows no interrelations to the overall network of the MCU.

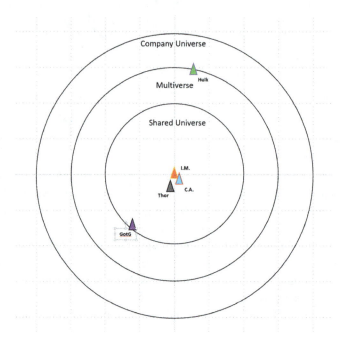

With merely one interrelation, this *Narrative Entity* can only have a distant relationship with other *Narrative Entities* within the network. While the explicit use of the same *Index Manifestation* rules out a Company Universe relation, the Guardians of the Galaxy Narrative barely breaches into a Shared Universe relationship as, at this point, it only shows a direct relation to the Thor Narrative.

3.1.1.2.6   Avengers: Age of Ultron (2015)

As a team narrative, *Avengers: Age of Ultron*, like *The Avengers*, represents a *Manifestation* without its own *Narrative Entity* but is constructed from the *Index Manifestations* of established *Narrative Entities*. As such, it similarly functions as a connective node within the overall network. In contrast to the first MCU's team narrative, *Avengers: Age of Ultron* also

---

67   *Thor: The Dark World*. Directed by Alan Taylor. Performances by Chris Hemsworth, Tom Hiddleston, Natalie Portman, and Christopher Eccleston. Marvel Studios, 2013. 01:45:32

takes on an aspect of renegotiation, as it deals with a greater number of potential *Trigger Waves* from previously released *Manifestations*.

The function of interrelating the involved *Narrative Entities* operates on a similar level as in the previous team narrative. *Avengers: Age of Ultron* relates the three *Narrative Entities* of Thor, Iron Man, and Captain America to one another by having the main characters portrayed by the same actors, bearing the same *semiotic cues*, interact with one another. The second team narrative expands on this interaction by including other *Index Manifestations* from each *Narrative Entity*. Don Cheadle's James "Rhodey" Rhodes appears during an Avenger's party, in the final conflict as his alter ego War Machine, and as a member of the new Avengers at the end of the movie. Specifically in the latter two instances, the character's representation matches the one established in *Iron Man 2*. Stellan Skarsgard reprised his role as Dr. Erik Selvig, helping Thor to ascertain the future. The halls of Asgard and Idris Elba's Heimdall appear in the vision Elizabeth Olsen's Wanda Maximoff induces in Thor. Anthony Mackie's Sam Wilson, who was introduced in *Captain America: The Winter Soldier*, also appears at the Avengers party, in the film's final battle, and as a member of the new Avengers team. As with the character War Machine, Sam Wilson/The Falcon retains his representation from his previous appearance. Additionally, Hayley Atwell's Peggy Carter appears in Steve Roger's vision induced by Wanda Maximoff[68].

Avengers: Age of Ultron's aspect of renegotiation arises mostly through connection via *Trigger Waves*. Hereby, the renegotiation of *Index Manifestations* is not with an altered state of the world as in the first three films of Phase 2 but takes place between *Index Manifestations* of different *Narrative Entities* and, thereby, renegotiates or reiterates the relationships between the network's *Narrative Entities*. Tony Stark's entire motivation and actions in the first half of *Avengers: Age of Ultron* relate to *The Avengers* and *Iron Man 3*. When Elizabeth Olson's Wanda Maximoff induces a hallucination of his greatest fear, he sees the aliens he encountered in *The Avengers* floating above his dead teammates. This vision reiterates the fear of loss and helplessness created in *The Avengers* and constantly referenced in *Iron Man 3*. His Iron Legion, a collection of Iron Man-esque robots, is an extension of his need to tinker and build something to protect everything he holds dear. The same motivation carried over from *Iron Man 3* leads him to create the film's antagonist, Ultron[69]. This need to create technology for universal protection and control directly contradicts Steve Rogers's experience of government overreach and reliance on automated technology in *Captain America: The Winter Soldier*. Rogers and Stark are placed in a specific relationship with one another when Steve Rogers questions the Avengers' morals by comparing them to S.H.I.E.L.D., and Tony Stark reminds the team of the out-worldly dangers they might face[70]. This disagreement rises to a physical conflict when Tony Stark tries to complete Ultron's experiment to the Avengers' benefit[71]. This specific renegotiation of *Index Manifestations* relates the two *Narrative Entities* (Captain America & Iron Man) involved even more closely to one another by the changes made to their *Index Manifestations*

---

68 For screenshots of all these *Index Manifestations* within the film consult https://marvelcinematicuniverse.fandom.com/wiki/Avengers:_Age_of_Ultron/Gallery
69 *Avengers: Age of Ultron*. Directed by Joss Whedon. Marvel Studios, 2015. 00:18:41
70 *Avengers: Age of Ultron*. Directed by Joss Whedon. Marvel Studios, 2015. 00:34:48
71 *Avengers: Age of Ultron*. Directed by Joss Whedon. Marvel Studios, 2015. 01:31:05

in the course of their own films, effectively drawing a line across *index* transformations through a course of *Trigger Waves*. In other words, such an occurrence organizes, potentially forces, a series of smaller transformations into a linear order, which later could form a *Shared Narrative*, which would interrelate the involved *Narrative Entities* even more.

While not as prominent, *Avengers: Age of Ultron* also renegotiates the relationship between other Index Manifestations. Chiefly, the character Thor (and, with him, his *Narrative Entity*) is drawn away from the MCU's Iron Man and Captain America Narrative and somewhat related to *Index Manifestations* with a decisively cosmic overtone. In contrast to the former example, Thor does not carry an altered view of the intradiegetic world into the team narrative because the renegotiation of *Index Manifestations* in *Thor: The Dark World* focused on mitigating the number of changes due to *The Avengers*. As the MCU network is constructed chiefly around three basic *Narrative Entities* – the MCU's Captain America, Iron Man, and Thor Narrative – at this point, it also cannot offer any *Index Manifestation* with the same potential impact (meaning with a *Narrative Entity* of its own) to counter Thor's (potential) position and create a similar conflict as in the case of Iron Man and Captain America. As such, *Avengers: Age of Ultron* operates as a layover for the MCU Thor Narrative. This increased distance to the other two *Narrative Entities* and the focus on a future MCU Thor *Manifestation* are prominent in the different fear visions each hero receives. While Steve Rogers and Tony Stark have visions fueled by events of their respective past, Thor receives a vision of the future unattached to any *Transformation Trigger* or currently active *Trigger Wave*. Additionally, he retreats from the team for a significant part of the film's second act (1:02:10–1:32:18) to investigate his premonition, lessening his interaction with the *Index Manifestations* of other *Narrative Entities*. During his absence, Thor discovers the danger of the Infinity Stones, which specifically tie back to *Thor: The Dark World*, in which one of them plays a prominent role. As a neutral character in the previously mentioned conflict, Thor's return to the team postpones the conflict between Steve Rogers and Tony Stark. Finally, he leaves Earth to find out who has been revealing/pursuing the Infinity Stones. Leaving Earth creates an imagined distance between the MCU Thor Narratives and the other Narrative Entities and moves him closer to *Index Manifestations* associated with a cosmic aspect like the Infinity Stones, namely the Guardians of the Galaxy Narrative. As such, Thor ends up in an unaware or uninterested position concerning the brewing conflict between the MCU's Iron Man and Captain America Narrative. Instead, the MCU's Thor Narrative begins an association with the MCU network's cosmic-oriented elements.

In contrast to *The Avengers*, *Avengers: Age of Ultron* sets up a new *Narrative Entity*. The film alludes to the Black Panther Narrative by mentioning the fictitious African nation Wakanda and by including Andy Serkis's Ulysses Klaue. Either *index* is directly related to that *Narrative Entity* (Black Panther) and later appears in the *Manifestation Black Panther*. Ulysses Klaue retains the same design except for a new artificial hand, an alteration due to a *Transformation Trigger* in *Avengers: Age of Ultron*[72]. However, while these connections exist, they only place the Black Panther Narrative in a Company Universe relationship

---

72 For screenshots of this character in either film consult https://marvelcinematicuniverse.fandom.com/wiki/Ulysses_Klaue/Gallery

with the rest of the network, as the *indices* used do not necessitate future incorporation of the entire *Narrative Entity* at this point.

All the intricate connections mentioned earlier make this team narrative even more reliant on previous *Manifestations* than *The Avengers*. *Avengers: Age of Ultron* reiterates the relationship between the MCU's first three Narrative Entities (Captain America, Iron Man, and Thor) by relying heavily on information from their *Manifestations*. Thor, Steve Rogers, and Tony Stark's vision under the influence of Wanda Maximoff/Scarlet Witch leans on knowledge of their respective films. This reliance contrasts with Natasha Romanoff/Black Widow's vision, in which the character relives her oppressive training as a child, containing references to her initiation ceremony. Due to this vision's 'unattached' nature, it requires a direct explanation within the film[73]. The non-existence of S.H.I.E.L.D. requires knowledge from *Captain America: Winter Soldier*. Thor's presence on Earth is only explained in *Thor: The Dark World*. Entire motivations and snippets of dialogue throughout *Avengers: Age of Ultron* hinge on *Transformation Triggers* from other *Manifestations*. For example, the initial hunt for Hydra and a conversation between Steve Rogers and Sam Wilson relate to *Transformation Triggers* created at the end of *Captain America: Winter Soldier*. To comprehend all of the character's actions and behavior as well as specific relationships, a film, traditionally, would have to include exposition. However, with the multitude of complex *Index Manifestations*, this would severely expand the movie's length. As such, this team narrative relies heavily on an audience with knowledge of the singular *Narrative Entities' Manifestations*.

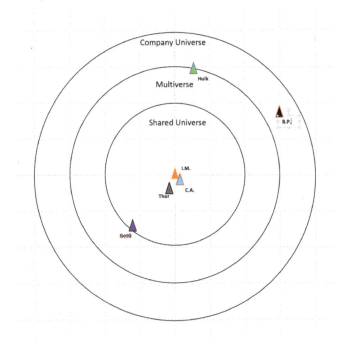

---

73   *Avengers: Age of Ultron*. Directed by Joss Whedon. Marvel Studios, 2015. 01:07:42

The combination of interacting *Index Manifestations*, *Trigger Wave* effects, and *Narrative Reliance* changes the overall relationship in the network only slightly but significantly. All *Narrative Entities* are drawn closer together due to the film's reliance on each of their *Manifestations*. This close relationship is reiterated through the interaction of diverse *Index Manifestations* from each *Narrative Entity*. However, the altered interaction due to different *Trigger Waves* significantly draws the Captain America Narrative and the Iron Man Narrative towards one another. At the same time, the Thor Narrative is slightly pulled away. This slight shift in relation is significant because it implies which *Narrative Entities* potentially may form a *Shared Narrative* and what form these might take.

3.1.1.2.7 Ant-Man (2015)

The final film of Phase 2, *Ant-Man*, is the second new *Narrative Entity* introduced to the network. In contrast to *Guardians of the Galaxy*, which enters the network with relative autonomy, *Ant-Man* firmly relates to established *Narrative Entities* within the MCU, chiefly the Captain America and the Iron Man Narrative. These relationships are established through the mention or appearance of *Index Manifestations* related to these two *Narrative Entities*. Michael Douglas's Hank Pym appears in a discussion with Hayley Atwell's Peggy Carter (from the Captain America Narrative)[74] and John Slattery's Howard Stark (from the Iron Man Narrative)[75] at the film's beginning. In the case of the latter, it is notable that the *Manifestation* uses the actor who played Howard Stark in *Iron Man 2* instead of using an aged version of Dominic Cooper, who played the character in *Captain America: The First Avenger*. Using Dominic Cooper would not have changed the plot but would have altered the MCU Ant-Man Narrative's relationship within the network, as that manifestation of this particular *index* would also relate more to the MCU's Captain America Narrative. The film further relates to *Captain America: The Winter Soldier*, when a still-under-construction version of the Triskelion is shown in the same scene. Additionally, Anthony Mackie's Sam Wilson/The Falcon appears in the film's post-credit scene and guards Avengers' Headquarters. Hank Pym also compares the Ant-Man suit to the Iron Man armor in dialogue[76].

Ant-Man also places its *Narrative Entity* firmly into the network by referring to the Avengers and reacting to *Transformation Triggers* from *Avengers: Age of Ultron*. Presented with the chief conflict of *Ant-Man*, Paul Rudd's Scott Lang mentions that their "first move should be calling the Avengers". Later in the film, he attempts to break into a Stark warehouse, only to discover that it is the new Avengers' headquarters. The status of the warehouse as the new Avengers HQ directly relates to the destruction of Avengers' Tower in *Avengers: Age of Ultron* and the establishment of a new base at the end of the same film. The appearance and description of Sam Wilson as an Avenger equally goes back to changes established in *Avengers: Age of Ultron*, in which he is shown as a member of the new team.

---

[74] For screenshots of all Peggy Carter's appearances in the MCU consult https://marvelcinematicuniverse.fandom.com/wiki/Peggy_Carter/Gallery

[75] For screenshots of Howard Stark's appearances (Slattery and Cooper) in the MCU consult https://marvelcinematicuniverse.fandom.com/wiki/Howard_Stark/Gallery

[76] *Ant-Man*. Directed by Peyton Reed. Performances by Paul Rudd, Michael Douglas, and Evangeline Lilly. Marvel Studios, 2015. 00:45:42

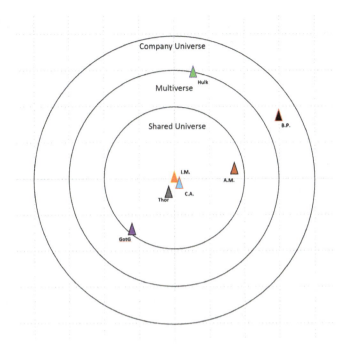

As such, the Ant-Man Narrative, in contrast to *Guardians of the Galaxy*, appears firmly embedded into the network, as it holds ties to the MCU's Captain America and Iron Man Narrative as well as acknowledges the team narrative. Interestingly, this only creates a low level of *Narrative Reliance*: *Ant-Man* does not continue or hinge on any *Trigger Wave*. While the appearance of transposed *Index Manifestations* builds a relationship, the film itself does not rely on information from another *Manifestation*. The respective scenes in which transposed *Index Manifestations* appear only convey aspects directly related to *Ant-Man*'s plot. Recognizing the *Index Manifestation* only increases the enjoyment of an informed audience but does not derail a casual one. Peggy Carter and Howard Stark could have been replaced with any representation of a S.H.I.E.L.D. executive when Hank Pym quits the organization, accusing them of stealing his work. Scott Lang could have fought any Avenger when breaking into their headquarters, including the non- or less-attached ones like Scarlet Witch or The Vision. The *Manifestation* does not rely on previous knowledge for the comprehension of its overall plot.

Overall, the Ant-Man Narrative directly appears in a distant Shared Universe relationship with the network's central *Narrative Entities*. A connection to the MCU's Captain America and Iron Man Narrative chiefly defines this relationship.

3.1.1.3 Phase 3

In contrast to the previous two phases, each comprising six films, the third phase contains eleven movies. Excluding *Captain America: Civil War*, two of the eleven are team narratives in the form of *Avengers: Infinity War* and *Avengers: Endgame*. Four of the remaining nine films introduce new *Narrative Entities*, while another four continue *Narrative Entities* established in previous phases. The remaining *Manifestation* is *Spider-Man: Far From Home*, the second *Manifestation* of the MCU's Spider-Man Narrative, which is the only *Narrative Entity* with two films in this phase.

3.1.1.3.1 Set up

Dually escalating the expansion of the MCU network, the third phase has to manage the introduction of new material and the continued development of existing *Narrative Entities*. Concerning the latter, continuing *Narrative Entities* cannot entirely ignore or remove themselves from the collection of *Trigger Waves* started in the previous phases. As such, they have to react to the increasing state of interrelation and, more so, continually renegotiate the position of their *indices* within the larger network. In the case of *Narrative Entities* introduced in the second phase, the renegotiation efforts are comparable to those seen in the first three Phase 2 *Manifestations* – *Iron Man 3*, *Thor: The Dark World*, and *Captain America: The Winter Soldier*. Each reacts to the changes affecting them, repositioning their *Index Manifestations* within the larger network. *Narrative Entities* with a notable presence within the network (due to either a high number of *Manifestations* or frequent use of its *Index Manifestations* within the overall network) have to incorporate aspects of previous renegotiations or eventually end their potential to influence change on the network. The MCU solves the latter by completing the 'overarching plot' of a *Narrative Entity* and removing a more significant part or all of its *Index Manifestations*. Similar to the introduction of the MCU's Ant-Man Narrative and Guardians of the Galaxy Narrative in Phase 2, new *Narrative Entities* have two means to enter the network in Phase 3. They can either appear greatly removed from other *Narrative Entities* in the network or acknowledge existing *Index Manifestations* and *Transformation Triggers*.

3.1.1.3.2 Captain America: Civil War (2016)

Revolving around a conflict between different hero characters, *Captain America: Civil War* – despite its designation as a *Manifestation* of a specific *Narrative Entity* – involves many transposed *Index Manifestations*. As such, it interconnects several *Narrative Entities* directly. The titular heroes from the MCU's Iron Man, Black Panther, Spider-Man, and Ant-Man Narratives appear, played by the same actors and using the same designs for their costumes and props as in their respective films. Notably, if we refer to the publication order, two of these characters connect to established *Narrative Entities* (Iron Man, Ant-Man), while the other two connect to *Narrative Entities* with upcoming *Manifestations* (Black Panther, Spider-Man). *Captain America: Civil War* also includes several *Index Manifestations* associated with multiple *Narrative Entities* which are not the namesake hero. The MCU's Iron Man Narrative is further intertwined via the use of Don Cheadle's James "Rhodey" Rhodes. Despite never appearing in the same clothing as in previous films, he is also active as War Machine, whose representation has remained consistent since its first appearance in *Iron Man 2*. John Slattery reprises his role as Howard Stark, which marks Slattery's first appearance as the character in a *Manifestation* of the MCU's Captain America Narrative[77]. Other *Index Manifestations* of the Black Panther Narrative

---

77   For screenshots of the mentioned *Index Manifestations* consult https://marvelcinematicuniverse.fandom.com/wiki/Captain_America:_Civil_War/Gallery

are introduced via Martin Freeman's Everett K. Ross[78], John Kani's T'Chaka[79], and Florence Kasumba's Ayo[80], who later reappear in *Black Panther*. As *Black Panther* expands on the secretive fictional culture of Wakanda, the latter two reappear with slightly different designs but retain their respective *semiotic cues*. In contrast to the MCU's Iron Man and Black Panther Narrative, the Spider-Man Narrative offers only one additional *Index Manifestation* outside its titular hero in the form of Marisa Tomei's May Parker[81]. *Captain America: Civil War* also uses William Hurt's Thaddeus "Thunderbolt" Ross, who last appeared in *The Incredible Hulk*. Additionally, the third *Manifestation* of the MCU's Captain America Narrative makes use of unaffiliated (or primarily Avengers-affiliated) *Index Manifestations*: Elisabeth Olsen's Wanda Maximoff/Scarlet Witch, Paul Bettany's The Vision, and Brett Renner's Clint Barton/Hawkeye, who all mostly appeared within the team *Manifestations*. Here, equally played by the same actors and actress, displaying the same *semiotic cues*. This abundance of *Index Manifestations* from different *Narrative Entities* makes *Captain America: Civil War* a connective node similar to a team narrative.

However, while *Captain America: Civil War* might connect *Narrative Entities* in the same manner a team narrative does, the reason the MCU's Captain America Narrative could adopt an *index* network of transposed *Index Manifestations* seems more critical regarding the management of such a network as the MCU. A combination of *Trigger Waves* led to the collection of *Index Manifestations* in *Captain America: Civil War*. As with *Captain America: The First Avenger*, the end of *Captain America: The Winter Soldier* employs a *Transformation Trigger*, which removes most of the film's *indices* from its *index* network. The fall of the fictional organization S.H.I.E.L.D. naturally alters the status of each *Index Manifestation* associated with it. As shown in the analysis of *Captain America: The Winter Soldier*, nearly every new *index* associated with the MCU's Captain America Narrative was related to S.H.I.E.L.D. in some form. While removing an organization is not as harsh as relocating the hero to an entirely new setting, either change favors the retention of *Index Manifestations* that share some additional meaningful relationship with the hero character. In the case of *Captain America: The Winter Soldier*, the two retained characters have additional connections other than the era and the war. Peggy Carter is presented as a founder of S.H.I.E.L.D.; Buchanan 'Bucky' Barnes was put through an alternate super soldier program and spent time in cryo-stasis like Steve Rogers. Additionally, he also was the hero character's childhood friend. In other words, the fall of S.H.I.E.L.D. makes it unlikely for *Index Manifestations* to reappear in the MCU's Captain America Narrative if they do not include another aspect connecting them to the overall *Narrative Entity*. This assertion bears out in *Captain America: Civil War*, as the only recurring *Index Manifestations* attached to *Captain America: The Winter Soldier* are Anthony Mackie's Sam Wilson/The Falcon, Scarlett Johansson's Natasha Romanoff/Black Widow, and Frank Grillo's Brock Rumlow/

---

78 For screenshots of this character's appearances within the MCU consult https://marvelcinematicuniverse.fandom.com/wiki/Everett_Ross/Gallery
79 For screenshots of this character's appearances within the MCU consult https://marvelcinematicuniverse.fandom.com/wiki/T'Chaka/Gallery
80 For screenshots of this character's appearances within the MCU consult https://marvelcinematicuniverse.fandom.com/wiki/Ayo/Gallery
81 For screenshots of this character's appearances within the MCU consult https://marvelcinematicuniverse.fandom.com/wiki/May_Parker/Gallery

Crossbones. Of these three, only the last was solely connected to the overall narrative via an association with S.H.I.E.L.D. Brock Rumlow is gravely wounded and disfigured at the end of *Captain America: The Winter Soldier* and vows revenge against Steve Rogers. While Crossbones appears in the third Captain America Manifestation, he kills himself in an attempt to harm Captain America roughly 14 minutes into the movie, removing this *Index Manifestation* from the narrative belatedly. In contrast, Sam Wilson/The Falcon was also introduced in *Captain America: The Winter Soldier*, but not via S.H.I.E.L.D. Instead, he appears as a fellow veteran with similar morals and viewpoints to Steve Rogers, who could help take down S.H.I.E.L.D. from the outside. As such, the *Transformation Trigger* of the second Captain America *Manifestation* did not affect the character in the same manner as those associated with the organization, allowing Sam Wilson to return unencumbered. Additionally, the character became part of the new Avengers team in *Avengers: Age of Ultron*, giving him an additional connection to the MCU's Captain America Narrative. Natasha Romanoff/Black Widow similarly holds the latter advantage. As she appears in *The Avengers* and *Avengers: Age of Ultron*, she also holds an additional connection to the Captain America Narrative. Due to providing a venue for relationships between characters, *Avengers: Age of Ultron* is of similar importance to *Captain America: Civil War* as *The Avengers* was to *Captain America: The Winter Soldier*: Either team narrative brought the 'index-starved' hero (and therefore the MCU's version of the *Narrative Entity*) in contact with a potential source of *indices*. While *The Avengers* provided an organization for Steve Rogers to join, *Avengers: Age of Ultron* offers a set of otherwise unattached *Index Manifestations* in the form of Elizabeth Olsen's Wanda Maximoff/Scarlet Witch, Paul Bettany's The Vision, and Jeremy Renner's Clint Barton/Hawkeye. Additionally, it provides a venue for the MCU's Captain America Narrative to adapt *Index Manifestations* from other *Narrative Entities* into a prominent position within its temporary *index* network. The most prominent example is the use of Tony Stark/Iron Man as the film's antagonist. Despite the film's superficial appearance as a team narrative, due to the application of several transposed *Index Manifestations*, *Captain America: Civil War* primarily remains a *Manifestation* of the MCU's Captain America Narrative. Its node-like position within the MCU network does not arise from an attempt to engage multiple *Narrative Entities* but from the *Narrative Entity's* pattern of removing its *index* network at the end of each film and replacing it by passing through a team *Manifestation*.

Recreating an *index* network by adapting transposed *Index Manifestations* forces the MCU's Captain America Narrative to engage with *Trigger Waves* from *Manifestations* of other *Narrative Entities* because the different *Index Manifestations* carry changes from other *Manifestations* into the new *index* network. Aside from relating to a *Trigger Wave* from *Captain America: The Winter Soldier*, *Captain America: Civil War* prominently picks up *Trigger Waves* from *Iron Man 3*, *Avengers: Age of Ultron*, and *Ant-Man*. Additionally, it starts a *Trigger Wave* for *Spider-Man: Homecoming* and *Black Panther* (both discussed in their respective chapters). Concerning the MCU's Iron Man narrative, *Captain America: Civil War* directly continues Tony Stark's fear of uncontrolled super-powered threats established in *Iron Man 3* and *The Avengers*. This fear re-emerges as the fear of a super-powered alien threat in *Avengers: Age of Ultron*, where Tony Stark gives the eventuality of an alien attack as the reason for his (accidental) creation of Ultron. His support for regulating super-powered individuals is a continuation of the *Trigger Wave* passing through either of the previous films. This purposely sets the character at odds with Captain America, who, during *Captain America: The Winter Soldier*, learned to distrust governmental oversight, as the film's plot revolves around a potential danger of governmental surveillance and overreach. Another smaller *Trigger Wave* continued from *Avengers: Age of Ultron* is the absence of Thor and Bruce Banner. Both disappeared at the end of *Avengers: Age of Ultron*, and their unknown whereabouts, in combination with their perceived power, become a point of discussion and contention within *Captain America: Civil War*[82]. The appearance of Paul Rudd's Scott Lang directly relates to the presence of Anthony Mackie's Sam Wilson/The Falcon in *Ant-Man*. As such, the third *Manifestation* of the MCU's Captain America Narrative strengthens the relationship with several *Narrative Entities* by acknowledging the changes within their *Narrative Entity*-specific *Manifestations*.

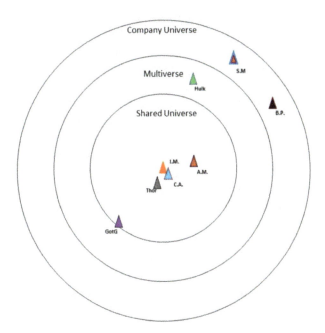

Using many *Index Manifestations* from across the MCU network, *Captain America: Civil War* relies to a greater degree on knowledge from other *Manifestations*. As such, the film relies on an informed audience, which has followed the MCU films. However, with the introduction of two *Narrative Entities* before the release of their respective *Manifestations*, the film also targets a lower tier of skilled audience, which either has or can ascertain information for future *Manifestations*. While an informed audience combined with the presence of various *Index Manifestations* and acknowledgment of different *Trigger Waves* firmly draws the MCU's Ant-Man Narrative and the MCU's Iron Man Narrative closer to the

---

82 *Captain America: Civil War*. Directed by Anthony Russo and Joe Russo. Performances by Chris Evans and Robert Downey Jr. Marvel Studios, 2016. 00:23:45

MCU's Captain America Narrative, the reliance on a lower-tier skilled audience indicates a more nuanced relationship between the MCU's Spider-Man Narrative, Black Panther Narrative, and Captain America Narrative. The presence of several *Index Manifestations* from the Spider-Man Narrative and Black Panther Narrative, as well as their direct interaction with the network of *indices* presented in *Captain America: Civil War*, would firmly move either *Narrative Entity* into a Shared Universe relationship with the MCU's Iron Man and Captain America Narrative. However, as the appearance of Spider-Man- and Black Panther-related *Index Manifestations* precedes the publication of *Narrative Entity*-specific *Manifestations*, neither has established a stable *Narrative Entity* within the MCU network. While the presence of these *Index Manifestations* implies the inclusion of material that will establish an entire network of *Index Manifestations*, which in turn will form a *Manifestation* that creates a presence within the MCU network, at this point, that has yet to happen. In other words, everything related to Spider-Man and Black Panther within *Captain America: Civil War* creates a connection to potentially emerging *Narrative Entities*, but as these have not yet emerged, because their films are still upcoming, they appear (or remain) in a Company Universe relationship within the visual representation of the MCU network at this point. Similarly, *Captain America: Civil War* alters the overall relationship of the network to the MCU's Hulk Narrative. The shift of *rendition cues* between Edward Norton's version and Mark Ruffalo's version of the character, as well as the absence of other *Index Manifestations* from *The Incredible Hulk* in either team *Manifestation*, firmly solidified the Hulk Narrative presented in *The Incredible Hulk* between a Multiverse and a Company Universe relationship. At the same time, the MCU network operates with an unrelated *Index Manifestation* of the character Hulk in the team narrative. With the reappearance of William Hurt's Thaddeus "Thunderbolt" Ross, the MCU network marks a relation to its previous Hulk narrative. This *Index Manifestation* provides an interesting outlier because it is the only *Index Manifestation* from a *Narrative Entity* whose main character (either version) is not part of *Captain America: Civil War*. Hurt played the same character in *The Incredible Hulk*. However, while the character was presented as a U.S. Army General in its first representation within the MCU, this version appears as the United States' Secretary of State. The alteration in position coincides with changes to other *semiotic cues*. In *The Incredible Hulk*, the character appears exclusively in military fatigues or a military dress uniform. In *Captain America: Civil War*, he exclusively wears a suit[83]. While a continuation of Ross's career logically would explain the changes, and a mention of his military service[84] and his receiving the Congressional Medal of Honor[85] relate to the previous iteration, the *Manifestation* presents us with no direct or indirect *Transformation Triggers* showing these changes. Additionally, Thaddeus Ross does not remark on his previous relation to the Hulk Narrative. The inclusion of this *Index Manifestation* draws the MCU's Hulk Narrative over the border into a clear Multiverse relationship, as the strong semiotic nature

---

83   For screenshots of this character's appearances within the MCU consult https://marvelcinematicuniverse.fandom.com/wiki/Thaddeus_Ross/Gallery
84   *Captain America: Civil War*. Directed by Anthony Russo and Joe Russo. Performances by Chris Evans and Robert Downey Jr. Marvel Studios, 2016. 00:20:59
85   *Captain America: Civil War*. Directed by Anthony Russo and Joe Russo. Performances by Chris Evans and Robert Downey Jr. Marvel Studios, 2016. 00:27:52

of using the same actor in such a context at least implies that this version of Senator Ross has some direct relation to the General Ross seen in *The Incredible Hulk*. However, as the appearance of Senator Ross avoids the usage of any other *semiotic cue* related to General Ross in either representation or dialogue, the MCU's Hulk Narrative does not close into the network any further.

Aside from the adjustments of the *Narrative Entities* within the MCU network, it is necessary to acknowledge that *Captain America: Civil War* serves a pivotal role in the formation of the upcoming Phase 3 *Manifestations*. The film effectively creates a new status quo, similar to the end of *The Avengers*. Ending with half of the established heroes in hiding and the other half bound by new laws and regulations, the film effectively provides an explanation for the public absence of different heroes in upcoming *Manifestations*. This public absence not only frees Phase 3 Manifestations (to a degree) from needing to employ any of these *Index Manifestations* but also determines the type of upcoming publication. With the exception of the two Spider-Man films, the second Ant-Man film, and the team narratives, all *Manifestations* after *Captain America: Civil War* operate with a set of unique *Index Manifestations*, which are removed from the imitation of a human (or US) society built in the course of Phase 1 and 2. *Thor: Ragnarok* takes mostly place in outer space. *Guardians of the Galaxy Vol.2*[86] maintains its own space opera *index* network. *Doctor Strange* and *Captain Marvel* play on Earth but are removed from the established world, with *Doctor Strange* taking place in hidden dimensions created by a society of sorcerers and *Captain Marvel* playing in the 90s. The events of *Black Panther* formally also occur on Earth but are generally focused on establishing the fictional nation of Wakanda. In other words, while the third Captain America Narrative did not remove a more significant part of its *index* network in the same fashion its predecessors had, it still provided a *Transformation Trigger*, which created room for the introduction of new and the expansion of less established *Narrative Entities* within the network.

3.1.1.3.3 Doctor Strange (2016)

The second film of the third phase, *Doctor Strange*, establishes a new *index* network over creating an interrelation with other *Narrative Entities*. To that end, the *Manifestation* employs a similar strategy to *Guardians of the Galaxy Vol.1* and in contrast to the approach of *Ant-Man*. In other words, on a spectrum of introducing a new *Narrative Entity* with little connection and a clear relation to the overall network, *Doctor Strange* merely includes singular token elements, which imply a relationship. Aside from a post-credit scene connecting *Doctor Strange* to *Thor: Ragnarok*, the film refers allusively to *Captain America: Civil War*. The latter allusion arises from a snippet of dialogue within the film, in which Stephen Strange is offered a medical case involving "[...] a 35-year-old Airforce Colonel [who] crushed his lower spine in some kind of experimental armor [...]"[87]. This small line of dialogue most likely relates to the injuries Don Cheadle's James "Rhodey" Rhodes/War Machine suffered during *Captain America: Civil War*. The interaction between Benedict

---

86 *Guardians of the Galaxy Vol.2*. Directed by James Gunn. Performances by Chris Pratt and Zoe Saldana. Marvel Studios, 2017.

87 *Doctor Strange*. Directed by Scott Derrickson. Performances by Benedict Cumberbatch, Chiwetel Ejiofor, Mads Mikkelsen, Tilda Swinton and Rachel McAdams. Marvel Studios, 2016. 00:11:03

Cumberbatch's Dr. Strange and Chris Hemsworth's Thor in *Doctor Strange*'s post-credit scene is more substantial. While Thor appears without a greater part of his *semiotic cues* (he lacks his hammer and wears 'civilian' clothes), the sequence connects strongly to *Thor: Ragnarok*. In this case, *Doctor Strange*'s post-credit scene was lifted directly from the latter film[88]. As the appearance of Thor has no bearing on the changes occurring in *Doctor Strange*, this sequence rather indicates the importance of *Index Manifestations* from the MCU's Dr. Strange Narrative for *Thor: Ragnarok* than any bearing the MCU's Thor Narrative has on *Doctor Strange*. Independent from the direct relation, the appearance of Chris Hemsworth's Thor connects the two *Narrative Entities*. The connection, however, remains distant as this representation of Thor lacks a greater part of its usual *semiotic cues*, leaving Dr. Strange in a distant Shared Universe relationship with the more tight-knit section of the network on the side of the Thor Narrative.

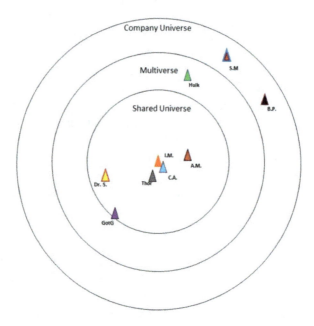

---

[88] For screenshots of Thor's appearances in the MCU including two scenes mentioned consult https://marvelcinematicuniverse.fandom.com/wiki/Thor/Gallery

3.1.1.3.4 Guardians of the Galaxy Vol.2 (2017)

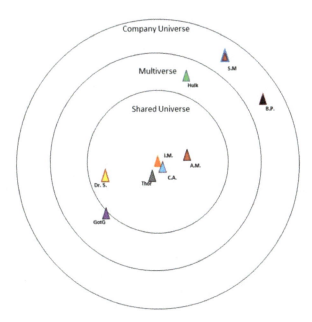

Interestingly, *Guardians of the Galaxy Vol.2* does not relate directly to any other *Narrative Entity* within the MCU network. Instead, the film operates mainly as a direct sequel to *Guardians of the Galaxy Vol. 1*, taking no cues or aspects from other *Manifestations* the network released between the two films. One potential exception is the appearance of an *Index Manifestation* from *Thor: Ragnarok*. Jeff Goldblum's The Grandmaster appears as a dancing emoji in the film's end credits. However, as this appearance is neither part of the *Manifestation*'s plot nor appears in any interaction with other *Index Manifestations*, it principally serves as a homage and does not rise to a connection.

The lack of further interrelation paired with the little interrelation of this *Narrative Entity*'s previous *Manifestation* raises an interesting question: Does the lack of a maintained relationship erode the interrelation with the rest of the network? Considering the aspect of *Narrative Reliance*, it becomes clear that the MCU's Guardian of the Galaxy Narrative is generally geared towards a casual audience up to its second *Manifestation*. Even the connection via Benicio del Toro's Taneleer Tivan/The Collector in the first *Manifestation* does not require previous knowledge. However, focusing on a casual audience entails a weaker connection, as there is no reliance on any other part of the network. As such, the Guardians of the Galaxy Narrative may slip further away from the rest of the network. The more important realization is that this may be the potential effect of avoiding any means of connection, namely the slow regression of a *Narrative Entity* from the network.

3.1.1.3.5 Spider-Man: Homecoming (2017)

While usually separate *Narrative Entities*, the Iron Man Narrative and the Spider-Man Narrative are directly intertwined in the MCU network. In *Spider-Man: Homecoming*, Robert Downey Jr.'s version of Tony Stark takes on the mantle of mentor to Tom Holland's Peter Parker. That these two characters operate in such a relationship is exemplified when Tony Stark lectures Peter Parker on his recklessness[89] and advises some more mentoring at the film's end[90]. This specific relationship continues their interaction in *Captain America: Civil War*, in which Tony Stark recruits Peter Parker in the conflict with Steve Rogers. Including the *Index Manifestation* of Tony Stark in such a manner within the *index* network of the MCU's Spider-Man Narrative transplants several *Index Manifestations* from the MCU's Iron Man Narrative to the first MCU's Spider-Man *Manifestation*[91]. Aside from Robert Downey Jr.'s Tony Stark, Harold "Happy" Hogan and Pepper Potts appear in *Spider-Man: Homecoming*. Jon Favreau plays Harold Hogan in each of the three MCU's Iron Man *Manifestations* and in *Spider-Man: Homecoming*. Equally, he appears in the classic black suit of a bodyguard and works in a security and organizational capacity for Tony Stark throughout all four movies[92]. Gwyneth Paltrow's Pepper Potts makes a cameo at the end of *Spider-Man: Homecoming*[93]. Her appearance continues a series of *Transformation Trigger*s, which started in *Iron Man* and concerns her romantic relationship with Tony Stark. They repurpose a press meeting meant to introduce Spider-Man as a new member of the Avengers to announce their engagement. The inclusion of the MCU Iron Man Narrative's *Index Manifestation* in *Spider-Man: Homecoming* also continues a *Transformation Trigger* from *Captain America: Civil War*, in which Tony Stark enlists Peter Parker's help in his conflict with Steve Rogers, providing his signature Spider-Man suit and bonding with him over a sense of responsibility. Aside from the MCU's Iron Man Narrative, *Spider-Man: Homecoming* indirectly relates to the MCU's Captain America Narrative. Chris Evan's Steve Rogers appears in public service announcements played at Peter Parker's school. In these announcements, he wears his costume from *The Avengers*. Specifically, one of the three announcements ties back to *Transformation Triggers* from *Captain America: Civil War*, when a gym teacher wonders if Captain America is considered a war criminal[94]. The connections with the MCU's Captain America Narrative are lighter than those to the MCU's Iron Man Narrative and serve mostly as a reminder of the connections created through Peter Parker's appearance in *Captain America: Civil War*.

---

89   *Spider-Man: Homecoming*. Directed by Jon Watts. Performances by Tom Holland, Michael Keaton, Zendaya, and Robert Downey Jr. Marvel Studios, 2017. 01:21:10

90   *Spider-Man: Homecoming*. Directed by Jon Watts. Performances by Tom Holland, Michael Keaton, Zendaya, and Robert Downey Jr. Marvel Studios, 2017. 01:59:13

91   For a collection of screenshots from the entire film depicted some of the transferred *Index Manifestations* consult https://marvelcinematicuniverse.fandom.com/wiki/Spider-Man:_Homecoming/Gallery

92   For screenshots of this character's appearances within the MCU network consult https://marvelcinematicuniverse.fandom.com/wiki/Happy_Hogan/Gallery

93   For screenshots of this character's appearances within the MCU network consult https://marvelcinematicuniverse.fandom.com/wiki/Pepper_Potts/Gallery

94   *Spider-Man: Homecoming*. Directed by Jon Watts. Performances by Tom Holland, Michael Keaton, Zendaya, and Robert Downey Jr. Marvel Studios, 2017. 00:26:45

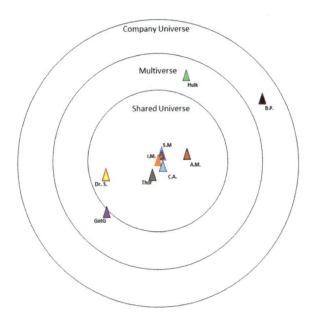

The use of transposed *Index Manifestations* and the use of *Transformation Triggers* significantly solidify the MCU Spider-Man Narrative's position within the overall MCU network. Simultaneously, the interrelation with the MCU's Iron Man Narrative goes further, as established aspects of the original (comic) Spider-Man Narrative are amended to strengthen the connection between the two *Narrative Entities*. While Peter Parker, similar to the comics, makes his own version of web-shooters and costume, Tony Stark provides his more recognizable Spider-Man outfit in the film. The costume is equally amended to contain *semiotic cues* usually associated with Iron Man's armor, particularly the inclusion of an artificial intelligence, which communicates with Peter Parker similarly to the onboard artificial intelligence of Tony Stark's armor. Aside from providing part of Spider-Man's equipment, Tony Stark is also integral to the antagonist's backstory and motivation. In contrast to the original version, Michael Keaton's Adrian Toomes is driven to his criminal enterprise because Tony Stark usurps his contract with New York City to dispose of the alien technology left behind after the 'Battle of New York'"[95] in *The Avengers*. In essence, *Spider-Man: Homecoming* provides as much a continuation of an Iron Man-related *Trigger Wave* (in a similar fashion, the character's function as an antagonist did in *Captain America: Civil War*) as it tells a story for the MCU's version of Spider-Man.

Within the visual representation of the MCU network, the combination of all these appearances creates a near overlap between the MCU's Spider-Man and Iron Man Narrative, specifically because this version of Spider-Man takes on *rendition cues* usually associated with an Iron Man Narrative. At the same time, the MCU's Spider-Man Narrative maintains a slightly greater distance from the MCU's Captain America Narrative, as the audience is merely reminded of that *Narrative Entity*'s presence in this world.

---

95 *Spider-Man: Homecoming*. Directed by Jon Watts. Performances by Tom Holland, Michael Keaton, Zendaya, and Robert Downey Jr. Marvel Studios, 2017. 00:02:30

3.1.1.3.6 Thor: Ragnarok (2017)

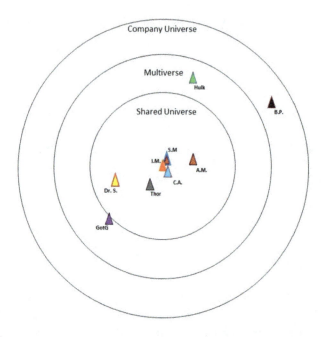

The third Thor film relates mainly to the MCU network by continuing *Trigger Waves* left off at the end of *Avengers: Age of Ultron*. Thor's reaction to the prophecy from the second team narrative leads him to search for and fight Surtur, who – according to Norse mythology and the film – is destined to destroy Asgard. The *Transformation Trigger* from *Avengers: Age of Ultron* effectively initiates the plot of *Thor: Ragnarok*. By challenging Clancy Brown's Surtur, Thor discovers that his brother Loki has usurped the throne of Asgard at the end of *Thor: The Dark World*. This relationship between the two films is even acknowledged at the beginning of *Thor: Ragnarok* when Chris Hemsworth's Thor relates his passage from the second Avengers film to his situation at the beginning of this film[96]. *Thor: Ragnarok* also picks up the thread of the Hulk's disappearance at the end of the second Avengers film. Bruce Banner's alter ego reappears as a Gladiator on an alien planet, explaining that he landed on the planet in the Quinjet he took at the end of *Avengers: Age of Ultron*.[97]

Outside of reacting to *Trigger Waves*, *Thor: Ragnarok* only relates to one other *Narrative Entity*, the MCU's Doctor Strange Narrative. In contrast to Thor's appearance in *Doctor Strange*, Benedict Cumberbatch's appearance in *Thor: Ragnarok* provides a stronger interrelation. Aside from a direct interaction between the two titular heroes, the sets, props,

---

[96] *Thor: Ragnarok*. Directed by Taika Waititi. Performances by Chris Hemsworth, Tom Hiddleston, and Cate Blanchett. Marvel Studios, 2017. 00:00:53

[97] *Thor: Ragnarok*. Directed by Taika Waititi. Performances by Chris Hemsworth, Tom Hiddleston, and Cate Blanchett. Marvel Studios, 2017. 01:04:04

and visual effects established in the MCU's Dr. Strange *Manifestation* reappear in the same form as the plot leads Thor to visit Dr. Strange's Sanctum Sanctorum[98]. As such, *Thor: Ragnarok* not only presents an abundance of *Index Manifestations* but equally uses all previously set *semiotic cues*. Additionally, the mid-credit scene from *Doctor Strange* reappears in the exact same form as the interaction between Thor and Dr. Strange, setting it into a larger context. A smaller allusion also relates *Thor: Ragnarok* to an *Index Manifestation* of *Guardians of the Galaxy Vol. 1*. Tessa Thompson's Valkyrie mentions that they would need to refuel on Xandar on their way to Asgard[99]. Xandar was the home planet of the Nova Corps and provided a stage for the final conflict of *Guardians of the Galaxy Vol.1*.

As such, the MCU's Thor and Dr. Strange Narrative move closer to one another, with the Thor narrative spinning lightly towards the Guardians of the Galaxy Narrative. However, this movement does not dislodge the *Narrative Entity* greatly from its previous relations, as *Thor: Ragnarok* focuses on an informed audience and continues *Trigger Waves* from previous MCU *Manifestations*.

3.1.1.3.7 Black Panther (2018)

Aside from a post-credit scene, in which Sebastian Stan's Bucky Barnes/The Winter Soldier recovers in Wakanda, which continues a *Trigger Wave* from *Captain America: Civil War*, *Black Panther* uses no *Index Manifestations* from other *Narrative Entities*. Instead, the film furthers the connection to *Captain America: Civil War* by elaborating on information revolving around Chadwick Boseman's Black Panther. These elaborations come partly in the form of explanations, which place the character's actions and abilities in its previous appearance in context, and partly in continuation of *Trigger Waves*. *Black Panther* revolves around T'Challa/Black Panther's ascension to the throne of Wakanda and his role as ruler of the fictional nation. As such, the plot arises as a direct continuation of his father's death in *Captain America: Civil War*. Additionally, Andy Serkis's Ulysses Klaue provides a connection to *Avengers: Age of Ultron*. Ulysses Klaue was introduced in the second Avengers film as an illegal arms dealer who sold vibranium. The character lost his left hand in the team narrative. Aside from retaining all of his previously established *semiotic cues*, the representation of the character in *Black Panther* acknowledges that *Transformation Trigger* by adding a mechanical left hand encasing a sonic weapon[100].

While *Black Panther* makes no effort to increase its entanglement with other *Narrative Entities* and slightly shifts away from the MCU's core network, as the film serves primarily a casual audience, its appearance as a *Manifestation* of the Black Panther Narrative establishes a clear Shared Universe relationship – a relationship reinforced by acknowledging the *Trigger Waves* from previous *Manifestations*.

---

98 For screenshots of this *Index Manifestation*'s appearance within this film consult https://marvelcinematicuniverse.fandom.com/wiki/Thor:_Ragnarok/Gallery

99 *Thor: Ragnarok*. Directed by Taika Waititi. Performances by Chris Hemsworth, Tom Hiddleston, and Cate Blanchett. Marvel Studios, 2017. 01:25:23

100 For screenshots of this character in either film consult https://marvelcinematicuniverse.fandom.com/wiki/Ulysses_Klaue/Gallery

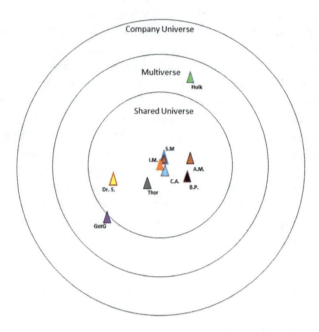

3.1.1.3.8 Avengers: Infinity War (2018)

Discussing the presence and representation of individual *Index Manifestations* from different *Narrative Entities* comprising this team narrative in the same fashion as *The Avengers* and *Avengers: Age of Ultron* would prove too extensive and would not significantly advance the purpose of this research. It is sufficient to say that as the next-to-last team narrative within the Infinity Saga, *Avengers: Infinity War* includes several *Index Manifestations*, first and foremost all hero characters of the various *Narrative Entities* from the overall MCU network. As in all previous cases, the *Index Manifestations* retain the MCU versions of their *semiotic cues*. The two exceptions in this regard are *Index Manifestations* of the MCU's Ant-Man Narrative and the MCU's Captain Marvel Narrative. *Manifestations* of either *Narrative Entity* were released between the third and fourth team narrative (*Avengers: Infinity War*, *Avengers: Endgame*), with the plot of the second Ant-Man *Manifestation* taking place during the events of *Avengers: Infinity War* and the Captain Marvel *Manifestation* introducing the Captain Marvel Narrative to the MCU network. A post-credit scene in *Avengers: Infinity War* alludes to the existence of the MCU's Captain Marvel Narrative. Based on the appearance of the different *Index Manifestations* alone, *Avengers: Infinity War* draws the *Narrative Entities* into a close-knit network[101].

However, the acknowledgment of multiple Trigger Waves from previous *Manifestations* is more significant in regard to interrelation. Aside from relying on the exposition and introduction from *Manifestations* focused on specific *Narrative Entities*, *Avengers: Infinity Wars* leans on the knowledge of certain *Transformation Triggers* from various films explaining the state and relationship of different characters. The third Avengers film mainly

---

101 For screenshots of the various involved *Index Manifestations* consult https://marvelcinematicunive rse.fandom.com/wiki/Avengers:_Infinity_War/Gallery

resolves changes made to *Index Manifestations* in *Captain America: Civil War* and *Thor: Ragnarok*. The latter sets the stage for the beginning of *Avengers: Infinity War*, as *Thor: Ragnarok* ends with Thor captaining an ark of Asgardians that survived the fall of Asgard. Thanos intercepted this ark in the post-credit scene of *Thor: Ragnarok*. Aside from explaining the circumstances of *Avengers: Infinity War*'s beginning, the third *Manifestation* of the MCU's Thor Narrative also provides all *Transformations Triggers* explaining the changes to Thor's *semiotic cues*. Of those changes, the most significant is the loss of Mjolnir – his mystical hammer – as the greater part of this character's actions within *Avengers: Infinity War* serve to create a stronger version of that lost *index* cue. The impact of *Captain America: Civil War* lies mainly in the lack of contact and interaction between *Index Manifestations* of different *Narrative Entities* and provides a *Transformation Trigger* explaining changes in the representation of some characters. Either aspect goes back to the conflict of the third MCU's Captain America *Manifestation*, which ended with the Avengers divided and all characters on Captain America's side in violation of the Sokovia Accords, which presumably at that point regulates superhero activity. The division explains their separate realization and approach to the threat Thanos poses, as the two sides hear about the threat singularly, and Tony Stark is reluctant to contact Steve Rogers[102] when he is warned about the impending attack. The violation of the accords also provides an implicit explanation for changes in different characters' representation and some characters' absence. The most notable alteration of representation comes in the form of Scarlett Johansson's Natasha Romanoff/Black Widow and Chris Evan's Steve Rogers/Captain America. Romanoff has changed her hair color, wears a more body-armor-type outfit, and now employs electric batons. Rogers still wears his uniform from *Captain America: Civil War*, but the star on his chest is barely visible, and its color has faded. Additionally, he has a beard and does not have his shield – which he left with Iron Man after their fight in *Captain America: Civil War*. As the characters went into hiding at the end of the third Captain America *Manifestation*, attempts at an altered appearance or indication of a rough life are presumable changes to their representation. The absence of Brent Renner's Clint Barton/Hawkeye and Paul Rudd's Scott Lang/Ant-Man also align with the *Transformation Trigger* of the third Captain America *Manifestation*, as it is mentioned that they struck a deal with the government to spare their families[103]. As such, *Avengers: Infinity War* does not only tie the different *Narrative Entities* closer together by relying on other *Manifestations* to explain certain characters but also by addressing the *Transformation Triggers* of two other films.

The importance of *Trigger Waves* in the third Avengers film goes even further, as they resolve or are part of *Manifestation*-spanning connections, namely the Captain America – Iron Man relationship and the whereabouts of the Infinity Stones. Either is discussed in a chapter of its own. However, the significance of either spanning series of *Transformation Triggers* further highlights the film's reliance on an informed audience. *Avengers: Infinity War* equally expects an informed audience for MCU *Manifestations* following it, as it ends with half of the universe's population dissolved. Such a far-reaching *Transformation Trigger* necessarily needs either addressing or some manner of circumvention by any *Manifestation* still operating in the MCU network.

---

102   *Avengers: Infinity War*. Directed by Anthony Russo and Joe Russo. Marvel Studios, 2018. 00:15:59
103   *Avengers: Infinity War*. Directed by Anthony Russo and Joe Russo. Marvel Studios, 2018 00:56:24

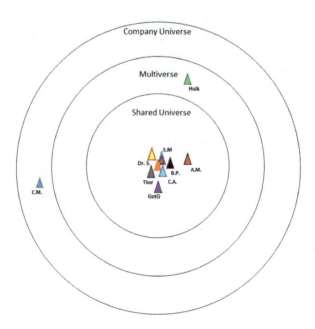

Taking the number of *Index Manifestations* from multiple *Narrative Entities*, the acknowledgment of different *Trigger Waves*, and the heavy reliance on an informed audience, *Avengers: Infinity War* holds a similar node function to the previous team narratives. However, the film fulfills the function on a larger scale, as *The Avengers* only had to combine four *Narrative Entities*, and *Avengers: Age of Ultron* only continued established relationships. Combining nearly all active *Narrative Entities* means *Avengers: Infinity War* draws all of them closely together.

3.1.1.3.9 Ant-Man and The Wasp (2019)

As the follow-up to *Avengers: Infinity War*, *Ant-Man and The Wasp*[104] do not use transposed *Index Manifestations*. Like *Black Panther*, interrelations are established through the acknowledgment of *Transformation Triggers*. The film presents Paul Rudd's Scott Lang/Ant-Man living under house arrest. The character's limited freedom relates to his involvement in *Captain America: Civil War*[105]. The alterations caused by *Captain America: Civil War* also influence the status of other *Index Manifestations* within *Ant-Man and the Wasp*, namely that Evangeline Lilly's Hope van Dyne/Wasp and Michael Douglas's Hank Pym have become fugitives under the Sokovia Accords[106]. Additionally, the film relates to the *Transformation Triggers* of *Avengers: Infinity War*, as its post-credit scene shows Michael Douglas's Hank Pym, Michelle Pfeiffer's Janet van Dyne, and Evangeline Lilly's Hope van

---

104 *Ant-Man and The Wasp.* Directed by Peyton Reed. Performances by Paul Rudd, Michael Douglas, Michelle Pfeiffer and Evangeline Lilly. Marvel Studios, 2018

105 *Ant-Man and The Wasp.* Directed by Peyton Reed. Performances by Paul Rudd, Michael Douglas, Michelle Pfeiffer and Evangeline Lilly. Marvel Studios, 2018. 00:07:48

106 *Ant-Man and The Wasp.* Directed by Peyton Reed. Performances by Paul Rudd, Michael Douglas, Michelle Pfeiffer and Evangeline Lilly. Marvel Studios, 2018. 00:15:33

Dyne disappear, leaving only the dust residue shown as a *semiotic cue* for Thanos's murder of half the universe's population in the previously released team narrative. The position of the latter *Transformation Triggers* in the post-credit scene also organizes the *Trigger Waves* of each film as occurring parallel to each other. The sudden death of characters from the MCU's Ant-Man Narrative due to the effect of the Infinity Stones necessarily aligns the ending of *Avengers: Infinity War* with the post-credit scene of *Ant-Man and The Wasp*. This alignment of *Trigger Waves* affords the additional benefit of providing a supplementary reason for the absence of specific *Index Manifestations* from each film.

While *Ant-Man and the Wasp* makes no effort to increase its entanglement with other *Narrative Entities* and slightly shifts away from the MCU's core network, as the film serves primarily a casual audience, it mitigates a more significant increase in distance by acknowledging the *Trigger Waves* from previous *Manifestations*.

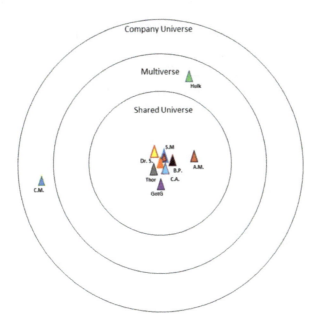

3.1.1.3.10 Captain Marvel (2019)

Set in 1995, *Captain Marvel*'s *Index Manifestations* and *Transformation Triggers* do not have a high potential of directly engaging with the overall MCU network. Formally taking place between *Captain America: The First Avenger*, which is set during the Second World War (excluding its post-credit scene), and the rest of the MCU films, general perceptions concerning the effects of time on most *Index Manifestations* would remove or alter established *semiotic cues*. While such changes do not entirely dissolve the potential for a connection via an *Index Manifestation*, it makes the prospect more unlikely. Because different transposed *Index Manifestations* appearing in *Captain Marvel* would most likely appear in a reinterpretation of its previous form, their level of similarity would most likely be much lower. In other words, because *Captain Marvel* takes place in the presumed past of the other already established *Narrative Entities*, all *Index Manifestations* have to appear in a version excluding all known *Transformation Triggers* and backstory *indices* of the established variety. The use of Samuel L. Jackson's Nick Fury and Clark Gregg's Phil Coulson in *Captain Marvel* follows this assertion. As *Index Manifestations* with their own series of *Transformation Triggers* and *Shared Narrative*, respectively, these characters should tie the MCU's Captain Marvel Narrative directly into the MCU network. However, the film uses a Nick Fury without his established *semiotic cues* other than the related actor. He wears no eyepatch (while the film explains how Fury's eye was injured), appears in a classic agent suit instead of his coat and military gear, and has hair and no beard instead of being bald with a trim beard. While this version uses the same actor, Samuel L. Jackson has been rejuvenated in post-production, equally altering the comparability of this *semiotic cue*. The representation of Phil Coulson does not diverge as much from the established version, giving the character mostly a period-appropriate hairstyle. The same principle applies to the appearance of *Index Manifestation* known from the *Guardians of the Galaxy*: While Djimon Hounsou appears as Korath in both films, the version in *Captain Marvel* serves in the Kree military (and as such wears their uniform) and lacks all cybernetic enhancement seen in the Guardians of the Galaxy *Manifestation*, lacking all *semiotic cues* other than the actor[107]. The representations of Lee Pace's Ronan the Accuser share more similarities than the other *Index Manifestations*. The character retains his war hammer in both iterations and his uniform. However, the representation within *Captain Marvel* lacks the dark war paint, which the character prominently wears in *Guardians of the Galaxy*[108]. While the overall representation is darker in *Guardians of the Galaxy*, the *Index Manifestation* retains dominantly the same design. The absolute exception to this divergence in representation comes in the form of the Tesseract. As the object never changes, it retains its representation. It connects the MCU's Captain Marvel Narrative to the larger network by interrelating it to *Captain America: The First Avenger* and *The Avengers*, in which the Tesseract plays a pivotal role[109].

As chronologically removed from the other *Manifestations*, *Captain Marvel* actively has to avoid negotiating changes due to *Transformation Triggers* or current *Trigger Waves*. The only connection possibly created via *Transformation Triggers* arises when the film replaces previous sections of an *Index Manifestation's* backstory with *Transformation Triggers* or adds to an existing series of *Transformation Triggers*. It does so regarding the Tesseract and Nick Fury. In the case of the latter, the film provides the *Transformation Trigger*, which creates the *semiotic cue* of his lost eye, a piece of personal backstory the character refers to on several occasions throughout the MCU network. The film also indicates how the close relationship between Clark Gregg's Phil Coulson and Nick Fury developed, as it portrays part of their partnership and shows Coulson as more loyal to Fury than to S.H.I.E.L.D. As Howard Stark found the Tesseract at the end of *Captain America: The First Avenger*, and

---

107 For screenshots of this character's appearances in the MCU consult https://marvelcinematicuniverse.fandom.com/wiki/Korath_the_Pursuer/Gallery

108 For screenshots of this character's appearances in the MCU consult https://marvelcinematicuniverse.fandom.com/wiki/Ronan_the_Accuser/Gallery

109 For screenshots of this *Index Manifestation's* appearances in the MCU consult https://marvelcinematicuniverse.fandom.com/wiki/Tesseract/Gallery

it is seen in the possession of S.H.I.E.L.D. at the end of *Thor*, *Captain Marvel* adds new interactions with the object, specifically its effect on newly introduced *Index Manifestations*, most notable as source of Brie Larson's Carol Danvers/Captain Marvel's abilities.

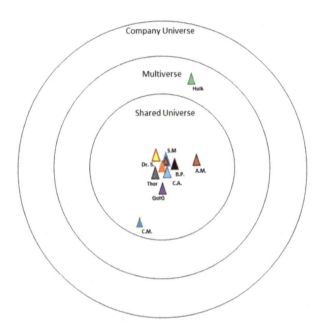

Positioning the MCU's Captain Marvel Narrative solely on the mentioned interrelations is tricky. Removed from the proceeding changes to the network in its intradiegetic representations automatically creates some distance to the other *Narrative Entities*. However, using a version of a long-established *Index Manifestation* in the form of Nick Fury does not make it utterly unrelated to the overall network. The same can be said about its contributions in the form of *Transformation Triggers*. The most likely position of the MCU's Captain Marvel Narrative in relation to the rest of the network would be in a Multiverse context. However, the film includes a post-credit scene directly connecting Captain Marvel's character with *Avengers: Endgame*. Including the actors who played Steve Rogers, Natasha Romanoff, Bruce Banner, and James 'Rhodey' Rhodes, respectively, the scene shows their reaction to a pager Nick Fury activated in the post-credit scene of *Avengers: Infinity Wars*. The pager presumably called Carol Danvers for help, continuing the *Trigger Wave*. Her appearance and short interaction with these *Index Manifestations* draw the *Narrative Entity* into a Shared Universe relationship, albeit a distant one.

3.1.1.3.11 Avengers: Endgame (2019)
As the direct continuation of *Avengers: Infinity War*, *Avengers: Endgame* provides a similar connective effect. By including the previously missing *Narrative Entities*, namely the MCU's Ant-Man and Captain Marvel Narratives, the film expands on the preceding *Avengers Manifestation*. As such, a precise analysis of *Index Manifestations* and their interrelating effect would be too expansive and yield little additional understanding

concerning the interrelation of the MCU's *Narrative Entities*. A precise analysis of *Index Manifestations* appears even more moot in light of the film's final conflict, in which nearly every significant hero character appears to battle the main antagonist, Thanos, and several characters of each *Narrative Entity* appear at Tony Stark's funeral[110].

Trigger Waves influencing *Avengers: Endgame* and exerting influence on *Manifestations* following it warrants, in contrast to *Index Manifestations*, a closer look. The film reacts directly to *Transformation Triggers* from two other *Manifestations*, *Avengers: Infinity War* and *Ant-Man and The Wasp*. As the fourth Avengers film directly continues the events of the third team narrative, the interconnection created between both Avengers films based on *Transformation Triggers* is inarguable. These *Trigger Waves* intersect with *Trigger Waves* from the MCU's Ant-Man Narrative: In the post-credit scene of *Ant-man and The Wasp*, Paul Rudd's Scott Lang/Ant-Man is stranded in the quantum realm when the characters operating the machinery disappear in reaction to the *Transformation Trigger* at the end of *Avengers: Infinity War*. Within the same scene, Michelle Pfeiffer's Janet van Dyne mentions the existence of time vortices within the quantum realm[111]. After the fourth team narrative establishes the new state of the world following the *Transformation Trigger* of *Avengers: Infinity War*, *Avengers: Endgame* begins a *Trigger Wave* to reverse that change by returning Scott Lang from the quantum realm. Providing a means of time travel, the character's return offers the option to undo the *Transformation Trigger* from the third MCU's Avengers *Manifestation*. As such, *Avengers: Endgame* effectively draws the effects of various *Trigger Waves* from multiple *Narrative Entities* together to produce its plot. The connecting effect of *Transformation Triggers* created at the end of the fourth team narrative has a similar bearing on the entire MCU network because they force the following *Manifestations* to acknowledge *Transformations Triggers* from *Avengers: Endgame*. Additionally, the film potentially removes two significant *Narrative Entities* from the network –the Captain America Narrative and the Iron Man Narrative. The reversal of Thanos's genocide to half the universe's population demands some form of recognition solely based on the scale and reach of the *Transformation Trigger*. Purely by its presentation in either of the final two Avengers films, it affected all known *Narrative Entities* and any *Narrative Entity* that has not yet appeared within the network. As such, future *Manifestations* (for a time) have to make note of the influence of this *Transformation Trigger*. Tony Stark's death and Steve Roger's disappearance/aging at the end of the *Avengers: Endgame* demands some reaction from future *Manifestations* because the disappearance of the hero character (in the case of most superhero narratives) calls the continuation of their respective *Narrative Entity* into question. As such, future *Manifestations* have to renegotiate (1) the removal of such a pivotal character, (2) a potential replacement of the associated *Narrative Entity* within the network, and (3) the place of remaining *Index Manifestations* from the respective *Narrative Entities*. Depending on the overall situation and potential for future *Manifestations*, these renegotiations may yield various results. Remaining *Index Manifestations* of a removed *Narrative Entity*, for example, might disappear, become unattached or attached to

---

110 For screenshots of the film showing the different *Index Manifestation* consult https://marvelcinematicuniverse.fandom.com/wiki/Avengers:_Endgame/Gallery

111 *Ant-Man and The Wasp*. Directed by Peyton Reed. Performances by Paul Rudd, Michael Douglas, Michelle Pfeiffer and Evangeline Lilly. Marvel Studios, 2018. 01:49:11

a different *Narrative Entity*, or transform into a hero character for a new *Narrative Entity*. Independent of the process and result of the renegotiations, they have to be addressed in future *Manifestations*.

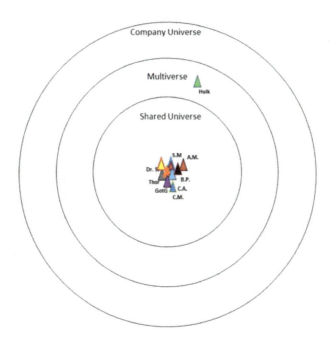

Concerning the relationships within the MCU network, *Avengers: Endgame* draws all involved *Narrative Entities* (except *The Incredible Hulk*) into a tight and close network, leaving most significantly the MCU's Captain America Narrative and the MCU's Iron Man Narrative in an even closer proximity. Despite removing two pivotal hero characters, Steve Rogers (who returns to his time) and Tony Stark (who dies in the final conflict), their associated *Narrative Entities* remain in the network for now because either case implied a legacy, which still needs to be resolved. Tony Stark's function as Peter Parker's mentor in *Spider-Man: Homecoming* sets up the latter as a potential inheritor of certain *Index Manifestations*. *Avengers: Endgame* creates a similar legacy pattern when Steve Rogers passes on his signature shield to Sam Wilson.

3.1.1.3.12 Spider-Man: Far From Home (2019)
As the final film of the Infinity Saga and the first film after *Avengers: Endgame*, *Spider-Man: Far From Home*'s primary purpose – within the notion of a Shared Universe – is to resolve the overall effect of the two universe-spanning *Transformation Triggers*. As such, its interrelation leans on dealing with the overall alterations created by the disappearance of half of the universe's population in *Avengers: Infinity War* (the Snap) and their subsequent return five years later in *Avengers: Endgame* (the Blip) as well as the death of Tony Stark/Iron Man. Concerning the latter, the interrelated nature between the MCU Spider-Man and the Iron Man Narrative created in *Spider-Man: Homecoming* puts the second Spider-Man

Manifestation in the position to address the effect of Tony Stark's death. *Spider-Man: Far From Home* does so by discussing a potential Iron Man legacy. This legacy arises mainly in dialogue, in which Peter Parker expresses doubts about his own ability. On the level of representation, *Spider-Man: Far From Home* adapts some of the MCU Iron Man Narrative's *Index Manifestations*. Jon Favreau's Harold 'Happy' Hogan reappears as Peter's liaison to Stark Industries and as a love interest for Marisa Tomei's Aunt May[112]. Aside from providing access to Stark Industries' technology (and thus other Iron Man *Index Manifestations*), Harold Hogan also serves as a dialogue partner for Peter Parker to discuss Tony Stark's demise and the path of a hero[113]. As with *Spider-Man: Homecoming*, Stark Industries' technology and resources explain Spider-Man's equipment and interweave *semiotic cues* of both characters with one another, specifically in the process of designing their suits. Here, the scene in which Peter Parker uses Stark Industries' technology to design a new suit uses sequences reminiscent of *Iron Man*, specifically slipping their hand into a holographic projection of a gauntlet and the use of a song by AC/DC, marking Spider-Man as a potential inheritor of an Iron Man legacy. The motivation of the film's antagonist also interrelates with an Iron Man heritage. Altered from the comic book version, Jake Gyllenhaal's Quentin Beck appears as a disgruntled ex-employee fired from Stark Industries after complaining about the misuse of technology he developed[114]. The antagonist wants to claim Tony Stark's legacy as his own, specifically a specialized drone army controlled by an advanced artificial intelligence called E.D.I.T.H., which Peter Parker inherited.

Spider-Man: Far From Home also addresses the disappearance and return of half the population across the MCU network. Dubbed 'the Blip' within the *Manifestation*, the *Transformation Trigger* is addressed at the beginning of the film in a video report from the news crew from Peter Parker's school (in which also the death of certain heroes as the end of *Avengers: Endgame* are reiterated). The extensive effect of the *Transformation Trigger* comes up regularly through Peter Parker's romantic rival, Brad Davis, played by Remy Hii. A new *Index Manifestation* to the MCU's Spider-Man Narrative, the character did not appear in *Spider-Man: Homecoming*. However, dialogue from the second MCU Spider-Man Narrative indicates that he was a "little kid who cried and got nosebleeds all the time[...]" in the previous Spider-Man film, and "suddenly [the lost population] blipped back and he's totally ripped and super nice, and all these girls are after him"[115] in *Spider-Man: Far From Home*. The representation and occurrence of this *Index Manifestation* is connected to the *Trigger Wave* from the last two Avengers films because people who disappeared at the end of *Avengers: Infinity War* and reappeared five years later at the end of *Avengers: Endgame* did not age. The frequent comments on Brad Davis's sudden shift in age attempt to acknowl-

---

112 For screenshots of this character's appearances within the MCU network consult https://marvelcinematicuniverse.fandom.com/wiki/Happy_Hogan/Gallery
113 *Spider-Man: Far From Home*. Directed by Jon Watts. Performances by Tom Holland, Jake Gyllenhaal, and Zendaya. Marvel Studios, 2019. 01:26:10
114 *Spider-Man: Far From Home*. Directed by Jon Watts. Performances by Tom Holland, Jake Gyllenhaal, and Zendaya. Marvel Studios, 2019. 01:02:04
115 *Spider-Man: Far From Home*. Directed by Jon Watts. Performances by Tom Holland, Jake Gyllenhaal, and Zendaya. Marvel Studios, 2019. 00:11:20

edge and renegotiate the effect of the *Avengers: Endgame*'s *Transformation Trigger* within the larger unified world.

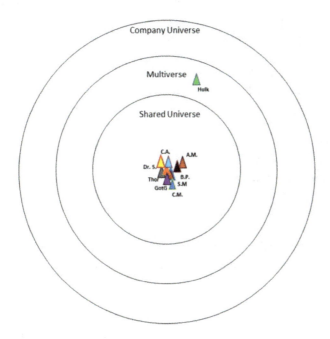

Addressing both *Transformation Triggers* deeply ties the MCU Spider-Man Narrative into the overall network. More importantly, the MCU's Spider-Man Narrative is directly connected to the MCU's Iron Man Narrative, not only via the continued presentation of Peter Parker as Tony Stark's inheritor but also by tying the film to an earlier version of the MCU's Iron Man via *Index Manifestations*. Aside from negotiating Tony Stark's legacy, *Spider-Man: Far From Home* also interrelates the two *Narrative Entities* through the appearance of nearly forgotten *Index Manifestations*, most notably Peter Billingsley's William Ginter Riva, who appears as a scientist in *Iron Man* and reappears as part of Quentin Beck's team in *Spider-Man: Far From Home*[116]. This strong interrelation allows the suggestion that *Spider-Man: Far From Home* effectively induces a replacement of the MCU's Iron Man Narrative within the overall network. Aside from relating to the Iron Man Narrative and *Avengers: Infinity War* and *Avengers: Endgame*, *Spider-Man: Far From Home* connects to the MCU's Captain Marvel Narrative through its post-credit scene. Ben Mendelsohn's Talos and Sharon Blynn's Soren, aliens associated with the MCU's Captain Marvel Narrative, are revealed to have impersonated Nick Fury and Maria Hill throughout *Spider-Man: Far From Home*[117].

---

116 For screenshots of this character in *Iron Man* and *Spider-Man: Far From Home* consult https://marvel cinematicuniverse.fandom.com/wiki/William_Ginter_Riva/Gallery
117 For screenshots of these characters' appearances throughout the MCU consult https://marvelcine maticuniverse.fandom.com/wiki/Soren/Gallery and https://marvelcinematicuniverse.fandom.co m/wiki/Talos/Gallery

3.1.1.4 Network Spanning Connections

Aside from the singular elements binding *Narrative Entities* together into a world-creating network, the MCU also employs *Index Manifestations* that span multiple *Narrative Entities*. These engage with the larger network as either a *Shared Narrative* or an overarching *Index Manifestation*. While *Index Manifestations* or acknowledgment and continuation of *Transformation Triggers* provide a direct interrelation between two specific *Narrative Entities*, *Shared Narratives* can tie an overall network closer together by spreading a plot across *Manifestations* of different *Narrative Entities*. Hereby, the connection is not only created by the recurrence of a stable *Index Manifestation* but also by the constant acknowledgment of a chain of changes through *Trigger Waves*. In contrast to the singular changes binding two *Narrative Entities* together, a *Shared Narrative* hinges on each alteration to an *Index Manifestation*, contributing to its larger plot. Combining a series of alterations across several *Manifestations* necessarily addresses an informed audience, which has the knowledge and engagement to perceive such a fragmented plot. The combination of a wandering *Index Manifestation*, chains of changes through a series of *Trigger Waves*, and the need for an (at least) informed audience marks the existence of a *Shared Narrative* as a technique that binds *Narrative Entities* more clearly into a Shared Universe relationship than singular connections potentially could. *Shared Narratives* provide strong connections by touching upon all connecting mechanics previously discussed. However, singular *Index Manifestations* can also wander across *Manifestations* from different *Narrative Entities* without necessarily creating a specific plot for themselves. These wandering *Index Manifestations* still change due to *Transformation Triggers*. Therefore, they facilitate *Trigger Waves* when they shift between different *Narrative Entities*, but their changes do not line up with the structure of a plot – potential examples of such are characters that remain (mostly) constant across appearances in different *Manifestations* or recurring objects without agency of their own. Still, these overarching *Index Manifestations* interrelate *Narrative Entities* with a larger network as they provide an identifiable constant, marking *Narrative Entities* as members of a specific network. Additionally, they can transport information and the effects of *Transformation Triggers* across a network. While these overarching *Index Manifestations* fulfill an essential purpose, they do not connect different *Narrative Entities* to the same degree that *Shared Narratives* do. Despite transporting the effects of *Transformation Triggers*, overarching *Index Manifestations* do not require an informed audience to unfold their potential. As their series of changes does not work towards the phases of a plot, knowing about such a series provides an informed audience with additional pleasure, but not knowing does not detract from potentially crucial aspects of a *Manifestation* or network. As such, *Shared Narratives* mark different *Narrative Entities* as part of a network but nearly automatically draw them into a closer Shared Universe relationship, while overarching *Index Manifestations* also mark a *Narrative Entity* as part of a network but merely draws *Narrative Entities* together in the same fashion any other wandering *Index Manifestation* would.

3.1.1.4.1 Shared Narrative

The MCU film network contains three significant *Shared Narratives*: (1) The *Shared Narrative* of Phil Coulson ties the *Manifestations* of the MCU's first phase together, helping to set its foundation. (2) The Black Widow *Shared Narrative* overlaps in several instances with the Captain America/Iron Man *Shared Narrative*, providing an important smaller plot within that larger *Shared Narrative*. (3) The *Shared Narrative* revolving around Captain America and Iron Man formally spans the entire Infinity Saga, giving the larger number of *Manifestations* a sense of order.

Agent Phil Coulson Within the six films of the first phase, the character of Phil Coulson, played by Clark Gregg, appears in four[118]. He is introduced in *Iron Man*, in which he wants to debrief Robert Downey Jr's Tony Stark – after that character escapes from Afghanistan – and later accompanies Gwyneth Paltrow's Pepper Potts to arrest Jeff Bridges's Obadiah Stane. Phil Coulson is revealed as an Agent of S.H.I.E.L.D. (The Strategic Homeland Interventions, Enforcement, and Logistic Division) at the end of the film. The character briefly reappears in *Iron Man 2*, where he discovers the prototype for Captain America's shield among Howard Stark's possessions and is sent to secure Thor's hammer, which he does in *Thor*. The character's final appearance within the MCU's first phase is in *The Avengers*. He is prominently featured throughout the movie, but most significantly, he is sent to collect Tony Stark, converses with Thor as a friend, and is shown as a fan of Steve Rogers, asking him to sign a set of Captain America collectible cards from the Second World War. Phil Coulson dies during *The Avengers*, serving as the catalyst for the protagonists to operate as a unit against a common enemy. All semiotic cues defining the character remain the same within these appearances. Clark Gregg plays the character throughout all installments with the same mannerisms and is dressed in a typical government suit.

Phil Coulson's combined appearances within the first phase show all the hallmarks of a *Shared Narrative*. He is a singular *Index Manifestation* that follows the structure of a plot across several *Manifestations* from multiple *Narrative Entities*. Applying the pattern set up for *Shared Narratives*, Coulson is introduced to the audience (*Exposition*) in *Iron Man* as a typical government agent with access to unusual technology and means of subterfuge[119]. He also serves as an introduction to the existence of S.H.I.E.L.D., as he is the only formal character from the organization we meet within the plot of the film – the definition of him as a typical S.H.I.E.L.D. Agent continues in *Iron Man 2*. While Phil Coulson only appears briefly in the film, the audience is reminded of his association with the organization. He then interweaves with various *Transformation Triggers* from the MCU's Thor Narrative's first *Manifestation* (*Rising Transformation*), increasing his tie to the different hero characters. Within *Thor*, S.H.I.E.L.D. and Coulson serve as primary obstacles for Thor to reach Mjolnir. Agent Coulson also stifles Erik Selvig's and Jane Foster's research, interweaving S.H.I.E.L.D. with other *Index Manifestations* from the Thor Narrative. The chief alteration in this instance is the close association of the *Index Manifestation* Phil Coulson with the Thor Narrative. The *Rising Transformation* continues in *The Avengers* as Coulson recruits Iron Man for the Avengers and constantly interacts with several members of the

---

118   For screenshots of Phil Coulson's appearances in the MCU consult https://marvelcinematicunivers e.fandom.com/wiki/Phil_Coulson/Gallery

119   *Iron Man*. Directed by Jon Favreau. Performances by Robert Downey Jr., Gwyneth Paltrow, Terrence Howard, and Jeff Bridges. Marvel Studios, 2008. 00:43:45

team. Here, the character also relates to Steve Rogers through his admiration for Captain America, represented in his vintage card collection of the superhero. As such, Agent Phil Coulson develops further relationships entangling him with superheroes. Coulson's increased entanglement with superheroes narratively leads to him standing his ground against the supervillain Loki[120], which serves as the *Shared Narrative*'s climatic *Transformation Trigger (Climax)*[121]. The *Climax* is resolved with Coulson's death and the subsequent rallying of the different heroes to form the Avengers[122] and save New York from an alien invasion[123] (*climax wave*). As such, the effect of the *Climax* on the *Index Manifestation* of the *Shared Narrative* relates to the *film's Climax*, which dually serves as the conclusion of the *Shared Narrative* of Phil Coulson (*Denouement*) and the MCU's first phase. Within this structure, the *Index Manifestation* of Phil Coulson first relates the foundational *Narrative Entities* with one another (foremost Iron Man and Thor) by passing through them. With the previous appearances, his death in *The Avengers* provides a reasonable rallying event for the hero characters and potentially an emotional resonance for an informed audience. Additionally, the *Shared Narrative* of the character necessarily organizes some of the previous films into a fixed order. The events of *Iron Man*, *Iron Man 2*, *Thor*, and *The Avengers* necessarily are arranged along Coulson's plotline.

Considering the management of a network of *Narrative Entities*, the *Shared Narrative* of Phil Coulson generally draws the initial *Narrative Entities* closer together during the overall formation of a Shared Universe relationship. The more minor involvement in either appearance makes this *Shared Narrative* less critical for the plot of the singular *Manifestations*. Still, the continued relationship with the different *Narrative Entities* primes an engaged audience towards the emotional payoff continued loyalty might yield when the character dies unexpectedly and significantly. As such, Phil Coulson's *Shared Narrative* provides a foundation for the Shared Universe on several levels: It provides the necessary connection between the new iterations of known *Narrative Entities*, and it subtly teaches a new (casual) audience how *Manifestations* of multiple *Narrative Entities* might interrelate. This *Shared Narrative* provides the latter by operating with a simple plot and a significant *Climax* to that plot.

Natasha Romanoff/Black Widow Scarlett Johansson's Natasha Romanoff/Black Widow appears in eight *Manifestations* throughout the 23 films of the Infinity Saga. Half of these appearances occur within the four Avengers films, marking her as an *Index Manifestation* that potentially can be associated with the overall MCU network over a specific *Narrative Entity*. Of the remaining four, one is a cameo in the post-credit scene of *Captain Marvel*. The final three are split between *Iron Man 2* and Captain America's second and third films[124]. As such, the character relates more to these two *Narrative Entities* than other

---

120 *The Avengers*. Directed by Joss Whedon. Marvel Studios, 2012. 01:23:59
121 *The Avengers*. Directed by Joss Whedon. Marvel Studios, 2012. 01:26:01
122 *The Avengers*. Directed by Joss Whedon. Marvel Studios, 2012. 01:29:20
123 *The Avengers*. Directed by Joss Whedon. Marvel Studios, 2012. 01:37:47
124 For screenshots of Natasha Romanoff/Black Widow's appearances within the MCU consult https://marvelcinematicuniverse.fandom.com/wiki/Black_Widow/Gallery

Narrative Entities within the network. This dual interrelation finds prominence in *Captain America: Civil War*, in which Captain America and Iron Man are in conflict with one another.

Like the *Index Manifestation* Phil Coulson, Natasha Romanoff/Black Widow follows a series of *Transformation Trigger*s forming a *Shared Narrative*. Introduced as a highly capable spy associated with the organization S.H.I.E.L.D. in *Iron Man 2*, the *Exposition* continues into *The Avengers*, which provides a general motivation for her heroism in the need to make amends for past sins[125]. As a connective node for the MCU network, *The Avengers* also interweaves this *Index Manifestation* with those of other *Narrative Entities* and influential *Transformation Trigger*s (*Rising Transformation*), altering the position of this *Index Manifestation* to others within the overall network. The interrelation with several *Narrative Entities* notably leads to the character's adoption into the *index* network of the MCU's Captain America Narrative. Natasha Romanoff/Black Widow plays an integral part in *Captain America: The Winter Soldier*, in which her actions motivate Steve Roger's suspicion of S.H.I.E.L.D.'s activity[126]. Her support of Rogers helps him uncover Hydra's infiltration of S.H.I.E.L.D., and her testimony finally helps bring the organization down. Within this context, Black Widow changes by shifting her loyalty from Nick Fury – who does not include her in his circle of trust when he fakes his death – to Steve Rogers – due to their shared struggle as fugitives. The *Rising Transformation* as a process of interrelation continues in *Avengers: Age of Ultron*. Set in relation to other of the larger network's *Index Manifestations*, dominantly Bruce Banner, with whom she shares most of her scenes, the character is further interwoven into the overall network. *Avengers: Age of Ultron* equally elaborates on her previously established motivation, adding to exposition through a hallucination sequence, which forces her to reveal aspects of her training in the Red Room. Adding an origin trauma/story heightens the relationship to Tony Stark/Iron Man and Steve Rogers/Captain America, whose own fears and traumas appear in hallucinations within the same sequence. In *Captain America: Civil War*, the *Transformation Trigger* of the Sakovia Accords, which specifically puts the *Narrative Entity* of Captain America and Iron Man at odds, places the *Index Manifestation* of Natasha Romanoff in a field of tension between their two positions based on her previous connection to either. Despite siding with Tony Stark, she constantly argues in favor of Steve Roger's safety, attempting to mitigate the effects of the Sakovia Accords on either side. Her association with Bruce Banner even comes up when asked how she would evaluate his position on the accords. All *Transformation Triggers* of *Captain America: Civil War* lead the *Index Manifestation* Natasha Romanoff to her climatic *Transformation Trigger* at the end of the fight between Roger's and Stark's forces. Having the option to stop Captain America and the Winter Soldier, she decides to help them escape, cementing her connections within the overall network to Steve Rogers. This alteration is resolved at the end of *Captain America: Civil War*, in which she leaves the Avengers, and in *Avengers: Infinity War*, in which the character (outside of action sequences in the final battle) only appears in scenes with Steve Rogers, often even in the same shot (*climax wave*). The *Shared Narrative* concludes at the beginning of *Avengers:*

---

125   *The Avengers*. Directed by Joss Whedon. Marvel Studios, 2012. 01:05:13
126   *Captain America: The Winter Soldier*. Directed by Anthony Russo and Joe Russo. Performances by Chris Evans, Scarlett Johansson, and Sebastian Stan. Marvel Studios, 2014. 00:13:53

Endgame when the character is confronted with the absolute and final consequence of her climatic decision. The movie begins right after the *Transformation Trigger*s of *Avengers: Infinity Wars* and reignites the conflict between Steve Rogers and Tony Stark, giving the appearance that Stark had been on the right side of the issue. This assertion solidifies when the remaining heroes go after Thanos to reverse his actions, only to discover that he destroyed the Infinity Stones. Here, Natasha Romanoff's *Shared Narrative* concludes (*Denouement*) because the inability to save the universe from Thanos presents the overall outcome of her previous choices. A new series of *Trigger Waves* forming a plot begins when *Avengers: Endgame* jumps five years into the future. Focused on the *Index Manifestation* of Black Widow, Freytag's structure restarts as the audience is presented with the character's place in the new world order (*Exposition*). She runs the Avengers with Steve Rogers, lost touch with Clint Barton and the Hulk, and desperately wishes for a way to save the world. Her new *Rising Transformation* begins when Scott Lang and his means of time travel surface, and she uses her previous connection to the different *Narrative Entities* and *Index Manifestations* to reassemble the Avengers. The *Rising Transformation* continues with the formulation of a plan to assemble the Infinity Stones by traveling into the past. The character's climax of this plot structure arises when she and Clint Barton discover that a sacrifice is required to retrieve the Soul Stone. Motivated by her established sense of guilt and need to balance her scale, she competes with Clint Barton to sacrifice herself. The *Climax Wave* occurs when the rest of the Avengers have to accept her death. The *Denouement* of her character arc within the film occurs when the team assembles the Infinity Stones and uses them to reverse the *Transformation Trigger* of *Avengers: Infinity War*. Formally speaking, the latter series of *Transformation Triggers* is a character arc within the plot of a *Manifestation* and not a *Shared Narrative*. However, its existence highlights that the previous longer *Shared Narrative* truly ends in the middle of a *Manifestation* and shows that the structure of a plot within a network, as presented here, can stretch across several *Manifestations* or be compressed to fit into a section of one.

Concerning the management of *Narrative Entities*, this *Shared Narrative* provides a prime example of using an *Index Manifestation* to influence a singular relationship within the overall network. By being introduced in one *Narrative Entity* and attaching itself to another, Natasha Romanoff/Black Widow subtly interrelated two singular *Narrative Entities* closely within a continually more complex network.

Captain America - Iron Man Shared Narrative The most interesting network and phase-spanning connection resides in the relationship between the *Index Manifestations* of Steve Rogers and Tony Stark and their respective *Narrative Entities*. Essentially, these two *Narrative Entities* interrelate by creating two separate *Shared Narratives*, which then interweave to form a third in the conflict of their respective positions and individual developments.

Robert Downey Jr.'s Tony Stark/Iron Man effectively spans the entirety of the Infinity Saga. The first MCU's Iron Man *Manifestation* starts the network, and the character's death in *Avengers: Endgame* and its mourning in *Spider-Man: Far From Home* formally concludes the Infinity Saga. Throughout the 23 *Manifestations* of the MCU network, the character appears in nine films (discounting post-credits scene appearances), three *Manifestations* focused on his *Narrative Entity*, four team narratives in the form of the Avengers films, and two transposed *Manifestations* with *Captain America: Civil War* and *Spiderman:*

Homecoming[127]. All of these appearances combine into an overall *Shared Narrative* relating the development of this character from a selfish megalomaniac to a sacrificial hero. Within the structure of a *Shared Narrative*, the first two Iron Man films and *The Avengers* serve as *Exposition*. While the character changes in the course of the singular films, within the complex of the MCU network, *Iron Man* (as the origin story) introduces and explains the character, while *Iron Man 2* contextualizes his appearance and existence to a society in which superheroes are not a regular occurrence. *The Avengers* contextualizes this character into a group of super-powered individuals and a more superhero comic-like society. The *Rising Transformation* begins with the final *Transformation Trigger*s of *The Avengers*, in which the character discovers the great danger of a superhuman and alien-populated universe. This *Rising Transformation* continues across *Iron Man 3*, *Avengers: Age of Ultron*, *Captain America: Civil War*, and *Spider-Man: Homecoming*. In all four movies, Tony Stark negotiates the dangers the world faces through super-powered threats with means to protect it from those dangers. In *Iron Man 3*, this struggle is personal, as he has to overcome PTSD and find a way to operate within a much more dangerous world. Additionally, the film highlights the danger created by super-powered individuals by employing the notion of super-powered terrorists. Within the negotiation between super-power threats and the means to combat them, Tony Stark accidentally creates Ultron in *Avengers: Age of Ultron* in an attempt to build a planetary defense system. Again, he cites his fear of an alien invasion to justify his actions. *Captain America: Civil War* revolves around the threat superpower individuals potentially pose to regular society. Within this context, Tony Stark sides with the regulation and oversight of the Avengers and other super-powered individuals, continuing his attempt at protecting the world from such threats. This notion remains in *Spider-Man: Homecoming*. Within his role as Peter Parker's mentor, Tony Stark encourages Peter to be a better hero, emphasizing the potential for collateral damage in their line of work. Tony Stark's *Shared Narrative* finds its *Climax* in *Avengers: Infinity War*. Despite all the character's efforts in previous *Manifestations*, he ultimately fails as Thanos 'kills' half of the universe's population, including Peter Parker. The realization of his failure begins the *Shared Narrative*'s *Climax Wave* at the beginning of *Avengers: Endgame*. In his first encounter with Captain America, after they fail to stop Thanos, he recounts their disagreement on the actions necessary to protect society. He symbolically gives up his Iron Man persona by handing over his Iron Man armor. While Tony Stark is shown to have settled down with Pepper Potts five years later, guilt over his failure – as with all the hero characters[128] – and the fear of loss[129] dominate all of his scenes up to the moment, he rejoins the Avengers. This dominant theme of the *Climax Wave*, guilt over personal failure and the attempt to rectify their mistake, guides Tony Stark in *Avengers: Endgame*'s final conflict. Tony Stark's *Shared Narrative* results in his sacrifice at the end of the *Climax Wave*, as his death is presented as the only means to rectify his previous failure. The *Denouement* finally takes place in *Spider-Man: Far From Home*, in which the meaning

---

127 For screenshots of Tony Stark/Iron Man's appearances within the MCU consult https://marvelcinematicuniverse.fandom.com/wiki/Iron_Man/Gallery
128 *Avengers: Endgame*. Directed by Anthony Russo and Joe Russo. Marvel Studios, 2019. 02:08:09
129 *Avengers: Endgame*. Directed by Anthony Russo and Joe Russo. Marvel Studios, 2019. 00:35:45

of Tony Stark's existence and death for the represented world is negotiated, and his role is symbolically handed over to Peter Parker.

Appearing in eight films of the 23 *Manifestations* included in the Infinity Saga, Steve Rogers/Captain America serves as a close second to Tony Stark as the defining character of the MCU network. Aside from the three *Manifestations* dedicated to his specific *Narrative Entity* – *Captain America: The First Avenger*, *Captain America: Winter Soldier*, and *Captain America: Civil War* – the character is featured prominently in all four Avengers films and appears indirectly in *Spider-Man: Homecoming*[130]. As with the *Shared Narrative* representation of Tony Stark, the question of the relationship between society/the government and the super-powered community underlines Steve Rogers's *Shared Narrative*. However, where Iron Man turns from a more personal viewpoint to a notion of the greater good, Captain America makes the alternate transition. In effect, the character starts with a dedication to the safety of the world as a whole and with a penchant for self-sacrifice – which the first Captain America film captures, when Steve Rogers dives onto a grenade to protect the people around him – but later distrust larger institutions/society, rather placing his faith in individuals[131]. The *Exposition* of Captain America's *Shared Narrative* stretches across *Captain America: The First Avenger*, in which the *Index Manifestation* is introduced, and *The Avengers*, in which the character is placed in relation to the modern world and the reality of other super-powered individuals. The *Exposition* extends into the first third of *Captain America: Winter Soldier* because his place in the modern world requires further negotiations and explanation, as the character still evaluates his place in it. Steve Rogers's *Rising Transformation* begins with his discovery of 'Project: Insight' – a form of government surveillance with the potential of preemptive elimination developed by S.H.I.E.L.D. – and Hydra's infiltration of S.H.I.E.L.D. With these two *Transformation Triggers*, the character's dedication to the American ideal turns into distrust for governmental institutions. The *Rising Transformation* continues in *Avengers: Age of Ultron*, in which Steve Rogers emphasizes personal moral decisions and the safety of all people over systemic protection protocols. The emphasis on personal morality becomes apparent in the character's refusal to sacrifice a city's population to save the world[132]. This contrasts him directly with Tony Stark, who attempts to construct a universal system of protection and reluctantly proposes the city's destruction as a solution. The *Rising Transformation* continues through the greater part of *Captain America: Civil War*. The character's distrust for governmental institutions continues with a distrust of the Sakovia Accords, which would regulate the Avengers and potentially the super-powered community. Instead, he promotes personal responsibility over government regulation[133]. The situation escalates when the accords prevent him from helping his friend Bucky Barnes, whom Steve Rogers

---

[130] For screenshots of Steve Rogers/Iron Man's appearances within the MCU consult https://marvelcinematicuniverse.fandom.com/wiki/Steve_Rogers/Gallery

[131] *Captain America: Civil War*. Directed by Anthony Russo and Joe Russo. Performances by Chris Evans and Robert Downey Jr. Marvel Studios, 2016. 02:14:57

[132] *Avengers: Age of Ultron*. Directed by Joss Whedon. Marvel Studios, 2015. 01:50:33

[133] *Captain America: Civil War*. Directed by Anthony Russo and Joe Russo. Performances by Chris Evans and Robert Downey Jr. Marvel Studios, 2016. 00:30:09

trusts to be a good person over the reports of his actions. The *Climax* of this *Shared Narrative* arrives in the direct conflict between Tony Stark and Steve Rogers at the end of *Captain America: Civil War*. Aside from fighting Tony Stark as a representation of increased governmental control, Steve Rogers actively decides to value a personal relationship and individual judgment over a judgment made by institutions of society. The *Climax Wave* begins directly after the fight, when he leaves his shield, symbolically dropping his governmentally created and issued superhero persona. This notion continues with the letter he leaves Tony Stark, in which Steve Rogers explains that he never really fit into any institution but always believed in individuals. While the character does not directly appear in *Spider-Man: Homecoming* – as his presence is limited to a Public Service Announcement (PSA) videos played for the students at Peter Parker's High School – the representation of the character within the film is significant for the *Shared Narrative*'s *Climax Wave*. Because the version in the PSAs wears the Captain America uniform from *The Avengers*, the representation is reminiscent of the MCU's Captain America before *Captain America: The Winter Soldier*, meaning before the *Transformation Triggers*, which incited the *Rising Transformation*. These reminiscent PSA appearances highlight the character's altered position within the world order due to the *Transformation Triggers* of *Captain America: Civil War*. The gym teacher's comment regarding Steve Rogers's legal standing[134] indicates the altered status. The *Climax Wave* of the *Shared Narrative* continues in *Avengers: Infinity War*. Steve Rogers reappears in the uniform he wore at the end of *Captain America: Civil War*, but the star, which usually adorns his chest, is gone, with only an outline suggesting its former presence. Instead of retrieving or receiving the shield associated with Captain America, Steve Rogers obtains alternative claw shields provided by T'Challa/Black Panther, highlighting the increased difference from his previous representation. *Avengers: Endgame* provides the *Denouement* for this *Shared Narrative*, as Steve Rogers has given up on his Captain America persona. Outside of the time travel sequence, in which he pretends to be his past self, and the final conflict, the character does not don his uniform. He is uncertain about accepting his shield[135] when Tony Stark returns it to him. When he encounters his former self, we can identify the later version by the fact that he does not wear the full costume in contrast to his former self. Additionally, the future Steve Rogers uses underhanded tactics – which appear counter to the honorable character presented earlier – to collect Loki's spear from Hydra (pretending to be a Hydra Agent) and defeat his past self (emotional manipulation). A certain disdain for his former self appears hidden in a joke when, after tricking him, the future Steve Rogers looks down on his past self and says: "That is America's ass"[136]. In this instant, he underhandedly judges his former morality and belief in institutions. In addition, Steve Rogers chooses to remain in the past to live out his life with Peggy Carter, which contradicts the pennant for self-sacrifice established in *Captain America: The First Avenger*. All these actions indicate that he has stepped away from the role as a representation of the US government and its defense as a pinnacle of moral authority, leaning more toward the value of individuality. The greater

---

134 *Spider-Man: Homecoming*. Directed by Jon Watts. Performances by Tom Holland, Michael Keaton, Zendaya, and Robert Downey Jr. Marvel Studios, 2017. 00:26:45)
135 *Avengers: Endgame*. Directed by Anthony Russo and Joe Russo. Marvel Studios, 2019. 00:47:25
136 *Avengers: Endgame*. Directed by Anthony Russo and Joe Russo. Marvel Studios, 2019. 01:23:32

emphasis on individual responsibility is finalized when he chooses his successor as Captain America himself (instead of letting the government make that choice).

As such, the *Shared Narrative* of Captain America mirrors the *Shared Narrative* of Iron Man, placing them into direct opposition as they always represent the other side of a specific argument and the ideal of superheroism. This leads to a combination of these two *Shared Narratives* into a hybrid third. As mentioned in their singular *Shared Narratives*, Tony Stark and Steve Rogers represent two sides of the potential morality of a superhero. While their stance alters during their *Shared Narratives*, they create the ends of a hero spectrum on which other characters related to them can be identified, specifically when they are closely related to either. This spectrum finds some semblance of importance within the ideas represented in *Captain America: Civil War*, but also within new *Narrative Entities* introduced in connection with these characters. *Ant-Man* introduces its *Index Manifestations* in relation to both the MCU's Captain America and Iron Man Narrative, but throughout the film, it focuses on defining Ant-Man in detraction to Iron Man. Spider-Man is developed as a potential continuation of the MCU's Iron Man Narrative. In the course of *Captain America: Civil War*, Black Panther makes a transition from a revenge-seeking character to a moralistic protector, which carries over into *Black Panther*, in which he wonders about Wakanda's position and moral responsibility. Such later definition along a spectrum between the MCU's Iron Man and Captain America Narrative is only possible because they have a developing relationship across the MCU network's *Manifestations*. Aside from films in which the two main characters interact directly with each other (which include three of the four Avengers films and *Captain America: Civil War*), the relationship between the two *Narrative Entities* is negotiated in *Iron Man*, *Iron Man 2*, and *Captain America: The First Avenger*. The *Exposition* of this interlaced *Shared Narratives* plays out across *Iron Man*, *Iron Man 2*, *Captain America: The First Avenger*, and *The Avengers*. The two *Narrative Entities* are linked to one another through the use of *Index Manifestations* formally associated with the other *Narrative Entity*. A prototype of Captain America's shield appears in the two Iron Man films, and Dominic Cooper's Howard Stark appears in *Captain America: The First Avenger*. The setup of a relationship between Tony Stark and Steve Rogers via Howard Stark is played out in *The Avengers*, in which Tony Stark comments on his father's stories of Steve Rogers. Within the first team narrative, their relationship is then directly tied to the idea of the Avengers. After Coulson's death, Nick Fury gives his "there was an idea"[137] - speech (only) to Tony and Steve. The relationship between Steve Rogers and Tony Stark finds some balance after the death of Phil Coulson, visible in their conversation after Nick Fury's speech. In it, they still show differences in the evaluation of the situation (specifically pertaining to Coulson's death and their role in the grand scheme of things) but find common ground in a distrust of Nick Fury and in playing off one another in figuring out Loki's plan[138]. This short equilibrium is also shown in the fight against the Chitauri at the end of *The Avengers*, in which Tony Stark defers to Steve Rogers's expertise

---

137 "*There was an idea, Stark knows this, called the Avengers Initiative. The idea was to bring together a group of remarkable people, see if they could become something more. See if they could work together when we needed them to fight the battles we never could.*"
138 *The Avengers*. Directed by Joss Whedon. Marvel Studios, 2012. 01:35:37

concerning an imminent battle strategy,[139] and the two characters communicate more with each other than with the other Avengers. The later aspects solidify a connection, as the dialogue between them mostly confirms the situation and determines an imminent course of action. As presented in their respective *Shared Narratives* and the analysis of the respective *Manifestations*, both characters change due to the *Transformation Triggers* of *The Avengers* before the *Shared Narrative* of their friendship continues in *Avengers: Age of Ultron*. The *Rising Transformation* of the *Shared Narrative* begins as the characters are placed in opposition concerning initial notions of protecting the world. Their initial friendly relationship is solidified in the first half of the film through banter between them in the raid on the last Hydra compound, the party celebrating their victory, and their working off one another in search of Ultron. The *Rising Transformation* begins with the visions induced by the Scarlet Witch. In the case of Tony Stark, it is the fear already mentioned in *Iron Man 3* and at the beginning of *Avengers: Age of Ultron*. He fears losing the entire planet and his friends to an alien invasion. In the case of Steve Rogers, it is a reminder of what he personally has lost due to his service, namely Peggy Carter and his home, meaning his original place in time. These visions set the stage for their preferred future course of action. The *Rising Transformation* continues, as the two characters have their first fight after their visions, with Steve Rogers questioning Tony Stark's actions, Tony Stark questioning the purpose of the Avengers and Steve Rogers's lack of a dark side. The *Rising Transformation* continues in the film with a first physical confrontation over The Vision, which Tony Stark wants to create as a weapon against Ultron and in which Steve Rogers sees a dangerous repetition of recent mistakes. The *Rising Transformation* continues in *Captain America: Civil War*, in which the conflict leads to a separation of these characters due to Steve Rogers's split loyalty and his final decision to support Bucky Barnes over Tony Stark. The *Shared Narrative* finds its *Climax* in *Avengers: Infinity War* when Tony Stark refuses/hesitates to call Steve Rogers to inform him about Thanos and the Infinity Stones. While not a bombastic *Climax*, it reflects the accumulation of the change in their relationship due to the *Rising Transformation*. This hesitation leads to the *Climax Wave*, in which the Avengers operate in separate teams throughout *Avengers: Infinity War* instead of coordinating and operating as a whole to achieve a shared goal. This separation finally contributes to their defeat. The *Climax Wave* continues in *Avengers: Endgame*. Even after Steve Rogers acknowledges the consequence of their differences and Tony Stark re-enforces the idea that he needed him in the fight against Thanos, Steve Rogers leads a failed mission without Tony Stark to retrieve the Infinity Stones. The *Denouement* of this *Shared Narrative* begins when the two characters acknowledge that they need to work together. This happens when Tony mentions missing Steve Rogers's eternal optimism (in reference to the ability of the Avengers), and Steve Rogers comes to Tony Stark for help to complete their plan to retrieve the Infinity Stones. The *Denouement* finally plays out across the last two-thirds of *Avengers: Endgame*, when the team (in contrast to *Avengers: Infinity War*) collectively establishes and executes a plan and faces a second assault by Thanos together. Their relationship ends with Tony Stark's death and Steve Rogers's effective retirement.

Aside from allowing multiple high points and a variety of plot stages throughout the different MCU *Manifestations*, the combined *Shared Narrative* represents the poten-

---

139   *The Avengers*. Directed by Joss Whedon. Marvel Studios, 2012. 01:52:32

tial to guide the position and relation of multiple *Index Manifestations* within a more extensive network by coordinating their singular development along one another. In other words, this hybrid *Shared Narrative* does not only connect the *Narrative Entities* but provides a means to steer them into opposing positions necessary to manage relationships and larger *Manifestation*-spanning plot points.

3.1.1.4.2 Overarching Index Manifestations

In addition to the *Shared Narratives*, the MCU films contain three overarching *Index Manifestations*: The two characters, Nick Fury and Peggy Carter, appear throughout the network, relating the single *Narrative Entities* to one another. Additionally, the Infinity Stones provide *Index Manifestations* and a theme binding multiple *Narrative Entities* closer together. In contrast to previous examples, these overarching *Index Manifestations* do not develop their own plot across several *Manifestations*. While they change, these changes do not follow any definable larger order, leaving them as stable elements within the larger network.

Nicholas Joseph Fury Samuel L. Jackson's Nick Fury appears eleven times within the 23 MCU films of the Infinity Saga[140]. Within the first phase, the character appears in mostly smaller or singular scenes until he brings the titular superhero team together in *The Avengers*. He is in the post-credit scenes of *Iron Man*, *Thor*, and *Captain America: The First Avenger*. *Iron Man 2* provides a notable exception within the first phase, as Nick Fury appears in the second act and delivers the necessary knowledge for the main character to overcome his personal obstacle. As the director of S.H.I.E.L.D. and planning the creation of the Avengers, Nick Fury also has a more prominent role in *The Avengers*. Within the second phase, he is in two of the six films. The character has a more significant role in *Captain America: Winter Soldier*, in which S.H.I.E.L.D. is dissolved, and a smaller appearance in *Avengers: Age of Ultron*. In the former, he provides information on the inner operations and plans of the organization. In the latter, he does the same in his first short appearance, providing the Avengers with information on Ultron and his movements. He also serves as a deus ex machina at the end of *Avengers: Age of Ultron*, when he shows up with the means to save a city's population, thereby protecting Steve Rogers's integrity. Nick Fury is notably absent from all *Manifestations* between the second and third Avengers films. He returns at the end of the third phase in *Avengers: Infinity War*, *Captain Marvel*, *Avengers: Endgame*, and *Spider-Man: Far From Home*. The appearances in the third and fourth Avenger films are short cameos. In *Avengers: Infinity Wars*, the character disappears in a post-credit scene due to Thanos's use of the Infinity Gauntlet. In *Avengers: Endgame*, he has a short non-dialogue appearance at Tony Stark's funeral. The character's role is more substantial in *Captain Marvel* and *Spider-Man: Far From Home*. In the former, he makes contact with the titular hero, and the film shows how he becomes interested in the more unusual elements of this world. In the last of the Infinity Saga films, a version of Nick Fury passes on technology from Stark to Peter Parker and serves as a catalyst for the plot to unfold.

---

140 For screenshots of Nick Fury's appearances within the MCU consult https://marvelcinematicuniverse.fandom.com/wiki/Nick_Fury/Gallery

While not belonging to a specific *Narrative Entity*, Nick Fury draws several *Narrative Entities* closer together because he is used as a stable and recognizable *Index Manifestation*. Aside from a retention of the actor playing him, all iterations (except the one in Captain Marvel) use familiar semiotic cues: He maintains his eyepatch and his black attire. In most instances, he also appears with his long black coat. Especially the first phase uses this recognition to interrelate the different films, which might be why the character appears in every Phase 1 *Narrative Entity* except the Hulk Narrative. However, while the *Index Manifestation* is pivotal in singular *Manifestations*, the different appearances do not align with a *Shared Narrative*. One of the reasons for a lack of *Shared Narrative* is that the character always (except in *Captain Marvel*) provides information and support to the protagonist on an intradiegetic level or as a plot catalyst. These functions remain in place independently from the time the character appears on screen. In all his cameo appearances, the character merely hints towards another *Narrative Entity*. He mentions that Iron Man becomes part of a larger world (*Iron Man*); he introduces the Tesseract (*Thor*); he tells Steve Rogers that he has been asleep for 70 Years (*Captain America: The First Avenger*); he provides information on Ultron's activity (*Avengers: Age of Ultron*); and he uses a beeper to call Carol Danvers (*Avengers: Infinity War*). All of these appearances tease upcoming *Manifestations* or provide some form of exposition. While having a more substantial role, films in which Nick Fury plays a larger part do not stray from this function. In *Iron Man 2*, the character only appears to explain who Scarlett Johansson's Natasha Romanoff is, why Tony Stark has been acting erratic in the film's first act, and divulge Howard Stark's relationship with S.H.I.E.L.D. In *The Avengers*, Nick Fury elaborates on the Avengers Initiative, provides information concerning Loki and the Tesseract, and explains S.H.I.E.L.D.'s course of action. Here, he also serves as a catalyst or prompt for the formation of the team, as he orders the members assembled and gives them the motivation to work together. While having more screen time in *Captain America: The Winter Soldier*, Nick Fury serves a similar function: He introduces and explains 'Project Insight' and argues for its need. Additionally, he schools Steve Rogers on S.H.I.E.L.D.'s means and mode of operation, as well as on the fact that the organization has been compromised. As mentioned, he provides only support and information in *Avengers: Age of Ultron*. The same function as a catalyst and exposition device continues in *Spider-Man: Far From Home*. Nick Fury recruits Peter Parker for a mission in Europe and provides information on the overall situation. It should be mentioned that the Nick Fury in *Spider-Man: Far From Home* is revealed as an imposter at the end of the movie. However, the revelation of an imposter does not change the coherent function this unattached *Index Manifestation* provides within the singular *Manifestation*. In contrast to his other appearances, Nick Fury in *Captain Marvel* does not serve the exposition and catalyst function but serves as a soundboard for exposition. This *Manifestation* provides some new backstory for the character (how he lost his eye, how he encountered the unusual elements of this world, and how he came up with the Avengers.) However, the differing function is not the only distinction between the representations, as discussed in the chapter on *Captain Marvel*. It coincides with a very different representation of Nick Fury concerning his different *semiotic cues*. While *Transformation Triggers* alter a character's state, they mostly do so in relation to the explanation of its function within singular *Manifestations*. Nick Fury is universally informed about all events of the world up to the fall of S.H.I.E.L.D. in *Captain America: The Winter Soldier*. He mentions his lack of resources in *Avengers: Age of Ultron*, forcing them to act independently. Something similar occurs after the *Transformation Triggers* of *Avengers: Infinity War* and *Avengers: Endgame*, through which half the universe's population skipped five years. He mentions his sudden lack of information in *Spider-Man: Far From Home*, providing a reason Jake Gyllenhaal's Quentin Beck could trick him. However, in either case, he retains the same overall function. Specifically, in the last example, it is arguable that any deceit of the audience concerning the antagonist's true intentions relies on the trust it might have built towards Nick Fury's exposition function. In other words, the audience could only be deceived because they are used to trusting this character's information. The manner of its appearance marks Nick Fury's occurrence as greatly independent from one another, requiring only minimal knowledge to understand. As such, the *Index Manifestation* of Nick Fury does not form a *Shared Narrative* across its different appearances but does draw the *Narrative Entities* closer together. All of this leads to the realization that the *Index Manifestation* Nick Fury reoccurs with the clear narrative function of providing exposition and helping the plot along instead of strengthening the interrelation through a *Shared Narrative*.

Within the context of speculative fiction and, therefore, Shared Universe-based speculative *Narrative Entities*, a narrative has to provide necessary exposition. The MCU apparently outsourced part of each *Manifestation's* need for exposition to an unattached *Index Manifestation* in the form of Nick Fury. While such a character cannot (and probably) should not offer all exposition, having an *Index Manifestation* attached to a reasonable explanation for holding all necessary information and having a good reason for not sharing all of it provides a reasonable tool for different *Narrative Entities* to deliver necessary explanation without setting up an additional *Index Manifestation* of its own.

Agent Peggy Carter   In her comic book representation, the *Index Manifestation* Peggy Carter is generally associated with the Captain America Narrative. Therefore, Hayley Atwell's version of the character makes her first appearance in *Captain America: The First Avenger*. In *Captain America: The Winter Soldier*, Atwell was aged into her 90s via CGI for a scene with Chris Evans's Steve Rogers[141]. The character also finds mention in *Captain America: Civil War* but does not appear on-screen. The relation to the Captain America narrative holds in her appearances within the team narrative. She is part of Steve Rogers's vision in *Avengers: Age of Ultron*. Peggy Carter also appears in multiple time periods in *Avengers: Endgame*. However, all her appearances associate her with Steve Rogers: He sees her working in her office in 1970, and he travels back to 1940 to be with her at the end of the film. As such, she is marked as part of the Captain America *index*, even when her appearances occur in the team narrative[142].

Peggy Carter warrants special mention regarding the interrelation of different *Narrative Entities* because of the ABC series *Agent Carter* – which will be discussed in a later chapter – and her appearance in *Ant-Man*. In the latter, the character is aged into her

---

141   https://www.fxguide.com/fxfeatured/captain-america-the-winter-soldier-reaching-new-heights/, retrieved September 21st, 2021
142   For screenshots of all Peggy Carter's appearances in the MCU consult https://marvelcinematicuniverse.fandom.com/wiki/Peggy_Carter/Gallery

late 60s and is featured in the film's opening scene, which takes place in 1989. However, while Hayley Atwell plays the character in each instant, her appearance holds no other *semiotic cue* directly associated with her established representation. Additionally, she is never named within *Ant-Man*'s opening scene (in contrast to Howard Stark), leaving the *Index Manifestation* open for interpretation. Still, Hayley Atwell's presence in the scene alone without the use of other *semiotic cues* presents an interesting case for the strength of an actor/actress as a *semiotic cue* in the composition of an *Index Manifestation*. Despite the overall change in representation, specifically in *Ant-Man*, an informed audience will – due to context and previous representations – associate Hayley Atwell's presence with an older version of Peggy Carter, despite the absence of other *semiotic cues* associated with the *Index Manifestation*. Assuming an actor's or actress's position as a *semiotic cue* within an established context is accurate, audio-visual productions outside of animation have a unique advantage in the creation of a Shared Universe, as in some cases, the actor will provide a means of interrelation if the necessary context has been established.

Infinity Stones/Thanos All overarching *Index Manifestations* up to this point revolved around characters. However, as all *Index Manifestations* theoretically can interrelate *Narrative Entities*, using objects or McGuffins within an overarching interconnecting capacity is possible. Adapted from the Marvel Comic universe, the Infinity Stones are six gem-like objects, each representing a different characteristic of existence – power, reality, time, space, mind, and soul. Within the MCU, not everybody can wield an Infinity Stone, made apparent by Lee Pace's Ronan the Accuser's disbelief when Chris Pratt's Peter Quill/Star-Lord uses the Power Stone. Combining all six Infinity Stones in a specialized gauntlet effectively gives its bearer omnipotence. As such, an overarching series of *Transformation Triggers* spanning most of the MCU's three phases deals with the possession and location of each Infinity Stone and the parties interested in them. In their adaptation for the MCU, the Infinity Stones fused with other fantastical objects from the Marvel comics. These fusions lowered the number of McGuffins within the MCU network and created a greater potential for interrelating *Narrative Entities*, as each Infinity Stone could double as an *Index Manifestation* for a specific *Narrative Entity*[143].

As the name of the first 23 films ("The Infinity Saga") implies, the Infinity Stones should influence the interrelation of different *Narrative Entities*. The Space Stone is the MCU network's first and most prominent Infinity Stone. Fused with the Tesseract, the Space Stone appears in *Thor, Captain America: The First Avenger, The Avengers, Thor: Ragnarok, Avengers: Infinity War, Captain Marvel*, and *Avengers: Endgame*[144]. Up to being crushed into its original form in *Avengers: Infinity War*, the Tesseract retains its overall representation and *semiotic cues*. This *Index Manifestation* wanders through multiple *Manifestations* due to a continued change of ownership. The Tesseract's change of ownership connects several *Narrative Entities* across all phases, especially the MCU's Thor, Captain America, and Captain Marvel Narrative. Within the same vein, the Mind Stone is fused to another

---

143 For screenshots of the Infinity Stones in their gem form within the MCU consult https://marvelcinematicuniverse.fandom.com/wiki/Infinity_Stones/Gallery

144 For screenshots of this *Index Manifestation*'s appearances in the MCU consult https://marvelcinematicuniverse.fandom.com/wiki/Tesseract/Gallery

Index Manifestation within the MCU. In *Avengers: Age of Ultron*, Thor's vision reveals that the Mind Stone is hidden in Loki's scepter. The scepter appears in *The Avengers*, *Captain America: The Winter Soldier*, and *Avengers: Age of Ultron*. In the latter film, Ultron destroys the scepter, revealing the Mind Stone. Incorporated into the android Vision, the Mind Stone continues to appear in *Captain America: Civil War* and *Avengers: Infinity War*. Thanos retrieves the Mind Stone in *Avengers: Endgame*[145]. As this Infinity Stone's appearances relate exclusively to the MCU's Captain America and the team narratives, it does not provide much additional interrelation other than to the remaining Infinity Stones. Fused with the Aether, the Reality Stone appears as a fluid-like cloud in *Thor: The Dark World*. At the end of the film, the Aether is handed over to the Collector. It remains with the Collector until *Avengers: Infinity War*, in which Thanos retrieves it from him[146]. Appearing in only two *Manifestations*, the Reality Stone only binds the MCU's Thor Narrative somewhat to the MCU's Guardian of the Galaxy Narrative, as both of their *Manifestations* within the second phase deal with the existence and danger of an Infinity Stone. The Power Stone provides the direct McGuffin of *Guardians of The Galaxy* as all factions in the film attempt to retrieve it. As such, the orb containing the Power Stone changes hands frequently and ends up with the Nova Corps – an MCU's Guardians of the Galaxy Narrative's *Index Manifestation*. *Guardians of the Galaxy* also conveys crucial information on the Infinity Stones, explaining that they "can only be brandished by beings of extraordinary strength"[147], which becomes relevant in their use in *Avengers: Infinity War* and *Avengers: Endgame*. Thanos retrieves the Power Stone off-screen before the events of *Avengers: Infinity War*[148]. Thor mentions that Thanos "already has the Power Stone because he stole it last week when he decimated Xandar."[149] The Power Stone ties the MCU's Guardians of the Galaxy Narrative a little more to the other *Narrative Entities* through a presumed relationship between the different stones. Additionally, the scene in which the Collector explains the Infinity Stones contains shots of images of the Tesseract and the Aether, reiterating their existence and tying the different representations slightly closer together. The Time Stone sits within the Eye of Agamotto, a significant *Index Manifestation* of the Dr. Strange Narrative and usually a mark of his position as Sorcerer Supreme. It does not change status or place within the MCU until *Avengers: Infinity War*. However, the Eye of Agamotto reappears in *Thor: Ragnarok*, in which Dr. Strange wears it throughout his interactions with Thor. Like the Power Stone, the Time Stone ties a *Narrative Entity* (which otherwise has only a loose connection to other *Narrative Entities*) to others within the network through the relationship between the stones. The entire story and collection of the

---

145 For screenshots of this *Index Manifestation*'s appearances as scepter and as gem consult https://marvelcinematicuniverse.fandom.com/wiki/Scepter/Gallery and https://marvelcinematicuniverse.fandom.com/wiki/Mind_Stone/Gallery

146 For screenshots of this *Index Manifestation*'s appearances as cloud and as gem consult https://marvelcinematicuniverse.fandom.com/wiki/Reality_Stone/Gallery

147 *Guardians of the Galaxy*. Directed by James Gunn. Performances by Chris Pratt and Zoe Saldana. Marvel Studios, 2014. 00:57:35

148 For screenshots of this *Index Manifestation*'s appearances consult https://marvelcinematicuniverse.fandom.com/wiki/Power_Stone/Gallery

149 *Avengers: Infinity War*. Directed by Anthony Russo and Joe Russo. Marvel Studios, 2018. 00:33:31

Soul Stone is part of *Avengers: Infinity War*. As such, it has no relevance in the interrelation of the *Narrative Entities* within the 'Infinity Saga'.

Concerning the interrelating effect of the Infinity Stones, it is interesting to note that while the singular *Index Manifestations* of the specific stones have little influence on connecting different *Narrative Entities*, the relationship of the stones themselves serves as a low-level interrelation. This connection through separate *Index Manifestations* with a significant relationship is chiefly used to tie newer *Narrative Entities* with less overt and meaningful connections to the overall network (*Guardians of the Galaxy, Doctor Strange, Captain Marvel*). Additionally, it becomes clear that among the first *Narrative Entities*, Thor holds the strongest relation to the Infinity Stones, as the character has the most interaction with them across the 23 films. Aside from his connection to the Space and Mind Stone through *The Avengers* and *Avengers: Age of Ultron*, the Reality Stone appears, up to *Avengers: Infinity War*, solely in *Thor: The Dark World*. Additionally, Thor meets Dr. Strange, who is wearing the Time Stone, in *Thor: Ragnarok*. Despite the Power Stone's connection to the *Guardians of The Galaxy*, Thor tells the Guardians how Thanos came into its possession. In the course of different *Manifestations*, Thor presents some relationship to four of the six Infinity Stones. This relationship appears significant because from the three initial *Narrative Entities* forming Phase 1, two (Iron Man and Captain America) formed a complex *Shared Narrative* revolving around Earth's entry into a more expansive, more dangerous universe. Without such a *Shared Narrative*, the MCU's Thor Narrative garners significance for the management of the Shared Universe by effectively creating a second overarching 'storyline' following the appearance of the Infinity Stones. Both later cumulate into the larger conflict presented in *Avengers: Infinity War* and *Avengers: Endgame*.

The Infinity Stones exemplify that the association between *Index Manifestations* can interrelate *Narrative Entities*. Despite never appearing in their *Manifestations*, the Power Stone, for example, connects the MCU's Captain Marvel and the Dr. Strange Narrative to the MCU's Guardians of the Galaxy Narrative solely by an established relationship between the different stones. Furthermore, their existence shows how touching upon a splintered set of *Index Manifestations* can elevate the importance of a *Narrative Entity*, in this case, the MCU's Thor Narrative.

3.1.1.5 MCU-conclusion

Within a network, singular *Manifestations* appear to take on various degrees of responsibility for the entanglement of *Narrative Entities*. The most apparent and minor approach is the inclusion of post-credit scenes, which ideally create anticipation and interest in upcoming films via the use of foreign – meaning not usually associated with that specific *Narrative Entity* – *Index Manifestations*. The simple use of foreign *Index Manifestations* can rise to not only an appearance but even an essential function within the main plot of a *Manifestation*. Acknowledging different changes within the overall fabric of the network as well as its overall setting equally supports the interrelation of *Narrative Entities*. Here, simple single *Transformation Triggers* hint at interconnections. At the same time, *Trigger Waves* and *Shared Narratives* indicate and help organize the ever more complex relationships and causalities between multiple *Narrative Entities* and their *Manifestations*. If not consciously conceived in a manner detached from these processes, each following *Manifestation* increasingly relies on previously released material for its network of *Nar-*

rative Entities. Every Manifestation within a network that relies on another Manifestation (to some degree) serves an informed audience. However, how the MCU employs the different techniques discussed here indicates the potential of controlling and gradually increasing such interdependence between Manifestations and their Narrative Entities. With only an informed or skilled audience in mind, such a gradual increase appears engaging but overall impractical. Suppose such a gradual application of Narrative Reliance is related to the notion of a casual audience. In that case, the education of that audience to an informed one is conceivable and – from the producers' point of view – desirable. In other words, it is possible that by gradually increasing the interdependence of Manifestations, the MCU network established a manner to transform a casual audience into an informed one. Interestingly, the first Manifestations hinging on connections greater than mere allusion appears only after the first team narrative, *The Avengers*. With the beginning of Phase 2, even Manifestations for specific Narrative Entities begin to rely on an informed audience. Despite the advantageous process for creating an informed audience, films, due to their relatively high production cost, might need to engage a subset of a casual audience to remain financially successful. The need to engage both audience types necessitates a delicate balance between films with a limited-to-non-existent Narrative Reliance and those with high levels of interdependency, independent from the existence of an informed audience. This connects to the different usages of wandering Index Manifestations but also to the various applications of Transformation Triggers, Trigger Waves, and Shared Narratives. With an escalation in the interrelation of established Narrative Entities, the need to please a casual audience demands the use of Manifestations with a lesser relation to the overall network to avoid recreating the avant-garde elitism associated with the superhero comic book. *Doctor Strange* and *Guardians of the Galaxy* avoid any Narrative Reliance, merely using allusion and post-credit scenes (which exist outside of the film's plot structure) to please informed audiences, but ultimately allow a casual audience to engage with the film without any need to engage with previous parts of the network. The combination of these approaches allows for the creation of Narrative Entities for casual audiences, which can initiate a process of making them informed ones, independent from their initial moment of engagement. It also provides the means of balancing a narrower, specialized viewer base with a broader, less engaged one.

On a mechanical level, Index Manifestations associated with a specific Narrative Entity wandering into the Manifestation of another Narrative Entity provide the foundation of interrelation. The specificity of the representation and the overall number of Index Manifestations involved in the crossing stabilizes such connections. Within the MCU's first phase, the transposition of Index Manifestations associated with a specific Narrative Entity remains low, mainly existing as hints or allusions. However, with continued progression, the use of transposed Index Manifestations becomes more and more commonplace within specific Manifestations and among various members of the overall network. The appearance of Manifestations constructed from Index Manifestations based on different Narrative Entities (i.e., a team narrative) serves as a clear indicator of a shared imaginary space or world created from the interaction of different Narrative Entities. As the balanced approach to audiences indicates, the escalated use of foreign Index Manifestations is not universal or level across the network. Each Narrative Entity appears to increase its interrelation with the network and/or another Narrative Entity independent from existing and progressing states of entanglement of the overall network. Aside from allowing different *Narrative Entities* to engage with the network regarding their individual needs, these independent levels of interaction allow new additions to be introduced to a network at any level of interconnection. The use of *Transformation Triggers* and *Trigger Waves* appear to follow a similarly escalating pattern as *Index Manifestations*. However, where wandering *Index Manifestations* appear early on in the formation of the MCU network, the interrelating effect of *Transformation Triggers* only takes hold with the first team narrative and initially becomes prominent after it. After this process of interrelation is established in Phase 2, it is used to a degree that allows for the creation of *Manifestations* geared dominantly to an informed audience or avoided to a degree that allows for the creation of *Manifestations* geared dominantly to a casual one.

Appearing as the pinnacle of interrelation via *Trigger Waves*, *Shared Narratives* do not follow the escalating expansion of *Index Manifestations* and *Transformation Triggers* in relation to connecting *Narrative Entities*. While they do interconnect *Narrative Entities*, they, more importantly, provide a semblance of order to the different *Manifestations* and the *Transformation Triggers* within them. This order extends to the gradual interdependency of *Narrative Entities* on one another. The *Shared Narrative* of Phil Coulson determines the order in which the different Manifestations occur and creates a line of gradual expansion concerning the overall Shared Universe. While informed audiences are chiefly aware of such an order, it also allows casual audiences to potentially 'discover' the way the different *Manifestations* are meant to be viewed, coaxing them into the process that could make them informed audiences.

In conclusion, the analysis of the whole network shows an escalation of interrelation within the network of *Narrative Entities*. The levels of interrelation of *Narrative Entities* are managed through the acknowledgment of *Transformation Triggers* and *Trigger Waves* as well as the usage of wandering *Index Manifestations*. Hereby, a *Manifestation*'s degree of *Narrative Reliance* on either determines the ideal audience for that *Manifestation*. An escalation of *Narrative Reliance* over an increasing number of *Manifestations* and *Narrative Entities* allows for the gradual education of a casual audience into an informed one. Within this complex of escalation, *Shared Narratives* imply an order among the *Manifestations*.

3.1.2 The Marvel Netflix Universe (MNU)

The second network of *Narrative Entities* within this paper consists of the Marvel Series released on the streaming platform *Netflix*. Containing six series – *Daredevil, Jessica Jones, Luke Cage, Iron Fist,* and *The Punisher* – with two or three seasons each, the Netflix series form intricate interrelations. According to the different producers, the Netflix series and the MCU films are meant to relate to one another in some fashion[150].

Within the context of this analysis, it should be noted that the techniques presented and used here could also be used to describe the relationship of singular episodes within

---

150 Hibberd, Jane. "Daredevil: 7 things we learned about Netflix's new series". *Entertainment Weekly*. December 29th, 2014. https://ew.com/article/2014/12/29/daredevil6/?hootPostID=86d97ba533da5 f593b1f0d7aca86d91, retrieved September 21st, 2021

the season of a series. As *Manifestations* formally can describe a single episode and the relationship between episodes also hinges on the retention of *Index Manifestation*, acknowledgment of *Transformation Triggers*, and singular episodes' reliance on previous ones, the collection of all episodes within and across different seasons formally connect into the traditional structure of an overarching series. As this research focuses on the creation of a network of *Narrative Entities*, the analysis presented here takes the interrelation of the singular episodes within the season of a series as a given. Additionally, it describes complete seasons as one *Manifestation* and focuses on the relationships between the different seasons of different *Narrative Entities*. As within a multi-season series, *Index Manifestations* reoccur from episode to episode and season to season, the research equally assumes a connection between the seasons of the same series. As the research is not concerned with the connections between *Manifestations* of the same *Narrative Entity*, such interrelations generally are not mentioned within the following analysis.

The MNU series and MCU films are analyzed as separate networks, as the unity of medium and producer makes a stronger interrelation among the Netflix series and the cinematic films likely to be more prominent than between them. Beddows and Harvey already described that recipients of transmedia products tend to remain within the medium of their original reception[151]. In other words, an audience that encountered Star Wars in film first is more likely to follow the franchise within the medium of film predominantly, neglecting other iterations from television, novelization, or comic books. Jenkins and Harvey mention this as a difficulty of transmedia storytelling's audience engagement. Within this research, an audience's tendency to consume a franchise along the same medium provides a reason for examining the networks of the series and the films singularly first, in contrast to any other means of organizing the material. Later, the different networks are interrelated to one another.

As the material – concerning its entire viewing hours – is more extensive than the MCU film material, the following description avoids the direct reference to singular scenes in favor of a grander overview of the applied techniques. As such, the following description mentions aspects covered across the entire *Manifestation* or cites singular episodes over specific scenes. Hereby, singular episodes are quoted as a whole when the aspect referenced appears across a single or several episodes but are quoted with a specific time stamp when the mentioned aspect only appears once within an episode.

Collectively, the six series adapted from Marvel Comics for the streaming platform Netflix are often (but not universally) referred to as the Marvel Netflix Universe (MNU). This network contains thirteen seasons, with all but two seasons running for 13 episodes. As with the analysis of the previous network, the MNU analysis describes connections in the order of the *Manifestations*' release.

3.1.2.1 Daredevil, Season 1 (2015)

As the first *Manifestation* of the MNU network, *Daredevil*[152] S1 sets up several *Index Manifestations* and *Transformation Triggers* later used to interrelate multiple *Narrative Entities*. All of these are discussed in the section on overarching connections, as they are used to

---

151 Harvey, Colin. *Fantastic Transmedia*. London: Palgrave Macmillian, 2015, p.128ff
152 *Daredevil*. Created by Drew Goddard. Marvel Television/ABC Studios. 2015–2018

interrelate more than two *Narrative Entities*. Otherwise, *Daredevil S1* does not include any *Index Manifestation* associated with another *Narrative Entity*.

Following the setup of the MCU film network analysis, the MNU's version of Daredevil provides the center of the network with the other *Narrative Entities* placed in relation to it.

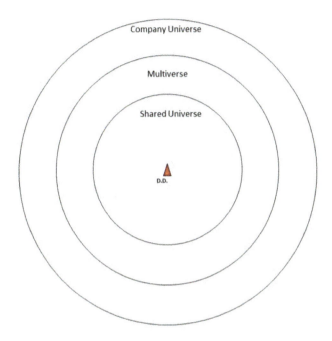

3.1.2.2 Jessica Jones, Season 1 (2015)

The first season of the MNU's second series connects to a Luke Cage Narrative through the introduction of that *Narrative Entity*'s hero character and part of his backstory. In a fashion similar to *Captain America: Civil War*, *Jessica Jones*[153] S1 introduces Mike Coulter's Luke Cage, weaving the character into the plot of the series[154]. Luke Cage's appearances indicate some of the character's backstory but leave the more significant part of it to its own *Manifestation*. Kyrsten Ritter's Jessica Jones stalks and protects Luke Cage, feeling guilty for killing his lover, Parisa Fitz-Henley's Reva Conners. Jessica Jones discovers that Cage has powers just like her. The discovery of their similar and unique situation brings them closer together, while the revelation of Jessica Jones's involvement in Reva's murder emotionally separates them again. The series' antagonist, David Tenant's Kilgrave, later utilizes Luke Cage in conflict with Jessica Jones. In addition to introducing a transposed *Index Manifestation*, *Jessica Jones S1* begins a series of *Transformation Triggers* revolving around the discovery of Luke Cage's and Reva Conners's past. It begins with the reve-

---

153 *Jessica Jones*. Created by Melissa Rosenberg. Marvel Television/ABC Studios. 2015–2019
154 For screenshots of the character's appearances within the overall network consult https://marvelcinematicuniverse.fandom.com/wiki/Luke_Cage/Gallery

lation that the titular character murdered Reva under the influence of her mind-controlling nemesis, Kilgrave. Kilgrave originally was after a USB stick containing information on human experimentation. Reva's connection to human experimentation continues in *Luke Cage*[155] *S1* and *S2*. All *Transformation Triggers* here do not alter the *Index Manifestation* but gradually reveal the backstory related to other *Index Manifestations* by unearthing a link between Luke Cage, Kilgrave, and Jessica Jones.

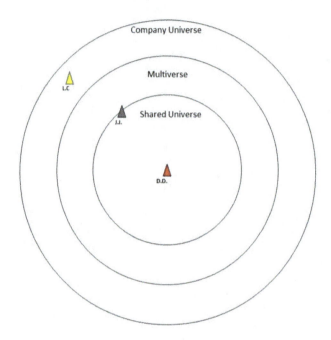

In addition to a connection with the MNU's Luke Cage Narrative, the character Samantha Reyes ties the MNU's Jessica Jones to the MNU's Daredevil Narrative[156]. As the character has a total of seven appearances, and six of them occur in *Manifestations* associated with Daredevil, she is an *Index Manifestation* of that *Narrative Entity*. Portrayed by Michelle Hurd, Samantha Reyes is marked by her position as a New York District Attorney. Aside from her profession, she retains a consistent hairstyle throughout her appearances (except in her final one). While consistently professional, her wardrobe changes frequently throughout *Daredevil S2*, devaluing it as a *semiotic cue*. Within *Jessica Jones S1*, Samantha Reyes is the District Attorney in the episode "AKA Smile"[157], wanting to prosecute Jessica Jones for the murder of Kilgrave. *Jessica Jones S1* also relates to the

---

155   *Luke Cage*. Created by Cheo Hodari Coker. Marvel Television/ABC Studios. 2016–2018
156   For screenshots of the character's appearances within the overall network consult https://marvelcinematicuniverse.fandom.com/wiki/Samantha_Reyes/Gallery
157   "AKA Smile". *Jessica Jones*. Created by Melissa Rosenberg. Season 1, episode 13. Marvel Television/ABC Studios. 2015–2019. 00:46:00

previous *Daredevil S1* via the appearance of Rosaria Dawson's Claire Temple, who appears throughout the episode "AKA Smile"[158].

The MNU's Jessica Jones Narrative ties closely to the MNU's Luke Cage Narrative, whose main character appears in seven episodes of *Jessica Jones S1*'s 13 episodes. In contrast, the connection with the MNU's Daredevil Narrative is tangential, leaning on a singular appearance of a significant *Index Manifestation*, Claire Temple, and on an obscure one in the form of Samantha Reyes. As such, the Jessica Jones Narrative starts on the border between a Shared Universe and a Multiverse relationship with the MNU's Daredevil Narrative but has a clear Shared Universe relationship with the MNU's Luke Cage Narrative, which in itself remains in a Company Universe position due to it receiving its own *Manifestation* (and therefore establishing its own *Narrative Entity*) later on in the process.

3.1.2.3 Daredevil, Season 2 (2016)

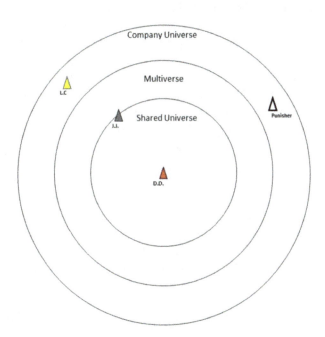

The second season of *Daredevil* repeats the technique employed by *Captain America: Civil War* and *Jessica Jones S1*. Introducing Jon Bernthal's Frank Castle/The Punisher[159], the MNU's Daredevil Narrative connects directly to the later-released series *The Punisher*[160]. The connection between Frank Castle/The Punisher and Matthew Cox's Matt Murdock/Daredevil follows a similar structure as the one between Jessica Jones and Luke Cage. As

---

158 For screenshots of Claire Temple's appearances within the overall network consult https://marvel cinematicuniverse.fandom.com/wiki/Claire_Temple/Gallery

159 For screenshots of Frank Castle/The Punisher's appearances within the overall network consult ht tps://marvelcinematicuniverse.fandom.com/wiki/Punisher/Gallery

160 *The Punisher*. Created by Steve Lightfoot. Marvel Television/ABC Studios. 2017–2019

with Luke Cage, the audience discovers enough about the Punisher to inform his position within the Daredevil narrative, but the character is fleshed out in his own *Manifestation*. Additionally, *Daredevil S2* introduces Danny Johnson's Benjamin Donovan[161], who later reappears in both seasons of *Luke Cage* and *Daredevil S3*. The character is established with several *semiotic cues*, grey temples and a plum of grey hair above his forehead. Additionally, he has a thin mustache in all appearances. In Donovan's function as a lawyer for affluent criminals, a suit and tie also appear as weaker *semiotic cues*. In contrast to other lawyer characters, his clothing is not kept fully coherent throughout different representations. Benjamin Donovan appears in two episodes of *Daredevil S2*, "Seven Minutes in Heaven"[162] and "The Man in the Box"[163]. As mentioned in the previous chapter, Michelle Hurd's Samantha Reyes[164] connects the *Narrative Entities* of the MNU's Daredevil and Jessica Jones. She was introduced in the final episode of *Jessica Jones S1* before appearing in six episodes of *Daredevil S2*.

Daredevil S2 directly ties into the *Transformation Triggers* of *The Defenders*. At the end of the second season, Élodie Yung's Elektra is shot and placed in a resurrection coffin. These *Transformation Triggers* are later addressed in the team narrative and continue a *Trigger Wave* in regard to her relationship with Matthew Cox's Matt Murdock/Daredevil.

As with *Jessica Jones S1* and the character Luke Cage, the introduction of its main character attaches the MNU's Punisher Narrative to a Shared Universe relationship with the MNU's Daredevil Narrative. The appearance of Samantha Reyes does not influence the relationship between the established *Narrative Entities*, as the *Index Manifestation*'s effect has been established. Ben Donovan will draw the MNU's Daredevil Narrative and Luke Cage Narrative closer together after his appearance in *Luke Cage S1*.

3.1.2.4 Luke Cage, Season 1 (2016)

Due to a previously established connection, the first season of the MNU's Luke Cage Narrative relates mainly to the MNU's Jessica Jones Narrative. Appearing in 38 of the 39 episodes of *Jessica Jones*, Rachael Taylor's Trish Walker unequivocally is part of an MNU Jessica Jones *index* network. The character reiterates the connection between Luke Cage and Jessica Jones via the radio show 'Trish Talk'. An episode of the show discussing the merits and dangers of Luke Cage's presence in Harlem appears as a voice-over at the beginning of "Suckas Need Bodyguards". Within this voice-over, the show is identified by name and Rachael Taylor's voice[165]. *Luke Cage S1*, to some degree, relies on the introduction of its hero character in a previous *Manifestation* as well as a fair share of *Transformation Triggers* from *Jessica Jones S1* (relationships with certain characters, revelations about

---

161 For screenshots of this character's appearances within the overall network consult https://marvelcinematicuniverse.fandom.com/wiki/Benjamin_Donovan/Gallery

162 "Seven Minutes in Heaven". *Daredevil*. Created by Drew Goddard. Season 2, episode 9. Marvel Television/ABC Studios. 2015–2018. 00:02:11/00:06:43

163 "The Man in the Box". *Daredevil*. Created by Drew Goddard. Season 2, episode 10. Marvel Television/ABC Studios. 2015–2018. 00:20:20

164 For screenshots of the character's appearances within the overall network consult https://marvelcinematicuniverse.fandom.com/wiki/Samantha_Reyes/Gallery

165 "Suckas Need Bodyguards". *Luke Cage*. Created by Cheo Hodari Coker. Season 1, episode 6. Marvel Television/ABC Studios. 2016–2018. 00:01:24

the past, injuries sustained...) to move the narration forward. While the character Jessica Jones does not appear in *Luke Cage S1*, Reva Conners's backstory continues in the series.

The MNU's Luke Cage Narrative prominently connects to the MNU's Daredevil Narrative via the *Shared Narrative* of Claire Temple[166]. Rosaria Dawson's Claire Temple appears in eight episodes of either's *Manifestation* before the team narrative. The exact nature of her *Shared Narrative* is discussed later, but she unequivocally interrelates the two *Narrative Entities*. Danny Johnson's Benjamin Donovan[167] strengthens the relationship between the MNU's Luke Cage and Daredevil Narrative. He retains his *semiotic cues* of grey temples and a grey plum of hair above his forehead and appears in the episodes "Manifest", defending Mahershala Ali's Cornell 'Cottonmouth' Stokes[168], and "Blowin' up the Spot", interfering with the interrogation of a witness[169].

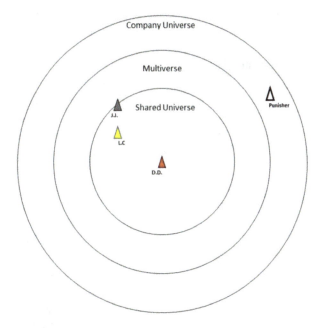

Marquis Rodriguez's Darryl is mainly featured in the first season of *Iron Fist*[170], in which he is a promising student of Colleen Wing's Chikara Dojo and a member of The

---

166 For screenshots of Claire Temple's appearances within the overall network consult https://marvel cinematicuniverse.fandom.com/wiki/Claire_Temple/Gallery
167 For screenshots of this character's appearances within the overall network consult https://marvel cinematicuniverse.fandom.com/wiki/Benjamin_Donovan/Gallery
168 "Manifest". *Luke Cage*. Created by Cheo Hodari Coker. Season 1, episode 7. Marvel Television/ABC Studios. 2016–2018. 00:01:41
169 "Blowing up the Spot". *Luke Cage*. Created by Cheo Hodari Coker. Season 1, episode 8. Marvel Television/ABC Studios. 2016–2018. 00:19:06
170 *Iron Fist*. Created by Scott Buck. Marvel Television/ABC Studios. 2017–2018

Hand. Appearing in five episodes of *Iron Fist S1*, the character presents as an *Index Manifestation* of that *Narrative Entity*. As a general representation of the youths recruited by The Hand, Darryl carries no specific signifying *semiotic cues*, which help to interrelate *Narrative Entities*. However, Marquis Rodriguez makes a cameo appearance in the *Luke Cage* episode "Take It Personal"[171], when the police shake down the residence of Harlem for Luke Cage's whereabouts. However, outside of using the same actor, no indication is given that the boy in Luke Cage is meant to be the character later shown in *Iron Fist S1*, making this more of an allusion or interrelation solely for skilled audiences[172].

The combination of *Index Manifestations* and *Narrative Reliance* leaves the MNU's Luke Cage Narrative closest to the MNU's Jessica Jones Narrative, followed by the MNU's Daredevil Narrative. While a potential *Index Manifestation* from the MNU's Iron Fist Narrative appears, it has merely a few seconds on screen and does not carry any identifying *semiotic cues* other than using the same actor. Assuming that only a skilled audience would make the connection, the MNU's Iron Fist Narrative would barely appear in a Company Universe relationship with the MNU's Luke Cage Narrative at this point.

3.1.2.5 Iron Fist, Season 1 (2017)

The last *Narrative Entity* introduced to the MNU network before the team narrative, Iron Fist's primary connections comes in the form of three transposed *Index Manifestations*, Rosaria Dawson's Claire Temple, Wai Ching Ho's Madame Gao, and Carrie-Anne Moss's Jeri Hogarth. All three form longer overarching connections and, as such, are discussed in detail in their own chapter but should be briefly mentioned here for the purpose of immanent interrelation between specific *Narrative Entities*. Claire Temple appears in eight episodes of *Daredevil* and *Luke Cage* at the beginning of *Iron Fist S1*, relating her firmly with either *Narrative Entity*. She takes part in six of the *Iron Fist S1*'s 13 episodes[173]. *Daredevil* also introduced Madame Gao, who is in six episodes of the series and takes part in nine episodes of the first Iron Fist *Manifestation*[174]. The *Index Manifestation* Jeri Hogarth ultimately appears in 34 of the 36 episodes of *Jessica Jones*, meaning she is firmly associable with that *Narrative Entity*. The character appears in three episodes of *Iron Fist S1*[175]. All other connections solely exist as mentions of *Index Manifestations* in dialogue. A veiled reference by Rosaria Dawson's Claire Temple in "The Blessing of Many Fractures"[176] relates to Luke Cage's status as an inmate of Seagate Penitentiary, to which he was sent at the end of *Luke Cage S1*. Claire Temple also uses Luke Cage's catchphrase 'Sweet Christmas' on

---

171 "Take it Personal". *Luke Cage*. Created by Cheo Hodari Coker. Season 1, episode 10. Marvel Television/ABC Studios. 2016–2018. 00:15:11

172 For screenshots of this character's appearances within the overall network consult https://marvelcinematicuniverse.fandom.com/wiki/Darryl/Gallery

173 For screenshots of Claire Temple's appearances within the overall network consult https://marvelcinematicuniverse.fandom.com/wiki/Claire_Temple/Gallery

174 For screenshots of Madame Gao's appearances within the overall network consult https://marvelcinematicuniverse.fandom.com/wiki/Madame_Gao/Gallery

175 For screenshots of this character's appearances within the overall network consult https://marvelcinematicuniverse.fandom.com/wiki/Jeri_Hogarth/Gallery

176 "The Blessing of Many Fractures". *Iron Fist*. Created by Scott Buck. Season 1, episode 8. Marvel Television/ABC Studios. 2017–2018. 00:17:04

occasion. The series relates to the MNU's Daredevil Narrative in several instances. Tom Pelphrey's Ward Meachum compares Finn Jones's Danny Rand to Daredevil in "Eight Diagram Dragon Palm"[177]. Wai Ching Ho's Madame Gao mentions the previously established moniker 'Devil of Hell's Kitchen' (Daredevil) and refers to "the man with unbreakable skin" (Luke Cage) in "Felling Tree with Roots"[178]. She also states their names, using the superhero alias in the case of Daredevil, in the episode "The Mistress of All Agonies"[179]. The two series also connect via mentions of the Dogs of Hell biker gang. One of three criminal organizations targeted by the Punisher in *Daredevil S2*, the Dogs of Hell are mentioned when Madame Gao discusses plans to distribute a new drug in "Felling Tree with Roots"[180]. Additionally, the New York Bulletin editor-in-chief Mitchell Ellison and reporter Karen Page are mentioned when a reporter makes a call in "Eight Diagram Dragon Palm"[181]. Karen Page is a permanent part of Daredevil's *Index Manifestations*, appearing in all 39 episodes of *Daredevil* and relating to the main character as a love interest, friend, and ally. She also becomes a reporter at the New York Bulletin at the end of *Daredevil S1*, bringing her constantly in contact with its editor-in-chief Mitchell Ellison. *Iron Fist S1* also includes a vague allusion to Jessica Jones when Jessica Stroup's Joy Meachum mentions hiring a private investigator who "was worth every penny...when she was sober"[182], alluding to Jessica Jones's profession and her constant drinking in the series.

While the first Iron Fist *Manifestation* pursues connections to all other *Narrative Entities* within the network, it mostly confirms its existence in a similar imaginary space via the three transposed *Index Manifestations*. Without the existence of three network-spanning connections, Claire Temple, Madame Gao, and Jeri Hogarth, the *Narrative Entity* would have no apparent relationship with the rest of the network, as the different allusions only work in the context of established *Index Manifestations*. Hereby, the MNU's Iron Fist Narrative has the closest relationship with the MNU's Daredevil Narrative, which holds associations via Claire Temple and Madame Gao, followed by the MNU's Luke Cage Narrative through Claire Temple. Appearing in only three episodes, Jeri Hogarth provides a connection to the MNU's Jessica Jones Narrative but is also the weakest interrelation in comparison.

---

[177] "Eight Diagram Dragon Palm". *Iron Fist*. Created by Scott Buck. Season 1, episode 4. Marvel Television/ABC Studios. 2017–2018, 00:02:32

[178] "Felling Tree with Roots". *Iron Fist*. Created by Scott Buck. Season 1, episode 7. Marvel Television/ABC Studios. 2017–2018, 00:28:47

[179] "The Mistress of All Agonies". *Iron Fist*. Created by Scott Buck. Season 1, episode 9. Marvel Television/ABC Studios. 2017–2018, 00:10:18

[180] "Felling Tree with Roots". *Iron Fist*. Created by Scott Buck. Season 1, episode 7. Marvel Television/ABC Studios. 2017–2018, 00:34:51

[181] "Eight Diagram Dragon Palm". *Iron Fist*. Created by Scott Buck. Season 1, episode 4. Marvel Television/ABC Studios. 2017–2018, 00:39:20

[182] "The Blessing of Many Fractures". *Iron Fist*. Created by Scott Buck. Season 1, episode 8. Marvel Television/ABC Studios. 2017–2018, 00:31:06

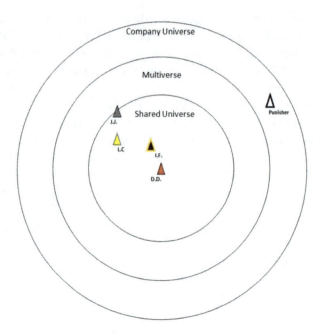

3.1.2.6 The Defenders (2017)

The Defenders[183] is Netflix's equivalent to the MCU's *The Avengers* (note the title similarity). In the series, all heroes from the other shows – namely Charlie Cox's Matt Murdock/Daredevil, Krysten Ritter's Jessica Jones, Mike Colter's Luke Cage, and Finn Jones's Iron Fist – band together to defeat a greater enemy than any of them could take on alone. Within this frame, a number of each *Narrative Entity*'s *Index Manifestations* appear in this team *Manifestation*[184]. Support characters of each series interact with one another when they are brought to the 29th Precinct Police Station, where Simone Missick's Detective Mercedes Kelly 'Misty' Knight (an *Index Manifestation* from the MNU's Luke Cage Narrative appearing in all 26 episodes of *Luke Cage*) is stationed. As with all the Avengers narratives, *The Defenders* depends on knowledge from previous *Narrative Entity*-specific *Manifestations* as the series continues and refers to crucial *Transformation Triggers*. Matthew Cox's Matt Murdock has given up his Daredevil persona at the end of *Daredevil S2*, needing to rediscover it in the course of *The Defenders*. Luke Cage and Jessica Jones's previous relationship explains their sudden alliance. Additionally, their conflict from *Jessica Jones S1* is resolved. The alteration of Foggy Nelson's appearance in *The Defenders*, in contrast to his appearance in *Daredevil S1/S2*, directly relates to his employment by Jeri Hogarth's law firm at the end of *Daredevil S2*. As such, *The Defenders* serve an informed or a skilled audience, which has a high level of knowledge from the other *Manifestations*, over a casual one.

---

183   *The Defenders*. Created by Douglas Petrie and Marco Ramirez. Marvel Television/ABC Studios. 2017
184   For screenshots of the entire series consult https://marvelcinematicuniverse.fandom.com/wiki/The_Defenders/Gallery

One specific use of *Index Manifestations* contrasting the MNU network from the MCU network is the more significant use of sets. The MCU films do not employ sets to interrelate different *Narrative Entities* significantly. As a *Manifestation* leaning on existing *Index Manifestations*, the Avengers films could have reused the sets from its contributing *Narrative Entities* in the same manner they used established characters and props. However, each Avengers film generally creates new ones for its team narrative, notably avoiding sets established in *Narrative Entity*-specific *Manifestations*. *The Avengers* takes place on the newly introduced Helicarrier and the recently completed Stark Tower, which appears in none of the Iron Man films. *Avengers: Age of Ultron* introduces Clint Barton's family home and the fictional nation of Sakovia, only reusing Stark Towers from the previous Avengers film. *Avengers: Infinity War* proves an exception as some events of the film take place in Dr. Strange's Sanctum Sanctorum – which is introduced in *Doctor Strange* and reappears in the same form in *Thor: Ragnarok* – and Wakanda – which was introduced in *Black Panther*. Otherwise, the third Avengers film creates new sets or reuses sets established in previous Avengers films. As the plot of *Avengers: Endgame* calls for a return to previous events via time travel, the use of already established *Index Manifestations* in the form of sets is more prominent. However, even here, only two places from *Narrative Entity*-specific *Manifestations* make an appearance: Thor's Asgard and the Planet Morag from *Guardians of the Galaxy*. Hereby, places are only relevant when they – like any other *Index Manifestation* – appear with their specific *semiotic cues*. Formally speaking, Dr. Strange's Sanctum Sanctorum makes an appearance in *Avengers: Endgame*. However, the film only shows the previously unseen roof instead of the previously established rooms. While the MCU films' team narratives (and all its *Manifestations*) avoid using sets for interrelation, the MNU series applies them to that end in their team narrative. Several different, unchanged sets reappear in *The Defenders*: Misty Knight's home precinct, the 29th Police Precinct Police Station[185], introduced in *Luke Cage S1*, appears in five episodes and houses several *Index Manifestations* from different *Narrative Entities* in "Take Shelter"[186] and "Fish in the Jailhouse"[187]. Colleen Wing's Chikara Dojo[188], a vital set of the MNU's Iron Fist Narrative, serves as a neutral meeting place between Luke Cage and Danny Rand/Iron Fist in the episode "Worst Behavior"[189]. The only other place aside from the 29th Police Precinct and Chikara Dojo that directly houses transposed *Index Manifestations* is Soledad Temple's Apartment. This set already made appearances in *Luke Cage S1* and *Iron Fist S1*. In the series' final episode, Elden Henson's Franklin Percy "Foggy" Nelson, who is associated with the MNU Daredevil Narrative appearing in 38 of 39 episodes, comes to the apartment to inform Luke Cage and Claire Temple about their legal situation in the episode "The

---

185   For screenshots of this *Index Manifestation*'s appearances within the overall network consult https://marvelcinematicuniverse.fandom.com/wiki/29th_Precinct_Police_Station/Gallery
186   "Take Shelter". *The Defenders*. Created by Douglas Petrie and Marco Ramirez. Season 1, episode 5. Marvel Television/ABC Studios. 2017
187   "Fish in the Jailhouse". *The Defenders*. Created by Douglas Petrie and Marco Ramirez. Season 1, episode 7. Marvel Television/ABC Studios. 2017
188   For screenshots of this *Index Manifestation*'s appearances within the overall network consult https://marvelcinematicuniverse.fandom.com/wiki/Chikara_Dojo/Gallery
189   "Worst Behavior". *The Defenders*. Created by Douglas Petrie and Marco Ramirez. Season 1, episode 3. Marvel Television/ABC Studios. 2017

Defenders"[190]. Several other recognizable sets appear in *The Defenders*, serving the interconnecting nature of a team narrative. However, while the Alias Investigation Office from *Jessica Jones*, Matt Murdock's Apartment, Pop's Barber Shop from *Luke Cage*, and several other places appear, they solely appear with their usually associated *Index Manifestations*. While their presence strengthens the interrelation between the different *Narrative Entities*, they only do so by being in the same series instead of potential interactions with another *Narrative Entity*'s *Index Manifestation*.

As the team narrative, *The Defenders* draws all *Narrative Entities* within the network closer together, ensuring a clear Shared Universe relationship.

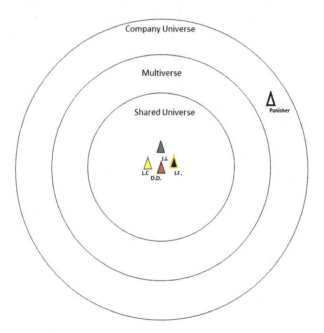

3.1.2.7 The Punisher, Season 1 (2017)

While rising out of *Daredevil S2*, *The Punisher S1* avoids most direct interrelation with other MNU Narratives. Deborah Ann Woll's Karen Page[191] and the *Index Manifestations* surrounding her (The New York Bulletin, Mitchell Ellison) appears in five episodes of the series, which maintains a relationship to the Daredevil narrative. Equally, Frank Castle's high regard for her is based on *Transformation Triggers* of *Daredevil S2* and requires some knowledge from that *Manifestation*. Otherwise, no *Index Manifestation* from another *Narrative Entity* even finds mention in the series, meaning that the MNU's Punisher Narrative merely retains a connection to the MNU Daredevil Narrative. Even regarding

---

190 "The Defenders". *The Defenders*. Created by Douglas Petrie and Marco Ramirez. Season 1, episode 8. Marvel Television/ABC Studios. 2017. 00:41:50

191 For screenshots of this character's appearances within the overall network consult https://marvel cinematicuniverse.fandom.com/wiki/Karen_Page/Gallery

Daredevil S2, the series avoids creating a *Shared Narrative* across the two *Manifestations*, as Frank Castle's first pursuit of revenge ends in *Daredevil S2*. That end is reiterated at the beginning of *The Punisher S1*, in which Frank Castle kills the last of the remaining Dogs of Hell and then retires his Punisher persona until an ex-NSA hacker reignites his quest with new evidence, effectively starting a new series of *Transformation Triggers*. As such, the series avoids a *Shared Narrative*, clearly ending the connection via *Transformation Triggers* with the MNU's Daredevil Narrative.

Within the complex of the MNU network, this *Manifestation* sets this *Narrative Entity* into a Shared Universe relationship with the MNU's Daredevil Narrative due to previously established and reiterated connections. Still, it holds a clear distance to the otherwise close network created within *The Defenders*.

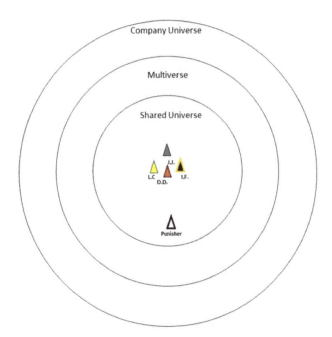

3.1.2.8 Jessica Jones, Season 2 (2018)

While close to the other *Narrative Entities* after the team narrative, the second season of *Jessica Jones* barely acknowledges any relationship with other *Narrative Entities* within the same network. The series recognizes the MNU's Daredevil Narrative through the appearance of Foggy Nelson in "AKA Sole Survivor"[192]. To some degree, the series shows an awareness of the MNU's Iron Fist Narrative through mentions of Rand Enterprises, the company owned by Finn Jones's Danny Rand/Iron Fist.

Jessica Jones S2 barely acknowledges or reacts to the *Transformation Triggers* or *Trigger Waves* from the larger team narrative. This lack of recognition partly arises due to a lim-

---

192 "AKA Sole Survivor". *Jessica Jones*. Created by Melissa Rosenberg. Season 2, episode 3. Marvel Television/ABC Studios. 2015–2019. 00:11:50

ited effect the *Transformations Triggers* of *The Defenders* has on the *Index Manifestations* of the MNU's Jessica Jones Narrative. However, it still shows a notable independence from the overall network, as the series can continue without any specific reliance on another *Narrative Entity*. This contrasts the *Manifestations* to those following the team narrative in the MCU, which showed a conscious reaction to the sudden interrelation created by their first team narrative. With only the bare minimum of acknowledgment of other *Narrative Entities* and no effect from the larger team narrative, the MNU's Jessica Jones Narrative slightly moves away from the tight-knit internal network, mostly maintaining a relationship to the MNU's Daredevil Narrative.

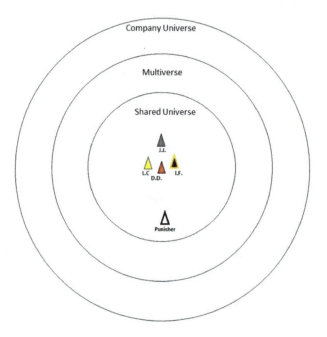

3.1.2.9 Luke Cage, Season 2 (2018)

In contrast to *Jessica Jones S2*, *Luke Cage S2* actively uses the *Index Manifestations* from other *Narrative Entities*. Most prominently, Finn Jones's Danny Rand/Iron Fist[193] accompanies the titular hero, Luke Cage, throughout the episode "The Main Ingredient"[194]. Within this appearance, the series acknowledges their interaction from *The Defenders*, mainly in a mutual agreement to protect Manhattan. They also mention each *Narrative Entity* that took part in the team narrative. Another *Index Manifestation* from the MNU's Iron

---

193   For screenshots of Danny Rand/Iron Fist's appearances in the overall network consult https://marvelcinematicuniverse.fandom.com/wiki/Iron_Fist/Gallery

194   "The Main Ingredient". *Luke Cage*. Created by Cheo Hodari Coker. Season 2, episode 10. Marvel Television/ABC Studios. 2016–2018.

Fist Narrative, Jessica Henwick's Colleen Wing[195], appears in "Wig Out"[196]. She helps Simone Missick's Misty Knight, who lost her arm during *The Defenders*, regain her confidence. Misty Knight also receives a bionic arm from Rand Enterprises, Danny Rand/Iron Fist's company, in the episode "All Souled Out"[197], indicated by the Rand Enterprise Logo on the computer used to calibrate the arm. The arm's origin is later also mentioned in dialogue. In addition to the MNU's Iron Fist Narrative, *Luke Cage S2* also relates to the *Narrative Entity* of Daredevil through Elden Henson's Foggy Nelson[198]. The character appears in several episodes, helping Luke Cage to deal with a lawsuit against him. Danny Johnson's Benjamin Donovan, who was featured in *Daredevil S2* and *Luke Cage S1*, appears more prominently in this *Manifestation* than the previous two[199]. Carrying the same *semiotic cues*, he represents a criminal suing Luke Cage for damages in "All Souled Out"[200]. The character also maintains its *semiotic cue* of protecting affluent criminals in "If It Ain't Rough, It Ain't Right"[201], when he gets Alfre Woodard's Mariah Dillard released from interrogation and legally advises Theo Rossi's Hernan 'Shades' Alvarez, an associate of Maria Dillard, until he discovers that his employer has lost all her assets. He returns to Mariah Dillard's services in "The Main Ingredient" and serves as her lawyer in all capacities until her death in "They Reminisce Over You"[202]. With 14 appearances in total, Stephen Rider's Blake Tower is in twelve episodes of *Daredevil*, firmly associating him with that *Narrative Entity*[203]. Marked by his position as a lawyer in the District Attorney's office, the character appears in the final episode of *Luke Cage S2*, "They Reminisce Over You"[204], in which he prosecutes Mariah Dillard. The connecting effect of his presence is undercut by his lack of glasses, which the character wore in every previous appearance and used in every subsequent appearance outside of the episode "Please"[205] from *Daredevil S3*, removing one of his few *semiotic cues*. Henry Yuk's Hai-Qing Yang appears in eight

---

195   For screenshots of this character's appearances within the overall network consult https://marvelcinematicuniverse.fandom.com/wiki/Colleen_Wing/Gallery
196   "Wig Out". *Luke Cage*. Created by Cheo Hodari Coker. Season 2, episode 3. Marvel Television/ABC Studios. 2016–2018. 00:24:41/00:30:25
197   "All Souled Out". *Luke Cage*. Created by Cheo Hodari Coker. Season 2, episode 5. Marvel Television/ABC Studios. 2016–2018. 00:09:08
198   For screenshots of this character's appearances within the overall network consult https://marvelcinematicuniverse.fandom.com/wiki/Foggy_Nelson/Gallery
199   For screenshots of this character's appearances within the overall network consult https://marvelcinematicuniverse.fandom.com/wiki/Benjamin_Donovan/Gallery
200   "All Souled Out". *Luke Cage*. Created by Cheo Hodari Coker. Season 2, episode 5. Marvel Television/ABC Studios. 2016–2018. 00:01:30
201   "If it ain't Rough, It ain't Right". *Luke Cage*. Created by Cheo Hodari Coker. Season 2, episode 8. Marvel Television/ABC Studios. 2016–2018.
202   "They Reminisce Over You". *Luke Cage*. Created by Cheo Hodari Coker. Season 2, episode 13. Marvel Television/ABC Studios. 2016–2018.
203   For screenshots of this character's appearances within the overall network consult https://marvelcinematicuniverse.fandom.com/wiki/Blake_Tower/Gallery
204   "They Reminisce Over You". *Luke Cage*. Created by Cheo Hodari Coker. Season 2, episode 13. Marvel Television/ABC Studios. 2016–2018. 00:00:50
205   "Please". *Daredevil*. Created by Drew Goddard. Season 3, episode 2. Marvel Television/ABC Studios. 2015–2018.

episodes within the MNU network[206]. Six of these appearances occur within *Manifestations* of the MNU's Iron Fist Narrative, associating him with that *Narrative Entity*. As the leader of a criminal organization, the character is marked by his interest in maintaining and expanding the heroin trade in New York. His appearance alters to include a beard after the first season of *Iron Fist*, which the character retains in all further representations. The bearded Hai-Qing Yang appears in two episodes of *Luke Cage S2*, "The Creator"[207] and "Can't Front on Me"[208]. In "The Creator", he is shown in Mariah Dillard's office, where they discuss running heroin through Harlem. When Maria Dillard negotiates with the head of the other crime families in "Can't Front on Me", Hai-Qing Yang supports her position. *Luke Cage S2* creates a light connection to *The Punisher S2* through the recurrence of a set. Rob Morgan's Turk Barrett interrelates several *Narrative Entities* (discussed in overarching connections) as a street-level criminal. Within the context of *Luke Cage S2*, he has opened a shop to provide Marijuana dispensaries with the necessary equipment. The shop is marked in its appearance by the presence of several bongs and other Marijuana-related equipment. Additionally, it is hidden in a closed area without windows and one sole entrance. Aside from appearing in *Luke Cage S2*'s episode "The Main Ingredient", the shop is also seen in *The Punisher S2*'s "One-Eyed Jacks"[209], where the Russian mob tries to set up Frank Castle.

In contrast to *Jessica Jones S2*, the second season of *Luke Cage* actively uses its position within a network of *Narrative Entities*, primarily by filling exchangeable support characters with established transposed *Index Manifestations*. However, it also connects more to the MNU's Iron Fist Narrative via the use of two prominent *Index Manifestations* of that *Narrative Entity* while acknowledging *Transformation Triggers* from the team narrative. Additionally, the series acknowledges the existence of the MNU's Punisher Narrative, even if only tangentially through the character of Turk Barrett. As such, the series maintains its current connections to all but two *Narrative Entities* – the MNU Jessica Jones and Daredevil Narrative – within the network. It draws closer to the MNU's Iron Fist Narrative and very lightly closer to the MNU's Punisher Narrative. The latter change in relationship only occurs because this is the first and only acknowledgement each *Narrative Entity* makes of the other. More importantly, *Luke Cage S2* repeats the pattern from the MCU, in which *Manifestations* following the team narrative re-evaluate their network of *Index Manifestations* in relation to their newly formed relationships with other *Narrative Entities*. In this case, the ability of characters to find support and help from *Index Manifestations* is associated with the MNU's Iron Fist Narrative.

---

206 For screenshots of this character's appearances within the overall network consult https://marvel cinematicuniverse.fandom.com/wiki/Hai-Qing_Yang/Gallery

207 "The Creator". *Luke Cage*. Created by Cheo Hodari Coker. Season 2, episode 11. Marvel Television/ ABC Studios. 2016–2018. 00:22:18

208 "Can't Front Me". *Luke Cage*. Created by Cheo Hodari Coker. Season 2, episode 12. Marvel Television/ ABC Studios. 2016–2018. 00:07:06

209 "One-Eyed Jacks". The Punisher. Created by Steve Lightfoot. Season 2, episode 5. Marvel Television/ ABC Studios. 2017–2019

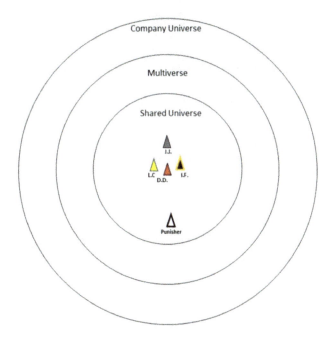

3.1.2.10 Iron Fist, Season 2 (2018)

The interrelation between the MNU's Iron Fist and Luke Cage Narrative continue with the prominent use of Simone Missick's Misty Knight[210] in *Iron Fist S2*. Usually associated with the MNU's Luke Cage Narrative, appearing in all 26 episodes of that series, she is in six of the *Iron Fist S2*'s ten episodes. Marked by wearing her afro-textured hair naturally and carrying her NYPD badge before the final episode of *The Defenders*, in which she lost her right arm, the *Index Manifestation* receives a bionic prosthetic from Rand Enterprises in *Luke Cage S2* as an additional *semiotic cue*. Retaining all these *semiotic cues*, Misty Knight enters *Iron Fist S2* in "Target: Iron Fist"[211] and remains part of the show up to its end. Aside from her presence building a connection between the *Narrative Entities*, she also relates to the final *Transformation Trigger* of *Luke Cage S2*, when she mentions Luke Cage's new position as mob boss and implies that she will enlist Jessica Henwick's Colleen Wing's help to fight him in the future[212].

Solely focused on the MNU's Luke Cage Narrative, the MNU's Iron Fist Narrative moves even closer towards that *Narrative Entity*, maintaining its relationship to the other parts of the MNU network via its acknowledgement of *Transformation Triggers* of the team narrative and its appearance in the *Luke Cage S2*. Notably, however, the second MNU's

---

210 For screenshots of this character's appearances within the overall network consult https://marvel cinematicuniverse.fandom.com/wiki/Misty_Knight/Gallery

211 "Target: Iron Fist". *Iron Fist*. Created by Scott Buck. Season 2, episode 4. Marvel Television/ABC Studios. 2017–2018.

212 "A Duel of Iron". *Iron Fist*. Created by Scott Buck. Season 2, episode 10. Marvel Television/ABC Studios. 2017–2018. 00:25:28

Iron Fist *Manifestation* equally redefines itself in the wake of the team narrative. This redefinition partly arises from its now close relationship with the MNU's Luke Cage Narrative and from the repositioning of the titular hero's motivation. The season begins with Finn Jones's Danny Rand/Iron Fist trying to take on Daredevil's position of fighting criminals and protecting the city as he stops the robbery of an armored truck in the first episode[213]. As the character has shown no inclination to fight crime in this manner – generally focusing on his task as 'The Mortal Enemy of the Hand' and regaining control of his family's company in the first season – this new mission (or motivation) appears to arise out of the knowledge that Daredevil fulfilled such a task before he died in *The Defenders*.

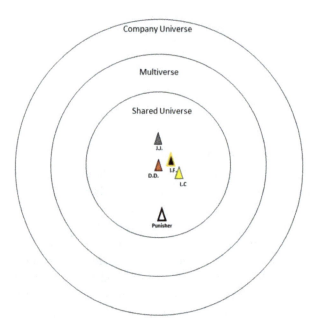

3.1.2.11 Daredevil, Season 3 (2018)

The final season of *Daredevil* connects directly to *Luke Cage* via the *Index Manifestation* Benjamin Donovan. The character appears previously in both seasons of *Luke Cage*. Retaining his *semiotic cues*, he re-enters the MNU's Daredevil Narrative as the main antagonist's lawyer[214]. Throughout *Daredevil S3*, he helps Fisk cut a deal with the FBI and collects information for him, appearing in that capacity in four episodes, "Resurrection"[215], "No Good

---

213 "The Fury of Iron Fist". *Iron Fist*. Created by Scott Buck. Season 2, episode 1. Marvel Television/ABC Studios. 2017–2018
214 For screenshots of this character's appearances within the overall network consult https://marvelcinematicuniverse.fandom.com/wiki/Benjamin_Donovan/Gallery
215 "Resurrection". *Daredevil*. Created by Drew Goddard. Season 3, episode 1. Marvel Television/ABC Studios. 2015–2018

Deed"[216], "The Perfect Game"[217], and "Reunion"[218]. Additionally, the season acknowledges *Transformation Triggers* from the team narrative. Notably, the presumed death of Matthew Cox's Matt Murdock/Daredevil colors a greater part of the season's interaction between characters.

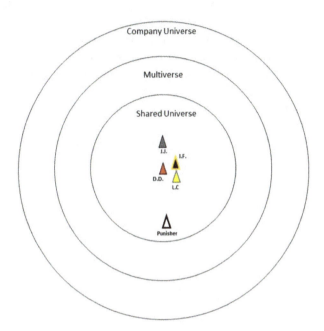

The acknowledgment of *Transformation Triggers* maintains the connection to the other MNU *Narrative Entities* with the exception of the MNU's Punisher Narrative, which did not take part in the team narrative. Danny Johnson's Benjamin Donovan draws the MNU's Luke Cage Narrative slightly closer to the MNU's Daredevil Narrative. While acknowledging the team narrative and its effects on the overall *Narrative Entity*, Daredevil S3 does not attempt to redefine or reposition the MNU's Daredevil Narrative in the wake of the shared world created by the team narrative. Instead, the *Manifestation* applies a similar strategy to *Thor: The Dark World*, mitigating the causal relation of changes created by the team narrative to focus more on the elements of its own *Narrative Entity*.

3.1.2.12 The Punisher, Season 2 (2019)

The second season of The Punisher does not attempt to alter its interrelation with the other *Narrative Entities*. Instead, it mainly retains its connection to the MNU's Daredevil

---

216 "No Good Deed". *Daredevil*. Created by Drew Goddard. Season 3, episode 3. Marvel Television/ABC Studios. 2015–2018

217 "The Perfect Game". *Daredevil*. Created by Drew Goddard. Season 3, episode 5. Marvel Television/ABC Studios. 2015–2018

218 "Reunion". *Daredevil*. Created by Drew Goddard. Season 3, episode 11. Marvel Television/ABC Studios. 2015–2018

Narrative by utilizing Deborah Ann Woll's Karen Page[219], who appears in "The Abyss", where she helps John Bernthal's Frank Castle/The Punisher flee the hospital. *The Punisher S2* also lightly connects to *Luke Cage S2* through the recurrence of Turk Barrett's Marijuana shop. Rob Morgan's Turk Barrett interrelates several *Narrative Entities* as an overarching connection, which is discussed in a later chapter. Within the context of *Luke Cage S2*, Barrett has opened a shop to provide Marijuana dispensaries with the necessary equipment. The shop is marked by its appearance by the presence of several bongs and other Marijuana related equipment. Aside from appearing in *Luke Cage S2*'s episode "The Main Ingredient", in which Luke Cage seeks out Turk Barrett to shake him down for information, the shop also is in *The Punisher S2*'s "One-Eyed Jack", in which it is used as a decoy meeting space.

With its use of one transposed *Index Manifestation*, the *Punisher S2* only reiterates its start in the MNU's Daredevil Narrative and the existence of the remaining network, freezing its distant relations to the overall tighter network in place.

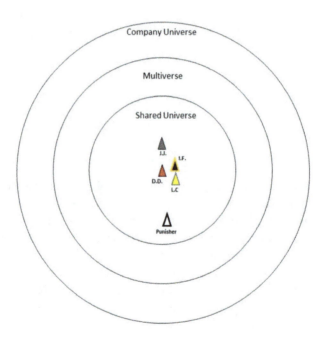

3.1.2.13 Jessica Jones, Season 3 (2019)

The third season of *Jessica Jones*, and the final show of the MNU network, only reiterates the interrelation with MNU's Luke Cage Narrative. Luke Cage returns in the final episode of the season and helps the main character to make a difficult decision[220]. Otherwise, this

---

219 For screenshots of this character's appearances within the overall network consult https://marvel cinematicuniverse.fandom.com/wiki/Karen_Page/Gallery

220 For screenshots of the character's appearances within the overall network consult https://marvelc inematicuniverse.fandom.com/wiki/Luke_Cage/Gallery

final *Manifestation* makes no attempt at reminding audiences of its place in a network of *Narrative Entities*.

3.1.2.14 Network Spanning Connections

As with the MCU, the MNU network does not solely rely on the singular exchange of *Index Manifestations* to connect its *Narrative Entities* within its network. Network-spanning connections in the form of *Shared Narratives* and overarching *Index Manifestations* equally appear throughout the network. Hereby, the MNU employs one *Shared Narrative* focused on the *Manifestations* up to the team narrative. The *Shared Narrative* serves the same function as the first *Shared Narrative* of the MCU, tying the early *Narrative Entities* together to create a reasonable foundation for a team narrative. A series of larger and smaller overarching *Index Manifestations* also interrelate the *Narrative Entities* of the MNU. It is noticeable that the MNU network employs more overarching *Index Manifestations* than the MCU while making less use of *Shared Narratives*.

3.1.2.14.1 Shared Narrative

Claire Temple   The only *Shared Narrative* appears prominently within the first six *Manifestations* of the MNU network. Introduced in the first season of *Daredevil*, Rosaria Dawson's Claire Temple is in six episodes of each *Iron Fist* and *The Defenders*, eight episodes of *Daredevil*, eleven *Luke Cage* episodes, and finally one episode of *Jessica Jones*. With the exception of three episodes of the *Luke Cage S2*, all her appearances occur before or during the team narrative[221].

Like Phil Coulson, the *Shared Narrative* of Claire Temple follows the character's ascension into the world of heroes. Introduced as a night-shift nurse living in Hell's Kitchen – Daredevil's area of operation – in *Daredevil S1*, Claire Temple provides Matt Murdock with medical assistance and information off the streets. After discovering the injured Daredevil in a dumpster, she helps him recover and discovers that he has superhuman senses. The *Transformation Trigger* of their encounter, witnessing his approach to fighting crime (including torture) and her ability to provide assistance, contextualizes the character to affordances of a superhero life within the presented *Narrative Entity* (*Exposition*). The *Shared Narrative*'s *Rising Transformation* begins when she tells Matthew Cox's Matt Murdock/Daredevil that some residents appreciate his vigilante actions and when she supports torturing a member of the Russian mob. Her involvement continues when the Russian mafia kidnaps her, and Daredevil saves her. Despite the experience, she continues helping Matt Murdock, chiefly by providing medical aid. The *Rising Transformation* continues into *Jessica Jones S1*. In the episode "AKA Smile", the injured Luke Cage requires medical attention, which Claire cannot provide directly due to his impenetrable skin. She outmaneuvers his powers, giving her experience with superhuman physiology. Her deepening entanglement with superheroes continues in *Daredevil S2*. She admits patients Daredevil freed from the mysterious and occult organization The Hand into Metro General Hospital. To avoid discovery, Temple hides these patients in an abandoned wing

---

221   For screenshots of Claire Temple's appearances within the overall network consult https://marvel cinematicuniverse.fandom.com/wiki/Claire_Temple/Gallery

of the hospital. Her actions create a direct encounter between her and Daredevil's enemies. She shows a penchant for the moral standards associated with superheroes when she sacrifices her job to protest the cover-up of her coworker's death. At the end of *Daredevil S2*, Claire Temple leaves Hell's Kitchen for Harlem. The *Rising Transformation* of her *Shared Narrative* continues in *Luke Cage S1*, in which Temple reconnects with the titular hero and actively injects herself into Luke Cage's cause. Aside from providing moral support, she helps him to defend Harlem, takes on a criminal organization, and braves gunfights. She also helps him discover the origin of his powers, increasing her knowledge of superhuman physiology. In the final episode of *Luke Cage S1*, she picks up a flyer for self-defense classes at the dojo of Jessica Henwick's Colleen Wing, which implies a continuation of the *Rising Transformation* as she is preparing for further violent encounters. Taking lessons in Colleen's dojo sets up her encounter with Finn Jones's Danny Rand/Iron Fist. Due to the *Transformation Triggers* of *Daredevil S2*, Claire Temple already views herself as an opponent of the Hand (an antagonistic organization to the MNU's Daredevil and Iron Fist Narrative). She becomes involved in Danny Rand's fight against the organization, even following him and Colleen Wing to China in pursuit of their enemy. In contrast to her previous appearances, she acts more of an equal to the other hero characters, Colleen Wing and Danny Rand, advising on a course of action and fighting alongside them. Displaying the accumulated experience from other series as an equal to the hero characters implies the near completion of the *Rising Transformation*. For one, *Iron Fist S1* is the final *Manifestation* before the team narrative, indicating that this *Index Manifestation*'s interrelation with the overall network is completed. Secondly, the sequence indicates that she has "caught up" to the necessary heroic abilities to become part of the superhero community. Within *Iron Fist S1*, Wai Ching Ho's Madame Gao spells out the course of Claire Temple's *Shared Narrative* in a dialogue with the character in the episode "Mistress of all Agonies"[222], accusing Claire Temple of hoping to become special herself by associating with special people. The *Rising Transformation* of this *Shared Narrative* runs throughout the greater part of *The Defenders*, in which her widespread entanglement helps to form alliances between the different hero characters. It continues in the realization of Luke Cage's and Claire Temple's romantic relationship at the beginning of the series. Through the romantic entanglement, she reaches the pinnacle of her inclusion into the superhero community and the greatest potential to draw the present hero characters together. Throughout the series, she uses her experience and status across the *Narrative Entities* to negotiate the situation and enlist the help of various characters. The *Shared Narrative*'s *Climax* occurs when she is included among the heroes as an equal in the final decision concerning their conflict with the antagonistic organization and her involvement in the final assault. The *Climax Wave* formally begins at the end of the team narrative, in which the presumed death of Matthew Cox's Matt Murdock/Daredevil and the injury to Simone Missick's Mercedes 'Misty' Knight highlight the potential cost of belonging to this hero community. The *Climax Wave* continues into *Luke Cage S2*, in which the titular character

---

[222] "The Mistress of All Agonies". *Iron Fist*. Created by Scott Buck. Season 1, episode 9. Marvel Television/ABC Studios. 2017–2018. 00:10:05

has difficulty accepting Claire Temple's status as an equal[223], fearing she may suffer a similar fate as Misty Knight due to her lack of powers. His neglect of her status, abilities, and advice in his crusade creates a rift in their relationship. The *Shared Narrative*'s *Denouement* arrives when Claire Temple exits the series and her relationship with Luke Cage in "Wig Out". While Claire Temple is mentioned in two further episodes of *Luke Cage S2*, Rosaria Dawson does not appear again within any *Manifestation* of the network. She has no direct dialogue or is involved in further *Transformation Triggers*.

Overall, the *Shared Narrative* of Claire Temple offers ties to all of the *Narrative Entities* of the MNU, with the exception of the MNU's Punisher Narrative. It does so specifically across the first six *Manifestations*, effectively performing a similar function to the *Shared Narrative* of Phil Coulson in setting up the foundation of an interconnected network needed for the team narrative. Within this context, the *Index Manifestation* is removed, like Coulson, at the end of the *Shared Narrative* instead of taking on a new function within the overall network.

3.1.2.14.2 Overarching Index Manifestations

The MNU network uses several overarching *Index Manifestations* targeted towards interrelating several *Narrative Entities*. Hereby, the importance of each *Index Manifestation* is counter-proportional to its spread. In other words, the more relevant to the plot of a *Manifestation* or the more significant within the overall network of *indices* a *Manifestation* appears to be, the lower the number of *Narrative Entities* it directly interrelates. Like the MCU, the MNU uses an organization and one of its members to interrelate most *Narrative Entities*. In contrast to the MCU, this network also employs a significant number of support and background characters for a similar purpose.

The Hand   Within the MNU network, The Hand is a secret and mystical organization that infiltrated many layers of society (primarily corporations and criminal organizations) in pursuit of control and the excavation of a dragon's corpse beneath Manhattan. In contrast to S.H.I.E.L.D. (which is represented through one or two significant characters across different MCU *Manifestations*), The Hand offers several *Index Manifestations*, perceived interests, and smaller operations across the different MNU *Manifestations*. Revealed gradually, these strains form a coherent representation within *The Defenders*.

This gradual process of revelation makes describing The Hand within the framework of the defined terminology difficult. As The Hand is not a singular *Index Manifestation* but a composition of several, it cannot follow the pattern of a *Shared Narrative*. For the same reason, *Trigger Waves* cannot interlink the numerous mentions and appearances of the organization, as *Transformation Triggers* apply to specific *Index Manifestations* within the organization but not to the organization as an *Index Manifestation*. *Transformation Triggers* – concerning The Hand and within the context of interrelating multiple *Manifestations* – serve to reveal new aspects of the organization. Each *Transformation Trigger* revealing a new facet of the organization does not interrelate the *Manifestations* via a traceable transformation of an *Index Manifestation* but via a series of revelations geared toward an in-

---

223   "Soul Brother #1". *Luke Cage*. Created by Cheo Hodari Coker. Season 2, episode 1. Marvel Television/ABC Studios. 2016–2018. 00:38:45

formed or skilled audience. As such, this type of interrelation works through the engagement of an informed audience, which follows the path of revelations in the order of publication, encountering the *Transformation Triggers* revolving around The Hand with either dramatic irony or in suspense for another piece of the puzzle. Set as a series of revelations means that The Hand as a binding element does not universally draw the *Narrative Entities* closer together to the same degree a *Shared Narrative* or the continued appearance of the same *Index Manifestation* would. Instead, the appearance of The Hand closes the distance between many *Narrative Entities* in accordance with its *Narrative Reliance*. When the information given requires knowledge from another *Manifestation* or *Narrative Entity* (previous or upcoming), the distance between the *Narrative Entities* shortens. When the representation of the Hand can stand on its own within a given *Manifestation*, the distance to the involved *Narrative Entities* increases. The distance between *Narrative Entities* uninvolved with The Hand remains unchanged. As a direct analysis of each individual *Index Manifestation* and each piece of information would overextend the range of this paper (and some parts of that analysis have been performed in the discussion of the specific seasons), the analysis of The Hand will focus on the information revealed across *Manifestations*.

Analyzed within this frame, the gradual revelation of The Hand's interests, key members, and abilities across different *Narrative Entities* necessarily form a dependent interrelation between *Daredevil S1&S2*, *Iron Fist S1*, and *The Defenders*. In order of appearance, the information revealed about the Hand is (1) an association with organized crime, (2) their use of devoted followers, (3) the concept of the Black Sky, (4) their interest in a specific region of Hell's Kitchen in *Daredevil S1*; (5) their ability to resurrect the dead and create longevity, (6) the identity of a specific Black Sky, (7) the existence of a counter organization (The Chaste) in *Daredevil S2*; (8) the existence of different factions within the organization, (9) its use of larger corporations, (10) its relations to the Iron Fist in *Iron Fist S1*; and (11) the source of their mastery over death, (12) the final members in leadership, (13) the reason for their schemes in *The Defenders*. Within this list of information, the ability to resurrect the dead and the relation to organized crime from *Daredevil S1* and *S2* are carried into *Iron Fist S1* through David Wenham's Harold Meachum. The connection between Harold Meachum and the Hand's ability to resurrect the dead arises when his son kills him. Despite being stabbed repeatedly, Harold Meachum awakes unharmed a day later. No explanation is given other than that The Hand healed him after he had fallen mortally ill years ago, relying to a degree on information given in previous *Manifestations*. *Iron Fist S1* creates dramatic irony reliant on previous knowledge from *Daredevil S2*, in which the organization's mastery over death and its limitations were already explained. The relationship between the Iron Fist, K'un Lun (a mystical place where the Iron Fist is trained), and The Hand is hinted at in *Iron Fist S1* through Madame Gao's vivid description of the place and Bakuto's need to capture Danny Rand/Iron Fist. The latter aspect reappears in *The Defenders*. Aside from revealing that the leadership of The Hand was cast out of K'un-Lun because they sought immortality[224], it is also revealed that a critical ingredient in their resurrection and longevity is dragon bone. However, a magical barrier protects a dragon's remains underneath Manhattan, and only the Iron Fist can open it.

---

224 "Royal Dragon". *The Defenders*. Created by Douglas Petrie and Marco Ramirez. Season 1, episode 4. Marvel Television/ABC Studios. 2017. 00:27:58

This information given in *The Defenders* places motivations and actions in *Iron Fist S1* into context. It explains Bakuto's designs toward Danny Rand as well as Madame Gao's hesitation to kill him. It also informs either character's unusual understanding of the Iron Fist's purpose and abilities. Due to the revelation of the Hand's scheme and motivation, *The Defenders* also relate back to both *Daredevil S1* and *S2*. A source of conflict in *Daredevil S1* is The Hand's attempt at acquiring a specific set of buildings in Hell's Kitchen. To this end, they use the reach of the criminal organizations under their control. In *The Defenders*, it is revealed that underneath the specific region of Hell's Kitchen, where The Hand erected a high-rise named Midland Circle, is the entrance to a dragon's grave. This information gives the vigorous pursuit of control over that specific building in *Daredevil S1* context. The process and ability of resurrection, intimate knowledge of the Iron Fist, and the reason for the relentless pursuit of real estate in Hell's Kitchen are only three specifically overt examples highlighting the *Narrative Reliance* created through the mysterious organization between the three *Narrative Entities*. Other smaller aspects also, to a degree, rely on information given in other *Manifestations*. For example, Madame Gao's entire presence, skill, and authority in Daredevil are informed by revelations about her in later *Narrative Entities*, specifically *Iron Fist S1*.

Madame Gao With nearly even distribution, Wai Ching Ho's Madame Gao appears in six episodes of *Daredevil* and *The Defenders* and nine episodes of *Iron Fist*[225]. Rather than being associated with any specific *Narrative Entity*, the *Index Manifestation* relates to The Hand, as her appearances coincide with revelations concerning the organization. Her mysterious behavior and extensive understanding and knowledge mark the character. In the *Daredevil S1* episode "Shadows in the Glass"[226], she states that she speaks every language. Throughout the season, she displays an uncanny understanding of the secretive Wilson Fisk. In the *Iron Fist S1* episode "Immortal Emerges from Cave"[227], she reveals a clear understanding of the Iron Fist, the rituals surrounding his existence, and vast knowledge of the mystical K'un-Lun. Visually, the character is consistently identifiable by her strict hairstyle, her cane, and her modern Asian-type clothing.

While the character is in *The Defenders*, she primarily connects the MNU's Iron Fist and Daredevil Narrative as she appears prominently in each's first Manifestation. The team narrative does not provide any additional interrelation regarding this specific Index Manifestation because, except for the final conflict, Madame Gao never interacts with any of the hero characters. Instead, she is used to introduce the leader of The Hand, Sigourney Weaver's Alexandra Reid, and give greater insight into the organization's inner workings. Her connective status between *Iron Fist* and *Daredevil* is specifically maintained as she interacts equally with an *Index Manifestation* associated with either *Narrative Entity*, Ramón Rodriguez's Bakuto for *Iron Fist* and Élodie Yung's Elektra Natchios for *Daredevil*.

---

225 For screenshots of Madame Gao's appearances within the overall network consult https://marvelcinematicuniverse.fandom.com/wiki/Madame_Gao/Gallery

226 "Shadows in the Glass". *Daredevil*. Created by Drew Goddard. Season 1, episode 8. Marvel Television/ABC Studios. 2015–2018.

227 "Immortal Emerges from Cave". *Iron Fist*. Created by Scott Buck. Season 1, episode 6. Marvel Television/ABC Studios. 2017–2018

Turk Barrett Rob Morgan's Turk Barrett is a generally overlooked character concerning the interrelation of the different *Narrative Entities*. Appearing in singular episodes of each *Jessica Jones*, *Iron Fist*, and *The Defenders* as well as two episodes of *The Punisher*, three episodes of *Luke Cage*, and seven episodes of *Daredevil*, the character covers all of the MNU's *Narrative Entities*, providing a permanent indication for their interrelation[228]. However, aside from retaining the same actor playing the character, Turk Barrett's appearances use very few consistent *semiotic cues*. He always has a beard, which appears patchy but varies in thickness. His clothing is usually understated and kept in dark, earthy colors, with him mostly wearing a shirt underneath a black jacket. Beginning with his appearance in *Luke Cage S1*, the character always wears a black beanie up to *Luke Cage S2*, in which he retains the beanie, but the color pattern of his clothes changes, becoming lighter. The lighter color pattern remains until his final appearance in *The Punisher S2*. He also exchanges the beanie for a flat cap, beginning with *Iron Fist S2*. The character changes his beard to a mustache and soul patch in *Iron Fist S2*. The previous style of beard returns in *The Punisher S2*. Aside from maintaining the same actor, the more stable *semiotic cue* associated with the character is his association with the illegal sale of firearms. His love for guns is established in *Daredevil S1*[229]. His appearances in *Daredevil S2*[230], *Jessica Jones S2*[231], and *Iron Fist S2*[232] are all tied to the sale of illegal firearms. Specific *Transformation Triggers* do not explain the alteration to this *Index Manifestation*, negating any *Narrative Reliance* concerning it. The low *Narrative Reliance* combined with the constant shift in *semiotic cues* leaves the discovery of the interrelation created by Turk Barrett to a skilled audience or potentially to an informed one. While the retention of the actor and position of the character as a low-level criminal, dealing primarily with weapons and information, preserves the connective effect of this *Index Manifestation*, the continued alteration to other *semiotic cues* weakens that connective effect. Still, his presence in several *Manifestations* ties all *Narrative Entities* lightly together.

Turk Barrett appears in the first, third, and fifth episodes and the season finale of *Daredevil S1*. In each appearance, he works in some capacity for the season's main antagonist, Wilson Fisk, and is arrested by the FBI at the end of that season. The character reappears in the first and last episode of *Daredevil S2*. In the former, he tries to sell guns illegally and, after explaining that he was released on parole, provides the titular hero with information. In the latter, The Hand abducts him, and he is saved by Daredevil. Turk Barrett reappears in *Luke Cage* S1 episodes "Code of the Street"[233] and "Soliloquy of

---

228 For screenshots of the character's appearances within the overall network consult https://marvelcinematicuniverse.fandom.com/wiki/Turk_Barrett/Gallery
229 "Rabbit in a Snow Storm", *Daredevil* S1E3, 00:01:33
230 "Bang". *Daredevil*. Created by Drew Goddard. Season 2, episode 1. Marvel Television/ABC Studios. 2015–2018. 00:30:50
231 "AKA Pray for my Patsy". *Jessica Jones*. Created by Melissa Rosenberg. Season 2, episode 12. Marvel Television/ABC Studios. 2015–2019. 00:27:00
232 "War Without End". *Iron Fist*. Created by Scott Buck. Season 2, episode 9. Marvel Television/ABC Studios. 2017–2018. 00:19:45
233 "Code of the Street". *Luke Cage*. Created by Cheo Hodari Coker. Season 1, episode 2. Marvel Television/ABC Studios. 2016–2018

Chaos"[234]. Within the former episode, he and other characters allude to his connection to the MNU's Daredevil Narrative by mentioning his association with Hell's Kitchen[235]. Here, it is important to mention that, like Harlem, Hell's Kitchen is an actual part of New York. However, within Marvel Comics and the MNU, Hell's Kitchen is more prominently Daredevil's area of operation. In the latter episode, the antagonist of *Luke Cage S1*, Erik LaRay Harvey's Diamondback, wants to use Turk's connections to sell his arms and invites him to discuss the proposition. Later in the same episode, Luke Cage tracks Turk down and scares him into giving up the antagonist's location. As with many other *Index Manifestations* from various *Narrative Entities*, Turk Barrett appears in *The Defenders*. In the episode "Mean Right Hook"[236], he gives Luke Cage information on the man recruiting kids off the street. The *semiotic cue* of Turk as an illegal arms dealer on the street brings him into contact with Frank Castle in the *Punisher S1*. Looking for guns, the Punisher tries to rob Turk Barrett's illegal stash in "Resupply"[237]. The character appears in *Jessica Jones S2* once again as an arms dealer, selling Carrie-Anne Moss's Jeri Hogarth a revolver[238]. When the character reappears in *Luke Cage S2*, he has opened a supply store for weed dispensaries. However, he still knows what is going on in the criminal world and provides Luke Cage with information in "The Main Ingredient"[239]. The character is back to arms dealing in *Iron Fist S2*, in which he sells Tom Pelphrey's Ward Meachum and Alice Eve's 'Typhoid Mary' Mary Walker guns in "War Without End"[240]. The character then makes his final appearance within the MNU in *The Punisher S2*. Despite claiming to have gone straight, Frank Castle tricks Turk into setting up a meeting with Russian criminals in "One-Eyed Jack". Here, the character provides an additional connection between the MNU's Punisher and Luke Cage Narrative, as his supply store for weed dispensaries also makes a brief appearance[241].

As he is in all *Narrative Entities*, Turk Barrett interrelates all of them to a degree. However, the constant change of his appearance and switches in his intradiegetic function in society lower his recognition value for audiences. Additionally, the character undergoes small changes from appearance to appearance, which are merely hinted at in dialogue or left unexplained, detaching this *Index Manifestation* from any transformation by specific *Transformation Triggers*. The absence lowers the connective value of the *Index Manifestation*

---

234 "Soliloquy of Chaos". *Luke Cage*. Created by Cheo Hodari Coker. Season 1, episode 12. Marvel Television/ABC Studios. 2016–2018
235 "Code of the Street", *Luke Cage S1E2*, 00:51:27
236 "Mean Right Hook". *The Defenders*. Created by Douglas Petrie and Marco Ramirez. Season 1, episode 2. Marvel Television/ABC Studios. 2017. 00:25:15
237 "Resupply". *The Punisher*. Created by Steve Lightfoot. Season 1, episode 4. Marvel Television/ABC Studios. 2017–2019. 00:02:30
238 "AKA Pray for my Patsy". *Jessica Jones*. Created by Melissa Rosenberg. Season 2, episode 12. Marvel Television/ABC Studios. 2015–2019. 00:27:00
239 "The Main Ingredient". *Luke Cage*. Created by Cheo Hodari Coker. Season 2, episode 10. Marvel Television/ABC Studios. 2016–2018. 00:34:40
240 "War Without End". *Iron Fist*. Created by Scott Buck. Season 2, episode 9. Marvel Television/ABC Studios. 2017–2018. 00:19:45
241 "One-Eyed Jacks". *The Punisher*. Created by Steve Lightfoot. Season 2, episode 5. Marvel Television/ABC Studios. 2017–2019. 00:37:20

because the explanations for the changes are missing within any *Manifestation*. Independent from the character's connective value, the *Index Manifestation partially* holds a similar function to the MCU's Nick Fury in that Turk Barrett's interconnected position is used in an information transit capacity. While unwillingly, the character still provides information to each of the hero characters, propelling the plot forward in a similar fashion Nick Fury does in many of his appearances.

Jeri Hogarth The character of Jeri Hogarth interrelated four of the six *Narrative Entities* within the MNU network. Prominently, she is an *Index Manifestation* of the MNU's Jessica Jones Narrative, appearing in 34 of the series overall 39 episodes. Additionally, she shows up in three episodes of *Iron Fist S1* and in one episode of *Daredevil S2* and *The Defenders*, respectively[242]. Played by Carrie-Anne Moss throughout her MNU appearances, the character retains a few clear *semiotic cues*. She always appears with a professional short haircut and always wears a black, professional dress. Additionally, outside of the entirety of *Jessica Jones*, her appearances all relate to her profession as a lawyer. Outside of *Jessica Jones*, Jeri Hogarth appears in "A Cold Day In Hell's Kitchen" of *Daredevil S2* when she offers Eldon Henson's Foggy Nelson a place at her firm[243]. Earlier in the season, the character is mentioned in conversation. She reappears in *Iron Fist S1* in the episode "Rolling Thunder Cannon Punch"[244], in which it is revealed that she shares a past with the titular hero. Within the episode, she agrees to help Danny Rand regain control of his company. This process also marks her appearance in the following episode, "Eight Diagram Dragon Palm"[245]. Jeri Hogarth's final appearance in *Iron Fist S1* is in the episode "Dragon Plays with Fire"[246]. Again, she appears as a lawyer, helping Danny Rand fight criminal charges against him. In *The Defenders*, the character warns Jessica Jones to avoid a federal case in "Mean Right Hook"[247]. In the same episode, she then provides an additional connection to the *Narrative Entity* Daredevil as she relegates the task of isolating her law firm from Jessica Jones to Elden Henson's Foggy Nelson[248], a prominent *Index Manifestation* from the MNU's Daredevil Narrative. While several *Transformation Triggers* within *Jessica Jones* alter the character of Jeri Hogarth, none of them have a significant impact on the *Index Manifestation*'s interrelating effect, as all Jeri Hogarth's appearances in other *Narrative*

---

242 For screenshots of this character's appearances within the overall network consult https://marvelcinematicuniverse.fandom.com/wiki/Jeri_Hogarth/Gallery
243 "A Cold Day In Hell's Kitchen". *Daredevil*. Created by Drew Goddard. Season 2, episode 13. Marvel Television/ABC Studios. 2015–2018. 00:08:05
244 "Rolling Thunder Cannon Punch". *Iron Fist*. Created by Scott Buck. Season 1, episode 3. Marvel Television/ABC Studios. 2017–2018
245 "Eight Diagram Dragon Palm". *Iron Fist*. Created by Scott Buck. Season 1, episode 4. Marvel Television/ABC Studios. 2017–2018
246 "Dragon Plays with Fire". *Iron Fist*. Created by Scott Buck. Season 1, episode 13. Marvel Television/ABC Studios. 2017–2018
247 "Mean Right Hook". *The Defenders*. Created by Douglas Petrie and Marco Ramirez. Season 1, episode 2. Marvel Television/ABC Studios. 2017
248 "Mean Right Hook". *The Defenders*. Created by Douglas Petrie and Marco Ramirez. Season 1, episode 2. Marvel Television/ABC Studios. 2017. 00:31:40

Entities take place between *Jessica Jones S1* and *Jessica Jones S2*, leaving the *Index Manifestation*'s state between the two seasons as the recognizable one for interrelation purposes. Additionally, with each appearance in other *Narrative Entities* focused more on her motivation and personality, none of her *Transformation Triggers* alter the character's *semiotic cues* outside of *Jessica Jones*. As such, Jeri Hogarth functions as a clear connecting element between the four *Narrative Entities* within the MNU network.

Foggy Nelson Tied to the MNU's Daredevil Narrative, Elden Henson's Franklin Percy "Foggy" Nelson appears in 38 of Daredevil's 39 episodes. Like Carrie-Anne Moss's Jeri Hogarth, he ties three other *Narrative Entities* deeper into the MNU network. This *Index Manifestation* manifests in episodes of *Luke Cage S2*, *Jessica Jones S2*, and in a greater part of *The Defenders*[249]. Aside from a flashback in the first season, the character maintains a few specific *semiotic cues* throughout *Daredevil S1* and *S2*. The character consistently wears chin-long hair and a suit with a lightly patterned shirt and a tie containing some form of print. These *semiotic cues* alter before the *Index Manifestation* is used to interrelate different *Narrative Entities*. With the *Transformation Trigger* of his resignation from Nelson & Murdock and his employment at Hogarth, Chao and Benowitz in "A Cold Day in Hell's Kitchen"[250], he changes to a cleaner, more professional haircut. Additionally, the character alters from his formerly 'cheaper' suits to more professional ones. However, even his more professional appearance retains a patterned shirt and a patterned tie, whereas in a more stylish fashion. As the *Transformation Trigger* takes place at the end of *Daredevil S2*, the altered *Index Manifestation* makes its first appearance in *The Defenders* episode "The H Word"[251]. In the episode, he gets Mike Colter's Luke Cage out of prison, connecting the *Index Manifestation* to the MNU's Luke Cage Narrative. The character reconnects with the MNU's Luke Cage Narrative in the team narrative's final episode when he helps Luke Cage out of a legal predicament and reminisces about the death of Matthew Cox's Matt Murdock/Daredevil[252]. Foggy Nelson interacts briefly with Jeri Hogarth in *The Defenders* "Mean Right Hook" when she relegates the task of isolating her law firm from Jessica Jones to him[253]. Within all other appearances in the team narrative, the character interacts solely with *Index Manifestations* from the MNU's Daredevil Narrative, even though he appears on the same set with *Index Manifestations* from other *Narrative Entities* in the MNU network. The connection with the MNU's Luke Cage Narrative is reaffirmed when Foggy Nelson takes part in the plot of "All Souled Out"[254], providing the titular hero with

---

249 For screenshots of most of this character's appearances within the overall network consult https://marvelcinematicuniverse.fandom.com/wiki/Foggy_Nelson/Gallery
250 "A Cold Day In Hell's Kitchen". *Daredevil*. Created by Drew Goddard. Season 2, episode 13. Marvel Television/ABC Studios. 2015–2018. 00:08:05
251 "The H Word". *The Defenders*. Created by Douglas Petrie and Marco Ramirez. Season 1, episode 2. Marvel Television/ABC Studios. 2017. 00:08:15
252 "The Defenders". *The Defenders*. Created by Douglas Petrie and Marco Ramirez. Season 1, episode 8. Marvel Television/ABC Studios. 2017. 00:41:50
253 "Mean Right Hook". *The Defenders*. Created by Douglas Petrie and Marco Ramirez. Season 1, episode 2. Marvel Television/ABC Studios. 2017. 00:31:40
254 "All Souled Out". *Luke Cage*. Created by Cheo Hodari Coker. Season 2, episode 5. Marvel Television/ABC Studios. 2016–2018

legal counsel. The character reaffirms a connection to the MNU's Jessica Jones Narrative when he reappears in *Jessica Jones S2* "AKA Sole Survivor"[255].

Thembi Wallace   Tijuana Ricks's Thembi Wallace is a reporter for WJBP-TV, a fictional news station within the MNU network. While mainly in the background, Thembi Wallace does appear in three episodes of *Jessica Jones*, two episodes of *Iron Fist*, and seven episodes of *Luke Cage*[256]. Within the framework of the MNU, Thembi Wallace is only significantly marked with the attributes of her profession. When shown, she either conducts an interview or reports on a recent event within the network. Hereby, the interviews occur within the series, while the reports often enter the scene through a television in the background. Her clothing and hairstyle match a representation of her profession but are not as uniform as in other characters. As this *Index Manifestation*'s *semiotic cues* are limited to a profession and an actress, the connecting effect is overall limited. Introduced in the *Luke Cage S1* episode "Suckas need Bodyguards"[257], Thembi Wallace conducts a live interview with Alfre Woodard's Mariah Dillard. The character reappears in "Now You're Mine"[258], in which she reports on a hostage situation, and in "Soliloquy of Chaos"[259], in which she reports on Luke Cage's escape and the subsequent manhunt. Within the latter episode, the report appears on a muted television in the background. Thembi Wallace stands among the crowd, watching the final confrontation of *Luke Cage S1*, and interviews the crowd later in "You Know My Steez"[260]. The character's function as reporting on the current public perception to reiterate or provide information continues in *Iron Fist S1* in "Under Leaf Pluck Lotus"[261] and "Dragon Plays with Fire"[262]. In either instance, the character provides news reports on various aspects of the series. Serving the same function in the *Luke Cage S2* episode "The Main Ingredient"[263], she reports on the events of a previous episode. In "They Reminisce Over You"[264] of the same season, Thembi Wallace reports on the deteriorating situation in Harlem, also contextualizing and reiterating the current state of

---

255 "AKA Sole Survivor". *Jessica Jones*. Created by Melissa Rosenberg. Season 2, episode 3. Marvel Television/ABC Studios. 2015–2019. 00:11:50
256 For screenshots this character's appearances within the overall network consult https://marvelcinematicuniverse.fandom.com/wiki/Thembi_Wallace/Gallery
257 "Suckas Need Bodyguards". *Luke Cage*. Created by Cheo Hodari Coker. Season 1, episode 6. Marvel Television/ABC Studios. 2016–2018. 00:22:05
258 "Now You're Mine". *Luke Cage*. Created by Cheo Hodari Coker. Season 1, episode 11. Marvel Television/ABC Studios. 2016–2018
259 "Soliloquy of Chaos". *Luke Cage*. Created by Cheo Hodari Coker. Season 1, episode 12. Marvel Television/ABC Studios. 2016–2018. 00:31:05
260 "You Know My Steez". *Luke Cage*. Created by Cheo Hodari Coker. Season 1, episode 13. Marvel Television/ABC Studios. 2016–2018
261 "Under Leaf Pluck Lotus". *Iron Fist*. Created by Scott Buck. Season 1, episode 5. Marvel Television/ABC Studios. 2017–2018. 00:31:29
262 "Dragon Plays with Fire". *Iron Fist*. Created by Scott Buck. Season 1, episode 13. Marvel Television/ABC Studios. 2017–2018. 00:00:30
263 "The Main Ingredient". *Luke Cage*. Created by Cheo Hodari Coker. Season 2, episode 10. Marvel Television/ABC Studios. 2016–2018. 00:01:30
264 "They Reminisce Over You". *Luke Cage*. Created by Cheo Hodari Coker. Season 2, episode 13. Marvel Television/ABC Studios. 2016–2018.00:05:50

the *Narrative Entity*'s setting within the episode. In "AKA Pray from my Patsy"[265] from *Jessica Jones S2*, Thembi Wallace convinces Rebecca De Mornay's Dorothy Walker to speak about her daughter on camera. The character has her final appearance in *Jessica Jones S3* when she conducts a formal interview with Jessica Jones in "AKA Camera Friendly"[266] and reappears later in the episode among a collection of reporters questioning the titular hero.

Similar to other unattached *Index Manifestations*, the character of Thembi Wallace provides an additional function within the network of *Narrative Entities*. As with Nick Fury and Turk Barrett, the function relates primarily to transporting information. Defined in the context of the network as a reporter, this *Index Manifestation*, in most appearances, either reiterates existing information or provides a new context.

Brett Mahoney Royce Johnson's Brett Mahoney is an *Index Manifestation* of the MNU's Daredevil Narrative, appearing in 17 of the show's 36 episodes. Mainly used to reiterate the strong interrelation between the MNU's Daredevil and Punisher Narrative, the character also appears in eight episodes of *The Punisher*. Otherwise, he is in one episode of *Jessica Jones*[267]. Introduced as a police officer in *Daredevil S1*, Brett Mahony is marked with the *semiotic cues* of his profession. Within the season, he appears solely in uniform and within the capacity of a police officer. Holding these *semiotic cues*, the character reappears in the *Jessica Jones S1* episode "AKA Top Shelf Perverts"[268] as one of the officers controlled by Kilgrave, remaining mostly in the background. In *Daredevil S2*, Brett Mahoney is promoted to detective after arresting the Punisher. This *Transformation Trigger* alters his *semiotic cues*. They remain in line with his profession but adjust to his new status. Instead of a NYPD uniform, the character appears in a grey suit, wearing a tie and his badge. The *Index Manifestation* reconnects the MNU's Daredevil Narrative with the MNU's Punisher Narrative after this alteration in representation. He is the lead detective investigating a shooting involving Jon Bernthal's Frank Castle/The Punisher and Deborah Ann Woll's Karen Page in *The Punisher S1* "Virtue of the Vicious"[269]. This representation of Brett Mahoney then has a more significant role in *The Punisher S2* as the lead detective hunting Ben Barnes's Billy Russo/Jigsaw, a prominent enemy of the titular hero.

3.1.2.15 MNU Conclusions

Within the context of creating a network of several *Narrative Entities*, the MNU generally applies similar strategies to the MCU when viewed in the context of entire seasons. *Index Manifestations* associated with a specific *Narrative Entity* appear in the *Manifestation*

---

[265] "AKA Pray for my Patsy". *Jessica Jones*. Created by Melissa Rosenberg. Season 2, episode 12. Marvel Television/ABC Studios. 2015–2019. 00:08:10

[266] "AKA Camera Friendly". *Jessica Jones*. Created by Melissa Rosenberg. Season 3, episode 8. Marvel Television/ABC Studios. 2015–2019

[267] For screenshots this character's appearances within the overall network consult https://marvelcinematicuniverse.fandom.com/wiki/Brett_Mahoney/Gallery

[268] "AKA Top Shelf Perverts". *Jessica Jones*. Created by Melissa Rosenberg. Season 1, episode 7. Marvel Television/ABC Studios. 2015–2019

[269] "Virtue of the Vicious". *The Punisher*. Created by Steve Lightfoot. Season 1, episode 4. Marvel Television/ABC Studios. 2017–2019

of another. *Transformation Triggers* create a relation between different plots within multiple *Manifestations*. *Shared Narratives* interrelate many *Narrative Entities* and place their *Manifestations* in order. However, the two networks differ in the number and strength of these techniques: While the MCU, especially in the beginning, hinges significantly on direct connections between two *Narrative Entities* through the appearance of singular transposed *Index Manifestations*, the MNU uses such connections rarely, visible in the overall shorter chapters on the specific *Manifestations*. In contrast, the MNU network employs more overarching connections, which simply appear in several *Manifestations* of the overall network. The representation of these *Index Manifestations* is oddly understated and lacks distinctive, easily recognizable *semiotic cues*. While Samuel L. Jackson's Nicholas Fury is easily identifiable across several *Manifestations* with his eye-patch and penchant for black coats, Turk Barrett is easily overlooked because he does not retain a prominent identifiable *semiotic cue* but relies mainly on a recognition of the actor. In the same vein, the MCU network uses several *Shared Narratives*, tying their appearances into some form of coherent narrative, thereby creating connections and reliance between their films. The MNU network, in contrast, has one *Shared Narrative*, which is removed after the character fulfills its function in laying the groundwork for the team narrative. Otherwise, the MNU network avoids *Trigger Waves*, making the related series overall more independent from one another. *The Defenders* is the notable exception because, as a team narrative, it has to take note of *Transformation Triggers* informing the *Index Manifestations* from various *Narrative Entities*. While the MNU's team narrative informs aspects of the *Narrative Entity*-specific *Manifestations* following it, these interdependencies are downplayed compared to the MCU relations. This lack of interdependence extends even to relationships created outside the team narrative, as in the case of the *Daredevil/The Punisher* relation, in which the effects of the *Transformation Triggers* from *Daredevil S2* are completed and separated from the rest of the series at the beginning of *The Punisher S1*. Something similar occurs with the connection between *Jessica Jones* and *Luke Cage*. While Mike Colter's Luke Cage is introduced in *Jessica Jones S1*, *Luke Cage S1* does not refer to the former series or its *Transformation Triggers*, even relegating information given about the character Reva Connors to a narrative extension. In contrast, *Black Panther* refers to the main character's previous appearance in *Captain America: Civil War* and its *Transformation Triggers* in a dialogue between Chadwick Boseman's T'Challa and Martin Freeman's Everett K. Ross[270]. *Spider-Man: Homecoming* more prominently uses the *Transformation Triggers* from *Captain America: Civil War* to set up the relationship between the MCU's Iron Man and Spider-Man Narrative. Within the MNU, the notable exception to this is the character Mercedes 'Misty' Knight, who follows a line across *Trigger Waves* concerning her arm. She loses it in *The Defenders*, receives a bionic replacement in *Luke Cage S2*, and appears as a supporting character with her bionic arm in *Iron Fist S2*. The MNU's avoidance of connections via *Transformation Triggers* directly influences any notion of *Narrative Reliance*. Most of the MNU's *Manifestations* require no direct knowledge of any other *Narrative Entity*, allowing them to function on their own, providing only pleasure for skilled audiences, which rec-

---

270   *Black Panther*. Directed by Ryan Coogler. Performances by Chadwick Boseman, Michael B. Jordan, and Lupita Nyong'o. Marvel Studios, 2018. 00:44:04

ognize the transposition of minor *Index Manifestations*, or, in some instances, informed audiences, which can trace major characters across maybe two or three *Manifestations*.

3.1.3 The ABC Series

The third and final network proclaimed as part of the overall Marvel Cinematic Universe included in this research initially aired on the American Broadcasting Company (ABC) channel of Walt Disney Television. *Agents of S.H.I.E.L.D.*[271] is the longer running of the two series, with 136 episodes spread across seven seasons. Considerably shorter, *Agent Carter*[272] has 18 episodes spread across two seasons. In contrast to the previous two networks, the interrelated ABC series has no commonly used name. As such, this research will refer to the network simply as the ABC network. In line with the research into the MNU network, the analysis will assume that the seasons of the same series are interrelated and, as such, connections via *Transformation Triggers* and *Index Manifestations* exist. However, as the focus lies on the interrelation between *Narrative Entities*, the research will ignore interconnections of singular episodes within the same series.

3.1.3.1 Agents of S.H.I.E.L.D. (2013–2020)

Agents of S.H.I.E.L.D. began in 2013 as a direct spin-off out of the MCU films and ran until 2020. The series interlinks mostly with one of its ABC counterparts, *Agent Carter*. This interrelation arises from the use of two *Index Manifestations* from the ABC's *Agent Carter* Narrative and later through several mentions of *Index Manifestations* and *Transformation Triggers*. Agent Carter's first notable transposed *Index Manifestation* is the titular character herself[273]. Hayley Atwell's Peggy Carter appears in flashbacks in the *Agents of S.H.I.E.L.D.* episodes "Shadows"[274] and "The Things We Bury"[275]. As the series *Agent Carter* was released after these episodes[276] were aired, the *semiotic cues* identifying the character are more in line with her appearance in *Captain America: The First Avengers*. Within the film, the uniform of the British Royal Military outside of battle and a dark-brown leather jacket over her military shirt and tie in battle mark the character. She appears with the latter *semiotic cues* in "Shadows", in which she is also addressed by name, and with the earlier ones in "The Things We Bury". A picture of Hayley Atwell as Peggy Carter in her uniform

---

271 *Agents of S.H.I.E.L.D.* Created by Joss Whedon, Jed Whedon, and Maurissa Tancharoen. Marvel Television/ABC Studios. 2013–2020

272 *Agent Carter.* Created by Christopher Markus and Stephen McFeely. Marvel Television/ABC Studios. 2015–2016

273 For screenshots of Peggy Carter's appearances in the MCU consult https://marvelcinematicuniverse.fandom.com/wiki/Peggy_Carter/Gallery

274 "Shadows". *Agents of S.H.I.E.L.D.* Created by Joss Whedon, Jed Whedon, and Maurissa Tancharoen. Season 2, episode 1. Marvel Television/ABC Studios. 2013–2020. 00:02:12

275 "The Things We Bury". *Agents of S.H.I.E.L.D.* Created by Joss Whedon, Jed Whedon, and Maurissa Tancharoen. Season 2, episode 8. Marvel Television/ABC Studios. 2013–2020. 00:12:30

276 *Agents of S.H.I.E.L.D.*; S2E1: "Shadows", Original Air Date: September 23, 2014; *Agents of S.H.I.E.L.D.*, S2E8: "The Things We Bury", Original Air Date: November 18, 2014; *Agent Carter* S1E1: "Now is Not the End", Original Air Date: January 6, 2015

also appears in "Heavy is the Head"[277], and another picture of her appears in a newspaper in "Emancipation"[278]. While these appearances interrelate the two series, the interconnection is somewhat weakened due to changes to the character when she switches from her position as a military agent to a civilian agent at the beginning of *Agent Carter*. The character also finds mention in "Meet the New Boss"[279], which indicates that she oversaw the construction of S.H.I.E.L.D.'s current base of operation. Enver Gjokaj's Daniel Sousa is the second significant *Index Manifestation* interrelating the two *Narrative Entities*. Appearing in all 18 episodes, Daniel Sousa firmly relates to *Agent Carter*. Within the series, the character is marked by his need for a crutch, due to a war injury. He uses the implement throughout *Agent Carter*. Daniel Sousa appears in *Agents of S.H.I.E.L.D.*'s seventh season[280]. Played by the same actor, the character enters the series in "Alien Commies from the Future"[281]. In detraction to his previous appearances, he uses a cane instead of a crutch. A minor connection between the two *Narrative Entities* arises in the form of the fictional chemical compound called Nitramene[282]. Stolen from its developer, Howard Stark, Nitramene is mentioned and later appears in the *Agent Carter* episodes "Now is Not the End"[283] and "Bridge and Tunnel"[284]. Within the narrative, a constant orange glow marks this *Index Manifestation*. The substance reappears in *Agents of S.H.I.E.L.D.*'s "Watchdogs"[285] when an antagonistic organization employs an advanced version of a compound with the same name and orange glow. Finally, the two *Narrative Entities* relate via *Agents of S.H.I.E.L.D.*'s backstory. Within the series and the MCU films, different characters mention that the S.S.R. (Strategic Scientific Reserve) was the precursor to S.H.I.E.L.D. and that several of S.H.I.E.L.D.'s installations previously housed sections of the S.S.R. Specifically, the training compound for S.H.I.E.L.D. scientists shown in "Seeds"[286] is referred to as an old S.S.R. installation. Additionally, Phil Coulson's new base of operation – introduced in "Beginning of the End"[287] and prominently featured for several seasons – is

---

277 "Heavy is the Head". *Agents of S.H.I.E.L.D.* Created by Joss Whedon, Jed Whedon, and Maurissa Tancharoen. Season 2, episode 2. Marvel Television/ABC Studios. 2013–2020. 00:10:27
278 "Emancipation". *Agents of S.H.I.E.L.D.* Created by Joss Whedon, Jed Whedon, and Maurissa Tancharoen. Season 3, episode 20. Marvel Television/ABC Studios. 2013–2020. 00:01:08
279 "Meet the New Boss". *Agents of S.H.I.E.L.D.* Created by Joss Whedon, Jed Whedon, and Maurissa Tancharoen. Season 4, episode 2. Marvel Television/ABC Studios. 2013–2020. 00:19:08
280 For screenshots of this character's appearances in the overall network consult https://marvelcinematicuniverse.fandom.com/wiki/Daniel_Sousa/Gallery
281 "Alien Commies From the Future". *Agents of S.H.I.E.L.D.* Created by Joss Whedon, Jed Whedon, and Maurissa Tancharoen. Season 7, episode 3. Marvel Television/ABC Studios. 2013–2020
282 For screenshots of this *Index Manifestation*'s appearances in the overall network consult https://marvelcinematicuniverse.fandom.com/wiki/Nitramene/Gallery
283 "Now is Not the End". *Agent Carter*. Created by Christopher Markus and Stephen McFeely. Season 1, episode 1. Marvel Television/ABC Studios. 2015–2016
284 "Bridge and Tunnel". *Agent Carter*. Created by Christopher Markus and Stephen McFeely. Season 1, episode 2. Marvel Television/ABC Studios. 2015–2016
285 "Watchdogs". *Agents of S.H.I.E.L.D.* Created by Joss Whedon, Jed Whedon, and Maurissa Tancharoen. Season 3, episode 14. Marvel Television/ABC Studios. 2013–2020.
286 "Seeds". *Agents of S.H.I.E.L.D.* Created by Joss Whedon, Jed Whedon, and Maurissa Tancharoen. Season 1, episode 12. Marvel Television/ABC Studios. 2013–2020. 00:04:27
287 "Beginning of the End". *Agents of S.H.I.E.L.D.* Created by Joss Whedon, Jed Whedon, and Maurissa Tancharoen. Season 1, episode 22. Marvel Television/ABC Studios. 2013–2020

referred to as an old SSR base, overseen by Peggy Carter, in several instances across the series.

Concerning the degree of interrelation, it is clear that ABC's Agents of S.H.I.E.L.D. and Peggy Carter Narrative exist in a Shared Universe relationship. However, the relation is not genuinely close, as the number of crossing *Index Manifestations* compared to the series' overall runtime is small. This limited interaction arises due to the imaginary separation of their *index* networks via time, as *Agent Carter* takes place shortly after the Second World War, while *Agents of S.H.I.E.L.D.* has a contemporary setting. However, within the understanding of the Universe Model, the formal separation between the two *Narrative Entities* is spatial and not temporal. The spatial difference arises due to a unity of overall representation within each series' *index* network, which creates the sense of a unique space within each. This uniqueness of either representation demands additional effort by a transposed *Index Manifestation* to breach. *Agents of S.H.I.E.L.D.* undertakes some extra effort when they include the *Transformation Trigger* of time travel to adapt part of its *Index Manifestations* to the very different general representation of *Agent Carter's index* network.

3.1.3.2   Agent Carter (2015–2016)

Within the first season, Agent Carter offers little to no connection to *Agents of S.H.I.E.L.D.* other than the knowledge that the S.S.R. will someday become S.H.I.E.L.D. Considering that *Agent Carter* is meant to take place in *Agents of S.H.I.E.L.D.*'s past, a limitation to an interrelation of both series through coinciding aspects of the former with the latter's backstory can be expected. There is little reason for *Index Manifestations* of *Agents of S.H.I.E.L.D.* to appear in *Agent Carter* directly. One aspect created during the second season of *Agent Carter*, which later reappears in *Agents of S.H.I.E.L.D.*, is a semi-mystical energy with varying properties from another dimension. A larger part of *Agent Carter's* second season deals with the accidental discovery of this *Index Manifestation*, referred to as Zero Matter. It appears in *Agents of S.H.I.E.L.D.* "The Only Light in the Darkness"[288] and "Parting Shots"[289]. However, while the energy is called Zero Matter in *Agent Carter*, it is referred to as Darkforce in *Agents of S.H.I.E.L.D.* This difference in naming is addressed in a short dialogue in *Agents of S.H.I.E.L.D.* "The Good Samaritan"[290], which also refers to *Transformation Triggers* from the *Agent Carter* series. During the dialogue, characters indicate that a document refers to the *Index Manifestation* by both names. While the alteration in the name is leveled out, the representation of the Zero Matter/Darkforce in either series is also not comparable. Aside from the fact that they use a notion of darkness within each, none of the representations is truly the same[291]. In *Agents of S.H.I.E.L.D.*, the Darkforce appears as a dark, cloudy shadow and a set of dark beams. In *Agent Carter*, Zero Matter appears as a dark rift in the sky, dark matter flowing through the air, a dark cloud,

---

288   "The Only Light in the Darkness". *Agents of S.H.I.E.L.D.* Created by Joss Whedon, Jed Whedon, and Maurissa Tancharoen. Season 1, episode 19. Marvel Television/ABC Studios. 2013–2020

289   "Parting Shots". *Agents of S.H.I.E.L.D.* Created by Joss Whedon, Jed Whedon, and Maurissa Tancharoen. Season 3, episode 13. Marvel Television/ABC Studios. 2013–2020

290   "The Good Samaritan". *Agents of S.H.I.E.L.D.* Created by Joss Whedon, Jed Whedon, and Maurissa Tancharoen. Season 4, episode 6. Marvel Television/ABC Studios. 2013–2020. 00:28:22

291   For screenshots of this *Index Manifestation*'s appearances in the overall network consult https://marvelcinematicuniverse.fandom.com/wiki/Darkforce/Gallery

a dark scar across a character's face, and so on. Within this context, the alteration of appearance and name limits the connecting effect of this specific *Index Manifestation* because only a skilled audience would assume the two interrelate and maybe discover similar aspects from the source material. Vigilant informed audiences might also find the interrelation if they encountered articles in which the show's producers explained that Zero Matter was meant to be the Darkforce before it received its more common name.

With only one potential and weak moment of interrelation, Agent Carter does not change the relationship between the two *Narrative Entities* significantly.

3.1.3.3 Conclusion ABC Series

Containing fewer *Narrative Entities* than the other networks, the interrelation within the ABC series is simple and direct. Due to the imaginary chronological relation between the series, all relations align along *Agent Carter* providing *Transformation Trigger*s for *Agents of S.H.I.E.L.D.*'s backstory. The one exception is the appearance of Daniel Sousa in *Agents of S.H.I.E.L.D.*'s seventh season when the series employs time travel and engages with an *Index Manifestation* associated with *Agent Carter*.

3.1.4 The Marvel Relationships

As the relationships between the different *Narrative Entities* of three networks on the level of their medium of release have been established, these smaller networks can be placed in context with one another. As the overall network started with the MCU network, the MCU films will serve as the focal point. Instead of going from *Manifestation* to *Manifestation* as in the previous chapters, the interrelation between the networks is discussed in broader strokes, focusing on elements appearing across the *Manifestations* from all involved *Narrative Entities*. For organizational purposes, each of the three potential relationships (MCU/MNU; MCU/ABC; MNU/ABC) are discussed in individual chapters.

3.1.4.1 MNU/MCU Relationship

In December 2014, Jeph Loeb, the then Head of Marvel Television, explained:

> "Within the Marvel universe there are thousands of heroes of all shapes and sizes, but the Avengers are here to save the universe and Daredevil is here to save the neighborhood … It does take place in the Marvel Cinematic Universe. It's all connected. But that doesn't necessarily mean that we would look up in the sky and see [Iron Man]. It's just a different part of New York that we have not yet seen in the Marvel movies."[292]

The quote indicates the producers' intention to create a series related to the MCU films while maintaining independence from them. As such, the MNU network has a stated relationship with the MCU network. However, while the producers' intention might prime an audience to search for interrelations, it does not guarantee that these texts share a

---

[292] Quoted in Hibberd, Jane. "Daredevil: 7 things we learned about Netflix's new series". *Entertainment Weekly*. December 29th, 2014. https://ew.com/article/2014/12/29/daredevil6/?hootPostID=86d97ba533da5f593b1f0d7aca86d91, retrieved September 21st, 2021

connection. Excluding allusions, the direct connection between the MCU and MNU networks via crossing or interrelated *Index Manifestations* or *Transformation Triggers* is limited. The one notable *Index Manifestation* concerning a relationship with the MCU in the MNU network are issues of the New York Bulletin – a fictional newspaper publication – hanging in the background of Vondie Curtis-Hall's Ben Urich's and later Deborah Ann Woll's Karen Page's office. Either front page refers to a *Transformation Trigger* from the MCU films' first phase. One titled 'Harlem Terror' refers directly to the final battle of *The Incredible Hulk*, mentioning the Hulk by name. The second one, titled 'Battle of NY', refers to the end of *The Avengers*. In either case, screenshots from the original films provide the covers for each paper, necessarily introducing pictures of MCU *Index Manifestations* into the MNU network[293]. However, while they exist, the plot never focuses on either of the papers, leaving them in the background and, therefore, as a subtle way of interrelation.

Another potential transposed *Index Manifestation* within the MNU network is the company Hammer Industries. In *Iron Man 2*, Hammer Industries is introduced as a competing weapons manufacturer to Stark Industries. Within the film, the company and its founder, Sam Rockwell's Justin Hammer, are marked by a certain level of incompetence. They are unable to replicate the Iron Man Armor; they need help from the film's main antagonist – Mickey Rourke's Ivan Vanko/Whiplash – to build their military drones (which they lose control of); their hallmark weapon 'The Ex-Wife' proves ineffective. Concerning interrelation, the Hammer Industries logo provides a directly recognizable link. Appearing mostly in the background in several scenes of *Iron Man 2*, the logo is visible behind Justin Hammer holding a speech at the Stark Expo[294]. Crates with the same logo, bearing the same font, appear in the *Luke Cage S1* episode "Moment of Truth"[295]. Arms produced by the company are part of an illegal sale, and one of the characters argues the weapon's effectiveness by using Justin Hammer's name. While the logo (or any other visual marker) of Hammer Industries does not appear in any other instant of the MNU network, many high-end weaponries is associated with the company through dialogue. However, no other specific detail concerning the company is given within the series. Sam Rockwell's Justin Hammer makes no appearance, nor do any of his employees from the film. Incidentally, the significant *Transformation Triggers* of *Iron Man 2* concerning this *Index Manifestation* – neither Justin Hammer's presence at the Senate hearing nor the incident with his drones at the Stark Expo – are mentioned within the series. The result of these *Transformation Triggers* is equally never discussed. With merely the logo and the fact that the company is a weapons manufacturer as detailed links between the two representations, the connecting effect of this *Index Manifestation* remains relatively low.

---

[293] For screenshots of these specific *Index Manifestations* consult *Epsiode1.12 The Ones We leave Behind* and the background of *Episode 1.10: Nelson v. Murdock* from https://marvelcinematicuniverse.fandom.com/wiki/Ben_Urich/Gallery

[294] *Iron Man 2*. Directed by Jon Favreau. Performances by Robert Downey Jr., Gwyneth Paltrow, Don Cheadle, Sam Rockwell, and Mickey Rourke. Marvel Studios, 2010. 01:32:23

[295] "The Moment of Truth". *Luke Cage*. Created by Cheo Hodari Coker. Season 1, episode 1. Marvel Television/ABC Studios. 2016–2018. 00:18:14

While direct interrelation through an exchange of *Index Manifestations* or shared *Transformation Triggers* is virtually non-existent, the MNU alludes to *Index Manifestations* from the MCU films. In the *Daredevil S1* episode "In the Blood", Tobey Leonard Moore's James Wesley alludes to the existence of Iron Man and Thor[296]. Frank Whaley's Rafael Scarfe also alludes to Thor's hammer[297] in the *Luke Cage S1* episode "Who's Gonna Take the Weight?". Luke Cage alludes to the Hulk in a conversation with Jessica Jones[298] in *Jessica Jones S1* "AKA It's Called Whiskey". She, in return, implies the existence of Captain America and the Hulk[299] in "AKA 99 Friends". Of all the notable *Index Manifestations* from the MCU films, only Tony Stark and Captain America are directly mentioned by name in MNU's *Manifestations*: Tony Stark is mentioned in the *Luke Cage S1* episode "Moment of Truth" (with further references to other Avengers)[300] and as his superhero persona in a song[301] performed intradiegetically by the rapper Method Man in "Soliloquy of Chaos". Captain America is referred to directly in the *Jessica Jones S2* episode "AKA Sole Survivor" by the son of the main character's building supervisor[302]. As typical for allusions, they hinge on the audience's cooperation or acceptance of the producer's intent. The texts give little indication that these allusions, even the use of character names, directly refer to the *Index Manifestations* presented in the films instead of another potential manifestation of these *indices*. Except for the newspapers in the background, each reference or allusion within the MNU has no necessary relation to the films but, at this point, merely indicates that a version of these *Narrative Entities* exists within the world presented within the MNU series. In other words, while the MNU network implicitly contains some version of Tony Stark, Captain America, Thor, and the Hulk, the only indication that these are the renditions from the MCU films, in contrast to some others, relies on two newspaper covers in the background of one set and the stated producer's intent. Hereby, it is notable that one of the two newspaper covers connects the MNU to *The Incredible Hulk*, which also has a tenuous connection to the overall MCU film network.

The one grand *Transformation Trigger*, which carries great influence into each of the three networks, is the end of *The Avengers*. The conflict between the newly formed Avengers and Loki's Chitauri army reverberated throughout each network, creating several *Trigger Waves*. Any physical representation of the *Transformation Trigger* within the MNU is limited to the newspaper article in Ben Urich's and Karen Page's office. The end

---

[296] "In the Blood". *Daredevil*. Created by Drew Goddard. Season 1, episode 4. Marvel Television/ABC Studios. 2015–2018. 00:08:20

[297] "Who's Gonna Take the Weight". *Luke Cage*. Created by Cheo Hodari Coker. Season 1, episode 3. MarvelTelevision/ABC Studios. 2016–2018. 00:41:57

[298] "AKA It's Called Whiskey". *Jessica Jones*. Created by Melissa Rosenberg. Season 1, episode 3. Marvel Television/ABC Studios. 2015–2019. 00:04:15

[299] "AKA 99 Friends". *Jessica Jones*. Created by Melissa Rosenberg. Season 1, episode 4. Marvel Television/ABC Studios. 2015–2019. 00:35:52

[300] "The Moment of Truth". *Luke Cage*. Created by Cheo Hodari Coker. Season 1, episode 1. Marvel Television/ABC Studios. 2016–2018. 00:10:25

[301] "Soliloquy of Chaos". *Luke Cage*. Created by Cheo Hodari Coker. Season 1, episode 12. Marvel Television/ABC Studios. 2016–2018. 00:29:51

[302] "AKA Sole Survivor". *Jessica Jones*. Created by Melissa Rosenberg. Season 2, episode 3. Marvel Television/ABC Studios. 2015–2019. 00:31:36

of *The Avengers* informs a greater part of each MNU's *Manifestations*' backstory. *Daredevil S1*'s "Into the Ring"[303] alludes to the destruction caused by an event like the 'Battle of New York' as the reason for massive rebuilding efforts within the city. In the *Iron Fist S1* episode "Shadow Hawk Takes Flight"[304], such an event is mentioned as the cause for a rise in a new form of delusion, in which people believe they have superpowers. A greater fear of enhanced people is pervasive in *Luke Cage* and *Jessica Jones*. A change to overall society, criminal society, and the process of policing is often mentioned within *Luke Cage*. Alfre Woodard's Mariah Dillard decries the actions of "freaks in our neighborhood" and refers to the super-powered individuals in her public speeches. A direct series of *Transformation Triggers* potentially linking *Luke Cage* to *The Avengers* lies in the appearance of the Judas Bullets. A prototype firearm ammunition capable of penetrating Luke Cage's bulletproof skin, the Judas Bullet is introduced in "Just to Get a Rep". In the episode, the bullet's extraordinary capabilities are related to an alien metal left behind during an alien attack on New York[305]. Aside from more minor sequences in which the main character of *Jessica Jones* deals with fear towards her extraordinary strength, the subplot of "AKA 99 Friends" revolves around a direct reaction to an event such as the 'Battle of New York'. In the episode, Jessica Jones accepts a case of a cheating husband. Jones tracks the husband to a rendezvous with his alleged girlfriend. As it turns out, the wife solicited the case to trap and kill Jessica Jones because Jones is a superpowered individual. This *Transformation Trigger* links to the 'Battle of New York', as the wife blames super-powered individuals for her mother's death, who died specifically during that event. While these connections to the end of *The Avengers* exist, they straddle the line between a clear interrelation and a mere allusion. Each moment provides hints, but none makes clear that this underlying backstory necessarily coincides with the 'Battle of New York' as it was presented in *The Avengers*. A difference in terminology underscores this ambiguity. While this *Transformation Trigger* goes by 'Battle of New York' in the MCU films, the MNU – except for the New York Bulletin's front page – refers to it as 'The Incident'. The lack of a coherent reference creates distance between the two networks concerning this *Transformation Trigger*. Additionally, MNU *Manifestations* avoid giving direct descriptions of the actual battle. Instead, the dialogue just hints at an alien attack, greater levels of destruction, and the appearance of a version of the Avengers. In contrast, the MCU films employ their established reference to the *Transformation Triggers* (Battle of New York) comparatively seldom but regularly reiterate actual parts of the battle, specifically *Iron Man 3* and *Avengers: Age of Ultron* are notable in that regard. Additionally, the influence of the 'Battle of New York' decreases after the first season of every *Narrative Entity* in the MNU, as all examples stem from the first seasons.

While the 'Battle of New York' – or a version of it – at the end of *The Avengers* informs a greater part of the MNU's backstory and flows into smaller *Trigger Waves*, a lack of clear,

---

303 "Into the Ring". Daredevil. Created by Drew Goddard. Season 1, episode 1. Marvel Television/ABC Studios. 2015–2018.
304 "Shadow Hawk Takes Flight". *Iron Fist*. Created by Scott Buck. Season 1, episode 2. Marvel Television/ABC Studios. 2017–2018. 00:52:00
305 "Just to get a Rep". *Luke Cage*. Created by Cheo Hodari Coker. Season 1, episode 5. Marvel Television/ABC Studios. 2016–2018. 00:27:05

detailed connections seems notable. The MNU does not present any *Index Manifestation* transferred from the films. The heavy emphasis on allusions over *Index Manifestations* directly wandering between the networks creates an odd limbo concerning their connection, especially at the latter stages of each network. While a connection exists, the clarity of its existence hinges on parts of the setting in the background and some goodwill on the side of the audience. As the only part of the MNU displaying verifiable *Index Manifestations* of the MCU films, the newspapers form the only tangible proof of an interrelation. All other mentions of the MCU films boil down to the audience's receptiveness to the producers' stated intent of interrelating the two networks. With even the allusions dying away with the series' progression, the meager interrelation has to compete with a more significant number of *Manifestations* without any link to the MCU. Notably, this research only mentions connections flowing from the MCU films to the MNU series, but none in the other direction. The reason is that the MCU does not refer to any part of the MNU network. No part of the series' *Index Manifestation* appears or finds mention in the films. The films show no changes or acknowledgment of the MNU's *Transformation Triggers*.

As such, the MNU maneuvers into a situation in which it relates to the rest of the MCU primarily by the producers' intention. It is clear that the series shares a world with characters similar to those in the film. Also, a large *Transformation Trigger* similar to the end of *The Avengers* and the final battle of *The Incredible Hulk* exist. The *Manifestations*, however, give only one background hint, indicating that the allusions are direct references to the versions of the *Index Manifestations* presented in the MCU films. That hint draws the MNU and MCU network into a Multiverse, maybe a distant Shared Universe, relationship. The series' lack of reliance on the films and the films' absolute non-reliance on the series pushes the two networks further apart. While it is easy to presume that there is, at least, an imagined dependency of the series on the films, the films require no knowledge of the series. Even this imagined dependence is not strong, as accepting a backstory involving large-scale superhero conflicts is sufficient to contextualize most references to 'The Incident'. The series could occupy any version of a Marvel Superhero Universe containing these characters, which had a significant, large-scale event in New York (the number of qualified options from comics is astounding). The lack of necessary interrelation opens the MNU network to a casual audience. While an informed audience migrating from the MCU may see or enjoy these largely narrative extensions alluding to the films, the interrelation mainly targets a skilled audience, which has previous knowledge concerning the interrelation of all involved *Narrative Entities* within the comics. This accessibility to a casual audience, due to not requiring specific knowledge from the films, pushes the two networks further apart, placing them into a clear Narrative Multiverse relationship.

The distance between the MCU and MNU network raises an interesting question concerning the different audience types within the Universe Model. The existence of *Shared Narratives* and the introduction of *Index Manifestations* within their own shows for later use in a team narrative indicate that not all parts of the MNU network can operate with a purely casual audience. However, as the previous discussion on the interrelation of either network implies, the MNU does not require an informed audience from the MCU network. The recognition of several types of informed audiences resolves this apparent contradiction. Informed audiences necessarily have to be associated with specific networks or sets of *Narrative Entities*. To understand the application and range of interrelating techniques, it is necessary to differentiate between three types of informed audiences in this instant: an overall MCU-informed audience, an MNU-informed audience, and an MCU films-informed audience. The first engages with the films and the MNU series, carrying knowledge of most of the Shared Universes. The third engaged mainly (only) with the films, only knowing the MCU film network. The second informed audience grows from solely engaging with the MNU network. It appears foolish to assume that the MNU-informed audience has absolutely no knowledge of the MCU films, but their engagement can be rudimentary. A distinction between these three types of informed audiences indicates that the MNU network, equal to the MCU network, contains a process to educate a casual audience into an informed one, which then recognizes and enjoys the connections between the different *Narrative Entities* within that network.

3.1.4.2 ABC/MCU Relationship

In contrast to the MNU, both ABC series were created directly related to the MCU films. *Agents of S.H.I.E.L.D.* continues the story of Clark Gregg's Phil Coulson, who provides a *Shared Narrative* for the MCU films. Equally, *Agent Carter* explores the life of Hayley Atwell's Peggy Carter, a character established in *Captain America: The First Avenger*, and equally serves as an interconnecting *Index Manifestation* for the films. As the series grew out of the MCU films, *Agents of S.H.I.E.L.D.* and *Agent Carter* necessarily begin with a strong relation to the MCU films, expressed in a greater reliance on the MCU film's *Index Manifestations* and *Transformation Triggers*.

The most apparent *Index Manifestations* interrelating the MCU films with the ABC series are each series' main character. Clark Gregg's Phil Coulson appears in the first episode of *Agents of S.H.I.E.L.D.* and in 123 of the series' 136 episodes. The character's initial appearance in the series continues its representation from the film[306]. Marked by a government man aesthetic, Phil Coulson wears a dark, non-descript suit. The series retains this representation for most of the first two seasons. Specific *Transformation Triggers* alter the character's style of clothing temporarily. At the beginning of the third season, the representation of Phil Coulson replaced the suit with a more casual summer jacket, a simple shirt and pants, and he lost the tie, removing the *Index Manifestation* somewhat from the version seen in the films. The previous color scheme remains. The alteration arises from a *Transformation Trigger*, which also gives the character a new prosthetic hand as an additional *semiotic cue*. With a few exceptions due to the course of the series, the representations of Phil Coulson adhere to this new version up to the end of season four. Due to another *Transformation Trigger* (being held captive by aliens), the representation of Phil Coulson shifts for half of the fifth season. The *Index Manifestation* is generally dirtier, unshaved, and wears a summer pullover instead of a shirt. The prosthetic hand remains. Again, the shift creates distance between the representations of the character in the films. After the season's midpoint, the character returns to a version of its former representation, which finds them back on earth. Except for specific *Transformation Triggers*, this representation remains in place until the character dies in the sixth

---

306 For screenshots of Phil Coulson's appearances in the MCU consult https://marvelcinematicuniverse.fandom.com/wiki/Phil_Coulson/Gallery

episode of the sixth season. Clark Gregg returns as alternate versions of Phil Coulson, but these are different characters. One has aspects of Coulson but isn't him, and the other is a robotic copy of the original. The latter of these two versions begins in the suit-and-tie representation of the character but shifts to a version more akin to the character's earlier representation at the end of the season. However, within the series, the copy is continually marked as not-Coulson through dialogue and the inclusion of different abilities and knowledge to the original.

While Hayley Atwell's Peggy Carter appears in fewer episodes of the ABC network than Phil Coulson, as *Agent Carter* ran only for 18 episodes, the character provides a stronger connection between the two networks. In contrast to Coulson, Peggy Carter does not have a clear unity of representation within either network[307]. Instead, the character appears throughout *Agent Carter* in a variety of dresses and hairstyles from the show's era (whereas her hairstyle remains stable within seasons). Something similar can be said about her representation within the films. While the character's general style remains the same, suited to the era in which the *Narrative Entity* takes place, the constant shifts in outfit lower the comparability when contrasted with Phil Coulson. Therefore, Peggy Carter's connection leans mainly on the consistent use of the actress Hayley Atwell within the context of the MCU and a particular type of fashion, hair, and makeup as *semiotic cues*. However, while Phil Coulson and Peggy Carter directly intersect with the MCU films nearly the same number of times, Peggy Carter ties the two networks closer together, as her appearances are spread out across the MCU's different phases. Hayley Atwell is introduced as the character in the first phase (*Captain America: The First Avenger*), appears in three films of the second phase (*Captain America: The Winter Soldier, Avengers: Age of Ultron, Ant-Man*), and shows up in the next-to-last film of the third phase (*Avengers: Endgame*). These spread-out appearances serve as constant reminders of the *Index Manifestation*'s existence and significance, strengthening the relationship between the networks. Phil Coulson, in contrast, appears five times within the MCU network. However, with the exception of *Captain Marvel*, which takes place before the events of *Iron Man*, all the character's MCU appearances fall into the first phase. This more concentrated use of Phil Coulson helps to tie the first films together but also allows for a clear distinction between the *Index Manifestation* shown in the second half of *Agents of S.H.I.E.L.D.* and the version shown in the films, as the new version (and a reminder of the series) is never established in the MCU network. While Phil Coulson's inclusion in *Captain Marvel* serves as a reminder of the character and the series, the version used in the Captain Marvel *Manifestation* relates more to one presented in earlier films than the version from later in *Agents of S.H.I.E.L.D.*, as *Captain Marvel* ignores all *Transformation Triggers* from the series. As such, the two main characters of *Agents of S.H.I.E.L.D.* and *Agent Carter* relate the ABC and MCU networks to one another. However, the relationship grows weaker with the rise of *Transformation Triggers* in the case of Phil Coulson. Equally, the relation created through Peggy Carter is nebulous through the character's shifting visual representation but stabilized through her spread-out appearance.

---

307   For screenshots of Peggy Carter's appearances in the MCU consult https://marvelcinematicuniverse.fandom.com/wiki/Peggy_Carter/Gallery

Aside from Clark Gregg's Phil Coulson and Hayley Atwell's Peggy Carter, other characters connect the MCU films and the ABC series by appearing in both – Samuel L. Jackson's Nick Fury, James D'Arcy's Edwin Jarvis, Cobie Smulders's Maria Hill, Maximiliano Hernández's Agent Jasper Sitwell, Powers Boothe's Gideon Malik, Toby Jones's Arnim Zola, Henry Goodman's Doctor List, Jamie Alexander's Sif, and William Sadler's President Matthew Ellis. The most notable is Samuel L. Jackson's Nick Fury's inclusion in *Agents of S.H.I.E.L.D.*[308]. Jackson's interpretation of the character makes a guest appearance in the episode "0-8-4"[309] and is briefly seen in "The Magical Place"[310]. He returns in the season finale, "Beginning of the End". The consistency of visual cues between the films and the series is remarkable. Within the films, Nick Fury retains a standard appearance containing his eye patch, long black coat, and mostly black clothing. After the fall of S.H.I.E.L.D. at the end of *Captain America: The Winter Soldier*, the character alters his outfit. He replaces his eye patch with sunglasses and exchanges his coat for a dark jacket. In *Agents of S.H.I.E.L.D.*, the character retains his former visual cues in the previous two episodes, which concerning the influence of *Trigger Waves* occurs before the fall of S.H.I.E.L.D., while appearing in his latter form in the season's finale, acknowledging the changes to the *Index Manifestation* due to the *Transformation Triggers* of *Captain America: The Winter Soldier*. In contrast, the character of Jarvis provides a lighter connection between the two networks[311]. Edwin Jarvis, portrayed by James D'Arcy, appears as Howard Stark's butler in all 18 episodes of *Agent Carter*. In several instances, the dialogue implies that the person in the series inspired J.A.R.V.I.S., the artificial intelligence underlying Iron Man's armor until *Avengers: Age of Ultron*. More significantly, James D'Arcy shows up in *Avengers: Endgame* implicitly as an older version of the same character[312]. Like the character Peggy Carter, the connection created relies solely on recognizing the actor within the context of the MCU, as other visual cues change between appearances. While *Agent Carter* merely provides one other *Index Manifestation* interrelating the different networks, *Agents of S.H.I.E.L.D.* has several instances of wandering *Index Manifestations*. As the series revolves around the organization S.H.I.E.L.D., some of the characters affiliated with the organization who appeared in the films also appear in the series. Aside from Nick Fury, Cobie Smulders's Maria Hill is among the most prominent[313]. Introduced in *The Avengers*, the character appears in *Captain America: The Winter Soldier*, *Avengers: Age of Ultron*, *Avengers: Infinity War*, *Avengers: Endgame*, and *Spider-Man: Homecoming*. She also is in

---

308 For screenshots of Nick Fury's appearances within the MCU consult https://marvelcinematicuniverse.fandom.com/wiki/Nick_Fury/Gallery
309 "0-8-4". *Agents of S.H.I.E.L.D.* Created by Joss Whedon, Jed Whedon, and Maurissa Tancharoen. Season 1, episode 2. Marvel Television/ABC Studios. 2013–2020. 00:39:41
310 "The Magical Place". *Agents of S.H.I.E.L.D.* Created by Joss Whedon, Jed Whedon, and Maurissa Tancharoen. Season 1, episode 11. Marvel Television/ABC Studios. 2013–2020. 00:33:55
311 For screenshots of this character's appearances in the overall network consult https://marvelcinematicuniverse.fandom.com/wiki/Edwin_Jarvis/Gallery
312 *Avengers: Endgame*. Directed by Anthony Russo and Joe Russo. Marvel Studios, 2019. 01:46:26
313 For screenshots of this character's appearances within the MCU consult https://marvelcinematicuniverse.fandom.com/wiki/Maria_Hill/Gallery

three episodes of *Agents of S.H.I.E.L.D.*, "Pilot"[314], "Nothing Personal"[315], and "The Dirty Half Dozen"[316]. Within the films, the character appears dominantly in two forms: She is dressed in her S.H.I.E.L.D. uniform up to the infiltration and fall of the organization in *Captain America: The Winter Soldier*. After the fall of S.H.I.E.L.D., she interviews for a job at Stark Industries and starts at the company. The *Transformation Triggers* alters her *semiotic cues*. Forthwith, she appears dominantly in situation-appropriate civilian attire[317]. As with the character Nick Fury, the changes are mirrored in the character's appearance in the series. In "Pilot", Maria Hill is shown in her S.H.I.E.L.D. uniform, reflecting her introduction in *The Avengers*. She shifts to civilian clothing for the episode "Nothing Personal", which takes place after *Captain America: The Winter Soldier*, wearing a business suit, leaving her office and more practical clothes when she accompanies the military to one of S.H.I.E.L.D.'s former bases. As the character retains the actress as well as displays her relationships and status within the overall network in most interactions as a fixed *semiotic cue*, this *Index Manifestation* provides a tangible connection.

The connection between the networks via S.H.I.E.L.D. employees continues with lesser-known characters. Maximiliano Hernández's Agent Jasper Sitwell appears in smaller roles across the MCU films, but the character also is prominently featured in *Agents of S.H.I.E.L.D.*[318]. Debuting in *Thor*, he reappears in *The Avengers* and *Captain America: The Winter Soldier*, where he is killed. The character also is in three episodes of *Agents of S.H.I.E.L.D.*, "The Hub"[319], "Yes Men"[320], and "End of the Beginning"[321]. In all appearances, the character is presented as the classic agent in a non-descript suit. Equally, each visual representation of Jasper Sitwell within the MCU films and the ABC series shows him bald and wearing glasses. Despite dying in *Captain America: The Winter Soldier*, Jasper Sitwell appears twice after that *Transformation Trigger*, once in *Avengers: Endgame*, in which the heroes travel back in time, and in the fifth season's episode "Rise and Shine"[322] of *Agents of S.H.I.E.L.D.* However, the latter has no bearing on the connection between the networks, as it shows the character at a younger age in a previously

---

314 "Pilot". *Agents of S.H.I.E.L.D.* Created by Joss Whedon, Jed Whedon, and Maurissa Tancharoen. Season 1, episode 1. Marvel Television/ABC Studios. 2013–2020

315 "Nothing Personal". *Agents of S.H.I.E.L.D.* Created by Joss Whedon, Jed Whedon, and Maurissa Tancharoen. Season 1, episode 20. Marvel Television/ABC Studios. 2013–2020.

316 "Dirty Half Dozen". *Agents of S.H.I.E.L.D.* Created by Joss Whedon, Jed Whedon, and Maurissa Tancharoen. Season 2, episode 19. Marvel Television/ABC Studios. 2013–2020. 00:40:00

317 The end of the *Avengers: Age of Ultron* is a notable exception as she temporarily returns to her role as S.H.I.E.L.D. agent.

318 For screenshots of this character's appearances within the MCU consult https://marvelcinematicuniverse.fandom.com/wiki/Jasper_Sitwell/Gallery

319 "The Hub". *Agents of S.H.I.E.L.D.* Created by Joss Whedon, Jed Whedon, and Maurissa Tancharoen. Season 1, episode 7. Marvel Television/ABC Studios. 2013–2020

320 "Yes Men". *Agents of S.H.I.E.L.D.* Created by Joss Whedon, Jed Whedon, and Maurissa Tancharoen. Season 1, episode 15. Marvel Television/ABC Studios. 2013–2020. 00:06:57

321 "End of the Beginning". *Agents of S.H.I.E.L.D.* Created by Joss Whedon, Jed Whedon, and Maurissa Tancharoen. Season 1, episode 16. Marvel Television/ABC Studios. 2013–2020

322 "Rise and Shine". *Agents of S.H.I.E.L.D.* Created by Joss Whedon, Jed Whedon, and Maurissa Tancharoen. Season 5, episode 15. Marvel Television/ABC Studios. 2013–2020

unknown version. As the secret organization Hydra forms S.H.I.E.L.D.'s main antagonist and equally appears in the ABC and MCU networks, *Index Manifestations* associated with Hydra also connect both networks.

Powers Boothe's Gideon Malik is introduced in *The Avengers* as a member of the World Security Council, which supervises S.H.I.E.L.D. Powers Boothe continues his depiction of Gideon Malik in eleven episodes of *Agents of S.H.I.E.L.D.*'s third season[323]. While the same actor portrays the character in either iteration, the connective effect is limited as the version shown in *The Avengers* only appears as one of four shadowy figures on a screen within the scene. This representation allows for very few *semiotic cues*, leaving only the actor within a specific context as a connecting element, similar to Peggy Carter and Edwin Jarvis. One Hydra-associated character connecting the two networks via *Agent Carter* is Toby Jones's Arnim Zola[324]. Featured in *Captain America: The First Avenger*, Arnim Zola later reappears as a computer program in *Captain America: The Winter Soldier*. The character is also in the *Agent Carter* episode "Valediction"[325]. One *semiotic cue* tied to the character is his round glasses. These appear with each iteration portrayed by Toby Jones and are even used to identify the foggy representation of him as a computer program. When Arnim Zola appears in *Agent Carter*, the character only retains his glasses as a *semiotic cue*, relying otherwise on the actor within the context of the series. While the character shows no continuity in clothing throughout his appearance in *Captain America: The First Avenger*, his representation in prison relies on the *Transformation Trigger* of his capture at the end of the MCU's first Captain America *Manifestation*.

Another *Index Manifestation* creating a connection via the use of the same actor in the same role comes in the form of Henry Goodman's Doctor List[326]. Doctor List is particularly interesting because the character's appearances in *Captain America: The Winter Soldier* and *Avengers: Age of Ultron* frame his presence in three episodes of *Agents of S.H.I.E.L.D.* Not marked visually outside of the actor, as he wears a lab coat in either movie and a black suit in the series, Doctor List is marked through his direct relation to Thomas Kretschmann's Wolfgang von Strucker. With the exception of three short sequences, the two characters interact in all their movie appearances. Additionally, Wolfgang von Strucker is mentioned in nearly every conversation with or even about Doctor List in *Agents of S.H.I.E.L.D.*, effectively making Doctor List a stand-in for the more famous Hydra leader. List's interest and motivation in the series are equally tied to the movies. In either instance, he is mainly concerned with creating enhanced individuals. The constancy of Doctor List's relationship with Strucker and the coherence in his motivation, which folds into the plot of the series as he appears right after the introduction of the super-powered Inhumans, creates a strong interrelation between the series and films.

---

[323] For screenshots of this character's appearances within the MCU consult https://marvelcinematicuniverse.fandom.com/wiki/Gideon_Malik/Gallery

[324] For screenshots of this character's appearances within the MCU consult https://marvelcinematicuniverse.fandom.com/wiki/Arnim_Zola/Gallery

[325] "Valediction". *Agent Carter*. Created by Christopher Markus and Stephen McFeely. Season 1, episode 8. Marvel Television/ABC Studios. 2015–2016. 00:41:08

[326] For screenshots of this character's appearances within the MCU consult https://marvelcinematicuniverse.fandom.com/wiki/List/Gallery

However, the connection also hinges significantly on a skilled audience, which recognizes not only the *Index Manifestation* but also the interrelated order of its appearance with little direct hints in either *Manifestation*.

Agents of S.H.I.E.L.D. also uses *Index Manifestations* not directly or indirectly associated with S.H.I.E.L.D. Jamie Alexander's Sif, who is prominently featured in *Thor* and *Thor: The Dark World*, appears in "Yes Men" from *Agents of S.H.I.E.L.D.*'s first season and returns in the second season's "Who You Really Are"[327]. In contrast to most of the previous examples, Sif retains her *semiotic cues*[328]. Due to the movies, the character is associated with a silver armor, a small shield, and a sword. While the design of these items changes between the movies slightly, Jamie Alexander wears her outfit and uses her weapons shown in *Thor: The Dark World* in "Yes Men". In the greater part of "Who You Really Are", she operates without the *semiotic cue* of her armor but retains her sword. However, the character is shown with her full *semiotic cues* at the end of the episode. The appearance of Jamie Alexander's Sif generates a stronger connection between the films and the series because of the retention of clear markers. Additionally, this *Index Manifestation* does not naturally associate with *Index Manifestations* of *Agents of S.H.I.E.L.D.* in the same manner the previously mentioned do, highlighting its transposed nature. As Phil Coulson and Sif knew one another from *Thor* and Coulson presumably died at the end of *The Avengers*, Sif's familiarity with Coulson and her surprise at his presence rely on information given in the MCU films, strengthening the connection between series and films due to a degree of reliance.

A further non-S.H.I.E.L.D. related *Index Manifestation* connecting the two networks comes in the form of William Sadler's President Matthew Ellis[329]. As the United States presented in the MCU films and the ABC series presumably are the same fictional version of the nation, the U.S. President should also be the same. President Matthew Ellis is introduced in *Iron Man 3*, in which he is a damsel-in-distress. A quote from the character is also part of the Captain America display at the Smithsonian in *Captain America: The Winter Soldier*[330]. More significantly, Matthew Ellis appears in three episodes of *Agents of S.H.I.E.L.D.* and is mentioned in several others. In "Laws of Nature"[331], he is shown on a television screen addressing the nation on the emergence of Inhumans. The character appears directly in "Bouncing Back"[332] to discuss the overall situation with Phil Coulson. He

---

327 "Who You Really Are". *Agents of S.H.I.E.L.D.* Created by Joss Whedon, Jed Whedon, and Maurissa Tancharoen. Season 2, episode 12. Marvel Television/ABC Studios. 2013–2020.
328 For screenshots of this character's appearances within the MCU consult https://marvelcinematicuniverse.fandom.com/wiki/Sif/Gallery
329 For screenshots of this character's appearances within the MCU consult https://marvelcinematicuniverse.fandom.com/wiki/Matthew_Ellis/Gallery
330 *Captain America: The Winter Soldier*. Directed by Anthony Russo and Joe Russo. Performances by Chris Evans, Scarlett Johansson, and Sebastian Stan. Marvel Studios, 2014. 00:18:24
331 "Laws of Nature". *Agents of S.H.I.E.L.D.* Created by Joss Whedon, Jed Whedon, and Maurissa Tancharoen. Season 3, episode 1. Marvel Television/ABC Studios. 2013–2020. 00:35:19
332 "Bouncing Back". *Agents of S.H.I.E.L.D.* Created by Joss Whedon, Jed Whedon, and Maurissa Tancharoen. Season 3, episode 11. Marvel Television/ABC Studios. 2013–2020. 00:04:05

makes his final appearance in *Agents of S.H.I.E.L.D.* "Parting Shots"[333], in which he helps to insulate S.H.I.E.L.D. from an international incident. Aside from being portrayed by the same actor in all these appearances, the character also always wears a politician's suit with a pin of the star-spangled banner on his lapel.

Aside from characters, other *Index Manifestations* also intertwine the two networks: S.H.I.E.L.D.'s main headquarters in Washington DC, known as the Triskelion, is shown in the MCU films and in *Agents of S.H.I.E.L.D.*[334]. Mentioned throughout both, the building itself makes only four on-screen appearances. Within the MCU network, its construction is shown in *Ant-Man* and its presence and destruction in *Captain America: The Winter Soldier*. Footage of the building's destruction is later shown in *Captain America: Civil War* and the *Agents of S.H.I.E.L.D.* episode "Providence"[335]. The footage in either instance is lifted from *Captain America: The Winter Soldier*. After its destruction in the MCU films, the Triskelion reappears in five episodes of *Agents of S.H.I.E.L.D.*'s fourth season. As this version of the building is part of a simulated reality known as the Framework, it appears with key differences but still alludes to the original design.

Loki's Scepter is another *Index Manifestation* interrelating *Agents of S.H.I.E.L.D.* and the MCU films[336]. Introduced in *The Avengers*, the object appears in three further films: *Captain America: The Winter Soldier*, *Avengers: Age of Ultron*, and *Avengers: Endgame*. A vision and a computer design of the scepter are also featured in the *Agents of S.H.I.E.L.D.*'s "The Dirty Half Dozen"[337]. Aside from the final battle in *The Avengers*, the scepter never changes throughout its appearances. This consistency in visual representation is used in *Agents of S.H.I.E.L.D.* when a scene from *The Avengers* is blurred and repurposed as a vision and also allows for a weaker connection via a computer diagram.

Aside from tangible *Index Manifestations*, the two networks also employ grouped *Index Manifestations* to interrelate with one another. One of the more obvious ones is the use of the same alien races. Two alien races directly appear in both networks, the Asgardians and the Kree. Informally introduced in the episode "T.A.H.I.T.I."[338], the Kree appear in four MCU *Manifestations* and several episodes of *Agents of S.H.I.E.L.D.* While no specific individual member of the Kree crossed between the series and the films, these aliens interlink the networks through shared characteristics in representation. Most notable and stable across all representations is their dominantly blue skin and their greater physical capability compared to humans. Notable examples of these characteristics are *Index Manifestations* like Minn-Erva, Bron-Char, and Att-Lass from *Captain Marvel*, Ronan the

---

[333] "Parting Shots". *Agents of S.H.I.E.L.D.* Created by Joss Whedon, Jed Whedon, and Maurissa Tancharoen. Season 3, episode 13. Marvel Television/ABC Studios. 2013–2020. 00:31:24

[334] For screenshots of this *Index Manifestation*'s appearances within the MCU consult https://marvelcinematicuniverse.fandom.com/wiki/Triskelion/Gallery

[335] "Providence". *Agents of S.H.I.E.L.D.* Created by Joss Whedon, Jed Whedon, and Maurissa Tancharoen. Season 1, episode 18. Marvel Television/ABC Studios. 2013–2020.

[336] For screenshots of this *Index Manifestation*'s appearances within the MCU consult https://marvelcinematicuniverse.fandom.com/wiki/Scepter/Gallery

[337] "Dirty Half Dozen". *Agents of S.H.I.E.L.D.* Created by Joss Whedon, Jed Whedon, and Maurissa Tancharoen. Season 2, episode 19. Marvel Television/ABC Studios. 2013–2020. 00:39:57

[338] "T.A.H.I.T.I.". *Agents of S.H.I.E.L.D.* Created by Joss Whedon, Jed Whedon, and Maurissa Tancharoen. Season 1, episode 14. Marvel Television/ABC Studios. 2013–2020. 00:38:13

Accuser from *Guardians of the Galaxy*, the Kree Reapers from *Agents of S.H.I.E.L.D.*'s "Failed Experiment"[339], or several Kree individuals appearing throughout the first half of *Agents of S.H.I.E.L.D.*'s fifth season. The combination of these characteristics with consistency in naming implies a coherent heritage of all *Index Manifestations* associated with these aliens. Additionally, interaction and description of such a concept by a wandering *Index Manifestation* strengthens the existing interrelation. *Agents of S.H.I.E.L.D.* uses such a strategy when Sif lists the Kree as one of several blue-colored alien species in "Yes Men"[340] and when she interacts with Eddie McClintock's Vin-Tak, who only appears in "Who You Really Are". The Asgardians are presented in a similar fashion.

Aside from the wandering *Index Manifestation*, Sif, *Agents of S.H.I.E.L.D.* includes two further Asgardians. After this alien race was introduced in *Thor* and reiterated in *Thor: The Dark World*, Peter MacNicol's Elliot Randolph, and Elena Satine's Lorelei appear in the series. Asgardians are marked by displayed or mentioned characteristics like their physical durability, superhuman strength, and long lifespan, as they are presented with an average human appearance. Elliot Randolph is in "The Well"[341] and "Purpose in the Machine"[342]. Specifically, in the former episode, he is marked as an Asgardian due to presenting uncanny strength when he bends the blade of a knife, shows high resistance to harm, healing from near death, and indicates a long lifespan as it is revealed he lived on Earth for hundreds of years. Dialogue also makes note of his Asgardian heritage and relates the character to a notable Asgardian, Thor[343]. His second appearance further showcases the character's life span and strength. Lorelei equally acknowledges her association with Asgardians when she displays uncanny strength by tossing a man several feet with a backhand slap, and her long lifespan finds mention when her past crimes are described as being 600 years ago in "Yes Men". As with the Kree, the appearance and association with Sif strengthens the character relations to the concept of Asgardians. While the interrelation of the two networks via the concept of a fictional species occurs, it creates a far lesser degree of connection than the direct use of a specific *Index Manifestation*. For one, using a fictional species relies on the audience's comprehension of its existence and the ability to associate several different *Index Manifestations* via that concept, therefore relying on an informed or skilled audience. Additionally, as the characteristics of a fictional species often operate with a lesser degree of detail, connections via species often can be made beyond the original network. The characteristics of Asgardians and Kree easily connect the MCU films and ABC series, but equally with their comic book representations or even fictional races from other networks. While these connections exist in an intertextual sense, they alone do not draw *Narrative Entities* closer together.

---

339 "Failed Experiment". *Agents of S.H.I.E.L.D.* Created by Joss Whedon, Jed Whedon, and Maurissa Tancharoen. Season 3, episode 19. Marvel Television/ABC Studios. 2013–2020.

340 "Yes Men". *Agents of S.H.I.E.L.D.* Created by Joss Whedon, Jed Whedon, and Maurissa Tancharoen. Season 1, episode 15. Marvel Television/ABC Studios. 2013–2020. 00:14:15

341 "The Well". *Agents of S.H.I.E.L.D.* Created by Joss Whedon, Jed Whedon, and Maurissa Tancharoen. Season 1, episode 8. Marvel Television/ABC Studios. 2013–2020.

342 "Purpose in the Machine". *Agents of S.H.I.E.L.D.* Created by Joss Whedon, Jed Whedon, and Maurissa Tancharoen. Season 3, episode 2. Marvel Television/ABC Studios. 2013–2020.

343 "The Well". *Agents of S.H.I.E.L.D.* Created by Joss Whedon, Jed Whedon, and Maurissa Tancharoen. Season 1, episode 8. Marvel Television/ABC Studios. 2013–2020. 00:16:48

Something similar can be said about the application of the Red Room to interconnect the two networks. First mentioned in *Avengers: Age of Ultron* through flashbacks, The Red Room is the name given to a program where young girls are trained to become assassins. It is characterized by scenes showing how Natasha Romanoff was isolated, prepared for cruelty, and trained in combat. The idea of the Red Room is picked up in *Agent Carter* through Bridget Regan's Dottie Underwood. While never referred to by the same name, the image of girls being isolated and trained in espionage and combat arises in "The Iron Ceiling"[344]. Additionally, Dottie Underwood's fighting style shows similarities to that used by the Black Widow, again implying a similar origin. Even more than with the fictional alien species, this interrelation relies on an audience making the connection, as the connection is not as direct as the reoccurrence of an *Index Manifestation*. Finally, in regard to interrelating *Index Manifestations*, the ABC and MCU networks connect through the idea of Extremis[345]. Like the Zero Matter/Darkforce interrelation between *Agents of S.H.I.E.L.D.* and *Agent Carter*, Extremis provides a connection via the reoccurrence of semiotic cues outside a singular specific character or object. Described as an advanced form of genetic manipulation using nanotechnology, Extremis is introduced with a specific set of *semiotic cues* in *Iron Man 3*. As a primary part of the plot, this *Index Manifestation* is visualized through a veiny red glow underneath the skin and glowing eyes. The film also associates Extremis greatly with heat and fire. Extremis reappears in *Agents of S.H.I.E.L.D.* in two forms: It is re-introduced in "Pilot" with the same *semiotic cues*, also tying it back to its explosive nature from *Iron Man 3*. Extremis becomes relevant again in "The Girl in the Flower Dress"[346]. At the end of the episode, Extremis is stabilized. This *Transformation Trigger* removes all its *semiotic cues*. Furthermore, all future appearances show a version of Extremis mixed with other fictional substances. As such, developing a new set of *semiotic cues* for Extremis due to *Transformation Triggers* gradually marks it as an *index* of the ABC's *Agents of S.H.I.E.L.D.* Narrative, even up to the point the term Extremis is dropped for Centipede – the project that applied it. However, the inclusion of the *semiotic cues* for Extremis in using a new formula in "Rag Tag"[347] serves as a reminder of its origin. Similar to other concepts used across networks, Extremis creates a connection. While this connection is stronger than the one set up by the Red Room – as it has clearer *semiotic cues* associated with it – it does not connect to the same degree a wandering *Index Manifestation* would.

Aside from using more and less tangible *Index Manifestations*, the two networks are also interrelated through the acknowledgment of *Transformation Triggers*. *Agents of S.H.I.E.L.D.* relates significantly to the MCU's *Transformation Triggers* because its initial creation had to take stock of two larger *Transformation Triggers* in *The Avengers*, the death of Clark Gregg's Agent Phil Coulson and the 'Battle of New York'. Despite the character

---

[344] "The Iron Ceiling". *Agent Carter*. Created by Christopher Markus and Stephen McFeely. Season 1, episode 5. Marvel Television/ABC Studios. 2015–2016.

[345] For screenshots of this *Index Manifestation*'s appearances within the MCU consult https://marvelcinematicuniverse.fandom.com/wiki/Extremis/Gallery

[346] "The Girl with the Flower Dress". *Agents of S.H.I.E.L.D.* Created by Joss Whedon, Jed Whedon, and Maurissa Tancharoen. Season 1, episode 5. Marvel Television/ABC Studios. 2013–2020.

[347] "Rag Tag". *Agents of S.H.I.E.L.D.* Created by Joss Whedon, Jed Whedon, and Maurissa Tancharoen. Season 1, episode 21. Marvel Television/ABC Studios. 2013–2020.

being killed by Loki, Clark Gregg reprises the same role for the series. As such, *Agents of S.H.I.E.L.D.* had to acknowledge the *Transformation Trigger* of his death not to upset a change made to that *Index Manifestation*. The actual *Transformation Trigger* explaining Coulson's survival invokes two storylines through the subsequent *Trigger Waves*; one focused on the mystery of his survival, and a later one is based on the consequences that grow out of the means used to resurrect him. The first storyline forms an overarching plot for the first season, while the second kicks off an overarching plot for the second season. Either series of *Trigger Waves* necessarily ties back to Coulson's death at the end of *The Avengers*. The 'Battle of New York' influences the series, as it provides the reason for the existence of Coulson's team. As S.H.I.E.L.D. approaches a new way to deal with the world, Maria Hill specifically explains Grand Ward's reassignment with the *Transformation Trigger* from *The Avengers*:

Maria Hill:	"What does S.H.I.E.L.D. stand for, Agent Ward?"
Grant Ward:	"Strategic Homeland Intervention, Enforcement, and Logistics Division."
Maria Hill:	"And what does that mean to you?"
Grant Ward:	"It means someone really wanted our initials to spell out 'shield'."
Maria Hill:	"…"
Grant Ward:	"It means we're the line between the world and the much weirder world. We protect people from news they aren't ready to hear. And when we can't do that, we keep them safe. Something turns up, like this Chitauri neural link; we get to it before someone bad does."
Maria Hill:	"Any idea who Vanchat was planning to sell it to?"
Grant Ward:	"I'm more interested in how this Rising Tide group found out about it. I thought they were just hackers. What changed?"
Maria Hill:	"Everything's changing. A little while ago, most people went to bed thinking that the craziest thing in the world was a billionaire in a flying metal suit. Then aliens invaded New York and were beaten back by, among others, a giant green monster, a costumed hero from the '40s, and a god."
Grant Ward:	"I don't think Thor's technically a god."
Maria Hill:	"Well, you haven't been near his arms. The Battle of New York was the end of the world. This now is the new world. People are different. They have access to tech, to formulas, secrets they're not ready for."
Grant Ward:	"Why was I pulled out of Paris?"
Maria Hill:	"That you have to ask Agent Coulson."
Grant Ward:	"Uh, yeah. I'm clearance level 6. I know that Agent Coulson was killed in action before the Battle of New York. Got the full report."
Phil Coulson:	"Welcome to level 7."[348]

As this dialogue implies, the series' basic premise leans on a world changed by the end of *The Avengers*. While the 'Battle of New York' initiates the series, the *Transformation Trigger* from *Captain America: The Winter Soldier* has a far greater impact on it. In the film, Steve Rogers/Captain America and Natasha Romanoff/Black Widow discover that Hydra

---

[348] "Pilot". *Agents of S.H.I.E.L.D.* Created by Joss Whedon, Jed Whedon, and Maurissa Tancharoen. Season 1, episode 1. Marvel Television/ABC Studios. 2013–2020. 00:05:21

has infiltrated and corrupted S.H.I.E.L.D. They take down the entire organization in an armed conflict and by leaking all its secret files to the internet. Such a *Transformation Trigger* should affect a series titled *Agents of S.H.I.E.L.D.* within the same network. The revelation of S.H.I.E.L.D.'s infiltration by Hydra leads to several internal conflicts. These alter the alliances of all characters within the series. The *Transformation Trigger* of the organization's fall is part of Nick Fury's appearance in the "Beginning of the End". He acts upon the *Transformation Trigger* from *Captain America: The Winter Soldier* by making Coulson the new director of S.H.I.E.L.D., tasking him with rebuilding the agency. The appearance and actions of Nick Fury tie back to the *Transformation Trigger* in two ways: (1) It acknowledges S.H.I.E.L.D.'s fall proclaimed in the MCU films, but not entirely acknowledged in the series, which played out the internal conflict longer than the film. (2) By declaring that Coulson should rebuild S.H.I.E.L.D. slowly[349], the series introduced a *Transformation Trigger* that allowed it to continue with a smaller scope. This cements the notion that the series and films formally operate in an implied shared space but that their sphere of influence differs. This difference in reach and scope allows for a hierarchical influence of *Transformation Triggers* between the networks. As they are often world-spanning, *Transformation Triggers* of the MCU films can more easily influence the *Index Manifestations* of the series. In contrast, the series has to make a special effort to influence the *Index Manifestations* of the films from its smaller and more secretive network of *indices*. The effect of such hierarchical *Transformation Triggers* already occurred in episodes before the fall of S.H.I.E.L.D.: Thor's battle with the Dark Elves in London and Lorelei's escape from Asgard are *Transformation Triggers* related to *Thor: The Dark World*. At the end of the film, the final battle causes destruction to not only earthly structures but also creates debris of alien technology. At the beginning of the episode "The Well", Coulson's team is charged with collecting and classifying the alien technology. The series relates directly to the film by starting with clips from *Thor* and *Thor: The Dark World* and a voice-over initiating a joke on the mysticism inherent to the MCU's Thor Narrative. While the connection leads into a plot dealing with Northern Mythology and Asgardians, the remainder of the episode does not refer to the film's *Transformation Triggers*. The plot of the episode effectively does not even continue a *Trigger Wave*, meaning *Agents of S.H.I.E.L.D.* needed to acknowledge the films, while their own plot had no direct relation to it. Similarly, an earlier *Transformation Trigger* from *Thor: The Dark World* is used to explain the escape of Elena Satine's Lorelei from Asgard in "Yes Men". In the film, one of the antagonists allows himself to be captured to initiate a large-scale prison break. Lorelei escapes with the others held by the Asgardians in that prison[350]. However, while the explanation reminds the series' audience of the film, the film notably never acknowledges this hunt for escaped prisoners. *Thor: The Dark World* includes no sequence showing Elena Satine's Lorelei among the escapees, nor does the film include dialogue to the effect of her recapture. Again, the series shows the need to acknowledge the *Transformation Triggers* of the film, even if only in one line of dialogue, whereas the films do not show this need. Concerning this hierarchical influence

---

349 "Beginning of the End". *Agents of S.H.I.E.L.D.* Created by Joss Whedon, Jed Whedon, and Maurissa Tancharoen. Season 1, episode 22. Marvel Television/ABC Studios. 2013–2020. 00:37:23
350 "Yes Men". *Agents of S.H.I.E.L.D.* Created by Joss Whedon, Jed Whedon, and Maurissa Tancharoen. Season 1, episode 15. Marvel Television/ABC Studios. 2013–2020. 00:11:45

of *Transformation Triggers*, *Agents of S.H.I.E.L.D.*'s interrelation with *Avengers: Age of Ultron* presents an illuminating case. *Transformation Triggers* from the series carry the veneer of a direct influence on the film. At the end of "A Dirty Half Dozen", a prophecy predicts the *Transformation Triggers* of *Avengers: Age of Ultron*, and a short section of dialogue implies that Phil Coulson used parts of the *Transformation Triggers* within the episode to collect the location of Wolfgang von Strucker's Hydra base. It is even mentioned that Doctor List is on his way there. This snippet of dialogue relates to the beginning of *Avengers: Age of Ultron*, in which the Avengers attack said base. However, the film never acknowledges the series' contribution to the Avengers' initial actions, only mentioning that they have been looking for the scepter for a long time. Something similar occurs at the end of the film. In its climax, Nick Fury appears with a Helicarrier to bring civilians to safety the Avengers otherwise would have to sacrifice to avert global destruction. In dialogue, Nick Fury says that he "pulled her out of mothballs with a couple of old friends" and that "she's dusty, but she'll do"[351], implying that he had the Helicarrier stashed away. In contrast, the series had a continued mystery surrounding Phil Coulson running a secret operation known as Theta Protocol. In "Scars"[352], the series reveals that Theta Protocol referred to a project in which Phil Coulson was working on a Helicarrier for Fury. In dialogue, it is implied that the Helicarrier was used at the end of *Avengers: Age of Ultron*. A scene from the film's ending refurbished as a news clip shown in the episode supports that implication. However, the dialogue immediately veers away from that series of *Transformation Triggers* and refocuses on its own plotline. While the *Transformation Triggers* of the series mantle the film, a hierarchy between the networks remains. Where the series sees a need to acknowledge the more global *Transformation Triggers* of the MCU films, the films do not need to acknowledge *Transformation Triggers* of the series directly related to their own. This need even continues into the episode "Laws of Nature", in which the *Transformation Triggers* of *Avengers: Age of Ultron* serve as explanations for S.H.I.E.L.D.'s extreme actions in the containment of new Inhumans[353].

Another *Transformation Trigger* tying the ABC and MCU network together is the implementation of the Sakovia Accords. A set of legal documents designed to regulate the activities of enhanced individuals, the ratification of this document and the immediate fallout of it determine some of the plot of *Captain America: Civil War*. Mentions of the Sokovia Accords appear in a variety of other MCU films. The ratification of the Sokovia Accords also influences the *Transformation Triggers* of *Agents of S.H.I.E.L.D.*, specifically at the end of the third season, which focused on the Inhuman's origin and the effect of their emergence in society, and the fourth season, which initially sees S.H.I.E.L.D. under new leadership. At the beginning of "Emancipation", a news report reiterates the existence of the Sokovia Accords and some of the *Transformation Triggers* of *Captain America: Civil War*. The

---

351   *Avengers: Age of Ultron*. Directed by Joss Whedon. Marvel Studios, 2015. 01:51:28
352   "Scars". Agents of S.H.I.E.L.D. Created by Joss Whedon, Jed Whedon, and Maurissa Tancharoen. Season 2, episode 20. Marvel Television/ABC Studios. 2013–2020
353   "Laws of Nature". *Agents of S.H.I.E.L.D.* Created by Joss Whedon, Jed Whedon, and Maurissa Tancharoen. Season 3, episode 1. Marvel Television/ABC Studios. 2013–2020. 00:14:38

dialogues between Phil Coulson and Ming Na-Wen's Melinda May[354], as well as Phil Coulson and Adrian Pasdar's General Talbot, revolve around the effects the Sokovia Accords could have on the organization. Interestingly, the second dialogue of the scene also implies that adherence to the accords could reverse the status of S.H.I.E.L.D. as a secret organization established through the *Transformation Triggers* of *Captain America: The Winter Soldier* and the final episode of *Agents of S.H.I.E.L.D.*'s first season.

Glenn Talbot: "I'm here because the President sent me. The Sokovia Accords are the law of the land now, and he's concerned you may have some undocumented enhanced assets working for you."
Phil Coulson: "And why would he think that?"
Glenn Talbot: "Because he's not a moron. Come on, Phil. It's time for S.H.I.E.L.D. to come in from the cold. Re-legitimize."
Phil Coulson: "In exchange for revealing and registering any Inhumans we may have? Not gonna happen."[355]

The idea of legitimation and re-emergence through the Sokovia Accords arises again at the beginning of the fourth season in "The Ghost"[356] when dialogue implies that S.H.I.E.L.D. is actively searching and signing "enhanced individuals" to the Sokovia Accords. The accords are mentioned again in "Uprising"[357], in which an Anti-Inhuman group receives a list of Inhumans and hunts them down. In the same episode, the attack on an Inhuman is used to re-establish S.H.I.E.L.D. as a public law enforcement organization, moving it out of its clandestine position established after *Captain America: Winter Soldier*. The re-emergence of S.H.I.E.L.D. due to the acknowledgment of the Sokovia Accords warrants mention because the films take no note of it. While Jason O'Mara's Jeffery Mace has several public press appearances as the organization's new director, even revealing being an Inhuman himself in "Lockup"[358], the films released around and after the fourth season make no mention of S.H.I.E.L.D.'s return. Equally, *Transformation Triggers* caused by the emergence of Inhumans, like the "blackout of four cities in five hours, London, Los Angeles, Moscow, and Miami,"[359] find no mention in any of the films. *Agents of S.H.I.E.L.D.*'s acknowledgment of the Sokovia Accords and the MCU films' subsequent lack of acknowledgment of the *Transformation Triggers* within the series reinforce a hierarchical nature to their interrelation. Finally, while not interrelated with the *Transformation Triggers* of the films like *Agents of S.H.I.E.L.D.*, *Agent Carter*

---

354 "Emancipation". *Agents of S.H.I.E.L.D.* Created by Joss Whedon, Jed Whedon, and Maurissa Tancharoen. Season 3, episode 20. Marvel Television/ABC Studios. 2013–2020. 00:01:15
355 "Emancipation". *Agents of S.H.I.E.L.D.* Created by Joss Whedon, Jed Whedon, and Maurissa Tancharoen. Season 3, episode 20. Marvel Television/ABC Studios. 2013–2020. 00:02:15
356 "The Ghost". *Agents of S.H.I.E.L.D.* Created by Joss Whedon, Jed Whedon, and Maurissa Tancharoen. Season 4, episode 1. Marvel Television/ABC Studios. 2013–2020.
357 "Uprising". *Agents of S.H.I.E.L.D.* Created by Joss Whedon, Jed Whedon, and Maurissa Tancharoen. Season 4, episode 3. Marvel Television/ABC Studios. 2013–2020
358 "Lock Up". *Agents of S.H.I.E.L.D.* Created by Joss Whedon, Jed Whedon, and Maurissa Tancharoen. Season 4, episode 5. Marvel Television/ABC Studios. 2013–2020
359 "Uprising". *Agents of S.H.I.E.L.D.* Created by Joss Whedon, Jed Whedon, and Maurissa Tancharoen. Season 4, episode 3. Marvel Television/ABC Studios. 2013–2020. 00:11:05

still connects to one of the films, *Captain America: The First Avenger*. A significant part of Peggy Carter's motivation, the judgment she endures, and the praise she receives from others arise from *Transformation Triggers* from the film introducing her. Examples of this interconnection are the anger she displays when she discovers that Howard Stark kept a vial of Steve Rogers's blood in "The Blitzkrieg Button"[360], the familiarity with the Howling Commandoes in "The Iron Ceiling", as well as the assertion that she only was part of the secret operation because she was Captain America's "squeeze" in "Now Is Not The End".

The hierarchical nature of *Transformation Triggers* between the two networks points towards a similar hierarchical nature concerning *Narrative Reliance*. As shown, the films never expect an audience to acquire knowledge from the series. None of the *Agents of S.H.I.E.L.D.*'s *Transformation Triggers* affects the *Index Manifestations* of MCU films. Equally, *Index Manifestations* from the films appear in the series, but no *Index Manifestations* exclusively introduced in the series make their way back to the films. Conversely, the series operates with some necessary knowledge from the films. *Agent Carter* effectively continues the story of an *Index Manifestation* from one of the MCU films. *Agents of S.H.I.E.L.D.* does so too, in the form of Phil Coulson, but equally acknowledges later *Transformation Triggers* from various films. The MCU network is more geared towards a casual audience, which might engage with the overall network but may disregard the series. The ABC network, in contrast, relies to a degree on information from the films, gearing it more towards an informed audience. However, this dependency, especially in the case of *Agents of S.H.I.E.L.D.*, is not uniform. *Agents of S.H.I.E.L.D.*'s initial season relies significantly on the films. Its initial premise arises from an *Index Manifestation*'s (Phil Coulson's) demise in the previously released films. Within the first season, other films are constantly invoked and mentioned through *Index Manifestation* and *Transformation Triggers* from *Iron Man 3*, *Thor: The Dark World*, and *Captain America: The Winter Soldier*. The series maintains the use of *Index Manifestations* and *Transformation Triggers* in its second season in the use of Jamie Alexander's Sif from the MCU's Thor Narrative and acknowledging the *Transformation Triggers* of *Avengers: Age of Ultron*, but the degree of interrelation appears lower. With the third and fourth seasons, the films' *Transformation Triggers* only influence the series indirectly, using them as reasoning, but there is little direct transfer of *Index Manifestations*. This leads to an interesting aspect concerning the audience. Due to the earlier interrelation, the level of *Narrative Reliance* required an informed or skilled audience. With the progression of the series, the lowered degree of interrelation technically allows for a casual audience to engage with the series regarding the relationship between the networks. However, because *Agents of S.H.I.E.L.D.*'s audience started as an informed audience, it cannot become a truly casual one. Nevertheless, overlaid with the publishing dates of the films and the seasons, this transformation in audience type implies that *Agents of S.H.I.E.L.D.* could support an audience that stopped engaging with the films somewhere between *Captain America: The Winter Soldier* and *Captain America: Civil War*. For the interrelation of networks, this implies that the two networks gradually slipped apart as they continued to add unconnected *Manifestations*.

---

360 "The Blitzkrieg Button". *Agent Carter*. Created by Christopher Markus and Stephen McFeely. Season 1, episode 4. Marvel Television/ABC Studios. 2015–2016

A close link is undeniable concerning the interrelation of the ABC and MCU networks. While hierarchical, many elements of either network engage with one another and facilitate connections. However, the degree of interrelation gradually lowers, making each network more autonomous over time despite the initial deep connection. As *Agents of S.H.I.E.L.D.* and the MCU films (if viewed as a monolithic serial) are the longest-running parts of the overall network, this distance begs whether any close relationship between the two could have been maintained. And if not, what provided the most likely difference in their departure, medium (film/television), format (film/series), or focus (several subjects/one subject)?

Aside from the tangible interrelations, the ABC and MCU networks share a parallel introduction and engagement with specific themes and notions. The conflict concerning the regulation of Inhumans mirrors the conflict of the regulations of superheroes in the MCU films. The appearance of magical elements through the character Ghost Rider and the object The Darkhold mirrors the introduction of magic through *Doctor Strange*. The entire series' shift to outer space in the fifth season mirrors MCU's focus on cosmic events in its third phase. This parallelism in theme already begins with the inception of *Agents of S.H.I.E.L.D.*, as it and the MCU network's Phase 2 both revolve around the different *Narrative Entities* dealing with a weirder world. The notion of parallel themes continues past *Captain America: The Winter Soldier*, which leaves a world with a disgraced and destroyed S.H.I.E.L.D. As such, *Agents of S.H.I.E.L.D.*'s second and third seasons deal with the distrust within and towards the remaining organization when they engage with the secret and later emerging race of Inhumans. This mirrors the films' attempt to understand the position of the Avengers in a world without an institute like S.H.I.E.L.D., which culminates in the conflict of *Captain America: Civil War*. Both problems end with the acceptance and ratification of the Sokovia Accords, mentioned at the end of *Agents of S.H.I.E.L.D.*'s third season. The fourth season of *Agents of S.H.I.E.L.D.* explores supernatural and mystical concepts, which ties in with the release of *Doctor Strange*. Both represent the first instances of a magical aspect entering either network. In addition to the Darkhold, a magical book of sins, *Agents of S.H.I.E.L.D.* introduces Gabriel Luna's Robbie Reyes/Ghost Rider. Executive Producer Jed Whedon even explained in July 2016 in an *Entertainment Weekly* article that the previous tie-ins were sometimes "very direct", and other times "more thematic." "The tie this year will feel more of a reflection of [*Doctor Strange*], less an interweaving plot."[361] The episode "Deals with Our Devils"[362], aired after the release of *Doctor Strange*, shows a dimensional portal visually reminiscent of those used in the film, adding a potential connection via *Index Manifestation* to thematic parallelism. In November 2017, producer Jed Whedon explained that the fifth season moved the characters to space because *Guardians of the Galaxy Vol. 2* and *Thor: Ragnarok* explored

---

[361] Abrams, Natalie. "Agents of S.H.I.E.L.D. will cross over with Doctor Strange". *Entertainment Weekly*. September 16th, 2016. https://ew.com/article/2016/09/16/agents-shield-doctor-strange/, retrieved September 30st, 2021.

[362] "Deals with our Devils". *Agents of S.H.I.E.L.D.* Created by Joss Whedon, Jed Whedon, and Maurissa Tancharoen. Season 4, episode 7. Marvel Television/ABC Studios. 2013–2020

that part of the Shared Universe[363], continuing this parallel development. Finally, the seventh season of *Agents of S.H.I.E.L.D.* introduces time travel into the series, mirroring the notion of a time travel heist added by *Avengers: Endgame*. This parallel usage of theme implies the potential of interconnection on another level than practical narrative elements. However, while this may influence the interest and mindset of the audience, it is difficult to argue that it creates a connection between the networks other than intertextually or along the lines of genre expectations.

The relationship between these two networks produces two interesting aspects: (1) The notion of a hierarchical relationship between *Narrative Entities* and networks due to a one-sided use of connections and (2) a dilution of interrelation through the waning use of interconnecting elements. Overall, the ABC network, especially *Agents of S.H.I.E.L.D.*, generated such a significant amount of *Transformation Trigger*s and *Index Manifestation* detached from the MCU films that any reliance from one on the other waned altering the type of audience for the series. Within the larger network, the ABC series slipped further away from the MCU films, whereas the MNU network retained a similar distance. The greater distance here does not solely arise from the lack of new connections but from the lack of new connections in the face of a rise in the overall number of *Manifestations*. In other words, the increase in films and episodes from the beginning of the second to the end of the third phase gradually deludes the established connections because it enables an audience unfamiliar with the newer films to continue watching the series. The MCU film network and the ABC series effectively hold an ideational connection by broaching the same issues and themes. However, the ABC network is not directly subject to the *Transformation Trigger*s of *Captain America: Civil War*. *Agents of S.H.I.E.L.D.* dealt with similar themes to the MCU films on a more personal scale, but without directly leaning on any *Index Manifestation* or *Transformation Trigger* presented in the films after a certain point. This gradual separation becomes more prominent through the hierarchical nature of the interrelation, as all burden is placed on the series to maintain any connection. In contrast, the interrelations between *Narrative Entities* within the MCU network are more level, avoiding greater compromise to the *Manifestation*'s actual story.

3.1.4.3 MNU/ABC Relationship

Operating with the notion of a 'mothership' – to use Mittell's term – the MNU network and the ABC network stand in some relation to the MCU films, which started the overall network and serve as the most widely known of all three parts. However, as each part of the network is meant to be interlinked, this section takes a closer look at the elements interrelating the MNU with the ABC series. The *Index Manifestation* of Carl 'Crusher' Creel appears as the most overt connection between the ABC and MNU networks. Portrayed by Brian Patrick Wade, the character appears in nine episodes of *Agents of S.H.I.E.L.D.* While not on screen directly, a poster and bits of dialogue in *Daredevil S1* refer to the

---

363   Ching, Albert. "How Agents of S.H.I.E.L.D. Season 5 ties-in to the Marvel Studios Movies". *CBR.com*. November 30th, 2017. https://www.cbr.com/agents-of-shield-season-5-marvel-studios-movies *connection*/, retrieved September 30st, 2021.

character[364]. However, as with other *Index Manifestations* that only find mention in one network while appearing in the other, it is never entirely clear how the character in *Daredevil S1* relates to the *Index Manifestation* shown in *Agents of S.H.I.E.L.D.*, as identification solely hinges on the use of the name. In this specific case, an argument can be made that the mention of Carl 'Crusher' Creel in *Daredevil S1* could be to another *Index Manifestation*, as all mentions refer to a *Transformation Trigger* in Matt Murdock/Daredevil's childhood – approximately 20 years before the *Index Manifestation* of Creel appears in *Agents of S.H.I.E.L.D.* While neither *Manifestation* mentions the character's age, the actor portraying the *Index Manifestation* in *Agents of S.H.I.E.L.D.* was 36 when he first appeared as the character, indicating an age of 16 in *Daredevil S1*. While many explanations for the age discrepancy and the idea of a 16-year-old boxing professionally are imaginable, the notion of two separate versions of the character lingers within these representations. While not as prominent, several smaller connections between the two networks appear more straightforward. Prominently featured in *Luke Cage S1*, the Judas Bullet was made of alien metal and the only thing that could penetrate the main character's skin. In a demonstration video, the bullet is shown to drill into its target after hitting it and exploding. While never referred to by name, a projectile used in an assassination attempt in *Agents of S.H.I.E.L.D.* "The Patriot"[365] has the same *semiotic cues*, drilling into a podium and destroying it in an explosion. However, while the special nature of the bullet is discussed in the episode, its name is never mentioned, nor is its origin. The coherence of *semiotic cues* may forge a relation between the two networks for a skilled audience but provides little indication for others. Within the MNU network, the 'Dogs of Hell' are a criminal motorcycle club operating in New York. While the gang appears more prominently in the Netflix series, it was introduced in *Agents of S.H.I.E.L.D.*: The Dogs of Hell first appear in "Yes Men". In either iteration, members of the gang display visual cues associated with motorcycle clubs – leather vests with symbols on the back, casual clothing usually consisting of jeans and a black shirt, gruff exterior, and motorcycles. As the *Index Manifestations* presented in either series are meant to represent different chapters of the gang, the connection is weakened by a difference in the logos and an alteration to the surrounding *semiotic cues* (the Nevada desert vs. New York City). Another gang tying the MNU network and the ABC series together is the Aryan Brotherhood. First mentioned in the *Daredevil S2* episode "Seven Minutes in Heaven", the group first appears in *Agents of S.H.I.E.L.D.* "The Ghost", when they steal a box for another gang[366]. The gang reappears in *Punisher S2* "Flustercuck"[367]. It is revealed that one of the season's antagonists, Josh Stewart's John Pilgrim, is a former member of the gang. He returns to them to get

---

[364] For screenshots of the character and the poster reference consult https://marvelcinematicuniverse.fandom.com/wiki/Absorbing_Man/Gallery

[365] "The Patriot". *Agents of S.H.I.E.L.D.* Created by Joss Whedon, Jed Whedon, and Maurissa Tancharoen. Season 4, episode 10. Marvel Television/ABC Studios. 2013–2020. 00:03:21

[366] "The Ghost". *Agents of S.H.I.E.L.D.* Created by Joss Whedon, Jed Whedon, and Maurissa Tancharoen. Season 4, episode 1. Marvel Television/ABC Studios. 2013–2020. 00:13:58)

[367] "Flustercuck". *The Punisher*. Created by Steve Lightfoot. Season 2, episode 9. Marvel Television/ABC Studios. 2017–2019.

some information but is attacked for past digressions in "The Dark Heart of Men"[368]. As with the Dogs of Hell, the connection is light, as either series shows different smaller sections of a larger organization. The events of *Agents of S.H.I.E.L.D.* take place in Pasadena, California, while the events of *The Punisher S2* take place in New York City. Aside from a membership consisting solely of white men, members of the Aryan Brotherhood show no coherent uniform or symbol in either of their appearances, limiting the connecting effect to the use of a name. Another connection between the networks created through a nation-spanning organization is the use of the news station WZTM. Not a direct *Index Manifestation*, the news channel marks its presence with a logo in its news reports and on its microphones[369]. Microphones with a logo of the news organization appear as part of a set at a news conference in *Daredevil S1*'s "Shadows in the Glass"[370] and "Daredevil"[371] as well as in *Daredevil S3* "Reunion"[372]. The same microphones can be seen at a press conference in *Luke Cage S1*'s "Take It Personal"[373]. A news report bearing the station's logo is in *Daredevil S3*'s "One Last Shot"[374] and *Agents of S.H.I.E.L.D.*'s "Watchdogs"[375]. The connection across the networks is somewhat tedious in this case. While using the same letters implies a unity of *Index Manifestations*, the differences in logo, font, and color scheme call this connection into question. The news station might support a light interrelation in combination with clearer interrelations. Another potential interrelation relying solely on a reference is Saint Agnes Orphanage. Matt Murdock grew up at the orphanage after his father died, and Daisy Johnson was dropped off there when she was a baby but did not remain for long. The orphanage is mentioned and appears in *Daredevil S1* "Stick"[376] and throughout *Daredevil S3*. It is only mentioned in dialogue in *Agents of S.H.I.E.L.D.* and appears on a document in "The Only Light in the Darkness". However, the actual building is never shown in *Agents of S.H.I.E.L.D.* As such, the interrelating effect of this *Index Manifestation* falls into a similar category as the previously mentioned Dogs of Hell, Aryan Brotherhood, and WZTM News. The pure use of the name implies a potential interrelation, but it remains unclear if each iteration refers to the same *Index Manifestation* or even

---

368 "The Dark Heart of Men". *The Punisher*. Created by Steve Lightfoot. Season 2, episode 10. Marvel Television/ABC Studios. 2017–2019

369 For screenshots of these appearances consult https://marvelcinematicuniverse.fandom.com/wiki/WZTM_News/Gallery

370 "Shadows in the Glass". *Daredevil*. Created by Drew Goddard. Season 1, episode 8. Marvel Television/ABC Studios. 2015–2018. 00:49:30

371 "Daredevil". *Daredevil*. Created by Drew Goddard. Season 1, episode 13. Marvel Television/ABC Studios. 2015–2018. 00:32:36

372 "Reunion". *Daredevil*. Created by Drew Goddard. Season 3, episode 11. Marvel Television/ABC Studios. 2015–2018. 00:15:31

373 "Take it Personal". *Luke Cage*. Created by Cheo Hodari Coker. Season 1, episode 10. Marvel Television/ABC Studios. 2016–2018. 00:26:58

374 "One Last Shot". *Daredevil*. Created by Drew Goddard. Season 3, episode 12. Marvel Television/ABC Studios. 2015–2018. 00:40:59

375 "Watchdogs". *Agents of S.H.I.E.L.D.* Created by Joss Whedon, Jed Whedon, and Maurissa Tancharoen. Season 3, episode 14. Marvel Television/ABC Studios. 2013–2020. 00:03:26

376 "Stick". *Daredevil*. Created by Drew Goddard. Season 1, episode 7. Marvel Television/ABC Studios. 2015 2018

if the Saint Agnes Orphanage mentioned in *Agents of S.H.I.E.L.D.* is in New York, making the connection more allusive.

While the implication of connection via *Index Manifestation* exists between the MNU network and ABC series, these connections lack the clarity a wandering *Index Manifestation* or a *Trigger Wave* would provide. The use of the Judas Bullet seems the most unambiguous, as the *semiotic cues* of the projectile are unique to the MNU. However, its recognition requires an aware audience, meaning either a skilled one or an informed audience for both networks. Every other *Index Manifestation* retains some level of ambiguity concerning the nature of their sameness, leaving a direct interrelation between the MNU network and the ABC network disputable at best.

3.1.4.4 The Roxxon Corporation/Stark Industries

Two *Index Manifestations* arching across all three networks come in the form of the Roxxon Corporation and Stark Industries. With Roxxon presented as a large multinational corporation, the *Index Manifestations* lacks a singular character, set, or prop that identifies each appearance of the company. The singular comparable and, therefore, connecting aspect is the coherent use of its name and the recurrence of its logo[377]. The Roxxon Corporation appears in each Iron Man film, three episodes of *Agent Carter*, two episodes of *Agents of S.H.I.E.L.D.*, and two episodes of *Daredevil*. The company is also mentioned in *Iron Fist*. Established in the background of *Iron Man*[378], Roxxon's name appears shifted in the middle to form a stylized logo. However, the stylization is not coherent across the films. In *Iron Man*, the logo with enlarged Xs appears on the side of a truck, and the name is seen split atop a building in the background with a long line passing through both Xs. The latter version of the logo also appears on the side of a ship in *Iron Man 3*[379]. A similar version colored in red with a white outline adorns a gas station in *Agents of S.H.I.E.L.D.*'s episode "Repairs"[380]. In *Iron Man 2*, the unaltered name appears on the spoiler of a Formula One racing car[381]. The same version of the logo is shown throughout all of the company's appearances in *Agent Carter*, marking a refinery in "Now is Not the End"[382] as well as office buildings in "Bridge and Tunnel"[383] and "The Atomic Job"[384]. The Roxxon Corporation is

---

[377] For screenshots of this *Index Manifestation* across the overall network consult https://marvelcinematicuniverse.fandom.com/wiki/Roxxon_Corporation/Gallery

[378] *Iron Man*. Directed by Jon Favreau. Performances by Robert Downey Jr., Gwyneth Paltrow, Terrence Howard, and Jeff Bridges. Marvel Studios, 2008. 01:45:18/01:46:17/01:46:56

[379] *Iron Man 3*. Directed by Shane Black. Performances by Robert Downey Jr., Gwyneth Paltrow, Don Cheadle, Ben Kingsley, and Guy Pearce. Marvel Studios, 2013. 01:39:01

[380] "Repairs". *Agents of S.H.I.E.L.D.* Created by Joss Whedon, Jed Whedon, and Maurissa Tancharoen. Season 1, episode 9. Marvel Television/ABC Studios. 2013–2020. 00:01:32

[381] *Iron Man 2*. Directed by Jon Favreau. Performances by Robert Downey Jr., Gwyneth Paltrow, Don Cheadle, Sam Rockwell, and Mickey Rourke. Marvel Studios, 2010. 00:33:00

[382] "Now is Not the End". *Agent Carter*. Created by Christopher Markus and Stephen McFeely. Season 1, episode 1. Marvel Television/ABC Studios. 2015–2016. 00:33:18

[383] "Bridge and Tunnel". *Agent Carter*. Created by Christopher Markus and Stephen McFeely. Season 1, episode 2. Marvel Television/ABC Studios. 2015–2016. 00:12:59

[384] "The Atomic Job". *Agent Carter*. Created by Christopher Markus and Stephen McFeely. Season 2, episode 5. Marvel Television/ABC Studios. 2015–2016. 00:13:27

mentioned in the *Daredevil S1* episode "Nelson v. Murdock"[385] in a flashback, in which a former employee tries to sue the company for damages, and in *Daredevil S2* "Kinbaku"[386] when Élodie Yung's Elektra Nachios asks Charlie Cox's Matt Murdock/Daredevil for representation against the company. Roxxon also finds mention in *Agents of S.H.I.E.L.D.*'s "The Good Samaritan"[387] as the owner of a smaller company, which experimented with Zero Matter in the 40s. Stark Industries finds mention throughout most MCU films and is constantly represented through Robert Downey Jr.'s Tony Stark/Iron Man. Its presence comes mainly in the form of facilities owned by the company or technology designed and built by it. Aside from *Manifestations* of the MCU's Iron Man Narrative, the company appears in every MCU Captain America and Spider-Man *Manifestation*, in two of the four Avengers' films, as well as in one *Manifestation* of the MCU's Ant-Man and Hulk Narrative. In *The Incredible Hulk*, the Stark Industries logo flashes on the screen during the opening credit sequence and is on the Cyrosync container. Stark Industries is part of the 'World Exposition of Tomorrow' in *Captain America: The First Avenger*. Here, the Stark Industries logo is modified to suit the *index* network of the film, representing a 1940s time period. Stark Industries is in *The Avengers*, with Tony Stark opening Stark Tower. In *Captain America: The Winter Soldier*, Stark Industries redesigned the Helicarriers' propulsion systems. Cobie Smulder's Agent Maria Hill also applies for a position at Stark Industries at the end of the second Captain America *Manifestation*. In *Avengers: Age of Ultron*, Elisabeth Olsens's Wanda Maximoff/Scarlet Witch and Aaron Taylor-Johnson's Pietro Maximoff/Quicksilver reveal that a Stark Industries-manufactured mortar shell killed their parents. In *Ant-Man*, the Avengers' headquarters in Upstate New York is described as a former Stark Industries warehouse. In *Captain America: Civil War*, Tony Stark delivers a presentation at MIT to promote a Stark Industries program. In *Spider-Man: Homecoming*, Damage Control, which removed the debris after the end of *The Avengers*, is a joint venture between Stark Industries and the U.S. government. *Spider-Man: Far From Home* features a group of disgruntled former Stark Industries employees. As direct spin-offs from the MCU network, Stark Industry finds more mention in the ABC network than in *Manifestations* of the MNU network. *Agent Carter* frequently refers to Stark Industries through the presence of Dominic Cooper's Howard Stark. In the *Agents of S.H.I.E.L.D.* episode "Nothing Personal," Maria Hill is shown working for Stark Industries. Stark Industries only builds a connection with the MNU because the company finds mention at the top of a Forbes cover that reports Danny Rand's return in "The Mistress of All Agonies"[388].

While either company exists mostly in the background and without coherent *semiotic cues* presented across all three networks, Stark Industries and the Roxxon Corporation do help to imply that these networks exist within a shared imaginary space. However, their

---

[385] "Nelson v. Murdock". *Daredevil*. Created by Drew Goddard. Season 1, episode 10. Marvel Television/ABC Studios. 2015–2018. 00:33:46

[386] "Kinbaku". *Daredevil*. Created by Drew Goddard. Season 2, episode 5. Marvel Television/ABC Studios. 2015–2018. 00:23:40

[387] "The Good Samaritan". *Agents of S.H.I.E.L.D.* Created by Joss Whedon, Jed Whedon, and Maurissa Tancharoen. Season 4, episode 6. Marvel Television/ABC Studios. 2013–2020. 00:28:40

[388] "The Mistress of All Agonies". *Iron Fist*. Created by Scott Buck. Season 1, episode 9. Marvel Television/ABC Studios. 2017–2018. 00:22:59

background status and fluidity of representation also allow for the possibility of understanding the different mentions as one of multiple versions of the same *Index Manifestation*. As such, these *Index Manifestations* draw the networks only lightly together.

3.1.5 Lack of Connection

In multiple instances, the main producer of Marvel's television arm at the time, Jeph Loeb, broadcasted an interrelation between the television shows and the films, a sentiment mirrored by different actors and showrunners of either of the networks. While a closer look at the *Manifestations* shows some low-tier attempts at interrelation, the connection between the networks appears somewhat tedious. The MNU network does not share any apparent *Index Manifestation* with the MCU films, only mentioning notable sections of its *Index Manifestations*. The MNU does show some relation by using one significant *Transformation Trigger* from the MCU network as backstory, deriving a great deal of explanation from its occurrence. However, outside of this one *Transformation Trigger*, the MNU shows little relation to the MCU network. The use of one specific *Index Manifestation* and a few unspecific ones marks the connection between the ABC series and the MNU network. However, even here, the interrelations hinge greatly on allusion, assertions, and the audience's compliance, as all these aspects of connection never clarify if they are the same *Index Manifestations* or different versions of it. The most substantial interrelation of the networks exists between the MCU films and the ABC series, as the latter spun directly out of the former, taking some *Index Manifestations* with it and carrying the burden of existing *Transformation Triggers*. Especially the first season of *Agents of S.H.I.E.L.D.* exhibits a certain dependency on the MCU network. However, as the number of *Manifestations* dedicated to its own *Narrative Entity* rises, *Agents of S.H.I.E.L.D.* also gradually lost its reliance on the films. Overall, the networks do not share the same close and clear relationship the *Narrative Entities* within the networks themselves share. However, if set in relation to one another, the MNU network displays a greater distance to the MCU network than the ABC series, whereas the distance between the MNU network and the ABC series presents the greatest, as nearly every connection relies on a skilled or (well-)informed audience. While an interrelation through *Transformation Triggers* (especially between the MCU films and ABC series) cannot be denied, the dominantly unidirectional influence must be acknowledged. The impact of *Transformation Triggers* favors the films over either of the series, effectively creating a hierarchy between the networks. This hierarchy appears to extend to *Index Manifestations*, forcing either series to use or mention the film's *Index Manifestation*, while the films operate with no such constraint.

While this interconnection and hierarchy among the networks exist, *Transformation Triggers*, which should affect the entirety of the network, oppose it because they do not find mention in larger parts of the overall complex. The most notable examples within the presented *Manifestations* are the Snap and the Blip. The former refers to Thanos's destruction of half of the universe's population with the snap of a finger, while the latter refers to the sudden return of that half five years later. As the *Transformation Trigger* is described as a universe-wide alteration several times within *Avengers: Infinity War*, the absence of its effect is notable in the MNU network and, even more so, among the ABC series. Neither series in either network mentions the sudden disappearance of half of the population. Not addressing these *Transformation Triggers* calls the connections created due to allusions and smaller interrelations between the networks into question because it violates an established expectation. While the Snap and the Blip present the most prominent culprits in this regard, the *Transformation Triggers* are not singular in this opposition to the idea of interconnection between the three networks. The absence of S.H.I.E.L.D. in the MNU network is profound, as it significantly relates the MCU films and the ABC series to one another. This prominent presence in two networks generates a greater base of knowledge concerning this *Index Manifestation*, calling its absence even more into question. Because the MNU network does not share unambiguous markers with the other networks concerning the order of *Transformation Triggers*, it is difficult to relate S.H.I.E.L.D.'s changing level of publicity, sanction, and activity with the current state of the MNU's *Index Manifestation*. However, if we assume an overall interrelation, the *Transformation Triggers* of the MNU network began after *The Avengers*, as nearly all the series technically refer to the film's ending and base some of their own *Transformation Triggers* on it. As such, we can assume that Nick Fury's S.H.I.E.L.D. was active and worked with governmental goodwill at the MNU's inception (the overall first season of each *Narrative Entity*). Even after the *Transformation Triggers* of *Captain America: The Winter Soldier*, *Agents of S.H.I.E.L.D.* presents the organization actively working to identify, register, and, if necessary, contain enhanced individuals, especially beginning with its third season. Despite this mission statement and numerous implications of S.H.I.E.L.D. operatives working outside *Agents of S.H.I.E.L.D.'s* context, S.H.I.E.L.D. neither appears nor is mentioned within the MNU network, even though *Jessica Jones* and *Luke Cage* thematically bring up the subject of enhanced people in society. Additionally, the titular heroes of both MNU *Manifestations* use their powers publicly. In *Jessica Jones S1*, one of these displays initiates a series of *Trigger Waves* leading to a murder attempt on Krysten Ritter's Jessica Jones in "AKA 99 Friends". In the same season, several victims of David Tenant's Kilgrave report their encounter with his mind-controlling ability after a radio show asks for people with such an experience to come forward in "AKA It's Called Whiskey"[389]. In the same episode, the radio host gives the report of one of Kilgrave's victims credence by comparing its likelihood to an alien attack. This allusion to the end of *The Avengers* places a public discussion of an enhanced criminal in a time of S.H.I.E.L.D.'s continuous public operation. In the season finale of *Jessica Jones S1*, Carrie-Ann Moss's Jeri Hogarth even uses a public acknowledgment of Kilgrave's abilities to protect Jessica from jail. Mike Colter's Luke Cage's open use of his enhanced abilities makes him renowned and famous throughout Harlem by Luke Cage S2, leading to an app – the Harlem's Hero app – tracking his whereabouts. After he survives the blast of a ballistic missile, a camera operator films him as he punches his way out of the rubble in "Step in the Arena"[390]. He is also recorded testing the limits of his abilities in front of an audience in "Straighten It

---

[389] "AKA It's Called Whiskey". *Jessica Jones*. Created by Melissa Rosenberg. Season 1, episode 3. Marvel Television/ABC Studios. 2015–2019. 00:26:36

[390] "Step in the Arena". *Luke Cage*. Created by Cheo Hodari Coker. Season 1, episode 4. Marvel Television/ABC Studios. 2016–2018. 00:43:52

Out"[391]. Directly after this display, a Nike scout even approaches him. He publicly states his name after surviving an explosion in an internet post in "Soul Brother #1"[392]. A radio show openly discusses Luke Cage's abilities. At the same time, the residents of Harlem start to wear Hoodies with bullet holes in them to display their solidarity in "Soliloquy of Chaos", and Chaz Lamar Shepard's Raymond 'Piranha' Jones has a small museum of collectibles associated with Luke Cage in his office in "All Souled Out". While Danny Rand is not as acknowledged as Luke Cage or Jessica Jones, he does not shy away from telling everybody that he is the Iron Fist and openly uses his mystical abilities. He smashes out a metal door in view of a security camera in "Shadow Hawk Takes Flight"[393]. Taking over for Daredevil in "The Fury of Iron Fist"[394], he also smashes the engine of an armored truck, leaving the destroyed chassis on the street. Despite all these open uses of enhanced abilities, no agent of S.H.I.E.L.D. appears to take action in the MNU network. In contrast, within the MCU network, the organization establishes research, containment, and first contact with alien artifacts and their creators in *Thor*. They contact and evaluate enhanced individuals in *Iron Man* and *Captain America: The First Avenger*. They provide information and equipment for the capture of enhanced individuals in *The Incredible Hulk*. *Agents of S.H.I.E.L.D.* openly states that the search, registration, and, if necessary, containment of enhanced individuals is part of S.H.I.E.L.D.'s mission statement in "Repairs" and other episodes. This mission statement serves as the reason for the recruitment, training, and deployment of J. August Richards's Mike Peterson/Deathlok, which stretches across several episodes and even seasons, and equally informs the entirety of the Inhumans' storyline. In essence, the combination of S.H.I.E.L.D.'s activities in the MCU films, as well as *Agents of S.H.I.E.L.D.* contextualized with the open usage of powers in *Manifestations* of the MNU network, calls its absence into question and, therefore, the interrelation of these networks.

A similar effect occurs with the *Index Manifestation* of the Inhumans. While the emergence of Inhumans in *Agents of S.H.I.E.L.D.* causes a worldwide political debate, as seen in "The Inside Man"[395], their existence never finds mention in either the MCU or the MNU network. This oversight is specifically notable in *Doctor Strange*. Within the *Manifestation*, the main character seeks every potential treatment for the nerve damage in his hands, implicitly reaching for the most experimental procedures. However, while within the notion of a coherent shared imaginary space Inhumans with extraordinary abilities exist, *Doctor Strange* does not mention searching for an Inhuman with healing abilities. Equally, the film makes no hints at the procedures that saved Jessica Jones's and Luke Cage's life and gave them their abilities. Instead, Stephen Strange pursues a mystical option, which,

---

391 "Straighten It Out". *Luke Cage*. Created by Cheo Hodari Coker. Season 2, episode 2. Marvel Television/ABC Studios. 2016–2018. 00:01:40
392 "Soul Brother #1". *Luke Cage*. Created by Cheo Hodari Coker. Season 2, episode 1. Marvel Television/ABC Studios. 2016–2018. 00:45:40
393 "Shadow Hawk Takes Flight". *Iron Fist*. Created by Scott Buck. Season 1, episode 2. Marvel Television/ABC Studios. 2017–2018. 00:58:47
394 "The Fury of the Iron Fist". *Iron Fist*. Created by Scott Buck. Season 2, episode 1. Marvel Television/ABC Studios. 2017–2018. 00:02:25
395 "The Inside Man". *Agents of S.H.I.E.L.D.* Created by Joss Whedon, Jed Whedon, and Maurissa Tancharoen. Season 3, Episode 12. Marvel Television/ABC Studios. 2013–2020

in contrast to Inhumans, has not been proven as real within the context of the shared imaginary space. Concerning the absence of *Index Manifestations* and *Transformation Triggers*, these three are more prominent examples. On a smaller scale, the Netflix series fail to mention any specific landmark from the films. Neither Stark Tower nor the Triskelion appear in the MNU network. Equally, the films and *Agents of S.H.I.E.L.D.* make no mention of Rand Enterprises, Midland Circle, Harlem's Crispus Attucks Complex, or the law firm Hogarth, Chao, & Benowitz. While audiences can easily explain all these instances of overlooked *Index Manifestations* and *Transformation Triggers*, their absence equally creates fields of tension concerning interconnection. Missing an acknowledgment of important *Index Manifestations* while constantly hinting at an interrelation gives room for interpretation, allowing different audiences to perceive the relationship between the networks in accordance with their level of interest and engagement, leading to a complex grouping of audience types.

As discussed in the analysis of the singular networks, the greater part of each *Manifestation* plays to either a casual audience or an informed one, usually creating an informed audience by gradually educating a casual one. Hereby, *Manifestations* from the MCU network favor a casual audience more than the MNU network and ABC series, which rely on some knowledge from the films and lean on an audience's constant and repeated access to their singular episodes to 'get up to speed'. Ignoring the singular *Manifestations*, all networks focus on developing and pleasing an informed audience. While not every *Manifestation* relies on an informed audience, the complex of the smaller networks gravitates towards creating and pleasing such an audience by gradually increasing the *Narrative Reliance* within the network. Any notion of a casual audience disperses with a look at the larger network as a whole. Aside from understanding the reliance of singular episodes on one another (in the case of series) and the reliance of *Manifestations* and *Narrative Entities* on one another, an audience engaging with the entire network has to discover the non-reliant and reliant interrelations spread out across all *Manifestations*. As the analysis shows, these connections are singular and often hidden so as not to discourage audiences that did not engage with the entire network. Additionally, the audience of the entirety of the larger network has to contend with the absence of encompassing *Index Manifestations*. As such, the interrelation of the different networks targets mainly skilled audiences, which not only can identify singular allusive connections (like the Judas Bullet or Doctor List) but also engage with the ambivalent relationship between the smaller networks created through the tension between the lighter connections and the absence of encompassing and specific *Index Manifestations*. An informed audience created through thorough engagement with every element of the network might be able to identify such singular obscure connections and/or the absence of encompassing and specific *Index Manifestations* but cannot accept the ambivalence of such an interrelation. Meaning they are incapable of accepting that these aspects might hint at a connection but cannot serve as definite proof of one. This incapability arises out of the informed audience's adherence to their interpretation of the producer's intent, which leads them to evaluate the interrelation as either a success or a failure. Operating without the guidance of the producer's intent, the skilled audience evaluates the interrelation solely on the presence or absence of textual clues, accepting that future *Manifestations* might alter the current relationship with a rise of *Manifestations* void of obvious connection diluting the interrelation and the appearance of clearly identifiable wandering *Index Manifestations* strengthening these interrelations. However, while the scattered view on the various networks is inconsistent, this inconsistency allows for an overall wider audience and the potential sacrifice of one part without endangering the other.

As such, the MNU network stands in a Narrative Multiverse relationship with the MCU films and the ABC series. The ABC series started with a solid connection to the MCU films, firmly planting the two networks in a Shared Universe relationship. However, with the addition of *Manifestations*, the ABC series gradually moved away from the MCU films as the number of shared *Index Manifestations* slowly dropped. Despite these changes, the two networks remain in a Shared Universe relationship, as the series acknowledges the films up to *Captain America: Civil War*. Still, the ABC series moves closer to a Multiverse relationship with the MCU films because the interrelation is hierarchical. More importantly, the gradual distancing of the ABC series from the MCU implies that the already great distance of the MNU network could increase through the absence of connections in new *Manifestations*, indicating that the relationship could move to the distance of a Company Universe, eventually splitting off from the overall network.

3.2 Understanding the Mechanics of *The Marvel Cinematic Universe*

The analysis shows the different degrees of *Index Manifestations*, *Transformation Triggers*, *Trigger Waves*, *Narrative Reliance*, and *Shared Narratives* used to interrelate the singular elements of the MCU. While these processes are interesting, they, more importantly, reveal some overarching principles used to manage the overall network and control its development. The following chapter describes and attempts to universalize these principles. Hereby, the focus lies on (1) the process and structure of expansion within and of such a network, (2) the organization of a continually growing number of *Narrative Entities* and their *Index Manifestations*, (3) the processes involved in creating and maintaining an informed audience while remaining open to a casual one, and (4) finally the potential means of continuing such a network ad infinitum.

3.2.1 From Personal to Global to Cosmic and Beyond: Managing Expansion and Escalation

Expansion within the context of a Shared Universe network refers to a continual addition of meaning to the overall network. Such an expansion comes naturally with the addition of new *Narrative Entities* and new *Index Manifestations*, as either introduces new elements to the overall network. However, every change to an *Index Manifestation* and, therefore, any *Transformation Trigger* and every *Trigger Wave* equally adds new meaning by changing the familiar and creating new backstory. Because each technique contributes to the expansion, the process is tied to the addition of *Manifestations* to the overall material of a narrative network. In the simplest terms, a Shared Universe network expands with every additional film, novel, episode, and comic book officially contributed to that network and acknowledged as part of it. This notion of expansion applies equally to linearly produced worlds, such as those created by singular film franchises, novel series, or television series, through the process of seriality. In those cases, each new *Manifestation* adds new meaning via new *Index Manifestations* or changes to familiar ones. While seriality equally underlines the expansion of a narrative network as described by the Universe Model, the application of seriality in conjuncture with such a network demands additional considerations, as the endless continuation of characters and stories within a Shared Universe network necessitate the use of seriality on multiple levels.

The nature of a Shared Universe as composed of several *Narrative Entities* and *Manifestations* necessitates a dualistic view of seriality because every *Manifestation* released for the Shared Universe stands equally in a serial relationship with the *Narrative Entity* it is associated with and in a serial relationship with all *Manifestations* released for that specific network. *Manifestations* exclusively associated with one *Narrative Entity* relate to one another directly. They exist in a linear fashion typical of episodes of a series, issues of a comic book series, or singular films of a movie franchise. This linear seriality influences merely a specific line of *Manifestations* (usually) focused on one specific *Narrative Entity*. Within the Shared Universe of the MCU, the three Iron Man films or the three Thor films exist within a linear seriality, as each film relates to and builds on the previous *Manifestation* of the same *Narrative Entity*. However, as any *Index Manifestation* within a network of *Narrative Entities* can and is subject to *Trigger Waves* that originated in the *Manifestation* of another *Narrative Entity*, seriality equally appears in a fragmented form.

In their essay on authorization practices[396], Kelleter & Stein propose the notion of a 'multilinear seriality', which describes an overlapping, parallel, and media-independent seriality that relies on an audience's engagement and the addition of *Manifestations* via professional and non-professional contributors. While multilinear seriality shares many qualities presented within the Shared Universe model, it is too broad, as it purposely ignores any potential hierarchy between different *Manifestations* created through a producer's intent, general accessibility, and understanding of interrelation. To limit the scope of the term, multilinear seriality within this research is further discussed as limited by the confines of a presented network. Within this limitation, the interrelation of traditional linear seriality and multilinear seriality creates a shift in overall complexity. As pointed out by Urbanski in her analysis of the reboot experience, the complexity of any narrative increases by the additional number of *semiotic cues* created through previous *Manifestations*[397]. As such, the complexity of a singular episode at the end of a linear series necessarily increases with the length of that series because the latest episode operates with all *semiotic cues* established in the previous ones. In other words, the more *Manifestations* a *Narrative Entity* (in a serial) has accumulated, the more predetermined knowledge the latest episode potentially requires for engagement[398]. Networking several *Narrative Entities* with numerous *Manifestations* potentially raises the number of *semiotic cues* bearing down on any *Manifestation* later released into that network. While the inclusion of new *Narrative Entity*-specific *Manifestations* does not burden any other linear se-

---

[396] Kelleter, Frank und Daniel Stein. "Autorisierungspraktiken seriellen Erzählens". *Populäre Serialität: Narration–Evolution–Distinktion*. Frank Kelleter (Ed.). Bielefeld: transcript Verlag, 2012. 259–290
[397] Urbanski, Heather. *The Science Fiction Reboot*. London: McFarland & Company, 2013. Page 159
[398] Kelleter discusses a similar burden of such *Manifestations* in from of a "cumulative narrative" in his essay "Five Ways of Looking at Seriality".

rial than its own, it still adds additional information to the overall network, as each other *Narrative Entity* can interact with its *Index Manifestation* and/or acknowledge its *Transformation Triggers*. As such, *Manifestations* within a network exist with a shifting complexity. *Manifestations* have to take on an increased complexity created by material from their own *Narrative Entity*, but they can take on additional complexity by engaging with a multilinear seriality within the network. Depending on the singular *Manifestation*, the engagement with a network's multilinear seriality is overt – and as such potentially necessary for complete comprehension of specific *Manifestations* – or subtle – and therefore focused dominantly on an informed audience. The Marvel Cinematic Universe has several linear series, which, through their release dates, stand in an additional fragmented serial relationship with one another. While having no linear serial relationship to the Captain America Narrative, the film *Ant-Man*, for example, still acknowledges changes made to the overall Shared Universe through the fall of the agency S.H.I.E.L.D. in *Captain America: The Winter Soldier*. Team narratives, composed of *Index Manifestations* from several *Narrative Entities*, like *The Avengers*, necessarily rely on multilinear seriality, as all effects of the different linear series affect them directly and vice versa. Conversely, films like *Doctor Strange* actively avoid acknowledging established aspects of the network, thereby minimizing the influence of the collection of established *semiotic cues*. As such, the combination of linear and multilinear seriality creates particular circumstances concerning the expansion of a network. A new *Manifestation* not only introduces new *semiotic cues* to the network on an intersection of different existing materials but can decide if and to what degree it will acknowledge existing strains of multilinear seriality. Conversely, such new *Manifestations* introduce new elements, which not only add and transform a specific *Narrative Entity* but also could influence any *Narrative Entity* in the network.

The serialized nature of a network in the Universe Model determines that the expansion of the network is best understood via the addition of new *Manifestations* and their increasing degree of entanglement with other elements of the network. Basing the expansion of a Shared Universe network on its potential relation with its own existing and transposed *Manifestations* creates a natural break in the consideration of the process. During the inception of a network, it is free from self-produced *semiotic cues* and only has a low level of multilinear seriality, if at all, simply because it has no material to create either. After a number of *Manifestations* and some degree of entanglement, the continued expansion has no choice but to constantly negotiate the state of the network and its *Narrative Entities* in some form. As such, it appears useful to consider the process of expansion in two distinct phases: (1) a foundational phase, in which the basic network emerges, and (2) an expansion phase, which is the addition of new material after the creation of a foundation.

3.2.1.1 The Foundational Phase: Constructing a Network

With the construction and expansion of a Shared Universe network dependent on a *Manifestation*'s interrelation through the recognition of reoccurring elements, any attempt to describe the process requires a manner of formulating such potential recognitions. As the audience types derived in relation to the principle of *Narrative Reliance* operate on such an understanding, this chapter will rely on these audience types to discuss such dependence on *semiotic cues*. In other words, the process and degree of interrelation for the construction and expansion are related via the possibility of an audience type engaging with a *Manifestation*. Within this view, it is notable that very few *Manifestations* (especially considering the MCU films) serve the engagement of purely one audience type. The nature of increasing information within a Shared Universe network precludes the potential of a *Manifestation* solely constructed for a casual audience because a network necessitates some inclusion of a transposed *semiotic cue*. However, while a narrative geared towards a casual audience can (and within a narrative from a Shared Universe often does) include *Index Manifestations* hinting, re-enforcing, or establishing a connection to another *Narrative Entity*, these can be presented in a manner that makes them mostly superfluous to the plot or easily replaceable. Post-credit scenes represent a perfect display of this notion, as by their nature, they exist outside the *Manifestation*'s actual plot. *Manifestations*, which relegate their interrelation to a post-credit scene, offer a point of entry because the narrative gives information concerning the Shared Universe but requires little to no previous knowledge. As such, they often find use within the overall MCU network but are specifically notable in the MCU films' first phase. On the other end of the spectrum, economic reality combined with the cost of production may exclude *Manifestations* utterly beholden to an informed audience. Here, media choice concerning the form of *Manifestations* influences the development of a network. Due to their low production cost, comic books can and have ignored casual audiences; blockbuster movie productions may not have that luxury. To retain an appeal to a casual audience, these *Manifestations* may sacrifice a significant portion of their content in an otherwise strongly reliant plot to a spectacle as a source of pure entertainment. Such *Manifestations* can offer more non-narrative spectacles without sacrificing narrative complexity because such complexity arises from its interrelation with another *Manifestation*. Within the overall MCU network and in the superhero narrative at large, these spectacles often come down to superpowered individuals punching one another creatively. This narrative strategy comes somewhat natural to team *Manifestations*. They can sacrifice time for a greater spectacle because parts of necessary exposition and character development have been "outsourced" to *Narrative Entity*-specific *Manifestations*. Of course, this approach mostly satisfies a spectacle-oriented casual audience over one with a narrative interest but still allows for a film's needed larger total audience. While generally applicable in the process of expansion, these two extremes within a Shared Universe network potentially also mark the beginning and conclusion of a foundational phase with a first *Manifestation*, showing merely some hint at a larger universe, and a final *Manifestation*, which nearly entirely relies on an audiences' knowledge of some or most previously established *semiotic cues*. Presuming this range, the foundational phases within the overall MCU network usually range from the very first *Manifestation*, which hints at a larger universe and serves mainly a casual audience, to the first team narrative, which draws all previously introduced *Narrative Entities* together and focuses on an informed audience. For the MCU films, this encompasses the entire first phase, from *Iron Man* to *The Avengers*. For the MNU network, the range is similar, starting with *Daredevil S1* and ending with *The Defenders*. In either case, the first *Manifestation* hints at a larger world (*Iron Man* with a post-credit scene and *Daredevil* with various *Index Manifestations*), and the team narratives rely on all preceding material. As both *Narrative Entities* from the ABC network rely on their origin in the MCU films, that network appears to have no foundational phase.

Viewing the different *Manifestations* between these two ends, they gradually increase in interrelation and, therefore, the gradual shift from a casual to an informed audience is notable. In either network, each new *Manifestation* operates with a greater dependency on an additional *Narrative Entity* than the previous one, with the final *Manifestation* before the team narrative connecting to most other members of the network in some fashion. Hereby, the degree of interrelation differs between films and series, with the total amount of interrelation appearing lower in the series in relation to the total hours of material. Within this context, the team narrative appears as the pinnacle of interrelation, the final statement solidifying different *Narrative Entities* as members of one network and their *Index Manifestations* as smaller components of a composed imaginary world.

The gradual increase in *Narrative Reliance* also arises due to the use of a *Shared Narrative* across the foundational phase. Clark Gregg's Phil Coulson provides a *Shared Narrative*, spanning the first phase of the MCU, appearing in four of its six *Manifestations*, and Rosaria Dawson's Claire Temple serves a similar purpose within the MNU, appearing in each of the MNU's foundational *Manifestations*. In either case, other overarching *Index Manifestations* support the overarching connection the Shared Narrative provides. Notably, this support appears mainly in the form of organizations with S.H.I.E.L.D. and characters associated with it, which draw in *Manifestations* outside the Coulson *Shared Narrative*, and the Hand and characters associated with it, cementing interrelations established by the Temple *Shared Narrative*. However, while a *Shared Narrative* serves as a means of connecting different *Manifestations*, its ability to organize them via its inherent plot structure appears more relevant in the process of constructing a network. As mentioned, a *Shared Narrative* creates some form of order between the *Manifestations* of two or more *Narrative Entities*. As each *Manifestation* appears to present a step in the genesis of a unified world, understanding the order (if not following it) bears some influence on comprehending that world and the relationship of the *Narrative Entities* within its network. Additionally, these *Shared Narratives* provide a guide for an escalating interrelation, as each step towards their *Climax* demands a more significant role within the plot of each subsequent *Manifestation*. In other words, the plot structure of this narrative technique not only helps audiences follow the order laid out by producers but also provides a guide for the rising importance of the relationships between the texts within a network. Removing its *Index Manifestation* from the network underscores a *Shared Narrative*'s singular purpose. Phil Coulson prominently dies in *The Avengers*. While his story formally continues in the ABC network, the character notably only returns once to the MCU film network. However, his appearance in *Captain Marvel* shows a different version of the character, which predates any other representation. Similarly, Claire Temple leaves the MNU network after appearing in three episodes of *Luke Cage S2*, which also marks her only appearance after the team narrative. Other characters mention Claire Temple, but she never reappears within any *Manifestation* of the network. As such, the overall MCU network indicates a necessary use of a *Shared Narrative* within the foundational phase of a network of *Narrative Entities*.

This strategy of gradually increasing the reliance on *semiotic cues* from previous material is not a specific feature of a Shared Universe network but seems an overall feature of serialized fiction in most forms. The beginning of any series employs a slow construction of meaning for their *Narrative Entity* with gradual greater reliance on previously provided information. Similarly, each series' final episode appears to mark the end of that process and indicates a new status quo within the presented world. Within any series, the gradual progression serves several functions but dominantly allows an audience to discover, learn, and understand the associated *Index Manifestations* and their *semiotic cues*. The construction of a Shared Universe network apparently requires a similar gradual process to introduce the components of its *Narrative Entities*. However, the gradual nature also gives an audience time to realize there is a connection between different *Manifestations* – whereas it is obviously present between consecutive episodes of a series – and understand the relationship between them. While this gradual approach seems necessary in the construction of a Shared Universe network, an exact rate of increased interrelation between *Manifestations* is impossible to determine from merely two examples. However, it is presumable that the process of interrelation in such a foundational phase could move too quickly, giving audiences not enough time to discover and understand the situation, or move too slowly, delaying the expected and meaningful interaction between specific *Index Manifestations* (in this case the hero character) to a point at which the audience loses interest.

3.2.1.2 The Expansion Phase: Maintaining and Adding to the Network

With the first team narrative, a network of *Narrative Entities* formally declares its status as a unified world, a presumably coherent imaginary space in which their *Index Manifestations* coexist in some form. As each *Manifestation* in the foundational phase existed in service of gradually building such a unified imaginary space, its established state excludes a similar function for *Manifestations* within the network following the first team narrative. Instead, each new *Manifestation* has to serve a function in relation to the already existing notion of a unified world. Within this context, the overall MCU network indicates a need for three types of function: (1) the addition of a New *Narrative Entity*, (2) the re-contextualization of an established network of *Index Manifestations*, and (3) an increase in interrelation.

Instinctively, introducing a new Narrative Entity into an established network proceeds in the same fashion as introducing a new Narrative Entity in the foundational phase. Partly, this assumption appears correct. The *Manifestation* provides a new network of *Index Manifestations*, which interrelates with the rest of the network to some degree. However, where new *Narrative Entities* of the foundational phase could focus on relating to other *Narrative Entities*, new *Narrative Entities* have to consider their relationship not only to singular *Narrative Entities* within the network but to the network as a whole. *Manifestations* of the foundational phase created a network of *Index Manifestations*, which connected to other networks of *Index Manifestations*. New *Manifestations* of the expansion phase create a set of new *Index Manifestations* within an established tight-knit network, forming a world. As such, each new *Narrative Entity* has to enter the network, declaring its relationship to the existing network. Hereby, the overall MCU network presents two distinctive approaches: (1) a clear connection and dependence on existing material or (2) a nearly complete avoidance of the imaginary space with only minor interrelation. Within the MCU film network, *Spider-Man: Homecoming* and *Ant-Man* provide examples of the former strategy, while *Black Panther* and *Guardians of the Galaxy* are examples of the latter. The former two *Manifestations* intertwine their network of *Index Manifestations* directly into the unified world by interrelating noticeably with other *Narrative Entities* and acknowledging the unified space. *Ant-Man* ties the origin of Michael Douglas's Henry Pym to S.H.I.E.L.D., the Iron Man Narrative, and the Captain America Narrative, while *Spider-Man: Homecoming* makes multiple references to the current state of the superhero community, equally tying itself to the mentioned *Narrative Entities*. Conversely, *Black Panther* and *Guardians of the Galaxy* only acknowledge their relationship to a larger network through singular interrelations, the appearance of Sebastian Stan's Buchanan 'Bucky' Barnes/The Winter Soldier and Benicio del Toro's Taneleer Tivan/The Collector, respectively. The difference between *Black Panther* and *Spider-Man: Homecoming* is interesting in this regard, as the hero characters from either *Narrative Entity* were introduced before the publication of their own *Manifestations*, indicating that the technique used to add a new *Narrative Entity* operates somewhat[399] independently from processes of interrelation. Interestingly, the MNU and ABC networks also employed these strategies at their inception. As either of these networks came into existence after *The Avengers* and referred back to some version of its final *Transformation Trigger*, their inception apparently tries to negotiate some relationship with an established world. Similarly, they also present the use of either strategy. The ABC network starts deeply connected to the MCU films, using established *Index Manifestations* and acknowledging several *Transformation Triggers*, especially in *Agents of S.H.I.E.L.D.*, but also in *Agent Carter*. The MNU network operates with only an allusive connection to the MCU films and primarily focuses on establishing an independent network of *Narrative Entities*. The use of these approaches for singular *Narrative Entities* and the addition of smaller networks gives the impression that both options provide the chief manner in which *Manifestations* can introduce the whole network of *Index Manifestations* from a new *Narrative Entity*.

While the establishment of a world alters the process of introducing a new *Narrative Entity*, the sudden shift also affects previously introduced *Narrative Entities*. Because new networks of *Index Manifestations* appearing in the expansion phase are created with an existing world in mind, they come into existence with a defined relation to that world and the network creating it. *Narrative Entities* established in the foundational phase – while providing the components of this imaginary space – are conceived as autonomous entities connected to another *Narrative Entity* but not necessarily as part of a greater whole. The new state of the network requires that the formerly more autonomous *Narrative Entities* are re-contextualized regarding their position within the network and related to the newly established world. In other words, when they were created, the *Manifestations* of the foundational phase did not have to consider a relationship to a larger world. When they reappear in the expansion phase, they must determine their place within a more prominent network. As such, *Manifestations* of established *Narrative Entities* focus on defining or redefining their network of *Index Manifestation* in relation to the new status quo. Within the MCU film network, the first three films of the second phase, *Iron Man 3*, *Captain America: The Winter Soldier*, and *Thor: The Dark World*, appear as the most prominent examples of

---

399 *Black Panther* does not operate as independently as *Guardian of the Galaxy* does because part of its plot refers to a *Transformation Trigger* in *Captain America: Civil War*, in which the hero character was introduced.

such a redefinition. Hereby, their approach to such a re-contextualization varies. Adapting a greater part of its *Index Manifestations* from the network, *Captain America: The Winter Soldier*'s re-contextualization means replacing all but the most defining *Index Manifestations* with others from the overall network. The second MCU's Captain America *Manifestation* does this by folding *Index Manifestations* associated with S.H.I.E.L.D. into the narrative while only reusing four established characters, Chris Evan's Steve Rogers/Captain America, Sebastian Stan's Buchanan "Bucky" Barnes/The Winter Soldier, Hayley Atwell's Margaret "Peggy" Carter, and Toby Jones's Arnim Zola (whereas the final two appear in an altered form). *Thor: The Dark World*, in contrast, circumvents this need for re-contextualization. Hereby, the *Manifestation* leans on a prominent and highlighted difference between the *indices* of the MCU Thor Narrative and other parts of the newly established network to explain its reaction to the more prominent network. Some of the narrative's *indices* have a non-Earthly and mythological representation, as all Asgardians within the MCU appear as an advanced alien race that lives lightyears away from Earth. Intradiegetically, this explains the *Narrative Entity*'s unique stability concerning a re-contextualization, as events on Earth would only have a marginal influence on an intergalactic society. Within *Thor: The Dark World*, the re-contextualization mostly appears in the form of acknowledgment of the events of *The Avengers* and smaller changes to singular *Index Manifestations*. Despite this circumvention, the *Manifestation* is still forced to address the network's altered state, underscoring a need to react to the overall change in some fashion.

Iron Man 3 makes use of either technique. The hero character repeatedly mentions the altered state of the world, creating a notable acknowledgment of the new status quo. Additionally, Tony Stark's entire stance on protection and responsibility changes in the wake of *The Avengers*, acknowledging his place in a larger network. As such, the re-contextualization of the *Narrative Entity* takes place via changes to the namesake *Index Manifestation*. While *Iron Man 3* maintains a greater part of its established *Index Manifestations*, it also acknowledges the new state of the world by adding a thematically unusual threat. The previous two MCU Iron Man *Manifestations* focused on the antagonists' attempt to imitate, steal, or lay claim to Tony Stark's Iron Man technology. Jeff Bridges's Obadiah Stane steals Tony Stark's design; Sam Rockwell's Justin Hammer tries to build his own version of the armor; and Mickey Rourke's Ivan Vanko/Whiplash lays claim to the arc reactor technology powering the suit. The Extremis soldiers and the technology creating them introduce the notion of a super-powered threat, a type of antagonist usually reserved for hero characters from a thematically similar realm like the Hulk or Captain America.

A similar process of re-contextualization also takes place among the *Manifestations* of the MNU network. While *The Defenders* does not project an as overt *Transformation Trigger* as *The Avengers*, the team narrative still greatly alters the state of the network and requires that the *Narrative Entities* re-contextualize their relationship within it. Generally, each of the four previously established *Narrative Entities* displays some greater acknowledgment of a coherent world by employing a greater deal of transposed *Index Manifestations*. Here, the cross-*Manifestation* appearances of Elden Henson's Franklin Percy "Foggy" Nelson are notable. Otherwise, each *Manifestation* also uses one of the previously described techniques. *Jessica Jones S2* tackles the alteration in a similar fashion to *Thor: The Dark World*. The *Manifestation* circumvents direct changes to its own network of *In-*

dex *Manifestations* by acknowledging the larger network through mentions of the events of the team narrative and some transposed *Index Manifestations*, which never meaningfully engage with a greater part of the Jessica Jones Narrative's network of *Index Manifestations*. *Luke Cage S2* applies a similar tactic to *Iron Man 3*. Hereby, it is not the hero character who views the world differently, but the world that acknowledges Luke Cage as a hero. Additionally, the series makes use of the existence of other *Narrative Entities* in the same space, notably the MNU Iron Fist Narrative. Two characters – Jessica Henwick's Colleen Wing and Finn Jones's Danny Rand/Iron Fist – appear as friends and confidants within the series, and Danny Rand's company provides advanced, otherwise unattainable, technology. More importantly, the hero character's responsibility to work together and protect Manhattan[400] is a reminder of their shared imaginary space. The second season of *Iron Fist* approaches its re-contextualization similar to *Captain America: The Winter Soldier*. With the fall of The Hand at the end of *The Defenders*, the *Narrative Entity* lost its main antagonist and, therefore, a section of its network of *Index Manifestations*. *Iron Fist S2* elevates some of its established *Index Manifestations* to greater importance, but it also adds a character from another *Narrative Entity* to its network: Simone Missick's Misty Knight appears in a greater part of the series. Additionally, the hero character re-contextualized his mission statement from being "the sworn enemy of The Hand" to taking over for Daredevil, who (presumably) died in *The Defenders*. *Daredevil S3* naturally has to acknowledge the presumed death of its titular hero and rearrange the relationships and positions within the narrative to accommodate that *Transformation Trigger*. Concerning this process of re-contextualization, the greater acknowledgment of an established world within the films compared to the series is notable and should be acknowledged. However, the research can give no reason or insight on the difference. While this process of re-contextualization notably takes place after the first team narrative established a world, *Ant-Man and The Wasp* and *Spider-Man: Far From Home* indicate that such a re-contextualization also occurs within the expansion phase. Aside from being sequels for a specific *Narrative Entity*, each of these *Manifestations* also reacts to larger changes within the overall network. *Spider-Man: Far From Home* prominently negotiates the destruction and resurrection of half of the population from *Avengers: Infinity War* and *Avengers: Endgame*. Additionally, the film deals with the death of Tony Stark/Iron Man. Similarly, *Ant-Man and The Wasp* acknowledges not only the events of its own predecessor (*Ant-Man*) but also responds to *Transformation Triggers* from *Captain America: Civil War*, specifically Paul Rudd's Scott Lang/Ant-Man's participation in the superhero battle at the airport and the Sakovia Accords. Either of these cases implies that the function of redefining a *Narrative Entity* within the context of a network appears when a *Manifestation* is created in the wake of not only its own predecessor but also any network-encompassing *Trigger Wave*. *Guardians of the Galaxy Vol.2* supports this notion, as the *Narrative Entity* remains distant from the core of the network up until *Avengers: Infinity War*. This distance allows it to ignore the transformations created in either *Avengers: Age of Ultron* or *Captain America: Civil War*. Unencumbered by these *Manifestations*, *Guardians of the Galaxy Vol. 2* only engages with the

---

400 "The Main Ingredient". *Luke Cage*. Created by Cheo Hodari Coker. Season 2, episode 10. Marvel Television/ABC Studios. 2016–2018. 00:04:44

Trigger Waves from its predecessor, as it does not need to define its network of *Index Manifestations* within a new context. Presumably, the *Narrative Entity* will have to re-contextualize in its third installment, as it now is entangled with the overall network after the third and fourth team narrative. *Captain America: Civil War* continues the tale of Steve Rogers's life after the fall of S.H.I.E.L.D. in the *Narrative Entity*'s previous *Manifestation* but also re-contextualizes the different *Index Manifestations* in the context of the *Transformation Triggers* from *Avengers: Age of Ultron*, most notably the new Avengers team presented at the end of the movie and the fallout of the Avengers' battle in Sakovia. While *Thor: Ragnarok* also reacts to the combined *Transformation Triggers* of *Thor: The Dark World* and *Avengers: Age of Ultron*, specifically the vision of Asgard's demise. Overall, *Manifestations* with the function of redefining their *Narrative Entity* appear at the intersection of *Trigger Waves* from their predecessors and from *Manifestations* that greatly interrelate *Narrative Entities*. Hereby, they re-contextualize the relationship of the *Narrative Entity* by either redefining their *Index Manifestation(s)* into the new context or adapting transposed *Index Manifestations*.

The third function a *Manifestation* can have within a Shared Universe network is to increase the interrelation of its different components. Hereby, this function connects to the process of re-contextualization as larger changes to the network; therefore, the initiation of far-reaching *Trigger Waves* arises mostly (not exclusively) from *Manifestations*, which increase interrelation. Such a relationship is not surprising. As the definition of *Transformation Triggers* includes changes to *Index Manifestations*, the easiest way to spread their effects across a network is for the change to occur within a *Manifestation* with characters, props, and sets from various *Narrative Entities*. In other words, it is easier to alter several parts of the network in one *Manifestation* if that *Manifestation* contains a recognizable part from each section making up the network. The truth of the relationship between a sudden increase in interrelation and grand *Transformation Triggers*, which create *Trigger Waves* across the network, becomes apparent with a brief look at the MCU films' team narratives. Each of the Avengers films contains a grand alteration to the overall network: *The Avengers* transforms the network into a unified world and introduces each part of the network to aliens and enhanced individuals; *Avengers: Age of Ultron*[401] marks the entrance of artificial intelligence, the notion of enhanced individuals as an international threat, and the acknowledgment of the Infinity Stones as a rising threat; *Avengers: Infinity War* sees the death of half the universe's population; and *Avengers: Endgame* shows the resurrection of the lost half of the population as well as the death of Tony Stark and the retirement of Steve Rogers. Within this context, *Captain America: Civil War* also holds a sudden increase in interrelation, as a larger part of its network of *indices* is replaced with several unattached and transposed *Index Manifestations*. Equally, it contains a *Transformation Trigger*, which causes a far-reaching *Trigger Wave* in the form of the Sakovia Accords and the split of the superhero community. While the combination of a sudden increase in interrelation and the creation of a far-reaching *Trigger Wave* is clear, the purpose of this function within the overall network is less obvious. Within the context of a Shared

---

401 *Avengers: Age of Ultron* formally does not increase any interrelation but re-establishes existing ones. However, I mention it in this list because it is a team narrative and has a network-spanning impact. The odd outlier composition of this *Manifestation* is discussed in the following chapter.

Universe network, the purpose of adding new *Narrative Entities* in the process of expansion is self-evident. Equally, as it is a reaction to a combination of changes, which need to be acknowledged, the purpose of re-contextualizing also appears obvious. However, the sudden increase in interrelation and the subsequent *Trigger Waves* of such a *Manifestation* only have an immanent role at the end of the foundational phase. The absence of such increased interrelations in the ABC and MNU networks highlights this lack of necessity, as the former operates without a unifying team narrative, and the latter only has one at the end of its foundational phase. The notable difference appears to lie in the number of *Manifestations* and *Narrative Entities* within either network. While the ABC network consists of two *Narrative Entities* spread across nine *Manifestations* (counting each season as one *Manifestation*) and the MNU network consists of five *Narrative Entities* spread across 13 *Manifestations*, the MCU films have ten *Narrative Entities* spread across 23 *Manifestations*. Considering the larger number of *Narrative Entities*, using a sudden increase in interrelation is an economical path to draw the different parts of the network together. This appears particularly important in the context of the potential of introducing new *Narrative Entities* with a low interrelation within the larger network. The MCU's Guardians of the Galaxy and Dr. Strange Narratives entered the network with such autonomy that a gradual interrelation might have taken longer than the sudden appearance in the final two Avengers films. More importantly, such sudden increases in interrelation allow for a clear organization of the *Narrative Entities* within the network. *Avengers: Age of Ultron* reiterates the connection of all *Narrative Entities* from the foundational phase, clearly marking the MCU's Guardians of the Galaxy Narrative, the new *Narrative Entity* introduced right before the team narrative, as connected but separate from a presumed core network. A similar effect occurs with *Captain America: Civil War*, which draws the MCU's Ant-Man, Spider-Man, and Black Panther Narratives into this presumed core network, created by the founding *Narrative Entities*, but also marks the MCU's Guardians of the Galaxy and Dr. Strange Narrative as something (still) separate. The absence of the MCU's Thor Narrative from the third MCU's Captain America *Manifestation* may also serve such an organizational purpose as it separates the upcoming MCU's Thor *Manifestation* (to a degree) from the *Trigger Waves* created by the Sakovia Accords and the split of the superhero community. As such, the increase in interrelation serves dominantly an organizational purpose, which is utilized by drawing parts of a network together. Hereby, it usually creates network-spanning *Trigger Waves*, which demand a re-contextualization from *Manifestations* of established *Narrative Entities* following it.

In contrast to a classically linear franchise or even a transmedial franchise, the Shared Universe can grow to encompass *Narrative Entities*, which do not relate to one another 'naturally'. Using the previously mentioned aspects, producers of the Shared Universe can introduce, redefine, and relate *Narrative Entities* independently from their content. The functions used within an expansion phase allow for such a precise management of the network. Hereby, all these functions within the expansion phase have been discussed as separate and singular within a *Manifestation*. To a degree, *Manifestations* can perform some of these functions simultaneously. Specifically, an increase in interrelation may be part of nearly every *Manifestation* within a network of *Narrative Entities*. However, while *Manifestations* can combine several of these functions, I presume that they dominantly perform one within the context of all other *Manifestations* within the same network.

Tracking these dominant functions along the line of *Manifestations* in relation to their release dates should reveal a structural pattern organizing the *Manifestations* of a singular network.

3.2.1.3 The General Structure of Shared Universe Expansion

Understanding that *Manifestations* can take on a dominant function in the expansion of a Shared Universe allows for the determination of governing patterns or rules, which guide the creation of *Manifestations* within a Shared Universe context. To this end, each network is presented in a table that aligns the *Manifestations* with its U.S. release date and its dominant function. The date is included to justify a potential order of engagement and to highlight potential changes as a reaction to the content of other *Manifestations*. The reason for the determined function of each *Manifestation* follows below each table, as well as a short conception of its pattern.

Maintaining a view of the MCU films in the context of their own phase structure, a notable pattern emerges. As described, the foundational phase coincides with the first phase, with each *Manifestation* (except one) introducing a new *Narrative Entity* meant to become a part of the initial world. Within this process, the interrelation within the emerging network continuously escalates until the unified world is formed through a sudden increase in interrelation created by the first team narrative. The exception within this process is *Iron Man 2*. The break in pattern potentially occurred because Disney acquired Marvel at the end of 2009, bringing along changes due to previous negotiations and a change in management. Independent from the reason, *Iron Man 2* does not disturb the formation of a unified world, as it maintains the process of a slow interrelation in the same manner the *Manifestation* of a new *Narrative Entity* would. The inclusion of a sequel in the foundational phase shows that not each *Manifestation* has to introduce a new *Narrative Entity* before the establishment of a world. It also indicates that the number of *Manifestations* within the foundational phase is not fixed or determined by the number of *Narrative Entities* providing the basis of the network.

After the first team narrative has drawn the early *Narrative Entities* into a fixed unified world, creating a Shared Universe, the first expansion phase (or the MCU's second phase) begins with three sequels to *Manifestations* from the foundational phase. As discussed, these *Manifestations* re-contextualize their *Narrative Entity* with the changes created due to the increased interrelation and *Trigger Waves* created by the first team narrative. This phase expands the network by introducing two new *Narrative Entities*, with one tied closely to the network (*Ant-Man*) and the other holding a more distant relationship (*Guardians of the Galaxy Vol. 1*). A team narrative separates the two new *Narrative Entities*. Despite being a team narrative, *Avengers: Age of Ultron* does not function as a sudden increase of interrelation because it does not include any *Index Manifestations* from either of the new *Narrative Entities*. Instead, the *Manifestation* re-contextualizes the relationships between the established *Narrative Entities*, specifically the hero characters, in the wake of not only the first team narrative but also individual re-contextualization, most notably from *Iron Man 3* and *Captain America: The Winter Soldier*. The reality of this focus on re-contextualization becomes apparent with the second team narrative's position in all but one *Shared Narrative* and all overarching *Index Manifestations* from the MCU films. However, despite not suddenly increasing interrelation, it still creates *Trigger Waves*, which influence a significant portion of the overall network. *Avengers: Age of Ultron* shows that there is no necessary association between the function of an increased interrelation and team narrative or far-reaching *Trigger Waves*. The first expansion phase generally stabilizes the network by contextualizing established *Narrative Entities* within the new reality of the unified world. Actual expansion only occurs via New *Narrative Entities*, whereas notably, the closer related of these new introductions appears after all *Manifestations* focused on re-contextualization have all been released.

Manifestation	U.S. release date	Function
MCU's Phase One (Foundational phase)		
Iron Man	May 2, 2008	First Narrative Entity
The Incredible Hulk	June 13, 2008	New Narrative Entity
Iron Man 2	May 7, 2010	Maintain
Thor	May 6, 2011	New Narrative Entity
Captain America: The First Avenger	July 22, 2011	New Narrative Entity
Marvel's The Avengers	May 4, 2012	Increase in Interrelation (World Establishment)
MCU's Phase Two (Expansion phase I)		
Iron Man 3	May 3, 2013	Re-contextualize
Thor: The Dark World	November 8, 2013	Re-contextualize
Captain America: The Winter Soldier	April 4, 2014	Re-contextualize
Guardians of the Galaxy	August 1, 2014	New Narrative Entity (distant)
Avengers: Age of Ultron	May 1, 2015	Re-contextualize
Ant-Man	July 17, 2015	New Narrative Entity (close)
MCU's Phase Three (Expansion phase II)		
Captain America: Civil War	May 6, 2016	Increase in Interrelation/Re-contextualize
Doctor Strange	November 4, 2016	New Narrative Entity (distant)
Guardians of the Galaxy Vol.2	May 5, 2017	Maintain
Spider-Man: Homecoming	July 7, 2017	New Narrative Entity (close)
Thor: Ragnarok	November 3, 2017	Re-contextualize
Black Panther	February 16, 2018	New Narrative Entity (distant)
Avengers: Infinity War	April 27, 2018	Increase in Interrelation
Ant-Man and the Wasp	July 6, 2018	Re-contextualize
Captain Marvel	March 8, 2019	New Narrative Entity (close)
Avengers: Endgame	April 26, 2019	Increase in Interrelation
Spider-Man: Far From Home	July 2. 2019	Re-contextualize

While the process of expansion continues in the MCU's third phase, it follows a different pattern than the section preceding it. This alteration in process appears to arise from two factors: (1) the increased number of *Manifestations* and (2) a new mixture of new *Narrative Entities*, first sequels, and second sequels. The combined story of the final two team narratives, as well as *Captain America: Civil War*, frame most of this phase. The third MCU Captain America *Manifestation* is the only film within this structure, which notably performs two of the presented functions equally. Continuing the *Shared Narrative* of the Iron Man and Captain America relationship, the film has to re-contextualize the relationship of several characters as well as the view of the world on the Avengers in the wake of *Avengers: Age of Ultron*. Due to the conflict over the registration of superhumans and the separation of the Avengers into two teams, *Captain America: Civil War* also initiates *Trigger Waves* that alter significant parts of the unified world. These *Trigger Waves* are carried throughout the network because this Captain America *Manifestation* also increases interrelation. Hereby, the film draws established and upcoming New *Narrative Entities* into the core of the network. The final two Avengers films, in contrast, solely serve to suddenly increase the interrelation within the network, inarguably drawing all *Narrative Entities* into the unified world and, in the process, also creating a network-wide *Trigger Wave*, which no *Narrative Entity* within the MCU film network could ignore. Within this frame, this phase introduces four new *Narrative Entities*, of which two appeared previously, and two have not. More importantly, these new *Narrative Entities* appear alternating between a distant and close relationship to the overall network, independent of their previous establishment. This alternation continues from the previous phase, which started with a distant new *Narrative Entity* and followed up with a close one. Hereby, *Black Panther* is defined as a distant new *Narrative Entity* because the film itself contains only little reference to the larger network, despite the hero character's involvement in *Captain America: Civil War*[402]. This appears especially true if contrasted with *Spider-Man: Homecoming*, which adapts entire parts of the MCU's Iron Man Narrative. The second notable distinction between the four new *Narrative Entities* is on the level of content. The new *Narrative Entities* not tied to *Captain America: Civil War* both have an Infinity Stone interwoven into their plot. The connection to either the initial film or to the preparation of the Infinity Saga suggests that the introduction of more than two *Narrative Entities* into an already established and expansive network within a phase with several *Manifestations* requires either a noticeable setup – as, for example, the early appearance of the hero characters

---

402   *Black Panther* is notably more difficult to classify as close or distant than other *Manifestations*. It contains more connective elements than a post-credit scene, specifically because part of its *Index Manifestations* appeared previously (aside from the hero character, specifically the Dora Milaje and Martin Freeman's Everett K. Ross). Additionally, the plot continues *Transformation Triggers* from a previous film. The *Manifestation* is still classified as appearing distantly related to the network because these connections are mostly kept in the background within *Black Panther*. Essentially, the film caters, despite these connections, mostly to a casual audience, while *Manifestations* with a close relationship leans more into the relationship with the network by making part of it central to its setup. As such, I determined that *Black Panther* is below the threshold of interrelations for a close New *Narrative Entity*, despite being more connected than many other distant New *Narrative Entities*.

– or has to provide a significant *Index Manifestation* for the overarching story and the upcoming team narrative. As expected and previously described, sequels are focused on re-contextualizing their network of *Index Manifestations* created by intersecting *Trigger Waves*. The number of *Manifestations* creating *Trigger Waves* makes this action unsurprising. In each instance, the various sequels react to changes arising out of *Manifestations* from their own *Narrative Entity* and the changes arising from team narratives. In this context, *Thor: Ragnarok* requires attention, as it is the only *Manifestation* re-contextualizing in reaction to *Trigger Waves* started outside of the third phase. The film's redefinition of the *Narrative Entity*'s position within the network solely refers to material from the previous phase. Notably, it reacts to *Thor: The Dark World*, specifically Loki's usurpation of Asgard's throne, and *Avengers: Age of Ultron*, specifically the Hulk's disappearance and Thor's vision of Asgard's destruction. Every other re-contextualization reacts, at least in part, to *Trigger Waves* started within the third phase. The distinction is noticeable because it highlights the narrow dependency concerning the placement within the overall line of *Manifestations*. A *Manifestation* with the function of re-contextualization can be released at any point as long as it appears after the larger *Transformation Trigger* influencing it and before its new state interrelates with the rest of the network. A similar freedom is afforded to *Manifestations* that just have to contend with changes from their own predecessor. The network of *Index Manifestations* from *Guardian of the Galaxy Vol.2* has not been interrelated with the rest of the network. It, therefore, can ignore the *Trigger Waves* created by the preceding sudden increases in interrelation. This function of maintaining its status within the developing unified world, which constantly changes due to activity within the network, shows the potential of attached but independent *Narrative Entities* within such a Shared Universe network. Within this second expansion phase, the actual expansion of the network occurs along two lines. Primarily, the addition of new *Narrative Entities* increases the overall material within the network. On a second level, the network expands through the sudden interrelation of previously distant material. Here, the expansion does not transpire due to new material but by folding the additional *indices* introduced by these new materials, which constituted a world of its own, into the existing unified world. Similar to the formation of the world at the end of the foundational phase, the sudden increases in interrelation within *Manifestations* of the second expansion states unequivocally that the different *Narrative Entities* exist in a shared imaginary space. This statement forces the formation of a new unified world, which has assimilated the worlds the singular *Manifestations* have created for their own *Narrative Entity*. In other words, the sudden interrelation expands the unified world by forcing the formation of a new unified world, which combines the old unified world and the elements defining the newly added *Narrative Entities*. Where a notion of the mystical arts (magic) and fantastical science (science fiction) existed in loosely interlinked but mostly separate worlds before the appearance of *Avengers: Infinity War*, after the film's sudden increase in interrelation, they have to exist in tandem in a reformatted unified world. As such, expansion in this phase grows out of the addition of material and the progression of the base world, which determines the course of the network.

Manifestation	U.S. release date	Function
Foundational phase		
Daredevil Season 1	April 10, 2015	First Narrative Entity
Jessica Jones Season 1	November 20, 2015	New Narrative Entity
Daredevil Season 2	March 18, 2016	Increase in Interrelation
Luke Cage Season 1	September 30, 2016	New Narrative Entity
Iron Fist Season 1	March 17, 2017	New Narrative Entity
The Defenders	August 18, 2017	Increase in Interrelation (World Establishment)
Expansion phase		
The Punisher Season 1	November 17, 2017	New Narrative Entity (distant)
Jessica Jones Season 2	March 8, 2018	Re-contextualize
Luke Cage Season 2	June 22, 2018	Re-contextualize
Iron Fist Season 2	September 7, 2018	Re-contextualize
Daredevil Season 3	October 19, 2018	Re-contextualize
The Punisher Season 2	January 18, 2019	Maintain
Jessica Jones Season 3	June 14, 2019	Maintain

Overall, the MCU films' larger structure indicates that the actual order and number of *Manifestations* are not fixed. However, creating and expanding a Shared Universe network follows a general order. The network begins with setting up initial *Narrative Entities* and then draws them into a unified world. A general focus on re-contextualizing the different *Narrative Entities* to the new relationship follows. While some expansion occurs through the introduction of New *Narrative Entities*, the focus clearly lies on stabilizing the new world. Aggressive expansion then occurs after the stabilization is completed. Here, the expansion arises through a number of new *Narrative Entities* and the growth of the unified world, only broken by the need to re-contextualize established *Narrative Entities*.

In contrast to the MCU films, the MNU network is divided into a foundational and expansion phase. Despite not being marketed in phases as the films were, this clear distinction arises from the appearance of a singular team narrative, which creates a pivot point in the formation and management of the MNU's world.

Structurally speaking, the release of a singular season and its application in the creation of a Shared Universe mirrors the MCU films of the first phase, with one major exception. Where the one sequel in the foundational phase of the films merely maintains its position in the network, the one sequel in that phase of the MNU network provides a sudden increase in interrelation by introducing the hero character of a new *Narrative Entity* with an upcoming *Manifestation*. This specific increase in interrelation differs from other versions of this function on two levels: (1) It lacks the activation of a network-influencing *Trigger Wave*, and (2) it interrelates to a *Narrative Entity* outside of the foundational phase. The latter is significant because, despite the *Manifestation*'s sudden increase in interrelation by tying two *Narrative Entities* into one world, fulfilling this function does not disrupt the slow increase in connection of the foundational *Narrative Entities*. With *The Punisher S1* released after the team narrative, the network of *indices* forming the world specific to that *Narrative Entity* appears after the formation of a unified world and, therefore, has no bearing on that formation. However, the sudden interrelation creates some form of relationship with the then-created core of the network. Because the connection remains to one singular *Narrative Entity* within the network, the retroactive inclusion of this later introduced *Narrative Entity* into the unified world appears unlikely. Rather, the *Narrative Entity* retains the connection but exists as a parallel network of *indices* instead of an incorporated one. This assertion is supported by the fact that the first and second MNU Punisher *Manifestations* hold only a distant relationship to the unified world created by the team narrative and mainly maintain their connection through the MNU's Daredevil Narrative. Following the team narrative, the *Manifestations* of the expansion phase generally follow the pattern laid out in the MCU film network. A new *Narrative Entity* is introduced, and established *Narrative Entities* re-contextualize their network of *indices* in the wake of intersecting *Trigger Waves*. Hereby, the low level of re-contextualization within Jessica Jones S2 needs mentioning. In contrast to the other *Manifestations* of established *Narrative Entities*, which all greatly alter their network of *indices* to accommodate the effects of the newly formed unified world, Jessica Jones S2 merely acknowledges its inclusion in a larger world but maintains the formation of its own network of *indices*. This approach is similar to low-level re-contextualization in *Thor: The Dark World*, which also only acknowledged its presence in a unified world. In either case, re-contextualization takes place as a necessity but is performed to maintain their network of *indices* rather than adapting them to the new circumstance. Notably, the two sequels introduced after the re-contextualization process maintain their relationship with the network instead of engaging with it. Hereby, Jessica Jones S3 and *The Punisher* S2 mirror the reaction of *Guardians of the Galaxy Vol. 2*. They present a story purely focused on their *Narrative Entity*, avoiding a sudden increase in interrelation. Without a previous, more significant *Trigger Wave* carried throughout the network, neither has any need to re-contextualize their network of *indices*. With merely one new *Narrative Entity*, the expansion phase of the MNU network is one in name only. Instead, the phase stabilizes the unified world after using the same foundational process as the MCU film network. However, the MNU never uses this stabilized world, as it does not expand or release a further team narrative.

In the overall comparison of these three networks, the ABC network has an oddly differing structure concerning the function of its *Manifestations*. Because the *Narrative Entities* spun out of the foundational phase of the MCU films, the network has no foundational phase of its own, instead leaning on the unified world created with *The Avengers*. As such, the structure of this network does not operate on its own but rather as an alternate expansion phase to the MCU film's foundational phase.

Within the ABC network's different context, it still makes use of the same overall functions, dominantly the process of re-contextualization and the introduction of new *Narrative Entities*. However, the former operates differently from their counterparts from the other networks. With the unified world set, either *Narrative Entity* enters the network via its first *Manifestation*. Hereby, *Agents of S.H.I.E.L.D.* appears with a relatively close relationship to the MCU films' unified world, as its entire network of *indices* is built upon the understanding of its existence. *Agent Carter* has a distant relationship to the unified world, as the series constructs a world mostly connected to the one presented in *Captain America: The First Avenger* but has no direct relation to the unified world formed by the MCU's first team narrative. While both new *Narrative Entities* follow the pattern of this function within an expansion phase (setting up a network of *indices* in consideration of the established attributes within the new unified world), specifically *Agents of S.H.I.E.L.D. S1* also re-contextualizes its network of *indices* throughout its run. This additional function arises due to the differing manner of release between television series and films, as well as the series' dependency on the world created by the films. In other words, while the series was running, new films were released, which caused *Trigger Waves* that affected the series. Within this context, singular episodes of the series serve as means of re-contextualization, while the greater part of the first season primarily focuses on establishing the new *Narrative Entity*. The series holds a similar duality between re-contextualization and maintaining its status for the following two seasons. The presumption of such a duality arises because the series focuses on its own network of *indices* and its own *Transformation Triggers*, only singularly acknowledging the events from the films. While season five also alludes to the films, specifically *Avengers: Infinity War*, the *Manifestations* of *Agents of S.H.I.E.L.D.* after the third season mostly focus on their own development, maintaining their overall status. Having no immediate relationship with the *Transformation Triggers* of the MCU film network, *Agent Carter* only appears with a relationship to that network but then maintains its level of connection for its second season. The simple structure of this standalone expansion phase indicates how a network could come into being and operate from another foundational phase. However, it also indicates that a new *Narrative Entity*'s reliance on its source may dwindle with a rising number of *Manifestations*.

Universally, the order of *Manifestations* reveals small indications governing the mechanics of a Shared Universe. The three functions previously defined for the process of expansion – New *Narrative Entity*, sudden increase in interrelation, and re-contextualization – require two additions in the form of maintain and network wave. The latter describes a *Trigger Wave*, which reaches several *Narrative Entities* within a network and affects a greater part of the unified world created via the network. While the notion of a network wave was incorporated in the sudden increase in interrelation, and these two functions usually appear together, they can occur separately. Acknowledging their separate existence allows for the description of a team narrative that merely maintains the status of interrelation in the network and includes the potential of a *Manifestation* that suddenly increases the interrelation of *Narrative Entities* but does not cause a widespread change in the unified world. However, while the function of a network wave detaches from a sudden increase in interrelations, it still does not appear on its own. Network waves, sudden increases in interrelation, a new *Narrative Entity*, and re-contextualization all describe *Manifestations* that alter a network in some fashion, either proactively or in reaction to another function. The previously presented structure, however, shows that not every *Manifestation* alters the state of a network, but some specifically avoid changes, operating with the established order. These *Manifestations* effectively have the function of maintaining the status of the unified world. Concerning the organization of *Manifestations* with these functions, a look at the overall structure of the material reveals only an additional phase between the foundational and the expansion phases. After the unified world is set, each established *Narrative Entity* has to be re-contextualized within the overall new order to stabilize the new world. Both the MCU film and MNU networks focus on re-contextualization over expansion right after the first team narrative. Even one of the ABC series is greatly concerned with re-contextualizing itself in the subsequent changes made to the network. As such, the general structure for an emerging Shared Universe would have the pattern of a foundational phase – which gradually interrelates different *Narrative Entities* to combine them into a unified world with a team Narrative – followed by a stabilization phase – which mostly re-contextualizes the network and introduces a limited number of new *Narrative Entities* – and then an expansion phase – which gradually grows the network by adding new *Narrative Entities* and enlarging the unified world. Aside from specific causal relationships between different functions and on the level of content, *Manifestations* within the different phases apparently are not set in a fixed order.

Manifestation	U.S. release date	Function
MCU's Phase One (Foundational phase)		
Iron Man	May 2, 2008	First Narrative Entity
The Incredible Hulk	June 13, 2008	New Narrative Entity
Iron Man 2	May 7, 2010	Maintain
Thor	May 6, 2011	New Narrative Entity
Captain America: The First Avenger	July 22, 2011	New Narrative Entity
Marvel's The Avengers	May 4, 2012	Increase in Interrelation (World Establishment)
ABC's Expansion phase		
Agents of S.H.I.E.L.D. Season 1	September 24, 2013	New Narrative Entity (close)
Agents of S.H.I.E.L.D. Season 2	September 23, 2014	Re-contextualize (MCU films)
Agent Carter Season 1	January 6, 2015	New Narrative Entity (distant)
Agents of S.H.I.E.L.D. Season 3	September 29, 2015	Re-contextualize (MCU films)
Agent Carter Season 2	January 19, 2016	Maintain
Agents of S.H.I.E.L.D. Season 4	September 20, 2016	Maintain
Agents of S.H.I.E.L.D. Season 5	December 1, 2017	Maintain
Agents of S.H.I.E.L.D. Season 6	May 10, 2019	Maintain (decreased Interrelation)
Agents of S.H.I.E.L.D. Season 7	May 27, 2020	Increase in Interrelation/ Maintain

3.2.2 It's All Too Much: The Need for Clustering

The expansion of the MCU network in the stabilization as well as the expansion phase indicates that the different *Narrative Entities* within a Shared Universe network do not exist in an overall even relationship with one another. *Narrative Entities* like the Guardians of the Galaxy and Dr. Strange Narrative conspicuously exist outside of the strong interrelation of the foundational *Narrative Entities* within the MCU film network. The process of expansion described in the earlier chapter implies that this separation between a core network and satellite *Narrative Entities* is a natural phenomenon of a network's creation and growth. While that might be the case, a short look at the organization of superhero comics and the relationship of all three networks discussed here indicate that many *Narrative Entities* and *Manifestations* within the same network automatically organize into clusters. A cluster in this context refers to a collection of *Narrative Entities* that interact more frequently with one another than with other members of their network. In other words, in the visual presentation described for the Shared Universe network, these *Narrative Entities* would cluster together because they more frequently exchange *Index Manifestations*, more frequently acknowledge *Transformation Triggers*, and more likely have a *Shared Narrative* spread among them.

Shifting from the concept of a core within the network to multiple clusters seems important under the consideration of continued expansion. While technically, a network could continue to operate with a core/periphery view, a similarity in *Index Manifestations*, themes, and potential plot structures between different *Narrative Entities* in the network will raise their interaction naturally. In other words, while the core/periphery view works when most *Narrative Entities* play on Earth and deal with human enhancement and only singular ones deal with extraterrestrial, extradimensional, and mystical themes, a more even spread of those denominators within the network naturally will create several different clusters, instead of only one core. The truth of such an occurrence is visible in superhero comics. Outside of fixed relationships usually created through a team narrative, different *Narrative Entities* cluster together with their respective denominations. The Guardians of the Galaxy, Nova, and Silver Surfer Narratives from Marvel Comics are more likely to interact with one another because all of them operate in space and deal with cosmic threats, plotlines, and themes. The network of *indices* from Dr. Strange, Brother Voodoo, and Hellstorm will more likely interact because of their association with magic. The height of this effect arises with such *Narrative Entities* as Spider-Man, Scarlet Spider, Miles Morales: Spider-Man, Venom, Spider-Woman, and Silk. This natural preference does not invalidate the potential interactions between all *Narrative Entities* but only highlights simple associations within a network. Clusters do not have to form along such similarities in themes; the effect of audiences considering or thinking of *Narrative Entities* associated with one another appears to have a similar effect. The most notable example of this might be the Superman/Batman relationship. While these *Narrative Entities* do not share any direct denominations, they are often considered related to one another because of their status as first superhero and first vigilante hero, respectively. However, it is important that such clusters seem to appear within a Shared Universe network with a high number of *Narrative Entities*. This natural tendency to interact does not only arise with a greater number of *Narrative Entities* but equally appears to become more necessary in managing a Shared Universe network. If all *Narrative Entities* within a network relate equally to one another, predicting and understanding the potential interactions of *Index Manifestations* and the range and effects of *Trigger Waves* becomes difficult. Clusters essentially create smaller networks within a larger one, which allows for a more explicit definition and understanding of interactions between different *Narrative Entities*. This aspect of clusters allows us to maintain the sense of a larger complex Universe with endless possibilities while offering recipients manageable chunks to engage. Existing clusters also give recipients smaller units through which they can first "decide" to educate themselves on the aspects and mechanics of this unified world and later on add new clusters to receive a better overview of the overall network. As such, clusters appear as an important part of managing a network of *Narrative Entities* by organizing the overall network into smaller sections.

3.2.2.1 The Process of Clustering

The creation of clusters within a network of *Narrative Entities* purely hinges on the focused use of connective techniques between specific *Narrative Entities* over others. In other words, if a few *Narrative Entities* exchange *Index Manifestations* and react to each other's *Transformation Triggers* with a higher frequency than the rest of the network, they form a cluster. Due to this higher frequency of interrelation, association via chains of interaction[403] notably affects clusters more significantly than in other instances of the Shared Universe network, as *Index Manifestations* can trace their connection to one another across several lines of association. *Shared Narratives* support this higher frequency of engagement by providing a specific *Index Manifestation*, which engages with each *Narrative Entity* (ideally via the hero character), thereby creating a direct and visible line of association between different (relevant) *Index Manifestation*. The *Shared Narratives* of Phil Coulson and Claire Temple serve this function. Specifically, Claire Temple interacts with each hero character within its own *Narrative Entity* before the team narrative, clearly indicating that they exist in a somewhat closer relation to one another. While not as rigorous as *Shared Narratives*, overarching *Index Manifestations* also provide a potential shortcut for chains of interaction. Within the MNU, singular appearances of Turk Barrett throughout the different series help to draw the *Narrative Entities* closer. As such, the use of a *Shared Narrative*, the selected use of overarching *Index Manifestations*, and a more frequent use of different connection techniques form a cluster.

While the occurrence of clusters, as well as individual changes to their constellation within a network, operate along the use of the techniques discussed, more significant changes to clusters notably appear to alter the constellation of an overall network. Within this context, clusters can stabilize, shrink, grow, shatter, and form. Maintaining the current formation of clusters seems to require a continued reiteration of their interrelation and a maintained level of connection with other clusters in continuously published *Manifestations*. Existing connections can become diluted when an increasing number of *Manifestations* provide further interrelation with a *Narrative Entity* outside the cluster. As such, the stabilization of a cluster hinges on regularly reaffirming existing connections within the complex of an increasing number of *Manifestations*. The alteration of connections serves as the primary way to remove *Narrative Entities* from and add *Narrative Entities* to an existing cluster. Assuming a *Narrative Entity* is not meant to become 'clusterless', the

---

403 Spider-Man interacted with Iron Man; Iron Man interacted with Thor; Thor interacted with Groot. Ergo Spider-Man and Groot exist in the same network of *Narrative Entities*, despite never interacting with one another.

process requires the simultaneous dilution of connections to *Narrative Entities* of the existing cluster while increasing the connection to a new cluster. In effect, the *Narrative Entity* wanders from its old cluster to its new one via a shifted focus in engagement between *Narrative Entities*. The old cluster effectively shrinks, as it now has fewer *Narrative Entities*, while the new cluster effectively grows as it now has more *Narrative Entities*. Notably, both the growth and shrinkage of clusters can lead to the end of a cluster's existence. In case of shrinkage, the cluster could simply lose so many *Narrative Entities* that it no longer forms a cluster. Hereby, this might happen long before only a singular *Narrative Entity* remains, as the relationship with *Narrative Entities* outside the cluster has become more prominent. In case of growth, the cluster ceases to exist when it, in effect, contains all of the Shared Universe's *Narrative Entities* and, therefore, does not form a cluster anymore but effectively becomes the Shared Universe. The latter transpired in the MCU film network when all the *Narrative Entities* converged in *Avengers: Infinity War* and *Avengers: Endgame*, effectively dissolving any semblance of a 'core' network and some 'satellite' *Narrative Entities* within the Shared Universe. While the previous three describe relatively slow and controlled processes in the management of clusters, the latter two, shatter and formation, describe sudden changes. These changes rely less on the subtle use of narrative mechanics but usually follow a *Transformation Trigger*, which severs the existing connections between the *Narrative Entities* within the cluster or, conversely, draws *Narrative Entities* into a cluster. Formation occurs at the end of the foundational phase when a team narrative creates the sense of a Shared Universe by binding the first *Narrative Entities* together. The effects formally reoccur in the MCU film network with *Captain America: Civil War* and every team narrative except *Avengers: Age of Ultron*, when these draw new *Narrative Entities* into the core cluster of that network. Currently, no section of the MCU network provides a *Transformation Trigger* shattering a cluster. Within superhero comics, shattering usually occurs when smaller universes, which share some form of Genre Multiverse relationship with the main Shared Universe, dissolve and are partly folded into the main universe. A relatively recent case is the cancellation of Marvel Comics's Ultimate Universe in 2015. Instead of gradually transferring *Narrative Entities* from one cluster to another, the producers employed a *Transformation Trigger* that allowed for a redefinition of some relationships between *Narrative Entities* with the Secret Wars[404] storyline (I am disregarding the

---

404 The Secret Wars Narrative Event involves the destruction of the Marvel Universe and various other alternate universes (the Ultimate Universe and the 2099 imprints, the "Age of Apocalypse" storyline, the *Marvel 1602* universe, and the "House of M" storyline), with each universe's respective Earth combined into one Battleworld. At the end of the event, Marvel's Genre Multiverse is restored with slight changes to accommodate some *Narrative Entities* and singular *Index Manifestations* transferring to the company's main Shared Universe. The Miles Morales Narrative, a character that originated in the Ultimate Universe to take over the mantle of Spider-Man when the Ultimate Universe's Peter Parker died, migrated with its entire *Index Manifestation* to the "main" Marvel universe. The Maker, an evil Reed Richards, moved to the *Infamous Iron Man* comic book, where he became a part of the Dr. Doom Narrative, who temporarily had taken on the Iron Man persona. The hammer of the Ultimate Thor ends up in the *Unworthy Thor* miniseries and, as such, becomes part of a different Thor Narrative. Jimmy Hudson, the son of Ultimate Wolverine, appears in the X-Man Narrative of Marvel's main Shared Universe, most prominently in X-Men Blue.

Miles Morales Narrative's gradual transfer for the sake of argument[405]). This *Transformation Trigger*, in effect, shattered most of the clusters within the Narrative Multiverse and partly even within the Shared Universes, leaving them open for re-formation. In other words, where shrinkage and growth follow slow subtle transpositions of *Narrative Entities* through gradual alteration of the current connections, shatters and reformations use a singular (or a short chain of) *Transformation Triggers* to instantly alter relationships in a network.

The existence of clusters within more extensive Shared Universe networks and their potential to alter with additional Manifestations creates degrees of reliance. Clustering necessarily increases the reliance of each *Narrative Entity* on members of its cluster due to the greater interaction. In contrast, the reliance on the network as a whole decreases as the relationships between *Narrative Entities* inside and outside the cluster do not carry the same impact. Assuming the existence of several clusters within a singular network and a process of meta-clustering – meaning the clustering of established clusters – among them, a Shared Universe network through varying levels of *Narrative Reliance* would engage different types of audiences. The different levels of engagement created through clustering of interconnected text allow for a more multilayered audience within the framework of a casual, informed, and skilled audience. Within this framework, an informed audience can exist specifically for each cluster, for each potential collection of clusters, and for the entire network, creating an increasingly complex audience for a constantly expanding Shared Universe network. While the system of clustering does not multiply skilled and casual audiences in the same fashion, its notion within a larger Shared Universe highlights such a network's potential dependence on (highly specialized) informed and skilled audiences, as only either of these could successfully engage with any *Manifestation* from that network. This need for either of these two audience types is even more apparent when the potential for clusters altering their constellation is considered, as the *Narrative Entities* in a newly formed cluster in some form still relate to their previous connections. Despite the need for a well-informed audience, clusters may also serve as an entry point into an existing Shared Universe network, as discovering the needed information for a cluster is less daunting and laborious than doing the same for the entire network. A cluster allows casual audiences a point of entry without forcing them to educate themselves about the entire Shared Universe. Such a complex can also create evaluations of fan association or perceived legitimacy. Audiences engaged with a larger portion of a Shared Universe network or even all of it can declare themselves more legitimate fans within a larger fan base. Within the same vein of thought, producers may serve specific audience preferences to increase their audience base. In other words, the different clusters allow a Shared Universe network to cater to various age, socio-economic, and interest groups within the larger fan and non-fan community by having distinctive styles within the same network. The distinction of audience types

---

405 In contrast to the other *Index Manifestations* of the Ultimate Universe, Miles Morales's Spider-Man gradually connected to Marvel's main Shared Universe via its Spider-Man Narrative. The two *Narrative Entities* interact first in *Spider-Men* from 2012 and again in *Spider-verse* from 2014 establishing some connection, before the redefinition of Marvel's Multiverse in 2015 via *Secret Wars*.

within the framework created within this paper holds economic importance for producers of such vast interconnected narrative structures because it simultaneously engages an already interested customer pool, offers a new entry point for customers outside of the usual interest group, and allows different degrees of financial input in *Manifestations* without endangering the whole franchise. This economic potential, however, appears to seduce producers into regularly altering cluster composition, as each re-constellation inherently contains the possibility to introduce existing *Narrative Entities* to new audiences. The abuse of the balanced relationship between audience types, clustering, and network size may be one of the reasons the superhero comic has cultivated such an exclusive readership, as each cluster requires a great deal of knowledge to understand after constant re-constellation and the number of entry points via *Narrative Entities* with low attachments is limited.

3.2.2.2 Connecting Clusters

Understanding that clusters form within a network of *Narrative Entities*, which generally exist in a Shared Universe relationship, necessitates a connection between the different clusters, which also marks them as in Shared Universe relationships. In other words, if all the *Narrative Entities* exist in one type of relationship, the clusters they form must also exist in such a relationship. The significance of this association does not lie in its existence but in how it is conducted and maintained. The notion and mechanics of interrelation and clusters dictate that clusters potentially change if any of their *Narrative Entities* starts interrelating with another cluster within the same network. A glance at the constant changes in cluster constellation within superhero comics indicates that such a continuous shift is the norm in large-scale Shared Universes. However, if a network maintains its clusters, it also requires some means to interrelate them. Within the overall MCU network, the connections between clusters employ the same narrative techniques required for the interrelation of singular *Narrative Entities*. Hereby, each narrative technique used to connect clusters instead of singular *Narrative Entities* operates on one principle: A differentiation between the effectiveness of connections built within a cluster and those relating two or more clusters to one another. *Narrative Entities* within clusters create multiple points of interrelation by employing more connections than average within the given network. Such a stable and multilayered relationship generates a higher degree of interdependence among the different *Narrative Entities* within their cluster. The purpose of any narrative technique connecting clusters is to relate a *Narrative Entity* within a cluster to another outside of it without necessarily creating the same degree of interdependence. Hereby, the relationship of these two different interdependencies (the one within and the one between clusters) might be individual to each network, as the number of connective techniques used overall might differ between networks. The final determination of each singular *Narrative Entity* in a Shared Universe relationship arises in the form of a chain of interaction, which then relates the singular *Narrative Entities* within a cluster to others outside the cluster but within the same network. Assuming the three analyzed networks in this research operate as three clusters within a larger network, examples of such singular narrative techniques connecting potential clusters are the unnamed use of the Judas Bullet from the MNU's Luke Cage Narrative in *Agents of S.H.I.E.L.D. S4* and the Hammer Industries logo from the MCU's Iron Man Narrative in *Luke Cage S1*. In either case, a singular *Index Manifestation* (or hint at the existence of that *Index Manifestation*) relates two *Narratives Entities* within separate clusters. In the idealized view of the former case, ABC's Agents of S.H.I.E.L.D. Narrative is related to the MNU's Luke Cage Narrative, thus implying via chains of interaction that all elements of the MNU network and all elements of the ABC network exist in some relationship to one another. The Hammer Industries logo creates a similar implication for a relationship between the MNU network and the MCU film network. Within the context of interrelating clusters via these narrative techniques, two manners of interrelation emerge as prominent means of interrelating clusters: (1) unaffiliated *Index Manifestations* and (2) *Narrative Entities*, which operate as a tether between the clusters.

Without a direct association with any specific *Narrative Entity*, unaffiliated *Index Manifestations* provide a means to interrelate different networks via chains of interaction without creating a direct relationship between them. The most prominent examples within the networks researched here are Samuel L. Jackson's Nick Fury and Rob Morgan's Turk Barrett. In either case, the appearance of this *Index Manifestation* does not create any direct association between two *Narrative Entities* in the same manner the application of a *Narrative Entity*-specific *Index Manifestation* would. They maintain a perceived autonomy between the connected *Narrative Entities*, as they create an intermediate element for the interrelation. This intermediate status of an unaffiliated *Index Manifestation* can also create a link to the entire cluster rather than any specific *Narrative Entity* within the cluster. The application of Nick Fury within the MCU film universe shows such an effect, as the character appears in several MCU films. However, the *Index Manifestation*'s use in interrelating clusters is prominent in its connecting effect between the MCU films and *Agents of S.H.I.E.L.D.* Unaffiliated with any specific *Narrative Entity* from the MCU films, when Nick Fury appears in the ABC series, the character's presence automatically relates *Agents of S.H.I.E.L.D.* with all *Narrative Entities* within that cluster via a chain of interaction. However, as the connection is also limited to one chain of interaction, no direct relation between the different *Narrative Entities* occurs. Practically, this maintained distance allows the MCU films to ignore everything within the series, as all connecting effects (dominantly *Trigger Waves*) are filtered through the representations of Nick Fury. The series never affected the films simply because the different unaffiliated *Index Manifestations* (Fury and Hill) never mention any event or specific *Index Manifestation* from the series in the movies. Formally, this limitation operates bilaterally. However, *Agents of S.H.I.E.L.D.* unilaterally incorporated elements from the films and transposed *Index Manifestations* within the series to refer to elements of the film. Contrasted with any direct means of interrelation via the immanent transfer of *Index Manifestations* or acknowledgment of *Transformation Triggers*, using an unaffiliated *Index Manifestation* allows for the overall interrelation of clusters without potentially compromising the constellation of any cluster involved.

The use of a *Narrative Entity* as a tether between clusters operates and provides similar advantages to an unaffiliated *Index Manifestation*. It can similarly operate as an intermediate, maintaining the integrity of each cluster while providing a connection to the overall cluster via a chain of interactions. However, a *Narrative Entity* is itself a network of *Index Manifestations*, meaning that it has several venues to provide interrelation. As such, *Narrative Entities* connecting clusters can operate as a hub, in contrast to the usual singular line of interrelation provided by unaffiliated *Index Manifestations*. Without conducting a deeper analysis, it is easy to postulate that some of Marvel Comics's flagship series operate in a hub position within their main Shared Universe. *The Amazing Spider-Man*, for example, relies little on other *Narrative Entities* but regularly takes on or lends out *Index Manifestations* for specific storylines, leaning on Peter Parker/Spider-Man's presumed friendships (Johnny Storm/The Human Torch, Bobby Drake/Iceman) or his understanding of specialized expertise (Dr. Strange/Tony Stark/Reed Richards). These 'exchanges' seldom bear *Trigger Waves* or grander expressions of interrelation, thereby maintaining a general connection between different clusters without compromising their constellation. Within the networks analyzed, the MCU's Thor Narrative and ABC's *Agents of S.H.I.E.L.D.* provide a hub function for the MCU film network. The MCU's Thor Narrative effectively ties a cluster created via the Captain America–Iron Man *Shared Narrative* and the Black Widow *Shared Narrative* to the more out-worldly *Narrative Entities* within the MCU film network. The *Narrative Entity* begins this function after *The Avengers* and until *Avengers: Infinity War*. Aside from the *Narrative Entity*'s prominent position in the creation of the MCU film's Shared Universe, the interactions between the three different hero characters (Captain America, Iron Man, Thor) in *Avengers: Age of Ultron* restates the presence of each *Narrative Entity* in the same unified world, despite the Thor Narrative's absence from that cluster (most notably in the hero character's absence from *Captain America: Civil War*). Both sequels of the MCU's Thor Narrative connect to the singular two out-worldly *Narrative Entities* in the MCU film network, *Guardians of the Galaxy* and *Doctor Strange*. Neither relates to another *Narrative Entity* within the MCU film network before *Avengers: Infinity War*. As such, the MCU's Thor Narrative serves as an intermediary connection between the cluster and these two out-worldly *Narrative Entities*. This function of the Thor Narrative is reiterated when *Index Manifestations* associated with *Thor: Ragnarok* serve as the first point of contact between the characters from the cluster and *Index Manifestations* from either *Narrative Entity*. Mark Ruffalo's Bruce Banner/the Hulk appeared prominently in *Thor: Ragnarok* and established contact between Benedict Cumberbatch's Dr. Strange and Robert Downey Jr.'s Tony Stark/Iron Man in *Avengers: Infinity War*. Chris Hemsworth's Thor meets the Guardians of the Galaxy early in the third Avengers film; their knowledge of him and the information he has given them serves to establish a relationship with part of Earth's Avengers. ABC's *Agents of S.H.I.E.L.D.* also connects the MCU film network's cluster with the MCU's Guardian of the Galaxy Narrative and the MCU's Captain Marvel Narrative. Not as obvious, the connection relies on a 'longer' chain of interaction, specifically because it hinges on the existence of an alien race and not the direct interactions of specific *Index Manifestations*. *Agents of S.H.I.E.L.D.* relates to the cluster via several *Index Manifestations* and *Transformation Triggers* to the two films via the mention and appearance of the alien Kree. While no specific *Index Manifestation* related to the Kree crosses from one *Narrative Entity* into the other, the appearance of the race in *Manifestations* of all three *Narrative Entities* implies a shared imaginary space. The chain of interaction is longer because it only works with the assumption that each representation refers to the same version of the Kree and that the singular members of the alien race could meet under some circumstances[406]. Operating with similar principles, *Narrative Entities* employed as tethers are basically more expansive versions of unaffiliated *Index Manifestations* within this context. This greater expansiveness allows them to serve as an intermediary for several participants, connecting several clusters. It also creates the potential to draw different clusters together more immediately because it offers a space where usually difficult-to-relate *Index Manifestations* can interact.

3.2.2.3 Cluster Relationships (Shared Universes in a Multiverse Relationship)

The entire discussions of clusters up to now revolve around their formation within a Shared Universe relationship. Notably, the two relatively small networks (in comparison to superhero comic networks) with more than two *Narrative Entities* both operate with a structure of a singular cluster with singular *Narrative Entities* attached via the techniques discussed earlier. The relationship between the four Narratives combined in *The Defenders* and the MNU's Punisher Narrative follows a similar pattern as the relationships presented in the MCU film network. After the team narrative and *Shared Narrative* of Claire Temple formed the MNU's main cluster, the MNU Punisher Narrative connected via an unaffiliated *Index Manifestation*, Turk Barrett, and a tether created through the MNU's Daredevil Narrative. However, taking a step back, the relationship between the three analyzed networks could be viewed in a cluster context. In other words, instead of regarding the overall MCU network as three related networks, they could be viewed as three clusters of the same network. This shift in understanding allows for a quicker evaluation between the different networks, as the sole use of either an unaffiliated *Index Manifestation* or a *Narrative Entity* as tether allows for a more direct determination of their relationship. For example, the ABC and MNU networks' dominant use of unaffiliated *Index Manifestations* to connect to the other networks indicates a clear separation and active avoidance/limitation of influence between them. The use of affiliated *Index Manifestations* in the case of the ABC and MCU film connection (Peggy Carter, Sif) slightly augments the relationship between these two networks. More importantly, this view allows the Shared Universe model to describe the diverse relationships that different Shared Universes may have within a Genre Multiverse context.

Within superhero comics, collections of different series interact to create different versions of a main Shared Universe. Researched by Kukkonen and others, superhero comics have the tendency to create alternate realities representing different versions of their main Shared Universe. While most publications focus on alternate realities taking the form of limited series or singular graphic novels, there are instances of alternate realities with several running titles. In the case of Marvel superhero publications, two notable examples of the recent past are the Ultimate Universe, which ran from 2000 to 2015, and the MC2 Universe, which ran from 1998 until roughly 2010. In the former, the emergence of superheroes starts at the beginning of the 21st century (instead of the 1960s). As such, the two networks arise in a slightly different context intradiegetically

---

406 The Guardians of the Galaxy interacted with Ronan the Accuser; Ronan the Accuser **could potentially have** interacted with the House of Kasius; Taryan of the House Kasius interacted with Daisy Johnson, Agent of SHIELD. Ergo the Guardians of the Galaxy and Daisy Johnson **could potentially** exist in the same network of *Narrative Entities*, despite never interacting with one another.

and in terms of audience. Continuously running titles associated with the Ultimate Universe were *Ultimate Spider-Man*[407], *Ultimate X-Men*[408], *The Ultimates*[409], and *Ultimate Fantastic Four*[410], among others. The MC2 Universe depicts an alternate future timeline informed by the state of Marvel Comics's main Shared Universe at its current iteration in 1998. *Spider-Girl*[411], *A-Next*[412], *J2*[413], *Fantastic Five*[414], and *Wild Thing*[415] were prominent titles of the MC2 Universe, among others. With several *Narrative Entities*, these two alternate worlds functioned as self-contained Shared Universe networks. Initially, these Shared Universe networks only related to one another and the main Shared Universe via the application of reinterpretations of existing *Narrative Entities* and alternate renditions of their *Index Manifestations* but had no direct exchange. Due to the realities of intellectual property, all of these networks exist in a Company Universe relationship with one another. Without any direct interaction, it is simpler to view each of these as autonomous networks based on the same *Narrative Entities*. In most contexts, this separation and relationship is absolute and remains mostly unchanged, comparable to the relationship between adaptations or re-imaginations of the same singular, non-networked *Narrative Entity*. However, the notion of Genre Multiverse creates a venue for such different Shared Universe networks to engage with one another. With the potential for interaction, two differing interpretations of the relationship between these three networks arise. They can be viewed as closed-off, interacting and relating to other closed-off networks, or as clusters of the same network. The distinction alters the prescribed potential for change and transfer. In the case of a closed-off network, only the relationship between the networks is altered via connecting narrative techniques. While not limiting the variety of connecting narrative techniques, this view necessarily limits their number. Viewing the different worlds as clusters in a singular network allows for the alteration of the relationships between the singular *Narrative Entities* among the different clusters. This shifted potential for change dissolves a presumed sanctity of a singular and specific unified world created by the network of specific titles, the Ultimate Universe, the MC2 Universe, and Marvel's main Shared Universe in this case. The loss of sanctity or stability of these Universes allows for the different segments to alter their constellation or even dissolve and their components to reform into new clusters. In other words, viewing Marvel's main Universe, the Ultimate Universe, and the MC2 Universe as connected but autonomous networks retains the formation and sanctity of each unified world created via the singular Shared Universe networks. Viewing the three universes as clusters of

---

[407] *Ultimate Spider-Man*. Written by Brian Michael Bendis. Illustrated by Mark Bagely and Stuart Immonen. Ultimate Marvel, 2000–2014

[408] *Ultimate X-Men*. Created by Mark Miller. Ultimate Marvel, 2001–2009

[409] *The Ultimates*. Written by Mark Miller. Illustrated by Bryan Hitch. Ultimate Marvel, 2002–2004

[410] *Ultimate Fantastic Four*. Created by Mark Miller and Brian Michael Bendis. Ultimate Marvel, 2004–2009

[411] *Spider-Girl*. Written by Tom DeFalco. Illustrated by Ron Frenz and Pat Olliffe. MC 2, 1998–2006

[412] *A-Next*. Written by Tom DeFalco. Illustrated by Ron Frenz. MC 2, 1998–1999

[413] *J2*. Written by Tom DeFalco. Illustrated by Ron Lim. MC 2, 1998–1999

[414] *Fantastic Five*. Written by Tom DeFalco. Illustrated by Paul Ryan. MC 2, 1999–2000

[415] *Wild Thing*. Written by Tom DeFalco and Larry Hama. Illustrated by Ron Frenz and Ron Lim. MC 2, 1999–2000

the same network guarantees no such protection but also alters the potential for a direct relationship between different renditions of the same *Narrative Entity*.

The distinction between these two approaches is not purely philosophical. For one, determining the more applicable view describing the relationship between different networks may give insight into their future development, presumed significance, and/or producer assertion concerning specific audiences. More importantly, however, a shift of such a relationship from connected Shared Universes to clusters within the same Universe appears to precede the dissolution of an imaginary space and the incorporation of (some of) their *Narrative Entities* into another cluster or network. The process of these shifting views as steps towards dissolution is prominently visible in the cancellation of the Ultimate Universe. The producers of the Ultimate series did not connect these to the series of Marvel's main Shared Universe for most of the former network's existence. As such, the two networks existed in a mostly unconnected company relationship. This status changed with the limited series *Spider-Men*[416], in which several *Index Manifestations* of the Miles Morales/Spider-Man Narrative from the Ultimate Universe and the Peter Parker/Spider-Man Narrative from Marvel's main Universe interacted with one another. The publication connected the two Shared Universe networks. Still, it did not alter the overall constellation of *Narrative Entities* within them, creating a relationship closer to the notion of two connected but autonomous networks. This type of relationship altered with the "Cataclysm" storyline. Spread among several Ultimate Universe *Manifestations*, "Cataclysm" hinges on *Index Manifestations* of either network crossing over into the other. Notable, Galactus from Marvel's main Universe, as well as Miles Morales/Spider-Man and Reed Richards/The Maker from the Ultimate Universe, engage with a transposed network of *Index Manifestations*. This interaction of *Index Manifestations* from different *Narrative Entities* from either network already implies an understanding of each universe as a cluster of the same network, as the threat to the Ultimate Universe, as well as its solution, originated in Marvel's main universe, forcing more engagement between singular *Narrative Entities*. The notion of singular networks shifts to a complete notion of clusters with the new "Secret Wars" storyline from 2015. The escalation of a cosmic event, referred to as Incursion, destroys Marvel's Genre Multiverse. Victor von Doom from Marvel's Main Universe reforms a patchwork reality made of several altered elements collected from the Genre Multiverse. Several *Index Manifestations* created in the network from Marvel's main universe, and the Ultimate Universe survive the Genre Multiverse's destruction in a cosmic lifeboat. The mere premise of "Secret Wars" counters the notion of separate networks, as the storyline's *Transformation Triggers* enable a team narrative involving *Index Manifestations* from every version or every *Narrative Entity* Marvel ever created. As such, any notion of sanctity concerning the Ultimate Universe dissolves, leaving at this point merely a view of clusters within a network. At the conclusion of the storyline, the Genre Multiverse is restored, including the Ultimate Universe and Marvel's main Universe. However, all *Manifestations* directly related to the Ultimate Universe have been canceled. Only the Miles Morales/Spider-Man Narrative retains a *Manifestation* of its own. Aside from losing its Ultimate tagline, its network of *Index Manifestations* is altered to fit into Marvel's main Shared Universe network. Miles and Peter share the mantle of

---

416   *Spider-Men*. Written by Brian Michael Bendis. Illustrated by Sara Pichelli. Marvel Comics, 2012

Spider-Man. Peter is Miles's active mentor. Not Peter Parker's death but the death of a friend inspired Miles to take on the mantle of Spider-Man. Peter Parker's Spider-Man operates on a global level similar to Iron Man or Captain America, while the now-16-year-old Miles patrols Spider-Man's traditional area of operation, New York City. Initially, Miles and his loved ones have no memories of their origin in the Ultimate universe. Other singular *Index Manifestations* also enter the remaining Shared Universe network. In effect, "Secret Wars" shattered the cluster constituting the Ultimate Universe, folding one of its *Narrative Entities* into the larger network (and another smaller cluster) as well as relegating other *Index Manifestations* to different *Narrative Entities*. This shatter was only possible because the formerly autonomous network was first connected to other Shared Universe networks and then perceived as a cluster instead of a unified world of its own. This difference in view allowed for the application of techniques described in the management of clusters, which ultimately enabled Marvel Comics to retain some desirable *Narrative Entities* and *Index Manifestations* while relegating the Ultimate Universe from a Shared Universe network in a Multiverse relationship with its main Universe to merely a Genre Multiverse extension of existing *Index Manifestations*. Aside from providing a series of steps through which several Shared Universe networks may alter their overall relationship, the differentiation in views also underlines how clustering ultimately describes the relationships of different Shared Universes that can be related to one another and how they potentially can be related to one another.

While these relationships are described for the more complex and more *Narrative Entity*-abundant networks of Marvel superhero comics, the phenomenon has some bearing on the simpler MCU network described in this research. The potential to describe the MNU network's relationship with the MCU film network as separate Shared Universes over separate clusters of the same network highlights the autonomous nature of the MNU network, contrasting the presumed relationship marketed towards audiences. Hereby, a unity in medium within each network appears to support such an autonomous nature in the same manner the use of signifying titles supported the autonomous nature of the Ultimate Universe. Acknowledging the potential effect of a shared medium does not exclude the possibility of a fully integrated network with *Narrative Entities* appearing in either series or film. The relationship between the ABC series and the MCU films indicates the possibility of a relationship across different media. Similarly, newer material outside this research, namely the currently released Disney+ series, shows a potential for a close relationship between different *Narrative Entities* across media. However, the relationships within the overall MCU network indicate that medium can be an organizing *semiotic cue*, which influences the potential perception of a network's range of engagement and has to be overcome by the application of the appropriate narrative techniques, countering somewhat the egalitarian view on medium argued by transmedia storytelling.

3.2.3 Escalating the Network: Audience Creation and Maintenance

The notion of *Narrative Reliance* inherently creates a requirement for an audience versed in the specific Shared Universe network. However, relying on a natural and unprompted emergence of such an audience denotes a reaction model to the production of such a network. In other words, *Manifestations* relying on other material only occur when a sufficiently interested audience has already materialized. While the current reality of production (especially in film and television) dominantly applies such a reaction model concerning *Narrative Reliance* in general, the necessary foresight required in setting up and maintaining a Shared Universe network combined with the economic realities of film production and distribution might not allow for an engaged audience to materialize naturally. Instead, a Shared Universe network created in a more economically challenging medium has to rely on the existence of such an audience, or it has to educate a casual audience, transforming it into a sufficiently informed one.

Reliance on the existence of such an audience has been the economic basis for several adaptations, re-imaginations, continuations, and reboots of popular *Narrative Entities*, especially those usually associated with the science-fiction or fantasy genre. Fandoms, particularly, provide a large audience with a substantial and reliable knowledge base and an inherent interest in creating and using new information regarding a specific *Narrative Entity*. However, an audience with existing interest often has preconceived notions or, in the case of fandoms, absolute opinions on the 'correct' form of an *Index Manifestation* from 'their' *Narrative Entity*. The duality of an interested audience simultaneously makes it unreliable concerning long-term engagement with any newly created Shared Universe network. This unreliability does not even consider the contradictory interpretations of specific *indices* within a *Narrative Entity* created by large, multigenerational, and multicultural fan community discourses. Films based on the most prominent *Narrative Entities* from Marvel Comics (Spider-Man, X-Men, Fantastic Four, Hulk) created by a variety of film studios prior to the MCU hint at the difficulty of transferring an existing audience to a new rendition of a popular *Narrative Entity*. As such, relying on a potentially existing audience appears only marginally better than reacting to the emergence of an engaged audience concerning the creation of a Shared Universe network.

A Shared Universe network's need for an informed audience and the limited potential of one emerging naturally allows for the reasonable assertion that the structures creating and governing the network include mechanics and processes that transform a casual audience into an informed one. In other words, a Shared Universe network relies to such a degree on an informed audience that it has to contain some inherent features that allow for the indoctrination of an audience. Such an indoctrination is not unique to a world created via a network, as any form of fiction requires some process to educate its audience on fictional characters, institutions, societies, and so on. However, the split of such information across several *Manifestations* and the inherent possibility of a hypertextual engagement with them requires overarching structural elements dedicated to the creation of an informed audience. Such structural elements have to exist throughout the network, as an increase in *Manifestations* within a network generally increases the amount of information or knowledge new *Manifestations* can rely on, making each new *Manifestation* potentially more reliant on an informed audience.

3.2.3.1 Crafting Fandoms: Creating an Informed Audience

Relying on the analysis and understanding of the overall MCU network hints that educating an audience follows the pattern of foundation, re-establishment, and expansion. Hereby, the foundational phase's structure with low, but gradually rising, levels of interrelation hint at techniques that create venues for casual audiences to become informed ones. Hereby, the difference between interrelating *Narrative Entities* and *Narrative Reliance* is meaningful, as the potential of educating the audience and entertaining them necessarily requires a specific balance. With the focus on entertaining a casual audience, the foundational phase favors little to no *Narrative Reliance* in its *Manifestations* while including smaller means of interrelation to add value for an engaged audience and slowly guide them towards becoming an informed one. Within this structure, interrelation between *Narrative Entities* should gradually rise to give the existence of a network greater importance and prepare an audience for a *Manifestation* with a noticeable degree of *Narrative Reliance*. As such, while remaining low to inconsequential, the notion of *Narrative Reliance* also increases across the foundational phase with increasing interrelation. To accommodate this odd contradiction, these early *Manifestations* employ Narrative Reliance mostly outside their plot. The MCU film network and the MNU network use these strategies (interrelation without reliance, rise of interrelation and reliance). A casual audience, which encounters each *Manifestation* of a network in order of release, naturally begins their engagement with the 2008 *Iron Man* for the MCU or the 2015 *Daredevil S1* for the MNU. *Iron Man* notably hints at the existence of other *Narrative Entities* with its post-credit scene, only directly alluding to a Captain America Narrative, but relies in no form on knowledge from outside the actual text for the comprehension of its overall plot. *Daredevil S1* operates less obviously, setting up overarching *Index Manifestations*, namely the Hand, but equally has no reliance on any material outside the text. With the increase in interrelations, the foundational *Manifestations* of the MCU film network also gradually increase their *Narrative Reliance*. However, except for the *Shared Narrative*, any matter of *Narrative Reliance* up to the first team narrative is relegated to post-credit scenes within the MCU film network. Simply by their placement within a film, post-credit scenes cannot directly affect the *Manifestation*'s plot, only hinting at upcoming material or connecting different *Narrative Entities*. The foundational phase of the MNU focuses its increase in *Narrative Reliance* on overarching *Index Manifestations*. Overarching *Index Manifestations* can take on a function within a plot. However, within the foundational phase of the MNU, this function is not dependent on information given outside of the present text. For example, Jeri Hogarth's appearance in *Iron Fist S1* requires only accepting her profession as a lawyer but leans on no knowledge provided by her presence in *Jessica Jones S2*[417]. As such, the foundational phase provides initial exposure to the notion of interrelation without burdening an audience with *Narrative Reliance*. Gradually employing *Narrative Reliance* in overarching *Index Manifestations* or post-credit scenes introduces the notion of relying on information outside the given *Manifestation* without compromising the plot. While this approach trains an audience that has engaged with all *Manifestations* in order, it will ideally also entice latecomers to catch up on previous material. The gradually increasing exposure to *Narrative Reliance* trains a constantly engaged audience in recognizing and potentially anticipating relationships between the *Manifestations* of different *Narrative Entities*. The first

---

417 The MNU network includes a sudden increase in Narrative Reliance within its foundational phase. The introduction of Luke Cage in *Jessica Jones S1* creates some level of reliance of *Luke Cage S1* on the Manifestation of another *Narrative Entity*. An outlier to the overall structure, *Luke Cage S1* appears as an exception to the rule.

team narrative, which completes the foundational phase, tests if an informed audience has emerged from the structure by gauging the success of a heavily reliant *Manifestation*.

While the potential for a hypertextual engagement with the different *Manifestations* of the foundational phase certainly appears possible – specifically with the existence of recording mediums (DVDs) and streaming services – the process of educating a casual audience, turning it into an informed one, favors the maintenance of a specific viewing order. Producers may use contextual constraints (order of publication, systems of marketing, and fan guidance) to increase the chance of a casual audience engaging with the *Manifestations* in an intended order. A narrative technique to increase the chances of an orderly engagement is the application of a *Shared Narrative*. As mentioned, a *Shared Narrative* splits its plot structure across several *Manifestations*, creating an internal order among them. As such, a *Shared Narrative* serves not only as a suitable means to increase a notion of *Narrative Reliance* within a *Manifestation* but also provides a means within the text for engaged audiences to discover the intended order. This potential for deducing the 'producers' design' might create an additional draw for early casual audiences[418]. This importance of a *Shared Narrative* as an organizing tool is underscored by the singular presence of one in either foundational phase. The notion that they serve solely to organize the *Manifestations* of that phase arises with the acknowledgment of their removal within or shortly after the team narrative has ended the process of establishing a unified world and concluded the 'education process'.

The gradual increase in *Narrative Reliance* marks a text-inherent attempt at creating an informed audience for a Shared Universe network. Ideally – from the producer's point of view – a casual audience 'discovers' the initial *Manifestation* starting the network and is drawn into engaging with the subsequent material. Because this casual audience engages with all *Manifestations* within a singular network, they gradually learn about the storytelling mechanics of *Narrative Reliance*. As such, they (theoretically) become an informed audience by the end of the foundational phase. In other words, they become an audience whose knowledge of the Shared Universe the producers can rely on. While this process encompasses how a specific network attempts to create its own informed audience, it is unlikely that every informed audience arises out of this pattern. Later emerging informed audiences are more likely to emerge from interacting with an existing informed audience, engaging with the *Manifestations* after the fact, or simply transferring their understanding of *Narrative Reliance* from another network. The latter specifically requires only information to become an informed audience but can also understand reliant *Manifestations* within the network due to their experience with similar networks. In effect, audiences with an understanding of *Narrative Reliance* but lacking information on a specific network constitute a skilled audience. Skilled audiences warrant mention because they somewhat exist outside of the casual audience-informed audience relationship created via the structure of the foundational phase. Instead, a skilled audience can freely engage any part of the network and use their understanding of *Narrative Reliance* to become an informed audience at their own pace.

---

418   Jenkins discusses what might draw an audience into engaging with a larger media franchise in *Convergence Culture*. Within his analysis of different franchises, he also mentions an audience's urge to uncover the producers' design (and potentially spoil it).

3.2.3.2 Making Everybody Happy: Balancing Audience Types

Remaining in the previous structure, *Manifestations* following the foundational phase may cater exclusively to their informed audience, relying on their knowledge of previously introduced *Index Manifestations* and *Transformation Triggers*. Specifically, sequels to the *Manifestations* of the foundational phase can rely on and reward an existing knowledge base. However, relying solely on an informed audience may impede a Shared Universe network's continuation. Depending on genre popularity, media engagement, and economic realities, the continued growth of a Shared Universe network may require the frequent engagement of a casual audience in addition to the stable interest of an informed one. As such, while only releasing *Manifestations*, which reward the informed audience's knowledge base, might generate a constant interest in new material and re-enforce the formation of an exclusive group, it would also limit the potential expansion of the network, as casual audiences are excluded from participating with the new material. This highlights a general problem of serialized narratives in particular, be it transmedial, a Shared Universe, or even a network of adaptations. The creation and existence of an informed audience guarantees a specific number of interested recipients. However, their knowledge of the earlier material requires *Manifestations* within such serialized products that acknowledge, engage, and reward the informed audience's dedicated effort. A more precise analysis of this aspect is part of Henry Jenkins's principle of *participatory culture* and his overall understanding of transmedia storytelling. Even if we exclude the shift in media in Jenkins's concept and focus on a singular medium, the need to create narratives to engage a knowledgeable audience still garners the problem of possibly excluding any audience without the necessary knowledge base. It could be argued that a similar process across a longer period of time created the highly specialized readership usually associated with the superhero comic. However, while the comic industry can survive by focusing, engaging, and cultivating an exclusive audience, the movie industry cannot. In other words, due to financial consideration alone, a Shared Universe network such as the MCU films or even the MNU series cannot solely rely on the sustained interest of an informed audience but equally has to engage a casual one to some degree.

Two strategies allow a Shared Universe network to balance a casual and an informed audience. *Manifestations* following the foundational phase can either exclusively cater to one of the two audience types or attempt to recreate *Manifestations* of the foundational phase structurally. In the case of the former, *Manifestations* focused on an informed audience would use *Narrative Reliance* indiscriminately, while those focused on a casual audience would avoid any form of it. Imitating *Manifestations* of the foundational phase in this instance suggests the inclusion of *Narrative Reliance* but independent from the film's plot. The MCU film network dominantly favors two types of *Manifestations* in this regard. Sequels, team narratives, and a few new introductions (*Ant-Man*, *Spider-Man: Homecoming*) rely heavily on basic knowledge of the existing network. Other new introductions (*Guardians of the Galaxy*, *Doctor Strange*, *Black Panther*) to the Shared Universe use some *Narrative Reliance* but move it outside their plot structure, leaving a greater part of the *Manifestations* accessible to a casual audience. The MNU network makes use of all three approaches with both *Manifestations* of the MNU's Punisher Narrative operating without any *Narrative Reliance*, three *Manifestations* (*Daredevil S3*, *Iron Fist S2*, *Luke S2*) relying to various degrees on other *Narrative Entities*, and either Jessica Jones *Manifestation* following the team narrative including *Narrative Reliance* with no bearing on the plot. By its nature, the ABC network is steeped in *Narrative Reliance*, and its earlier seasons do not function without a degree of outside knowledge. Aside from limiting the degree of *Narrative Reliance*, *Manifestations* of a Shared Universe network can emphasize a spectacle to engage casual audiences. Following the Merriam-Webster definition of spectacle as "something exhibited to view as unusual, notable, or entertaining" or "an eye-catching or dramatic public display"[419], a spectacle[420] within a *Manifestation* is meant to be understood as grand and impressive displays of action and aesthetic, which inherently do not have to include a significant narrative function. The classic versions of such a spectacle in film are long fight scenes, stretched-out kiss sequences, and excessive comedic interludes, which all target an audience's emotional response but often could be shortened concerning their value for the plot. While every *Manifestation* of the MCU film network uses such spectacles, their length, number, and grandeur particularly increase in films with a higher degree of *Narrative Reliance*. Notably, most team narratives include spectacles in a more prominent form. Considering that spectacles within the superhero genre usually come in the form of fight scenes, *The Avengers* has a long battle with aliens in New York, a fight between Thor, Captain America, and Iron Man, as well as a fight between Thor and the Hulk, while Iron Man and Captain America try to save the Helicarrier. *Avengers: Age of Ultron* begins with an extended fight scene when the team invades an enemy compound. It also has a long party sequence in the first third of the movie, which mitigates some effects of interrelation but serves no purpose for the film's plot and ends with the Avengers fighting legions of robots. They equally combat legions of robots at the end of the film while saving the population of a city sitting on a makeshift meteor threatening to destroy humanity. As the plot of the third Avengers film focuses on the villain's constant pursuit of a universe-ending weapon, it essentially is a series of spectacles, leaning on *Narrative Reliance* to give many scenes meaning. Assuming its final battle sequence at the end of the film begins with the Avengers' use of the Infinity Gauntlet and ends with Iron Man's death, *Avengers: Endgame* dedicates more than 1/6th of its entire runtime to that one spectacle, which is not the only spectacle in the movie. Other *Manifestations*, such as *Captain America: Civil War*, also use spectacles to counteract the high degree of *Narrative Reliance*. Spectacles dominantly appear in *Manifestations* with less space to potentially relieve some *Narrative Reliance* within the plot, while a diverse use of *Narrative Reliance*, as well as its relegations outside the plot, appear universal across the network. In the case of the latter, each network within this research generally favors using non-plot-relevant *Narrative Reliance* over using none.

---

[419] https://www.merriam-webster.com/dictionary/spectacle, retrieved October 14th, 2021

[420] I am aware of the critical term 'spectacle' developed by Guy Debord and prominently used by Bernays, Adorno, Marx, and Lukács. As Debord's version of spectacle discusses "the autocratic reign of the market economy which had acceded to an irresponsible sovereignty, and the totality of new techniques of government which accompanied this reign", that version of the term is not applicable in the context of this research. (Debord [1988] *Comments on the Society of the Spectacle*, II)

3.2.3.3 Limited Audience: The Escalation of Expansion

The different approaches of balancing *Narrative Reliance* allow the formation and re-formation of a Shared Universe network. Hereby, *Jessica Jones S2/S3 and the Punisher Manifestations from the MNU network* indicate that a constant and static *Narrative Reliance* within a Shared Universe network is possible. In other words, after the unified world is formed, an increase in overall *Narrative Reliance* within singular *Manifestations* or the overall network is not predetermined. However, a constant increase of *Narrative Reliance* can create a more coherent unified world instead of promoting the notions of different regions of the same world. The MCU film network constantly escalates its interrelation and *Narrative Reliance* with sudden increases in interrelation, giving the impression of a singular imaginary space. After the foundational phase, the network advances its core cluster with *Captain America: Civil War*. At the end of the Infinity Saga, this core cluster incorporates every *Narrative Entity* within the MCU, necessarily creating some degree of *Narrative Reliance* among the different members of that network. As mentioned, such an increase in reliance favors an informed audience, with *Manifestations* focused on larger spectacles to maintain a section of a casual audience. However, the sudden increase in *Narrative Reliance* combined with spectacle creates a greater awareness of a unified world. This greater awareness ties different *Narrative Entities* within a network together beyond their representation in *Manifestations*, as the larger discourse surrounding them, carried by the casual audience, ties different *Narrative Entities* together. In other words, the casual audience will discuss several *indices* from different *Narrative Entities* as one component of a spectacle, tying these *Narrative Entities* closer together in an overall public discourse. While such an increased relation between different *Narrative Entities* has no direct bearing on the use of *Narrative Reliance* within an upcoming *Manifestation*, the discourse surrounding the different *Narrative Entities* creates expectations concerning interrelation and interaction. As such, the combination of higher levels of *Narrative Reliance* and spectacle might create the need for future *Manifestations* of established *Narrative Entities* to include a higher degree of *Narrative Reliance*, while the lack of reliance on a spectacle in *The Defenders* allows following *Manifestations* to regulate their *Narrative Reliance* more freely.

The expectation of a degree of *Narrative Reliance* within a Shared Universe network dictates the development of a network towards exclusively serving an informed audience. The increased interrelation of the MCU film network, as well as the current state of superhero comic books, indicate the truth of such a development. However, with the need to engage a large audience, the MCU network cannot focus on an exclusive audience. Instead, it regularly introduces new *Narrative Entities* void of an expectation of *Narrative Reliance*. *Guardians of the Galaxy Vol.1* and *Vol.2* are prime examples of this strategy, as is *Doctor Strange*. Combining spectacles in highly reliant *Manifestations* and non-reliant new *Narrative Entities* allows a Shared Universe network, such as the MCU film network, to simultaneously cater to a secure informed audience and a larger casual audience. While a viable method of balancing audiences, this particular combination of strategies constantly expands the network, as each use of it increases the number of *Narrative Entities* within the network. The constant addition of new *Narrative Entities* necessarily increases the complexity of the overall network. A constant use of this pattern creates an escalation of expansion, forcing a Shared Universe network to add new *Narrative Entities* as venues for casual audiences to engage with it and potentially become an informed audience.

However, the constant expansion also creates a complexity even an engaged informed audience might be unable to manage at some point.

An unchecked use of *Narrative Reliance* and spectacle, which leads to an escalation of expansion, imaginably is one of the causes of the current state of the superhero comic book Shared Universe. However, as the announcement of its fourth phase already includes seven new *Narrative Entities* (three films/four series), the MCU sharing a similar fate is equally imaginable. If it does not find a way to counter or balance its own constant expansion, the MCU film network or even the MCU network overall might steer towards its own expiration due to focusing on a too narrow audience.

3.2.3.4 Bigger Threats: The Escalation of Spectacles

While spectacles within the system of a Shared Universe network serve as means of countering *Narrative Reliance*, they appear within the dynamic of specific structures. Hereby, the assertion that audiences expect something bigger and better from a sequel appears to determine the development of *Manifestations* within a Shared Universe network as it would in a regular franchise. However, as the sequels within a network do not operate along a singular line of escalation, the increase of spectacles equally follows a more diverse pattern. Within the confines of the superhero genre, the escalation of spectacles overlaps with an increase in the range and danger of perceived threats. As conflicts within the genre connect to physical altercations, an increased prominence of its spectacles coincides with a more difficult, more prominent threat to overcome. As such, viewing the escalation of threat within the superhero genre as presented in the medium of film allows for a universal understanding of the escalation of spectacles within a Shared Universe network. As one of the strategies to balance audience types relies on spectacles, their application and development indicate potential tendencies Shared Universe networks may display, generally.

Focusing on the MCU film network, the development of threats along *Manifestations* of a network appears to follow two general lines of escalation. As the general tagline associated with the Avengers – "To fight the foes no single hero could withstand!" – implies, a team narrative within the superhero genre exists to engage with conflicts that require *Index Manifestations* of different *Narrative Entities* to overcome. This assertion necessarily implies that conflicts within the *Narrative Entity*-specific *Manifestations* differ from those in team narratives in some form. While such a difference may appear in scope, it more likely arises in specificity towards the network of *indices* underlining a *Narrative Entity*. In other words, conflicts of specific *Narrative Entities* appear in a form that not only precludes the involvement of other heroes but also reasonably associates with the titular hero in some manner. Iron Man fights enemies who use/abuse technology; Captain America deals with a Nazi-esque organization and its descendants; Thor stands against creatures related to Norse Mythology. This relationship between the threats in the *Manifestation* of singular *Narrative Entities* and the team narrative points towards a relation to two different lines of seriality: the one focused on one *Narrative Entity* (*Iron Man*, *Iron Man 2*, *Iron Man 3*) and the one for the overall order of *Manifestations* within the Shared Universe network. *Manifestations* focused on singular *Narrative Entities* within the first phase employ conflicts specific to their underlining network of *indices*. In either case, these threats do not endanger or engage other portions of the Shared Universe network. This restrain within the foundational phase preserves the potential for a greater or larger danger, which then invokes the need for a team narrative. In *Iron Man* and *Iron Man 2*, the larger threats are attempts to undermine Tony Stark's control of his company and technology; the physical conflict or spectacle merely endangers a section of Stark's company, a section of street (*Iron Man*), and the Stark Expo ground (*Iron Man 2*). *The Incredible Hulk* focuses on Bruce Banner's search for a cure and the fear of a creature such as the Hulk weaponized by the military. The physical confrontation at the end of the movie is limited to Harlem, New York. *Thor*'s and Loki's attempt to prove their worthiness to Odin provide the general conflict in *Thor*. The physical altercation at the end of the film remains in a small town in New Mexico and on Asgard. As the first Captain America movie takes place during the Second World War, its threat automatically is removed from the other *Narrative Entities*, which all employ networks of *indices* associated with a fictional notion of the contemporary United States. An alien invasion led by an Asgardian god in *The Avengers* supersedes the previous dangers, creating a larger threat in scope and spectacle. However, the first team narrative still limits the region of influence intradiegetically by focusing on New York, preserving the potential for a greater (and more spectacular) danger in later team *Manifestations*. The MCU film network implies that threats within the foundational phase escalate once noticeably within the team narrative, leaving a singular and linear relationship between the threat of the first team narrative and the other *Manifestations*. Only the relationship between the two MCU Iron Man *Manifestations*, in which the sheer number of opponents mostly increases, indicates a secondary line of threat escalation. As a continued linear increase of threats similar to the foundational phase would quickly lead a Shared Universe network to the limit of a reasonable conflict within its specific genre, sequels of specific *Narrative Entities* have to increase their threat in relation to their previous *Manifestation*, instead of continuing the level of threat linearly from the team narrative. In other words, the risks, conflicts, and threats in *Iron Man 3* should not (and do not) stand in comparison to *The Avengers* but to *Iron Man 2*. This allows *Manifestations* to draw back on the overall spectacle within singular *Manifestations* in relation to the overall network while still raising the stakes meaningfully for a specific narrative. Pulling back on the risk and threat does not mean that *Transformation Trigger*s created by them cannot influence the overall Shared Universe. Within the MCU film network, *Iron Man 3* and *Captain America: The Winter Soldier* follow this notion. Following *The Avengers*, *Iron Man 3* refocuses on the theme of terrorism and an attack on Stark's company/legacy, initiating parts of a *Trigger Wave* leading to the conflict in *Captain America: Civil War*. Equally, while the *Transformation Trigger*s of *Captain America: The Winter Soldier*, specifically the fall of S.H.I.E.L.D., affect other *Narrative Entities* within the network, the film's threat does not call for the hero characters of other *Narrative Entities* to get involved. As the team narrative of the stabilization phase, the threat of *Avengers: Age of Ultron* supersedes the conflicts of each singular *Narrative Entity*. However, the danger within the film (and, therefore, the spectacle) also supersedes its namesake predecessor. Instead of a city, the Avengers defend a nation; instead of one villain with an army, they engage three villains with an army; instead of staying in place to defend against the enemies, they hunt them across the globe. As such, the increase of threat within a Shared Universe follows two different lines of escalation, one following the linear seriality of the specific *Narrative Entities* and a second following the linear seriality of the team narrative. However, in their interaction, these two paths of escalating threats create a sense of a continuously increasing threat to the overall Shared Universe.

The dual increase of threats entails a potential endless escalation of spectacle for the entire network. As each line of threat rises on its own, the overall threat to the network equally rises, leading to a general expectation for larger spectacles from *Manifestations* of the network. However, the use of new *Narrative Entities* helps to manage the threat escalation within a Shared Universe network. Hereby, new *Narrative Entities* restart the process of escalation within their *Manifestations* by having a comparatively lower level of danger and, therefore, a smaller spectacle. Not directly part of the existing escalation process and, thus, not directly accountable to existing levels of spectacle, the *Manifestations* of new *Narrative Entities* can repeat the low-level danger of *Manifestations* from the foundational phase. As such, new *Narrative Entities* start new lines of escalating threats, which have the potential to increase while existing *Manifestations* have to run their course. Within the MCU film network, *Ant-Man*, *Spider-Man: Homecoming*, and *Black Panther* provide such a pull-back to the overall threat expectation of the network, with each focused on a danger specific to their network of *indices*, which endangers the *Index Manifestations* of the overall network tangentially, but do not spill directly into other *Narrative Entities*. On the other end of the spectrum, some existing and new *Narrative Entities* present grander or as grand spectacles as the previous team narrative. Hereby, the spectacles remain confined to the *Narrative Entity*'s network of *indices*. Including a threat that supersedes the team narrative automatically creates lines of escalation above the previous ones. Providing a grander spectacle or pronounced threat, these *Narrative Entities* force team narratives following them to adapt or exclude them from their *Manifestations*. An example of this process is *Guardian of the Galaxy Vol.1*, which endangers an entire planet with a grand space battle involving a planetary defense force in its climax but is prominently absent from the following *Avengers: Age of Ultron*. This exclusion and invitation to increase its level of spectacle allow the use of *Manifestations* to prepare an audience for the pinnacle threat to the team narrative. *Doctor Strange*, *Guardians of the Galaxy Vol.2*, and *Thor: Ragnarok* indicate this potential within the MCU film network. In either case, the overly powerful individual enemy threatens the entire cosmos in some fashion. More significantly, despite a grand spectacle displaying a physical conflict, these grand threats are not beaten in a straightforward fight and require personal sacrifice on the side of the hero character. Dr. Strange forces Dormammu to retreat by trapping himself and his enemy in a time loop; Peter Quill defeats Ego the Living Planet by tapping into the latter's cosmic power, sacrificing any potential future use; and Thor can only overcome Hela by destroying his home Asgard. These types of threats set up the expectation of a team narrative with an enemy that will provide a grand spectacle and whose defeat will not be straightforward and require great sacrifice. *Avengers: Infinity War* and *Avengers: Endgame* then provide such an enemy and the accompanying spectacle. In the former, Thanos fights his way through several characters of the MCU film network to get the Infinity Stones and destroys half the universe's population. No straightforward approach can stop him. In the latter, the remaining heroes travel through time to reverse Thanos's act of destruction. Ultimately, Iron Man has to sacrifice himself to beat this enemy. The use of threats and spectacle within the MCU film network indicates that it is more useful to think of escalating threats within a Shared Universe network as multiple instead of dual. The potential of different

Narrative Entities to hold various levels of spectacle and threat creates multiple lines of escalation. These lines can flow solely through one specific or several *Narrative Entities*. More importantly, team narratives operate with a threat that supersedes the threat of each individual *Narrative Entity* within its formation but leaves the individual escalation of that *Narrative Entity* apparently untouched. Hereby, the team narrative also supersedes the threat of its own predecessor if the same *Narrative Entities* are part of either *Manifestation*. The present material does not indicate if a team narrative within the same network constructed from entirely different *Narrative Entities* would still be beholden to its predecessor. However, the variability of threat within individual series of *Narrative Entities* implies similar variability within team narratives constructed from different *Narrative Entities*. This multilinear development of threats allows for alternative types and ranges of spectacle within the same unified world, opening up different passages of pleasing and engaging multiple audience types.

3.2.4 Endings and Beginnings Forever

The overall structure within the researched material implies that the continued growth of a Shared Universe network helps to maintain its existence. While the MCU film network continues beyond the scope of the material within this research, as several films and series based on established *Index Manifestations* have been slated for the foreseeable future, the other two networks have ended. Assuming contextual factors and not textual ones determined the faith of the MNU and ABC network, the lack of expansion within either network remains notable. The ABC network briefly attempted to expand with the series *Inhumans*, which was canceled after one season, and the MNU network only expanded via *The Punisher*. Because *Agents of S.H.I.E.L.D.* effectively kept the ABC network alive for seven years, a lack of expansion does not imply the immediate end of a network. However, the expansion of the network facilitates the renewal of an audience base through a restart of threats, the creation of manageable clusters, and new material for casual audiences, implying the expansion's need for the continued development of such a network. As such, a running Shared Universe has an economic interest in continued growth and renewal to maintain its informed audience while gradually renewing it with a steady flow of to-be-educated casual audiences. Hereby, the continued expansion of a Shared Universe network appears primarily limited by economic realities. Market forces in relation to the affordances of the specific media production determine the viability of a Shared Universe network's continued expansion. Independent from any direct expansion via the addition of new *Narrative Entities*, the constant release of new *Manifestations* based on the current state of a network increases the amount of required knowledge for the comprehension of the entire network, gradually limiting the accessibility for new casual audiences and, therefore, creating the basis for its eventual demise. In other words, while a constant expansion allows a Shared Universe network to extend its shelf life by potentially bringing in new audiences, the same process gradually makes the network more inaccessible to this vital new audience. As such, if a Shared Universe network plans on a continuous release of *Manifestations*, a process that diminishes or removes established *Index Manifestations*, *Transformation Triggers*, and the knowledge associated with them has to balance the process of constant expansion.

Effectively, Shared Universe networks have two means of lowering the knowledge threshold for engaging with it. (1) The superhero comic network has the tendency to renew the entire Shared Universe through the process of reboots. (2) The MCU film network appears to approach the problem by regularly removing *Narrative Entities* from the network, thereby creating a constantly manageable level of knowledge threshold. Using the terminology developed in this research, a reboot would immediately replace all *Manifestations* of (a network of) *Narrative Entities* with a new rendition of the same (network of) *Narrative Entities*. In other words, superhero comics end the existing rendition of their network and replace it with a new version of the same network. Hereby, the degree of inclusion of the previous version's *Transformations Triggers* (and its subsequent change to the *Index Manifestations*) into backstory of the new rendition appears dependent on the attempted balance between an existing informed audience and a to-be-gathered casual audience. The reboot seems to bank somewhat on established readers' ability and enjoyment in comparing the old with the new while opening up the network to new audiences by circumventing the need to know the content of a long backlog. Replacing the entire Shared Universe with a new version of itself holds the advantage of retaining popular *Index Manifestations* and acknowledging famous *Transformation Triggers* while decreasing the entry threshold for new readers. However, as Stein's research into authorization practices shows, deeply invested informed audiences (i.e., fans) may revolt against the changes made in a new rendition. A reboot can also cause the creation of an entirely different *Narrative Entity*, effectively separating the reboot from the original, according to Urbansik's discussion of reboot practices. Similarly, Geoff Klock's notion of misprision indicates that, contrary to its intent, this practice can unwillingly increase the complexity of a Shared Universe network, raising the knowledge threshold for new audiences. Within the context of balancing the constant expansion of a Shared Universe network, the reboot's greatest advantage appears to lie in its potentially immediate implementation. Therefore, reboots allow the Shared Universe network of superhero comics to push their expansion to the limit their audience is willing to tolerate by giving them a venue to react to sudden changes in the market. As Dittmer points out for superhero comics, "the usual economic model is one of never-ending narrative, with its demise unplanned and at the hands of market forces."[421] The reboot effectively allows superhero comics to operate with this specific economic model by allowing it to restart its entire network when the current one has expanded beyond favorable market conditions. This reactive application of the reboot arises out of the comic's means of production, which is relatively cheap, monthly, and can continue independently of any specific person.

Formally speaking, a Shared Universe network created in an audio-visual medium could attempt a similar process of renewal. Operating with a higher cost of production, however, a Shared Universe network in television and film depends on a greater number of contextual factors. Specific actors may contribute as a *semiotic cue* to a character; specific sets and props may have altered the expectations of an *index*; the style and tone of a previous *Manifestation* may now define a *Narrative Entity*. While all of these factors influence the reboot process in superhero comics as well, maintaining or altering these

---

[421] Dittmer, Jason. "Serialization and Displacement in Graphic Narrative." *Serialization in Popular Culture*. Ed. Rob Allen and Thijis van den Berg. New York: Routledge, 2014. 125–140, Page 125

aspects requires an ignorable logistic and financial effort in comics. Recreating a *Narrative Entity* and dealing with its earlier iterations demands a more significant amount of overall effort in audio-visual media. The exchange of actors, sets, style, and tone not only requires facilitation but also may endanger existing expectations and loyalty or undermine the introduction of a new audience. More importantly, these mistakes are not as easily rectified as in the medium of comics, which may reboot again or decide to add or dismiss an alteration on a whim, a process known as 'retconning'. Reboots effectively provide a restart of a Shared Universe network. Another means of counterbalancing the continued expansion of a network is the regular removal of established *Narrative Entities*. Removing singular *Narrative Entities* from the network and replacing them with new ones allows rewarding informed audiences and lowers the threshold for casual audiences to engage with new *Manifestations*. In contrast to reboots, replacing *Narrative Entities* does not require a redefinition of established *Narrative Entities* within the network. In the context of film production, such an approach avoids the conflicting *semiotic cues* a recast of actors and remaking props would create. Instead, a new *Narrative Entity* may carry on the function of a fading one, allowing the reuse of existing *Index Manifestations* within a different network of *indices* or simply ignoring every *semiotic cue* of this fading *Narrative Entity*. Hereby, the use of existing *Index Manifestations* and *semiotic cues* from a fading *Narrative Entity* in the *Manifestation* of a new one may equally follow market forces. As such, replacing *Narrative Entities* allows producers to steer the network without necessarily engaging with any baggage of the fading material. In reaction to higher costs and logistically more complex means of production, a Shared Universe network in audio-visual media – specifically films – seems to engage market forces with the more organized approach of replacing *Narrative Entities* instead of rebooting the entire network. In contrast to their comic counterparts, they (can) only employ a more limited number of *Narrative Entities* within their Shared Universe network and have to cope with the realities of film production. As such, Shared Universes in film could only maintain their network over a longer period of time when they allow *Narrative Entities* to end and introduce new ones to replace them. Both the removal of *Narrative Entities* and the addition of *Narrative Entities* have to happen without disrupting the makeup and current flow of the existing Shared Universe to retain a sense of overall coherence.

3.2.4.1 Levels of Ending

As reboots alter everything within a network, a clearer understanding of ending a *Narrative Entity* is not required. The process of replacing, on the other hand, demands a more nuanced approach to defining the ending of a *Narrative Entity*'s presence within a network. The simplest assertion is to tie the presence of a *Narrative Entity* to the continued production of dedicated *Manifestations*. However, *Narrative Entities* can contribute to the network and continue developing outside of *Manifestations* dedicated to them. Meaningful *Index Manifestations* of a *Narrative Entity* continue to find mention, appearance, and change long after their final dedicated *Manifestation*. The entangled nature of *Index Manifestations* and *semiotic cues* within a Shared Universe network makes the removal of a *Narrative Entity* a potentially gradual process. Even removing the main *Index Manifestation* – via either death or destruction – usually leaves parts of a *Narrative Entity*'s network of *Index Manifestations* intact, which can continue to interact with the larger network. The prime example of the latter is the appearance of props and characters from the MCU Iron Man Narrative in the MCU Spider-Man Narrative after the death of Tony Stark in *Avengers: Endgame*. As such, removing a *Narrative Entity* from a Shared Universe network has several levels, which lie between the discontinued production of *Narrative Entity*-specific *Manifestations* and the disappearance of all its *indices* from the network.

The potential for a *Narrative Entity* to exist in a Shared Universe network without its own *Manifestations* raises the question of *index* association. Determining the relationship of an *Index Manifestation* to a specific *Narrative Entity* appears relatively easy if dedicated *Manifestations* present their network of *Index Manifestations*. In other words, audiences can identify the network of *Index Manifestations* associated with a *Narrative Entity* when they appear together in a *Manifestation*. However, with the ability to use *Index Manifestations* across the network, clear associations can become more difficult, as the relationship between different *indices* can become more nuanced. Within the overall MCU network, association with a specific *Narrative Entity* is created by presenting these elements of the network repeatedly in *Narrative Entity*-specific *Manifestations* with an added reliance on the source material. Additionally, such associations are strengthened via presented interconnections within team narratives. Pepper Potts's connection to the MCU Iron Man Narrative exemplifies this process. The character appears in all three MCU Iron Man Narratives, and her appearances in *The Avengers*, *Spider-Man: Homecoming*, *Avengers: Infinity War*, and *Avengers: Endgame* are directly tied to other elements of the MCU Iron Man Narrative, specifically Tony Stark/Iron Man. On the other end of the spectrum, the overall MCU network avoids tying some *Index Manifestations* to specific *Narrative Entities* by spreading their appearance (more or less evenly) across the *Manifestations* of several *Narrative Entities* or by mainly using them in a network of *indices* associated with the team narrative. Nearly all overarching *Index Manifestations* and *Shared Narratives* are examples of the former. Characters such as Paul Bettany's The Vision, Elizabeth Olsen's Wanda Maximoff, and Brent Renner's Clint Barton/Hawkeye provide examples of the latter. The association of an *Index Manifestation* via the prominence of its use within a Shared Universe network suggests the potential for *Index Manifestations* to transition from one status to the other. Equally, if a transition from one specific network of *Index Manifestations* to an autonomous existence and a transition from autonomous existence to a specific network of *Index Manifestations* is possible, an *Index Manifestation* must correspondingly be able to transfer from one network of *Index Manifestations* to another. The latter potentially occurs in the character of Harold 'Happy' Hogan. Jon Favreau's version of the character enters the MCU film network associated with the MCU Iron Man Narrative but appears to undergo a transfer to the MCU Spider-Man Narrative through his use in both of its *Manifestations*. This potential for *Index Manifestations* to alter their associations is crucial because it allows for ending a *Narrative Entity* without removing all of its *indices* and while leaving a residual presence. As with clustering, *Index Manifestations* preserve the existence of a *Narrative Entity* by maintaining a network of *indices* associated with that *Narrative Entity*. Similarly, clusters dissolve when each of their *Narrative Entities* has created more meaningful connections after a series of *Transformation Triggers*; a *Narrative Entity* technically can end when all its *Index Manifestations* create stronger associations with other parts of the overall network. Within this context, the *Narrative Entity* leaves an echo of its existence in the network as its re-associated *Index Manifestations* are still present, even if they do not directly associate with one another anymore.

The combined possibility of ending the direct representation of a network of *Index Manifestations*, removing *Index Manifestations* from the network, and re-associating *Index Manifestations* creates four degrees of ending to a *Narrative Entity* within a Shared Universe network: (1) without a direct *Manifestation*, (2) remaining *Index Manifestations*, (3) echo of its existence, and (4) complete removal. After the production of *Manifestations* specifically dedicated to the *Narrative Entity* has ceased, its network of *Index Manifestations* may continue to operate within the larger complex of the Shared Universe. The *Index Manifestations* in question still form a network, as they are associated with one another in their appearances. Hereby, the network does not have to contain a large number of elements. Within the MCU network, the continued existence of the MCU Iron Man Narrative provides the best example of this stage of ending. After *Iron Man 3*, Tony Stark/Iron Man, Pepper Potts, James "Rhodey" Rhodes, Harold 'Happy' Hogan, and Stark Industries continue to appear in MCU *Manifestations*. Each of these *Index Manifestations*' appearances is related to the MCU Iron Man Narrative in some fashion, usually via a connection to the namesake main character or his company. As these *Index Manifestations* mostly retain a direct relationship with one another, even within team narratives, the network creating the *Narrative Entity* is maintained even with no specific *Manifestations* released. The MCU's Hulk Narrative, in contrast, retains *Index Manifestations* within the Shared Universe but without these maintaining any direct relations to one another. After *The Incredible Hulk*, two *Index Manifestations* from the Hulk Narrative appear in other *Manifestations* of the MCU film network. Ignoring the difficulty of alterations to the character's *semiotic cues*, Bruce Banner/The Hulk is in every Avengers film and the third MCU Thor *Manifestation*. William Hurt's Theodor 'Thunderbolt' Ross takes part in *Captain America: Civil War* and the final two Avengers films. While these two characters appear within the network, they operate independently from one another. They never share a scene or mention any specific association with one another. In the MCU's third Captain America Narrative, Ross mentions the Hulk but gives no indication of their past relationship. In effect, these *Index Manifestations* operate independently from one another but do not form a coherent *Narrative Entity*, only alluding to its previous existence and its potential meaning for the current state of the Shared Universe. The remains of ABC's Agent Carter Narrative within the MCU film network provide another example of remaining *Index Manifestations* without a connection. Hayley Atwell's Peggy Carter appears prominently within different *Manifestations* of the MCU film network, and James D'Arcy's Edwin Jarvis is briefly in *Avengers: Endgame*. The relationship between these two characters formed a foundation of ABC's Agent Carter Narrative. While their presence in the MCU film network alludes to the *Narrative Entity*, the *Index Manifestations* show no direct relationship in the films, standing on their own within the complex of the MCU film network at that point. *Spider-Man: Far From Home*, through its application of Harold 'Happy' Hogan, whose gradual adaptation to the MCU Spider-Man Narrative began in *Spider-Man: Homecoming*, provides the only indication for a transferred *Index Manifestation* and the echo of its previous *Narrative Entity*. However, as the film makes heavy use of *semiotic cues* related to the MCU's Iron Man Narrative, the presence of the relation between the *Index Manifestation* and the echo of its *Narrative Entity* remains debatable. Equally, the association of 'Happy' Hogan to either *Narrative Entity* is potentially arguable, especially as his association with the MCU's Iron Man Narrative never ceases, despite his clear use as a part of the Spider-Man Narrative's network of *Index Manifestations*. Despite removing all *Index Manifestations* from a network being the most unambiguous means of ending a *Narrative Entity*, the entire MCU network provides no direct example of such a strategy. However, as the other degrees of ending do occur within the network, the complete removal of a *Narrative Entity* is likely to occur in the future development of the overall network. Concerning the removal of a *Narrative Entity* from the representations used in this research's analysis, it seems useful to keep *Narrative Entities* within the network until it only occurs as an echo. In the previous stages, its *Index Manifestations* still represent the *Narrative Entity* and can create interrelations with others. When the *Narrative Entity* only exists as an echo, its re-associated *Index Manifestations* will serve as a means of interrelation for its new *Narrative Entity*. As such, the *Narrative Entity* cannot alter its relationships anymore, as it has no direct bearing on the future development of the Shared Universe network.

3.2.4.2 Types of Endings and Beginnings

Consciously applying the degrees of ending a *Narrative Entity* and their potential reversal as a means of introduction, the MCU films provide three specific techniques for a Shared Universe to add, remove, and replace *Narrative Entities* within its network. As these techniques have been observed solely in the film network, film-editing terms are used to refer to them, specifically *Cut*, *Fade*, and *Transitions*.

Similar to the film technique described in Phillips[422], *Cuts* offer clear endings and beginnings to *Narrative Entities*. This transition ends *Narrative Entities* by removing the *Index Manifestations* from the Shared Universe. Hereby, a *Cut* does not have to remove all *Index Manifestations* from a *Narrative Entity*, only enough to make established constellations obsolete. As such, this transition appears to coincide with the clear end of a story connecting the different *Manifestations* of the *Narrative Entity*. An example of cutting out a greater part of *Index Manifestations* at the end of a connecting story arises in the form of the MCU's Thor Narrative. All three Thor films, to some degree, deal with Thor's ascension to the throne of Asgard. The first film revolves around Chris Hemsworth's Thor learning that he is still unworthy of his birthright and the powers bestowed upon him. At the film's end, the character proves himself worthy of his power but not entirely of the throne. The theme continues in *Thor: The Dark World*. While the plot mostly builds around the rise of an ancient evil in the form of the Dark Elves, it is framed by the question of Thor's ascension. Anthony Hopkins's Odin mentions that the nine realms look to Thor for leadership. The matter comes up again at the end when Thor outright refuses to take the mantle of king. The second and third acts of *Thor: Ragnarok* deal with Cate Blanchett's Hela's – who in this version is Odin's spurned daughter – claim to the throne and Thor's subsequent challenge to that claim. The film ends with Thor's ascension to the ruler of all remaining Asgardians. The third film completes the overall story of Thor's ascension, leading the *Narrative Entity* to a potential end. More importantly, a greater part of the Thor Narrative's *Index Manifestations* is destroyed in the course of this story's completion:

---

422 Phillips, William H. *Film: An Introduction (Third Edition)*. Boston: Bedford/St. Martin's. 2005.

Asgard's armies, including the Warriors Three, are killed; Odin dies; the relationship between Thor and Jane Foster is dissolved; Hela shatters Mjolnir; Surtur destroys Asgard; and several *semiotic cues* for the character Thor are altered. In the end, only Idris Elba's Heimdall, Tom Hiddleston's Loki, a few Asgardian extras, and the main character remain from the original network. The removal of *Index Manifestations* somewhat continues in *Avengers: Endgame*, when Thanos kills Loki. Depending on the network of *Index Manifestations*' state after the *Cut*, ending a *Narrative Entity* in this manner does not exclude its remains from appearing within the Shared Universe network or even restarting with a new story and a new network of *Index Manifestations*. The MCU Thor Narrative has set up a potential for the latter by introducing new *Index Manifestations* to replace the lost ones in *Thor: Ragnarok*. The continued association of these, most prominently Tessa Thompson's Valkyrie, implies the formation of a new network of *Index Manifestations*. However, while these elements might be part of another story within a new *Narrative Entity* (of the same name), the presumable conclusion of an overarching theme clarifies an end to that specific *Narrative Entity*. The MCU's Captain America Narrative equally employs Cuts to separate the different versions of the *Narrative Entity* presented in its singular *Manifestations*, removing a greater part of the network of *Index Manifestations* and replacing it with a new one in each film. *Cuts* used as an introduction conversely present a *Narrative Entity* without relying on any network of *Index Manifestations*. Any connection built to the larger Shared Universe appears in the form of short references, which neither interfere with the plot nor might confuse audiences unfamiliar with the Shared Universe context. A good example of the introduction of a *Narrative Entity* through a *Cut* is the MCU Dr. Strange *Manifestation*. While there are small indications of connection to a larger Shared Universe, such as a reference to an injury sustained in another *Narrative Entity*, the limited connection to the rest of the Shared Universe is notable. In this case, the lack of references to other *Narrative Entities*' medical and healing applications is particularly striking, as seeking treatment for his injured hands is a central theme of the film's first act. While the protagonist's search mentions unnamed experimental procedures, the montage is oddly void of any attempted recreation of the healing abilities of the super soldier serum (Captain America Narrative), gamma radiation (The Hulk Narrative), or new technology (Iron Man Narrative). Stephen Strange's desperate search does not include any attempt at collecting alien or Asgardian technology (The Avengers or Thor) before directly steering towards sorcery, which had not been a defining part of any *Narrative Entity* in the MCU. Mentioning one of these options might have related the MCU Dr. Strange Narrative closer to the larger Shared Universe, but it might also have detracted from the *Narrative Entity*'s uniqueness and, therefore, might have limited its potential to establish not only itself but also the aspect of magic, into the Shared Universe. Using a *Cut* as an introduction to a *Narrative Entity* allows the Narrative to stand on its own first in contrast to the other transitions, while its application to end a *Narrative Entity* allows for the instant removal of all or many *Index Manifestations*.

As the name implies, *Fades* introduce and remove *Narrative Entities* gentler than *Cuts*. Essentially, *Fades* move through the different degrees of ending a *Narrative Entity*, allowing networks of *Index Manifestations* to form or dissolve by running through the previously discussed levels of ending. Introducing a *Narrative Entity* with a *Fade* works by including singular *Index Manifestations* of the *Narrative Entity* within the *Manifestation* of another

Narrative Entity, relating these singular *Index Manifestations* to one another, and later releasing a *Manifestation* solely focused on that *Narrative Entity*. *Index Manifestations* of the MCU Black Panther Narrative appear early in the Shared Universe network, with vibranium appearing in *Captain America: The First Avenger*. Initially, the fictional metal exists as part of the MCU Captain America Narrative until it is linked to the fictional nation of Wakanda in *Avengers: Age of Ultron*, which also introduces Andy Serkis's Ulysses Klaw. The character is directly linked to the metal and the nation, shifting aspects of the MCU Black Panther Narrative from a singular *Index Manifestation* to a potentially small network, which lays the groundwork for the *Narrative Entity*. Chadwick Boseman's T'Challa/The Black Panther is then introduced in *Captain America: Civil War*, in which he is directly linked to Wakanda. Additionally, the (unnamed) Dora Milaje advances the network of *Index Manifestations*. A *Manifestation* specific to this *Narrative Entity* then enlarges the network and completes the process of fading it into the network. The appearances of the narrative's aspects allow the audience to gather rudimentary information and garner interest in the *Narrative Entity* without clearly defining it. Ending a *Narrative Entity* with a *Fade* follows the same steps in reverse. After a final *Manifestation*, a *Narrative Entity* continues as a network of *Index Manifestations* within the Shared Universe. At some point, the different *Index Manifestations* begin to appear regularly without their usual relationships and are finally absorbed into another *Narrative Entity* or disappear from all future *Manifestations*. None of the networks presented in this research employ a *Fade* in this manner. However, the existence of the Iron Man Narrative as an independent network of *Index Manifestations* without a dedicated *Manifestation* after *Iron Man 3*, as well as the independent application of *Index Manifestations* from the Hulk Narrative after *The Incredible Hulk*, implies that ending a *Narrative Entity* via a *Fade* is possible. Employing this manner of removal would allow dispersing *Index Manifestations* (and within them necessary *semiotic cues* and ideas) across the Shared Universe network, making their further use possible without necessarily holding on to their *Narrative Entity* of origin.

While the former two techniques either end or introduce a *Narrative Entity*, *Transitions* create a link between an emerging *Narrative Entity* and a fading one. Aside from allowing the immediate transfer of *Index Manifestations*, *Transitions* also transplant the 'spirit' of one *Narrative Entity* to another by intertwining them fundamentally. Instead of creating a complete network of *Index Manifestations*, the emerging *Narrative Entity* employs a section of the fading *Narrative Entity*'s *Index Manifestations*. Hereby, this 'borrowed' section of the network takes on a function for the emerging *Narrative Entity*, which may be similar or completely different from its original use. Currently, the MCU employed a *Transition* once. While usually separate *Narrative Entities*, the MCU's Iron Man and the Spider-Man Narratives connect their respective networks of *Index Manifestations* in *Spiderman: Homecoming*. This entanglement informs parts of *Avengers: Infinity War* and *Avengers: Endgame*. In contrast to their relationship within the 'original' comics, Tony Stark/Iron Man takes on the function of Spider-Man's mentor/father figure, somewhat replacing the Uncle Ben character. This alteration necessarily draws other *Index Manifestations* of the Iron Man network into the Spider-Man Narrative but also leads to an adaptation of specific *semiotic cues*. While Peter Parker, similar to the comics, makes his own version of web-shooters, web-fluid, and costume, Tony Stark provides his more recognizable superhero outfit. This outfit is amended to contain *semiotic cues* associated with Iron Man's armor, particularly the inclusion of advanced technology and artificial intelligence. Tony Stark is also linked to the actions and motivation of the film's villain. In contrast to the original version, Michael Keaton's Adrian Toomes/The Vulture is driven to his criminal enterprise because Stark Industries usurps his contract with New York City to dispose of alien technology after the 'Battle of New York' in *The Avengers*. The entanglement of the two networks continues with the use of Jon Favreau's Harold "Happy" Hogan, who continuously questions Peter Parker's ability to be a hero and displays the need to monitor his activities, functionally replacing the representation of newspapers and society from the comics. The use of *Index Manifestations* from the MCU's Iron Man Narrative was so prominent that marketing for the film emphasized the connection within the film. Most posters, for example, contain Iron Man in some capacity, with one even including Happy Hogan. *Transitions* allow for the continuation of some aspects of a fading *Narrative Entity* into a new one, maintaining elements the Shared Universe network requires while allowing a *Narrative Entity* to end. Hereby, the emerging *Narrative Entity* benefits but is also burdened with the genesis and development of the former *Narrative Entity*, which naturally means that it is automatically, to some degree, geared towards an informed audience.

While easily categorized, none of these transitions appear to operate completely separate from one another. The character Spider-Man is introduced via a quick *Fade* before the release of a dedicated *Manifestation*. Similarly, a more significant part of the Iron Man Narrative's network of *indices* began to end via a *Fade* before being used in a *Transition*. Independent from singular or combined usage, these transitions allow a Shared Universe network to retain its endless seriality by gradually replacing *Narrative Entities* without rebooting the entire network.

3.2.4.3 Continuing Forever

In conclusion, a Shared Universe network attempting to continue beyond the natural lifespan of its component *Narrative Entities* has two main approaches to sustain itself: (1) Superhero comics generally appear to favor a universal renewal of their entire network when it reaches a stage at which it becomes (or is perceived as) unmanageable. At this point, the producers of superhero comics reboot the Shared Universe to lower the overall complexity and provide new entry points for new readers. (2) The MCU, as an example of a successful Shared Universe in an audio-visual medium, indicates a favor for replacing a limited number of *Narrative Entities* with others by employing transitions to phase out older ones and introduce newer ones, leaving the overall network intact while ensuring its continuation. Using reboots to cycle through *Narrative Entities* is more direct and allows for a universal redefinition/rebranding of a Shared Universe, phasing old *Narrative Entities* out and phasing new ones in retains the Shared Universe overall without any notable breaks or necessary rebranding. While either medium technically could (and potentially does) make use of either approach, passing the torch, so to speak, from one *Narrative Entity* to another seems immeasurably more important within the medium film, as it only operates with a limited number of *Narrative Entities* at the time, due to the higher financial and logistical requirements of production.

4 Reflections

4.1 Reflection on Practice: A short look at other Universes

With its focus on the MCU's Shared Universe, the Universe Model might appear self-serving and unduly limited to a singular, unique phenomenon. However, as mentioned throughout previous chapters, the MCU is not the only attempt at a 'cinematic' universe and not the only Shared Universe constructed within an audio-visual medium. Several film production companies attempted to launch their own Shared Universe franchises with varying degrees of success: Universal's Dark Universe, 20th Century Fox's X-Men Universe, Warner Brothers's DC Extended Universe, New Line Cinema's The Conjuring Universe, and Legendary Entertainment's MonsterVerse are currently the most prominent. With the parallel release of new interconnected shows, Star Wars and Star Trek arguably also attempt a Shared Universe approach on the small screen, following the success of the CW's Arrowverse. Even within print media, Shared Universes are not limited to comic books and the superhero genre, as the Black Library book series from Games Workshop revolves around two distinct Universes, and Terry Pratchett's Discworld series equally creates a unified world via several singular book series. The existence of all of these franchises not only shows the spread of this phenomenon but also provides the potential for further definition and clarification of the Shared Universe terminology, as well as allows for refinement of the model itself.

While this publication cannot provide additional research into other variations of a potential Shared Universe structure, it appears useful to point toward notable objects, which might provide new insight into the development and application of the Universe Model. To this end, the following chapter will introduce three self-declared Shared Universes and explain their significance for further research.

4.1.1 The Arrowverse: Keeping the Comic Structure

The Arrowverse emerges from several interconnected television series based on properties from DC Comics, primarily airing on the American television channel 'The CW' and its sister channel 'CW Seed'. Employing common plot elements and *Index Manifestations* across seven live-action television series and two animated series established a network of *Narrative Entities*, which eventually formed a Shared Universe. The franchise debuted in October 2012 with the series *Arrow*[1], based on DC's Green Arrow Narrative. *The Flash*[2] and the animated web series *Vixen*[3] followed in 2014 and 2015, respectively. The second season of *Arrow* introduced *Index Manifestations* of the former, namely the main character Grant Gustin's Barry Allen/The Flash. In January 2016, *Legends of Tomorrow*[4] added a team narrative to the network, as the series employed *Index Manifestations* established and associated with previous *Narrative Entities*. The same year, CBS's *Supergirl*[5], which had already crossed over with *The Flash*, moved to The CW for its second season. A second animated web series, *Freedom Fighters: The Ray*[6], was released in 2017. The main character, Ray Terrill/The Ray, made a live-action appearance during that year's crossover event "Crisis on Earth-X". With stronger ties established between Supergirl and the Arrowverse, a fifth, *Batwoman*[7], and a sixth series, *Superman & Lois*[8], were added to the list of *Narrative Entities* in 2019 and 2021, respectively.

Since 2014, the Arrowverse's live-action series included a yearly crossover event, which spread a story across singular episodes of different series. Among these, the most notable are 2016's "Invasion" for employing all live-action series for the first time; 2017's "Crisis on Earth-X" for presenting an alternate version of the Shared Universe, which is not separated by a Genre Multiverse; and 2019's "Crisis on Infinite Earths" for rearranging the overall relationships within the network of *Narrative Entities*. "Elseworlds" and "Crisis on Infinite Earths" expanded the overall Arrowverse network by retroactively adding past DC series and films to the franchise's Genre Multiverse, including another previously separately running series, *Black Lightning*[9].

Research into the Arrowverse's approach may yield interesting insights into the formation of a Shared Universe network on two accounts: (1) the overlapping use of Genre Multiverse and Narrative Multiverse and (2) a better distinction between the use of team narratives and crossovers relating to the formation of a Shared Universe network. As already mentioned, the application of a Multiverse as part of a *Narrative Entity* and its application as a denominator of the relationship between different *Narrative Entities* are decidedly different. While these may occur in concert with one another, with the notion of traversing the Multiverse being used to connect otherwise clearly separated *Narrative Entities*, at the time of this writing, such an approach is exceedingly rare outside of comics.

---

1 *Arrow*. Created by Greg Berlanti, Marc Giggenheim, and Andrew Kreisberg. Warner Bros Television. 2012–2020

2 *The Flash*. Created by Greg Berlanti, Andrew Kreisberg, and Geoff Johns. Warner Bros Television. 2014-ongoing

3 *Vixen*. Created by Greg Berlanti, Marc Giggenheim, and Andrew Kreisberg. Warner Bros Animation. 2014–2016

4 *Legends of Tomorrow*. Created by Greg Berlanti, Marc Giggenheim, Andrew Kreisberg, and Phil Klemmer. Warner Bros Television. 2015-ongoing

5 *Supergirl*. Created by Greg Berlanti, Ali Adler, and Andrew Kreisberg. Warner Bros Television. 2016-ongoing

6 *Freedom Fighter: The Ray*. Created by Greg Berlanti, Marc Giggenheim, and Sam Register. Warner Bros Animation. 2017–2018

7 *Batwoman*. Created by Caroline Dries. Warner Bros Television. 2019-ongoing

8 *Superman&Lois*. Created by Greg Berlanti and Todd Helbing. Warner Bros Television. 2021-ongoing

9 *Black Lighting*. Created by Salim Akil. Warner Bros Television. 2018–2021

The foundational iteration of the Arrowverse formally established that none of the *Index Manifestations* of DC's two most recognized *Narrative Entities*, Superman and Batman, existed within its world[10]. This stated characteristic of the emerging network formally excluded any immediate relations with the Supergirl Narrative broadcasted on a different network, as the *Narrative Entity* is inherently linked to a Superman Narrative. This clear separation is bridged via *The Flash*, which included a notion of Genre Multiverse in its network of *Index Manifestations*. The previously established ability to transverse different universes allowed connecting the growing Arrowverse and the Supergirl Narrative via the episode "World's Finest"[11] from the latter's series. While the initial interaction apparently only occurred as a fun allusion to existing connections between the source material and different actors on each show, the continued use of this explanation in later episodes and events allowed for an overlap between a Genre Multiverse and Narrative Multiverse within the overall network. A closer look at *Narrative Entities* connected based on a Genre Multiverse conception may provide insight into the exact relationship between specific *indices* as well as the potential for forming and developing a Shared Universe network. The latter appears significant in the case of the Arrowverse, as the initial notion of a Genre Multiverse serves to rearrange the relationships between established *Narrative Entities* within the network[12] and add past interpretations of known *Narrative Entities*[13] to it.

More significant than the influence of content on structure within the formation and development of a Shared Universe network may be the different positions and applications of the team narrative in relation to the MCU. While the Arrowverse has a team narrative in the form of *Legends of Tomorrow*, it only reiterates existing relationships between *Narrative Entities* of the network. In contrast to the team narratives of the MCU, *Legends of Tomorrow* does not produce far-reaching and world-changing *Trigger Waves* that influence the overall network. While the time-traveling premise of the *Narrative Entity* would allow for such an application, the team's mission to protect time expressly circumvents the creation of meaningful *Trigger Waves*, as it implies that everything has to happen or will be restored at some point. Within a Shared Universe solely constructed from television series, the production of *Trigger Waves*, which influence a significant portion of the network, appears to fall to crossover events. Understanding crossover events in this instance as a singular concise plot spread across singular episodes of different series, these appear with the potential to create network-shaping *Trigger Waves* for the same reason the team narrative carries this ability. They provide *Transformation Triggers* within a context in which the *Index Manifestations* of several different *Narrative Entities* interact. However, while the potential exists, crossover events within the Arrowverse are seldom used for

---

10   Indeed, Stephen Amell's Oliver Queen/Arrow takes on many characteristics traditionally associated with Batman, while Grant Gustin's Barry Allen/The Flash does the same for Superman.
11   "World's Finest". Supergirl. Created by Greg Berlanti, Ali Adler, and Andrew Kreisberg. Season 1, episode 18. Warner Bros Television. 2016-ongoing
12   The previously 'separate' worlds of *Supergirl* and *Black Lighting* were incorporated into the unified world created by the networked cluster of *Arrow*, *The Flash*, and *Legends of Tomorrow*. The incorporation of *Supergirl* created the potential to draw *Batwoman* and *Superman & Lois* into the network.
13   Due to "Crisis on Infinity Earths" and "Elseworld", the Arrowverse network potentially incorporates the 1966's *Batman* television series, the 1989 *Batman* film, the 1990 *The Flash* series, the 2001 *Smallville* series, 2002's *Birds of Prey* television series, and the 2006 *Superman Returns* film.

the purpose of such a universal change. Because these crossover events usually occur in the middle of each series' season, they naturally intersect with each series' season's running storyline. The crossover event usually halts these regular storylines, which resume normally afterward. Still, crossover events such as "Crisis on Infinite Earths" indicated that they can have the same transformative impact. While this potential for impact to the intersection of networks of *Index Manifestations* relates crossover events to the function of team narratives, its ad hoc definition indicates parallels to the process of a *Shared Narrative*. However, this mode of interrelating *Narrative Entities* and altering the network does not completely operate as either. A closer look at its influence might allow for adding to the Universe Model or adjusting some of its existing elements.

While the interrelation of these different television productions within the Arrowverse mirrors many processes described in the overall MCU network, its emergence in dominantly one medium and the application of a specific index to its advantage creates uniquely different mechanics in its maintenance and development. Taking a closer look at these may allow for the advancement of the Universe Model.

4.1.2 DCEU: Working without a Foundation

The financial and critical success of the MCU has prompted other attempts at creating a similar Shared Universe network. None has garnered a similar success or renown at the time of this writing. Among these attempts, Warner Brothers's DC Extended Universe (DCEU) appears of particular interest, considering potential applications and adjustments of the Shared Universe model. A specific focus on the DCEU is warranted because it is based on similar source material, with DC comics being Marvel's chief competitor in the publication of superhero comics. Secondly, the approach of the DCEU actively violates many of the structural guidelines excavated within this research, potentially even raising the question of whether the franchise can be considered a Shared Universe as defined here or if the Universe Model is overall too limited. Based on *Narrative Entities* owned by DC Comics, the DCEU includes comic books, short films, novels, and video games but forms dominantly around a collection of films. Originally planned to center around five films directed by Zack Snyder, the production company downplayed the shared nature of the universe after the sobering reception of *Justice League*[14] in 2017 – an adaptation of DC's version of The Avengers – and a notably positive acknowledgment of *Wonder Woman*[15], a *Manifestation* focused on a singular *Narrative Entity*. In 2021, after the successful re-release of a four-hour cut of *Justice League* on HBO Max, Warner Media reversed course and announced the attempt to interrelate future *Manifestations*. This franchise began with

---

14   *Justice League*. Directed by Zack Snyder. Performances by Henry Cavill, Ben Affleck, Gal Gadot, Ezra Miller, and Jason Mamoa. Warner Bros Pictures, 2017

15   *Wonder Woman*. Directed by Patty Jenkins. Performances by Gal Gadot and Chris Pine. Warner Bros Pictures, 2017.

Man of Steel[16]. *Batman v Superman: Dawn of Justice*[17], *Suicide Squad*[18], *Wonder Woman*, *Justice League*. *Aquaman*[19], *Shazam!*[20], *Birds of Prey*[21], and *Wonder Woman 1984*[22] followed in that order. The franchise expanded onto HBO Max with the four-hour Snyder cut[23] of *Justice League*[24] and added another *Manifestation* with *The Suicide Squad*[25] in 2021. The exact relationship of the two different iterations of a Justice League Narrative within the complex of all DCEU *Manifestations* is, as of now, undetermined. Warner Media announced five further additions to the overall list: *Black Adam* (2022), *The Flash* (2022), *Aquaman: The Lost Kingdom* (2022), Batgirl (2022) and *Shazam! Fury of the Gods* (2023).

The order in which *Manifestations* of the DCEU were released already indicates a significant divergence from the MCU model. Instead of beginning with a set of *Manifestations* focused on singular *Narrative Entities*, three of the first five films contain characteristics of a team narrative. Only *Man of Steel* and *Wonder Woman* construct a set of *Index Manifestations* from and for a singular *Narrative Entity*. In contrast, *Batman v Superman: Dawn of Justice*, *Suicide Squad*, and *Justice League* operate with a network of *Index Manifestations* constructed from several *Narrative Entities* – most prominently a Batman Narrative, a Wonder Woman Narrative, an Aquaman Narrative, and a Flash Narrative – which were not established previously. Any classification as team narrative in this instance is only possible because the different *Index Manifestations* exist as singular *Narrative Entities* within the designated source material. In other words, an audience can only identify the inclusion of separate *Narrative Entities* in *Batman v Superman: Dawn of Justice* because they

---

16   *Man of Steel*. Directed by Zack Snyder. Performances by Henry Cavill, Amy Adams, and Michael Shannon. Warner Bros Pictures, 2013
17   *Batman v Superman: Dawn of Justice*. Directed by Zack Snyder. Performances by Henry Cavill, Ben Affleck, and Jesse Eisenberg. Warner Bros Pictures, 2016
18   *Suicide Squad*. Directed by David Ayer. Performances by Margot Robbie, Will Smith, and Jared Leto. Warner Bros Pictures, 2016
19   *Aquaman*. Directed by James Wan. Performances by Jason Mamoa and Amber Heard. Warner Bros Pictures, 2018
20   *Shazam!*. Directed by David F. Sandberg. Performances by Zachery Levi and Mark Strong. Warner Bros Pictures, 2019
21   *Birds of Prey*. Directed by Cathy Yan. Performances by Margot Robbie and Ewan McGregor. Warner Bros Pictures, 2019
22   *Wonder Woman 1984*. Directed by Patty Jenkins. Performances by Gal Gadot, Chris Pine, Kirsten Wiig, and Pedro Pascal. Warner Bros Pictures, 2020
23   The theatrical version of Justice League, released in 2017, suffered a difficult production. In May 2017, Snyder stepped down as director during post-production following the death of his daughter. Joss Whedon took over, completing the film as an uncredited director. In accordance with a mandate from the production company, Whedon oversaw reshoots, cutting down the runtime significantly as well as incorporating a brighter tone and more humor. The theatrical version received mixed reviews and bombed at the box office. Many fans expressed interest in an alternate cut more faithful to Snyder's vision. This interest galvanized into a petition demanding the release of the 'Snyder Cut'. In May 2020, Snyder announced that Warner Media agreed to release his original cut on the streaming service HBO Max as Zack Snyder's Justice League.
24   *Zack Snyder's Justice League*. Directed by Zack Snyder. Performances by Henry Cavill, Ben Affleck, Gal Gadot, Ezra Miller, and Jason Mamoa. Warner Bros Pictures, 2021
25   *The Suicide Squad*. Directed by James Gunn. Performances by Margot Robbie, Idris Elba, and John Cena. Warner Bros Pictures, 2021

know that Batman, The Flash, and Wonder Woman exist as separate *Narrative Entities* with their own *Manifestations* in the 'original' comic form and are not part of the general Superman Narrative. Considering this reliance on the source material, the DCEU, up to and including the first *Justice League*, arguably does not operate as a Shared Universe in the sense of a unified world constructed through the interaction of several separate networks of *Index Manifestations*. Instead, it operates more as a regular series, in which an established network of *Index Manifestations* is expanded with each entry and in which singular *Index Manifestations* receive a spin-off. The presumably original conception of the DCEU's foundation as five films from a singular director, of which two were canceled and replaced with singular, less attached films after the poor reception of *Batman v Superman: Dawn of Justice*, supports this view of its structure. As such, this 'type' of foundation cannot employ an increasing interrelation with future *Manifestations* but instead seems to grow the network of *Index Manifestations* to create viable spin-off material. While this approach excludes the classification of the DCEU as a Shared Universe network in the manner presented in this research, it also implies the possibility that a Shared Universe network may grow out of one clear *Narrative Entity*. Most *Manifestations* following *Justice League* focus on adapting a specific *Narrative Entity*. Four of these follow *Index Manifestations* introduced in the previous foundational films, but the remaining five focus on singular *Narrative Entities*, which could interrelate via the mechanics employed in other Shared Universe constructions. Aside from implying an alternative structure to the creation of a network of *Narrative Entities*, the DCEU approach may also indicate a different collection of general techniques. The need and use for such things as a *Shared Narrative*, *Narrative Reliance*, and the education of a casual audience into an informed one may be very different within such an approach.

Another prominent difference of the DCEU is the lack of any process of escalation, notably the escalation of threat. Aside from often threatening the world or the universe at large, threats appear uneven across the different *Manifestations*. The first film, *Man of Steel*, endangers the entire world with a Kryptonian terraforming invasion, including several Superman-like enemies. The conflict in this first film destroys an entire major metropolis and a small town. A single monster created from Kryptonian and human DNA, solely created to destroy Superman, in *Batman v Superman: Dawn of Justice* appears as a more personal threat in the second *Manifestation*. *Suicide Squad* then escalates the threat again with a pair of demonic siblings who transform a city's population into monsters and want to destroy all humankind. *Wonder Woman*, in contrast, provides the concept of war and modern warfare, including its personification of the Greek god Ares as a threat. *Justice League* repeats the general threat of *Man of Steel* with a singular villain with a set of faceless monsters, who in service of an unseen master want to terraform earth. This uneven development of threats, which do not appear to build on one another, generally continues throughout the films. While the franchise attempts to level out these differences with intradiegetic explanations, the odd presentation of threats concerning their overall order and the relation to the presumed hero contradicts the potential sensation of a unified world, in which certain problems by nature would 'activate' specific heroes or naturally explain the sudden emergence of a team. Noting the lack of a controlled escalation does not imply that one is needed but that this attempt at something like a Shared Universe operates without it. As with the altered structure, such a difference calls for a closer look at the potential mechanics governing the DCEU and their relation to the structure of the MCU.

As the concept of an extensive network of interrelated *Narrative Entities* to form a unified world is relatively new within the medium of film, there are several different approaches to its creation. More so, the loose use of the term Shared Universe to describe different media franchises implies the existence of several means to create such a phenomenon. While each of these may carry varying levels of success, analyzing their individual approaches can inform the Universe Model or even open discussion of a differing classification. For this purpose alone, the differences in the DCEU should be researched more closely and added to the overall discourse on the matter. However, it also should be noted that the MCU and DCEU are not the only film franchises creating unified worlds.

4.1.3 Discworld: Shared Universe in Novels

The research in this paper focused mainly on the medium of comics and film. However, the discussion concerning the reproducibility of *Index Manifestations* implies that while the choice of medium is important, no medium or combination of media is excluded from the potential of carrying a Shared Universe. Hereby, differences between representation practices and capabilities of different media influence the spread of the network and the relationship between different *Narrative Entities*. Still, no combination necessarily excludes the creation of a Shared Universe. While such a statement may appear obvious, arguments for and against the medium of comic regarding its unique potential to create a unified world from a network of different *Narrative Entities* has been made in several instances. The rise of the MCU offset the general acceptance of that notion. However, Shared Universes as networks of different *Narrative Entities* outside of comics have existed for some time. Terry Pratchett's Discworld series appears as a prominent example. A humorous fantasy book series, it debuted in 1983 with *The Colour of Magic*[26] and ended after forty-one books, following Pratchett's death, with *The Shepherd's Crown*[27] in 2015. The series has been adapted for graphic novels, theatre, video and board games, and television. While taking place predominantly in one coherent world created by one author, the book series employs Shared Universe techniques to establish and expand this world. Generally, the Discworld novels are considered seven separate series and some standalone novels, which employ a specific network of *Index Manifestations*. Overall, the books employ a form of linear narrative time in relation to one another. Characters' ages change to reflect the passing of years, and some novels refer to events from other novels. To interrelate, different *Index Manifestations* briefly appear within another network of *Index Manifestations*. Some main characters may provide a connection as transposed *Index Manifestations* in other novels, such as Carrot Ironfoundersson and Angua from the City Watch novels,[28] who appear briefly in the Moist von Lipwig books *Going Postal*[29], *Making*

---

26   Pratchett, Terry. *The Colour of Magic*. Berkshire: Colin Smythe Publishing, 1983
27   Pratchett, Terry. *The Shepherd's Crown*. UK: Penguin Random House, 2015
28   *Guards! Guards!* (1989), *Men at Arms* (1993), *Feet of Clay* (1996), *Jingo* (1997), *The Fifth Elephant* (1999), *Night Watch* (2002), *Thud!* (2005) and *Snuff* (2011)
29   Pratchett, Terry. *Going Postal*. UK: Penguin Random House, 2004

Money[30], as well as the stand-alone novel *Unseen Academicals*[31]. The most notable connecting *Index Manifestation* is the personification of death. Death is most notably marked by the capitalization of his direct speech, indicating the supernatural nature of his voice. The character appears in all but two Discworld novels, as he always picks up the souls of the recently deceased. Several unattached *Index Manifestations*, such as staff members of the Unseen University, the city Ankh-Morpork, the assassin's guild, and Lord Vetinari, appear in many different *Manifestations* without having specific storylines of their own. The meetings of various characters from different narrative threads (e.g., Ridcully and Granny Weatherwax in *Lords and Ladies*[32], Rincewind and Carrot in *The Last Hero*[33]) relate different events within the world to one another, maybe indicating the existence of *Shared Narratives*. Aside from the prominent difference in medium, Terry Pratchett's Discworld novels additionally point out the potential of a purely auteur Shared Universe, as all *Narrative Entities*, which finally make up this world, are the sole creation of one author.

Prominently created in the written form, the network of *Narrative Entities* that make up the Discworld would also provide an exciting combination of the Universe Model and the notion of media-mix. While film and play adaptations transfer the *Narrative Entity* to another medium, influencing an audience's perception, games such as *Discworld Noir* actually provide a new *Narrative Entity*. However, this network appears as one of the few Shared Universes that originated in novels, not only in its creation but also in the audience's dominant perception of it. The origin of a purely written medium for its creation may have altered the overall structure of the network. Additionally, the lack of directly adapted material, which had already created a semblance of a *Narrative Entity* in the public's consciousness, may also give the book series a unique application of the techniques presented within the Universe Model.

4.1.4 Other Universes

The advent of the MCU has prompted academia to realize that expansive complex universes derived from different *Narrative Entities* can exist outside the medium of comics. Academia, however, failed to realize that the notion of a Shared Universe has existed outside of comics for some time, especially within popular culture. The rise of such a complex world within the medium of film highlights this blind spot within scholastic research, but film is only now joining the fray as mainstream audiences gradually become accustomed to the idea. As such, there are complex networks, unified worlds, and issues not yet explored because we did not have the tools to understand these works in their expansive complexity. The Arrowverse, the DCEU, and Terry Pratchett's Discworld series provide only the most prominent examples for expanded research into the formation of unified worlds through a network of *Narrative Entities*. However, popular culture provides a great deal of objects for such research. The collection of Black Library[34] books (and

---

30   Pratchett, Terry. *Making Money*. UK: Penguin Random House, 2007
31   Pratchett, Terry. *Unseen Academicals*. UK: Penguin Random House, 2009
32   Pratchett, Terry. *Lords and Ladies*. UK: Penguin Random House, 1992
33   Pratchett, Terry. *The Last Hero*. UK: Penguin Random House, 2001
34   The Black Library is a division of the board and roleplay game development company Games Workshop. This division is devoted to the publication of novels and audiobooks set in the Warham-

other publishers focused on the publication of novels based on worlds initially created for games) helped create a universe originally conceived for board or roleplaying games. Star Trek offers one of the most expansive processes of creating and altering a unified world through different *Narrative Entities*. This process is notably ongoing, with several recently released and upcoming *Manifestations* expanding on existing material and creating entirely new concepts. While speculative genres appear most prominent in the creation of unified worlds, more grounded fiction also attempts to interconnect its series via the use of techniques described here. The NCIS Universe is a good example of a largely underdiscussed attempt at interrelation. Containing multiple *Manifestations* (*JAG*, *NCIS*, *NCIS: Los Angeles*, *NCIS: New Orleans*, *Hawaii Five-O* (2010), *Scorpion*, *MacGyver* (2016), *Magnum P.I.* (2018)), this network only exists via singular minor interactions. In addition to all these "professional" creations, independent creators have attempted to produce singular *Manifestations*, which connect into some form of a Shared Universe. Notable in this regard may be the YouTube channel *Crypt TV*[35]. Focused on developing, producing, and distributing horror-themed digital content with an emphasis on monsters, *Crypt TV* created several *Narrative Entities* that interconnect into a Shared Universe. Conscious attempts at creating a network to form a coherent world appear even in fiction that are not meant to create a unified world, as the existence of the Pixar Theory[36] shows.

4.2 Reflection on Theory: Researching Universes

While the construction of the theoretical frame and the subsequent analysis of the narrative techniques within Shared Universes focus on the MCU and its comic source material, the narrative techniques unearthed and discussed here may have broader implications for academic research. This goes beyond the analysis of declared Shared Universes as the ones mentioned in the previous chapter. The systemized view of *Narrative Entities* and *Manifestations* as a network offers an overarching perspective on complex interactions among different texts. Its application may help unearth common structures governing the development and formation of texts from a shared, but otherwise unrelated, cultural or production background. Combined with narratology, the creation of such a formalized network may yield unexpected narrative patterns, which manage the formation of a *Manifestation* in relation to other narrative products of its time. In other words, the application of the Universe Model may help to give insight into the influence of a current textual environment – meaning the *Manifestations* currently and recently published, which dominate the discourse of several *Narrative Entities* – on the perception of newly released *Manifestations* and their *Narrative Entities*. Applying such an approach to adaptation studies may allow for a systematic look at the correlation of *Narrative Entity*, *Manifestation*, and

---

mer Fantasy Battle and Warhammer 40,000 universes. Some of Black Library's best-known titles include the *Gaunt's Ghosts* and *Eisenhorn* series by Dan Abnett and *the Gotrek and Felix* series by William King and Nathan Long. The authors of Black Library novels created original storylines and characters that are based on playable armies in the main Warhammer 40,000 game and its many spin-offs. The result provides a fusion between tabletop gaming and speculative fiction writing.

35 https://www.youtube.com/c/Crypttv/playlists
36 https://www.thepixartheory.com

the interaction of different media representations, offering a new viewpoint on shifts in genre, re-imagination over time, and transposition in media. Within this process of shifts and changes, the Universe Model permits a better definition of characteristics considered essential for parts of different *Narrative Entities* and a *Narrative Entity* as a whole, as it provides tools to classify differences in its representation via a distinction between *index cues, rendition cues*, and *media cues*. Generally, systemizing the network of texts and classifying the different relationships between them, even if they are not intentional, will generate a map of relationships through which researchers may discover overarching principles governing the formation and creation of new stories in a constantly media and fiction producing environment – as the one currently dominating most, if not all, first world countries. In such an approach, the Universe Model can and should be combined with various theoretical conceptions concerned with the mechanics of long-term storytelling, like seriality, and the relationship of media, such as Media Mix. Incorporating these theoretical viewpoints may allow for greater insights into differences between aspects of seriality within a coherent series of *Manifestations* and seriality shifting along several different representations of the same *Narrative Entity*. Similarly, such research could compare systematic differences between linear franchises and MCU-style Shared Universes, alterations through different levels of engagement and different types of audiences, as well as changes through the application of other storytelling principles. Combinations with other theories focused on the systematic mapping of literature surely can also benefit from the use of the Shared Universe principle, as it, in essence, allows the comparison of singular works of literature and extensive networks of literature across different forms of representation.

While developed mainly for a network of *Narrative Entities*, which create a unified world, the tools and terminology also lend themselves to the description of other relationships between *Manifestations* and *Narrative Entities*. Not contrary to the notions of intertextual or adaptation research, but by focusing on their principles, organizing different adaptations of the same *Narrative Entity* in a Shared Universe network model opens a global perspective on their relationships and development. Such a global perspective unearths potential paths of development between the texts and potentially unexpected similarities between otherwise as mostly unrelated perceived texts. Determining the relationship between narrative text in a network by comparing the similarities in their *Index Manifestations*, considering real-world events and *Transformation Triggers*, and revealing unwilling potential *Shared Narratives*, in effect, codifies the notion of Intertextuality to some degree and evaluates as well as ranks the different relationships. This allows for a new overarching perspective on the development of the different texts and the potential discovery of unexpected similarities.

4.2.1 Value for Aesthetic Analysis

The Shared Universe approach offers a pre-set system to construct (potential) interrelations of several texts and formulate these as a network. Constructing a network as a map for other researchers provides potential advantages in the research across larger bodies of text. Such networks can function as direct data; in the same manner, questionnaires illicit data from larger audiences, not only providing numbers on the use and production of specific genres, themes, and types but also showing how these aspects relate to one another across texts. Applying the Shared Universe approach to texts that were not built as a Shared Universe allows for a more precise determination of contrasts across a wider range of material and automatically highlights the strength and the type of interrelation. It allows for the systemization of the interrelations between different texts. While such interrelations are easily constructed in between singular works, I believe building networks of *Narrative Entities* and networks of *Manifestations* opens up a new venue for literary research, a venue mirroring quantitative studies in the social sciences or forming a meta-analysis type research in the correlation of widespread aspects in the narration, which may or may not connect through author, genre, time, place of publication, or any other system used to form a corpus. Examples of such a network may be fairly straightforward, such as a network of all usages and appearances of Sherlock Homes within literature across nationalities and literary traditions, including all number of indices associated with the Sherlock Homes *Narrative Entity* beyond the titular character. Such a network may allow researchers to trace the transformation of the Sherlock Homes Narrative across traditions, cultures, and mediations. On a more abstract level, the Universe Model may be used to trace the similarities and differences of texts using similar tropes or motives on a larger scale than direct comparison may allow. While the development of such a model would provide research benefits, the formation of a useful network for such a purpose requires some intricate knowledge of different *Narrative Entities* and the content of their *Manifestations*. The need for such established knowledge across larger bodies of work is mostly visible in research into superhero comics. Many parts of the research conducted in this paper and articles on the cultural impact of the MCU hinged on my already existing knowledge of the material at hand, which, aside from providing a good basis, allowed me to tap into the collective knowledge base of different fan communities. Building the theory and the network of the MCU was partly possible because I had a chance to follow the process from its inception, remained vigilant across its expansion, and participated in discussions with non-academic fans knowledgeable on the network's content. With the current development, as with the larger Shared Universe in superhero comics, even the most avid fan may lose sight of all the interrelations and degrees of connection with an ever-expanding network. Researchers introduced later to the large volume of material forming a network have little chance of gaining a good overview. However, as shown, influences and intricacies between the texts of such Shared Universe echo far beyond literary science's usual systems of organizing corpi, and the academic discourse runs the danger of overlooking interconnections built across different *Manifestations*. Such deliberate networks, despite their complexity, were constructed to interrelate. As such, finding relationships between a collection of texts not directly meant to be interrelated may require a far deeper knowledge of its *Narrative Entities* and content than it is required for constructed networks. Acknowledging that no single researcher can have the complete knowledge to see the potential interrelations between all text in a field, especially in fields in which new *Manifestations* still add to the formation and perception of the *Narrative Entity*, the formation of a text-relating database appears useful for such overarching research. Existing systems of collaborative knowledge collection and production indicate the viability of creating one or several networks of literary material for specific inquiries. Such pre-constructed networks could point researchers towards overarching developments, give them an idea of the different parallel, serial narratives told across a period of time, and generally provide good access points to a researcher's inquiries. As such, such a network allows researchers to take a closer look at culturally, narratively, or otherwise important aspects within such a larger network. More importantly, employing such a form of data collection to create a network gives researchers without fan knowledge meaningful access to the material, allowing its complex narrative structures and connections to enter academic discourse. Similarly, it may give literary and cultural researchers an overview of material a singular researcher could seldom achieve. In other words, if employed systematically to construct and maintain a useful database networking different Manifestations, the Shared Universe approach counteracts Jenkin's postulated need for a fan researcher to evaluate the academic validity of serialized popular fiction and include it more meaningfully into academic discourse. Additionally, it may allow for the interaction of separate fields within literary science in a more direct and potentially more meaningful way. Overall, the Shared Universe approach might have the potential to further bridge the divide between academic research and contemporary popular literature by allowing researchers without a fan status to analyze the content without the need for the absolute devotion of a fan to get all the material and a focus on specific fields of inquiry.

4.2.2 Value for Cultural Analysis

While applying the Shared Universe approach is useful in conjunction with theories focused on text structure, the academically most useful application lies in conjunction with cultural theories. Different fields have argued for literature as a keyhole to understanding the culture and society that consumes and produces it. However, current approaches to literary studies focused on culture tend to analyze a small sample of material, often choosing a relatively small number of *Manifestations*. Even analysis with a larger body of work seldom accounts for the relationship between the text and potential assertions hidden in the text's overarching development outside the original inquiry. Due to a tradition of close reading and an assumed binary between the precise analysis of a text's singular features and a more global analysis of texts' makeup and structure, such approaches are understandable. However, meaning and cultural assertions can be hidden in processes and notions spread across long, serial developments across many *Manifestations*, especially in large networks. This potential problem once again is easily visible in general approaches to the network of superhero comics. Classic analysis discovers unifying themes, assertions, and classic structures within the superhero genre. Still, it overlooks assertions and assumptions hidden in long-term developments, the interconnectedness of societies and cultures, as well as the multiplicity of viewpoints inherent in a unified world constructed from multiple *Narrative Entities*. In other words, traditional approaches will not only have difficulty unearthing how the variety of viewpoints and relationships operate and change within such a complex network but also have difficulties relating these aspects to the culture that produces and consumes them. The latter dominantly arises from the audience's ability to selectively engage with parts of an extensive network and identify as varying degrees of an informed or casual audience. While the aspect of selective reading may have provided an argument for such research only serving a better comprehension of fan culture, a mainstream audience's acceptance of the MCU indicates not only a greater current need to understand such a network but also that these structures may have gradually penetrated the larger culture for years. As such, the analysis of more extensive complex networks may become more prevalent in current and potentially future literary research focused on cultural issues.

That the Shared Universe approach addresses a deficiency in the current cultural research surrounding such large complex narratives becomes evident in the focus of the research surrounding superhero comics and the current MCU. Notable research into superhero comics often neglects the expansive world on a direct analytical level, using the Shared Universe mainly as an argument for fan behavior or as a reason for highly specialized and limited audiences. Research into the cultural and social habits of fans, like works by Pustz, Jenkins, Stein, and Kelleter, explain how the overall complexity of superhero comics forms specific cultural characteristics of fan culture, but they seldom work out the individual ideas presented within such Shared Universes. The unilateral criticism of superhero comics' representation of women, for example, partly grows out of current cultural studies practices to analyze smaller segments of a vaster network. Most recently, Cocca's evaluations of female representation in superhero comics supplemented these findings, which supports the consensus[37]. Generally, feminist research on superheroes has rightfully pointed out the objectification of the female body within the overall genre. However, all the analysis focuses on the visual representation and specific singular functions of female characters in a short subsequence of material or specific graphic novels, usually applying Laura Mulvey's Male Gaze theory. While this approach brings up valid and important criticism, it neglects shifting representation, shifting interactions, and the necessary shift in characters' function when they move through different *Narrative Entities* of a network. The previous focus on visual representation in the case of feminist analysis and other cultural studies approaches in light of the large and complex body of work superhero comics present is not surprising, as even the most avid fan sometimes loses track of a singular character's story arc and their change in function across multiple titles. However, such approaches may reveal necessary and interesting aspects of cultural and societal development. These developments may present shifting views on such issues over time or even reveal shifting views on specific social groups in relation to context. Here, the existence of a database, which helps map out the engagement and representations of different *Narrative Entities* and *Index Manifestations*, may help create an overview of such developments. Aside from expansive interrelations, the narrative techniques governing these relationships may also provide insight into notions of a producing culture. Specifically, the manner in which *Narrative Entities* are introduced and removed from a network and the exact techniques used to interrelate them may unearth unconscious assertions about the audience's perspective of and on society.

Applying these ideas in a simplified manner to the MCU film network mapped out in this research, different potentials for interpretation may become more apparent. To this end, the following section looks at different interpretations of Tony Stark's motivations in *Iron Man 3*, when *The Avengers* is included and disregarded. It considers the manner

---

37 Cocca, Carolyn. *Superwomen: Gender, Power, and Representation*. New York: Bloomsbury, 2016

of introduction used for specifically the first black-led *Narrative Entity* and criticizes the female empowerment moment of *Avengers: Endgame*.

Arguably, one of the themes of the three MCU's Iron Man *Manifestations* is personal responsibility. The character reacts to the revelation that terrorists use his technology by shutting down his company's weapon research and manufacturing department. Discovering the illegal use of his weapons to threaten civilians initiates the public introduction of his hero persona. The theme continues in *Iron Man 2* when Tony Stark neglects the possibility that others could develop a similar weapon to his Iron Man armor and refuses to share his technology with the U.S. Government. The responsibility for his father's legacy, who never credited a Russian scientist for essential discoveries that made the Iron Man armor possible, supplements this theme of personal responsibility. In both films, Tony Stark takes responsibility for the ramifications of his (and his father's) choices and the technology created in their wake. The third film shifts the theme from personal responsibility for one's actions to responsibility for one's society. Technology remains the main focal point concerning this shift, but the notion of 'classic' military-style technology is replaced with the weaponization of people through human augmentation. While a connection between Tony Stark and these weaponized humans is established via a scene in which he corrects the base formula required to create them, the danger emerges outside of the *Narrative Entity*'s usual network of *indices*, as it has no resemblance or direct relation to the Iron Man armor – in contrast to the previous two films – and someone else developed and advanced the technology. While the idea of personal responsibility for your actions is touched upon, it is not the subject of dialogue or discussion within the film in the same manner it was in the previous two. Instead, the film shifts from a sense of personal responsibility to the responsibility of protecting your own. Tony Stark's fear of being incapable of providing this protection emerges throughout the film, notably in scenes depicting his PTSD and conversations with Pepper Potts.

Without a Shared Universe approach, in other words, with a traditional focus on the three movies of the same franchise, the analysis indicates a mostly romantic reason for the refocus of the responsibility theme. The significant *Transformation Triggers* from the second movie in this regard are the initiation of Pepper Potts's and Tony Stark's relationship as well as her promotion from his personal assistant to the CEO of Stark Industries. Shifting Pepper Potts's position to his equal and beginning a personal relationship give Tony Stark a tangible personal attachment, which he previously lacked. Assuming the full development appears in these three *Manifestations*, the shifting view of responsibility and sudden fear of loss boils down to the emergence of a meaningful 'connection', dominantly in the form of a relationship. A grander cultural interpretation here would indicate that the Iron Man franchise, therefore, implies that American/Western culture emphasizes a proactive approach to changing the world, in which one disregards the consequences of, but takes responsibility for, one's actions until one has something to lose; at which point responsibility shifts towards dominantly protecting one's personal social group.

While this viewpoint may be reasonable, it disregards the factor of a changing unified world and the influence of *Transformation Triggers* within the overall network. Merely including two *Transformation Triggers* from *The Avengers* – namely Tony Stark's near-death experience and the world's introduction to the threat of superhumans and aliens – alters the reason for the sudden shift in theme. Instead of the appearance of a romantic personal connection, the encounter of a significant unknown becomes the driving force behind the alteration. Considering *The Avengers*, Tony Stark's PTSD displays fear of a new world order, which has moved beyond the character's sense of control or general comprehension. Prior to the team narrative, Tony Stark – as the smartest man in every room – generally appears as his own worst enemy. Except for betrayal, only his own technology, something he understands and has some degree of control over, threatens his world. The Iron Monger armor from *Iron Man* is based on the Iron Man armor, and Ivan Vanko's technology from *Iron Man 2* is based on the Ark reactor that keeps Tony Stark alive and powers his suit. The Hammer drones are an attempt at imitating Stark's achievements. Using genetically altered, super-powered terrorists in *Iron Man 3* indicates not only a general new world order but also presents Tony Stark with an enemy that operates outside his previously controllable realm of experience. While any previous threat within the MCU's Iron Man Narrative arose solely from inside its network of *indices*, the threat after the foundational phase suddenly takes on *semiotic cues* usually associated with other *Narrative Entities*, mimicking the sense of dread towards an unknown outside force. As such, including the first team narrative not only alters the overall meaning of Tony Stark's PTSD but also provides a meaningful context to the choice of villains. The interpretation of the shift in themes suddenly is not that Western cultures become protective when they attain a personal connection, but rather the sudden protectiveness arises from discovering that the world is far bigger, more complex, and contains aspects that operate outside our realm of experience. This second interpretation is supported by Tony Stark's motivation in later *Manifestations* of the MCU network, in which he constantly invokes the danger of an alien invasion or attack. This view of the films indicates that American/Western society perceives a sudden shift to a protective view of responsibility as reasonable – maybe even necessary – in the wake of discovering a new unknown to one's understanding and experience.

While it is doubtful that anyone would conduct an analysis of the Iron Man films without regarding the influence of *The Avengers*, this example shows how failing to acknowledge such a direct influence can alter the overall understanding gained from such an analysis. This may appear even more relevant, considering the existence of less obvious interrelations, even within a Shared Universe network. Acknowledging the importance of interrelations for the value of a *Narrative Entity* within a network also comes to bear in evaluating the prominence of a *Narrative Entity* for its producing culture. Certain ideas attached to a *Narrative Entity* can be hidden in how it may have been introduced to or removed from an established network. Within the frame of this research, only two *Narrative Entities* used some form of *Fade* to enter the MCU film network: the Spiderman Narrative and the Black Panther Narrative. *Captain America: Civil War* introduces the hero characters and some related *Index Manifestations* of each *Narrative Entity* before either receives their own dedicated *Manifestation*. Arguably, the application of a *Fade* for the Spider-Man Narrative was directly related to negotiations concerning ownership and publication rights at the time, as well as the fact that this *Narrative Entity*'s origin story had been told twice in the 14 years prior to the character's appearance in the MCU[38]. These

---

38   Spider-Man's origin story received the cinematic treatment in 2002 as part of Sam Raimi's trilogy and in 2012 in Marc Webb's *Amazing Spider-Man*.

external circumstances lowered the need for a singular *Manifestation* to explain the character's origin as well as prompted a quick use of the *Narrative Entity* within the MCU.

The Black Panther Narrative, in contrast, does not share such external considerations. Longer than the *Fade* of the Spider-Man Narrative, the *Fade* of the Black Panther Narrative includes the appearance of additional *Index Manifestations* before its notable introduction in the third Captain America film. Aspects of the *Narrative Entity* appear in *Avengers: Age of Ultron*, particularly in the fictional nation Wakanda is mentioned. Additionally, one of its villain characters, Ulysses Klaue, and the fictional metal vibranium appear. Considering the *Fade* of the Black Panther Narrative, the exclusive use of this form of introduction for the only black *Narrative Entity* within the network could be connected to systemic distrust concerning the mainstream viability of black-led superhero *Manifestations*. In other words, the producers of the MCU did not trust that a purely black superhero *Narrative Entity* would prove successful in a mainstream market. In this view, they decided to introduce it gradually to either test the viability of this particular narrative or prime the audience for its potential appearance. Initially, the MCU avoids the racial component in *Avengers: Age of Ultron* as the one character from the Black Panther Narrative is a male Caucasian, and all other *Index Manifestations* are props. Merely mentioning an African dialect hints at the upcoming racial aspect. *Captain America: Civil War* then includes *Index Manifestations* with the racial component, either testing the general appeal of such a network of *indices* or simply preparing an audience for its potential arrival. *Black Panther* then presents an inverse of a (generally perceived as typical) racial distribution from *Captain America: Civil War* with dominantly black characters and two caucasians. Here, the *Fade* is not only used to introduce a new *Narrative Entity* but also to introduce the 'racial divergence' inherent in this *Narrative Entity*. This strategy is notable because, with the exception of a contested property, the *Fade* is singularly used for the one dominantly Black *Narrative Entity* within the MCU film network. A phenomenon repeated in the MNU with the Luke Cage Narrative, which is the only black-led and faded-in *Narrative Entity* of that network's foundational phase. In contrast, *Narrative Entities* containing far more unusual or from the established understanding divergent *indices* – such as the Guardian of the Galaxy Narrative and the Dr. Strange Narrative – enter the network without such a process of preparation, namely via a *Cut*. Equally, the one female-led *Narrative Entity*, *Captain Marvel*, enters the network directly[39]. Generally, the *Fade* appears as a good technique to create a gradual contact between new additions to a network and its audience. The choice of application can give insight into a culture's assumptions when such a gradual contact is perceived as being required.

Looking at the MCU film network implies that producers believe that audiences have to adjust to the idea of a superhero film with a predominantly black cast rather than a superhero film with an alien raccoon and an alien tree as part of its main cast. Within a network of *Narrative Entities*, contextualization of singular elements to the overall network, such as the comparison of narrative techniques used to introduce a *Narrative Entity*, allows for the critical assessment of otherwise lauded representations. The MCU's Black

---

[39] To be fair, *Captain Marvel* was released after *Wonder Woman* had shown that a female superhero film could be successful at the box office.

Panther Narrative, which was celebrated for its racial empowerment, is one of these examples. Another is the MCU's female power moment from *Avengers: Endgame*. In the final battle of the film (and arguably the three phases), beginning at 2:27:00, all present female superheroes work together to defeat a large section of the opposing force. Clearly meant as a female empowerment sequence, the scene has been equally criticized and lauded for its pursuit of highlighting the female superheroes in the MCU. The scene attempts to highlight the gender diversity within the network and shield it from some of the general criticism all superhero movies faced at the time. While the scene 'proves' that the MCU film network contains its share of female heroes, it glosses over the position these specific *Index Manifestations* have within the overall network. Applying the Shared Universe model highlights these characters' dependencies and relations to male-led *Narrative Entities*. Except for Brie Larson's Carol Danvers/Captain Marvel, none of the celebrated heroines are the central *index* in a *Narrative Entity*. Danai Gurira's Okoye and Letitia Wright's Shuri firmly relate to the Black Panther Narrative; the Thor Narrative contributes Tessa Thompson's Valkyrie; Gwyneth Paltrow's Pepper Potts famously rises out of the Iron Man Narrative; Elizabeth Olsen's Wanda Maximoff/Scarlett Witch appears as an unattached *Index Manifestation* in the Avengers films; the Guardians of Galaxy Narrative provides Pom Klementieff's Mantis, Zoe Saldana's Gamora, and Karen Gillian's Nebula; and Evangeline Lilly's Hope van Dyne/Wasp is part of the Ant-Man Narrative. Recognizing this relationship between the presented *Index Manifestations* and the *Narrative Entities*, which form the network, re-enforces an assumed dependency between female and male heroes. While this unified world produces powerful women, they apparently can only enter the unified world as part of a team's network or as part of a male hero's network. In other words, women can achieve such heights when men have brought them into the conversation. The fact that in a total of ten *Narrative Entities*, which manifested into 23 films, only one *Narrative Entity* and one film constructs its network of *indices* around a female hero highlights the truth of such an assumption. The insidiousness of a token scene celebrating a particular group within a network of *Narrative Entities* obfuscates the network's lack of representation, as it focuses attention on notable singular examples, avoiding the grander situation.

While each of the three examples merely provides a brief analysis of the MCU film network with potentially rather obvious results, each demonstrates a valuable application of the Shared Universe model in a cultural analysis capacity. It offers a unique opportunity to apply literary theories focused on cultural issues to larger, complex, popular, and/or serialized works of literature in a new and comprehensive manner.

While intertextuality has introduced the idea of all texts relating to one another in one manner or another, the theory does not offer any tools to define and, therefore, understand the strength of different relationships between texts. I would argue that taking not only a more global view of different texts produced within a culture but also focusing on their connections and the degree of their relationship can offer new and more detailed insight into the cultures that produced them. Understanding the relationship of texts from different cultures to one another using the Universe Model might also allow a better understanding of the unseen relationships between those cultures. As such, the Shared Universe approach might offer a new or additional tool for literary research focused on cultural studies. While the Shared Universe model provides the tools for such an analysis and potentially alleviates the need for a complete overview of the material, any research into a more extensive network of *Narrative Entities* would mostly fall to fan researchers. As such, the creation of a physical database that catalogs the relationship between *Manifestations* may prove equally valuable for researching the cultural phenomenon hidden within the interrelation of different texts, as it may circumvent the need for a complete in-depth knowledge of each *Manifestation* and *Narrative Entity* involved in a network. As a great deal of the cultural implications of such a network stand in relation to singular representation, which may hide a larger systemic assumption, such a database may even prove more beneficial to cultural than aesthetic research.

Afterword

In the end, the construction and maintenance of a Shared Universe relies on a few simple narrative techniques and their application in a specific form across several *Manifestations* from a larger whole. Hereby, a unified *Index Manifestation*, the acknowledgment of "larger" *Transformation Triggers*, and the application of *Shared Narratives* appear to form the basic building blocks. The slow escalation in creating and expanding a Shared Universe allows a balancing act between engaging a casual audience and rewarding an informed audience. This focus on a slow escalation and a gradual process of interrelations also offers a potential venue to transform casual audiences into informed ones, providing a pathway to an emerging fandom – something every expensive and expansive franchise may require to remain sustainable. Finally, the ability to remove *Narrative Entities* and introduce new ones gives a Shared Universe the ability to maintain the network without relying on singular fixed properties. Cycling *Narrative Entities* permits a Shared Universe to circumvent the danger of repetitiveness associated with endlessly running serial narratives by allowing narratives to end and re-telling similar stories in a different context. While these principles form the essential mechanics managing a Shared Universe network, they do not appear to cover the totality of aspects influencing the success of this phenomenon. Some aspects outside the textual structure appear to hold significance over its continued function and operation. The meta-narrative – in this instance, meaning the story told around the formation and creation of the network itself – appears to have some bearing on not only the perception of the network as a unified whole but equally the evaluation of its singular components. Concerning the former, the notion of a respected guiding force behind the network arises as an important factor. While a collective of people seems appropriate for such a guiding force as a Shared Universe network invites its emergence as a collective effort, the overall MCU network somewhat implies a single person as its benevolent auteur. Other than an association with most of the source material, Stan Lee made no creative contribution to the MCU films, neither providing scripts nor directing any part of the movies. However, his constant presence through cameos reminded (or introduced) audiences to his presumed status in the creation of the 'original' Marvel Comics universe, potentially creating the illusion of a mastermind or a figurehead audiences could pin a notion of originality on: Stan Lee offered the idea of an organized Shared Universe that now transferred to film. Independent from Stan Lee's actual involvement in the creation of the overall MCU network, his association with it appeared to provide a seminal function in broadcasting the notion of a coherent idea, which bound the different *Manifestations* together and gave the impression of a grand plan in its course and formation. Aside from providing an extradiegetic connective between all the *Narrative Entities* in the network, the perception of an auteur of a previous original appeared to insulate the actual makers of singular *Manifestations* from some public interest as well as criticism concerning the films. However, the MCU was and is not insulated from overall criticism. Fringe criticism of a more inclusive progression of the universe, most notable in reactions to *Captain Marvel*, highlights that fact. Aside from attacks against singular actors, complaints seem to target a faceless collective, apparently imagined as film executives or Disney's board of directors. The use of this strategy appears equally among several political and cultural affiliations, giving audiences something to blame without directly questioning persons or aspects associated with the overall network or singular films within it. This phenomenon arose noticeably in criticism of *Avengers: Age of Ultron*. Somewhat disparaged for its inclusion of 'unnecessary' scenes and the lack of straightforward entertainment provided by *The Avengers*, the responsibility for the film's final form was widely discussed. This discourse created a narrative in which faceless film executives stifled Joss Whedon's vision for the film, effectively absolving the director from any responsibility for its perceived shortcomings in the eyes of the audience. As an aspect operating exclusively outside of the actual text, the Shared Universe network developed in this research does not consider the advantages or disadvantages such a control over perceived responsibilities and influence on the final *Manifestations* might have or even if their existence may provide a necessity. However, they appear to be an important component to the success or failure of an overall network. Inarguably, the DCEU partly survived up to now solely on a perceived conflict between Zach Snyder's vision and an interfering corporate entity in the background, as well as a perceived auteur status of its other directors. Other aspects of the meta-narrative – such as the notion of independent production, the sense of direct influence on the Shared Universe's development, and maintaining a sense of discovery in relation to the Shared Universe's formation and later development – seem to have a similar influence on the operation and potential success of this type of narrative structure. The importance of such aspects appears partly prevalent in the lack of success other attempts at Shared Universes, as defined in this research, had in the wake of the MCU. As these aspects stand outside the actual textual formation of the phenomenon, the meta-narrative was not part of the structure formed here. However, their potential importance may call for further research.

Aside from understanding such a structure as presented in the overall MCU network, I hope this research advances the views within adjacent fields. First and foremost, scholarly research in the formation of fictional worlds – may they follow Ryan's storyworld principle or Wolf's concept of imaginary world – should consider not only the possibility that worlds may come together through the interaction of different sources but also that these sources do not necessarily have to rest on general unified assumptions. Furthermore, the system of interaction and manner in which *semiotic cues* influence potential relationships calls the core-periphery model and the egalitarian view of media use propagated by the Unified Transmedia Approach into question. Hereby, those views should not be ultimately dissolved but potentially amended to include an understanding of the hierarchy between different media within such a network and the understanding that while a core may exist, it is neither absolute nor necessarily stable. In contrast to the Unified Transmedia Approach, the Shared Universe model works with a network of individual relationships between the different elements that contribute to the Shared Universe. In clarifying these individual relationships, the model focuses on the narrative techniques presented in this research but places them in relation to the influence on media, audience engagement, and outside circumstances that contribute to changes in the text. The approach allows for a more fluid view of the different texts and their contribution to a unified world, providing terminology to define the different relationships singular texts might have with one another. Additionally, the Shared Universe model acknowledges the idea of continued changes by assuming some form of seriality. As such, it includes the potential to define the interrelations between different texts precisely and at different stages within the serial process. The combination of a more egalitarian view of the text and the acknowledgment of alteration over time allows a global view of the network's interrelation and focused research and analysis across not only a material axis but also a time axis. This approach may permit the inclusion of specific singular interactions between texts into more general understandings of fictional worlds and media, therefore allowing the advancement of these principles.

The inherent question for any research this paper hopes to prompt is the continued emergence of Shared Universe networks. While the MCU has been financially successful, attempted imitations of a 'Shared Universe' in film have produced mixed results. However, I would contend that these Shared Universes mostly adapted the moniker without employing the broader ideas or systems discussed here, usually sticking to a small number of *Narrative Entities*, which can hardly form a network (Legendary's Monsterverse), or creating a singular world by adapting several *Narrative Entities* into singular *Manifestations* (DCEU). As such, the larger literature-producing industry may not have tapped into the potential of the Shared Universe network yet. However, *Manifestation*-producing companies have a vested economic interest in creating a singular fandom for their products, expanding their properties without endangering the larger whole, and continuously enhancing the size of their audience. Employing the Shared Universe network contains the potential to provide all of these effects. While these processes are primarily based on narrative techniques and the expression of an interesting world, the creation and maintenance of a Shared Universe will be more driven by economic factors over artistic interest the more expensive the production of a *Manifestation* is. Media with a much higher cost of production, therefore, produce a Shared Universe equally more out of an economic motive. However, this economic motivation, the need to secure a larger audience and greater profit with rising costs of production, will most likely incentivize film companies to employ Shared Universes as a natural progression from the traditional film franchise. As this approach (in economics speak) diversifies assets while ensuring a general increase in profitability of the whole, the emergence of more Shared Universes in film, television, and novels appears inevitable if the board of faceless film executives figure out how to employ this structure beyond the initial success of the Marvel Cinematic Universe. As such, scholarly research should be prepared to employ such a structure to approach the analysis of such phenomena.

References

Primary Sources

Film

A Funny Thing Happened on The Way to Thor's Hammer. Directed by Leythum. Marvel Studios, 2011

Ant-Man and The Wasp. Directed by Peyton Reed. Performances by Paul Rudd, Michael Douglas, Michelle Pfeiffer and Evangeline Lilly. Marvel Studios, 2018

Ant-Man. Directed by Peyton Reed. Performances by Paul Rudd, Michael Douglas, and Evangeline Lilly. Marvel Studios, 2015

Aquaman. Directed by James Wan. Performances by Jason Mamoa and Amber Heard. Warner Bros Pictures, 2018.

Avengers: Age of Ultron. Directed by Joss Whedon. Marvel Studios, 2015

Avengers: Endgame. Directed by Anthony Russo and Joe Russo. Marvel Studios, 2019

Avengers: Infinity War. Directed by Anthony Russo and Joe Russo. Marvel Studios, 2018

Back to the Future Part II. Directed By Robert Zemeckis. Performances by Michael J. Fox and Christopher Llyod. Amblin Entertainment and Universal Pictures, 1989

Back to the Future Part III. Directed By Robert Zemeckis. Performances by Michael J. Fox and Christopher Llyod. Amblin Entertainment and Universal Pictures, 1990

Batman Begins. Directed by Christopher Nolan. Performances by Christian Bale and Liam Neeson. Warner Bros. Pictures, 2005

Batman v Superman: Dawn of Justice. Directed by Zack Snyder. Performances by Henry Cavill, Ben Affleck, and Jesse Eisenberg. Warner Bros Pictures, 2016

Batman. Directed by Tim Burton. Performances by Michael Keaton, Jack Nicholson, and Kim Basinger. Guber-Peters Company. 1989

Birds of Prey. Directed by Cathy Yan. Performances by Margot Robbie and Ewan McGregor. Warner Bros Pictures, 2019

Black Panther. Directed by Ryan Coogler. Performances by Chadwick Boseman, Michael B. Jordan, and Lupita Nyong'o. Marvel Studios, 2018

Captain America: Civil War. Directed by Anthony Russo and Joe Russo. Performances by Chris Evans and Robert Downey Jr. Marvel Studios, 2016

Captain America: The First Avengers. Directed by Joe Johnston. Performances by Chris Evans, Haley Atwell, and Hugo Weaving. Marvel Studios, 2011

Captain America: The Winter Soldier. Directed by Anthony Russo and Joe Russo. Performances by Chris Evans, Scarlett Johansson, and Sebastian Stan. Marvel Studios, 2014

Caravan of Courage: An Ewok Adventure. Directed by John Korty. Lucasfilm and Korty films. 1984

Doctor Strange. Directed by Scott Derrickson. Performances by Benedict Cumberbatch, Chiwetel Ejiofor, Mads Mikkelsen, Tilda Swinton and Rachel McAdams. Marvel Studios, 2016

Guardians of the Galaxy Vol.2. Directed by James Gunn. Performances by Chris Pratt and Zoe Saldana. Marvel Studios, 2017

Guardians of the Galaxy. Directed by James Gunn. Performances by Chris Pratt and Zoe Saldana. Marvel Studios, 2014

House of Frankenstein. Directed by Erle C. Kenton. Universal Pictures Company, Inc. 1944

Iron Man 2. Directed by Jon Favreau. Performances by Robert Downey Jr., Gwyneth Paltrow, Don Cheadle, Sam Rockwell, and Mickey Rourke. Marvel Studios, 2010

Iron Man 3. Directed by Shane Black. Performances by Robert Downey Jr., Gwyneth Paltrow, Don Cheadle, Ben Kingsley, and Guy Pearce. Marvel Studios, 2013

Iron Man. Directed by Jon Favreau. Performances by Robert Downey Jr., Gwyneth Paltrow, Terrence Howard, and Jeff Bridges. Marvel Studios, 2008

Justice League. Directed by Zack Snyder. Performances by Henry Cavill, Ben Affleck, Gal Gadot, Ezra Miller, and Jason Mamoa. Warner Bros Pictures, 2017

Man of Steel. Directed by Zack Snyder. Performances by Henry Cavill, Amy Adams, and Michael Shannon. Warner Bros Pictures, 2013

Mask of the Musketeers. Directed by Luigi Capuano. Jonia Film. 1963

Pride + Prejudice + Zombies. Directed by Burr Steers. Lionsgate. 2016

Return of the Jedi. Directed by Richard Marquand. Performances by Carrie Fisher, Harrison Ford, and Mark Hamil. Lucasfilm Ltd. 1983

Rogue One: A Star Wars Story. Directed by Gareth Edwards. Lucasfilm Ltd. 2016

Shazam!. Directed by David F. Sandberg. Performances by Zachery Levi and Mark Strong. Warner Bros Pictures, 2019.

Spider-Man. Directed by Sam Raimi. Performances by Tobey Maguire, William Defoe, and Kirsten Dunst. Sony Pictures Releasing, 2002

Spider-Man: Far From Home. Directed by Jon Watts. Performances by Tom Holland, Jake Gyllenhaal, and Zendaya. Marvel Studios, 2019

Spider-Man: Homecoming. Directed by Jon Watts. Performances by Tom Holland, Michael Keaton, Zendaya, and Robert Downey Jr. Marvel Studios, 2017

Star Trek. Directed by J.J. Abrams. Spyglass Entertainment and Bad Robot Productions. 2009

Star Wars: The Last Jedi. Directed by Rian Johnson. Performances by Carrie Fisher, Adam Driver, and Mark Hamil. Lucasfilm Ltd. 2017

Suicide Squad. Directed by David Ayer. Performances by Margot Robbie, Will Smith, and Jared Leto. Warner Bros Pictures, 2016

Superman Returns. Directed by Bryan Singer. Performances by Brandon Routh and Kevin Spacey. Warner Bros. Pictures, 2006

Superman: The Movie. Directed by Richard Donner. Performance by Christopher Reeves and Gene Hackman. Warner Bros. 1978

The Amazing Spider-Man. Directed by Marc Webb. Performances by Andrew Garfield, Emma Stone, and Rhys Ifans. Sony Pictures Releasing, 2012

The Avengers. Directed by Joss Whedon. Marvel Studios, 2012

The Dark Knight. Directed by Christopher Nolan. Performances by Christian Bale, Heath Ledger, and Maggie Gyllenhaal. Warner Bros. Pictures. 2008

The Empire Strikes Back. Directed by Irvin Kershner. Performances by Carrie Fisher, Harrison Ford, and Mark Hamil. Lucasfilm Ltd. 1980

The Incredible Hulk. Directed by Louis Leterrier. Performances by Edward Norton, Liv Tyler, William Hurt, and Tim Roth. Marvel Studios, 2008

The Suicide Squad. Directed by James Gunn. Performances by Margot Robbie, Idris Elba, and John Cena. Warner Bros Pictures, 2021

Thor. Directed by Kenneth Branagh. Performances by Chris Hemsworth, Tom Hiddleston, and Natalie Portman. Marvel Studios, 2011

Thor: Ragnarok. Directed by Taika Waititi. Performances by Chris Hemsworth, Tom Hiddleston, and Cate Blanchett. Marvel Studios, 2017

Thor: The Dark World. Directed by Alan Taylor. Performances by Chris Hemsworth, Tom Hiddleston, Natalie Portman, and Christopher Eccleston. Marvel Studios, 2013

Wonder Woman 1984. Directed by Patty Jenkins. Performances by Gal Gadot, Chris Pine, Kirsten Wiig, and Pedro Pascal. Warner Bros Pictures, 2020

Wonder Woman. Directed by Patty Jenkins. Performances by Gal Gadot and Chris Pine. Warner Bros Pictures, 2017.

Zack Snyder's Justice League. Directed by Zack Snyder. Performances by Henry Cavill, Ben Affleck, Gal Gadot, Ezra Miller, and Jason Mamoa. Warner Bros Pictures, 2021

Series

Agent Carter. Created by Christopher Markus and Stephen McFeely. Marvel Television/ABC Studios. 2015–2016

Agents of S.H.I.E.L.D. Created by Joss Whedon, Jed Whedon, and Maurissa Tancharoen. Marvel Television/ABC Studios. 2013–2020

Arrow. Created by Greg Berlanti, Marc Giggenheim, and Andrew Kreisberg. Warner Bros Television. 2012–2020

Avatar: The Legend of Korra. Created by Michael Dante DiMartino and Bryan Konietzko. Nickelodeon Animation Studio, 2012–2014

Batman: The Animated Series. Created by Eric Radomski and Bruce Timm. DC Entertainment and Warner Bros. Animation. 1992–1995

Batwoman. Created by Caroline Dries. Warner Bros Television. 2019-ongoing

Black Lighting. Created by Salim Akil. Warner Bros Television. 2018–2021

Daredevil. Created by Drew Goddard. Marvel Television/ABC Studios. 2015–2018

Freedom Fighter: The Ray. Created by Greg Berlanti, Marc Giggenheim, and Sam Register. Warner Bros Animation. 2017–2018

Iron Fist. Created by Scott Buck. Marvel Television/ABC Studios. 2017–2018

Jessica Jones. Created by Melissa Rosenberg. Marvel Television/ABC Studios. 2015–2019

Legends of Tomorrow. Created by Greg Berlanti, Marc Giggenheim, Andrew Kreisberg, and Phil Klemmer. Warner Bros Television. 2016-ongoing

Luke Cage. Created by Cheo Hodari Coker. Marvel Television/ABC Studios. 2016–2018.

Spider-Man (Japanese: スパイダーマン*)*. Created By Shozo Uehara and Susumu Takaku. Toei Company. 197–1979

Star Trek: The Original Series. Created by Gene Roddenberry. Norway Corporation, Desilu Production and Paramount Television, 1966–1969

Supergirl. Created by Greg Berlanti, Ali Adler, and Andrew Kreisberg. Warner Bros Television. 2016 ongoing

Superman&Lois. Created by Greg Berlanti and Todd Helbing. Warner Bros Television. 2021-ongoing

The Adventures of Superman. Written by George Putnam Ludlam. Mutual Broadcasting System & Citadel Media, 1940–1951. (radio series)

The Defenders. Created by Douglas Petrie and Marco Ramirez. Marvel Television/ABC Studios. 2017

The Flash. Created by Greg Berlanti, Andrew Kreisberg, and Geoff Johns. Warner Bros Television. 2014-ongoing

The Punisher. Created by Steve Lightfoot. Marvel Television/ABC Studios. 2017–2019

Vixen. Created by Greg Berlanti, Marc Giggenheim, and Andrew Kreisberg. Warner Bros Animation. 2014–2016

Episodes

"0-8-4". *Agents of S.H.I.E.L.D.* Created by Joss Whedon, Jed Whedon, and Maurissa Tancharoen. Season 1, episode 2. Marvel Television/ABC Studios. 2013–2020

"A Better World". *Justice League*. Directed by Dan Riba. Season 2, episodes 11 & 12. Warner Bros. Animation, 2002

"A Cold Day In Hell's Kitchen". *Daredevil*. Created by Drew Goddard. Season 2, episode 13. Marvel Television/ABC Studios. 2015–2018.

"A Duel of Iron". *Iron Fist*. Created by Scott Buck. Season 2, episode 10. Marvel Television/ABC Studios. 2017–2018

"Abyss". *The Punisher*. Created by Steve Lightfoot. Season 2, episode 11. Marvel Television/ABC Studios. 2017–2019

"AKA 99 Friends". *Jessica Jones*. Created by Melissa Rosenberg. Season 1, episode 4. Marvel Television/ABC Studios. 2015–2019

"AKA Camera Friendly". *Jessica Jones*. Created by Melissa Rosenberg. Season 3, episode 8. Marvel Television/ABC Studios. 2015–2019

"AKA It's Called Whiskey". *Jessica Jones*. Created by Melissa Rosenberg. Season 1, episode 3. Marvel Television/ABC Studios. 2015–2019

"AKA Pray for my Patsy". *Jessica Jones*. Created by Melissa Rosenberg. Season 2, episode 12. Marvel Television/ABC Studios. 2015–2019

"AKA Smile". *Jessica Jones*. Created by Melissa Rosenberg. Season 1, episode 13. Marvel Television/ABC Studios. 2015–2019

"AKA Sole Survivor". *Jessica Jones*. Created by Melissa Rosenberg. Season 2, episode 3. Marvel Television/ABC Studios. 2015–2019

"AKA Top Shelf Perverts". *Jessica Jones*. Created by Melissa Rosenberg. Season 1, episode 7. Marvel Television/ABC Studios. 2015–2019

"All Souled Out". *Luke Cage*. Created by Cheo Hodari Coker. Season 2, episode 5. Marvel Television/ABC Studios. 2016–2018

"Bang". *Daredevil*. Created by Drew Goddard. Season 2, episode 1. Marvel Television/ABC Studios. 2015–2018.

"Beginning of the End". *Agents of S.H.I.E.L.D.* Created by Joss Whedon, Jed Whedon, and Maurissa Tancharoen. Season 1, episode 22. Marvel Television/ABC Studios. 2013–2020

"Blowing up the Spot". *Luke Cage*. Created by Cheo Hodari Coker. Season 1, episode 8. Marvel Television/ABC Studios. 2016–2018

"Bouncing Back". *Agents of S.H.I.E.L.D.* Created by Joss Whedon, Jed Whedon, and Maurissa Tancharoen. Season 3, episode 11. Marvel Television/ABC Studios. 2013–2020

"Brave New Metropolis". *Superman: The Animated Series*. Directed by Curt Geda. Season 2, episode 12. Warner Bros. Animation, 1997

"Bridge and Tunnel". *Agent Carter*. Created by Christopher Markus and Stephen McFeely. Season 1, episode 2 Marvel Television/ABC Studios. 2015–2016

"Can't Front Me". *Luke Cage*. Created by Cheo Hodari Coker. Season 2, episode 12. Marvel Television/ABC Studios. 2016–2018

"Code of the Street". *Luke Cage*. Created by Cheo Hodari Coker. Season 1, episode 2. Marvel Television/ABC Studios. 2016–2018

"Daredevil". *Daredevil*. Created by Drew Goddard. Season 1, episode 13. Marvel Television/ABC Studios. 2015–2018

"Deals with our Devils". *Agents of S.H.I.E.L.D.* Created by Joss Whedon, Jed Whedon, and Maurissa Tancharoen. Season 4, episode 7. Marvel Television/ABC Studios. 2013–2020

"Dirty Half Dozen". *Agents of S.H.I.E.L.D.* Created by Joss Whedon, Jed Whedon, and Maurissa Tancharoen. Season 2, episode 19. Marvel Television/ABC Studios. 2013–2020

"Dragon Plays with Fire". *Iron Fist*. Created by Scott Buck. Season 1, episode 13. Marvel Television/ABC Studios. 2017–2018

"Eight Diagram Dragon Palm". *Iron Fist*. Created by Scott Buck. Season 1, episode 4. Marvel Television/ABC Studios. 2017–2018

"Emancipation". *Agents of S.H.I.E.L.D.* Created by Joss Whedon, Jed Whedon, and Maurissa Tancharoen. Season 3, episode 20. Marvel Television/ABC Studios. 2013–2020

"End of the Beginning". *Agents of S.H.I.E.L.D.* Created by Joss Whedon, Jed Whedon, and Maurissa Tancharoen. Season 1, episode 16. Marvel Television/ABC Studios. 2013–2020

"Failed Experiment". *Agents of S.H.I.E.L.D.* Created by Joss Whedon, Jed Whedon, and Maurissa Tancharoen. Season 3, episode 19. Marvel Television/ABC Studios. 2013–2020

"Felling Tree with Roots". *Iron Fist*. Created by Scott Buck. Season 1, episode 7. Marvel Television/ABC Studios. 2017–2018

"Fish in the Jailhouse". *The Defenders*. Created by Douglas Petrie and Marco Ramirez. Season 1, episode 7. Marvel Television/ABC Studios. 2017

"Flustercuck". *The Punisher*. Created by Steve Lightfoot. Season 2, episode 9. Marvel Television/ABC Studios. 2017–2019

"Heavy is the Head". *Agents of S.H.I.E.L.D.* Created by Joss Whedon, Jed Whedon, and Maurissa Tancharoen. Season 2, episode 2. Marvel Television/ABC Studios. 2013–2020

"If it ain't Rough, It ain't Right". *Luke Cage*. Created by Cheo Hodari Coker. Season 2, episode 8. Marvel Television/ABC Studios. 2016–2018

"Immortal Emerges from Cave". *Iron Fist*. Created by Scott Buck. Season 1, episode 6. Marvel Television/ABC Studios. 2017–2018

"In the Blood". *Daredevil*. Created by Drew Goddard. Season 1, episode 4. Marvel Television/ABC Studios. 2015–2018

"Into the Ring". *Daredevil*. Created by Drew Goddard. Season 1, episode 1. Marvel Television/ABC Studios. 2015–2018

"Just to get a Rep". *Luke Cage*. Created by Cheo Hodari Coker. Season 1, episode 5. Marvel Television/ABC Studios. 2016–2018

"Kinbaku". *Daredevil*. Created by Drew Goddard. Season 2, episode 5. Marvel Television/ABC Studios. 2015–2018

"Laws of Nature". *Agents of S.H.I.E.L.D.* Created by Joss Whedon, Jed Whedon, and Maurissa Tancharoen. Season 3, episode 1. Marvel Television/ABC Studios. 2013–2020

"Legends". *Justice League*. Directed by Dan Riba. Season 1, episodes 18 & 19. Warner Bros. Animation, 2002

"Lock Up". *Agents of S.H.I.E.L.D.* Created by Joss Whedon, Jed Whedon, and Maurissa Tancharoen. Season 4, episode 5. Marvel Television/ABC Studios. 2013–2020

"Mean Right Hook". *The Defenders*. Created by Douglas Petrie and Marco Ramirez. Season 1, episode 2. Marvel Television/ABC Studios. 2017

"Meet the New Boss". *Agents of S.H.I.E.L.D.* Created by Joss Whedon, Jed Whedon, and Maurissa Tancharoen. Season 4, episode 2. Marvel Television/ABC Studios. 2013–2020

"Nelson v. Murdock". *Daredevil*. Created by Drew Goddard. Season 1, episode 10. Marvel Television/ABC Studios. 2015–2018

"No Good Deed". *Daredevil*. Created by Drew Goddard. Season 3, episode 3. Marvel Television/ABC Studios. 2015–2018

"Nothing Personal". *Agents of S.H.I.E.L.D.* Created by Joss Whedon, Jed Whedon, and Maurissa Tancharoen. Season 1, episode 20. Marvel Television/ABC Studios. 2013–2020

"Now is Not the End". *Agent Carter*. Created by Christopher Markus and Stephen McFeely. Season 1, episode 1 Marvel Television/ABC Studios. 2015–2016

"Now You're Mine". *Luke Cage*. Created by Cheo Hodari Coker. Season 1, episode 11. Marvel Television/ABC Studios. 2016–2018

"One Last Shot". *Daredevil*. Created by Drew Goddard. Season 3, episode 12. Marvel Television/ABC Studios. 2015–2018

"One-Eyed Jacks". *The Punisher*. Created by Steve Lightfoot. Season 2, episode 5. Marvel Television/ABC Studios. 2017–2019

"Paradise Lost". *Agents of S.H.I.E.L.D.* Created by Joss Whedon, Jed Whedon, and Maurissa Tancharoen. Season 1, episode 16. Marvel Television/ABC Studios. 2013–2020

"Parting Shots". *Agents of S.H.I.E.L.D.* Created by Joss Whedon, Jed Whedon, and Maurissa Tancharoen. Season 3, episode 13. Marvel Television/ABC Studios. 2013–2020

"Pilot". *Agents of S.H.I.E.L.D.* Created by Joss Whedon, Jed Whedon, and Maurissa Tancharoen. Season 1, episode 1. Marvel Television/ABC Studios. 2013–2020

"Please". *Daredevil.* Created by Drew Goddard. Season 3, episode 2. Marvel Television/ABC Studios. 2015–2018.

"Providence". *Agents of S.H.I.E.L.D.* Created by Joss Whedon, Jed Whedon, and Maurissa Tancharoen. Season 1, episode 18. Marvel Television/ABC Studios. 2013–2020

"Purpose in the Machine". *Agents of S.H.I.E.L.D.* Created by Joss Whedon, Jed Whedon, and Maurissa Tancharoen. Season 3, episode 2. Marvel Television/ABC Studios. 2013–2020

"Rabbit in the Snow". *Daredevil.* Created by Drew Goddard. Season 1, episode 3. Marvel Television/ABC Studios. 2015–2018

"Rag Tag". *Agents of S.H.I.E.L.D.* Created by Joss Whedon, Jed Whedon, and Maurissa Tancharoen. Season 1, episode 21. Marvel Television/ABC Studios. 2013–2020

"Repairs". *Agents of S.H.I.E.L.D.* Created by Joss Whedon, Jed Whedon, and Maurissa Tancharoen. Season 1, episode 9. Marvel Television/ABC Studios. 2013–2020

"Resupply". *The Punisher.* Created by Steve Lightfoot. Season 1, episode 4. Marvel Television/ABC Studios. 2017–2019

"Resurrection". *Daredevil.* Created by Drew Goddard. Season 3, episode 1. Marvel Television/ABC Studios. 2015–2018

"Reunion". *Daredevil.* Created by Drew Goddard. Season 3, episode 11. Marvel Television/ABC Studios. 2015–2018

"Rise and Shine". *Agents of S.H.I.E.L.D.* Created by Joss Whedon, Jed Whedon, and Maurissa Tancharoen. Season 5, episode 15. Marvel Television/ABC Studios. 2013–2020

"Rolling Thunder Cannon Punch". *Iron Fist.* Created by Scott Buck. Season 1, episode 3. Marvel Television/ABC Studios. 2017–2018

"Royal Dragon". *The Defenders.* Created by Douglas Petrie and Marco Ramirez. Season 1, episode 4. Marvel Television/ABC Studios. 2017

"Seeds". *Agents of S.H.I.E.L.D.* Created by Joss Whedon, Jed Whedon, and Maurissa Tancharoen. Season 1, episode 12. Marvel Television/ABC Studios. 2013–2020

"Seven Minutes in Heaven". *Daredevil.* Created by Drew Goddard. Season 2, episode 9. Marvel Television/ABC Studios. 2015–2018

"Shadow Hawk Takes Flight". *Iron Fist.* Created by Scott Buck. Season 1, episode 2. Marvel Television/ABC Studios. 2017–2018

"Shadows in the Glass". *Daredevil.* Created by Drew Goddard. Season 1, episode 8. Marvel Television/ABC Studios. 2015–2018

"Shadows". *Agents of S.H.I.E.L.D.* Created by Joss Whedon, Jed Whedon, and Maurissa Tancharoen. Season 2, episode 1. Marvel Television/ABC Studios. 2013–2020

"Soliloquy of Chaos". *Luke Cage.* Created by Cheo Hodari Coker. Season 1, episode 12. Marvel Television/ABC Studios. 2016–2018

"Soul Brother #1". *Luke Cage.* Created by Cheo Hodari Coker. Season 2, episode 1. Marvel Television/ABC Studios. 2016–2018

"Step in the Arena". *Luke Cage.* Created by Cheo Hodari Coker. Season 1, episode 4. Marvel Television/ABC Studios. 2016–2018

"Straighten It Out". *Luke Cage*. Created by Cheo Hodari Coker. Season 2, episode 2. Marvel Television/ABC Studios. 2016–2018

"Suckas Need Bodyguards". *Luke Cage*. Created by Cheo Hodari Coker. Season 1, episode 6. Marvel Television/ABC Studios. 2016–2018

"T.A.H.I.T.I.". *Agents of S.H.I.E.L.D.* Created by Joss Whedon, Jed Whedon, and Maurissa Tancharoen. Season 1, episode 14. Marvel Television/ABC Studios. 2013–2020

"Take it Personal". *Luke Cage*. Created by Cheo Hodari Coker. Season 1, episode 10. Marvel Television/ABC Studios. 2016–2018

"Take Shelter". *The Defenders*. Created by Douglas Petrie and Marco Ramirez. Season 1, episode 5. Marvel Television/ABC Studios. 2017

"Target: Iron Fist". *Iron Fist*. Created by Scott Buck. Season 2, episode 4. Marvel Television/ABC Studios. 2017–2018

"The Atomic Job". *Agent Carter*. Created by Christopher Markus and Stephen McFeely. Season 2, episode 5. Marvel Television/ABC Studios. 2015–2016

"The Blessing of Many Fractures". *Iron Fist*. Created by Scott Buck. Season 1, episode 8. Marvel Television/ABC Studios. 2017–2018

"The Blitzkrieg Button". *Agent Carter*. Created by Christopher Markus and Stephen McFeely. Season 1, episode 4. Marvel Television/ABC Studios. 2015–2016

"The Creator". *Luke Cage*. Created by Cheo Hodari Coker. Season 2, episode 11. Marvel Television/ABC Studios. 2016–2018

"The Dark Heart of Men". *The Punisher*. Created by Steve Lightfoot. Season 2, episode 10. Marvel Television/ABC Studios. 2017–2019

"The Defenders". *The Defenders*. Created by Douglas Petrie and Marco Ramirez. Season 1, episode 8. Marvel Television/ABC Studios. 2017

"The Fury of the Iron Fist". *Iron Fist*. Created by Scott Buck. Season 2, episode 1. Marvel Television/ABC Studios. 2017–2018

"The Ghost". *Agents of S.H.I.E.L.D.* Created by Joss Whedon, Jed Whedon, and Maurissa Tancharoen. Season 4, episode 1. Marvel Television/ABC Studios. 2013–2020

"The Girl with the Flower Dress". *Agents of S.H.I.E.L.D.* Created by Joss Whedon, Jed Whedon, and Maurissa Tancharoen. Season 1, episode 5. Marvel Television/ABC Studios. 2013–2020

"The Good Samaritan". *Agents of S.H.I.E.L.D.* Created by Joss Whedon, Jed Whedon, and Maurissa Tancharoen. Season 4, episode 6. Marvel Television/ABC Studios. 2013–2020

"The H Word". *The Defenders*. Created by Douglas Petrie and Marco Ramirez. Season 1, episode 2. Marvel Television/ABC Studios. 2017

"The Hub". *Agents of S.H.I.E.L.D.* Created by Joss Whedon, Jed Whedon, and Maurissa Tancharoen. Season 1, episode 7. Marvel Television/ABC Studios. 2013–2020

"The Inside Man". *Agents of S.H.I.E.L.D.* Created by Joss Whedon, Jed Whedon, and Maurissa Tancharoen. Season 3, episode 12. Marvel Television/ABC Studios. 2013–2020

"The Iron Ceiling". *Agent Carter*. Created by Christopher Markus and Stephen McFeely. Season 1, episode 5. Marvel Television/ABC Studios. 2015–2016

"The Magical Place". *Agents of S.H.I.E.L.D.* Created by Joss Whedon, Jed Whedon, and Maurissa Tancharoen. Season 1, episode 11. Marvel Television/ABC Studios. 2013–2020

"The Main Ingredient". *Luke Cage*. Created by Cheo Hodari Coker. Season 2, episode 10. Marvel Television/ABC Studios. 2016–2018

"The Mistress of All Agonies". *Iron Fist*. Created by Scott Buck. Season 1, episode 9. Marvel Television/ABC Studios. 2017–2018

"The Moment of Truth". *Luke Cage*. Created by Cheo Hodari Coker. Season 1, episode 1. Marvel Television/ABC Studios. 2016–2018

"The Only Light in the Darkness". *Agents of S.H.I.E.L.D.* Created by Joss Whedon, Jed Whedon, and Maurissa Tancharoen. Season 1, episode 19. Marvel Television/ABC Studios. 2013–2020

"The Patriot". *Agents of S.H.I.E.L.D.* Created by Joss Whedon, Jed Whedon, and Maurissa Tancharoen. Season 4, episode 10. Marvel Television/ABC Studios. 2013–2020

"The Perfect Game". *Daredevil*. Created by Drew Goddard. Season 3, episode 5. Marvel Television/ABC Studios. 2015–2018

"The Things We Bury". *Agents of S.H.I.E.L.D.* Created by Joss Whedon, Jed Whedon, and Maurissa Tancharoen. Season 2, episode 8. Marvel Television/ABC Studios. 2013–2020

"The Well". *Agents of S.H.I.E.L.D.* Created by Joss Whedon, Jed Whedon, and Maurissa Tancharoen. Season 1, episode 8. Marvel Television/ABC Studios. 2013–2020

"They Reminisce Over You". *Luke Cage*. Created by Cheo Hodari Coker. Season 2, episode 13. Marvel Television/ABC Studios. 2016–2018

"They Reminisce Over You". *Luke Cage*. Created by Cheo Hodari Coker. Season 2, episode 13. Marvel Television/ABC Studios. 2016–2018

"Under Leaf Pluck Lotus". *Iron Fist*. Created by Scott Buck. Season 1, episode 5. Marvel Television/ABC Studios. 2017–2018

"Uprising". *Agents of S.H.I.E.L.D.* Created by Joss Whedon, Jed Whedon, and Maurissa Tancharoen. Season 4, episode 3. Marvel Television/ABC Studios. 2013–2020

"Valediction". *Agent Carter*. Created by Christopher Markus and Stephen McFeely. Season 1, episode 8. Marvel Television/ABC Studios. 2015–2016

"Virtue of the Vicious". *The Punisher*. Created by Steve Lightfoot. Season 1, episode 4. Marvel Television/ABC Studios. 2017–2019

"War Without End". *Iron Fist*. Created by Scott Buck. Season 2, episode 9. Marvel Television/ABC Studios. 2017–2018.

"Watchdogs". *Agents of S.H.I.E.L.D.* Created by Joss Whedon, Jed Whedon, and Maurissa Tancharoen. Season 3, episode 14. Marvel Television/ABC Studios. 2013–2020

"Who You Really Are". *Agents of S.H.I.E.L.D.* Created by Joss Whedon, Jed Whedon, and Maurissa Tancharoen. Season 2, episode 12. Marvel Television/ABC Studios. 2013–2020

"Who's Gonna Take the Weight". *Luke Cage*. Created by Cheo Hodari Coker. Season 1, episode 3. Marvel Television/ABC Studios. 2016–2018

"Wig Out". *Luke Cage*. Created by Cheo Hodari Coker. Season 2, episode 3. Marvel Television/ABC Studios. 2016–2018

"World's Finest". *Supergirl*. Created by Greg Berlanti, Ali Adler, and Andrew Kreisberg. Season 1, episode 18. Warner Bros Television. 2016-ongoing

"Worst Behavior". *The Defenders*. Created by Douglas Petrie and Marco Ramirez. Season 1, episode 3. Marvel Television/ABC Studios. 2017

"Yes Men". *Agents of S.H.I.E.L.D.* Created by Joss Whedon, Jed Whedon, and Maurissa Tancharoen. Season 1, episode 15. Marvel Television/ABC Studios. 2013–2020

"You Know My Steez". *Luke Cage.* Created by Cheo Hodari Coker. Season 1, episode 13. Marvel Television/ABC Studios. 2016–2018

Comics

Amazing Spider-Man #518. Written by J. Michael Straczynski. Illustrated by Mike Deodato Jr. Marvel Comics, 2005

Amazing Spider-Man #529. Written by J. Michael Straczynski. Illustrated by Ron Garney. Marvel Comics, 2006

Amazing Spider-Man #532-#538. Written by J. Michael Straczynski. Illustrated by Ron Garney. Marvel Comics, 2006–2007

Amazing Spider-Man (Vol.2) #31–#38. Written by J. Michael Straczynski. Illustrated by John Romita Jr. Marvel Comics, 2001

A-Next. Written by Tom DeFalco. Illustrated by Ron Frenz. MC 2, 1998–1999

Captain America #22-#24. Written by Ed Brubaker. Illustrated by Mike Perkins. Marvel Comics, 2006–2007

Civil War. Written by Mark Millar. Illustrator Steve McNiven. Marvel Comics, 2006–2007

Civil War: Frontline #1-#11 "Embedded". Written by Paul Jenkins. Illustrated by Ramon Bachs. Marvel Comics, 2006–2007

Civil War: Frontline #1-#11 "The Accused". Written by Paul Jenkins. Illustrated by Steve Lieber. Marvel Comics, 2006–2007

Civil War: Warzone. Written by Charles Soule. Illustrated by Leinil Francis Yu. Marvel Comics, 2016

Fallen Son: The Death of Captain America – Avengers. Written by Joeb Loeb. Illustrated by Ed McGuinness. Marvel Comics, 2007

Fallen Son: The Death of Captain America – Iron Man. Written by Joeb Loeb. Illustrated by John Cassaday. Marvel Comics, 2007

Fallen Son: The Death of Captain America – Spider-Man. Written by Joeb Loeb. Illustrated by David Finch. Marvel Comics, 2007

Fantastic Five. Written by Tom DeFalco. Illustrated by Paul Ryan. MC 2, 1999–2000

Fantastic Four #538-#541. Written by J. Michael Straczynski. Illustrated by Mike McKone. Marvel Comics, 2006

Iron Man #13-#14. Written by Daniel and Charles Knauf. Illustrated by Patrick Zircher. Marvel Comics, 2006–2007

J2. Written by Tom DeFalco. Illustrated by Ron Lim. MC 2, 1998–1999

Kingdome Come. by Mark Waid. Illustrated by Alex Ross. DC Comics 2008 (1996)

New Avengers #21-#25. Written by Brian Michael Bendis. Marvel Comics, 2006–2007

New Avengers #1-#3. Written by Brian Michael Bendis. Illustrated by David Finch. Marvel Comics, 2004

New Warriors #1-#6. Written by Zeb Wells. Illustrated by Skottie Young. Marvel Comics. 2005–2006

Spider-Girl. Written by Tom DeFalco. Illustrated by Ron Frenz and Pat Olliffe. MC 2, 1998–2006

Spider-Men. Written by Brian Michael Bendis. Illustrated by Sara Pichelli. Marvel Comics, 2012

Superman: Secret Identity. Written by Kurt Busiek. Illustrated by Stuart Immonen. DC Comics. 2004

Superman: Speeding Bullets. Written by J.M. DeMatteis. Illustrated by Eduardo Barreto. DC Comics, 1993

The Incredible Hercules #113-#141. Written by Greg Pak and Fred van Lente. Marvel Comics 2008–2010

The Ultimates. Written by Mark Miller. Illustrated by Bryan Hitch. Marvel Comics, 2002–2004

Thor #80-#85. Written by Michael Avon Oeming and Daniel Berman. Illustrated by Andrea DiVito. Marvel Comics, 2004

Ultimate Fantastic Four. Written by Mark Miller and Brian Michael Bendis. Marvel Comics, 2004–2009

Ultimate Spider-Man. Written by Brian Michael Bendis. Illustrated by Mark Bagely and Stuart Immonen. Ultimate Marvel, 2000–2014

Ultimate X-Men. Created by Mark Miller. Marvel Comics, 2001–2009

Wild Thing. Written by Tom DeFalco and Larry Hama. Illustrated by Ron Frenz and Ron Lim. MC 2, 1999–2000

Wonder Woman #31. Written by James Robinson. Illustrated by Carlo Pagulayan. DC comics, 2017

World War Hulk. Written by Greg Pak. Illustrated by John Romita Jr. Marvel Comics, 2007–2008

Books

McDonagh, Tim. *Star Wars: Galactic Atlas*. Egmont UK Limited, 2016
Pratchett, Terry. *Feet of Clay*. UK: Penguin Random House, 1996
Pratchett, Terry. *Going Postal*. UK: Penguin Random House, 2004
Pratchett, Terry. *Guards! Guards!*. UK: Penguin Random House, 1989
Pratchett, Terry. *Jingo*. UK: Penguin Random House, 1997
Pratchett, Terry. *Lords and Ladies*. UK: Penguin Random House, 199
Pratchett, Terry. *Making Money*. UK: Penguin Random House, 2007
Pratchett, Terry. *Men At Arms*. UK: Penguin Random House, 1993
Pratchett, Terry. *Night Watch*. UK: Penguin Random House, 2002
Pratchett, Terry. *Snuff*. UK: Penguin Random House, 2011
Pratchett, Terry. *The Colour of Magic*. Berkshire: Colin Smythe Publishing, 1983
Pratchett, Terry. *The Fifth Elephant*. UK: Penguin Random House, 1999
Pratchett, Terry. *The Last Hero*. UK: Penguin Random House, 2001
Pratchett, Terry. *The Shepherd's Crown*. UK: Penguin Random House, 2015
Pratchett, Terry. *Thud!*. UK: Penguin Random House, 2005
Pratchett, Terry. *Unseen Academicals*. UK: Penguin Random House, 2009
Robinson, Ben and Marcus Riley. *Star Trek Shipyards: 2294 to the Future – The Encyclopedia of Starfleet Ships*. Hero collector, 2021

Rowling, Joanne. *Fantastic Beasts and Where to Find Them*. London: Arthur A. Levine Books, 2001

Internet

https://www.youtube.com/c/Crypttv/playlists, retrieved January 5th, 2022
https://www.thepixartheory.com, retrieved January 5th, 2022

Secondary Sources

Abrams, Natalie. "Agents of S.H.I.E.L.D. will cross over with Doctor Strange". *Entertainment Weekly*. September 16th, 2016. https://ew.com/article/2016/09/16/agents-shield-doctor-strange/, retrieved September 30st, 2021.

Bacon-Smith, Camille. *Enterprising Women: Television Fandom and the Creation of Popular Myth*. Philadelphia: University of Pennsylvania Press, 1991

Barthes, Roland. "An Introduction to the Structural Analysis of Narrative". *New Literary History, Vol. 6, No. 2, On Narrative and Narratives*. 1975. 237–272

Bolter, Jay-David and Richard Grusin. *Remediation: Understanding New Media*. Cambridge: The MIT Press, 1999

Chatman, Seymour. *Story and Discourse: Narrative Structure in Fiction and Film*. Cornell: Cornell University Press, 1978

Ching, Albert. "How Agents of S.H.I.E.L.D. Season 5 ties-in to the Marvel Studios Movies". *CBR.com*. November 30th, 2017. https://www.cbr.com/agents-of-shield-season-5-marvel-studios-movies-connection/, retrieved September 30st, 2021

Cocca, Carolyn. *Superwomen: Gender, Power, and Representation*. New York: Bloomsbury, 2016

DeForest, Tim. "Faster than a Speeding Bullet: Superman". *Storytelling in the Pulps, Comics, and Radio: How Technology Changed Popular Fiction in America*. McFarland, 2004, 168–172

Dittmer, Jason. "Serialization and Displacement in Graphic Narrative." *Serialization in Popular Culture*. Ed. Rob Allen and Thijis van den Berg. New York: Routledge, 2014. 125–140

Felski, Rita. "Comparison and Translation: A Perspective from Actor-Network Theory." *Comparative Literature Studies, Vol. 53 no. 4*, 2016, p. 747–765. Project MUSE muse.jhu.edu/article/648800

Fiske, John. *Understanding Popular Culture*. Routledge; 1989

Fludernik, Monika. *Towards a 'Natural Narratology'*. London and New York: Routledge, 1996

Ford, Sam and Henry Jenkins. "Managing Multiplicity in Superhero Comics: An Interview with Henry Jenkins". *Third Person: Authoring and Exploring Vast Narratives*. Edited by Pat Harrigan and Noah Wardrip-Fruin. MIT Press, 2009. 303–311

Freytag, Gustav. *Technique of the Drama*. Translated by E.J. McEwan. Scott, Foresman and Company, 1900. https://archive.org/details/freytagstechniqu00freyuoft/page/124/mode/2up?q=125

Gordon, Ian. Superman: *The Persistence of an American Icon*. New Jersey: Rutgers University Press, 2017

Harvey, Colin. *Fantastic Transmedia*. London: Palgrave Macmillian, 2015

Harvey, Colin. "A Taxonomy of Transmedia Storytelling". *Storyworlds across Media*. USA: University of Nebraska Press, 2014. 278–294

Hassler- Forest, Dan. "The Walking Dead: Quality Television, Transmedia Serialization and Zombies". *Serialization in Popular Culture*. Ed. Rob Allen and Thijs van den Berg. New York: Routledge, 2014. 91–105

Hassler-Forest, Dan. "Transmedia Politics: Star Wars and the Ideological Battlegrounds of Popular Franchises". *The Routledge Companion to Transmedia Studies*. Edited by Matthew Freeman and Renira Rampazzo Gambarato. Routledge, 2018. 297–305

Herman David. "Narrative Ways of Worldmaking". *Narratology in the Age of Cross-Disciplinary Narrative Research*. Ed. Sandra Heinen and Roy Sommer. Walter de Gruyter GmbH. Berlin: 2009. 71–87

Herman, David. *Storytelling and The Science of Mind*. Cambridge: MIT Press, 2013

Herman, David. *The Basic Elements of Narrative*. London, Wiley- Blackwell: 2009

Hibberd, Jane. "Daredevil: 7 things we learned about Netflix's new series". *Entertainment Weekly*. December 29th, 2014. https://ew.com/article/2014/12/29/daredevil6/?hootPostID=86d97ba5 33da5f593b1f0d7aca86d91, retrieved September 21st, 2021

Howe, Sean. "Avengers Assemble!". *Slate*. Sept 28, 2012. https://slate.com/business/2012/09/marvel comics-and-the-movies-the-business-story-behind-the-avengers.html, retrieved September 21st, 2021

Hutcheon, Linda. *A Theory of Adaptation*. Routledge; Auflage: 2. 2012

Jeffries, Dru. "The Worlds Align: Media Convergence and Complementary Storyworlds in Marvel's *Thor: The Dark World*". *World Building. Transmedia, Fans, Industries*. Marta Boni (ed.), Amsterdam University Press, 2017. 287–303

Jenkins, Henry. *Convergence Culture*. New York: New York University Press, 2006

Jenkins, Henry. *Textual Poachers: Television Fans & Participatory Culture*. New York: Routledge, 1992

Johnston, Sarah Iles. "The Greek Mythic Story World." *Arethusa*, Vol. 48 no. 3, 2015, p. 283–311. Project MUSE, doi:10.1353/are.2015.0008

Kelleter, Frank und Daniel Stein. "Autorisierungspraktiken seriellen Erzählens". *Populäre Serialität: Narration–Evolution–Distinktion*. Frank Kelleter (Ed.). Bielefeld: transcript Verlag, 2012. 259–290

Kelleter, Frank. "Five Ways of Looking at Seriality". *Media of Serial Narratives*. Kelleter (Eds.). Columbus: Ohio University Press. 2017. 7–34

Kilgore, Christopher D. "Rhetoric of the Network: Toward a New Metaphor." *Mosaic: a journal for the interdisciplinary study of literature*, Vol. 46 no. 4, 2013, p. 37–58. Project MUSE, doi:10.1353/mos.2013.0044

Klock, Goeff. *How to Read Superhero Comics and Why*. New York: The Continuum International Publishing Group Inc. 2002

Kukkonen, Karin. *Studying Comics and Graphic Novels*. Singapore: Wiley Blackwell, 2013

Latour, Bruno. *Reassembling the Social: An Introduction to Actor-Network-Theory*. Oxford: Oxford University Press, 2005

Lindner, Christoph. "Foreword". *Serialization in Popular Culture*. Rob Allen and Thijis van den Berg (Ed.). New York: Routledge 2014

McBean, Sam. "The Queer Network Novel." *Contemporary Literature*, Vol. 60 no. 3, 2019, p. 427–452. Project MUSE muse.jhu.edu/article/763824

Mitchell, Kurt and Roy Thomas. *American Comic Book Chronicles: 1940–1944*. TwoMorrows Publishing, 2019

Mittell, Jason. "Strategies of Storytelling on Transmedial Television". *Storyworlds across Media*. USA: University of Nebraska Press, 2014. 253–277

Packard, Stephan. "Closing the Open Signification: Forms of Transmedial Storyworlds and Chronotopoi in Comics". *StoryWorlds: A Journal of Narrative Studies, Volume 7, Number 2*. University of Nebraska Press, 2015. 55–74

Phillips, William H. *Film: An Introduction (Third Edition)*. Boston: Bedford/St. Martin's. 2005

Prince, Gerald. *Dictionary of Narratology*. Nebraska: University of Nebraska Press, 2003

Pustz, Matthew. *Comic Book Culture: Fanboys and True Believers*. University Press of Mississippi, 1999

Rippl, Gabriele and Lukas Etter. "Intermediality, Transmediality, and Graphic Narratives". *From Comic Strips to Graphic Novels*. Göttingen: De Gruyter, 2013. 191–218

Ryan, Marie-Laure and Jan-Noel Thon. "Introduction". *Storyworlds across Media*. USA: University of Nebraska Press, 2014. 1–24

Ryan, Marie-Laure. "Interactive Drama: Narrativity in a Highly Interactive Environment." *MFS Modern Fiction Studies*, Vol. 43 no. 3, 1997, p. 677–707. Project MUSE, https://doi:10.1353/mfs.1997.0065

Ryan, Marie-Laure. "Semantics, Pragmatics, and Narrativity: A Response to David Rudrum." *Narrative*, Vol. 14 no. 2, 2006, p. 188–196. Project MUSE, https://doi:10.1353/nar.2006.0006

Ryan, Marie-Laure. "Story/World/Media – Tuning the Instruments of a Media-Conscious Narratology". *Storyworlds across Media*. USA: University of Nebraska Press, 2014. 25–49

Ryan, Marie-Laure. "The Aesthetics of Proliferation". *World Building. Transmedia, Fans, Industries*. Marta Boni (ed.), Amsterdam University Press, 2017. 29–46

Stein, Daniel and Jan-Noel Thon. "Introduction: From Comic Strips to Graphic Novels". *From Comic Strips to Graphic Novels*. Göttingen: De Gruyter, 2013. 1–26

Stein, Daniel. "Superhero Comics and the Authorizing Function of the Comic Book Paratext". *From Comic Strips to Graphic Novels*. Göttingen: De Gruyter, 2013. 155–190

Steinberg, Marc. *Anime's Media Mix: Franchising Toys and Characters in Japan*. Minneapolis: University of Minnesota Press, 2012

Thon, Jan-Noel. "Subjectivity across Media: On Transmedial Strategies of Subjective Representation in Contemporary Feature Films, Graphic Novels, and Computer Games". *Storyworlds across Media*. USA: University of Nebraska Press, 2014. 67–102

Thon, Jan-Noel. "Transmedia Character: Theory and Analysis". *Frontiers of Narrative Studies, vol.5, no.2*, 2019. 176–199. https://doi.org/10.1515/fns-2019-0012, retrieved February 17th ,2023

Tomabechi, Nao. *Supervillain Comics: The Significance of Supervillains in American Superhero Comics*. forthcoming.

Urbanski, Heather. *The Science Fiction Reboot*. London: McFarland & Company, 2013

van Dijk, Teun A. "Action, Action, Description and Narrative". *New Literary History*. Vol. 6, No. 2, On Narrative and Narratives, 1975, pp. 273–294

van Oenen, Gijs. "Interpassive Agency: Engaging Actor-Network-Theory's View on the Agency of Objects." *Theory & Event*, Vol. 14 no. 2, 2011. Project MUSE, https://doi:10.1353/tae.2011.0014.

Wolf, Mark J.P. *Building Imaginary Worlds: The Theory of Subcreation*. New York: Routledge, 2012

Wolf, Werner. Lyric Poetry and Narrativity: A Critical Evaluation, and the Need for "Lyrology". *Narrative*, Vol. 28 no. 2, 2020, p. 143–173. Project MUSE, https://doi:10.1353/nar.2020.0008

Wolf, Werner. "Narratology and Media(lity): The Transmedial Expansion of a Literary Discipline and Possible Consequences". *Selected Essays on Intermediality by Werner Wolf*. Ed. Walter Bernhart. Boston, 2018. p. 501–532

Zipfel, Frank. "Fiction Across Media: Towards a Transmedial Conception of Fictionality". *Storyworlds across Media*. USA: University of Nebraska Press, 2014. 103–125

Internet

http://cultureandcommunication.org/galloway/network-pessimism, retrieved July 29th, 2021

http://henryjenkins.org/blog/2012/03/how_to_ride_a_lion_a_call_for.html, retrieved July 8th, 2021

https://www.toonopedia.com/universe.htm, retrieved August 24th, 2021

https://dictionary.cambridge.org/dictionary/english/allusion, retrieved September 2nd, 2021

https://dictionary.cambridge.org/dictionary/english/denouement?q=Denouement, retrieved August 30th, 2021

https://literarydevices.net/denouement/, retrieved August 30th, 2021

https://marvelcinematicuniverse.fandom.com/wiki/29th_Precinct_Police_Station/Gallery, retrieved November 16th, 2021

https://marvelcinematicuniverse.fandom.com/wiki/Absorbing_Man/Gallery, retrieved November 19th, 2021

https://marvelcinematicuniverse.fandom.com/wiki/Arnim_Zola/Gallery, retrieved November 19th, 2021

https://marvelcinematicuniverse.fandom.com/wiki/Avengers:_Age_of_Ultron/Gallery, retrieved November 5th, 2021

https://marvelcinematicuniverse.fandom.com/wiki/Avengers:_Endgame/Gallery, retrieved November 8th, 2021

https://marvelcinematicuniverse.fandom.com/wiki/Avengers:_Infinity_War/Gallery, retrieved November 5th, 2021

https://marvelcinematicuniverse.fandom.com/wiki/Ayo/Gallery, retrieved November 5th, 2021

https://marvelcinematicuniverse.fandom.com/wiki/Ben_Urich/Gallery, retrieved November 19th, 2021 https://marvelcinematicuniverse.fandom.com/wiki/Benjamin_Donovan/Gallery, retrieved November 16th, 2021

https://marvelcinematicuniverse.fandom.com/wiki/Black_Widow/Gallery, retrieved November 8th, 2021

https://marvelcinematicuniverse.fandom.com/wiki/Brett_Mahoney/Gallery, retrieved November 17th, 2021

https://marvelcinematicuniverse.fandom.com/wiki/Captain_America:_Civil_War/Gallery, retrieved November 5th, 2021

https://marvelcinematicuniverse.fandom.com/wiki/Chikara_Dojo/Gallery, retrieved November 16th, 2021

https://marvelcinematicuniverse.fandom.com/wiki/Claire_Temple/Gallery, retrieved November 16th, 2021

https://marvelcinematicuniverse.fandom.com/wiki/Collector/Gallery, retrieved November 16th, 2021

https://marvelcinematicuniverse.fandom.com/wiki/Colleen_Wing/Gallery, retrieved November 16th, 2021

https://marvelcinematicuniverse.fandom.com/wiki/Daniel_Sousa/Gallery, retrieved November 18th, 2021

https://marvelcinematicuniverse.fandom.com/wiki/Darkforce/Gallery, retrieved November 18th, 2021

https://marvelcinematicuniverse.fandom.com/wiki/Darryl/Gallery, retrieved November 16th, 2021

https://marvelcinematicuniverse.fandom.com/wiki/Edwin_Jarvis/Gallery, retrieved November 19th, 2021

https://marvelcinematicuniverse.fandom.com/wiki/Erik_Selvig/Gallery, retrieved November 16th, 2021

https://marvelcinematicuniverse.fandom.com/wiki/Everett_Ross/Gallery, retrieved November 5th, 2021

https://marvelcinematicuniverse.fandom.com/wiki/Extremis/Gallery, retrieved November 19th, 2021

https://marvelcinematicuniverse.fandom.com/wiki/Foggy_Nelson/Gallery, retrieved November 16th, 2021

https://marvelcinematicuniverse.fandom.com/wiki/Gideon_Malick/Gallery, retrieved November 19th, 2021

https://marvelcinematicuniverse.fandom.com/wiki/Hai-Qing_Yang/Gallery, retrieved November 16th, 2021

https://marvelcinematicuniverse.fandom.com/wiki/Happy_Hogan/Gallery, retrieved November 5th, 2021

https://marvelcinematicuniverse.fandom.com/wiki/Hawkeye/Gallery, retrieved November 16th, 2021

https://marvelcinematicuniverse.fandom.com/wiki/Howard_Stark/Gallery, retrieved November 5th, 2021

https://marvelcinematicuniverse.fandom.com/wiki/Infinity_Stones/Gallery, retrieved November 8th, 2021 https://marvelcinematicuniverse.fandom.com/wiki/Iron_Fist/Gallery, retrieved November 16th, 2021

https://marvelcinematicuniverse.fandom.com/wiki/Iron_Man/Gallery, retrieved November 8th, 2021

https://marvelcinematicuniverse.fandom.com/wiki/Jasper_Sitwell/Gallery, retrieved November 19th, 2021

https://marvelcinematicuniverse.fandom.com/wiki/Jeri_Hogarth/Gallery, retrieved November 16th, 2021

https://marvelcinematicuniverse.fandom.com/wiki/Karen_Page/Gallery, retrieved November 16th, 2021

https://marvelcinematicuniverse.fandom.com/wiki/Korath_the_Pursuer/Gallery, retrieved November 8th, 2021

https://marvelcinematicuniverse.fandom.com/wiki/List/Gallery, retrieved November 19th, 2021

https://marvelcinematicuniverse.fandom.com/wiki/Loki/Gallery, retrieved November 16th, 2021

https://marvelcinematicuniverse.fandom.com/wiki/Luke_Cage/Gallery, retrieved November 16th, 2021

https://marvelcinematicuniverse.fandom.com/wiki/Madame_Gao/Gallery, retrieved November 16th, 2021

https://marvelcinematicuniverse.fandom.com/wiki/Maria_Hill/Gallery, retrieved November 16th, 2021

https://marvelcinematicuniverse.fandom.com/wiki/Matthew_Ellis/Gallery, retrieved November 19th, 2021

https://marvelcinematicuniverse.fandom.com/wiki/May_Parker/Gallery, retrieved November 5th, 2021

https://marvelcinematicuniverse.fandom.com/wiki/Mind_Stone/Gallery, retrieved November 8th, 2021

https://marvelcinematicuniverse.fandom.com/wiki/Misty_Knight/Gallery, retrieved November 17th, 2021

https://marvelcinematicuniverse.fandom.com/wiki/Mj%C3%B8lnir/Gallery, retrieved November 16th, 2021

https://marvelcinematicuniverse.fandom.com/wiki/Nick_Fury/Gallery, retrieved November 8th, 2021

https://marvelcinematicuniverse.fandom.com/wiki/Nitramene/Gallery, retrieved November 18th, 2021

https://marvelcinematicuniverse.fandom.com/wiki/Peggy_Carter/Gallery, retrieved November 5th, 2021

https://marvelcinematicuniverse.fandom.com/wiki/Pepper_Potts/Gallery, retrieved November 5th, 2021

https://marvelcinematicuniverse.fandom.com/wiki/Phil_Coulson/Gallery, retrieved November 8th, 2021

https://marvelcinematicuniverse.fandom.com/wiki/Power_Stone/Gallery, retrieved November 8th, 2021

https://marvelcinematicuniverse.fandom.com/wiki/Punisher/Gallery, retrieved November 16th, 2021

https://marvelcinematicuniverse.fandom.com/wiki/Reality_Stone/Gallery, retrieved November 8th, 2021

https://marvelcinematicuniverse.fandom.com/wiki/Ronan_the_Accuser/Gallery, retrieved November 8th, 2021

https://marvelcinematicuniverse.fandom.com/wiki/Roxxon_Corporation/Gallery, retrieved November 19th, 2021

https://marvelcinematicuniverse.fandom.com/wiki/Samantha_Reyes/Gallery, retrieved November 16th, 2021

https://marvelcinematicuniverse.fandom.com/wiki/Scepter/Gallery, retrieved November 8th, 2021

https://marvelcinematicuniverse.fandom.com/wiki/Sif/Gallery, retrieved November 19th, 2021

https://marvelcinematicuniverse.fandom.com/wiki/Soren/Gallery, retrieved November 8th, 2021

https://marvelcinematicuniverse.fandom.com/wiki/Spider-Man:_Homecoming/Gallery, retrieved November 5th, 2021

https://marvelcinematicuniverse.fandom.com/wiki/Steve_Rogers/Gallery, retrieved November 8th, 2021

https://marvelcinematicuniverse.fandom.com/wiki/Talos/Gallery, retrieved November 8th, 2021

https://marvelcinematicuniverse.fandom.com/wiki/T'Chaka/Gallery, retrieved November 5th, 2021

https://marvelcinematicuniverse.fandom.com/wiki/Tesseract/Gallery, retrieved November 8th, 2021

https://marvelcinematicuniverse.fandom.com/wiki/Thaddeus_Ross/Gallery, retrieved November 5th, 2021

https://marvelcinematicuniverse.fandom.com/wiki/The_Defenders/Gallery, retrieved November 16th, 2021

https://marvelcinematicuniverse.fandom.com/wiki/Thembi_Wallace/Gallery, retrieved November 17th, 2021

https://marvelcinematicuniverse.fandom.com/wiki/Thor/Gallery, retrieved November 5th, 2021

https://marvelcinematicuniverse.fandom.com/wiki/Thor:_Ragnarok/Gallery, retrieved November 5th, 2021

https://marvelcinematicuniverse.fandom.com/wiki/Thor:_The_Dark_World/Gallery, retrieved November 16th, 2021

https://marvelcinematicuniverse.fandom.com/wiki/Triskelion/Gallery, retrieved November 19th, 2021

https://marvelcinematicuniverse.fandom.com/wiki/Turk_Barrett/Gallery, retrieved November 17th, 2021

https://marvelcinematicuniverse.fandom.com/wiki/Ulysses_Klaue/Gallery, retrieved November 5th, 2021 https://marvelcinematicuniverse.fandom.com/wiki/William_Ginter_Riva/Gallery, retrieved November 8th, 2021

https://marvelcinematicuniverse.fandom.com/wiki/WZTM_News/Gallery, retrieved November 19th, 2021

https://www.dictionary.com/browse/entity, retrieved August 25th, 2021

https://www.fxguide.com/fxfeatured/captain-america-the-winter-soldier-reaching-new-heights/, retrieved September 21st, 2021

https://www.merriam-webster.com/dictionary/multiverse, retrieved July 12th, 2021

https://www.merriam-webster.com/dictionary/spectacle, retrieved October 14th, 2021

GPSR Authorized Representative: Easy Access System Europe, Mustamäe tee
50, 10621 Tallinn, Estonia, gpsr.requests@easproject.com